(Continued on back endsheets)

Dictionary of Literary Biography® • Volume One Hundred Fifty-Four

The British Literary Book Trade, 1700–1820

The British Literary Book Trade, 1700–1820

Edited by
James K. Bracken
Ohio State University
and
Joel Silver
Indiana University

A Bruccoli Clark Layman Book
Gale Research Inc.
Detroit, Washington, D.C., London

Printed in the United States of America

The paper used in this publication meets the minimum requirements
of American National Standard for Information Sciences–Permanence
Paper for Printed Library Materials, ANSI Z39.48-1984. ∞ ™

Copyright © 1995 by Gale Research Inc.
835 Penobscot Building
Detroit, MI 48226

Library of Congress Cataloging-in-Publication Data

The British literary book trade, 1700–1820 / edited by James K. Bracken and Joel Silver.
   p. cm. – (Dictionary of literary biography; v. 154)
"A Bruccoli Clark Layman book."
Includes bibliographical references and index.
ISBN 0-8103-5715-1 (alk. paper)
   1. Literature publishing – Great Britain – History – 18th century. 2. Literature publishing – Great
Britain – History – 19th century. 3. Publishers and publishing – Great Britain – Biography – Dictionaries.
4. Literature publishing – Great Britain – History – 18th century – Bibliography. 5. Literature
publishing – Great Britain – History – 19th century – Bibliography. 6. Booksellers and bookselling
– Great Britain – Biography – Dictionaries. 7. Printers – Great Britain – Biography – Dictionaries.
8. Book industries and trade – Great Britain – History – 18th century – Bibliography. 9. Book industries
and trade – Great Britain – History – 19th century – Bibliography. I. Bracken, James K., 1952– .
II. Silver, Joel, 1951– . III. Series.
Z326.B666 1995
070.5'0941 – dc20   95-4825
                                                             CIP

10 9 8 7 6 5 4 3 2 1

Contents

Plan of the Series

. . . Almost the most prodigious asset of a country, and perhaps its most precious possession, is its native literary product — when that product is fine and noble and enduring.

Mark Twain*

The advisory board, the editors, and the publisher of the *Dictionary of Literary Biography* are joined in endorsing Mark Twain's declaration. The literature of a nation provides an inexhaustible resource of permanent worth. We intend to make literature and its creators better understood and more accessible to students and the reading public, while satisfying the standards of teachers and scholars.

To meet these requirements, *literary biography* has been construed in terms of the author's achievement. The most important thing about a writer is his writing. Accordingly, the entries in *DLB* are career biographies, tracing the development of the author's canon and the evolution of his reputation.

The purpose of *DLB* is not only to provide reliable information in a convenient format but also to place the figures in the larger perspective of literary history and to offer appraisals of their accomplishments by qualified scholars.

The publication plan for *DLB* resulted from two years of preparation. The project was proposed to Bruccoli Clark by Frederick C. Ruffner, president of the Gale Research Company, in November 1975. After specimen entries were prepared and typeset, an advisory board was formed to refine the entry format and develop the series rationale. In meetings held during 1976, the publisher, series editors, and advisory board approved the scheme for a comprehensive biographical dictionary of persons who contributed to North American literature. Editorial work on the first volume began in January 1977, and it was published in 1978. In order to make *DLB* more than a reference tool and to compile volumes that individually have claim to status as literary history, it was decided to organize vol-

*From an unpublished section of Mark Twain's autobiography, copyright by the Mark Twain Company

umes by topic, period, or genre. Each of these freestanding volumes provides a biographical-bibliographical guide and overview for a particular area of literature. We are convinced that this organization – as opposed to a single alphabet method – constitutes a valuable innovation in the presentation of reference material. The volume plan necessarily requires many decisions for the placement and treatment of authors who might properly be included in two or three volumes. In some instances a major figure will be included in separate volumes, but with different entries emphasizing the aspect of his career appropriate to each volume. Ernest Hemingway, for example, is represented in *American Writers in Paris, 1920-1939* by an entry focusing on his expatriate apprenticeship; he is also in *American Novelists, 1910-1945* with an entry surveying his entire career. Each volume includes a cumulative index of the subject authors and articles. Comprehensive indexes to the entire series are planned.

With volume ten in 1982 it was decided to enlarge the scope of *DLB*. By the end of 1986 twenty-one volumes treating British literature had been published, and volumes for Commonwealth and Modern European literature were in progress. The series has been further augmented by the *DLB Yearbooks* (since 1981) which update published entries and add new entries to keep the *DLB* current with contemporary activity. There have also been *DLB Documentary Series* volumes which provide biographical and critical source materials for figures whose work is judged to have particular interest for students. One of these companion volumes is entirely devoted to Tennessee Williams.

We define literature as the *intellectual commerce of a nation:* not merely as belles lettres but as that ample and complex process by which ideas are generated, shaped, and transmitted. *DLB* entries are not limited to "creative writers" but extend to other figures who in their time and in their way influenced the mind of a people. Thus the series encompasses historians, journalists, publishers, and screenwriters. By this means readers of *DLB* may be aided to perceive literature not as cult scripture in the keeping of intellectual high priests but firmly positioned at the center of a nation's life.

DLB includes the major writers appropriate to each volume and those standing in the ranks immediately behind them. Scholarly and critical counsel has been sought in deciding which minor figures to include and how full their entries should be. Wherever possible, useful references are made to figures who do not warrant separate entries.

Each *DLB* volume has a volume editor responsible for planning the volume, selecting the figures for inclusion, and assigning the entries. Volume editors are also responsible for preparing, where appropriate, appendices surveying the major periodicals and literary and intellectual movements for their volumes, as well as lists of further readings. Work on the series as a whole is coordinated at the Bruccoli Clark Layman editorial center in Columbia, South Carolina, where the editorial staff is responsible for accuracy of the published volumes.

One feature that distinguishes *DLB* is the illustration policy – its concern with the iconography of literature. Just as an author is influenced by his surroundings, so is the reader's understanding of the author enhanced by a knowledge of his environment. Therefore *DLB* volumes include not only drawings, paintings, and photographs of authors, often depicting them at various stages in their careers, but also illustrations of their families and places where they lived. Title pages are regularly reproduced in facsimile along with dust jackets for modern authors. The dust jackets are a special feature. of *DLB* because they often document better than anything else the way in which an author's work was perceived in its own time. Specimens of the writers' manuscripts are included when feasible.

Samuel Johnson rightly decreed that "The chief glory of every people arises from its authors." The purpose of the *Dictionary of Literary Biography* is to compile literary history in the surest way available to us – by accurate and comprehensive treatment of the lives and work of those who contributed to it.

The *DLB* Advisory Board

Introduction

The two volumes of the *Dictionary of Literary Biography* that treat British literary publishers from 1821 to 1965, *DLB 106* and *DLB 112*, include in their titles the phrase *British Literary Publishing Houses*. *Publishing house*, is, however, too specialized and modern an expression for the subjects of the present volume. The book trade in the early part of the period covered here – 1700 to 1820 – still included many people who combined the functions of printer, bookseller, and publisher, but the publishing picture was about to change significantly. Changes in the book trade, such as an increase in the number of printers, improvements in distribution systems, and specialization and cooperation in printing and publishing, as well as larger changes in Britain in general, such as the rise in readership produced by an improved education system, and the increased mechanization of production that constituted the industrial revolution, made the publishing industry at the end of the period a much different world than it had been just over a century before. That world – the world of 1700 – would have been quite familiar to a printer of the early sixteenth century.

The period 1700 to 1820 was a time of transition for the British book trade that saw the emergence of some of the great names of the trade, including Longman, Murray, and Collins; but it was also a time when publishing firms most often were still controlled by single individuals, who, like independent publishers today, made judgments based on literary merit, political alliances and pressures, friendships, or the prospect of high profits. Some of the people treated in this volume got rich, some died paupers; many led adventurous lives, a few suffered tormented ones; and most participated in the production of some of the best-known works in British literature.

This volume is not a comprehensive dictionary of the eighteenth-century and early–nineteenth century British book trade; there were far too many figures active in various capacities in the trade to include all of them here. What is presented here is a selective cross section of members of the literary book trade, from large publishers such as William

Strahan and Archibald Constable to lesser-known figures such as John Almon and James Roberts. As in *DLB 106* and *DLB 112*, a broad definition has been adopted for the term *literary*, and there has been an attempt to include representative specialists such as William Lane's Minerva Press for popular fiction, Robert Foulis for scholarly editions of the classics, Thomas Davies for theatrical books, William Blake for artistically innovative editions of his own works, John Newbery and William Godwin for children's books, and Horace Walpole's Strawberry Hill Press for publications of the private rather than commercial press. The volume also includes publishers, such as William Blackwood, John Murray, and Smith, Elder, whose greatest periods of activity took place later than 1800: they are found here because their firms had begun operations by 1820 and so were not included in *DLB 106* or *DLB 112*. Still other printers and publishers, such as Jacob Tonson and the university presses at Oxford and Cambridge, were quite active and influential in the eighteenth century but were already in operation in 1700. These figures are not found here but will be included in a future *DLB* volume covering the pre-eighteenth century British literary book trade, along with an entry on the Stationers' Company of London.

The book trade in Britain evolved slowly. When William Caxton brought printing to England in 1476, some twenty years after the Gutenberg Bible was published, Caxton himself combined the functions of printer, publisher, and bookseller, as well as author, editor, and translator. Caxton and his contemporaries worked in small shops, using individually founded movable type, single sheets of hand-produced paper, and bindings that were also made by hand, one at a time. A British printer of the early 1700s such as Benjamin Motte Jr. worked in exactly the same way. By the 1820s printing and publishing were becoming mechanized, with increasing use of machine-made paper, improved and automated presses, and cloth bindings mass-produced by machine. While most early printer-publishers were not nearly as literate as Caxton, the pattern established in the fifteenth century of a publisher acting also as printer and seller remained the dominant one in England for some time to come. In 1700 it was still likely that a printer was also engaged in book-related activities other than printing. Printers such as Samuel Richardson and George Faulkner often acted as publishers, assuming some or all of the financial risk of publications that they or others were producing, and they might also participate in the sales of other books and pamphlets. Many booksellers stocked a variety of new books, and it was certainly not unknown for printers such as Foulis or James Edwards to deal in antiquarian books as well. The involvement of Edwards and his family in the binding trade demonstrates how closely related bookbinding was to the activities of printing and publishing: today the bookbindings of Edwards of Halifax are far better known than most of his many publications.

Like Caxton and other earlier bookmen, literary publishers of the eighteenth and early nineteenth centuries were also attracted by the pleasures and rewards of authorship, and one does not have to search far to find examples. Richardson's first composition, *The Apprentice's Vade Mecum; Or, Young Man's Pocket Companion,* was produced by his own press in 1733 and followed by a succession of works including *Pamela* (1740), *Familiar Letters* (1741), *Pamela II* (1741), *Clarissa* (1747), and *Sir Charles Grandison* (1753–1754). Almon's political pamphlets, Davies's theatrical biographies, Robert Dodsley's poetry, Lane's fictional works, the children's books published by Godwin and Newbery, and the beautiful books written and published by Blake and Walpole all serve as evidence that this involvement in both authorship and production was still flourishing several centuries after Caxton.

The apparent simplicity of the traditional arrangement, in which an author also acts as printer and/or publisher, was by the early 1700s increasingly becoming the exception rather than the rule. One motivation for Richardson's interest in printing and publishing his own works was to prevent their control by booksellers. He joined the Society for the Encouragement of Learning, founded in 1736 to print works that other London publishers would not produce. Likewise, Richardson's involvement in editing, printing, and publishing periodicals, and that of Ralph Griffiths in the *Monthly Review,* Constable in the *Edinburgh Review,* and Murray and Blackwood later in the period, provided secure and dependable sources of work and revenues.

One indication of the complexity of publishing and selling arrangements in this transitional period is evidenced by the imprints on the title pages of many eighteenth-century books and pamphlets. The long lists of names of publishers and booksellers look much like the "tombstone" announcements that fill today's financial press. The imprint of the first edition of Samuel Johnson's *A Dictionary of the English Language* (1755) reads "Printed by W. Strahan, For J. and P. Knapton; T. and T. Longman; C. Hitch and L. Hawes; A. Millar; and R. and J. Dodsley," while the 1783 edition of *The Works of Henry Fielding* was "Printed for W. Strahan, J. Rivington and Sons, S. Crowder, T. Longman, J. Robson, C. Dilly, G. Kearsley, G. Robinson, T. Cadell, T. Lowndes, R. Baldwin, W. Cater, G. Nicoll, S. Bladon, J. Murray, W. Flexney, T. Evans, W. Otridge, J. Sewell, W. Lane, J. Bowen, & W. Fox." Dodsley shared publications with at least sixty-nine London, Oxford, and Cambridge booksellers. A cooperative of forty London booksellers was organized in 1777 to publish a new edition of Johnson's *Lives of the Most Eminent English Poets* (1781), successfully negotiating with the previous copyright owners as well as with Johnson, the engravers, paper suppliers, and printers.

Imprint statements reveal much about cooperation among book-trade members, but records of the valuation of literary properties found in business accounts and personal correspondence, and especially in trade sale catalogues, are even more telling. Whereas formerly only whole or remaining publishers' and booksellers' stocks were offered for sale, by the mid 1700s the sale of parts of current stocks and shares of literary properties was commonplace. In one 1757 trade sale, for example, James Rivington offered a 1/32 share of Tobias Smollett's *The Adventures of Roderick Random* (1748) and half of a 3/32 share of Daniel Defoe's *Robinson Crusoe* (1719). With publishers facing increased costs, as well as the threat of piracy (publication of unauthorized editions), spreading the risk through cooperative ventures became more commonplace. Publishers had regularly cooperated before, but beginning in the 1680s these arrangements became more frequent and much more extensive. John Feather has written about the operation of the "congers" – groups of book-trade members who banded together for mutual benefit in ownership of copyrights, printing, and wholesaling. The membership of a conger could change with each title or transaction. Various-sized shares in publications were bought and sold, and not only did such arrangements allow the publication of titles that might have been too expensive for many publishers to pay for themselves, but they also decreased the likelihood that a pirated edition could be easily distributed.

Another device much used to lessen the financial risk of a publication was publication by subscription, which allowed the publisher to gauge the market and recover some of the costs before the work was published. The lists of subscribers included in such works provide valuable material for scholars.

While London had been the center of British printing and publishing since Caxton established his press in Westminster, by 1557, when the Stationers' Company of the City of London was incorporated, printing had been introduced into Scotland and Ireland, and there had also been limited printing activity in a few English towns. For more than a century, however, the officially chartered Stationers' Company effectively limited printing to London, Oxford, and Cambridge. But a diminishing of the prominence of printer-publishers and a corresponding ascendance of bookseller-publishers within the Stationers' Company, coinciding with government deregulation of the press and the development of the notion of author copyright, caused the power of the London company to wane in the late seventeenth century. With the final lapse in 1695 of the Licensing Act governing printing came a greater spirit of entrepreneurship, a much wider variety of publications, and increased activity by the provincial press.

Most indicative of this new variety was the periodical. Journals and newspapers became increasingly important in the book trade, and many of the entries in this volume demonstrate the deep involvement of printers and publishers in the periodical press, from Griffiths with the *Monthly Review* to Richardson with the *True Briton.* The turbulent politics of the period, coupled with intense business and personal rivalries, ensured a steady supply of political and literary magazines filled with government support or satire, flagrant and subtle personal attacks, and a great deal of good writing about the news and culture of the day. Such periodicals provided an outlet for the opinions of the publisher (as well as the publisher's friends) and provided regular work for printing houses. Attacks on the government, however, often brought on the suppression of the offending publications, producing financial hardship and temporary loss of liberty for those involved. The careers of Almon and William Bingley reveal the tribulations of the crusading periodical publisher. Not all of the period's periodicals were controversial: Joseph Johnson started the *London Medical Journal* in 1783, as well as other journals that addressed theology and literature, and Newbery started the *Lilliputian Magazine,* the first children's periodical in England, in 1751.

It was not until the eighteenth century that improved communication and transportation allowed the provincial press to thrive. One of the staples of the provincial press, as well as of many London printers and publishers, was the newspaper. The year 1702 saw the publication in London of the *Daily Courant,* the first daily newspaper, and also of the first regular newspaper outside London; by 1760 some 150 newspapers had appeared.

A great deal of research has been done on British publishing history by scholars in many disciplines, but there is much more to do. The papers of only a few members of the trade survive, and many of the standard surveys of printing and studies of the work of individuals during the period are out of date. There are, however, some positive recent developments. The *English Short Title Catalog* (*ESTC*), which includes titles from 1475–1700 and is available online through the Research Libraries Information Network (RLIN), has made routine a variety of research activities that could easily have consumed decades before its establishment. With this database one can trace the appearance of individual names in imprints or establish a chronology of printing activity by publisher or location. It is also fortunate for researchers that *The Bowyer Ledgers* – the extensive records of the printing business of the father and son William Bowyer – have finally been published. Covering most of the eighteenth century, these ledgers, edited by Keith Maslen and John Lancaster and published jointly in 1991 by the Bibliographical Society and the Bibliographical Society of America, make possible the detailed study of the production of several thousand imprints of the period. It is to be hoped that the surviving ledgers of the printer William Strahan will also be made available. Together with the forthcoming revision of *The New Cambridge Bibliography of English Literature,* with its sections on printing and the book trade, and the cooperatively produced *History of the Book in Britain* that is well under way, these sources will spur further research into eighteenth-century British printing, publishing, and reading.

Acknowledgments

This book was produced by Bruccoli Clark Layman, Inc. Karen L. Rood is senior editor for *The Dictionary of Literary Biography* series. Philip B. Dematteis was the in-house editor.

Production coordinator is James W. Hipp. Photography editor is Bruce Andrew Bowlin. Photographic copy work was performed by Joseph M.

Bruccoli. Layout and graphics supervisor is Penney L. Haughton. Copyediting supervisor is Laurel M. Gladden. Typesetting supervisor is Kathleen M. Flanagan. Systems manager is George F. Dodge. Julie E. Frick is editorial associate. The production staff includes George Anderson, Phyllis A. Avant, Charles D. Brower, Ann M. Cheschi, Melody W. Clegg, Patricia Coate, Denise Edwards, Joyce Fowler, Stephanie C. Hatchell, Erica Hennig, Rebecca Mayo, Kathy Lawler Merlette, Jeff Miller, Pamela D. Norton, Laura S. Pleicones, Emily R. Sharpe, William L. Thomas Jr., Jonathan B. Watterson, and Jennie Williamson.

Walter W. Ross and Robert S. McConnell did library research. They were assisted by the following librarians at the Thomas Cooper Library of the University of South Carolina: Linda Holderfield and the interlibrary-loan staff; reference-department head Virginia Weathers; reference librarians Marilee Birchfield, Stefanie Buck, Cathy Eckman, Rebecca Feind, Jill Holman, Karen Joseph, Jean Rhyne, Kwamine Washington, and Connie Widney; circulation-department head Caroline Taylor; and acquisitions-searching supervisor David Haggard.

Dictionary of Literary Biography® • Volume One Hundred Fifty-Four

The British Literary Book Trade, 1700–1820

Dictionary of Literary Biography

John Almon

(London: 1763 – 1805)

Champion of the freedom of the press and unrivaled as the chief opposition bookseller of the second half of the eighteenth century, John Almon was born in Liverpool on 17 December 1737 to John and Isabella Almon. His father joined the navy in 1743 and was apparently lost at sea; his mother died in a shipwreck in 1744 while returning from a visit to her in-laws in Ireland. Almon and his only surviving sibling (three others had died in infancy), his twelve-year-old brother Francis, went to live with their grandmother in Lancashire, where Almon probably received his education at Warrington. When Almon was fourteen, his brother disappeared on a voyage to the West Indies and was given up for dead. In March 1751 Almon was apprenticed to the Liverpool bookseller, binder, and printer Robert Williamson, who is best known for his *Liverpool Advertiser and Mercantile Chronicle.*

In September 1758 Almon left Liverpool and toured the Continent; in 1759 he settled in London, where he married Elizabeth Jackson on 27 October 1760. During these years he worked as a journeyman printer for one of the most important printing houses in the city, that of John Watts in Wild Court, Lincoln's Inn Fields. (Watts had lent William Caslon money to start his great foundry and had once employed Benjamin Franklin.)

Almon was frequently employed as a political pamphleteer. His first acknowledged work, *The Conduct of a Late Noble Commander Examined* (1759), went through two editions. It dealt with the alleged cowardice of Lord George Sackville during the August 1759 battle of Minden, where Sackville repeatedly delayed executing orders for the British cavalry to advance against the French. Almon's work is believed to have influenced public opinion toward Sackville, who was court-martialed the following year.

Charles Green Say, the printer and proprietor of the liberal journal *Gazetteer,* needed a writer to compete with Oliver Goldsmith, who was contributing to the *Public Ledger.* Say hired Almon in January 1761 to write political letters under such signatures as "Independent Whig" and "Lucius."

Precisely at the point when Almon began writing, the country was about to undergo one of its most politically chaotic periods. The decade following the accession of George III in 1760 was marked by many ministerial changes. William Pitt, having conducted the Seven Years' War brilliantly, wanted to continue the hostilities; but John Stuart, third earl of Bute, the king's favorite, who had become secretary of state in 1761, insisted on negotiating an end to the war. When Pitt and his brother-in-law, Richard Grenville, first earl Temple, learned that peace was at hand, they resigned on 5 October 1761.

Almon championed Pitt's cause in his *Review of Mr. Pitt's Administration* (1762), which ran through five editions and was translated into French and German. Almon's career as a political bookseller began when his chronicle of Pitt's activities aroused the interest of the wealthy politician to whom it was dedicated, Lord Temple, whose chief delight was to stir up faction. Almon, ever eager to capitalize on his opportunities, aligned his interests squarely with Temple's. As Robert Rea puts it in *The English Press in Politics 1760–1774* (1963), the "same press which made Temple a factor to be reckoned with in politics enabled John Almon to become a country gentleman." Until he met Temple, Almon was just another hack journalist; after making Temple's acquaintance he started to emerge as a significant political writer and publisher. Almon's association with Temple would end only with Temple's death in 1779. Through Temple, Almon met such powerful members of the opposition as Pitt; Thomas Pelham-Holles, first duke of Newcastle; and Charles Watson-Wentworth, second marquis of Rockingham.

In the fall of 1763 Temple and other prominent Whigs helped Almon establish himself at 178

3

John Wilkes, the radical politician whose association with John Almon led to the publisher's first trial for libel; engraving by W. Dickenson after a drawing by R. E. Pine

Piccadilly, across from Burlington House, where Almon converted the ground floor of his dwelling into a bookshop. Situated so advantageously, Almon soon became London's chief opposition publisher and his shop an important center for opposition activity.

Almon's business increased significantly as he began to publish works by important eighteenth-century figures such as Temple, Charles Townshend, Horace Walpole, Christopher Smart, George Grenville, William Knox, John Hall Stevenson, Charles Lloyd, and John Wilkes. Within a year of establishing his bookshop Almon, through Temple's influence, was appointed official bookseller to what was soon to become one of the most important opposition groups, the Coterie, the Whig club that met at Wildman's Tavern on Albermarle Street.

Temple introduced Almon to Wilkes just when Wilkes was becoming increasingly radical. Almon and Wilkes would be the best of friends

until Wilkes's death in 1797, and Almon's publishing activities on behalf of Wilkes were extensive.

In 1763 Wilkes used his private press to print number 45 of his journal, the *North Briton,* in which he attacked George III for showing "blind favour and partiality," and to print *An Essay on Woman,* the pornographic takeoff on Alexander Pope's *An Essay on Man* (1733–1734) that is generally attributed to Thomas Potter. Wilkes was charged with both seditious and obscene libel. *A Letter to J. Kidgell Containing a Full Answer to His Narrative* (1763), Almon's response to the Reverend John Kidgell's pamphlet attack on *An Essay on Woman,* charged that by publishing extracts of the work, Kidgell had made public a work that had been intended for a private audience.

Wilkes was convicted of both charges; when he failed to appear at his sentencing because he had been wounded in a duel, he was expelled from Parliament and declared an outlaw. In late December 1763 he fled to France. Shortly thereafter Almon

Wilkes in the Tower of London, June 1763, awaiting trial for seditious and obscene libel for material he published in his journal, the North Briton; *engraving by Bickham*

published *A Letter Concerning Libels* (1764), an examination of Wilkes's trial. There has been much conjecture about the identity of "Father of Candor," the pseudonymous author of *A Letter Concerning Libels;* but it was Almon who, as publisher of the tract, was prosecuted for libel. The pamphlet included lengthy arguments about two of the most controversial issues of the time, the legality of general warrants and the notion of libel as set out by William Murray, first earl of Mansfield, the lord chief justice. The tract also called into question Mansfield's alteration of a passage in the record of Wilkes's trial.

Almon's trial began on 1 May 1765. The defense contended that it was prejudicial to dispense with a jury and try Almon before Mansfield's colleagues. Due to a technicality the trial was delayed, and in July 1765, when Rockingham took office as prime minister, the charges were dropped.

Realizing that public support was essential if Wilkes was to obtain a pardon, Almon made sure that he was not forgotten at home. In May 1767 Almon published the first number of the *Political Register,* a monthly vehicle for Wilkite propaganda that scored an instant success. Almon also republished Wilkes's *A Letter to His Grace the Duke of Grafton* (1767), an attempt to reestablish himself at the forefront of English politics that had originally been published in Paris in 1764. Although several papers printed extracts, Almon published a fuller (though by no means complete) version, which placed him in considerable danger of prosecution.

On 19 December 1769 the thirty-fifth in a series of letters to the king written under the pseudonym "Junius" appeared in Henry Sampson Woodfall's *Public Advertiser.* In this letter Junius not only criticized the policies and conduct of the king but went so far as to recommend that he be deposed. Although the letter was reprinted in nearly every newspaper and magazine in the nation, the attorney general pressed libel charges against only six

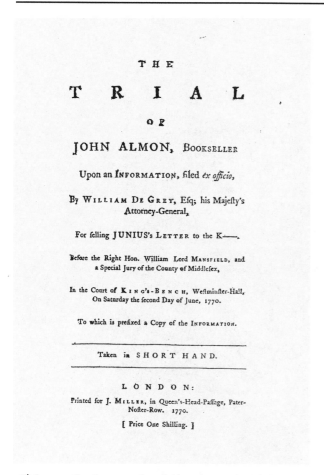

THE

T R I A L

O F

JOHN ALMON, BOOKSELLER

Upon an INFORMATION, filed *ex officio,*

By WILLIAM DE GREY, Efq; his Majefty's
Attorney-General,

For felling JUNIUS's LETTER to the K——.

Before the Right Hon. William Lord MANSFIELD, and
a Special Jury of the County of Middlefex,

In the Court of KING's-BENCH, Weftminfter-Hall,
On Saturday the fecond Day of June, 1770.

To which is prefixed a Copy of the INFORMATION.

Taken in SHORT HAND.

LONDON:

Printed for J. MILLER, in Queen's-Head-Paffage, Pater-
Nofter-Row. 1770.

[Price One Shilling.]

*Title page for the transcript of Almon's second trial for libel,
in which he was convicted*

publishers, of whom only Almon was convicted. Almon was tried on 2 June 1770 in the Court of King's Bench before Lord Mansfield. In libel trials the jury was limited to deciding whether the innuendo – in this case, that "K---" represented *King* – would be readily apparent to the average reader and whether the defendant published the work in question; only the court was empowered to determine whether the defendant was guilty of libel. Both sides agreed that the letter contained sufficiently clear innuendo; but Sergeant Glynn, Almon's lawyer, argued that John Miller, the printer of the *London Museum,* had inserted his client's name on the magazine's imprint without Almon's knowledge. Miller confirmed this contention in an affidavit.

The most important aspect of the crown's case against Almon was based on the principle that sale was equivalent to publication. Glynn argued that the offending magazine had been supplied to Almon's shop by Miller and sold by a servant, all unbeknownst to Almon, but Mansfield instructed the jury to disregard Almon's intention, to hold him responsible for his servant's actions, and to consider sale as tantamount to publication. After hearing unrefuted testimony that the magazine had been purchased at Almon's shop, the jury had no choice but to declare that the Junius letter contained an abundance of easily recognizable innuendo and that Almon had published it. Almon was, consequently, found guilty of libel.

Legally defining publication to include sale would make the bookseller accountable for the content of everything in his shop; as Almon complained in his *Memoirs of a Late Eminent Bookseller* (1790), it was "not in his power to read every book that is published." This responsibility would obviously have a bearing on the type of work that booksellers would be willing to sell and, consequently, on the kind of literature produced.

Almon was sentenced to pay a small fine and to put up eight hundred pounds to ensure his good behavior for two years. Almon realized that his sentence was meant to dictate the nature of his publications; as he said in his memoirs, "*that* was the sole object; for, if he will print no more political pamphlets, he suffers nothing from the sentence." Until the expiration of his sentence Almon devoted himself primarily to his popular literary collections, *The New Foundling Hospital for Wit: A Collection of Fugitive Pieces* (1768–1773) and *An Asylum for Fugitive Pieces* (1776–1779).

Almon's collections were compiled to disseminate political ideas in a lighthearted manner and an economical format. Since the literature in the collections is dependent on eighteenth-century politics, it has, for the most part, become obscure, even though much of it is by major eighteenth-century figures. For example, Almon's collections include Wilkes's "The Thane of Bute," Horace Walpole's "On Admiral Vernon," David Garrick's "Advice to the Marquis of Rockingham," and Thomas Gray's "Inscription for the Villa of a Decayed Statesman" (on Henry Fox, first Baron Holland) and "Jemmy Twitcher" (on John Montagu, fourth earl of Sandwich).

Thus, although Almon published few serious political works from 1770 to 1772, he retained a lively interest in politics. His role in reporting the debates in Parliament further demonstrates that he never fully relinquished his political activities during this time. Although the House of Commons had renewed its ban on publishing its proceedings in 1728 and had made its resolution more comprehensive in 1738, monthly magazines had continued printing the debates in transparently veiled form. But open defiance by newspapers began only in 1768, when Almon started anonymously reporting the debates in the *London Evening Post;* other papers quickly followed suit. In the "Printer's Case" of 1771 Almon was presented with the opportunity to press his view that Parliament had no right to prevent the publication of its proceedings. Parliament ordered the printers of eight London newspapers to appear before it, but Almon and Wilkes persuaded Miller, the printer of the *London Museum,* to disobey the summons. When a messenger arrived to take Miller into custody, Almon and Wilkes, by prearrangement with officials of the City of London, had the messenger arrested for assault. Several members of Parliament who were also magistrates announced that if any messengers were brought before them under similar circumstances, they would imprison the messengers. Parliament was finally forced to allow publication of its debates.

In addition to his role in the Printer's Case, Almon filled a gap in the records of parliamentary proceedings by publishing a summary (1766–1775) that covers the period from 1742, when Richard Chandler's reports end, until 1774, after which Almon's monthly *Parliamentary Register* (1775–1780) begins.

In the summer of 1767 Almon had published the first English edition of *The Examination of Doctor Benjamin Franklin, Relative to the Repeal of the American Stamp Act,* an account of Franklin's testimony of 13 February 1766 before the House of Commons. In 1774 Franklin persuaded Almon to publish *An Appeal to the Justice and Interests of the People of Great Britain in the Present Dispute with America,* a work attributed to Arthur Lee. Franklin also encouraged fellow colonists to send tracts to Almon to be reprinted in England. In addition, Franklin, along with Lee and William Bollan, authenticated Almon's version of the petition to the crown from the Continental Congress over a rival edition. Almon also corresponded with the pro-American member of Parliament and political philosopher Edmund Burke, supplying Burke with intelligence gleaned from his dealings with American printers. In 1777 Almon collected and published *The Letters of Valens.* These pieces, which had appeared in the *London Post* in 1775–1776, discussed affairs in Ireland and America and condemned Britain's attempt to retain the American colonies. Almon later attributed them to Burke's brother Richard, with the assistance of Edmund and their other brother, William. Almon also published *Substance of the Speeches Made in the House of Commons* (1779), a summary of Burke's first speech

THE

FUGITIVE MISCELLANY.

BEING A

COLLECTION of such

FUGITIVE PIECES,

In PROSE and VERSE, as are not in any other Collection.

With many PIECES never before publiſhed.

LONDON:

Printed for J. ALMON, oppoſite Burlington-houſe, in Piccadilly.

M.DCC.LXXIV.

Title page for one of the literary collections edited by Almon

on economic reform. From 1775 to 1784 he published the journal the *Remembrancer* to preserve ephemeral documents related to the American Revolution.

In June 1781 the Almons moved to Hertfordshire because of Elizabeth Almon's ill health. John Debrett, who at one point had been Almon's partner, bought his business. Elizabeth Jackson Almon died on 31 August 1781. In September 1784 Almon returned to London and married the widow of William Parker, who had been the owner and printer of the *General Advertiser.* Almon took over the paper, establishing his business at 183 Fleet Street. He served as a city councilman from 1784 to 1786.

Almon courted both the government and the opposition, receiving subsidies for his paper from both. It was not long, however, before he published two libels on William Pitt the Younger in the *General Advertiser,* thereby announcing his support for the opposition. Pitt sued Almon, who was assessed a comparatively small fine.

Almon's probable purpose in libeling Pitt was to ingratiate himself with the politician Charles James Fox. He was successful in doing so, and from 1787 to 1789 he received subsidies from the Foxite Whigs. Taking their part by arguing for the Prince of Wales's claims to an immediate regency, Almon was again tried for libel in 1788 for remarks concerning the king's insanity that had appeared in the *General Advertiser.* After his conviction he sold his paper, declared bankruptcy, and fled from London. He was outlawed for failing to appear for sentencing. Almon's whereabouts from 1789 until 1792 are uncertain; his memoirs were written and published while he was being sought as an outlaw, and revealing specific information would have been dangerous. During this period Almon also wrote *Anecdotes of the Life of the Right Hon. William Pitt, Earl of Chatham* (1792), apparently to appease the younger Pitt. After the publication of this work Almon surrendered; he was held in the King's Bench Prison from March 1792 to April 1793, when the outlawry charge was reversed.

Almon spent his remaining years in Box Moor and never resumed his bookselling and printing activities. He also withdrew from the current political scene, returning to earlier concerns. His *Biographical, Literary, and Political Anecdotes,* published in three volumes in 1797, feature previously unpublished pieces on such friends, acquaintances, and enemies as Temple; Mansfield; Townshend; Franklin; Burke; Grenville; David Hartley; Augustus Henry Fitzroy, third duke of Grafton; Sir Charles Pratt, first earl of Camden; and Josiah Wedgwood.

During this period Almon also compiled the first complete collection of Wilkes's letters, *Correspondence of the Late John Wilkes, with his Friends, Printed from the Original Manuscripts, in Which Are Introduced Memoirs of his Life* (1805). Almon worked quickly on the project since he had reason to believe that a rival edition was being contemplated.

Almon had published one of the first collections of the Junius letters near the beginning of his career; as his final venture he compiled *The Letters of Junius* (1806), a complete edition of the works of the notorious satirist. Like so many others of his day, Almon attempted to identify Junius, whom he vigor-ously contended was the Irish essayist Hugh Macaulay Boyd. Basing his work on Woodfall's edition of 1772 and adding letters to which Junius had responded, Almon edited, annotated, and wrote a preliminary essay for his collection. Almon did not live to see the publication of his edition; he died at Box Moor on 12 December 1805.

References:

John Almon, *Memoirs of a Late Eminent Bookseller* (London, 1790; facsimile reprint, New York: Garland, 1974);

Terry Belanger, "A Directory of the London Book Trade, 1766," *Publishing History,* 1 (1977): 7–48;

Robert Haig, *The Gazetteer 1735–1797* (Carbondale: Southern Illinois University Press, 1960);

"Mr. Almon," *Public Characters of 1803–1804,* 6 (1804): 120–138;

"Obituary, with Anecdotes of Remarkable Persons," *Gentleman's Magazine,* 75 (December 1805): 1179–1180;

Robert Rea, "Bookseller as Historian," *Indiana Quarterly for Bookmen,* 5 (1949): 75–95;

Rea, *The English Press in Politics 1760–1774* (Lincoln: University of Nebraska Press, 1963);

Rea, "John Almon: Bookseller to John Wilkes," *Indiana Quarterly for Bookmen,* 4 (1948): 20–28;

Deborah D. Rogers, *Bookseller as Rogue: John Almon and the Politics of Eighteenth-Century Publishing* (New York: Peter Lang, 1986);

George Rudé, *Hanoverian London 1714–1808* (Los Angeles: University of California Press, 1971);

Peter D. G. Thomas, "The Beginning of Parliamentary Reporting in Newspapers, 1768–1774," *English Historical Review,* 74 (October 1959): 623–636;

Thomas, "John Wilkes and the Freedom of the Press (1771)," *Bulletin of the Institute of Historical Research,* 33 (May 1960): 86–98;

Lucyle Werkmeister, *The London Daily Press, 1772–1797* (Lincoln: University of Nebraska Press, 1963).

Papers:

John Almon's papers are at the British Library, the Perkins Library of Duke University, and the New York Historical Society.

– Deborah D. Rogers

William Bingley

(London: 1767 – 1783)

Radical Wilkite printers and publishers active in London from the late 1760s through the middle of the 1770s included John Almon, the publisher of the periodical *London Museum* and of several of John Wilkes's works; William George Edmunds, one of the printers and publishers of the radical *Middlesex Journal* during its early months from late 1769 through early 1770; Isaac Fell, the publisher of *Freeholder's Magazine,* begun in late 1769, who was also involved in the *Middlesex Journal;* John Wheble, the printer of the *Middlesex Journal* after June 1770; John Miller, the printer of the *London Evening Post;* and Henry Sampson Woodfall, proprietor of the *Public Advertiser,* who printed the Junius letters. All of these men frequently faced harassment and prosecution at the hands of George III's ministers for publishing materials the government considered libelous or for printing the debates of the House of Commons, which that body had traditionally forbidden. But it is doubtful that any of these printers and publishers exhibited more courage in defending the freedom of the press, or paid a higher price for doing so, than did William Bingley. He was sent to prison for nearly two years for refusing to reveal the sources of material he published, and he suffered more financial hardship than perhaps any other radical publisher of the Wilkite years. By refusing to bow to the pressure of the court Bingley set an example for others who, though sometimes doubtful of his wisdom, never questioned his dedication to his principles.

Bingley was born in 1738 in New Romney, Kent. No information seems to have survived about his apprenticeship or training; the first trace of his work as a London bookseller and publisher comes in 1767, when his name is found in the imprint of Joseph Phipps's *Observations on a Late Anonymous Publication, Intituled, A Letter to the Author of a Letter to Dr. Formey, Etc., in Vindication of R. Barclay, and the Principles of the People Called Quakers.* Phipps wrote several tracts in defense of the Quakers, and Robert Barclay was a seventeenth-century Quaker apologist; whether Bingley had a particular interest in the sect is not known. The first of his several periodicals that attacked abuses of power, the *Monitor; or, Green-Room Laid Open,* appeared on 17 October 1767; in its second number, for 24 October, the title was changed to the *Theatrical Monitor.* Though the first two issues came out on consecutive weeks, the *Theatrical Monitor* was later published on an occasional basis; it concluded with number 18 on 16 April 1768. Bingley was only associated with the first fifteen numbers of the periodical; after the fifteenth was published on 5 March 1768, Samuel Bladon took over as publisher. The *Theatrical Monitor* focused on the analogy between theater and politics and exposed the venal hack writers who prostituted themselves to the theater powers. Hugh Kelly and his newspaper, the *Public Ledger,* were attacked in the *Theatrical Monitor* in 1767 for supporting David Garrick and the London theater establishment.

Bingley's next project soon turned out to be the source of his contemporary fame as well as the cause of private misery: publishing the new series of the *North Briton,* possibly the most significant political periodical of its time. Wilkes had started the journal in 1762 (its first number appeared on 5 June) to oppose the politics of John Stuart, third Earl of Bute, the king's favorite, who had become secretary of state in 1761. Bold in its opposition, the *North Briton* went too far when Wilkes in number 45, published on 23 April 1763, accused the monarch of showing "blind favour and partiality." George III's ministers obtained a general warrant directing officers to seize the "Authors, Printers & Publishers of a Seditious, & Treasonable Paper intitled, The North Briton, Number 45." Wilkes fled to France on 24 December 1763. Expelled from Parliament and found guilty of libel, Wilkes remained in exile, except for two brief visits to test the political waters in 1766, before returning to England for good in February 1768.

When Bingley published the first number of what he termed "Part II" of the *North Briton* on 10 May 1768, the tensions caused by Wilkes's return to the political arena were running high. Wilkes had been elected member of Parliament for Middlesex earlier in the spring and had voluntarily submitted to the courts so that the legal actions stemming from *North Briton* number 45 might be brought to a conclusion. But the lord chief justice, William Murray, first Earl of Mansfield, refused to pass judgment; and the

O! Liberty thou choicest treasure,
Seat of Virtue, source of pleasure,
Life without thee knows no blessing,
No endearment worth possessing.

William Bingley (Courtesy of Providence Public Library)

king was adamant that Wilkes not be seated in Parliament, which met on the very day issue number 47, the first of Bingley's new series of the *North Briton,* was published. By denying Wilkes bail Mansfield kept him from attending Parliament, which would soon adjourn until the fall. The fiftieth number of the *North Briton,* for 28 May 1768, was an open letter to Mansfield, rebuking him for his treatment of Wilkes. The writer claimed that the recent unrest in the city of London had been caused by Mansfield's lack of "lenity and indulgence" toward Wilkes, who had made many efforts to placate the ministry and had tried to calm his angry followers, and condemned Mansfield for blatantly favoring the court position.

In early June, William De Grey, the attorney general, secured an attachment against Bingley for both numbers 50 and 51, the latter because it defended the charges leveled against Mansfield in number 50 and further maintained that Mansfield might consider the truth itself a "scandalous libel." By 12 June, Bingley had been committed to Newgate Prison. On 23 August, Mansfield set the ab-

surdly high bond of twelve hundred pounds. Unable to raise bond and refusing steadfastly to answer interrogatories concerning numbers 50 and 51, Bingley languished in Newgate until he was removed to King's Bench Prison on 7 November. Desperate, Bingley submitted to the House of Lords a closely argued appeal of some twelve pages, probably written with the assistance of counsel, asking for release from prison and a jury trial. The petition, which forms the bulk of *North Briton* 75, for 12 November 1768, was unsuccessful.

There is some evidence that Bingley was released for brief periods, and it was perhaps during those times that he was able to attend to his business ventures. While still in Newgate he launched the *Constitutional Magazine; or Weekly Treasure of Politics and Literature,* which made its first appearance in late July 1768. An advertisement in *North Briton* number 60, for 6 August, noted that the second number of the *Constitutional* was available and that if the subscribers did not approve of the work, their money would be refunded. The seventh number was advertised in *North Briton* number 71, for 22 October 1768, where it was stated that the *Constitutional* was now a monthly that cost one shilling. Essays and letters expressing a radical viewpoint on political issues comprised much of the fare of the journal.

In *North Briton* number 81, for 23 December 1768, Bingley published an address to the public in which he responded to "maliciously propagated" charges that he had submitted to interrogatories that had compromised Wilkes. He traced these charges to the *Public Ledger,* a key pro-George III organ edited by his old enemy, Kelly. Bingley printed in *North Briton* number 91, for 18 February 1769, an oath that he had not submitted, nor would he submit, to interrogatories "without torture." The statement was reprinted in several London newspapers, suggesting that Bingley's fellow printers and publishers understood the importance to the freedom of the press of Bingley's stance.

In number 92, for 21 February, Bingley advertised his folio edition of the original *North Briton,* which excluded the notorious number 45. The edition was available only to subscribers, at a cost of ten shillings sixpence. The advertisement promised that the subscriber list would be kept "as secret as possible," an indication of the fear that permeated the London radical community during Wilkes's imprisonment.

Having failed in his appeal to the Lords, Bingley addressed a petition to the House of Commons that was printed on 11 May 1769 in *North Briton* number 106. Bingley complained that he ought not to be forced to incriminate himself nor be "compelled to become an informer" and asked that the House of Commons not force him to "remain a perpetual prisoner without a trial, conviction, or sentence." Bingley's effort was again ineffectual, but as political propaganda these petitions must be viewed as small victories for the London radicals. Some sense of the financial hardship from which Bingley was suffering because of his imprisonment is indicated by a story in the *Daily Advertiser* for 18 June 1769 that mentions him being taken to the Court of Common Pleas for an action of debt.

Bingley had evidently developed a business relationship with John Meres sometime in the spring of 1769; the Meres family had been associated with London newspapers since the 1730s, and John Meres managed the *Daily Post* until 1772. Whether this relationship was a partnership cannot be ascertained, but Meres began to sell both the *North Briton* and the *Constitutional Magazine,* which printed its ninth number on 30 June; the fact that it had only appeared twice since October 1768 suggests that the periodical had not attracted a sufficient audience.

The tenth number was scheduled for publication on 1 August, at which time Bingley also promised to print an index to the magazine's first volume. Whether the index ever appeared is not clear, and the magazine itself seems to have suddenly disappeared.

North Briton number 128, for 30 September, advertised the appearance of a new evening paper, the *Independent Chronicle, or, Freeholders Evening Post,* to be published on Mondays, Wednesdays, and Fridays. In justifying the existence of another newspaper, Bingley claimed that "Never was there since the Revolution so interesting or so critical an epoch as the present. Party contest was never at so great a height at home; nor were ever the objects in dispute of such general importance – The debate is no less than our Liberties! our Constitution! our Property!" He went on to assure "all the friends of Liberty and the Constitution" that the paper's publishers "shall not fail . . . to watch over the invaluable rights and privileges of the subject. . . ." But in *North Briton* number 165, for 26 May 1770, Bingley charged that he had been betrayed by the "original Projectors" of the paper, who had turned out to be "Scotch Jacobites" instead of the defenders of liberty Bingley had thought them to be. By the seventh number, Bingley claimed, the paper, which he said was under the secret direction of "Guthrie and others of the same Jacobitical stamp," had shown its proprietors' true conservative ideology. Bingley believed that William Guthrie and Archibald Hamilton – editor and publisher, respectively, of the conservative *Critical Review* – were the real powers behind the *Independent Chronicle* and that he had been deceived and manipulated into publishing a work contrary to his own political beliefs. Nevertheless, Bingley vowed to carry on the paper himself.

The *Middlesex Journal* of 26–29 May 1770 announced Bingley's release from the King's Bench Prison, which occurred on 28 May. The reasons for his liberation are not clear; Bingley wrote in *North Briton* number 167, for 9 June, that his "sudden and unexpected release" had plunged him into his business, which he had found in "very great confusion." A report in the *Daily Advertiser* for 29 May described him as a bankrupt. While he was in prison his business had been located in the Strand, but after his release he published at 31 Newgate Street; it is not clear whether his financial difficulties influenced this move. Instead of pursuing his plan to continue the *Independent Chronicle,* and evidently undaunted by his financial troubles, Bingley announced a new paper, *Bingley's Journal; Or, The Universal Gazette,* which he intended to publish every Saturday. He hoped to gather all the "interesting particulars of every week" and present them from "one point of view," thus avoiding the "many contradictions that must necessarily happen in the publication of a daily paper." In the first number of *Bingley's Journal,* for 9 June 1770, Bingley advised his readers in the country to send their orders to the "clerks of the different Roads at the General Post-Office," showing that he was conscious of the need to establish a broad readership beyond the confines of London.

In a 16 June advertisement he vowed to avoid fictitious reports, claiming that in other newspapers there were "false rumours and fictitious articles of intelligence trumpt up, almost every day, by *stock-jobbers* and *others,* in order to carry on private views." He asserted that his new paper would avoid printing long postscripts, which in other papers were made lengthy by a paragraph writer employed to compose material stemming from the "fruits of his imagination only."

Whereas during his two years in the King's Bench Prison Bingley appears to have dealt exclusively with political publications, after his release he seemed ready to extend the scope of his business to nonpolitical subjects aimed at nonurban audiences. In *Bingley's Journal* for 23 June he advertised for two shillings, bound, an anonymous work titled *The Country-Man's Repository of Useful Knowledge,* which dealt with the management of cattle, sheep, horses, and rabbits. Also in June Bingley advertised the *Musical Magazine; or Compleat Pocket Companion.* This was the first mention of the magazine in any of Bingley's periodicals; two other men active in the London booktrade were listed as involved in its publication: Thomas Bennett, who printed and sold musical publications from his Holborn shop; and Thomas Simpson, an engraver and printseller in the Strand. By June 1770 the magazine had already begun its fourth volume; the first three volumes were also advertised for sale, as were individual back numbers. It is unclear how long Bingley's association with the periodical lasted; no further advertisements for it appeared in the *Journal.*

Meanwhile, *Bingley's Journal* itself was thriving. In the number for 7 July Bingley thanked the public for its support of his new periodical, giving special thanks to those who had provided "generous patronage." Throughout its early years the *Journal* lacked the kinds and amounts of revenue-producing advertising that sustained most London papers. The few advertisements the paper did print were for the publications of other radical booksellers, such as Almon; in no issue did there appear the advertisements for real estate, auctions, and consumer goods that supported the established newspapers. That the paper carried only rare references even to any of Bingley's own publications suggests that he was concentrating on periodicals rather than on books or pamphlets. The paper changed its title to *Bingley's Weekly Journal* beginning with number 10, for 11 August 1770, but in the 23 February/2 March 1771 number the newspaper announced that it would revert to the original title. Accompanying that change was a shift in policy: the paper would from then on not just depend on extracts from other journals but would also offer, when appropriate, "original matter." Bingley maintained that the success of the *Journal* had made this shift in policy possible, noting that the paper had "near Two Thousand Subscribers in different parts of Great Britain and Ireland." Henry Sampson Woodfall's *Public Advertiser* had a circulation of roughly three thousand at this time, but it was a daily and had been publishing for several years. Given the recent appearance of Bingley's paper, its extremely partisan political viewpoint, and its relative absence of advertising, one must conclude that it was a reasonably successful enterprise.

But financial hardships may have plagued Bingley through the winter of 1770–1771, for in its number for 22–24 January 1771 the radical *Middlesex Journal* had printed a notice of a 22 January meeting at which the Wilkite Society for the Supporters of the Bill of Rights (SSBR) had voted on the issue of whether to raise funds for other radicals, such as Bingley, who had suffered financially in the service of liberty or to confine its financial support to Wilkes. Among these distressed radical publishers Bingley received the most press attention during the debate, but the vote was won by those who wished to support Wilkes only. As a consequence, many of the principal subscribers to the SSBR withdrew. Bingley's financial stress, then, is one reason the London radical movement suffered some divisiveness in 1771–1772. In its 12–14 February number the *Middlesex Journal* noted that the SSBR had changed its mind and voted in favor of raising five hundred pounds for the support of Bingley; later it voted to support other radical publishers and printers. The issue of support for others besides Wilkes remained confusing through the spring of 1771, for in its 23–25 April number the *Middlesex Journal* listed members who left the society because of its exclusive support of Wilkes to found a new organization, the Constitutional Society, that was pledged to aid Bingley and others. That the radical movement split over this issue suggests that for some radicals Bingley's well-being was crucial.

In *North Briton* number 214, for 13 April 1771, Bingley announced the necessity of incorporating that paper into the *Journal*. He blamed the paper's decline on "corrupt and arbitrary Ministers" who wished to prevent its circulation: he was unable to distribute the *North Briton* as readily and as cheaply as newspapers were circulated because the postal authorities refused to classify it as a newspaper. He acknowledged support from the SSBR but claimed that his publication never had the "advantages of a number of opulent proprietors, whose purses might have in some measure indemnified the Publisher." He promised to maintain the "same intrepid spirit of independency, for which it hath been hitherto so eminently distinguished." On 11 May 1771, with number 218, the *North Briton* died as an independent publication.

The first number of the *North Briton* to be printed as part of the *Journal* appeared in the 11–18 May issue; it was an address to the king, criticizing him for having "given the reins of authority out of " his hands, suggesting that he had not yet assumed the true character of king but had engaged in "elegant trifling," and implying that he had often been misguided by bad ministers. But the *North Briton* did not endure in its new mode of presentation: the last number was printed in the *Journal* for 15–22 June. In the following issue Bingley announced that because a great many subscribers to the *Journal* disliked the inclusion of the *North Briton* and had, as a consequence, refused to take the paper, the *North Briton* would be discontinued for the future. The periodical's eclipse could no longer be attributed to ministerial opposition; rather the lengthy and often tediously argued essays that made up the bulk of the work were not suited to a newspaper audience, which wanted a greater variety of matter presented in a more concise form. Thus ended the run of one of the most important political periodicals published in the eighteenth century.

In the *Journal* for 3–10 August, Bingley reported his bankruptcy, the notice of which had first appeared in the 5 August number of the *London Gazette*. He assured his readers that the newspaper would carry on as before, and, indeed, it seemed unaffected by its publisher's second bankruptcy in little more than three years. On 3 September Bingley's effects, including beds, window curtains, books, stationery items, and the lease on his house at 31 Newgate Street, were sold, and on 20 September his creditors were paid and public notice given that his debts were absolved. In a brief notice to the readers in the 14–21 September number of the *Journal* Bingley noted that in the future the paper would

be published at a new address, number 80, at the corner of Bull-Head Court, where he would accept letters, but only those that were postpaid. In the 21–28 September issue Bingley announced another change of address for his business, to 3 Chapterally, St. Paul's Churchyard. Bingley once again shifted his business, as reported in the 23–30 November *Journal,* to Crane-Court, Fleet-Street, although the paper was still to be sold at 3 Chapterally.

In the 14–21 December issue Bingley announced his intention to publish an index to the *Journal;* that no such index seems to have been completed may indicate the degree of Bingley's financial stress, and in the same notice he reminded new readers who mailed in their subscriptions that they, not he, were "to pay the postage of the letters . . . or they would not be received." Such a policy of frugality had not been evident during the paper's earlier existence. Bingley took an unusual and creative step in the 4–11 January 1772 number when he began to list on the masthead booksellers in small towns throughout the country where the paper could be obtained.

The 25 January–1 February *Journal* printed a copy of Bingley's letter to Richard Oliver, treasurer of the Constitutional Society, thanking the society for its donation of five hundred pounds, half of which he had already received. He continued: "I know I should have received [the money] sooner but for the opposition of a gentleman from whom I had the least reason to expect it, because the publication of a paper in his defence, was the crime originally imputed to me, and which produced my punishment." The "gentleman" here accused of ingratitude was, of course, Wilkes himself.

Apart from the bitterness toward Wilkes, the letter to Oliver reflects defiance toward the court and its ministers, whom he accused of using "unjust power" against him. This defiance is accompanied by a sense that he had suffered not merely for himself but for all Englishmen. After acknowledging the suffering of his family caused by the government's attack on him, he places his case in a larger, more impersonal framework: "Nothwithstanding I rejoice in my sufferings, since my perserverance of refusal to submit to this dreadful and dangerous usurpation has exposed, and thereby most probably defeated, their attempt on the rights of Englishmen." Clearly, Bingley comprehended the historical significance of his role in defending the freedom of the press.

Yet the courage and defiance that enabled Bingley to resist the ministers of George III did not stand him in good stead when those traits brought

Caricature by William Hogarth of the radical politician John Wilkes on trial for libel for criticizing King George III in 1763 in his paper, the
North Briton. *Wilkes was tried after returning from exile in France in 1768; that same year Bingley started a "second series"*
of the North Briton *and was also charged with libel.*

him into conflict with his fellow London booksellers. Soon after his letter to Oliver, Bingley addressed booksellers in Great Britain, Ireland, and America, complaining of the "combination entered into by many of the booksellers of London, to raise the prices of books. . . ." Appearing on the front page of the *Journal* for 8–15 February, the notice may suggest why so few London booksellers ever advertised in his papers. They could not have been pleased by Bingley's accusing them of endangering "the liberty of the press" and of placing "an incumbrance on literature in general." Nor could they have been happy to read that Bingley would oppose their raising of prices by offering booksellers outside of London whatever they required at prices lower than those of his competitors: "I offer you my services, for ready money, to procure and remit you

such goods . . . for five per cent. agency, charging you, in every article, the same price as is paid by the retail trade of London." After Bingley's death John Nichols would write in his *Literary Anecdotes of the Eighteenth Century* (1812–1815) that Bingley possessed an "irritability of temper" and spent a good bit of time "making apologies for mistakes which a slight consideration would have prevented." Bingley's attack on his fellow London booksellers may not have been caused by irritability, but certainly a "slight consideration" might have prevented him from alienating them at a time when he needed all the friends he could muster.

Bingley's attempt to win election to the post of clerk to the London Commissioners of Land Tax on 24 April 1772 resulted in his not receiving a single vote. Later in the spring he seems to have formed some sort of alliance with S. Woodgate, a female publisher doing business near the Chapter Coffee-House in St. Paul's; Woodgate's address appeared on the masthead of the 13–20 June issue of the *Journal* as the paper's sole London retail outlet. In a front-page address to the public in the 22–29 August issue Bingley announced that since his bankruptcy of August 1771 his paper had been controlled by others; but now, because of the "liberality of some public spirited gentlemen, and the generosity of a very benevolent, though unknown friend, I have lately been enabled to re-purchase the property of my Journal; and indeed, it is the only property I am at present possessed of." The address goes on to rehearse yet again the persecution he had suffered at the hands of Lord Mansfield, whom he calls the "tyrannical Scotch Chief Justice," and laments the consequences of his unfair treatment, which has "reduced me from a comfortable independency, to the want of the necessaries of life, with an afflicted family." Now, however, Bingley says, he has the chance to improve his financial condition by augmenting the *Journal* with an additional sheet, or "Supplement," which will review new books and pamphlets, provide a digest of political and literary essays that have recently appeared elsewhere, and report the speeches and votes in Parliament. Perhaps mindful of his audience's hostility to the inclusion of the *North Briton,* Bingley reassures his readers that the *Journal* will not be altered and that the "Supplement" need not be ordered should any reader "think it either expensive or unnecessary." The entire paper, including the "Supplement," will cost "no more than one guinea per annum."

But in a "Postscript" for the issue of 3–10 October, Bingley decries what he terms the suppression of his "Supplement" by the General Post Office, which apparently refused to send it free, as other newspapers were sent, on the grounds that it did not qualify as a legitimate newspaper since it was not stamped. Bingley promises that he will attempt to convey the "Supplement" in another fashion, but evidently he was unsuccessful.

In the 5–12 December 1772 issue of the *Journal* Bingley proposed to resume the *Independent Chronicle,* the paper that he had published from September 1769 to May 1770 and that he charged had been secretly directed by "Scotch Jacobites." Bingley probably confused the readers of the *Journal* by saying: "As I have the orders of many gentlemen for the Supplement, had it continued, I shall take the liberty to discontinue the Journal at Christmas next, and send the Chronicle, twice a week, unless ordered to the contrary . . . ." Many readers wrote to protest the cessation of *Bingley's Journal,* and in the 19–26 December issue Bingley promised that there would be "no alteration whatever of the *Journal*"; rather, "the *Independent Chronicle* will be an entire new paper, and is calculated to accommodate those gentlemen who would be glad to be furnished with a greater quantity . . . than the *Weekly Journal* affords." A biweekly, the paper was to be published on Mondays and Fridays. The new venture evidently lasted at least through number 106, published on 3 January 1774, the latest issue now extant.

Although the revived *Independent Chronicle* probably did not last much beyond early 1774, *Bingley's Journal* did endure, and Bingley was involved with it at least through 1785. Nichols claims that Bingley fled to Ireland soon after his declaration of bankruptcy, but he was still publishing his periodicals in London as late as January 1773, a year and a half after his bankruptcy. The actual date of his exile to Ireland is uncertain, but after returning to England in 1783 he joined Nichols's printing house. Among the works he published were two written by himself, *A Sketch of English Liberty* (1793) and *An Examination into the Origin of the Discontents in Ireland* (1799). The former rehearses, at a distance of more than twenty years, the trials and tribulations associated with his publishing the libelous numbers of the *North Briton;* it also repeats Bingley's attack on Wilkes's supporters for failing in the early 1770s to support publishers associated with radical politics. The latter work assesses recent Irish problems from a radical perspective.

Little is known of Bingley's final years. On 18 June 1796 he lost his wife of thirty-six years, with whom he had three daughters (who, according to Nichols, had married respectably). Bingley remarried on 21 January 1798 and died on 23 October 1799.

As Bingley left no business records apart from the addresses to his readers in his periodicals, it is difficult to determine how effective a businessman he was. Little information is available concerning his income, number of employees, or the frequency with which he wrote for his periodicals. Few advertisements ever appeared in Bingley's periodicals; no issue contained more than one or two, compared to, say, the one hundred advertisements per issue in the *Gazetteer and New Daily Advertiser.* Bingley had to pay a great deal of attention to his subscribers, since they were practically his sole source of revenue. Bingley was, indeed, sensitive to his audience, but it is not clear whether catering to his readers would have been sufficient for him to achieve success as a publisher; the financial problems that were caused by his political and legal difficulties cannot be distinguished from those that might have been produced by ineffective business practices. It is, therefore, difficult to arrive at final judgments concerning Bingley's business acumen.

One can, however, estimate his courage and contribution to the struggle to establish a free press. Nichols proposed an epitaph for Bingley:

> Cold is the heart that beat in Freedom's cause,
> The steady advocate of all her Laws.
> Unmov'd by threats or bribes his race he ran,
> And lived and died the Patriot! – the Man.

Bingley's courage in support of the freedom of the press is unparalleled among his professional contemporaries; certainly no other publisher of his era willingly suffered more personal misfortune in upholding this principle. His periodicals contributed to the expansion of democratic values and democratic discourse on the eve of the American and French Revolutions.

References:

S. E., "A Forgotten Journalist," *Athenaeum* (20 May 1899): 626;

John Nichols, *Literary Anecdotes of the Eighteenth Century: Comprizing Biographical Memoirs of W. Bowyer, and Many of His Learned Friends; an Incidental View of the Progress and Advancement of Literature during the Last Century, and Biographical Anecdotes of a Considerable Number of Eminent Writers and Ingenious Artists; with a Very Copious Index,* 9 volumes (London: Nichols, Son & Bentley, 1812–1815), III: 632–633.

– Robert R. Bataille

William Blackwood and Sons, Ltd.

(Edinburgh: 1804 – 1840; Edinburgh and London: 1840 – 1982)

Blackwood, Pillams and Wilson

(Edinburgh and London: 1982 – 1990)

Pillams and Wilson, Ltd.

(Edinburgh: 1990 –)

Sir Walter Scott, George Eliot, Charles Lever, Anthony Trollope, R. D. Blackmore, and Joseph Conrad are but a few of the well-known writers whose work was published by William Blackwood and Sons, Ltd., in its 178 years of operation. As general publishers from 1804 to 1982 the firm printed scholarly treatises, textbooks, and books on travel, sport, Scottish history, and the history of the British Empire's armed forces. *Blackwood's Magazine,* a politically conservative but broad-based monthly, was one of the best-known English periodicals of the nineteenth century and the firm's most prominent publication for 163 years.

William Blackwood was born in Edinburgh, Scotland, in November 1776. At fourteen he entered an apprenticeship with the booksellers Bell and Bradfute, where he gained experience with antiquarian bookselling in London, Glasgow, and Edinburgh. In 1800 he formed a partnership with Robert Ross, and in 1804 he set himself up in Edinburgh as a buyer and seller of rare books and private libraries. At the time Blackwood was establishing himself, Scotland was developing a great literary culture of its own, fostering a healthy climate for the publishing industry. Edinburgh and Glasgow were becoming centers of literary production as publishing firms such as Oliver and Boyd, Black, Blackie, Collins, Nelson, and Constable were establishing their reputations and breaking the long-established London publishing monopoly.

In 1810 the London publisher John Murray selected Blackwood as his Edinburgh publisher after a disagreement with the Ballantyne firm over financial matters. Murray was literary agent for the poet George Gordon, Lord Byron, and Blackwood joined Murray and John Cumming of Dublin in publishing Cantos I and II of Byron's *Childe Harolde's Pilgrimage* (1812). Blackwood also appeared as one of the publishers on the title page of Percy Bysshe Shelley's *Prometheus Unbound* (1820)

and William Hazlitt's *Table-Talk* (1821). Also in 1810 Blackwood was one of the founders of the *Educational Encyclopedia* (also known as the *Edinburgh Encyclopedia*), edited by David Brewster. This project would represent one of Blackwood's major publications when it was completed twenty years later. In 1811 Blackwood independently brought out the Reverend Thomas McCrie's *The Life of John Knox,* the first attempt to present the influence of Knox from both religious and secular perspectives. The considerable attention the study attracted made it an important work for the burgeoning firm. Also in 1811 Blackwood published the first volume of Robert Kerr's eighteen-volume *A General History and Collection of Voyages and Travels, Arranged in Systematic Order* (1811–1817), the kind of work that would be featured in the firm's catalogues and magazine for the next 170 years.

The 1812 Blackwood catalogue listed more than fifteen thousand volumes, placing Blackwood in a preeminent position as a seller of rare books. In 1816 he brought out Sir Walter Scott's four-volume *Tales of My Landlord.* After 1817 Blackwood began publishing more works by authors who had contracts exclusively with his firm. Early titles included Thomas Chalmers's popular *The Evidence and Authority of the Christian Revelation* (1814), which quickly went through five editions, and John Gibson Lockhart's translation of Friedrich Schlegel's *Lectures on the History of Literature, Ancient and Modern* (1818). Between 1820 and 1834 Blackwood's new publications included legal, medical, scientific, theological, and adventure books, as well as the journals of learned societies, including the *Law Journal* and the productions of the Scottish Highland Society.

It was the *Edinburgh Monthly Magazine,* begun in April 1817, that firmly established Blackwood as a publisher, and for years it was the focal point of the business. The magazine was commonly referred to as *Blackwood's,* and in 1905 its name would be

*William Blackwood, founder of William Blackwood and Sons; etching by
F. Huth after a painting by Sir William Allan*

changed to *Blackwood's Magazine.* Blackwood founded the periodical as a response to Thomas Constable's *Edinburgh Review* (1802–1829), which by 1817 had been the dominant Whig voice for fourteen years. Representing the positions of the Tories, *Blackwood's* supported the established church and government, a position it would maintain for the next 162 years. Edited by James Cleghorn and Thomas Pringle, the first six issues mixed poetry, criticism, and articles on Greek sculpture and sugarcane production in the United States with detailed records of births and deaths and pieces on such topics as animal magnetism and an "Account of the remarkable Case of Margaret Lyall, who continued in a state of sleep nearly six weeks." Sales were disappointing, amounting to fewer than twenty-five hundred copies per issue. Blackwood dismissed the editors because, as he wrote to his London agents on 23 July 1817, they "have done lit-

tle in the way of writing or procuring contributions" and hired Lockhart and John Wilson, who, along with Blackwood himself, were the architects of the successful version of the magazine.

The seventh issue of *Blackwood's* (October 1817) included the "Caldee Manuscript," a biting parody of Old Testament language attributed to Lockhart that attacked, among others, the publisher and staff of the *Edinburgh Review.* Threatened with charges of libel, Blackwood deleted the parody in a second printing. The issue also included the first of Lockhart's many attacks on the "Cockney School of Poetry," as he referred to a group of liberal writers, mostly from London, including Hazlitt, Leigh Hunt, and the "less important members" of the group, "the Shelleys, the Keatses, and the Webbes." When Hunt threatened to sue for libel, Blackwood professed that he had little control over his editor. Hunt dropped the suit, but the magazine was assailed in correspondence and in an anonymous pamphlet, *Hypocrisy Unveiled and Calumny Detected in a Review of* Blackwood's Edinburgh Magazine. In a review in the August 1818 issue Lockhart, by then called "The Scorpion" for his scathing criticism, attacked John Keats's *Endymion* (1818) as "drivelling idiocy, the product of an able mind reduced to insanity" and urged the poet to quit writing before he starved. (Shelley blamed Lockhart's invective for hastening Keats's death in 1821.) The review provoked a duel between Lockhart's friend Jonathan H. Christie and John Scott, editor of the short-lived *London Magazine,* who was mortally wounded.

After the early issues the tone of *Blackwood's* was moderated; as it slowly acquired respectability, it secured a wide audience and wielded greater influence. In addition to Wilson and Lockhart, Walter Scott and William Maginn were among its contributors. Blackwood was pleased to have Thomas De Quincey come to Edinburgh in 1822 to write for the magazine; but De Quincey was an unreliable contributor, and their relationship became strained. The two corresponded for years, however, with De Quincey's long letters communicating his many anxieties, explanations for missed deadlines, and requests for more funds, while Blackwood's letters frequently expressed his exasperation. De Quincey's anonymous political tracts, historical narratives, and essays for the magazine included some of his finest compositions. Blackwood added a footnote to De Quincey's "On Murder as One of the Arts," in the February 1827 issue, reminding readers that it was satire by noting its Swiftian qualities. *Blackwood's* also published De Quincey's "Revolt of the Tartars" (July 1837), "The Household Wreck" (January 1838), and "The Avenger" (August 1838), as well as his well-known essay on literary theory, "Style," published serially in July, September, and October 1840.

Among the magazine's early readers was Edgar Allan Poe. An editor himself, Poe closely followed *Blackwood's* to stay abreast of current literary trends, and critics have suggested that it influenced his artistic development. In 1830, for example, the magazine carried a short story, "The Iron Shroud," to which one of Poe's most celebrated stories, "The Pit and the Pendulum" (1842), would bear a striking resemblance. When confronted with the similarities, Poe added a subtitle to his piece: "A Tale Neither In Nor Out of Blackwood." Later, as a result of the accusations, he wrote a comical piece, "How to Write a Blackwood Article." (Charles Whibley revisited the controversy in the March 1917 centenary issue of *Blackwood's*).

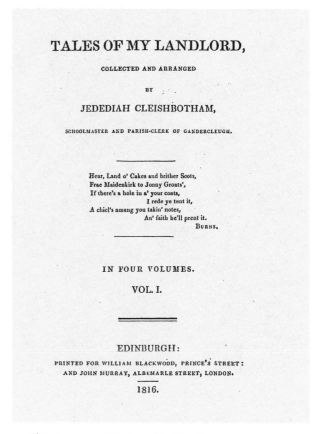

TALES OF MY LANDLORD,

COLLECTED AND ARRANGED

BY

JEDEDIAH CLEISHBOTHAM,

SCHOOLMASTER AND PARISH-CLERK OF GANDERCLEUGH.

Hear, Land o' Cakes and brither Scots,
Frae Maidenkirk to Jonny Groats',
If there's a hole in a' your coats,
    I rede ye tent it,
A chiel's amang you takin' notes,
    An' faith he'll prent it.
                                    Burns,

IN FOUR VOLUMES.

VOL. I.

EDINBURGH:

PRINTED FOR WILLIAM BLACKWOOD, PRINCE'S STREET:
AND JOHN MURRAY, ALBEMARLE STREET, LONDON.

1816.

Title page for a Blackwood publication, a pseudonymous work by Sir Walter Scott

In 1827 the magazine's circulation reached sixty-three hundred copies. Samuel Taylor Coleridge, who had several articles published in it, wrote Blackwood in 1832 that "*Blackwood's Magazine* is an unprecedented Phenomenon in the world of letters, and forms the golden – alas! the only – remaining link between the Periodical Press and the enduring literature of Great Britain." By 1833 *Blackwood's* had been molded into the shape it would have for more than one hundred years – a mixture of articles on exploration and discovery, essays on social concerns and conservative politics, book reviews, and short fiction.

Blackwood died in 1834 and was succeeded by his sons Alexander, Robert, and John; Alexander took over as business manager and editor of the magazine. The sons wanted to expand the firm's market by establishing a London office, and after the death of Thomas Cadell Jr. in 1836 they tried unsuccessfully to purchase his firm; instead, in 1840, they opened an office at Pall Mall, where the business consisted primarily of bulk book and magazine sales. In 1841 the firm published Samuel

Robert and John Blackwood, two of the three sons who succeeded William Blackwood as heads of the firm in 1834 (left: etching by Huth after a painting by R. Scott Lauder; right: etching after a photo image)

Warren's *Ten Thousand a-Year,* which had been serialized in the magazine beginning in October 1839; the comic tale went through several editions and became a popular stage play. From 1833 to 1842 William Blackwood and Sons, published Archibald Alison's ten-volume *History of Europe.* In 1845 Robert Blackwood acquired the *Berwick Warder,* a country newspaper. A year later the brothers purchased printing machinery from the proprietor of *Tait's Magazine,* opened an Edinburgh printing office, and from then on produced *Blackwood's* on the firm's own presses.

John Blackwood became head of the business in 1852 and guided a tremendous expansion of the firm. Also in 1852, Wilson and Lockhart made their last contributions to *Blackwood's,* and both died in 1854. Lockhart, who had launched his career with the firm, had come to enjoy a high reputation in English letters. Books written by him and published by Blackwood included *Peter's Letters to His Kinsfolk* (1819), *Some Passages in the Life of Mr. Adam Blair* (1822), and *Ancient Spanish Ballads* (1823). Edward Bulwer-Lytton translated works by Friedrich Schiller for the magazine that were collected in two volumes as *The Poems and Ballads of Schiller* (1844). Bulwer-Lytton became one of Blackwood's most successful authors; his scholarly historical novels at-tracted several generations of readers. His *The Caxtons: A Family Picture* (1849), with characters modeled on Laurence Sterne's *Tristram Shandy* (1760–1767), appeared serially in *Blackwood's* before being published in book form, as did his *"My Novel," by Pisistratus Caxton: or, Varieties of English Life* (1853) and *What Will He Do With It?* (1858).

In June 1850 Sir Edward Hamley wrote to John Blackwood that his brother, a military officer, would feel at home in *Blackwood's,* as "There was always a warlike trumpet-tone about the Magazine." During the Crimean War from 1853 to 1856 the firm emphasized articles and books on military subjects and assembled an accomplished staff of military writers. The magazine provided in-depth coverage of the conflict, including Hamley's frequent dispatches from the front, published under the title "The Story of the Crimea," and opinion pieces on military affairs. By publishing such articles as "The State of the Army," "Military Education," "The Punjab Mutiny," "Fleets and Navies," and "Ironclad Ships of War," as well as books such as Hamley's *Operations of War* (1866), which became standard reading for generations of military students, the firm established a reputation for superior war reportage and military analysis. "The Military Staff of Blackwood," as John Blackwood called his military contributors, included George Chesney, Garnet Wolseley, Archibald Alison, Henry Brackenbury, and Herbert Kitchener (later Lord Kitchener), as well as Hamley.

In 1856 John Blackwood received from George Henry Lewes, an occasional writer for the magazine, the manuscript for a short tale, "The Sad Fortunes of the Rev. Amos Barton," written by Lewes's friend Marian Evans. Although Blackwood thought that the story had a weak conclusion, he described it as "unquestionably very pleasant reading." He wrote Lewes that he was reluctant to publish a work by an unknown author; but he included the tale, in two parts, in the January and February 1857 issues of the magazine and thereby became George Eliot's publisher. (The nom de plume was first used in a letter from Evans to Blackwood.) Blackwood published two more stories by Eliot in the next nine issues and collected all three in June 1858 as *Scenes of Clerical Life.* While the collection was not a popular success, Blackwood paid the author handsomely, and the work was well received by the critics. Eliot's *Adam Bede* (1859) was a tremendous success, and Blackwood sent her a large and unexpected cash bonus. By the time *The Mill on the Floss* (1860; the title had been suggested by Blackwood) was completed, Eliot's popularity had grown considerably; she refused to allow the work to be printed serially in *Blackwood's* because, as she wrote Blackwood, "The Magazine edition would be devoured, and would sweep away perhaps 20,000 – nay, 40,000 – readers who would otherwise demand copies of the complete work from the libraries." Blackwood employee Margaret Oliphant would later write that the matter "produced with other causes a temporary *refroidissement* between writer and publisher. . . . Mr. John and the Major [William Blackwood II], it seems, said little but felt indignant." The rift was resolved by 1861, and Blackwood wrote to Eliot, "I have read the MS. you have sent of *Silas Marner* with great admiration. The first hundred pages are very sad, almost oppressive, but relieved by the most exquisite touches of nature and natural feelings. . . ."

In 1862 Eliot disappointed John Blackwood again when she gave *Romola* (1863) to a competitor, George Smith of Cornhill Publishing. Blackwood handled the loss of his greatest asset with his typical diplomacy:

> I am of course sorry that your new novel is not to come out under the old colours, but I am glad to hear that you have made so satisfactory an arrangement. Hearing of the wild sums that were being offered to writers of much inferior mark to you, and I thought it highly probable that offers would be made to you, I can readily imagine that you are to receive such a price as I could not make remunerative by any machinery that I could resort to. Rest assured that I feel satisfied of the extreme reluctance with which you would decide upon leaving your old friend for any other publishers, however great the pecuniary consideration might be, and it would destroy my pleasure in business if I knew any friend was publishing with me when he could, or thought he could, do better for himself by going elsewhere. . . .

Perhaps as a result of Blackwood's tact, Eliot reestablished her association with the firm with *Felix Holt, The Radical* (1866), which was serialized in *Blackwood's,* and in 1868 she contributed *The Spanish Gypsy: A Poem.* Her masterpiece, *Middlemarch,* was published by Blackwood in 1871. The correspondence between Blackwood and Eliot reveals that the publisher was regularly troubled by Eliot's realism and often advised her to soften her descriptions – a suggestion the author just as often rejected.

In 1861 the Irish novelist Lever convinced Blackwood to publish his *Tony Butler* in serial form. Author and publisher exchanged letters as the installments appeared, and Blackwood is credited with helping to develop the characters and the carefully constructed plot. When the novel was published anonymously in 1865 in three volumes, Lever's popularity had diminished, and the book form did not sell well. William Blackwood and Sons also published Lever's novel *Cornelious O'Dowd upon Men and Women and Things in General* in three volumes in 1864–1865. The author contributed to the magazine articles on foreign life and European politics, such as "Italian Brigandage" (May 1863), "Hero-Worship and Its Dangers, a Story" (June 1865), and "The Greek Massacre, from Our Own Commissioner's Report" (August 1870).

When William Blackwood II died in 1861 his eldest son, William Blackwood III, joined the firm as John Blackwood's assistant. Under his guidance the firm published the first of the eight volumes of A. W. Kinglake's *The Invasion of the Crimea* in 1863; the final volume appeared in 1887.

Anthony Trollope arranged to have *Nina Balatka: The Story of a Maiden of Prague* and *Linda Tressel* published serially in *Blackwood's;* the novels appeared in book form in 1867 and 1868, respectively. When the firm started an inexpensive series, Ancient Classics for English Readers, in 1868, John Blackwood persuaded Trollope to abridge Julius Caesar's seven-volume *Commentaries on the Gallic War* for it; the abridgment was published in 1870 as *The Commentaries of Caesar.* Trollope wrote that he en-

*Major William Blackwood II, who joined his father's firm in
1845; etching by Huth after a photo image*

joyed the project and gave Blackwood the copyright
to the work as a birthday gift. The series grew
steadily under the editorship of Lucas Collins. Another series, Blackwood's Foreign Classics, was inaugurated by Oliphant in 1877, growing to seventeen volumes by 1881.

Three years after Blackmore's *Lorna Doone*
(1869) was published by Low and Marston, he sent
Blackwood chapters from *The Maid of Sker.* Blackwood wrote the author that though his small handwriting was bothersome and the old fisherman character seemed one-dimensional, he would publish the
book. It appeared in 1872 and was later judged to
be one of the best of Blackmore's thirteen novels.

When John Blackwood died in the fall of
1879, Eliot wrote: "He has been bound up with
what I most cared for in my life for more than
twenty years and his good qualities have made
many things easy for me that without him would
often have been difficult." William Blackwood III
became the head of the publishing firm and fourth
editor of *Blackwood's.* Whereas his uncle John had a
reputation for prompt correspondence, William was
less reliable: there are letters, for instance, from
George Bernard Shaw and Arthur Conan Doyle in-

quiring about the status of manuscripts that had
been with the firm for months. Doyle wrote Blackwood three letters over a period of four months trying to find out whether his "A Physiologist's Wife"
would be used; finally, after nearly a year, he asked
to have the manuscript returned. Blackwood eventually did publish the story but rejected several others. In 1891, shortly after what would be his last rejection by *Blackwood's,* Doyle's *The Adventures of Sherlock Holmes* began running in the *Strand Magazine.*

William Blackwood III was an autocratic manager. As an editor he could be attentive and nurturing on one occasion and insensitive on another, annoying authors with suggestions for substantial
changes to their manuscripts. On 3 July 1880 Oliphant, a longtime contributor and employee of the
firm, wrote to complain that one of her pieces had
been brutally cut and cautioned the new editor that
his methods would alienate authors. In rejecting a
story by Robert Louis Stevenson, Blackwood
wrote,

> The heroine would be more apt to stir up the prejudices
> than the sympathies of my readers . . . the Ghastly pas-
> sages are very thrilling, but the abruptness of the change
> from commonplace incident to the supernatural rather
> jars upon me, and I am inclined to doubt its success with
> the public. . . .

Like previous Blackwood editors, William
had a strong interest in military affairs and an admiration for military life, and such titles as *The River
Column* (1885), by Brackenbury; *Fifteen Years of
"Army Reform"* (1884), by "an Officer"; *Sport, Travel,
and Adventure in Newfoundland and the West Indies*
(1885), by Captain William R. Kennedy; and *England and Russia Face to Face in Asia* (1887), by Lt. Arthur C. Yate, reflect this preoccupation. In 1883 the
firm published the forty-volume *Public Accounts and
General Statutes.* It continued to add titles to the Ancient Classics for English Readers series and in
1886 initiated a twelve-volume series, Philosophical
Classics. Under William III the magazine continued
in the established tradition but included more
strongly worded articles promoting his conservative
politics. Titles such as "The Unloaded Revolver –
A Diplomacy of Fanaticism," "Ireland's Fate –
Britain's Warning," and "Government by Fraud
and Giving Way" are among many staunchly Tory
articles intended to arouse the conservative elector-
ate.

In December 1894 Blackwood commissioned
Oliphant to compile a history of the firm. The novelist and biographer had been associated with William Blackwood and Sons since John Blackwood

published her novel *Katie Stewart* in 1853. The first two volumes of *Annals of a Publishing House,* subtitled *William Blackwood and His Sons, Their Magazine and Friends,* were published in 1897, but Oliphant died before the third volume was written. Blackwood asked his cousin Mrs. Gerald Porter, John Blackwood's daughter, to complete the work, and the third volume, *John Blackwood,* was published in 1898.

In 1899 *Blackwood's Magazine* celebrated its one thousandth edition with a special issue. That year *Lord Jim,* by Conrad – whose first publication with the firm, "Karein," had appeared in *Blackwood's* in 1897 – began to be serialized in the magazine. On 13 or 14 July 1900, Conrad wrote William Blackwood:

> The last word of *Lord Jim* is written, but before I retire to rest I must with the same impulse, the same dip of the pen as it were, say a word to you. Whatever satisfaction I have now or shall have out of the book I owe very much to you – not only in the way of material help, but in the conditions which you have created for me to work in by your friendly and unwearied indulgence.

Correspondence between Blackwood and Conrad continued until 1903, and Conrad's last contribution to the magazine, "Initiation: A Discourse on the Names of Ships and the Character of the Sea," appeared in 1905. Conrad's biographer Jocelyn Baines contends that Blackwood misconceived the art underlying the author's adventure stories, regarding them merely as examples of the sort of masculine tales he favored for the magazine; Baines also contends, however, that Conrad's attempts to have his work accepted by the magazine led to the creation of his celebrated narrator, Marlow. From 1900 to 1904 the firm published George Saintsbury's three-volume *A History of Criticism and Literary Taste in Europe from the Earliest Texts to the Present Day.*

Alfred Noyes began to have his patriotic poems published in the magazine in 1903, and his popular epic poem *Drake* appeared serially in *Blackwood's* from 1906 to 1908. Ian Hay (pen name of John Hay Beith) had his first story published in the magazine in 1907; he became a regular contributor, and several of his novels, including *"The Right Stuff"* (1908), *A Man's Man* (1909), and *A Safety Match* (1911), were serialized in it. In 1907, 1908, and 1909, respectively, the firm published Maud Diver's novels *Captain Desmond, V.C., The Great Amulet,* and *Candles in the Wind.* In 1907 Blackwood turned down a book by H. G. Wells, calling it well written but overpriced. Under William Blackwood III the firm also published many schoolbooks.

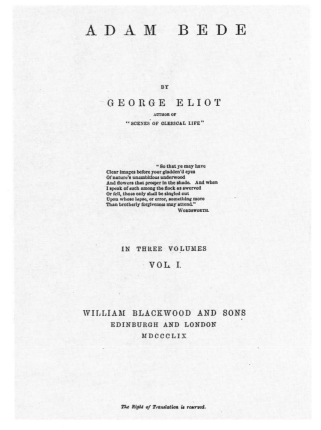

ADAM BEDE

BY

GEORGE ELIOT

AUTHOR OF
"SCENES OF CLERICAL LIFE"

"So that ye may have
Clear images before your gladden'd eyes
Of nature's unambilious underwood
And flowers that prosper in the shade. And when
I speak of such among the flock as swerved
Or fell, those only shall be singled out
Upon whose lapse, or error, something more
Than brotherly forgiveness may attend."
WORDSWORTH.

IN THREE VOLUMES
VOL. I.

WILLIAM BLACKWOOD AND SONS
EDINBURGH AND LONDON
MDCCCLIX

The Right of Translation is reserved.

Title page for the best known of the George Eliot novels published by Blackwood

In 1912 George William Blackwood became the head of the firm and editor of *Blackwood's.* Works in the firm's catalogues between 1910 and 1914 increasingly deal with the events that were leading to World War I, and after the outbreak of the war in 1914 many Blackwood publications dealt with the conflict. Notable titles included Hay's bestsellers *The First Hundred Thousand* (1915) and *Carrying On – After the First Hundred Thousand* (1917), and J. S. Clouston's *The Spy in Black* (1917). The magazine focused on articles from the fronts, as well as on opinion pieces on the war. Books about the war appeared for years after it was over, including *The Story of Our Submarines* (1920), by Klaxon (pen name of John Graham Bower), and Alan Bott's *Eastern Nights – and Flights* (1920). Throughout the 1920s the firm continued to produce adventure stories, books on military subjects, novels, and textbooks. In 1926 a general strike briefly suspended book publishing, but the magazine continued to be printed by members of the Blackwood family.

In 1936 the magazine was reporting on the Fascists in Germany and the Spanish Civil War,

The Blackwood offices at 45 George Street, Edinburgh

and in 1940 on Dunkirk and the fall of France. Prior to World War II William Blackwood and Sons was the fifth largest publishing house in the United Kingdom, with a catalogue of nearly one hundred pages. In December 1940, however, Paternoster Row, the center of the London publishing trade, was destroyed by firebombs during an air raid; all that was salvaged from Blackwood's London branch was an office safe and two brass door plates. James Hugh Blackwood, George Blackwood's brother, established a new London headquarters at Soho Square in May 1941.

More destructive to the firm in the long run was the country's paper shortage. The government rationed paper to publishers based on their output for 1939, which had been Blackwood's slowest year in twenty-five years. In place until after the war, the rationing system meant that the firm was unable to acquire even half the paper it had used previously for printing books; what paper was available was used primarily to reprint the work of established authors and to print a backlog of manuscripts that had been accepted before the war. For the magazine the size of type and the number of pages had to be drastically reduced. As a consequence, many manuscripts were turned away, and promising authors went elsewhere.

George Blackwood died in 1942, and James succeeded him. James's son, George Douglas Blackwood, became the head of the firm and the seventh editor of *Blackwood's* after the retirement of his father in 1948. During the 1950s the firm published J. B. Salmond's *The History of the 51st Highland Division, 1939–1945* (1953); textbooks; reports and materials from organizations such as the Institute of Bankers in Scotland, the Church of Scotland, the Agricultural Society, and the Scottish Text Society; and scholarly studies from Saint Andrews University. In 1954 Blackwood published *The House of Blackwood, 1804–1954: The History of a Publishing*

Firm, by Frank D. Tredrey, to commemorate the 150th anniversary of the firm. While the last chapter wistfully summarizes the firm's accomplishments, it dwells on the mounting financial pressures publishers were facing.

Because of such difficulties, the London office was closed in 1972. John Michael Blackwood, great-great-great-grandson of the founder, became head of the firm and editor of *Blackwood's* in 1979. For the last twenty years of its existence the magazine struggled for survival against competition from other popular magazines, evolving tastes of entertainment, and an audience that was less comfortable with the written word. A century-old tradition made format experimentation difficult, and circulation steadily declined. The last issue of *Blackwood's* was printed in December 1980, the magazine's 163rd year; to the very end of its run it was recognized for its superior writing. In an effort to strengthen the company, in 1982 William Blackwood & Sons, merged with Pillams and Wilson, another family-operated business, to form Blackwood, Pillams and Wilson. In 1987 the company became a subsidiary of Color Graphic PLC. The subsidiary was sold in 1990 and is now Pillams and Wilson, a contract printer in Edinburgh.

References:

Jocelyn Baines, *Joseph Conrad: A Critical Biography* (Westport, Conn.: Greenwood Press, 1960);

Colin Clair, *A History of Printing in Britain* (New York: Oxford University Press, 1966);

Gordon Haight, *George Eliot: A Biography* (New York: Oxford University Press, 1968);

Margaret Oliphant and Mrs. Gerald Porter, *The Annals of a Publishing House,* 3 volumes (Edinburgh: Blackwood, 1897–1898);

Frank D. Tredrey, *The House of Blackwood, 1804–1954: The Story of a Publishing Firm* (Edinburgh: Blackwood, 1954).

Papers:

In 1942 the main archives of William Blackwood and Sons, through 1900 were given in trust to the National Library of Scotland in Edinburgh. Indexing the collection of more than eighty thousand letters by some twenty thousand correspondents was completed in 1954. Selected twentieth-century letters and documents of the firm were auctioned in 1973. The remaining archives of William Blackwood and Sons, were placed on permanent loan to the National Library of Scotland by George Douglas Blackwood.

– Alan Pratt

William Blake

(London: 1784 – 1827)

See also the Blake entry in *DLB 93: British Romantic Poets, 1789–1832, First Series.*

William Blake was born on 28 November 1757 at 28 Broad Street, Westminster. His father, James Blake, was a hosier who made a comfortable living at his trade. William was the third son of seven children, of whom only five survived infancy. He appears to have received no formal elementary education but was taught to read and write, probably by his mother, Catherine Harmitage Blake. His parents noticed early that their son had a talent for drawing and sketching, and they sent him in 1767 to Henry Pars's drawing school in the Strand. It was not deemed practical for Blake to train as an artist, so in 1772 he was apprenticed to the engraver James Basire at 31 Great Queen Street.

Basire's speciality was the engraving of antiquarian and architectural drawings: he was the official engraver to the Society of Antiquaries and to the Royal Society. Part of Blake's training involved drawing ecclesiastical statuary in the local churches, including Westminster Abbey, to be engraved by Basire. This early emphasis on technical architectural drawing may have influenced Blake's continually stated preference for designs with strong, bold outlines rather than the tonal effects achieved with the chiaroscuro and mezzotint techniques popular with British engravers of the period.

Blake's apprenticeship ended in 1779, leaving him qualified as a journeyman engraver whose work would consist of engraving the designs and drawings of others. Blake seems to have been dissatisfied with his relatively low status and prospects, and on completing his apprenticeship in 1788 he enrolled at the Royal Academy Schools, where training in anatomy, perspective, architecture, painting, and drawing (both from plaster casts and from life) was available free of charge. In 1780 he exhibited his first painting at the Royal Academy, and he continued to exhibit there at irregular intervals for the next twenty years.

Beginning in 1779 the printer and bookseller Joseph Johnson of 72 St. Paul's Churchyard regularly commissioned the young man to engrave illustrations for his publications, including Sarah Fielding's *The Adventures of David Simple* (1782; first published in 1744), from the designs of another of Blake's friends, the artist Thomas Stothard. It is possible that Blake met some of the leading radicals of the period in the rooms above Johnson's shop, including Thomas Paine, William Godwin, Joseph Priestley, and Mary Wollstonecraft (whose *Original Stories from Real Life* Blake was to engrave in 1791, when it was published by Johnson). Through a fellow student at the Royal Academy, John Flaxman, a sculptor and draughtsman, Blake was introduced to a more cultured and genteel circle than he had previously known, including the Reverend Henry Mathew and his wife, Harriet. The Mathews held weekly soirees in their home, and Blake may have met such intellectuals as Anna Laetitia Barbauld and Hannah More there. In 1783 the Mathews and Flaxman sponsored the printing by Johnson of fifty copies of Blake's juvenile verse, which he had been writing since the age of eleven, under the title *Poetical Sketches.* But despite his new acquaintance among the radical and cultured classes, when Blake married Catherine Boucher at St. Mary's Church, Battersea, in August 1782, his illiterate bride signed the church register with a cross.

The couple moved to 23 Green Street, off Leicester Fields. Blake taught his wife to read and write and used her as his engraver's assistant. Catherine shared not only in his work but also in the "visions" that produced it.

In July 1784 Blake's father died. With his inheritance, which was probably small, Blake and his wife moved to 27 Broad Street, next door to the house where Blake had been born. There Blake and James Parker, an engraver specializing in mezzotint whom Blake had met as an apprentice at Basire's, went into partnership as dealers in new and secondhand prints; Parker and his wife moved into the Broad Street house. The intention appears to have been for Parker and Blake to produce and publish original engravings of their own designs; but the business was not successful, and the partners appear to have published only two engravings – and these were not of their own designs but were engravings by Blake after paintings by Stothard. By Christmas 1785 the Blakes had

William Blake; portrait by Thomas Phillips (National Portrait Gallery, London)

moved to 28 Poland Street, and the partnership was dissolved.

For the next few years, alongside his work as a jobbing engraver for Johnson, Blake began to experiment with the engraving techniques with which he was to produce his own illuminated books. The method with which Blake was probably most familiar from his training with Basire was intaglio, in which the image to be engraved is cut in reverse into a copper plate using tools called gravers and burins; the plate is treated with an acid-proof resin or varnish to blank out areas of the surface and placed in a bath of dilute nitric acid. The acid deepens the lines cut into the plate, which is removed from the bath and covered with ink from a roller; the excess ink is wiped off, and the print is taken by pressing a sheet of paper onto the surface of the plate by means of an engraver's rolling press with a variable pressure control.

Blake's innovation was perhaps developed after conversations with George Cumberland, an amateur artist who was studying engraving with him; Blake claimed that his younger brother, Robert, who had died in February 1787, revealed it to him in a vision. Instead of indentations carved into a plate, the technique used an image raised up on the surface, which meant that printing did not require much pressure. The details of the technique are not completely clear, but for many years, following the investigations of G. E. Bentley Jr. and Geoffrey Keynes, it was thought that Blake began by soaking a sheet of paper in a soap solution and gum arabic and leaving it to dry and stiffen. Using a quill pen, Blake wrote his poetry on the paper using engraver's acid-proof varnish instead of ink. The sheet was then placed face down on a heated copper plate; paper and plate were pressed together through the engraver's press so that the paper stuck to the plate, and the image was transferred to the plate as a mirror image. Paper and plate were cooled and placed in a water bath; the paper floated off the plate, leaving the words written in varnish on the plate's surface. The plate was touched up with more varnish where necessary, and illuminations were drawn in reverse directly on the plate with varnish. The plate was then placed into the bath of dilute nitric acid for at least six hours. The acid corroded the unvarnished background, leaving word and image standing out slightly from the plate's surface. Designs and texts were further modified or retouched, and the plate was inked. Since a roller was likely to produce an overinked surface, Blake inked another copper plate and pressed it gently onto the etched plate. Image and text were then transferred from the etched plate to paper using the engraver's press, set at low pressure.

More recently, however, Joseph Viscomi has suggested that this method is unnecessarily onerous and that there is no reason why Blake should have used a transfer technique to avoid writing backward on the plate; after all, for a trained engraver, mirror writing is virtually second nature. Moreover, Viscomi has attempted to replicate the conditions under which Blake worked, and his experiments imply that Blake could not have produced the clarity of results using transfers of words or images from paper to plate. He suggests that Blake's methods were not so different from those of his contemporaries: Blake, he believes, created relief images directly on the plate, with the graver, acid-proof resin, and acid. According to Viscomi, it was the *attitude* to technique that was Blake's truly new achievement: for Blake there was no hierarchy of word and image; both were created simultaneously, and the completed conception was placed directly onto copper with no paper draft being necessary. The technique was felt to be as much part of the artistic process as the drawings and the words.

Blake also experimented with the use of colored inks, sometimes using two or more colors on a single plate. He – or Catherine, acting on his instructions – also used watercolor washes on the plates. The finished product was also touched up by hand with watercolors and inks, making each engraving unique.

Around 1788, using his new method, Blake produced the first of the illuminated texts for which he is now famous: *There Is No Natural Religion* (in two series) and *All Religions Are One*. Both are books of illuminated aphorisms, possibly influenced by John Caspar Lavater's *Aphorisms on Man*, which was translated in 1788 by Henry Fuseli and published by Johnson with a frontispiece engraved by Blake after a picture by Fuseli. (Viscomi dates the extant versions of these texts as 1794 and 1795.) In 1789 Blake wrote the first of his prophetic books, *Tiriel;* he probably intended to engrave and illuminate it later, but it remained in manuscript form at his

death. More important, that year he used his new method to engrave his *Songs of Innocence,* which consists of thirty-one plates with watercolor washes and colored inks; the lettering, although handwritten, is based on conventional roman type. Blake probably made about thirty copies during his life; the majority were probably produced in 1789, with three further printings in 1794, 1802, and 1811. Also in 1789 he engraved and printed *The Book of Thel,* made up of seven plates; further print runs were made in 1790, 1795, and 1818.

In the autumn of 1790 the Blakes moved to 13 Hercules Buildings, Hercules Road, Lambeth. Throughout the 1790s Blake continued his close association with Johnson, receiving commissions to engrave illustrations for Erasmus Darwin's *The Botanic Garden* (1791) and James Stuart and Nicholas Revett's *The Antiquities of Athens* (1762–1816) and to engrave the author's illustrations for Capt. John Stedman's *Narrative of a Five Years Expedition against the Revolted Negroes of Surinam, from the Year 1772 to 1777* (1796). A projected edition of John Milton's works had to be abandoned when the editor, William Cowper, suffered a mental breakdown.

Blake always read carefully the texts on which he worked, and he was influenced by what he read. Stedman's book may have furnished him with some of the themes of slavery and oppression of *Visions of the Daughters of Albion,* which Blake wrote and engraved in 1792 (seventeen complete copies are extant, mostly produced from 1793 to 1795, with a further printing in 1818). In 1793 he produced an emblem book, *For Children: The Gates of Paradise,* which consists of seventeen plates telling of the limitations of human life. Five copies of this text remain, most from between 1806 and 1818 (Viscomi says that all of the printing took place in 1793 and that only binding and endpapers come from the later period). His reading of Milton for the Cowper edition influenced the development of *The Marriage of Heaven and Hell,* consisting of twenty-seven plates, which he had been writing since 1789 and engraved in 1794: of the nine complete copies that remain, eight are probably from 1794 and one from 1818. *Songs of Experience* was begun in 1789, engraved in 1789, and printed in 1794 both as a separate book and in a collected edition with the earlier poems as *Songs of Innocence and Experience, Shewing the Two Contrary States of the Human Soul;* he also engraved *Europe* (of which twelve copies remain, all apparently from 1794) and the *Book of Urizen* (six of the seven copies extant are from 1794, one from 1818).

In the early 1790s Blake also wrote "Book the First" of "The French Revolution," the first of a projected seven books, and it was set in type by

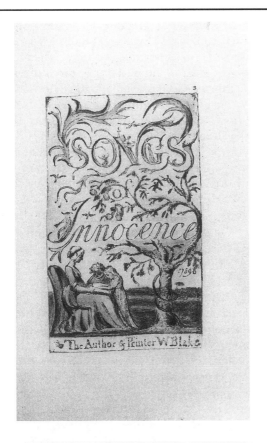

*Title pages, engraved by Blake, for three of his
self-published works*

Johnson, who appears to have commissioned the work. But either Blake or Johnson, who was notoriously timid about publishing radical works, withdrew from the project, and Blake wrote no more on the subject. In 1793 he wrote and engraved *America: A Prophecy* (of which he printed about fifteen copies), and in 1795 the *Song of Los* (of which five copies are extant), the *Book of Ahania,* and the *Book of Los* (the last two exist each only in one copy, and both were engraved by the intaglio, not the relief, method).

In 1795 Blake received one of his most important commissions when the publisher James Edwards asked him to design and engrave illustrations for Edward Young's *The Complaint, or, Night Thoughts on Life, Death and Immortality,* which had first appeared in 1742. This was a prestigious commission; other engravers regarded Blake as an odd choice, to say the least. Between 1795 and 1797 he designed more than five hundred watercolor illustrations, of which forty-three found their way into print in volume one of the work (1797). Owing to an economic crisis, Edwards did not publish the other three projected volumes, and the public largely ignored the designs.

In 1800 the poet and biographer William Hayley commissioned Blake to engrave the portrait of his dead son, and by July of that year he had invited Blake to live near him in the village of Felpham, Sussex. In the autumn the Blakes settled in a cottage belonging to the landlord of the local inn, where Blake worked on watercolor portraits of the poets for Hayley's library. Hayley also sent professional engraving work Blake's way, including the opportunity to engrave George Romney's portrait of Cowper and other illustrations for Hayley's life of the poet that was published by Johnson in 1804. Hayley even wrote, especially for Blake's benefit, a short book of poems, *Ballads Founded on Anecdotes Relating to Animals* (1805). Blake illustrated the text and was supposed to receive whatever profits it made. But Blake was finding it increasingly difficult to work for Hayley: the commissions he received through his patron's influence left him little time for his own work, but Hayley thought that the engraver was better off doing paid work than wasting his time illustrating his own visions and prophecies. In 1803 the Blakes returned to London, taking up residence at 17 New Molton Street.

For a while Blake remained on good terms with Hayley and worked on his behalf as a go-between with Richard Phillips, a London publisher and proprietor of the *Monthly Magazine,* for whom Hayley was producing a biography of the painter George Romney. Blake also received a commis-

sion from Robert Hartley Cromek, another engraver, to design and engrave illustrations for an edition of Robert Blair's *The Grave,* which had originally been published in 1743; the illustrated edition appeared in 1808 to mixed reviews. Cromek, however, had given the engraving work to Louis Schiavonetti and, according to Blake, also stole Blake's idea for a design of the pilgrims departing from the Tabard Inn in Geoffrey Chaucer's *The Canterbury Tales* that was eventually turned into a painting by Stothard, Blake's erstwhile friend, at Cromek's suggestion. (Stothard claimed not to have known that the original idea was Blake's.)

Blake was deeply resentful of Cromek's treatment of him, and this resentment may have spilled over into his relationships with his other friends and patrons; Flaxman, Fuseli, and Hayley withdrew their support and offered their commissions to younger engravers. Blake was, however, a man with a difficult temperament and was inefficient in his business dealings — he was, for example, notoriously slow to answer business letters — and his friends perhaps felt that he was taking too long to complete his commissions and was overcharging for them. By 1806 Blake's commercial work had virtually dried up, and for nearly ten years he appears to have had almost no paid engraving jobs. Instead, he relied on the goodwill of his friend Thomas Butts, for whom he painted several watercolors, and whose son, also called Thomas, he took as a drawing pupil for twenty-five guineas a year. Blake does not appear really to have earned this sum, and Butts seems to have acted more as a patron than as an employer.

Blake continued to try to make his name as an artist. In May 1809 he held a one-man exhibition of his watercolors at his brother's house, the old family home at 28 Broad Street. The admission of two shillings sixpence entitled the customer to a "Descriptive Catalogue" of the exhibits, written by the artist to explain his reason for putting on the exhibition (because the Royal Academy no longer accepted watercolors) and attacking prevailing taste in art. The exhibition did not attract many visitors, though it stayed open until the spring of 1810. Probably in 1810 Blake had a prospectus printed for his version of the initial stages of *The Canterbury Tales* in which he attacked Stothard's version as geographically inaccurate and a flawed interpretation of Chaucer's pilgrims. Blake's engraving was published on 8 October 1810, but it was not a success in competition with the engraving by Schiavonetti and James Heath after Stothard's painting.

Blake had begun to write *Jerusalem and Milton* perhaps as early as 1804. *Jerusalem* bears that date on its title page; Viscomi suggests that it had reached a proof stage by 1807, but the engraving was not completed until 1820. The book consists of one hundred plates and exists in five copies printed by Blake himself (three copies were printed from his plates after his death), four of which are black and white and one of which is in colored ink and watercolor. *Milton* is also dated 1804 on its title page, but the four copies produced by Blake are on paper that bears a later watermark, and it is possible that the first printing did not take place until 1808. (Viscomi dates three of the four copies as having been produced in 1811.)

In 1814 Blake renewed his friendship with Flaxman, who immediately got him a commission to engrave Flaxman's illustrations for Hesiod's *Work and Days and Theogony*, which were published in 1817. Through Flaxman, Blake was also introduced to the Wedgwood family, who commissioned him to draw and engrave their china products for their sales catalogues from 1815 to 1816. More-satisfying work came in the shape of a commission to engrave a few illustrations for Abraham Rees's thirty-nine-volume *Cyclopaedia* (1819 to 1820).

In 1818 Blake met John Linnell, a young artist who was beginning to make a career for himself. The two men took to each other immediately, and Linnell busied himself getting work for Blake — when he could not get someone else to commission him, Linnell would commission Blake's work himself. In 1819 Linnell introduced his friend to Dr. Robert John Thornton; through this meeting Blake was commissioned to illustrate and engrave Thornton's school edition of *The Pastorals of Virgil* (1821) — the only known example of his using a wood-engraving technique. In 1820 Blake produced a frankly commercial portrait engraving of Mrs. Harriet Quentin, the mistress of the prince regent. In June of that year the Blakes moved to 3 Fountain Court, off the Strand and near the Savoy. They were clearly poor at this time; their new house was small and dark, and Blake had been selling portions of the print collection that he had begun before his apprenticeship. Linnell supported the Blakes as best he could; he applied on Blake's behalf for a grant from the Royal Academy in June 1822, and Blake was unanimously voted the sum of twenty-five pounds. Linnell also, at his own expense, commissioned Blake to design and engrave ten illustrations for the Book of Job in March 1823; the contract was a way of giving Blake a wage of about a pound a week without it appearing to be charity. It took Blake until 1826 to complete the engravings, and Linnell published them that year. Linnell also

wanted Blake to design and engrave illustrations for Dante's *Divine Comedy*. Blake made more than one hundred drawings for the project in 1826 and 1827 and had begun to engrave seven of them before he died on 27 August 1827, apparently of disease of the stomach and gallbladder.

Blake was not a publisher in the strict sense of the word. The books of poems and prophecies that he wrote and engraved himself were not really published works at all: the copies were not uniform, they had different color schemes, and occasionally even the order of the plates was altered. They were not, that is, productions of the craftsman but — Blake liked to believe — individual works of art. Moreover, the number of copies was always extremely small. It used to be thought that Blake's usual business method was to have a few completed plates at his home to be shown to potential customers, so that if they liked his work they could order complete copies; but Viscomi suggests that this view may need revision. He points out that printing from engraved plates is not only hard work but also expensive; consequently, it seems unlikely that Blake would have set up shop on an ad hoc basis. It is more probable that he produced small editions of his texts, which were not uniform in part because the plates were hand finished and in part because using more than one ink on a plate leads to variation of color and tone. The fact that Blake was a visionary artist, says Viscomi, does not mean that he would not have used the most efficient and simple methods of production. On the other hand, although Blake produced a prospectus in October 1793 of works currently available and forthcoming, in which he signaled his intention to print and publish his own work, nothing came of it. He may have had a practical attitude to production, but he was less sure of himself when it came to marketing. In the prospectus he commented:

> The labours of the Artist, the Poet, the Musician, have been proverbially attended by poverty and obscurity; this was never the fault of the Public, but was owing to a neglect of means to propagate such works as have wholly absorbed the Man of Genius. Even Milton and Shakespeare could not publish their own works.

Blake did not really publish his own works, either. There was no possibility of a mass market for his illuminated books, since not only were his ideas obscure and complex but, also, the books were expensive. In the 1793 prospectus *The Book of Thel* is listed at a cheap three shillings; but Blake was asking two guineas by 1818 and by the time of his death three guineas, a large sum for seven illuminated plates. This increase in price, Viscomi suggests, almost certainly occurred because the poet began to see his texts as a series of original engravings rather than as copies of books, and art has a higher monetary value than craft. Finally, not even other poets understood Blake's poetry and philosophy, so what hope was there for the public at large? His customers were a specialized few, and so the books for which Blake is now best known were not widely disseminated in his lifetime.

Interest in his work began with Alexander Gilchrist's *Life of William Blake: Pictor Ignotus* (1863). The poet Algernon Charles Swinburne wrote an appreciative essay on him in 1868, and the first more or less scholarly edition of his work was edited by Edwin John Ellis and William Butler Yeats in 1893. In other words, it was many years after his death before Blake's works were really published in the sense that they became available to a wide audience.

References:
G. E. Bentley Jr., *Blake Records* (Oxford: Clarendon Press, 1969);

Bentley and Martin K. Nurmi, *A Blake Bibliography: Annotated Lists of Works, Studies, and Blakeana* (Minneapolis: University of Minnesota Press, 1964);

Edwin John Ellis and William Butler Yeats, eds., *The Works of William Blake, Poetic, Symbolic and Critical,* 3 volumes (London: Quaritch, 1893);

David Erdman and Donald Moore, eds., *The Notebooks of William Blake* (London: Oxford University Press, 1973);

Alexander Gilchrist, *Life of William Blake: Pictor Ignotus,* 2 volumes (London: Macmillan, 1863; enlarged, 1880);

Geoffrey Keynes, *Blake Studies: Essays on His Life and Work,* second edition, revised and enlarged (Oxford: Clarendon Press, 1971);

Algernon Charles Swinburne, *William Blake* (London: J. C. Hotlen, 1868);

Joseph Viscomi, *Blake and the Idea of the Book* (Princeton: Princeton University Press, 1993).

– Ruth Robbins

Cadell

(London: 1767 – 1793)

T. Cadell and W. Davies

(London: 1793 – 1820)

Cadell, Jr.

(London: 1820 – 1836)

The first Thomas Cadell set up in a publishing and bookselling business on Wine Street, Bristol, in 1739, but the business was not particularly successful. It was left to his son, "born of poor parents," to gain the reputation as "the first in Great Britain, and perhaps in Europe," according to John Nichols, and to his grandson to carry the business into the nineteenth century. The first Thomas Cadell apprenticed his son, usually referred to as Thomas Cadell the Elder, to the London publisher Andrew Millar in 1758. Millar, according to Nichols, found in Cadell "an apprentice congenial to his most ardent wishes," who, "combining industry with intellect, relieved him in a great measure from the toil of superintending an immense concern," and he made Cadell his partner in 1765. They did business at 141 Strand, the Buchanan's Head (formerly the Shakespeare Head), "over against Catherine Street," as their imprint announced. Cadell thus began his career in an auspicious manner: Millar, who published works by Henry Fielding, James Thomson, David Hume, Samuel Johnson, and William Robertson, to mention but a few, was the best-known publisher in London after Robert Dodsley. Nichols called Millar and Jacob Tonson "the best Patrons of Literature" of their half-century; Cadell would prove a worthy successor to that reputation, maintaining Millar's standards of liberal treatment of authors.

When Millar retired in 1767 he left the business in the hands of Cadell, then twenty-five, and their invaluable assistant, Robin Lawless, described by Nichols as combining "the soundest integrity of mind" with excellent judgment and a pure spirit (a painting of this "servant" hung in Cadell's drawing room, a testimony to Cadell's affection for him). Cadell continued in occasional partnership also with William Strahan, as Millar had done, and with

his son Andrew after Strahan died in 1785. Much was expected of Cadell as Millar's heir – in a 1776 letter to Strahan, Hume thanked him for a presentation copy of the first volume of Edward Gibbon's *The History of the Decline and Fall of the Roman Empire* (1776–1788) and remarked that "There will be no books of importance now printed in London but through your hands and Mr. Cadell's."

Firmly established as a publisher and bookseller of the first or second degree, Cadell felt secure enough to marry the daughter of the Reverend Thomas Jones on 1 April 1769; the couple had two children: Thomas Jr., born in 1773, who would take over the firm; and a daughter, who would marry Dr. Charles Lucas Eldridge, chaplain to King George III. Cadell's wife died in 1786.

Cadell and Strahan had their first great success early on with their six-volume edition of *The History of the Decline and Fall of the Roman Empire*. Gibbon called the undertaking "a perilous adventure" that one publisher (Peter Elmsley) had declined; the work, Gibbon claimed, "derived more credit from the name of the shop than from that of the author." The book outsold several impressions and continued successfully through the second and third volumes, brought out on 4 April 1781, and the final three volumes, published on 8 May 1788 – the author's fifty-first birthday. Cadell held a dinner party in honor as much of the work's success as of its writer. The surviving records of the contract with Gibbon provide an example of the liberality with which Millar and later Cadell treated their authors: Gibbon received two-thirds of the sales profits, while Cadell and Strahan divided the remaining third between them.

At the same time, works by authors such as Hume, Robertson, Adam Smith, and Sir William Blackstone appeared frequently on Cadell and Stra-

Thomas Cadell the Elder (Courtesy of Providence Public Library)

han's booklists. An especially important moment, not only for Cadell and Strahan but for the literary world in general, is recorded in a 26 September 1777 letter from the bookseller Edward Dilly to James Boswell: the London booksellers wanted to print "an elegant and accurate edition of all the English poets of reputation, from Chaucer to the present time," with prefaces by Boswell's friend Dr. Johnson. About forty of the most respectable publishers met and selected Cadell, Thomas Davies, and Strahan "to wait upon Dr. Johnson, to solicit him to undertake the Lives." Johnson accepted and asked for a fee of only two hundred pounds. The publishers, who had been prepared to accept a request of a thousand or more pounds for the project, voluntarily raised the payment to four hundred pounds. Johnson's prefaces proved to be so extensive that they were published separately from the works of the poets in ten volumes as *Prefaces, Biographical and Critical, to the Works of the English Poets* (1779–1781).

In 1782 Cadell began to publish the works of Robert Burns, and the connections between Burns

and the house continued into the lifetime of Thomas Cadell Jr., forming, according to Theodore Besterman's history of the firm, "the most honourable and interesting chapter in the publishers' history." Cadell the Elder's name appears on the London edition of *Poems, Chiefly in the Scottish Dialect* (1787), along with those of Strahan and William Creech, and on the enlarged 1793 edition, this time with Creech only. Cadell's son would continue to work successfully with Burns, his biographer, and his family for some years.

Cadell the Elder had not trained his son in the business; Besterman suggests that Cadell recognized his day as the end of a golden age for publishers and booksellers. In 1793, however, Cadell wanted to retire, and he brought his son into the trade after all. To ensure the continued success of the business Cadell made his apprentice and assistant, Davies, his son's partner. Cadell then retired in confidence, "in the full possession of his health and faculties, and with an ample fortune," Nichols reports. Cadell the Elder was elected alderman of

Walbrook ward in London on 30 March 1798; he also served a term as sheriff from 1800 to 1801. While sheriff, he became a master of the Stationers' Company, and shortly before his death he presented a painted window to the company for its hall. Cadell the Elder died on 27 December 1802.

Thomas Cadell Jr. did not immediately become active in the publishing trade, but he left the running of the business largely to Davies. Most of the correspondence from 1793 until 1813, when Davies fell ill, is in Davies's hand and polite wording; the shift to Cadell's blunt, less formal, and occasionally irritable style is quite noticeable in later correspondence.

Nichols remarks that the "reputation the house had acquired for liberality, honour, and integrity" continued, at least while Davies lived. A contemporary bookseller quoted by Besterman noted that Cadell and Davies, with "a capital and stock unrivaled in this, or perhaps any other country," continued Cadell the Elder's success "for many years with high talent and respectability." The firm bought up many copyrights and engaged in risky and expensive ventures such as the publication of art and picture books, some of which had to be retailed at forty guineas to cover expenses; but as the bookseller points out, as much money as Cadell Jr. inherited, it would take even an incompetent some time to lose it.

Some contemporaries expressed disapproval of the firm in terms that are not applied to Cadell the Elder in any extant writings. One memoir says that Davies "became too adventurous and liberal in his literary purposes" and embarked "in such heavy undertakings as the times would hardly sanction, and which his partner, who survived him many years, prudently relinquished." In a 1797 letter George Steevens claimed that "your correspondents C[adell] and D[avies] in spite of all their boasts, are not allowed to be at the head of their trade in the line of publication" and called the publishers rude "priests of Mammon."

George Austen wrote on 1 November 1797 that he had a manuscript about the length of Fanny Burney's *Evalina* (1778): "As I am well aware of what consequence it is that a work of this sort should make its first appearance under a respectable name, I apply to you." Austen offered terms that put the author rather than the publisher at risk and ended, "Should you give any encouragement, I will send you the work." Cadell and Davies declined by return post even to look at the manuscript for Austen's daughter Jane's "First Impressions," which would be published in 1813 as *Pride and Prejudice*.

During this time Cadell and Davies had to deal with one of their few truly unsatisfactory publisher-author relationships, that with the Reverend Charles Dunster. Dunster's 1795 edition of John Milton's *Paradise Regained* (1671) had sold poorly; nevertheless, he wanted to publish an edition of Milton's *Samson Agonistes* (1671) at the firm's risk and expense to make up for his financial disappointment. When Cadell and Davies wisely refused, Dunster tried to recover his losses by accusing the firm of proposing contracts in a partner's name that were "completely nugatory and ridiculous." The reply, from 1799 (Dunster made his first proposal in 1797), is the only angry letter that survives in the firm's business documents: "You tell us that our Letter . . . is no answer. . . . *We* cannot help thinking that there is scarcely another Man living who would not consider it as a *compleat and satisfactory Answer* — We shall decline troubling ourselves to write further, except to demand payment in turn from Mr. Dunster." In general, Cadell and Davies had a reputation for fair and liberal dealings with authors; but as this exchange makes clear, they also had an expectation of fair and liberal treatment from the authors whose works they published.

One business transaction with which their names are still associated, however, earned Cadell and Davies an unjust reputation for unfair dealing. Bishop Thomas Percy, the editor of Oliver Goldsmith's works, began contractual negotiations with a publisher in Ireland in 1785; but when the publication was delayed he transferred the contract to Nichols in London. The work still did not appear, and around 1793 Percy transferred his contract to John Murray, retaining Nichols as his printer. The work still was not forthcoming, and in November 1795 an increasingly irate and impatient Percy turned to Cadell and Davies, who accepted the job on the same terms of remuneration as Nichols had offered. Percy agreed to the terms, then changed his mind in July 1797 and raised the amount he expected. Cadell and Davies at first insisted on the original contract, but they acquiesced at last to Percy's new terms. In 1800 Percy's edition of Goldsmith still had not been printed, and he changed the terms again to include a cash payment to the Goldsmith family. Not until 1801 did Percy's four-volume edition appear. In 1807 he wrote and published a statement charging the firm with the many delays in publishing and with editing the manuscript heavily without his assistance. Percy himself, however, brought on much of the delay by changing publishers and contracts several times over a seventeen-year period, and the interpolations made in the text

P O E M S,

CHIEFLY IN THE

SCOTTISH DIALECT.

B Y

R O B E R T   B U R N S.

THE THIRD EDITION.

L O N D O N:

PRINTED FOR A. STRAHAN; T. CADELL IN THE
STRAND; AND W. CREECH, EDINBURGH.

M DCC LXXXVII.

*Title page for the London edition of Burns's poems, published
by Cadell the Elder in conjunction with other publishers.
Thomas Cadell Jr. continued the relationship
with the poet.*

were minor. Cadell and Davies had not consulted Percy on the changes because they simply did not bother to deal with the uncooperative editor any longer, calling him a "devious, formal, and fussy collaborator."

In 1799 James Currie contracted with the firm to provide books for a newly constructed reading room for the Liverpool Athenaeum. The account was enormous and aroused the jealousy of the Liverpool booksellers. To avoid an antagonistic relationship with the "Brethren at Liverpool," Cadell and Davies wrote to Currie on 17 October 1799 to suggest that they be dropped from the account after the first shipment, which was already en route, and that further purchases be divided among the Liverpool booksellers. The willingness of the firm "most readily" to "forego the Gratification we had promised ourselves from the Supply of [your] institution, rather than be the Means of raising any unpleasant Sensations" among the Liverpool booksellers testifies to the liberal and gracious attitude that gov-

erned their business relationships with authors, printers, agents, and rival publishing houses.

In April 1800 the United States Congress appropriated five thousand dollars for the purchase of books and transmitted an order to Cadell and Davies, who thereby provided the core of the new Library of Congress. The bill of sale can be regarded as the first catalogue of the collection: it includes books, journals, maps, and a map case. The accompanying letter, dated 11 December 1800, closes with the words "We beg you to accept our best thanks for your obliging preference of us on this occasion."

In 1802 Cadell married Sophia Elizabeth Smith. They had a large family, of whom four daughters, Elizabeth, Rosa, Sophia, and Joanna, and at least one son, Henry, survived to marriageable age.

The firm's relationship with Dr. James Currie, Burns's literary executor, allowed it to purchase the copyright to all of Burns's works, whether previously published or not; and its care with these works provided fourteen hundred pounds to Burns's widow and trustees. Besterman credits the revival of Burns's work to Cadell and Davies's able management of the copyrights and manuscripts, and for the first half of the century their series of Burns's works was the only authorized version. Constantly troubled by piracies of the books, they sued in the House of Lords; by winning the suit they effectively changed copyright law to the advantage of publishers.

In 1805 Archibald Constable contracted to be the agent for Cadell and Davies in Edinburgh. Thirty-six letters from 1805 to 1825 document the firms' "honeymoon period," the tension that arose between them, and, finally, the collapse of Constable's firm. At first, enthusiasm and praise mark Davies's and Constable's letters, as when Davies writes on 31 May that "nothing shall be wanting on my Part to extend and strengthen such an Intercourse between our Houses." But Constable began to worry that other booksellers were also engaged with Cadell and Davies, to which Davies replied soothingly on 6 February 1806 that "there's Room enough in the World for all of Us"; and he also began, in between writing apologetic letters full of rationalizations and promises of improvement, to move into a competitive position regarding copyrights in Cadell and Davies's possession. A 19 September 1815 letter signed by Cadell and Davies but probably written by Cadell — the writing is more direct and forceful than Davies's usual and is not marked by the frequent capitalization common to Davies's style — to complain, "We are sorry . . . to observe that, amongst your earliest acts, is the expression of a desire to dispossess us of the management of many of the works in question which we have so long had in our care." The letter goes on to advise Constable to stick to his job as agent and limit his activity to making suggestions rather than decisions. Constable replied three days later with an indignant protest that they should know him well enough to trust him and an assertion that just because a publisher has managed certain contracts in the past does not mean that he will continue to manage them in the future. Several other letters press Constable to remit overdue moneys to Cadell and Davies.

Since 1813 Cadell had been left to run the business on his own during Davies's bouts with illness. It was, perhaps, Cadell's inexperience that led to the only recorded instance of the firm's treating an author unfairly – in fact, exploiting him. The firm offered the Reverend Henry Kaye Bonney, a new and rather naive author, a third of the profits from his work *The Life of the Right Reverend Father in God, Jeremy Taylor, D.D.* (1815), subject to his guaranteeing against loss; worse than offering this uncharacteristically low remuneration, the firm also estimated printing costs at two hundred pounds, a rather high sum. The firm botched another publisher/author relationship during this period by selling the copyright of Walter Scott's *Minstrelsy of the Scottish Border* (1802) to Longman and Hurst; Cadell and Davies had been Scott's first publishers but lost subsequent contracts when it gave up copyright.

One positive "partnership" that Cadell and Davies developed during this decade was with Samuel Taylor Coleridge. In 1815 Coleridge was considering translating works by either Miguel de Cervantes or Giovanni Boccaccio and wanted "a settled promise from some respectable publisher, such as Mr. Cadell, that he will purchase the manuscript when it is ready for press." Coleridge wrote to the Edinburgh publisher William Blackwood on 12 April 1819 to thank him for suggesting the firm (apparently, Coleridge had originally been hesitant to do any business with Cadell and Davies that involved *Blackwood's*). "I do indeed," he wrote, "feel myself much obliged to you for having made me acquainted with a man of such genuine worth and so much sound unostentatious good Sense." As Besterman says, "The picture of the poet calling on Cadell & Davies at any time that he chose with a little roll of manuscript and collecting his ten guineas for it, is certainly an agreeable one."

On 28 April 1820 (not, as erroneously stated in *The Dictionary of National Biography,* in 1819) Da-

vies died. Nichols says that "Those who knew him best never witnessed in him anything but the most liberal conduct as a friend, and a straightforward man of business, in which he was assiduous and attentive, always giving the most valuable advice, and acting with the utmost fairness and liberality in the position in which his good conduct had placed him." After Davies's death Cadell changed the name of the firm to Cadell, Jr.; moved the business to his home in Charlotte Street, Fitzroy Square; and ran it with no assistance except occasional help from his son, Henry.

In 1819 T. Cadell and W. Davies had entered into an agreement with Blackwood to become the London publisher of that firm's *Edinburgh Monthly Magazine,* generally known as *Blackwood's Magazine.* The attack by *Blackwood's* led by its editors, John Wilson and John Gibson Lockhart, on what they called the "Cockney School of Poetry," led by Leigh Hunt and William Hazlitt, created problems for Cadell. On 27 April 1823 Hazlitt, who had already sued Blackwood for two thousand pounds and received one hundred pounds in an out-of-court settlement, wrote to Cadell: "Sir, – Unless you agree to give up publication of Blackwood's Magazine, I shall feel myself compelled to commence an action against you for damages sustained from repeated slanders and false imputation in that work on me." Cadell attached a copy of the demand to his own letter to Blackwood, saying that "my feelings would not be of the most agreeable nature, were my name brought before the public by him as disseminator of slanderous and false imputations." The matter never came to court, so Blackwood must have placated Hazlitt. But by May Cadell was considering giving up the magazine. Blackwood visited Cadell in London, calmed his fears, and persuaded him to continue as publisher. Immediately thereafter Hunt brought suit against Cadell for libel. This suit, too, was smoothed over, and Cadell kept the magazine in the firm; but Blackwood's talent for mollifying offended authors would continue, until his death in 1834 caused connections between the houses to cease.

By the 1830s Cadell was a member of the court of assistants of the Stationers' Company. He did not achieve the standing of "master" that his father had, and his house's reputation had lost some of its luster in its last decade, when he ran it single-handedly. But when Cadell died on 23 or 26 November 1836 – due to a clerical error the date is not certain – he left a large fortune. His will required his executors to "sell and dispose of[,] round up and close my business" as soon as convenient, but not more than three years after his death; this arrangement explains the appearances of Cadell's imprint on books as late as 1840. After unsuccessful attempts to sell the whole of the stock, capital, and copyrights, Cadell's trustees auctioned off the goods piecemeal in the fall of 1840, and the seventy-three-year-old house of Cadell ended.

References:

Theodore Besterman, ed., *The Publishing Firm of Cadell & Davies: Select Correspondence and Accounts, 1793–1836* (London: Oxford University Press, 1938);

Frank A. Mumby, *Publishing and Bookselling. Part One: From the Earliest Times to 1780* (London: Cape, 1974), pp. 166, 173, 176–178;

Mumby, *The Romance of Bookselling: A History from the Earliest Times to the Twentieth Century* (Metuchen, N.J.: Scarecrow Press, 1967), pp. 253, 265, 270–273, 300;

John Nichols, *Minor Lives: A Collection of Biographies by John Nichols,* edited by Edward L. Hart (Cambridge, Mass.: Harvard University Press, 1971), pp. 265–270.

Papers:

Correspondence and other business documents of the Cadell firm are located in many places; there is no one complete record of them. Yale's Osborne Collection has 24 letters, and its Beinecke Library holds about 550 letters to the firm, 125 replies from the firm, and about 100 manuscripts. Harvard University has 29 letters by Thomas Cadell the Elder, 16 addressed to him, and two receipts. The British Museum has correspondence with Samuel Ireland. The Folger Library, Washington, D.C., has letters from various correspondents. One letter exists in the William Cowper Collection at Princeton, and the Bodleian Library, Oxford, has a collection of letters to the firm. The New York Public Library holds letters, largely in the Ford Collection. Finally, there are papers concerning Constable in the National Library of Scotland, Edinburgh.

– Cynthia Guidici

William Collins, Sons and Company
(Glasgow and London: 1826 - 1949)

Chalmers and Collins
(Glasgow: 1819 - 1826)

William Collins and Sons, Ltd.
(London, Glasgow, New York, Melbourne: 1949 - 1983)

William Collins PLC
(London, Glasgow, New York, Melbourne: 1983 - 1990)

HarperCollins Publishers
(London, Glasgow, New York, Melbourne: 1990 -   )

The firm of Chalmers and Collins was founded in Glasgow in 1819 by William Collins and Charles Chalmers. Collins, born in 1789, had been a millworker and the owner and operator of a successful seminary. Throughout his life he would be a reformer and a philanthropist; he would found the Scottish Temperance Society in 1829 and would be active in the Church Extension movement of the 1830s. Chalmers was the somewhat feckless brother of the great Evangelical divine Dr. Thomas Chalmers. Dr. Chalmers conceived the idea of the publishing venture and put up the money for it, largely to secure a dependable outlet for his own writings. The house quickly rose to a position of eminence in the thriving and competitive Glasgow publishing and stationery market.

Dr. Chalmers was the firm's most prolific and important author in the period from 1819 to 1846, during which he earned an estimated fourteen thousand pounds from the publication of his books, sermons, pamphlets, speeches, and introductions. Chalmers and Collins's first publication was the initial quarterly number of Dr. Chalmers's *The Christian and Civic Economy of Large Towns,* which appeared on 24 September 1819. Installments of the widely distributed series were printed in various editions until its completion in 1826, and Dr. Chalmers had considerable control over how the series was advertised and distributed. *A Series of Discourses on the Christian Revelation* (1817) had established Dr. Chalmers as a popular author, and Chalmers and Collins published several editions of the book in the early 1820s.

The firm became a leader in educational publications — another interest to which the house would remain true. Many publications from the early years were inseparably religious and pedagogical (or, at least, didactic). In 1821 Chalmers and Collins published its first schoolbook, *A System of Commercial Arithmetic for Use in Schools and Private Families.* A book list appended to the 1825 edition of William Mure's *The Historie and Descent of the House of Rowallane* advertises fifty-five entries in the series Select Christian Biography, Intended for Youth: the list includes works by or adapted from Dr. Chalmers as well as now-long-forgotten moral tales such as *Pious Grandson, or the History of James Anderson, The Widow of Rosenheath, a Lesson of Piety, Affectionately Dedicated to the Young,* and *Disobedience; or, the History of Henry and Mary Walford.* The firm published dictionaries as well, beginning in 1824 with a Greek/English dictionary and continuing to the present day with dictionaries both specialized and popular. In the 1830s and 1840s the firm would publish such educational series as James Leitch's Practical and Economical Readers and the first of the Ready Reckoners.

In 1822 Chalmers and Collins inaugurated the successful Cheap Edition of Select Christian Authors; by 1829 the series would consist of approximately fifty perennially popular works of divinity with prefaces by modern authors. Dr. Chalmers contributed many of the prefaces; foremost among

William Collins, who founded the firm of Chalmers and Collins with Charles Chalmers

other contributors were Edward Irving and the great reformer William Wilberforce. The latter wrote the introduction for John Witherspoon's "Essay on Regeneration" in his *Treatises on Justification and Regeneration* (1824), and the firm published Wilberforce's own immensely popular *A Practical View of the Prevailing System of Professed Christians in the Higher and Middle Classes in This Country Contrasted with Real Christianity* (1797) in the series in 1826. In 1945 the firm would purchase the rights to Sir Reginald Coupland's 1923 biography of the reformer.

Thomas Dick's *The Christian Philosopher* (1823) was a great success for the firm throughout the century; and religious or devotional works by Irving, Nathaniel Paterson, James Montgomery, and others further established Collins's strength in Christian publications. Montgomery was particularly active for the firm, editing the durable anthologies *The Christian Psalmist* (1825) and *The Christian Poet* (1827); he would also provide the introduction for

the firm's edition of John Milton's *Paradise Lost* in 1842.

Profits from Dr. Chalmers's early publications, in large part, enabled Collins to repay his initial investment, with interest, in April 1826. At the same time Collins bought out Charles Chalmers's interest in the business, and Chalmers left the firm.

Collins often used his press as a means of distributing books and pamphlets in support of causes in which he and Dr. Chalmers were involved. In 1830 he flooded the market with some five hundred thousand copies of temperance tracts — often transcriptions of his own speeches — and five years later he was publishing fifty thousand copies monthly of the Tracts on Religious Establishments, a series designed to promote Church Extension among the working class. Also in the 1830s Collins edited and published the *Temperance Society Record* and published several other pro-Extension periodicals.

Dr. Chalmers was temperamental and egotistical, and his relationship with Collins was marked

Charles Chalmers's brother, Dr. Thomas Chalmers, an Evangelical clergyman who financed the establishment of Chalmers and Collins to provide an outlet for his own writings; portrait by Sir John Watson Gordon (National Gallery of Scotland)

by an escalating abusiveness toward the publisher. He had been unhappy about the dissolution of the partnership of Collins and Chalmers, and the poor sales of his *Political Economy in Connection with the Moral State and Moral Prospects of Society* (1832) further irritated him. Collins sold eight thousand copies of Dr. Chalmers's 1838 London lecture series within twelve months, but in 1841 Dr. Chalmers, troubled by what he called in a 15 October journal entry the "neglect and inattention" of Collins, hired his son-in-law William Hanna to watch out for his interests.

In 1841 Collins secured a license to print the New Testament, thereby moving the firm in a direction that it would follow throughout its existence. Collins printed some thirty thousand copies of a single impression of the New Testament in 1841 and was printing complete Bibles by 1842. When the Disruption rent the Church of Scotland in 1843, Collins rounded up forty thousand subscribers for

his edition of the *Select Practical Writings of John Knox* (1845) as part of his efforts for the Free Church faction. Relations between Collins and Dr. Chalmers continued to be mutually profitable until 1846, at which time Chalmers, for reasons still not entirely clear, defected to the rival firm of Oliver and Boyd.

Collins's son, William Collins II, had been made a partner in the firm in 1843, and he assumed control of it on the death of his father in 1853. Like his father, the younger William was an astute businessman, a devout man, and a philanthropist; and like his father he was active in the temperance movement, earning the nickname "Water Willie" for his enthusiastic adherence to the doctrine he preached. He would be elected lord provost of Glasgow in 1877 and knighted in 1881.

The 1850s saw Collins moving into publication of scientific encyclopedias and atlases, both of which remain staples of the modern book list. The firm's prominence in educational publishing was

*The Trongate in Glasgow, location of the Collins offices, in
1837; lithograph by S. D. Swarbreck*

Moxon and published nineteen volumes of the series under the title The Grosvenor Poets; the series is noteworthy for its prefatory material by William Michael Rossetti, the lesser-known brother of Dante Gabriel and Christina Rossetti.

The era of William Collins II is noteworthy more for its expansion of the company in both domestic and foreign markets than for the breadth of its book lists. Under his guidance the firm opened or extended markets in Canada, Australia, New Zealand, India, and Africa and established itself as a world leader in stationery and publishing, with an annual output of about two million books by 1879. In that year Collins made what was then an unusual move when he bought out the partners he had brought in during the previous decade and formed a limited-liability company, selling shares and forming the firm's first board of directors. In 1881 the firm introduced the date-book-like "diaries" that were to prove durable breadwinners. In 1884 it brought out the first in a series of large-type primers; the series would sell almost three million copies in ten years. Collins introduced educational readers with colored illustrations in 1891. In 1892 the firm opened an American agency for the distribution of its Bibles, Testaments, and prayer books.

The firm's expansion continued under the short administration of William Collins III, who assumed control when his father died in 1895. An eccentric who paid his wife five pounds for each of his frequent failures to attend Sunday church services and who carried his own cuts of meat into his favorite restaurants, William III overhauled the old printing facilities at Glasgow and began to mine the South American market while strengthening the company's position in older markets, such as Jamaica and Trinidad. In 1903 he opened a large stationery factory in Sydney and two years later opened the William Collins Company office in New York to help distribute Collins Bibles and the new and extraordinarily successful Collins Illustrated Pocket Classics. This series of small and inexpensive reprints was to prove profitable for the firm until the outbreak of World War II, by which time it would consist of more than three hundred titles, including sturdy nineteenth-century favorites by Sir Walter Scott, Jane Austen, Charles Dickens, William Makepeace Thackeray, George Eliot, and the Brontë sisters, as well as works by contemporary authors such as Walter de la Mare and H. G. Wells. Between 1903 and 1948 the series would sell more than twenty-five million copies. The Collins edition of the works of William Shakespeare (1900), edited by H. G. Bell, proved to be another successful ven-

recognized in the early 1860s, when William Collins II was named publisher to the Scottish School Book Association and the Irish National Schools; in the first decade of his appointment Collins shipped more than two million schoolbooks to Ireland. During William II's administration dictionary sales boomed, and the firm published works in English literary and language studies, selling, for instance, more than five hundred thousand copies of A. M. Trotter's *A Manual of English Grammar* (1873). Collins published 571 different schoolbooks in 1865 and was publishing 920 titles annually by the middle of the following decade; in this period Collins was also publishing the costly but successful Science series. Under the management of William Collins II the firm printed Bibles, both cheap and expensive, in many types, sizes, and styles of binding, and by 1862 it was selling some three hundred thousand Bibles annually. In 1871 Collins purchased the Popular Poets series from the failing publisher Edward

ture into the reprint market: it included a preface by Henry Irving on the Francis Bacon debate and sold more than a million copies.

William Collins III restored to the Collins book list a diversity that was both consistent with the firm's origins and indicative of the direction in which it would move in future years. He continued the firm's commitment to schoolbooks, introducing the *World-Wide Readers* and the three-colored *New Graphic Readers*. William III's interest in original works is evident in the juvenile literature he promoted, which accounted for annual sales of more than one million copies by the early twentieth century. Among Collins's most important or prolific writers of children's fiction were Katherine Tynan, Andrew Lang, and Florence Dugdale – the future wife of Thomas Hardy. Collins editor Herbert Hayens proved a reliable contributor in this genre, writing entries for the firm's Play-Up series for boys that was designed to complement the Abbey Girls series of the same period.

Fortunately for the firm, William III brought his nephews William IV and Godfrey into the firm in the 1890s. The brothers assumed control when William III died in 1906 after falling down an empty elevator shaft and would rule in tandem until Godfrey's death in 1936. Of Godfrey, who would be knighted in 1919 and be appointed secretary of state for Scotland in 1932, Rose Macaulay would say, "Never did any publisher realise more fully than he the identity of interest of publisher and author"; and T. H. White would call William IV "the kindest and bravest publisher in England." Godfrey maintained the company's interest in reprints, introducing in 1907 the Sevenpenny series of previously published works by living writers. In the same period Collins began publishing the inexpensive Pocket Library series of eighty novels and the Penny Library series for schools, which included works by Jonathan Swift and John Ruskin. The brothers were fine businessmen, and four years after the death of their uncle the firm was producing some eighty-nine thousand books weekly. In 1913 Godfrey published the series The Nation's Library, commentary on significant political and social topics of the day. Francis Brett Young's comments about the firm during the late 1910s suggest that Collins was not at that time a publisher whom Young, at least, found particularly prestigious or efficient; but he was impressed by the profusion of photographs reproduced by Collins in Young's *Marching on Tanga* (1917). In 1917 Godfrey introduced the firm's new fiction list. A thorough revision of the schoolbook list after World War I brought the firm into the

William Collins II, who became head of the firm on his father's death in 1853

modern world of educational publishing, in which it continues to exert a significant presence.

Godfrey kept the higher profile of the duumvirs, after 1917 supervising the firm's publishing activities from the company's new offices at 48 Pall Mall, London, while his brother, as chairman, tended to the stationery branch and office management. Godfrey hired F. T. Smith as chief editor, and the brothers brought in outside experts in publicity and sales. The Novel Library and the Shilling Novels first appeared in 1928, the latter series selling about one million copies during its first year. Global expansion continued unabated; in a letter of 1 September 1921 Young marvels at having seen "a pile of 100 or more" of his *The Black Diamond* at a bookshop in Cape Town. An improved stationery factory was opened in Australia in 1929, and a Canadian office was established three years later. During

William Collins III, who headed the firm from 1895 until he fell to his death in an elevator shaft in 1906. He enlarged the international presence of William Collins, Sons and Company and increased the diversity of its lists.

and following Godfrey's reign, Collins purchased the British rights to many American novels; it acquired in 1934 the British rights to the lucrative Walt Disney catalogue.

Godfrey's administration is memorable for the firm's expansion in the area of original literature, an area overseen principally by Godfrey's nephew and William IV's son, William Collins V, generally known as W. A. R. Collins or "Billy." By the 1920s the company was focusing on original fiction and poetry, both popular and belletristic. An advertisement in the 1921 edition of Young's *The Black Diamond* displays an extensive list of "Mssrs COLLINS' Latest Novels" and promises "to send their book lists regularly to readers who will send name and address." Collins publications began to win prestigious literary prizes in 1921 with Romer Wilson's Hawthornden Prize for *The Death of Society* (1921); in 1922 de la Mare received the James Tait Black Prize for *Memoirs of a Midget* (1921), and Macaulay

was awarded the Stock Prize for *Dangerous Ages* (1921). Later prizewinners include Winifred Holtby's 1937 Black Prize for *South Riding* (1936) and Peter Quennell's 1950 W. H. Heinemann Foundation for Literature Award for *John Ruskin* (1949). Recognition for the new Collins list came in 1929 from the fledgling Book Society, which made Helen Beauclerk's *The Love of the Foolish Angel* its first selection. In the following decade the society would accord the same honor to another Collins publication, Stuart Cloete's *Turning Wheels* (1937), which made publishing history by being the first novel to secure both this endorsement and its American equivalent, the featured selection of the Book-of-the-Month Club.

Among the important writers whose works were published by Collins under Godfrey and Billy were Victoria Sackville-West, John Middleton Murry, Michael Arlen, Rosamond Lehmann, Rachel Field, Kenneth Roberts, Peter Cheyney, Howard

The brothers Godfrey Collins and William Collins IV, who ran the firm in tandem from 1906 until Godfrey's death in 1936. William continued until his own death in 1945.

Spring, and the poet laureate, John Masefield, whose *The Country Scene* and *Tribute to Ballet* appeared in 1937 and 1938, respectively. Spring would comment on the extensive distribution of his *O Absalom!* (1938) in March 1939 when he inscribed a copy of the book with a mock apology: "It is my profitable misfortune . . . to be unable to get hold of a first-edition of this book."

Publications by de la Mare, Holtby, and H. G. Wells strengthened the company's reputation. De la Mare compiled for the firm the juvenile-verse anthology *Tom Tiddler's Ground* (1932). Wells, more lucrative to Collins for his presence in the reprint catalogue than as an original author, contributed *Washington and the Hope of Peace* to the firm's list of original works in 1922. Although literary history has not been kind to her, Holtby was one of Collins's premier authors during the 1930s. She was lured from the publisher Jonathan Cape in 1931 by Collins's

advance of £350 for her *Mandoa, Mandoa!* (1933). Holtby clearly enjoyed being courted by the firm; in a 1931 letter she commented wryly but gently on her dealings with the business-minded "Old Sir Godfrey" and called Billy Collins "rather sweet" and "most flatteringly deferential." The partnership was ultimately more remunerative for Collins than for Holtby, who died six months before the publication of *South Riding* (1936), the original eight-shilling edition of which sold in excess of forty thousand copies, the American edition more than ten thousand, and the cumulative sales of which had reached seventy thousand by the end of the 1930s. (In 1974 Collins's Fontana imprint would publish the successful companion volume to Yorkshire Television's adaptation of *South Riding*.)

But it was crime and detective fiction that was to become the bulwark of the firm's original lists during the reigns of Godfrey and Billy Collins. The

45

firm had experimented with crime fiction in 1919 and during the following decades was generally willing to publish crime and detective novels as well as thrillers and Westerns. In 1930, bolstered by its early successes with Agatha Christie, the firm founded the Crime Club, which over the years published monthly selections by such authors as Philip MacDonald, Rex Stout, Nicholas Blake (Cecil Day Lewis), and Ngaio Marsh; membership in the club soon reached twenty thousand.

Christie was Collins's most important – and most demanding – author from 1926 to 1976. Dissatisfied with her publisher, The Bodley Head, Christie signed a three-book contract in 1924 in which Godfrey Collins agreed to pay an advance of £200 and a substantial royalty for each book. In her autobiography (1977) Christie would call *The Murder of Roger Ackroyd* (1926), her first novel with Collins, "my most successful to date"; and the partnership would be financially rewarding to both author and publisher for its duration. A new contract in 1928 called for six novels, each with an advance of £750 and royalties of 20 to 25 percent; by 1941 Christie was receiving advances of £1,000 and a royalty rate of 25 percent after the first three thousand sales. Collins managed to continue its advances to its prize author during the war and, buoyed by the strong sales of *The Moving Finger* (published in New York by Dodd, Mead in 1942 and by Collins in 1943), *Five Little Pigs* (1942), and *Towards Zero* (1944), doubled them to £2,000 in 1945. A surge in Christie's popularity in 1951–1952 had the firm paying Christie extraordinarily high royalties for her titles in the new Fontana paperback series. When Collins merged with Harper and Row in 1989, Harper would pay $9.6 million for the rights to the Christie catalogue.

Largely due to the tact of Billy Collins, the partnership with Christie weathered some dramatic, if increasingly predictable, storms. Christie often complained about the firm's editorial alterations of her prose, the sloppiness of its proofreading, the low quality of its paper, the wording of its publicity releases and dust-jacket blurbs, and the representations of her characters on the dust jackets. Annoyed by the depiction of her detective Hercule Poirot on the jacket of the 1947 collection *The Labours of Hercules,* Christie commented in a letter to her literary agent that the illustration "suggests Poirot going naked to the bath," or, more luridly, "Poirot gone peculiar in Hyde Park." Although the firm could be tough with Christie when it felt the need to be – as in its criticism of *They Came to Baghdad* (1951) and *Passenger to Frankfurt* (1970), and in its rejection of

the political novel *The Rose and the Yew Tree* (which was published by William Heinemann in 1948) – Billy Collins himself typically responded to his star's outbursts with apologies, tickets to Wimbledon, tennis balls (during the war, when rubber was scarce), invitations to parties, Christmas packages of food and books, and promises of increased authorial control and editorial vigilance. On balance the relationship between Christie and Billy Collins was a genial as well as a productive one, and there is no reason to doubt the sincerity of Christie's dedication of *Ordeal by Innocence* (1958) to Billy "with affection and respect" or of Billy's address at Christie's memorial service in 1976.

In 1936 Godfrey replaced the globe logo with Eric Gill's fountain colophon, the tasteful art deco design that adorns many of the firm's best-known publications and would be alluded to in the corporate logo designed in 1989 for HarperCollins Publishers. By the 1930s annual sales of Bibles, Testaments, and prayer books had reached six hundred thousand, and they would top one million by 1940.

During World War II German air raids on 29–30 December 1940 and 23 February 1944 devastated Collins's London offices and destroyed books and business records. But the war years were, nevertheless, productive ones for the firm. Arthur Bryant's sweeping history, *English Saga, 1840–1940,* published jointly with Eyre and Spottiswoode in 1940, sold briskly during and after the war, as did Thomas Armstrong's 1940 novel *The Crowthers of Bankdam.* Hesketh Pearson wrote his biography *Bernard Shaw* (1942) in cooperation with its subject. With fellow publishers Macmillan and Heinemann, Collins founded the Pan imprint in 1944; by the early 1980s each firm would own some 660,000 shares of this profitable business.

During the war Collins manufactured eleven million copies of the White Circle novel series at plants all over the world. Several important series were initiated during the war. The first volume of the inexpensive series Britain in Pictures appeared in 1941; the series was designed, in part, to provide a portrait for the world of Britain during these difficult years. Each volume included text, color plates, and illustrations. In keeping with wartime changes in the economics of publishing, Britain in Pictures was produced in cooperation with the external printers Adprint, Ltd. The New Naturalist series, conceived during the war and begun at its termination, featured titles edited by distinguished scientists such as Julian Huxley.

Collins's London offices after the German air raids of 29–30 December 1940

William Collins IV died in 1945, leaving Billy Collins in charge of the operation, then based at St. James's Place following the destruction of the Pall Mall facilities. Billy would supervise the firm during some of its finest years and through the worst of the recession of the 1970s. The firm went public in 1949, adjusting successfully to the postwar economy. Collins capitalized on the demand for war-related books that accompanied the return to peace: among the historical novels, personal accounts, and military biographies and histories that came out after the war, Eric Williams's *The Wooden Horse* (1949) and Desmond Young's *Rommel* (1950) sold particularly well. Successful series included the St. James Library — a reprint series initiated in 1950 — and the perenially popular Pocket and Field Guides, which catered to amateur naturalists. Approximately seventy million scriptural and liturgical publications had been sold between 1841 and 1950. In 1953 William Collins and Sons, Ltd., purchased Geoffrey Bles, Ltd., a house specializing in religious publishing; in this manner the works of C. S. Lewis passed into Collins's hands. Later in the decade the

Harvill Press was added to the Collins family, providing Collins with Boris Pasternak's best-selling *Doctor Zhivago* (1958). The purchase in 1956 of Hatchard's, London's oldest bookshop, added prestige and further revenue. Billy Collins kept the firm's lists diverse and exciting: Chester Wilmot provided histories, and Bernard Wall's translation of Pierre Teilhard de Chardin's *The Phenomenon of Man* (1959) proved a successful excursion into philosophy. Collins continued to be active in children's publishing, with such authors as Dr. Seuss, Richard Scarry, Gerald Durrell, and Michael Bond providing significant entries; and Joy Adamson's Elsa books began appearing on Collins booklists in 1960. From its old competitors Blackie and Sons of Glasgow, Collins purchased an extensive printing works and bindery in 1966; the complex at Bishopbriggs remains the production center of HarperCollins, U.K. Collins inaugurated the biennial Religious Book Award in 1969 in acknowledgment of the role of religious publications in the firm's history.

Simone de Beauvoir, Alistair MacLean, Giuseppe di Lampedusa, Hammond Innes, Victoria

Holt, and Judith Kerr were some of the novelists who took the firm from the war years through the 1970s. The Fontana imprint matured under the guidance of Billy Collins's second son, Mark, becoming by the 1970s one of Britain's three leading British imprints. In 1973 Collins secured the rights to Nobel Prize winner Aleksandr Solzhenitsyn's *The Gulag Archipelago,* which it published the following year.

After the lean years 1973 to 1975, the company earned £49 million in 1976. That year Billy Collins (who had been knighted in 1970) died, and his son Jan assumed the chairmanship. The *Good News Bible,* published that year, achieved sales of one million within three months. Nevertheless, the 1970s were difficult for Collins as for the industry in general, and the firm ended the decade reporting a year-end loss of £255,000 for 1979. But Collins quickly regained financial health. Sales of Fontana paperbacks, clearly established as the firm's cash cow, rose from £8.51 million in 1980 to £10.18 million in 1981 and £13.39 million in 1982; Fontana placed twelve titles in the *Sunday Times* year-end best-seller list of 1986, as did the Grafton imprint, acquired by Collins with the purchase of Granada 22 Publishing in 1983. Popular novels were largely responsible for this impressive rise in fortune, and the booklist was increasingly dominated by names like Jackie Collins, Sidney Sheldon, Ken Follett, Craig Thomas, and John Trenhaile. Soviet leader Mikhail Gorbachev's *Perestroika* was published jointly by Collins and Harper and Row in 1987. Bible publishing remained an important part of Collins's Education, Reference, and Professional Division.

But the 1980s will be remembered in Collins history not for its book lists but for the end of the firm as an autonomous and family-owned concern. In 1981 Jan Collins negotiated the sale of the Collins family interest to the Australian media magnate Rupert Murdoch's News Corporation International. In the ensuing power struggle Ian Chapman succeeded Jan Collins as chairman and, in cooperation with various Collins authors, endeavored to keep the company independent. Chapman reached an agreement with Murdoch in August 1981 that allotted News Corporation International two directors. During the negotiations Lady Collins, Billy's widow and the editor of the Collins religious list, resigned from the board; Mark Collins resigned his directorship in 1983, thereby ending the family's involvement. The firm, now William Collins PLC, quickly absorbed Granada, and added 50 percent of Harper and Row in 1987 and 60 percent of Multiple Sound Distributors in 1988. Murdoch had paid

$293 million for Harper in 1987, and in 1989 he paid $717 million for the remaining 75 percent of Collins. By the time of the sale William Collins and Sons was the largest independent book publishing and book manufacturing company in the United Kingdom, with more than two thousand employees in the British Isles, offices and outlets all over the world, and a weekly production rate of some 1.4 million books. On 29 May 1990 the company became HarperCollins Publishers.

References:

Vera Brittain, *Testament of Friendship: The Story of Winifred Holtby* (New York: Macmillan, 1940);

Stewart J. Brown, *Thomas Chalmers and the Godly Commonwealth in Scotland* (Oxford: Oxford University Press, 1982);

A. C. Cheyne, ed., *The Practical and the Pious: Essays on Thomas Chalmers (1780–1847)* (Edinburgh: St. Andrew, 1985);

Agatha Christie, *An Autobiography* (New York: Dodd, Mead, 1977);

David Keir, *The House of Collins: The Story of a Scottish Family of Publishers from 1789 to the Present Day* (London: Collins, 1952);

Janet P. Morgan, *Agatha Christie: A Biography* (New York: Knopf, 1985);

Frank Arthur Mumby and Ian Norrie, *Publishing and Bookselling,* fifth edition (London: Cape, 1974);

William Mure, *The Historie and Descent of the House of Rowallane* (Glasgow: Chalmers & Collins, 1825);

Norrie, *Mumby's Publishing and Bookselling in the Twentieth Century,* sixth edition (London: Bell & Hyman, 1982);

Charles Osborne, *The Life and Crimes of Agatha Christie* (New York: Rainbird-Holt, Rinehart & Winston, 1983);

Forrest Reid, *Walter de la Mare: A Critical Study* (London: Faber & Faber, 1929);

Jessica Brett Young, *Francis Brett Young: A Biography* (London: Heinemann, 1962).

Papers:

Unpublished letters from Howard Spring and Francis Brett Young to William Collins and Sons are at the Harry Ransom Humanities Research Center, University of Texas at Austin. Miscellaneous published and unpublished information about William Collins and Sons (Holding), Ltd., and HarperCollins Publishers is at the Collins archives, Glasgow, and at the library of HarperCollins, New York.

– Alexander Pettit

Archibald Constable and Company

(Edinburgh: 1795 – 1826)

Archibald Constable became Scotland's premier publisher in the early nineteenth century, a time when the country's literary and intellectual activity was at a peak. He published works by many of the most important authors of his day on topics ranging from religion to economics. He also published many important reference books, including the *Encyclopædia Britannica,* as well as the most significant journal of the age, the *Edinburgh Review.* Moreover, he presided over the great revival of interest in Scottish folklore, history, and poetry during the period. But the jewel in his crown was Sir Walter Scott, whose prolific writings — especially his hugely popular Waverley novels — made both publisher and author a fortune. But despite this prosperity, Constable allowed his business affairs to become overly reliant on an increasingly complex series of debts, and both he and Scott fell into bankruptcy in 1826.

Constable was born at Carnbee in Fifeshire on 24 February 1774 to Thomas Constable, a farmer who became land steward to John Francis Erskine, earl of Kellie, and Elizabeth Myles Constable. Constable attended the local parish school without especially distinguishing himself, though he maintained a lifelong friendship with his teacher, William Forfar. In an autobiographical fragment written in 1821 and published in his son Thomas's 1873 biography of him, he relates that he became interested in the book trade in 1786 when an Edinburgh bookseller, William Cockburn, opened a shop in the nearby village of Pittenweem. Constable and his schoolfellows would buy school supplies and browse among the picture books on display there, and after one visit to the shop Constable announced to his father his strong desire to become a stationer (the term then used for bookseller). His father set up an apprenticeship for him with the firm of Peter Hill in Edinburgh.

The apprenticeship began in February 1788. Constable performed the usual duties of a young apprentice, such as tying up parcels and running errands. In the autobiographical fragment he notes that his first assignment from Hill was to take an order to Andrew Bell for one hundred copies of the *Encyclopaedia Britannica*; Bell had to refuse the order,

as the edition was sold out. The incident may have influenced Constable's decision years later to buy the rights to publish the *Britannica.* He gradually rose to such a position of trust in the business that Hill sent him out to auctions with the power to make buying decisions. In his years with Hill, Constable was able to observe such members of the Scottish literary elite as Robert Burns, a friend of Hill's.

Hill was not especially interested in acquiring and selling old and rare books, but Constable was. When Hill received a large shipment of old books in trade from Francis, ninth earl of Moray, Constable gained permission to catalogue them. From then on this branch of the bookseller's business became more and more central to Constable; in later life he would become one of the country's leading authorities on the valuation of rare books. His apprenticeship ended in 1794, but he stayed on one more year as clerk to Hill. On 16 January 1795 he married Mary Willison, the daughter of David Willison, a well-to-do printer. His new father-in-law helped Constable set up his own business that same month.

Among his first actions as an independent bookseller was to go to London to learn more about the trade, to buy books for his shop, and, most important, to make connections among the publishers there; those connections would be extremely useful to him. During this trip he met his future partner, Robert Cadell. His father-in-law had given him three hundred pounds worth of books to trade in London, and he had borrowed some cash from friends, as well, so he returned to Edinburgh with considerable stock. He opened his shop in High Street, with the sign "Scarce Old Books" over the door, and in May 1795 he published his first sale catalogue. Traffic in his shop steadily increased.

Hill's first steps into publishing were tentative and cautious: several small pamphlets, most of whose authors bore most of the printing expense. The first was a theological tract that he later called a "contemptible publication": *Anecdotes of the False Messias* (1795), by a divinity student identified only as "Mr. Black." Constable did not put his own name on the title page. After some other pamphlets that did not have much success, an account by Gordon

Engraving by James Faed after a painting by Sir Henry Raeburn

Turnbull of the insurrection in Grenada (1795) turned a profit and encouraged Constable to continue.

In 1796 Constable became acquainted with John Graham Dalyell, and the two discussed the idea of producing some Scottish-oriented publications. Dalyell, on Constable's request, edited the diary of Robert Birrell and some other pieces in a successful volume titled *Fragments of Scottish History* (1798). Constable's first paid author, having been given between twenty and thirty pounds for his labors, Dalyell went on to become curator of the Advocates Library and, hence, a major customer for Constable's old law books. Constable would publish some dozen other titles by Dalyell over the years. Constable purchased his first copyright when he paid one hundred pounds for a volume of sermons by Dr. John Erskine. He began publishing periodicals in 1800 with the quarterly *Farmer's Magazine;* in 1801 he bought the more prestigious *Scots Magazine*. He would later print many professional

periodicals, including the journals of the Highland Society, the Royal Society of Edinburgh, and the Caledonian Horticultural Society, as well as journals in fields ranging from medicine to philosophy.

Constable's business was growing steadily, but the real turning point for him came in 1802. A set of young intellectuals had begun frequenting his shop; among them were Sidney Smith and Francis Jeffrey, men of liberal leanings who found a sympathetic ear in Constable. They agreed that Scotland – indeed, Great Britain – needed a periodical that would espouse the cause of reform in a powerful manner. In October 1802 Constable printed the first issue of the *Edinburgh Review,* which was to become arguably the most politically, socially, and aesthetically significant periodical in British history (it would thrive throughout the Victorian era and would not cease publication until 1929). Smith, its first editor, later recalled the social and political situation of 1802:

The Catholics were not emancipated. The Corporation and Test Acts were unrepealed. The Game Laws were horribly oppressive; steel-traps and spring-guns were set all over the country; prisoners tried for their lives could have no counsel. . . . Libel was punished by the most cruel and vindictive imprisonments. The principles of political economy were little understood. The laws of debt and conspiracy were on the worst footing. The enormous wickedness of the slave-trade was tolerated. A thousand evils were in existence, which the talents of good and able men have since lessened or removed; and these efforts have been not a little assisted by the honest boldness of the *Edinburgh Review.*

Literary historians would concentrate not on the political and social reforms the journal helped bring about but on the fiery reviews of contemporary poets and novelists that Jeffrey and his contributors wrote under the cover of an anonymity that gave their opinions the force of the magisterial *Edinburgh Review* itself. Some of these reviews, such as Jeffrey's treatments of William Wordsworth, have become legendary examples of wrongheadedness, but the majority were sound, often powerful analyses of contemporary or past writers. Some, such as the mocking review by Henry Peter Brougham in the January 1808 issue of George Gordon, Lord Byron's first book, *Hours of Idleness* (1807), were cruel attacks – but attacks that made the ravaged author rethink his or her work. Byron, for example, was so enraged that he wrote his first truly good poem, the angry satire *English Bards, and Scotch Reviewers* (1809). Not all the critical essays in the *Edinburgh Review* had so dramatic an impact, but their influence on literary opinion was great; and Constable's association with such a publication catapulted him into the forefront of publishers.

He saw the value of the periodical and did all he could to nurture it and add to its prestige. Contributions for the first three issues were written without pay, but thereafter he offered writers the unheard-of sum of sixteen guineas per printed sheet; soon he increased the fee to twenty guineas and gave Jeffrey, the second editor, virtually carte blanche to set terms with authors as he saw fit. The best writers were, therefore, attracted to the journal not only for its prestige but also for its princely pay. Constable's business benefited, and so did the prestige of his country, which was beginning to be seen as the center of a liberal reawakening.

During the same year that Constable launched the *Edinburgh Review* he also made his first professional connection with Scott. Constable bought a share of the copyright in the third edition of *Minstrelsy of the Scottish Border* (1802); the rest was owned

by the London firm of Longman and Rees, which had bought it from Cadell and Davies. This is Scott's first book to bear Constable's name on the title page. The publication (jointly with Longman and Rees in London) of Scott's edition of *Sir Tristrem* (1804) marked Constable's first business dealings with Scott's close friend and printer, James Ballantyne. Scott began to pressure Constable to send printing business Ballantyne's way; Ballantyne's work was excellent, but resentment began to smolder in Constable – resentment that would now and then break out, threatening his continued relationship with Scott. But it became clear early on that if the publisher wanted Scott, he had to take Ballantyne along with him.

In 1803, his business expanding rapidly, Constable took on a partner, Alexander Gibson Hunter. Constable frequently sent Hunter to London, where he proved most valuable in establishing and expanding business agreements with other publishers. Thomas Longman wrote to Constable on 31 December 1803, congratulating him on his new partner and the proposed arrangements between Constable's firm and his own: "The means and the connexions you now possess, conjoined with your own excellent understanding, will necessarily command all that is valuable in the literature of Scotland. We shall doubtless do the same in England, and by a liberal exchange of copyrights, and thus promoting and combining our interests, we shall infallibly raise our fortunes and our names infinitely higher and to a more important station than has yet been known in the annals of our profession."

Hunter was also valuable in telling Constable some hard truths, though they were not always heard clearly enough. As early as 1808 he was warning Constable that Ballantyne was a poor businessman and that Scott would manipulate Constable and force him to bail Ballantyne out of difficulties – prophecies that were to prove all too true. At one point Scott heard what Hunter was saying and, in the first of several rifts between publisher and author, indignantly threatened to cut his ties with Constable.

In 1802 Longman's firm had acquired the right to publish the *Edinburgh Review* in London (it relinquished the right in 1807 and bought it back in 1814), and it also published, together with Constable, Scott's first major original success, *The Lay of the Last Minstrel* (1805); by 1825 the book would have gone into its fourteenth edition and have sold well over thirty thousand copies. Constable saw that the success of the poem reflected a huge appetite for such works among the reading public, and in 1807 he offered Scott £1,000 in advance for his next major poem, *Marmion* (1808). Its sales, too, were phenomenal (Scott's biographer John Gibson Lockhart estimated in 1836 that more than fifty thousand copies had been sold), and Constable offered Scott £1,500 in advance for his edition of the works of Jonathan Swift (1814); it was far less of a gold mine than Scott's original poems had been, but it eventually turned out to be profitable. Constable's big advances were not limited to Scott: for example, he advanced Thomas Campbell £500 in 1804 for *Specimens of the British Poets,* which Campbell did not complete until 1819. These advances, like the generous payments to authors writing for the *Edinburgh Review,* endeared Constable to the literary community; they would ultimately cause him financial trouble, but for the moment his business was prospering. He wrote to the London publisher John Murray on 17 July 1808: "When in London I saw 5000 copies of the last Number of the Edinburgh Review bought and paid for on the same day; the first edition of Marmion was sold in three days, and the second edition was out of print in a fortnight; a third is just ready, and I apprehend, from the orders already received for it, will be gone in a month, which will then enable me to say that, within six months, three editions, amounting in whole to 8500 copies, have been disposed of. This is pretty well, is it not?"

With £11,500 in investment capital, Constable opened a shop in London in December 1808 under the name Constable, Hunter, Park, and Hunter; the other partners were John Park and Charles Hunter. In 1810 Alexander Gibson Hunter left the firm after coming into a large inheritance; Robert Cathcart and Robert Cadell were taken on as partners in 1811. Cathcart died in 1812, but Cadell stayed on until the bankruptcy of 1826.

Despite the excellent sales figures, relations with Scott had grown strained after the publication of *Marmion.* This estrangement was nominally due to Alexander Hunter's having said something indiscreet that wounded Scott's pride, but it was also due to a negative review of the poem in the *Edinburgh Review* (April 1808) in which Jeffrey accused Scott of being insufficiently sensitive to Scottish national pride — an accusation that particularly nettled the intensely nationalistic Scott. The review led Scott to join Murray in launching a rival, conservative periodical, the great *Quarterly Review,* in 1809; like its rival, the *Quarterly Review* would have a long and distinguished life, not ending its run until 1967. Scott also had political motivations: he was troubled about the increasingly strident liberal stance of the *Edinburgh Review,* especially with regard to the hostilities in the Iberian peninsula: Jeffrey was taking a strong antiadministration position and calling for nonintervention, an approach Scott saw as nearly traitorous.

Scott had another reason to break with Constable at this time: he was testing the waters for an entry into the publishing business himself, in partnership with James Ballantyne and Ballantyne's brother John. Scott wanted to remain a silent partner, but many, including Constable, could see well enough what was happening. The new firm was named John Ballantyne and Company, and it set up shop on Hanover Street. By 1813 the Ballantynes found themselves in serious trouble. The firm had had a smashing success with Scott's *The Lady of the Lake* (1810), which sold more than twenty thousand copies within a few months. But the few successes only served to increase the company's credit rating; and Scott and the Ballantynes took full advantage of the increased credit, going ever more deeply into debt. Profits were used to throw gala parties and to buy land to enlarge Scott's new estate, Abbotsford. Perhaps the fairest description of the situation is that of James Ballantyne, quoted in Lockhart's biography of Scott (1837–1838):

> My brother, though an active and pushing, was not a cautious bookseller, and the large sums received never formed an addition to his stock. In fact, they were all expended by his partners, who, being then young and sanguine men, not unwillingly adopted my brother's hasty results. By May 1813, in a word, the absolute throwing away of our own most valuable publications, and the rash adoption of some injudicious speculations of Mr. Scott, had introduced such losses and embarrassments, that after a very careful consideration, Mr. Scott determined to dissolve the concern.... This became a matter of less difficulty, because time had in a great measure worn away the differences between Mr. Scott and Mr. Constable, and Mr. Hunter was now out of Constable's concern. A peace, therefore, was speedily made up, and the old habits of intercourse were restored.

There were other reasons for Scott to try to patch things up with Constable. His poem *Rokeby* (1813), which would have been a major success for most other authors, was something of a disappointment by Scott's standards, and for the first time his work was not receiving universal acclaim: the first parody of his work, John Roby's *Jokeby* (1813), appeared, and Scott began to worry that the well of poetic inspiration (and financial plenty) was running dry. Constable was relieved to see Scott coming back to him, and he made peace on generous terms, buying up more than a fourth of Ballantyne's worthless stock for two thousand pounds — stock that included such unsalable items as a three-volume edition of the works of Anna Seward, a poet admired by few other than Scott himself. The company had published many such writers solely because Scott had decided to do so; often his decisions were based on friendship with the authors rather than on the works' value. Another great drain on the company was the two-volume *Edinburgh Annual Register,* which never gained sufficient readership to justify its continuation. This bailout set a pattern for the future: Constable would end up buying nearly all of the Ballantyne stock at great financial cost to his own company.

The Ballantynes and Scott were convinced that Archibald Constable and Company was a bottomless reserve of ready cash; probably many people would have thought so, based on the firm's huge sales figures and its prestigious titles and authors. But Constable's well-known largesse to his authors was beginning to take its toll, as were other expensive acquisitions. In 1812 he had bought the *Encyclopaedia Britannica* for just over £13,000 and conceived a scheme for a new edition, which would be the fifth. He engaged the philosopher Dugald Stewart to write a massive dissertation for the supplement to the edition, a dissertation intended to rival Jean d'Alembert's great "Discours" in the French *Encyclopédie* (1751–1780), and advanced Stewart £1,700 for it. The fees for many of the other contributors were similarly grand. The fifth edition, published in 1817, was a success, realizing more than £20,000 in profits by 1821. Constable came to believe ever more strongly that a publisher had a responsibility to help educate the public, and he projected similar works to try to reach the widest possible audience, such as an "Encyclopedia for Mechanics" and an "Encyclopedia for Youth." But his financial successes masked severe financial problems.

The credit system of the time allowed borrowers to use other people as guarantors; in turn, the guarantors could use their debtors as guarantors for their own loans. As Scott biographer Eric Quayle describes the system, "The methods then used allowed what were sometimes unsound commercial enterprises and impoverished private individuals to present a totally false picture of their real financial worth to the world at large; often living and trading by means of an increasing snowball of credit which grew with every passing month, then suddenly melted to reveal a hopelessly inadequate core of assets." To use another metaphor, the credit system was like a house of cards, with no firm foundation

of collateral to hold it up when a loan had to be repaid. The system worked with "acceptances," agreements to accept liability for another person's bills; these acceptances multiplied, so that business transactions were increasingly supported only by paper, not by cash. Cadell worked feverishly in 1813–1814 to refinance debts that had come due; but the relief was only temporary, for it involved even more borrowing, and after 1814 Archibald Constable and Company was increasingly occupied with averting disaster via one financial ploy after another.

During these years Constable published what are perhaps his most lasting contributions to world literature, Scott's Waverley novels. Scott had drafted the opening of a historical novel several years prior to the rapprochement with Constable but had put it aside. In 1813, in the crisis about his poetic abilities brought on by *Rokeby,* he rediscovered it and saw its worth — though even he could not have guessed how huge the sales were going to be. Like many of his era, he thought that novels were less dignified than other forms of literature; so he concocted a subterfuge, submitting the reworked opening chapters to Constable via James Ballantyne, who was instructed on no account to hint who the author was. Constable did not take long to catch on, however, and he quickly grew excited about the book's possibilities. *Waverley; or, 'Tis Sixty Years Hence* was published on 7 July 1814 to immediate and long-lasting success. In this book Scott virtually invented the historical novel, a genre that would grow in popularity well into the latter half of the century; its prestige with critics has never been especially high, but Scott's sales figures — as well as those of Harrison Ainsworth and G. P. R. James, his two most prolific imitators over the next few decades — show that the genre had an enormous audience. Scott could see that he had found a new well, and he would produce some two dozen historical romances in the following years.

Most of these works would be published by Constable. Scott sought out other publishers from time to time to increase his advances, though Constable was usually willing to pay top price if given the chance to bid; Scott also wanted to remain anonymous, and he feared if "the Author of 'Waverley'" (as the title pages read) were too closely associated with Constable, his secret would be revealed. Over the years, of course, the literary world guessed the identity of "the Great Unknown"; but Scott continued to maintain his anonymity, even to the point of directly lying about the matter to friends. Constable made many suggestions to Scott for possible topics and plot developments, and Scott called on Consta-

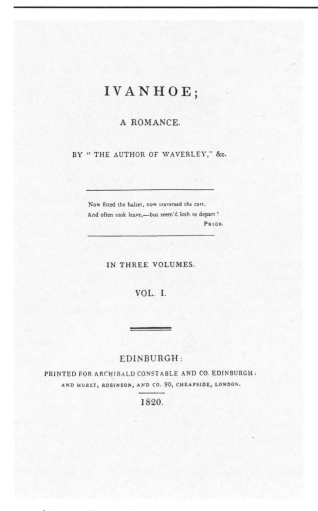

IVANHOE;

A ROMANCE.

BY " THE AUTHOR OF WAVERLEY," &c.

Now fitted the halter, now traversed the cart,
And often took leave,—but seem'd loth to depart !
PRIOR.

IN THREE VOLUMES.

VOL. I.

EDINBURGH:
PRINTED FOR ARCHIBALD CONSTABLE AND CO. EDINBURGH:
AND HURST, ROBINSON, AND CO. 90, CHEAPSIDE, LONDON.

1820.

Title page for one of the many Sir Walter Scott novels published by Constable

ble for historical and bibliographical data in constructing the novels. Constable was pleased when Scott wrote to him on 23 March 1822 that "They talk of a farmer making two blades of grass grow where one grew before, but you, my good friend, have made a dozen volumes where probably but one would have existed." Author and publisher became ever closer, and in March 1823 Scott made Constable a present of thirteen of his manuscripts, including those of some of his greatest novels, such as *Old Mortality* (1816), *The Antiquary* (1816), and *Rob Roy* (1817). The gift touched Constable deeply; he wrote on the back of the envelope: "The most kind and valuable letter I have ever received."

During the decade 1810 to 1820 Constable developed and maintained relationships with many other publishers, especially Longman and Murray. Some of the mutual respect in which the publishers held each other is indicated in a letter from Murray

to Constable of 29 September 1811: "I wish you would do me the favour to say if you think I have done well in inclining to [the Edinburgh publisher and a rival of Constable] James Blackwood's proposal to be my agent. He does now and then get a book or two to throw in one's way; but really no other person does, except your house, which gets all the rest." Constable also developed a relationship during this period with William Godwin, the aging London radical who had turned to publishing children's books under the pseudonym Edward Baldwin. Godwin arranged for the publisher to take on his son, Charles Clairmont, as an apprentice from 1811 to 1813. (Ironically, Godwin sought out Constable because he felt himself deficient in business sense and wanted his son to absorb the practical knowledge of running a book publishing firm so as to be able to help his father.) Godwin also negotiated with Constable to publish one of his last pieces of fiction, *Mandeville* (1817).

Constable worked out an apprenticeship for his own son David with Longman's firm in 1815. David Constable's real interest was in rare books, an interest his father shared, but the father always felt that the son was not quite competent. (His father's ruin in 1826 would unhinge David Constable, and he would suffer recurrent episodes of mental illness until his death in 1866.) Constable's wife died in 1814; in 1818 he married Charlotte Neale, the daughter of an Edinburgh merchant. That same year Cadell married Constable's daughter, but she died on 16 July.

The publication of Scott's *Ivanhoe* (1820), subtitled "A Romance," signaled a new literary direction for Scott – who at first wanted it to be printed without the designation "By the Author of 'Waverley,'" though he eventually gave in on this point. But the newness of *Ivanhoe* prompted Constable to work with Scott and Ballantyne to acquire special paper and type for the novel and, accordingly, a higher price – ten shillings per volume – was set. An even higher price, half a guinea per volume, was set for Scott's *Kenilworth* (1821), whose price and format are usually seen as inaugurating the "three-decker" novel format that would become the norm for the rest of the century.

In 1825 Constable developed a radical scheme that might have made him rich and would certainly have earned him a larger place in publishing history had he been able to carry it out. His belief in the publisher's role in transmitting knowledge as widely as possible led to the plan, which he expounded to Scott. According to Lockhart, he arrived, quite excited, at Scott's home one evening and burst forth:

"Literary genius may, or may not, have done its best; but printing and bookselling, as instruments for enlightening and entertaining mankind, and of course, for making money, are as yet in mere infancy. Yes, the trade are in their cradle." He went on to detail a plan for mass-produced books with cheap cloth covers that even the poorest people could afford. Scott told Constable that the scheme would make him "the grand Napoleon of the realms of print." Constable was, in effect, anticipating the great revolution in publishing known as railway editions, which would sell in the millions as the century progressed; perhaps it could be said that he was anticipating the twentieth-century paperback revolution initiated by Allan Lane and Penguin Books. He set to work on the great series, to be titled Constable's Miscellany.

One of the principal London firms with which Constable did business in the 1820s was Hurst, Robinson and Company; their relationship involved many acceptances and counteracceptances, so that the health of each firm depended on that of the other. In 1825 there was a flurry of stock-market investing in London, and many were getting rich quickly; but just as quickly the market crashed. The publisher J. O. Robinson was one who had overinvested: he had put more than forty thousand pounds in hops, which he suddenly could not unload. Hurst, Robinson and Company was in serious trouble that October, as a major creditor was demanding payment in real money rather than in acceptances. Constable came to London that same month to seek out funding for his Miscellany; he could not have arrived at a worse time, as banker after banker shut him out. At the same time, in Edinburgh, Cadell was being besieged by demanding creditors, and he, too, was finding the normal routes of payment by acceptance being closed off in the panic. Constable returned north in November and fell ill with dropsy; he was confined to his house, unable even to write letters.

He made another journey to London in January, but it was just as futile as the previous one; and on 17 January the word was out that Archibald Constable and Company could not meet its obligations. The Ballantynes and Scott also fell in the general collapse, as all their fortunes were so closely intertwined. Constable went bankrupt owing £256,000; Scott, too, went bankrupt, owing £116,838 (all of the Ballantynes' bills had been contracted by Scott, so he ended up taking their burden on top of his own). Cadell distanced himself quickly and adroitly from his father-in-law, setting up his own concern, Cadell and Company; on 23 January

Constable learned that Scott would thenceforth publish with Cadell. All of Constable's assets were put up for sale, including his home, furnishings, and personal library; one particularly sad note came when the thirteen manuscripts Scott had given him were sold at auction, fetching a mere £317. The Longman firm became the sole publisher of the *Edinburgh Review* and would remain so for the rest of the periodical's existence.

Constable tried to work, but the disaster had severely impaired his health. He weakened over the next year, dying on 21 July 1827. The only other person in the house at the time was Thomas, his youngest son by his first wife, who recorded Constable's last words: "Tom, I leave you very poor; had it pleased God to spare my life for a few years, it might have been otherwise; but I trust that at least you will find the name you bear no disadvantage." In 1873 Thomas Constable would publish a three-volume biography as testimonial to his father's good name.

The years after the crash were full of acrimony, as all parties fought over who was to blame. Lockhart's biography of Scott, his father-in-law, went to great lengths to blame primarily the Ballantynes and secondarily Constable. The Ballantynes fought back in pamphlets that blamed Scott and Constable. Thomas Constable's biography of his father tends to side with Lockhart while underplaying his father's role. Quayle's more recent study (1968) suggests that Scott was chiefly to blame because of his greed and shortsightedness. Clearly, all the individuals involved made bad business decisions, and all had motivations that were not of the purest. If a villain must be sought, perhaps it is best to blame the incredibly loose credit system of the time, which virtually guaranteed disaster for anyone unfortunate enough to get sufficiently entangled in it.

Thomas Constable founded his own printing company and was named printer to Queen Victoria in 1839; he sold out his stock in 1860 and devoted himself to writing. In 1890 Archibald Constable's grandson, also named Archibald, formed a new Archibald Constable and Company. He retired in 1893; in 1910 the firm became Constable and Company, Ltd., under which name it still does business.

Constable's contributions to literary culture were significant. The *Edinburgh Review,* the *Encyclopaedia Britannica,* and Scott's Waverley novels alone would guarantee a publisher a lasting place in literary history, but Constable also published the works of many of the best-known authors of his day, from Archibald Alison to Henry Mackenzie, from poets and philosophers to historians and divines. His plan to make books available to the masses marks him out as one who was ahead of his times.

References:

Ballantyne and Company, *The Ballantyne Press and Its Founders, 1796–1908* (Edinburgh: Ballantyne, Hanson, 1909);

John Buchan, *Sir Walter Scott* (London: Cassell, 1932);

Thomas Constable, *Archibald Constable and His Literary Correspondents: A Memorial,* 3 volumes (Edinburgh: Edmonston & Douglas, 1873);

Kenneth Curry, *Sir Walter Scott's* Edinburgh Annual Register (Knoxville: University of Tennessee Press, 1977);

Edgar Johnson, *Sir Walter Scott: The Great Unknown* (New York: Macmillan, 1970);

John Gibson Lockhart, *Narrative of the Life of Sir Walter Scott, Bart.* (7 volumes, London: Murray & Whittaker, 1837–1838; revised edition, 10 volumes, Edinburgh: Cadell / London: Murray & Whittaker, 1839); revised and abridged as *Narrative of the Life of Sir Walter Scott, Bart.* (Edinburgh: Cadell / London: Houston & Stoneman, 1848);

Jane Millgate, "Making It New: Scott, Constable, Ballantyne, and the Publication of *Ivanhoe,*" *Studies in English Literature,* 34 (Autumn 1994): 795–811;

Millgate, *Scott's Last Edition: A Study in Publishing History* (Edinburgh: Edinburgh University Press, 1987);

Stephen Parks, ed., *The Ballantyne-Lockhart Controversy, 1838–1839* (New York: Garland, 1974);

Eric Quayle, *The Ruin of Sir Walter Scott* (London: Hart-Davis, 1968);

Joanne Shattock, *Politics and Reviewers: The* Edinburgh *and the* Quarterly *in the Early Victorian Age* (London: Leicester University Press, 1989);

Richard Henry Stoddard, ed., *Personal Reminiscences by Constable and Gillies* (New York: Scribners, 1887).

Papers:

The bulk of Archibald Constable's surviving papers are in the National Library of Scotland, Edinburgh.

– Raymond N. MacKenzie

J. Coote

(London: 1758 – 1777)

J. Cooke and J. Coote

(London: 1757 – 1758)

The London bookseller, periodical proprietor, and publisher John Coote was born in Horsham, Sussex, probably in 1734. Coote was the author of an opera and five farces; while three of these works were printed, none was ever staged.

Without having been a Stationers' Company apprentice, Coote gained an entry into the London book trade in 1757 as the partner of John Cooke at the King's Arms in Great Turnstile, Holborn. Cooke, who later specialized in publishing books in weekly numbers, was then advertising jestbooks such as *The Prudent Jester* and chronicles of crime. By October 1757 Cooke had moved to the King's Arms, without Temple Bar, opposite Devereux Court in the Strand, and Coote's name appeared with his in newspaper advertisements; on 6 October they published *The Humours of the Old Bailey,* a collection of amusing trials. Late in 1757 Cooke and Coote moved a short distance to a shop opposite St. Clement's Church in the Strand. During the no more than six months that they were in partnership they continued to bring out works aimed for the most part at a low class of readers.

On 7 March 1758 Coote married Jane Weaver in the church of St. Clement Danes in the Strand; they would have seven children. Their eldest son, Charles, was sent to St. Paul's School in 1773 and matriculated at Pembroke College, Oxford, in 1778, where he took the degrees of B.A. in 1782, M.A. in 1785, and D.C.L. in 1789. He also served as editor of the *Critical Review* for some time.

Cooke and Coote separated early in 1758, perhaps about the time of Coote's marriage, and Coote set up shop in the environs of St. Paul's Cathedral, at the King's Arms (subsequently No. 16), Paternoster Row, on the north side of the street, near Queen's Head Passage. The two booksellers apparently continued an amicable relationship and may even have been related: a John Cooke married a Mary Coote on 17 December 1758 in the Church of St. Pancras-in-the-Fields. By 1766 Cooke's shop would be located at 17 Shakespeare's Head, Paternoster Row, next door to Coote's. No. 17 is the address from which Cooke's son Charles, beginning about 1793, would publish his well-known Pocket Editions of Select Novels, Sacred Classics, and Select Poets. Coote's earliest publications in his own name were political pamphlets, including Arthur Young's *The Theatre of the Present War in North America* (1758), for which Coote paid the author with books valued at ten pounds; the pamphlet's success prompted Coote to urge Young to write further works for him.

Soon after opening his shop Coote began to publish books and pamphlets aimed at a more sophisticated reading public. From 1759 to 1765 he brought out, two volumes at a time, an eight-volume anonymous translation "from the French of the last Paris Edition" of the letters of Madame Marie de Sévigné. The "last Paris edition" (1754) included 158 more letters than the first edition (1734–1737); this augmentation helped Coote's English translation sell well enough to prompt a ten-volume edition in a smaller format, which Coote began publishing in 1763.

In May 1759 Coote was granted a royal license to print the two-volume *A New Geographical Dictionary* (1759, 1760), a work in which he had invested, in the conventional words of his license petition, "very great Labour and expence in purchasing Books in various languages, and employing learned and ingenious Men, to write and compile." A royal license granted the petitioner the sole right to print and publish the specified work for fourteen years; the owners of works that included material likely to be illegally reprinted often used the license to forestall piracy. Coote's *London Chronicle* advertisement for the dictionary reveals why he went to the trouble and expense of obtaining a royal license: it announced that the work, to be brought out in one hundred sixpence numbers that would eventually make up two folio volumes, would be embellished with 150 copperplate engravings, which "exclusive of all other Expences, cost the Proprietors near

LETTERS

FROM THE

MARCHIONESS

DE SÉVIGNÉ,

TO HER DAUGHTER

THE

Countes DE GRIGNAN.

Tranſlated from the FRENCH of the laſt PARIS
EDITION.

VOLUME the THIRD.

She ſtrikes each point with native force of mind,
While puzzled learning blunders far behind.
Graceful to ſight, and elegant to thought,
The great are vanquiſh'd, and the wiſe are taught,
Her breeding finiſh'd, and her temper ſweet ;
When ſerious, eaſy ; and when gay, diſcreet ;
In glitt'ring ſcenes o'er her own heart ſevere,
In crowds collected, and in courts ſincere.   YOUNG.

LONDON:

Printed for J. COOTE, at the King's Arms
Pater-noſter-Row. M.DCC.LX.

Title page for one of the eight volumes of Marie de Sévigné's
letters published by John Coote from 1759 to 1765 (Courtesy
of the Lilly Library, Indiana University)

Eight Hundred Pounds." Such an investment merited protection.

Meanwhile, Coote had joined informally with a group of booksellers who were publishing works by the prolific author and journalist Tobias Smollett. The group included the partners James Rivington and James Fletcher Jr., Richard Baldwin Jr., William Johnston, George Kearsly (or Kearsley), and John Newbery. Coote worked most closely with Kearsly and Newbery. With Kearsly, who was becoming known as a publisher of plays, and Thomas Davies, Coote brought out four editions in 1760 and a fifth edition in 1761 of Samuel Foote's controversial comedy *The Minor,* an attack on George Whitefield and Methodism. In late April an advertisement stated that on 1 May would be published the first volume of a projected twelve volumes of Foote's *The Comic Theatre: Being a Free Translation of All the Best French Comedies,* printed by Dryden Leach for Coote, Kearsly, and Stanley Crowder; only five volumes ever appeared.

Besides investing in and publishing books, Coote became seriously involved in founding and

publishing periodicals, especially monthly magazines. In 1760 he would work with John Newbery in some of these endeavors, but it is clear that Coote had already established himself as an independent magazine proprietor before their collaborations began. He recognized that by the end of the 1750s magazines were proliferating as never before, that there was a vast readership for them, and that individual magazines could be tailored to appeal to specialized audiences. He commenced this branch of his profession rather grandly in May 1759 when he was granted a license "for the sole Printing, Publishing, and Vending" of the *Royal Magazine: or, Gentleman's Monthly Companion,* which first appeared in July 1759 and ran until December 1771, becoming the mainstay of Coote's periodicals. Typical of most general magazines, the *Royal Magazine* was informative rather than literary in its subject matter, although it included "Poetical Essays" and, in 1759 and 1760, an oriental tale and four essays by Oliver Goldsmith.

Coote followed up his initial magazine offering, which was aimed at men, with a petition in November 1759 to print a second, aimed at women: the *Female Magazine; or, Lady's Polite Companion,* for which he had "employed Mrs. Charlotte Lenox [*sic*] and other Learned and ingenious Persons to write and compile." The monthly magazine first appeared on 1 March 1760 and was conducted by the novelist Charlotte Lennox, but its title had become the *Lady's Museum,* and its publishers, according to the imprint, were Newbery and Coote. Coote's role in this periodical is unclear, but the license petition reveals that it was Coote, not Newbery, who first proposed it. The *Lady's Museum,* an essay-miscellany, survived for only eleven months, but it is noted for its originality, particularly as a vehicle for serializing Lennox's fiction. Meanwhile, in December 1759 Newbery and Coote petitioned for a license to print the *Christian's Magazine; or, A Treasury of Divine Knowledge,* edited by the Reverend William Dodd; it ran from May 1760 through January 1767.

The *British Magazine; or, Monthly Repository for Gentlemen and Ladies* first appeared on 1 January 1760, published by Rivington and Fletcher. Smollett, its founder and editor until mid 1763, was granted the royal license to print the magazine, but Newbery and Kearsly, neither of whose names appeared in its advertisements, owned shares in it; evidence points to Coote as an early shareholder, as well. Smollett included a significant amount of new fiction, notably his own novel *The Life and Adventures of Sir Launcelot Greaves,* which appeared in chapter-length installments from January 1760 through December 1761 – the first long work of prose fiction to be serialized before it was brought out in book form, an experiment in publishing that was not repeated until the nineteenth century. Coote and Kearsly acquired the copyright to *Sir Launcelot Greaves* from Smollett, most likely because they were already involved in the *British Magazine*. In March 1762 Coote's and Kearsly's names appeared together in advertisements for the first book-form edition of *Sir Launcelot Greaves,* but only Coote's name is on the title page.

The first number of the *Musical Magazine,* written "by Mr. Oswald, and other celebrated Masters" and published by Coote, came out on 1 February 1760. It included both letterpress and engraved songs, with music, and it must have survived at least into 1761: that year the *Royal Magazine* included several airs from the *Musical Magazine.*

Coote's ambitions extended to newspapers, but his single endeavor in that area proved futile. In May 1761 he was granted a warrant to establish the *Royal Gazette and Universal Chronicle;* the first number appeared on 22 May. A one-page advertisement for this "New Evening Paper," inserted with the outer blue paper wrapper of the *British Magazine* for May 1761, announced that it was "Printed for, and sold by R. Griffiths and J. Coote." Coote is not known to have had any other connection with Ralph Griffiths. In the advertisement Coote explained the rationale for establishing another London newspaper: there were currently five papers published on Tuesdays, Thursdays, and Saturdays, but only one on Mondays, Wednesdays, and Fridays; the *Royal Gazette and Universal Chronicle* was intended to help fill the gap. This rationale does not appear to have been a sufficient inducement to attract readers. On 19 June, with the thirteenth number, the title was simplified to the *Royal Gazette;* it is unknown how much longer the periodical continued, but it certainly did not survive into 1762: Audit Office records show an advertisement duty entry of £4.14.0 for the *Royal Gazette* in 1761 but no entry in the following year.

On 29 May 1762 Coote published the first number of Smollett's political weekly, the *Briton;* a week later Kearsly brought out the first number of the rival *North Briton.* Smollett wrote the *Briton,* which appeared until February 1763, to support the Tory ministry of John Stuart, third earl of Bute, during peace negotiations at the end of the Seven Years' War; John Wilkes and the satirists Charles Churchill and Robert Lloyd produced the ironically titled *North Briton* (Bute and Smollett were both Scots) in opposition to Smollett's periodical. Despite

the bitter quarrel between the two political camps, there is no indication that Coote and Kearsly severed their connection; indeed, they probably hoped to reap a mutual profit from the dispute. By mid 1763 Smollett had left England in ill health, and Coote had become one of Churchill's publishers: in June of that year Churchill's *An Epistle to William Hogarth* was printed for the author and sold by Coote. Churchill's *The Ghost: Book IV* came out in September, printed for John Coote, William Flexney, George Kearsly, G. Henderson, J. Gardiner, and John Almon. Although the order of their names in the imprints would vary, this group continued to publish Churchill's works until August 1764, when Kearsly's name was dropped and that of C. Moran added. Kearsly had been convicted of seditious libel for publishing number 45 of the *North Briton* in April 1763, whereupon he had fled the country and been declared bankrupt. Then in November 1764 Kearsly voluntarily returned to England to receive sentence and was discharged. He returned to business in late February 1765.

Thomas Mortimer's *The Universal Director* (1763), published by Coote, includes a "List of the Principal Booksellers of London and Westminster," with brief descriptions of each. The note on Coote reads: "Purchases any valuable Manuscripts that are offered him; and is a Proprietor in several considerable Copies [copyrights]." As early as 8 February 1759 his name had begun appearing occasionally among those of the prominent booksellers meticulously recorded in the margins of the Longman copies of the booksellers' trade sale catalogues. On that date, at Edward Wicksteed's sale, Coote bought three one-tenth shares of Edward Hoppus's *Practical Measuring Made Easy* (1759) and a one-tenth share of Charles Leadbetter's *The Royal Gauger* (1739). On 12 December 1761, although his identity was never revealed in the imprint, he purchased at auction six one-sixteenth shares of Smollett's best-selling *A Complete History of England* (1757–1758). But by and large Coote did not invest in "old" copyrights, preferring to hazard his money on promising new works that he probably commissioned, such as translations of recent well-received French books, and on new periodicals.

By 1767 Coote may have run into financial difficulties, forcing him to sell many of his copyright shares. While some of his property was not valuable – a receipt in the British Library shows that on 25 June 1767 he sold to Thomas Lownds one-fourth of the copyright of Foote's comedy *The Orators* (1762) for £2.12.6 – Coote clearly also owned shares, some of them substantial, in several

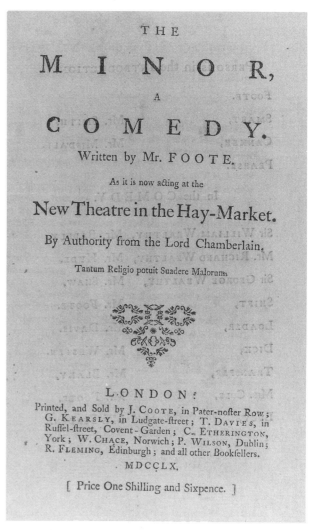

Mr Foote *in the Character of* Mrs Cole.

THE

M I N O R,

A

C O M E D Y.

Written by Mr. F O O T E.

As it is now acting at the

New Theatre in the Hay-Market.

By Authority from the Lord Chamberlain.

Tantum Religio potuit Suadere Malorum.

L O N D O N:

Printed, and Sold by J. COOTE, in Pater-noster Row;
G. KEARSLY, in Ludgate-street; T. DAVIES, in
Russel-street, Covent-Garden; C. ETHERINGTON,
York; W. CHACE, Norwich; P. WILSON, Dublin;
R. FLEMING, Edinburgh; and all other Booksellers.

MDCCLX.

[Price One Shilling and Sixpence.]

*Frontispiece and title page for one of the five editions of Samuel Foote's controversial comedy published by John Coote (Courtesy of
Special Collections, Thomas Cooper Library, University of South Carolina)*

lucrative works; the most valuable were still being printed when he sold them. According to receipts in the Manchester Public Library, on 23 July 1767 Coote received from George Robinson and John Roberts, up-and-coming wholesale booksellers, £1,000 for the copyright to and 180,000 copies of *The Christian's Family Bible* (1763–1767), by the Reverend William Rider, and the copyright to the "Stretch Bible," which has not been identified. On 26 August 1767 Coote sold to the same firm, for £100, three-fourths of the copyright to and 320 sets of the second edition of the *Letters* of Madame de Sévigné. He had brought out the first eight volumes of the second edition from 1763 to 1767, and Robinson and Roberts brought out volumes nine and ten in 1768. An advertisement in the *London Chronicle* in early March 1769 shows Robinson and Roberts offering for sale both de Sévigné's *Letters* and Smol-

lett's *Sir Launcelot Greaves;* the latter is not a new edition, so evidently Coote had sold them both his shares in, and his remaining copies of, his 1762 edition of the novel. On 30 May 1770, for £410.9.3, Coote sold Robinson and Roberts seven-sixteenths of the copyright and seven-sixteenths of the 12,776 remaining volumes of the English translation of Voltaire's works (1761–1770). Coote had been involved with this major publishing venture since it was first advertised. The translation, by Smollett and others, was originally projected to appear monthly, one duodecimo volume at a time, beginning in March 1761; it eventually reached thirty-seven volumes. Subscriptions were taken by Coote, Newbery, Kearsly, Davies, Richard Baldwin, Stanley Crowder and Company, and William Johnston. Possibly each of these booksellers owned at least a one-sixteenth share; and it is known that Newbery's

60

Salisbury business colleague Benjamin Collins also owned a one-sixteenth share, which he sold to Robinson and Roberts in July 1770. Coote's seven-sixteenths of the property thus suggests that he played a major role in launching the translation.

In 1766, when Coote's career was still at its height, Henry Dell wrote *The Booksellers,* a poem sketching the characters of one hundred London booktrade colleagues. Dell's encomium on Coote is notable:

> Ingenious *Coote* is ever forming schemes
> Unlike the alchymist's idle dreams;
> He plans with judgment, executes with spirit,
> And well deserves the just reward of merit.

Unfortunately, Dell does not specify what some of Coote's *schemes* – a neutral or even favorable term, analogous to *plans* or *projects* – may have been, but it is possible that he is referring not only to Coote's profitable book investments but also to his complicated role as a magazine proprietor and publisher. From 1759 through 1762 Coote can be identified through royal licenses as proprietor or coproprietor, and through imprints or advertisements as publisher or copublisher, of several London periodicals, including the *Royal Magazine,* the *British Magazine,* and the *Briton;* and, with the booksellers Davies and William Flexney, he had launched Robert Lloyd's *St. James's Magazine* in September 1762. Eight years later, however, except in the case of the *Royal Magazine,* he was either positioning his name in magazine imprints so that he appeared to be merely an agent who sold the periodical at his premises, or keeping his name off the imprints altogether. Thus, his proprietorships would have gone undetected by the public but for a lawsuit brought by Robinson and Roberts against John Wheble.

In July 1770 Coote had begun the *Lady's Magazine; or, Entertaining Companion for the Fair Sex,* hiring Wheble to serve as publisher; in other words, Wheble's name alone appeared in the imprint, but Coote was actually the proprietor. The magazine rapidly acquired a wide circulation – Robert D. Mayo notes that it "was to become the most successful publishing venture of its kind in the century" – and in 1771, after seven numbers had appeared, Coote sold it to Robinson and Roberts for five hundred pounds, a sum indicative of its profit-making potential. Dropped as publisher by the new owners, Wheble continued to bring out his own version of the magazine, later claiming that his name in the imprint had helped to establish the original magazine's popularity. Robinson and Roberts sued, and at the July 1771 trial several booksellers, including Coote,

testified about magazine ownership and the role of publishers in magazine production. Coote's testimony and Wheble's comments on it, all of which Wheble printed in the July 1771 issue of his magazine after the verdict went against him, divulge some of Coote's reasons for hiding his connections with the magazines.

The counsel for Robinson and Roberts explained how Coote had set up the *Lady's Magazine:*

> Mr. Coote intending to commence a new Magazine to be published monthly, did for the purpose engage the sort of assistance which the conduct of such a work required. He engaged proper persons to write in this pamphlet[;] himself was to receive, and to judge of such compositions as should be sent to him. . . . He engaged likewise proper engravers to embellish this work, proper printers to print it, and amongst others a publisher.

Coote had thus acted as both proprietor and editor, a form of control he probably also exercised over the *Royal Magazine,* an editor for which has never been identified. Asked to explain why he had employed Wheble instead of publishing the *Lady's Magazine* himself, Coote answered, "I was then Publisher of several Magazines, and it is a conceived notion amongst people, that if they do publish three or four, they are made up one of the other." In other words, according to Coote, the public was under the impression that the publishers and proprietors of magazines were one and the same, and if readers saw the same name in the imprints of two different magazines they would assume that the contents might be duplicated. Wheble's lawyer pushed Coote to reveal that he had had good reason to hide his ownership of the *Lady's Magazine:*

> Q. You said you was a publisher of some Magazines?
> A. I was not a publisher then.
> Q. No! then what can be your reason, if you were the publisher of no Magazine, what is the reason you could not do it?
> A. I was publisher and proprietor too.
> Q. You was publisher and proprietor of another?
> A. Yes.
> Q. So that the Public might suppose this intelligence, information and entertainment came from different sources, you put one in the hands of another person, that the public might not be undeceived?
> A. Yes, Sir, that was the way.

Writing up the trial in his magazine, Wheble characterized Coote as an "ingenious projector" and angrily revealed that he was even then the proprietor – that is, owner – of eight magazines: the *Royal Magazine; or, Gentleman's Monthly Companion;* the *Uni-*

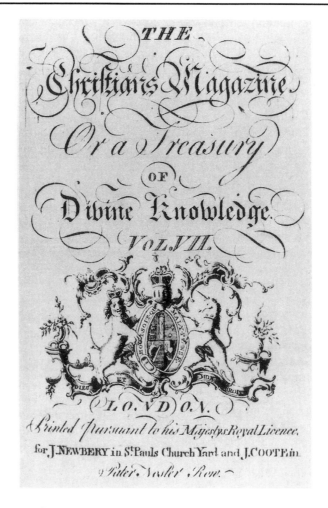

Title page for a volume of one of the many magazines
published or copublished by Coote. This one ran from
1760 to 1767.

versal *Museum and Complete Magazine of Knowledge and Pleasure*, begun in January 1762; the *Court Miscellany; or, Gentleman and Lady's New Magazine*, begun in July 1765; the *Oxford Magazine; or, University Museum*, begun in July 1768; the *Freeholder's Magazine; or, Monthly Chronicle of Liberty*, begun in September 1769; the *Court and City Magazine; or, A Fund of Entertainment for the Man of Quality*, begun in January 1770; the *Gentleman's Museum, and Grand Imperial Magazine*, begun in July 1770; and *Every Man's Magazine; or, The Monthly Repository of Science, Instruction and Amusement*, begun in July 1771. The title page of only one of these – the *Royal Magazine* – clearly identified Coote as the proprietor in 1771.

Coote had good reason to fear that readers might distrust him. As the owner of as many as eight magazines at a time, he faced each month the problem of filling each one. Probably first as a stopgap measure, but later as a regular tactic apparently unique to his periodicals, he had developed the practice of printing several articles concurrently in at least two magazines. For example, in their numbers for June, July, and August 1771 both the *Universal Museum* and the *Court Miscellany* carried a three-part anonymous tale, "The History of the Fair Ardelia." Purchasers of the two magazines would not be pleased at such duplication but would assume that it was coincidental. Were they to see that Coote was responsible for both magazines, however, they might suspect that the repetition was deliberate and stop buying any of his publications. Consequently, Coote kept himself hidden: according to their title pages for 1771, the *Universal Museum* was printed "by assignment from [Joseph] Johnson and [John] Payne for J. Smith," and the *Court Miscellany* was printed for William Richardson and Leonard Urquhart. Seeing no relationship between the magazines, readers were meant to – and probably did – infer that the duplicate articles were coincidental.

Coote had occasionally been printing articles concurrently at least as early as April 1762. In that month the *Royal Magazine* carried "Sir Walter Raleigh's Letter to his Wife after his Condemnation" and a "Copy of a genuine Letter from Mr. ADDISON to a Lady," while the *British Magazine* included "*Sir* Walter Raleigh's *Letter to his Wife after his Condemnation*" and a "*Copy of a genuine Letter from Mr. Addison to a Lady*." In December 1762 the magazines carried two other articles concurrently; in January 1763, three articles; in February 1763, seven. Each of those articles was separately set in type and printed for its respective magazine; but in April 1763, when a fourteen-page description of the city of Manila appeared in both magazines, Coote took an expedient shortcut: for the first seven pages each version was separately composed, but for the last seven pages sheets from the *British Magazine* were inserted in the *Royal Magazine;* the signatures were altered to conform to the *Royal Magazine,* but the pagination was not. In January 1764 the two magazines even shared the same monthly news column, "Domestic Intelligence." After Smollett, its founder and editor, left England in mid 1763, the *British Magazine* seriously decreased its offerings of original fiction and became more of a general-interest periodical, like the *Royal Magazine.* Its publisher from July 1761 until its demise in 1767 was Fletcher, accompanied for a time by his father, an Oxford bookseller; but the increasing incidences of concurrency with the *Royal Magazine* beginning in 1762 indicate that Coote was intimately connected with the *British Magazine* early on, exercised some control over its contents in 1763, and was perhaps even the successor to Smollett.

The exposure of Coote's periodical proprietorships in July 1771 probably contributed to the collapse of his business. The *Royal Magazine* ended with the December 1771 issue, and with the exception of the *Oxford Magazine,* which continued through 1776, his other magazines either failed or were deliberately brought to a close within eighteen months after the publication of Wheble's list: the *Freeholder's Magazine* in August 1771; the *Court Miscellany* and the *Gentleman's Museum* in December 1771; the *Court and City Magazine* and *Every Man's Magazine* in June 1772; and the *Universal Museum* in December 1772.

A commission of bankruptcy against Coote was sealed on 12 November 1772. He would, presumably, have had to vacate his shop, and after 1772 his name was no longer connected with Paternoster Row. The bookseller who succeeded Coote

at No. 16, the King's Arms, was Alexander Hogg, a former journeyman of Coote's erstwhile partner Cooke, whose shop was still next door to Coote's old premises. Mayo has described Hogg as "an aggressive and unscrupulous purveyor of cheap books," a man whose predatory practices as a magazine proprietor in the 1780s and 1790s make Coote's duplications within his own periodicals seem circumspect by comparison. Hogg would look for a current periodical with a wide readership and then launch his own version of it with the same title but with the addition of the word *New;* thus, in 1786 he brought out the *New Lady's Magazine,* intending to deceive readers into believing that it was a continuation of the *Lady's Magazine.* His ploy succeeded, and he repeated it many times with other magazines, to his considerable profit.

Like many other eighteenth-century booksellers, Coote survived bankruptcy and returned to business, but his output never again reached the level of the 1760s. His certificate was granted on 14 August 1773, and he paid dividends to creditors in June 1774 and July 1775. His location from late 1772 to 1776 is unknown. He may have been back in business by 1775: a receipt dated 14 April of that year shows that he sold Robinson the copyrights to Percival Proctor's four-volume *The Modern Dictionary of Arts and Sciences* and Watson's *Geographical Dictionary* for twenty-one pounds. The Proctor dictionary – actually the work of several hands – had been "Printed for the Authors; and sold by G. Kearsly" in 1774. The Watson dictionary was probably the same *New Geographical Dictionary* Coote had originally published in 1759; if so, the sale of its copyright indicates that he was not forced to relinquish all his property following his bankruptcy. Kearsly's name in the imprint of the Proctor work complicates the problem of dating Coote's return to business: it may simply mean that in 1774 Kearsly served as an agent for the authors, who held the copyright, and that in 1775 Coote acquired the copyright from the authors before he, in turn, sold it to Robinson; or it may mean that Coote held the copyright in 1774 and that Kearsly fronted for him. By 1776 Coote is found at 14 Red Lion (or Red-Lyon) Street, Clerkenwell, again publishing magazines and again, even more flagrantly, printing articles concurrently. E. W. Pitcher observes that from August 1776 the *Sentimental Magazine; or, General Assemblage of Science, Taste, and Entertainment* (begun in 1773) and the *Monthly Miscellany: or, Gentleman and Lady's Complete Magazine* (begun in 1774) occasionally ran articles concurrently, and from March through September 1777 "eighty to ninety percent

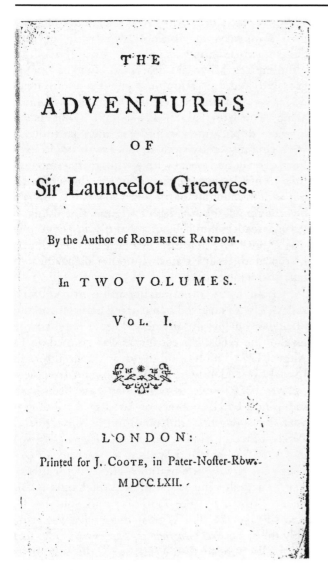

Title page for the book publication of Tobias Smollett's novel, which first appeared in installments in the British Magazine — *a periodical that was edited by Smollett and in which Coote was probably a shareholder. The work was the first novel by an important British author to be serialized in a magazine (Courtesy of the Lilly Library, Indiana University).*

of the contents of *The Monthly Miscellany* . . . duplicated what appeared in monthly parts of the same date in *The Sentimental Magazine.*" Both periodicals were "Printed for the Authors and sold by J. Coote" at the Red Lion Street address, and by October 1777 both were defunct. In 1777 Coote brought out an edition of Isaac Watts's *The Psalms of David* (1719) that included eight pages of music, "Tunes in the Tenor Part, fitted to the several metres."

Land Tax Records for Clerkenwell, Middlesex, dating only from 1780, reveal that Coote re-

sided in Compton Street from 1780 to 1781 and in St. John's Square from 1782 to 1787. Nothing further is known about Coote until his death on 20 October 1808 "in his 75th year," according to the *Gentleman's Magazine* obituary. He had outlived his wife and died intestate. Administration of his estate, valued at less than one hundred pounds, was granted to his eldest son, Charles, on 28 April 1809. At the time of his death Coote was living in White Lion Street, Pentonville, in the Parish of St. James, Clerkenwell. His name, however, does not appear in the register of burials for the parish.

In his *Dictionary of Printers and Printing* (1839) C. H. Timperley describes a change that occurred in the character of the Paternoster Row booktrade around 1774 – the year that saw the demise of perpetual copyright – "from old bookselling, or the issuing only of large and important new works by the principal houses, to general publishing, and particularly of periodicals." Coote's career epitomizes that change. He entered the London booktrade at a period when booksellers from outside the Stationers' Company were only beginning to make headway against its closed ranks. Although the source of his initial investment capital is unknown, he did not begin his business with inherited copyrights. Rather, he profited from his own ability to gauge what new works – whether books, such as translations and compilations, or periodicals – would appeal most to the reading public and which authors could best supply material for those works. While he worked well with established booksellers, no doubt learning from them and meeting through them such prominent authors as Smollett, Coote wanted to accomplish more than simply join other men's publishing ventures; and he saw that the burgeoning magazine market, in particular, offered a way to succeed. Not content with quietly holding shares in one or two established periodicals, Coote wanted to gamble, to initiate and control several magazines at once on the chance that at least one would quickly reap a large profit. His greatest success was the *Lady's Magazine,* but in the main Coote attempted more than he achieved. John Nichols's posthumous description probably comes closest to the mark: "Coote's talents rose above mediocrity; and he evinced fertility in the invention of schemes, but did not possess sufficient steadiness or patience to carry them into effect, or beneficial execution." Nevertheless, Coote was an important proprietor of monthly magazines during the 1760s and early 1770s, and his career throws light on the complicated interrelationships of many of the magazines during that period.

References:

A. Aspinall, "Statistical Accounts of the London Newspapers in the Eighteenth Century," *English Historical Review,* 63 (April 1948): 201–232;

Terry Belanger, "A Directory of the London Book Trade, 1766," *Publishing History,* 1 (1977): 7–48;

G. E. Bentley Jr., "Copyright Documents in the George Robinson Archive: William Godwin and Others 1713–1820," *Studies in Bibliography,* 35 (1982): 67–110;

Ronald S. Crane, Introduction to *New Essays by Oliver Goldsmith* (Chicago: University of Chicago Press, 1927), pp. xi–xli;

Barbara Laning Fitzpatrick, "The Text of Tobias Smollett's *Life and Adventures of Sir Launcelot Greaves,* the First Serialized Novel," dissertation, Duke University, 1987;

John G. Gazley, *The Life of Arthur Young, 1741–1820* (Philadelphia: American Philosophical Society, 1973);

Douglas Grant, ed., *The Poetical Works of Charles Churchill* (Oxford: Clarendon Press, 1956);

Charles Humphries and William Charles Smith, *Music Publishing in the British Isles from the Earliest Times to the Middle of the Nineteenth Century,* second edition (Oxford: Blackwell, 1970);

Frank Kidson, *British Music Publishers, Printers and Engravers: London, Provincial, Scottish, and Irish* (London: Hill, 1900; New York: Blom, 1967);

Ian Maxted, *The London Book Trades 1775–1800: A Preliminary Checklist of Members* (Folkestone: Dawson, 1977);

Robert D. Mayo, *The English Novel in the Magazines 1740–1815* (Evanston, Ill.: Northwestern University Press / London: Oxford University Press, 1962);

Thomas Mortimer, *The Universal Director; or, The Nobleman and Gentleman's True Guide to the Masters and Professors of the Liberal and Polite Arts and Sciences; and of the Mechanic Arts, Manufactures, and Trades, Established in London and Westminster, and Their Environs* (London: Coote, 1763);

John Nichols, "Obituary, with Anecdotes, of Remarkable Persons," *Gentleman's Magazine,* 78, part 2 (November 1808): 1041;

E. W. Pitcher, "Problems with Eighteenth-Century Periodicals: *The Monthly Miscellany,*" *Papers of the Bibliographical Society of America,* 80, no. 2 (1986): 233–237;

H. R. Plomer, G. H. Bushnell, and E. R. McC. Dix, *A Dictionary of the Printers and Booksellers Who Were at Work in England Scotland and Ireland from 1726 to 1775* (Oxford: Bibliographical Society, 1932 [i.e., 1930]);

Graham Pollard, "The Early Poems of George Crabbe and *The Lady's Magazine,*" *Bodleian Library Record,* 5 (1954–1956): 149–156;

C. H. Timperley, *Encyclopædia of Literary and Typographical Anecdote,* volume 2 (London: Bohn, 1842; New York: Garland, 1977);

Simon Trefman, *Sam. Foote, Comedian, 1720–1777* (New York: New York University Press, 1971);

John Wheble, "An Account of the Trial at Law, respecting the Right of Property in the Publication of the LADY'S MAGAZINE: With Observation on the Same," *Lady's Magazine,* 1 (July 1771): 41–52;

Charles G. S. Williams, *Madame de Sévigné* (Boston: G. K. Hall, 1981).

Papers:
Documents relating to the career of John Coote include "Booksellers' Trade Sale Catalogues, 1718–1768," in the British Library, London; Grants of Administration, Middlesex (DL/C/441), in the Greater London Record Office; State Papers, Domestic (SP36/142, f. 44,45; SP36/144, f.38), in the Public Record Office, Chancery Lane, London, and the George Robinson Archive in the Manchester Public Library.

– Barbara Laning Fitzpatrick

Joseph Cottle

(Bristol: 1791 – 1798)

Although Joseph Cottle's career as a publisher and bookseller spanned only eight years, he holds the distinction of being instrumental in publishing the early works of William Wordsworth, Samuel Taylor Coleridge, and Robert Southey. His publication of the works of the Lake Poets is remarkable on at least two counts: first, he was only in his twenties when he recognized the promise of these writers; second, he lived and worked in Bristol, far from London, the publishing center of England.

Cottle was born on 9 March 1770 to Robert Cottle, a tailor, and Sarah Cottle. He was educated at the school of Richard Henderson; Cottle attributed his taste in literature to Henderson's son John, who often tutored him. Cottle reportedly read more than a thousand volumes of English literature before the age of twenty-one.

Little of note occurred in Cottle's publishing career, which began in 1791, until 1794, when Robert Lovell introduced him to Coleridge and Southey. Lovell, Coleridge, Southey, and George Burnet planned to immigrate to America and establish a utopian colony called Pantisocracy, which was to be free of turmoil and governed by sound reasoning rather than laws, and were lodging in Bristol while awaiting funds to sail. Discussions of the project attracted Cottle and others, including Charles Lamb, Thomas Lovell Beddoes, Charles Lloyd, and Thomas Poole, many of whom became friends and clients of the young bookseller. In his *Early Recollections, Chiefly Relating to the Late Samuel Taylor Coleridge during His Long Residence in Bristol* (1837), Cottle quotes Coleridge's first letter to him, dated "Spring, 1795": "Can you conveniently lend me five pounds, as we want a little more than four pounds to make up our lodging bill, which is indeed much higher than we expected. . . ?" Cottle lent Coleridge the five pounds but encouraged him to have a volume of poetry published to forestall future financial problems. Coleridge replied that he had offered manuscripts of his poetry to several London booksellers, "who would not even look at them!" One had offered him six guineas for the copyright, an offer Coleridge had disdainfully rejected. Cottle offered thirty guineas for the proposed volume, to be paid "as your occasions re-

quire" instead of on completion of the volume, as was customary. Coleridge accepted Cottle's offer.

On meeting Southey, Cottle says, "I gave him at once the right hand of fellowship, and to the moment of his decease, that cordiality was never withdrawn." Cottle also offered Southey thirty guineas for a volume of his poetry, and Southey, like Coleridge, readily accepted. Cottle further offered fifty guineas for *Joan of Arc* (1796), the poet's work in progress; the bookseller had heard Southey read several books of the poem aloud. The two struck a bargain whereby Cottle would publish the work in quarto and give Southey fifty copies in addition to the fee.

In attempting to raise money for their venture Coleridge and Southey, aided by Cottle, launched a series of lectures in Bristol. Coleridge was to speak on moral and political issues, Southey on history. The first few lectures followed the plan, but when Coleridge, who had agreed to deliver one of Southey's lectures, failed to appear, Southey was incensed. Despite the efforts of Cottle and others, the friendship between the two poets deteriorated, and the rift sounded Pantisocracy's death knell. Although the two would marry sisters and would maintain a cordial relationship in later years, the mutual trust and support of their days as fledgling poets diminished considerably.

Cottle remained on good terms with both poets, but as Cottle and Southey were more like-minded, their relationship became stronger than that between Cottle and Coleridge. During these early years of his and Cottle's association, Southey's family disapproved of his abandoning his education and his relationship with Edith Fricker. With Cottle and his wife as witnesses, Southey secretly married Fricker on 14 November 1795, Cottle having lent him money to buy the license and the ring. Southey sailed for Lisbon immediately following the ceremony, leaving his bride to live with Cottle's sister, Mary, while he was abroad.

During his eight years of publishing, Cottle reportedly made a profit only on Southey's works. Cottle published Southey's *Poems* in 1797; when notified of a planned second edition, the poet wrote to Cottle on 2 May 1797 proposing to delete

66

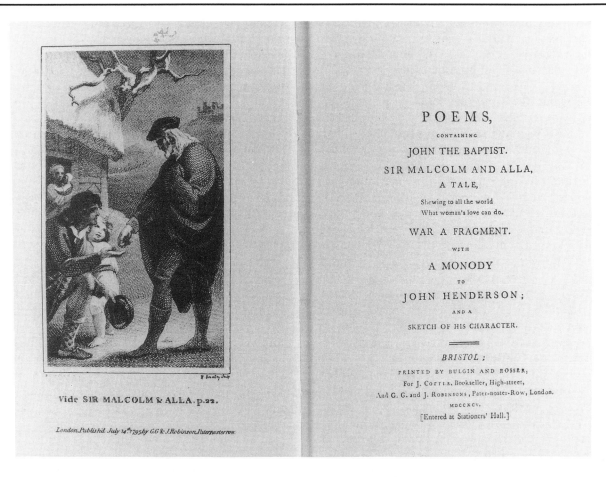

POEMS,

CONTAINING

JOHN THE BAPTIST.

SIR MALCOLM AND ALLA,

A TALE,

Shewing to all the world
What woman's love can do.

WAR A FRAGMENT.

WITH

A MONODY

TO

JOHN HENDERSON;

AND A

SKETCH OF HIS CHARACTER.

BRISTOL:

PRINTED BY BULGIN AND ROSSER,
For J. COTTLE, Bookseller, High-street,
And G. G. and J. ROBINSONS, Pater-noster-Row, London.
MDCCXCV.
[Entered at Stationers' Hall.]

Vide SIR MALCOLM & ALLA. p.22.

London, Publish'd July 14th 1795 by G.G & J.Robinson, Paternosterrow.

Frontispiece and title page for a collection of works by Joseph Cottle, published by himself

"Rosamund" and include "The Retrospect" in the new edition, although he admits his aversion to having different works in the two editions. He also discusses altering the format, revising and improving the poems, and including vignettes and a frontispiece by Gaspar Poussins. Southey admits, however, "I am indifferent concerning all this and merely suggest it as matter of consideration in the profit and loss way," revealing his trust in Cottle's judgment as publisher. In addition to *Poems* and *Joan of Arc* Cottle published Southey's *Letters Written During a Short Residence in Spain and Portugal. With some account of Spanish and Portugueze Poetry* (1797).

Cottle also attempted to provide financial security for Coleridge on several occasions. In addition to asking for advances against his future publications, Coleridge also asked Cottle for other considerations. After his marriage in October 1795 he wrote to Cottle requesting items such as candlesticks, tin spoons, a teakettle, a Bible, and various spices with which to begin housekeeping. On a later occasion Cottle acted as intermediary when

Thomas De Quincey wanted to alleviate Coleridge's financial state with an anonymous donation of five hundred pounds. Cottle suggested that De Quincey offer "a smaller sum, and which, if you see it right, you can at any time, augment." Cottle, although allegedly ignorant of Coleridge's opium problem at this time, was obviously aware of the poet's misuse of money.

At one juncture Cottle himself proposed a subscription of one hundred pounds per year for Coleridge's expenses, with the money to be dispensed without the poet actually having access to the funds. Southey objected, maintaining that Coleridge's problems were rooted in indulgence in opium and alcohol, not in lack of money. Cottle took Southey's advice, and the plan was dropped. Even after Cottle went out of business, Coleridge would continue to solicit funds from him under one pretext or another.

The bulk of the early correspondence between Cottle and Coleridge revolves around works Coleridge was to submit for Cottle's publication and shows Coleridge requesting advances and deadline extensions while Cottle pleads for more copy. Most of the correspondence occurred after Cottle published Coleridge's first book of poetry, *Poems on Various Subjects* (1796). In one letter, dated 22 February 1796, Coleridge says, "My happiest moments for composition are broken in upon by the reflection that I must make haste. I am too late! I am already months behind! I have received my pay beforehand!"

In a letter of 7 October 1795 to Poole, Coleridge says that his agreement with Cottle for "a guinea and a half for every hundred lines of poetry" after the first volume of poems is "perfectly sufficient for my maintenance." In the same letter he sets forth several reasons why he should not try to produce a periodical; yet five months later he disregarded his own advice and launched the *Watchman*.

Cottle expressed some surprise that Coleridge did not include him in the new enterprise, especially since several of their mutual friends, as well as Nathaniel Biggs, Cottle's printer, were involved. Coleridge explained that he had enough financial backing without calling on his publisher; he knew, he said, "how much money had been drawn from you lately." In *Early Recollections* Cottle would say, "Of all men, Mr. Coleridge was the least qualified to display periodical industry."

Coleridge later maintained that the *Watchman* ended after nine numbers; Cottle said that it lasted for ten. In his memoirs, *Biographia Literaria* (1817), Coleridge claims that Biggs pressed him for eighty to ninety pounds for printing the *Watchman* and that only the financial intervention of a third party kept the printer from having Coleridge jailed. In *Early Recollections* Cottle maintains that Biggs did not threaten Coleridge, that the printing cost only thirty-five pounds, and that Cottle advanced Coleridge the money for the paper, which cost more than the printing: "Mr. Coleridge paid me for the paper in fractions, as he found convenient, but from the falling off of his own receipts, I never received the whole." These discrepancies, however, were voiced years after the events. Meanwhile, Cottle published a revised volume of Coleridge's poetry under the title *Poems, by S. T. Coleridge, Second Edition. To Which Are Now Added Poems by Charles Lamb, and Charles Lloyd* (1797), and Coleridge and his wife, Sara Fricker Coleridge, whom he married on 4 October 1795, wrote poems honoring Cottle for his friendship.

For Cottle one of the most important outcomes of his association with Coleridge was gaining Wordsworth as a client. In *Early Recollections* Cottle

claims that Coleridge introduced him to Wordsworth during a visit by Cottle to Coleridge's home in the village of Nether Stowey in March 1798. Correspondence between Cottle and Wordsworth, however, predates the Nether Stowey visit. In a letter that Cottle, in *Early Recollections,* dates January 1796 Wordsworth acknowledges receiving from Cottle a copy of *Joan of Arc* and says that he will soon send Cottle a manuscript for his poem "Salisbury Plain." Other correspondence indicates that Cottle offered Wordsworth money in 1797 and that Wordsworth requested that the publisher send him a copy of Erasmus Darwin's *Zoonamia* (1794–1796) in early 1798. Perhaps the two men met in person for the first time during the Nether Stowey visit.

During that visit Wordsworth shared with Cottle some of the poetry that would appear in his and Coleridge's *Lyrical Ballads* (1798). In retrospect Cottle remarked about the poems, "I immediately perceived in them extraordinary merit, and advised him to publish them. I further said that he should be at no risk; that I would give him the same sum which I had given to Mr. Coleridge and to Mr. Southey." Cottle told Wordsworth that publishing his, Southey's, and Coleridge's works would be a "gratifying circumstance to me . . . such a distinction might never again occur to a Provincial bookseller." Wordsworth, who intensely disliked the publishing aspect of writing, declined the offer.

But Wordsworth's situation soon changed when his landlord leased Alfoxden House, Wordsworth's home near Nether Stowey, to another party, forcing Wordsworth and his sister, Dorothy, to find new lodgings. Coleridge suggested that the two families go to Germany for two years "to acquire the German language and to furnish ourselves with a tolerable stock of information in natural science." An annuity from Josiah and Thomas Wedgwood would cover the Coleridges' expenses on the trip, but Wordsworth lacked the resources for himself and Dorothy. Claiming that Wordsworth had asked him to do so, Coleridge wrote to Cottle, inquiring what the publisher would pay for a proposed tragedy by each of them, with short prefaces and analyses of their principal characters, in addition to Wordsworth's "Salisbury Plain," "Tale of a Woman," and several shorter poems by Wordsworth, all of which, Coleridge assured Cottle, would comprise a volume. Cottle countered with the suggestion that Wordsworth's long poems "Salisbury Plain" and *Peter Bell* appear in one volume and his shorter poems in a second volume. Although Cottle offered the poets thirty guineas each for the two tragedies, Wordsworth objected to having his poems published separately; he preferred that he and Coleridge collaborate on an anonymous book of poetry. Wordsworth was further determined that the two tragedies should not be published unless absolutely necessary to secure funds for their trip.

Cottle discussed the proposed publication on a visit to the two poets, and after much negotiation they decided that Coleridge's "The Rime of the Ancient Mariner" would open the volume, that only an extract of "Salisbury Plain" would be included, and that *Peter Bell* would be omitted. Against Cottle's recommendation the poets insisted on remaining anonymous, because, as Coleridge said, "Wordsworth's name is nothing – to a large number of persons mine *stinks*." Cottle's further recommendation that the volume be dedicated to the Wedgwoods was also declined by Wordsworth and Coleridge.

The publishing history of the first edition of *Lyrical Ballads* poses many problems, including varied claims about date of publication and publication rights and inconsistencies in cancellations, gatherings, pagination, title pages, and even in the paper of the earliest copies. Ascertaining the date of publication would seem to be an easy matter; with *Lyrical Ballads,* however, such is not the case. In a letter written in London and dated 13 September, Dorothy Wordsworth says that her brother's poems, "anonymously authored under the title 'Lyrical Ballads, with other Poems' have been printed but not yet published." William Wordsworth's biographers say that his poem "Lines Composed a Few Miles above Tintern Abbey, on revisiting the Banks of the Wye during a Tour, July 13, 1798" was composed during his and Dorothy's trip through the Wye Valley; was written down, without a line of revision, when they reached Bristol; and was immediately dispatched to Cottle for inclusion in *Lyrical Ballads,* which was already in the press. In *Early Recollections* Cottle gives the time of publication as midsummer 1798, which concurs with the title of the Tintern Abbey poem. Cottle, however, may have considered "publication" as occurring when the volume went to press. Robert W. Daniel, citing Dorothy's letter and records of Cottle's transactions with the London booksellers J. and A. Arch, estimates publication of the first edition occurred between 13 and 16 September.

Questions also surround publication rights to *Lyrical Ballads.* The day after Dorothy wrote her letter Wordsworth wrote to Joseph Johnson, a London publisher and bookseller who had published Wordsworth's *An Evening Walk* and *Descriptive Sketches* in 1793, asking him to deliver six copies of

POEMS

BY

ROBERT SOUTHEY.

SECOND EDITION.

BRISTOL:
PRINTED BY N. BIGGS, FOR
JOSEPH COTTLE, AND SOLD IN LONDON BY
MESSRS. ROBINSONS.
1797.

Title page for the second edition of Southey's poems. The poet made several suggestions for changes from the first edition but ultimately left the matter in Cottle's hands (Courtesy of the Lilly Library, Indiana University).

Lyrical Ballads to Wordsworth's brother, Richard. Wordsworth's letter does not mention Cottle, and the poet's request indicates that Johnson was in some way responsible for the publication of *Lyrical Ballads.* John E. Jordan conjectures that Wordsworth met Johnson in London and, thinking that the book would be more marketable there, agreed to have Johnson publish it. Before sailing for Germany from Yarmouth on 16 September, Wordsworth reportedly wrote to Cottle, telling him of the new arrangement and asking him to give the work to Johnson; this letter does not survive. On 2 October Cottle referred to the missing letter in correspondence with Johnson: "By the tenor of his letter I perceive clearly he is influenced, in this request, by an apprehension that the sale may not be such as to answer my purpose in publishing. . . . I however purchased them of him originally with the intention of being their publisher, and I still have the same wish, and accordingly have sent them to my Agent for that purpose."

Richard Wordsworth sent his brother a copy of Cottle's letter to Johnson, commenting, "This Business in my opinion also requires your immediate attention." Richard also enclosed a copy of a letter Cottle had written to James Tobin, a friend of the Wordsworth family, in which Cottle said that Wordsworth had merely "requested" that the poems be surrendered to Johnson. Pointing out that he had purchased the poems, Cottle criticized Wordsworth for entering into an agreement with Johnson before receiving Cottle's reply.

In any event Cottle could not have relinquished his publication rights to *Lyrical Ballads* to Johnson, because he had already contracted to sell the first edition to J. and A. Arch before he received Wordsworth's letter. Daniel suggests that Cottle sold the poems to Arch *"before he had published them at all,"* noting that the imprint on the title page reads, "Printed by Biggs and Cottle, for T. N. Longman." Speculating that Cottle assumed that Thomas Longman would buy the whole edition, as he had the second edition of Southey's *Joan of Arc,* Daniel maintains that Cottle "had not proclaimed himself the publisher at all; but, unasked, had ceded that honour to Longman." Wordsworth finally laid the dispute between Cottle and Johnson to rest in a letter dated 1 June 1799, in which he acknowledged Cottle's agreement with Arch; expressed regret over the "lost opportunity of connecting myself with Johnson"; and asked Cottle, who was in the process of selling his business, about disposal of the copyrights.

D. F. Foxon groups the publication problems posed by the variant copies of *Lyrical Ballads* into two categories: those generated by the cancellation of Coleridge's "Lewti; or, the Circassian's Love Chant" and those caused by the change in publisher, which necessitated a changed title page. The inclusion of "Lewti" threatened the authors' anonymity because it had been published in the *Morning Post* 13 April 1798; although Coleridge's name did not appear in the *Post* publication, it was widely known that he was the author. Whether publication of *Lyrical Ballads* occurred as early as midsummer or as late as mid September, the longest possible interval between the two dates is only five months, hardly enough time for Coleridge to have forgotten the poem's initial publication.

After the removal of "Lewti" someone, possibly Cottle, inserted a twenty-six-line poem titled "Domiciliary Verses. December 1795." in its place;

authorship of "Domiciliary Verses" has been attributed to Thomas Beddoes, the father of Thomas Lovell Beddoes. This poem, however, was replaced in turn by Coleridge's poem "The Nightingale." Copies including these adjustments appear to be nonexistent, but the British Library has a copy of *Lyrical Ballads* that originally belonged to Southey, in which the three canceled leaves with "Lewti" are inserted between "The Nightingale" and "The Female Vagrant."

The beleaguered publisher faced yet other changes in the text: in some copies page 97 has a revised line and page 98 a revised title; that leaf also has a larger and clearer typeface than that used in the rest of the book. Foxon and other bibliographers note other inconsistencies in pagination, gatherings, cancellations, and the paper's watermarks that likely reflect changes made after the volume went to press.

Perhaps the greatest mystery surrounding the *Lyrical Ballads* is its effect on Cottle's firm. Changes such as those incurred after *Lyrical Ballads* went to press are costly; Cottle owned the copyright to the poems and, as publisher, was presumably responsible for bearing these expenses. The unexpectedly high cost of publishing the *Lyrical Ballads* may have been one reason he went out of business in late 1798.

In *Reminiscences of Samuel Taylor Coleridge and Robert Southey* (1847), the revised version of his *Early Recollections,* Cottle relates that the first edition of *Lyrical Ballads* suffered from negative reviews and poor sales. Hence, Cottle claims, he was forced "at length, to part with, at a loss, the largest proportion of the impression of five hundred, to Mr. Arch, a London bookseller." Several scholars do not accept Cottle's explanation, however. Jordan claims that Cottle was a poor businessman who more often than not lost money on his publishing endeavors. Furthermore, he points out that Cottle's statement in *Reminiscences of Samuel Taylor and Robert Southey* "is certainly at odds" with Cottle's explanation to Johnson in 1798 about turning the book over to Arch. Jordan asserts that neither account furnishes a complete picture of what transpired; instead, Cottle may have sold the work to Arch because he anticipated, rather than experienced, a slow sale. Foxon also disputes both of Cottle's explanations of why he disposed of *Lyrical Ballads,* contending that the 1798 version was falsified to "conceal Cottle's financial troubles" at the time of publication. Foxon further speculates that *Lyrical Ballads* may not even have been published by Cottle in Bristol but may have only been circulated there to friends of Wordsworth, Coleridge, and Cottle. Daniel shares Foxon's reservations about Cottle's account, pointing out that, at the most, only six days passed between the publication and the sale to Arch; hence, "Cottle sold before he knew anything about either" the sales figures or the reviews. Like Foxon, Daniel suggests that Cottle "simply gave away a few copies" and had no intention of selling the book himself. The scarcity of surviving copies supports this theory: Southey owned one, as did Hannah More, and only twelve copies are known to survive.

Scholars who accept the theory that Cottle merely circulated copies to friends rather than actually putting *Lyrical Ballads* on the public market cite Cottle's financial problems in the fall of 1798 and hold that a pressing need for cash prompted the sale. In 1799 Longman and Rees, another Bristol publishing house, bought Cottle's business; the sale further obscures Cottle's involvement with *Lyrical Ballads,* because Longman and Rees returned the copyright of the volume to Cottle at his request, and Cottle, in turn, gave the copyright to Wordsworth and Coleridge.

Another possible reason for Cottle's sale of *Lyrical Ballads* concerns Southey. Thomas Hutchinson, who edited *Lyrical Ballads by William Wordsworth and Samuel Taylor Coleridge 1798* (1898), theorized that Cottle showed Southey an advance copy of the volume and that Southey urged Cottle to sell it as soon as possible. In a letter of 5 September 1798 to William Taylor, Southey mentions the volume's authors by name, despite their anonymity, and lambasts "The Rime of the Ancient Mariner" as "the clumsiest attempt at German sublimity I ever saw." The friendship of Southey and Cottle would explain how Southey knew who the anonymous authors of *Lyrical Ballads* were and how Southey would have an advance copy of the work, including variant pages. Some scholars speculate that Southey privately shared his assessment of *Lyrical Ballads* with Cottle: Southey, knowing of the precarious state of Cottle's business, probably would have wanted to spare the bookseller further financial embarrassment; and since Southey's stature as a literary critic was growing, Cottle would have been likely to take his friend's advice. The first of the negative reviews to which Cottle partly attributed his decision to sell the volume appeared in the *Critical Review* in November, almost a month after Cottle had turned the work over to Arch, and was written by Southey. Southey's review exhibits much of the same vehement criticism as that in his letter to Taylor. Speculation aside, one facet of the sale is clear; Cottle disposed of *Lyrical Ballads* before the volume had had

Title page for one of the first works written by Cottle after the demise of his firm

much public exposure. As Jordan says, "Why Cottle was in such a hurry to get rid of the *Lyrical Ballads* remains something of a mystery. Perhaps he did not value it very highly himself." If Cottle did not place much value on the volume, however, he was not alone: Longman would not have willingly parted with the copyright had he thought that *Lyrical Ballads* held much promise.

After Cottle's brief career as publisher and bookseller he wrote *Malvern Hills* (1798) and contributed some of his own poetry to Southey's *Annual Anthology* (1799, 1800), which also featured poems by Coleridge, Lovell, Charles Lamb, and several lesser-known writers. Cottle's *Alfred: An Epic Poem* appeared in 1801 and his *John the Baptist: A Poem* in 1802. Cottle and Southey collaborated on a three-volume edition of Thomas Chatterton's works that was published in 1803. Chatterton's sister had been tricked into giving up her brother's letters, and Cot-

LYRICAL BALLADS,

WITH

A FEW OTHER POEMS.

BRISTOL:
PRINTED BY BIGGS AND COTTLE,
FOR T. N. LONGMAN, PATERNOSTER-ROW, LONDON.
1798.

Title page for one of the variant printings of William Wordsworth and Samuel Taylor Coleridge's groundbreaking poems, a volume that may have helped to drive Cottle out of business (Courtesy of the Lilly Library, Indiana University)

tle and Southey undertook the edition to help the family. Cottle had, similarly, established a subscription for Robert Burns's wife and five children when Burns died in 1796, leaving his family financially pressed.

Southey acknowledged his own early debt to Cottle in a letter dated 28 April 1808. He thanked Cottle for publishing his works: "You bought them on the chance of success, what no London bookseller would have done. . . . Nay, if you had not published 'Joan of Arc,' the poem would never have existed," and continued: "The very money with which I bought my wedding ring, and paid my marriage fees, was supplied by you," adding that Cottle had provided him "a home when I had none."

Wordsworth and Southey wrote letters commending Cottle on his works; but after Cottle's *The Fall of Cambria* appeared in 1809, George Gordon, Lord Byron, ridiculed Cottle and his brother, Amos, who also wrote poetry, in his *English Bards, and Scotch Reviewers* (1809). Cottle's friends urged

him to disregard Byron's criticism. In a letter to Cottle, Lamb praised *The Fall of Cambria* and said of Byron: "I have a thorough aversion to his character, and a very moderate admiration of his genius; he is great in so little a way." Cottle's *Messiah* appeared in 1815. The fourth edition of *Malvern Hills,* published in 1829, includes an appendix with essays on John Henderson, the Rowley poems, and the fossils found in Oreston Caves near Plymouth; the latter essay illustrates Cottle's lifelong interest in paleontology. Cottle relates that he had acquired almost two thousand animal bones from these caves in 1822 and donated many of them to the Bristol Philosophical Institution.

Meanwhile, Cottle's relationship with Coleridge deteriorated after Cottle learned of the poet's opium habit. Cottle became less sympathetic about Coleridge's financial situation, urging him to renounce his habit and to turn to his family for help in his affliction. Cottle offered to defray all of Coleridge's expenses if he would return to Mrs. Coleridge and their children in Keswick. "And now let me conjure you . . . by the fear of God, and the awfulness of eternity, to renounce from this moment opium and spirits, as your bane!" Cottle wrote. Coleridge responded with an account of his addiction, to which Cottle replied that the poet should turn his back on Satan and be healed. The men exchanged much correspondence on the subject. In one letter Coleridge said that after his death "a full and unqualified narrative of my wretchedness and its guilty cause may be made public." After Coleridge's death in 1834, these letters provided Cottle with an excuse for making Coleridge's addiction a matter of public record in his *Early Recollections.* Cottle reproduced the correspondence in its entirety in his book.

Aghast when they learned of the intended disclosure, Coleridge's family attempted to suppress the information by urging Southey to intervene with Cottle. Before reading Cottle's manuscript, Southey asked him to omit any mention of Coleridge's addiction: in a letter to Cottle dated 10 October 1836 Southey advised, "A few omissions (one letter in particular, respecting the habit of taking opium,) would spare them great pain, and leave your book little the poorer, rich as your materials are." After reading Cottle's manuscript, however, Southey changed his position and agreed that any correspondence regarding Coleridge's addiction should be included.

But in 1837, after reading Cottle's recently released *Early Recollections,* Southey remarked, "The confusion in Cottle's 'Recollections' is greater than any one would think possible." In a letter to Caroline Bowles, who later became his second wife, Southey remarked that "unless you knew him thus thoroughly, you could not believe that such simpleheartedness and such inordinate vanity were to be found in the same person." The book provoked similar reactions from other contemporaries; in *A History of Booksellers, the Old and the New* (1873), Henry Curwen wrote that the *Quarterly Review,* one of the most prestigious periodicals of Cottle's time, responded to the book "with a howl of contemptuous abuse," accusing *Early Recollections* of being "'a refuse of advertisements and handbills, the sweepings of a shop, the shreds of a ledger, and the rank residuum of a life of gossip.'" One of the most frequently cited criticisms is that Cottle embellished his own role in his subjects' lives. Molly Lefebure, a Coleridge biographer, says that "Cottle . . . interpolated passages from one letter to another, altered days, inserted footnotes into the main body of text, printed fragments of letters as separate and complete entities and even did not hesitate to resort to improvisation of fact. . . ." Sometimes he penciled in dates on correspondences that he assumed should fit – as, for example, he did on his first letter from Wordsworth. In short Cottle's book jeopardized his credibility with his contemporaries and with future scholars as well.

The book is especially suspect in its claim that Cottle had no knowledge of Coleridge's opium habit until 1814, when he remarked to a friend about how much Coleridge's hands had quivered at a dinner party and the friend replied, "That arises from the immoderate quantity of opium he takes." In view of the long personal and professional relationship between the two, one wonders about Cottle's alleged surprise at this revelation. In 1798 Cottle had published Charles Lloyd's novel *Edmund Oliver,* which featured a hero who bore a remarkable resemblance to Coleridge and who was addicted to laudanum. Cottle actively edited his clients' works; therefore, he would be unlikely to be ignorant of the likeness between Coleridge and Edmund Oliver. James Gillman, who treated Coleridge while sharing living quarters with him for eighteen years, reacted to Cottle's book by composing his own biography of Coleridge.

In the preface to his book Cottle clearly anticipates a negative response to his account of Coleridge's opium addiction: "If the obligation to convey this undissembled fact, had not been imperative, I should gladly have consigned to oblivion, that one letter of Mr. Coleridge. . . ." Many of Cottle's contemporaries, however, questioned his

EARLY RECOLLECTIONS;

CHIEFLY RELATING

TO THE LATE

SAMUEL TAYLOR COLERIDGE,

DURING HIS LONG RESIDENCE IN BRISTOL.

BY JOSEPH COTTLE.

IN TWO VOLUMES.

VOL. I.

LONDON:
LONGMAN, REES & CO. AND HAMILTON, ADAMS & CO.

1837.

Title page for the first version of Cottle's memoirs, a book that called down a storm of abuse on its author (Courtesy of the Lilly Library, Indiana University)

self-proclaimed obligation to release this information. Coleridge's addiction would inevitably have been made public, but the manner in which Cottle did so – in a book ostensibly recounting memories of a longtime friend and business associate rather than in a serious biography – angered many readers. Other remembrances in Cottle's book received a negative reception, as well, and critics frequently echoed Southey's sentiments about Cottle's muddled account of events.

Despite the problems Cottle created for himself in disclosing the infamous "opium letters," as they came to be called, in 1847 he revised and enlarged the book. In the revised edition Cottle again tried to justify his actions, claiming that a biographer's duty is to present an accurate picture of his subject. He included Southey's 1836 letter supporting the disclosure, claiming that "This unqualified approval determined me to publish the whole of the opium letters."

A brief notice in the London *Times* on 10 June 1853 marked the eighty-four-year-old Cottle's death three days earlier at Fairfield House, near Bristol.

The obituary cited his friendships with the young Coleridge, Wordsworth, and Southey and provided what is probably Cottle's finest encomium: "He was extensively known by his own literary labours, and throughout his long life was greatly honoured and loved for his distinguished personal worth by all who had the privilege of his acquaintance."

Whether Cottle should have released the opium letters, whether he should have sold *Lyrical Ballads* to Arch, or whether he should have been more rigorous in composing *Early Recollections* are matters of opinion. What is not a matter of opinion, however, is that Cottle deserves the honor accorded him as the friend of Wordsworth, Coleridge, and Southey and as a publisher of verse that initiated a poetic revolution. His provincial location, his youth, and his inexperience certainly hindered what he was able to do. Whatever Cottle's shortcomings, they do not obviate the fact that he provided encouragement and support for these poets at a time when few recognized their talent and promise.

References:

Ernest Hartley Coleridge, ed., *Letters of Samuel Taylor Coleridge,* 2 volumes (London: Heinemann, 1895);

Basil Cottle, *Joseph Cottle of Bristol* (Bristol: Bristol Branch of the Historical Association, 1987);

Joseph Cottle, *Early Recollections, Chiefly Relating to the Late Samuel Taylor Coleridge During His Long Residence in Bristol,* 2 volumes (London: Longman Rees; Hamilton, Adams, 1837); revised as *Reminiscences of Samuel Taylor Coleridge and Robert Southey* (London: Houlston & Stoneman, 1847);

Kenneth Curry, *Southey* (London & Boston: Routledge & Kegan Paul, 1975);

Curry, ed., *New Letters of Robert Southey, Volume I: 1792–1810* (New York & London: Columbia University Press, 1965);

Henry Curwen, *A History of Booksellers, the Old and the New* (London: Chatto & Windus, 1873), pp. 478–483;

Robert W. Daniel, "The Publication of 'Lyrical Ballads,'" *Modern Language Review,* 33 (July 1938): 406–410;

Ernest de Selincourt, ed., *The Letters of William and Dorothy Wordsworth,* 5 volumes, revised and enlarged by Chester L. Shaver, Mary Moorman, and Alan G. Hill (Oxford: Clarendon Press, 1967–1988);

Malcolm Elwin, *The First Romantics* (London: Macdonald, 1947);

John Feather, *The Provincial Book Trade in Eighteenth-Century England* (Cambridge: Cambridge University Press, 1985);

D. F. Foxon, "The Printing of Lyrical Ballads, 1798," *Library,* fifth series 9 (December 1954): 221–241;

Thomas Hutchinson, ed., *Lyrical Ballads. By W. Wordsworth and S. T. Coleridge. 1798* (London: Dodsworth, 1898);

John E. Jordan, *Why the "Lyrical Ballads?": The Background, Writing, and Character of Wordsworth's 1798 "Lyrical Ballads"* (Berkeley: University of California Press, 1975);

Molly Lefebure, *Samuel Taylor Coleridge: A Bondage of Opium* (New York: Stein & Day, 1974);

Charles James Longman, *The House of Longman* (London: Longman, Green, 1936);

Mary Moorman, *William Wordsworth: A Biography, volume 1: The Early Years, 1770–1803* (Oxford: Clarendon Press, 1957; New York: Oxford University Press, 1957);

Cristopher Morley, "Joe Cottle, the Forgotten Man in a World of Centennials," *New York Times Book Review,* 29 July 1951, p. 5;

Thomas J. Wise, *Two Lake Poets; A Catalogue of Printed Books, Manuscripts and Autographed Letters by William Wordsworth and Samuel Taylor Coleridge* (London: Dawsons of Pall Mall, 1965).

Papers:

The British Museum holds Joseph Cottle's correspondence with Joseph Haslewood on the Rowley manuscripts; miscellaneous correspondence is held by the Ashmolean of Oxford University and by Cornell University.

— Sandra Spencer

William Creech
(Edinburgh: 1773 – 1781; 1790 – 1815)
Kincaid and Creech
(Edinburgh: 1771 – 1773)
Creech and Smellie
(Edinburgh: 1781 – 1790)

In a letter to the lawyer Gilbert Hutchison dated 28 September 1803, William Creech writes: "I believe I have published more Books and paid more money to Authors than any man of my profession in Scotland during my time." Creech is largely correct in his self-estimation; but, while he established connections with Scottish publishers in London – such as John Murray, William Strahan, and Robert Cadell – and even probed the American market through William Tod in Philadelphia, Creech remained an Edinburgh publisher whose influence in the trade was ultimately parochial. It would be Archibald Constable, the principal purchaser of Creech's stock in 1815, who would develop a house whose publishing interests were truly international.

Creech was born on 21 April 1745 at Newbattle, Midlothian; his father, William, a Presbyterian minister, died that same year. Creech and his mother, Mary Buley Creech, moved to Dalkeith, where Creech received a stellar preliminary education at the Dalkeith Academy under the guidance of James Barclay, a specialist in moral philosophy, and the Reverend John Robertson of Kilmarnock. It was at the academy that Creech first came into contact with the family of Lord Glencairn, through whom he would later meet Robert Burns and thus secure his most distinguished literary property. Creech entered the University of Edinburgh in 1761 with the intention of studying medicine, but while pursuing a course of study in the natural sciences Creech developed literary and philosophical interests that led him in 1764 to establish the Speculative Society, arguably the most important student organization in late-eighteenth-century Edinburgh. Through the society he made his initial contact with William Cullen and Hugh Blair, and associates of the society such as Alexander Duncan would enable Creech to continue connections with the medical community that eventually brought a steady stream of profitable if unremarkable titles to his publishing concern – not the least of these being the annual volumes of *Medical and Philosophical Commentaries* (1773–1795).

Also in 1764 Creech became an apprentice printer with the publishing and bookselling firm of Alexander Kincaid and John Bell. Kincaid, who was interested in the London trade, sent Creech to London in 1766 to introduce himself to the Scottish publishers and booksellers in the city. Creech remained away from Edinburgh until 1768, spending time in Holland and France in 1767. While he made purchases for Kincaid, Creech also developed connections of his own with the London booksellers that brought him back to London in 1769, 1770, and 1771 and would do so in 1772 and 1774. During these later visits Creech strengthened his ties especially with Cadell and Strahan, as indicated by the many dinner engagements with them recorded in his tour book for those years. Oddly, as often as Creech visited London early in his career, he would rarely venture out of Edinburgh after he was established as a publisher in the 1780s.

In 1770 Bell had parted with Kincaid, and Creech assumed the position of a junior partner in Kincaid's firm in May 1771 on returning from his third trip to London. Constable observes that "much of the literary connexion and respectability of Mr. Kincaid's trade accompanied" Bell when he set up business alone. Kincaid, who had been lord provost of Edinburgh and enjoyed the luxury of being the king's printer, was less inclined to publish new titles after Bell's departure and allowed some properties, notably the works of Henry Home, Lord Kames, to drift into Bell's control. As business declined, Creech encouraged Kincaid to retire, and he bought out his partner in 1773. While in partnership with Kincaid, Creech's important publications

William Creech (Courtesy of Providence Public Library)

included titles by Kames and James Beattie; thereafter, Creech and Bell sometimes appeared together on imprints, especially on later editions of Kames's *Elements of Criticism* (first published in 1762).

Creech's shop was ideally situated to become a center for his business and political activities: it stood at the eastern end of a block of buildings to the north of St. Giles Cathedral in the heart of the Old Town. Creech's shop could not have been more accessible, as Robert Chambers records: "He had a levee in his house [above the shop] till twelve every day, attended by literary men and printers. Between twelve and one he came to the shop, where the same flow of company lasted till four." Over the years Creech paid less and less attention to publishing and more to city politics; his major literary properties were all developed in the 1770s and 1780s: Beattie's *An Essay on the Nature and Immutability of Truth* (1770) and *The Minstrel* (1771, 1774); Andrew Erskine's *Town-Eclogues* (1773); Kames's *Sketches of the History of Man* (1774); William Cullen's

First Lines of the Practice of Physic (1777–1783); Henry Mackenzie's periodicals the *Mirror* (1779–1780) and the *Lounger* (1785–1787); William Smellie's *An Account of the Institution and Progress of the Society of Antiquaries of Scotland* (1782); the second edition of Burns's *Poems, Chiefly in the Scottish Dialect* (1787); and Hugo Arnot's *The History of Edinburgh* (1788). Creech also had a share in publishing Hugh Blair's *Lectures on Rhetoric and Belles Lettres* (1783).

While Creech amassed an impressive assortment of authors, beginning in the 1780s he also generated significant trade in reprints and republications. Along with titles in the classics, history, and the sciences both for popular and student readerships, Creech's catalogues list novels and popular entertainments such as *Evelina* (1778), by Frances Burney; *Chrysal; or, The Adventures of a Guinea,* by Charles Johnstone; and the anonymous *The Adventures of a Cork-Screw* (1775). Those lists indicate the sometimes surprising disparity between Creech as bookseller and as publisher: while the publisher began his career with an earnest intention to promote Scottish writers, the bookseller gradually became interested in catering to the growing demands of the popular reader. When Constable purchased Creech's stock in 1815 he would complain of its "thinness," referring to the superficiality of many of its titles. In addressing the demands of the common reader, however, Creech did not always pander to the lowest denominator: he consulted with Beattie in 1776 to put together the series of British Poets, which included a significant number of Scottish writers, and followed it with the series of Scottish Philosophy. Creech was also respected for the quality of his "cheap" editions and especially for the effort he made to supply new engravings and illustrations.

Creech was a conservative man whose business practices were seldom speculative. He was extremely protective of his own literary properties, and while much involved with London partners such as Cadell, Davies, Murray, and Strahan, he was wary of taking risks. He did not have many happy ventures with Murray, who blamed him for losses incurred on work by Gilbert Stuart, and he held back in offering shares in Lord Kames's works for which he held copyright. Constable criticizes Creech for mishandling his share in the London publication of Blair's *Sermons* (1813), which, "successful as the work was, he never made any effort to increase, nor did he think it worthwhile to print and publish the work in Edinburgh, as he ought to have done." In Constable's view Creech was always too submissive to his London partners; Constable seems particularly irritated by Creech's tendency "to write in his title-pages the names of the London booksellers before his own." Late in the history of his firm Creech witnessed the loss of Scottish authors to Constable because of this characteristic. Notable in this regard is Alexander Fraser Tytler, Lord Woodhouselee, who in 1812 offered the much enlarged third edition of his *Essay on the Principles of Translation* (1813; first published in 1791) to Constable after a lifetime of dealing with Creech. Woodhouselee's disenchantment with Creech can be directly traced to Creech's hesitation in securing an agreement with Murray in 1806 for the London edition of Woodhouselee's *Memoirs of the Life and Writings of the Honourable Henry Home of Kames* (1807).

Creech did much to make Edinburgh a modern middle-class city. As lord provost of Edinburgh from 1811 to 1813 he directed through the town council legislation that improved pensions for tradesmen, oversaw the construction of a new charity workhouse, and undertook an extensive survey and analysis of the city's water supply. But Creech also used his political authority to benefit his business interests, as when he took advantage of his position on the town council in 1783 to circulate two letters that undermined the publisher John Balfour and secured for Creech the position of publisher and bookseller to the Society of Antiquaries of Scotland.

In the 1790s Creech lobbied the Edinburgh Booksellers Society to form a corporation, modeled after the manner of the Stationers' Company in London, for the purpose of breaking a bookbinders' cartel. His first attempt, on 18 November 1790, came to nothing when the printer and publisher Smellie failed to advance the idea through his committee. In 1792 Creech put through a motion to form the Corporation of Booksellers, which continues to this day. Creech's elevation of self-interest over national interest was such that he remained silent during Alexander Donaldson's 1774 appeal to the House of Lords over the issue of perpetual copyright: fearing the loss of perpetual title to his own literary properties and having no desire to do anything to damage his connections with the London book trade, Creech was the only important Edinburgh publisher not to petition actively on Donaldson's behalf.

Smellie, who had edited the *Encyclopaedia Britannica,* operated a printing house in the Anchor Close and published titles under his own imprint from time to time; by the mid 1770s he had become Creech's favorite printer. Even by the lax standards of the day, however, Smellie was a poor businessman; and when he found his printing shop in financial jeopardy in 1781 he sold half of his firm to Creech. Smellie was thus able to satisfy his creditors, and Creech was able to save on printing costs. This union would, however, jeopardize Creech's relationship with Burns and would permanently and unfairly damage Creech's reputation as a publisher.

It was his exchanges with Burns that brought Creech his popular fame and ignominy. The Edinburgh edition of Burns's *Poems, Chiefly in the Scottish Dialect* was a complicated transaction that involved an elaborate subscription list, with at least two hundred of the subscribed texts being sold twice. This was possible because several of the major subscribers, such as Burns's patron Lord Glencairn, purchased as many as fifty copies, which they then declined and left for resale at a higher price in Creech's shop. The practice was a common means of "benefiting" a writer. Money from sales and subscriptions came in fits and starts over nearly two

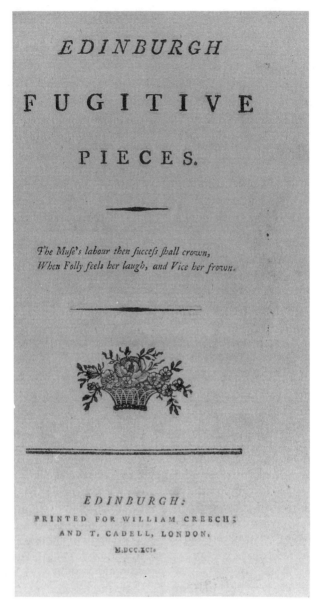

Title page for Creech's collected edition of his periodical
contributions (Courtesy of Special Collections, Thomas
Cooper Library, University of South Carolina)

years, during which Burns received regular small sums. Certainly Creech had, as usual, his own best interests foremost in mind, but he hardly deserved the much-quoted description of him recorded by Burns in his Edinburgh commonplace book as "a little upright, pert, tart, tripping wight / And still his precious self his chief delight." Creech's problems with Burns were, in truth, due to Smellie's faulty handling of his part in the transactions.

Correspondence between Creech and Smellie shows that the latter was responsible for significant mismanagement of the company books in the mid to late 1780s – especially during the crucial years when Burns wrote his many insulting letters about "Mr. Creech's ingenuous fair-dealing" and his being kept by Creech "hanging about Edinburgh from 7th August, 1787, until the 13th April, 1788, before he would condescend to give me a statement of affairs." The heated epistolary exchange between Smellie and Creech over the company's financial statements coincides with the dates given by Burns. Smellie was left in charge of the books while Creech was in London in 1787 (an absence that is the subject of Burns's short poem "Willie's Awa"), and

Creech complained in writing to Smellie on his return about being hampered in his access to the company's accounts for the period of his absence and about the "confused statements of accounts." Smellie took on even more responsibility for overseeing the business when Creech was appointed magistrate in 1788. As had happened a decade earlier with the demise of the *Edinburgh Magazine and Review*, Smellie escaped public suspicion for his part in this contretemps: Burns never altered his favorable opinion of his congenial drinking companion, Smellie, but his relationship with Creech soured. For his part, Creech declined to set the blame at his partner's door publicly or while defending himself in letters to Burns, but he dissolved the partnership with Smellie once matters were at a close with Burns. Burns received a settlement of £450 in March 1789, including the £100 Creech had promised him for the copyright; but recently discovered accounts of Creech's firm for the previous eighteen months show that Burns received a sum closer to £1,100 when the staggered receipts for subscription payments are included. Although Creech broke with Smellie in 1790, their financial entanglements continued until Smellie's death in 1795, and Creech had to settle against his former partner's estate in 1801. Creech took no more partners after Smellie.

Creech's correspondence is full of details about the growth and architecture of Edinburgh; he was aware of the unusual rapidity with which the city was becoming a sophisticated center for the arts. Creech's appreciation of the achievement of the designers and builders who reconceived the city and created, outside the Old Town walls, a new development that to this day rivals anything on the Continent clearly affected his determination as a publisher to raise international appreciation of Scotland as an intellectual force in Europe. This determination is particularly noticeable in Creech's correspondence with American colleagues in the late 1790s and early 1800s. Creech spent nearly ten years compiling *Letters, Addressed to Sir John Sinclair, Bart., Respecting the Mode of Living, Arts, Commerce, Literature, Manners, &c., of Edinburgh, in 1763, and since That Period* (1793) and *An Account of the Manners and Customs of Scotland* (1793), which were combined to form the proposal for the much more ambitious *A Statistical Account of Scotland*. Completed by Sir John Sinclair and sold by Creech and James Donaldson (the son of Alexander Donaldson), the work eventually ran to twenty-one volumes. Creech wrote to Sinclair in May 1792 that the "prosperity and happiness of every nation" largely depended upon the exhaustive compilation of statistical information.

Creech regularly contributed to the *Edinburgh Courant* sketches of Edinburgh life under the pseudonym "Theophrastus" and was the author of essays and pamphlets; among the latter is *An Account of the Trial of William Brodie, and George Smith, before the High Court of Justiciary, on Wednesday the 27th, and Thursday the 28th Days of August, 1788; for Breaking into, and Robbing, the General Excise Office of Scotland, on the 5th Day of March Last . . . by a Juryman* (1788). Creech, who knew Brodie well, seems to have been fascinated with the latter's double life as a respected businessman and city father, on the one hand, and master criminal à la Jonathan Wild, on the other; he wrote three pamphlets about Deacon Brodie and his cohorts. Brodie's activities captured the public imagination, and Creech made a reasonable profit out of the criminal lives he authored; but one cannot help speculating about the attraction of this businessman Jekyll and Hyde for the proper, upright, and thrifty Creech. Creech also contributed to the *Scots Magazine*. He collected and printed most of his periodical writing in *Edinburgh Fugitive Pieces* (1791). Creech wrote little after that date, with the exception of his statistical compilations, but *Edinburgh Fugitive Pieces* appeared in three separate printings in Creech's lifetime and was republished by G. Ramsay and J. Fairbairn in 1815, the year of Creech's death.

Late in his career Creech succeeded in a long-standing court battle with the Edinburgh printer John Robertson over the question of whether damages could be claimed for infringement on literary property where the contested works had not been entered in the Stationers' Hall. The issue had never been properly addressed in Scotland, where the copyright law was widely violated. The edition of Burns's poems published by Creech in 1793 included pieces that had not appeared in the earlier edition and had not been entered in the Stationers' Hall. In 1802 Robertson brought out a small selection of Burns's poetry that included some of the 1793 poems. The London firm of T. Cadell and W. Davies, which had jointly published with Creech an edition of Burns's poems in 1800, joined him in bringing a claim for damages in the Court of Session at Edinburgh on 16 May 1804. They lost, but they pursued their complaint to the House of Lords, which decided in their favor on 16 July 1811 and remanded the case to the Court of Session in Scotland. Damages were awarded on 24 January 1812, and Creech was credited with securing rights of literary property in Scotland fully equivalent to those recognized in England, in particular the entitlement "to prosecute for damages at common law . . . though works may not have been entered in Stationers' Hall."

Creech, who remained unmarried throughout his life, remained active in his trade until his death on 14 January 1815. His reputation has suffered because of the widely quoted, slanderous observations about his character and appearance in Burns's correspondence; he was, however, regarded with great respect by Lord Kames, Beattie, and Blair as a prime mover in the literary and civic maturation of Edinburgh in the late eighteenth century. Constable purchased the principal part of his stock for £2,750, a sum that is indicative of the dwindling of Creech's properties in the last decade, and especially the last five years, of his career. What was not purchased by Constable was dispersed through various Edinburgh booksellers, bringing in an additional £632.

References:

John C. Carrick, *William Creech, Robert Burns's Best Friend* (Dalkeith, Scotland: Lyle, 1903);

Robert Chambers, *A Biographical Dictionary of Eminent Scotsmen,* revised edition, 5 volumes (Glasgow: Blackie, 1855);

Thomas Constable, *Archibald Constable and His Literary Correspondents: A Memorial,* 3 volumes (Edinburgh: Edmonston & Douglas, 1873);

William Creech, *Letters, Addressed to Sir John Sinclair, Bart., Respecting the Mode of Living, Arts, Commerce, Literature, Manners, &c. of Edinburgh, in 1763, and since That Period* (Edinburgh, 1793);

J. De Lancey Ferguson, *Pride and Passion: Robert Burns* (New York: Oxford University Press, 1939);

Ferguson, ed., *The Letters of Robert Burns,* second edition, 2 volumes, edited by G. Ross Roy (Oxford: Clarendon Press, 1985);

Robert Kerr, *Memoirs of the Life, Writings, and Correspondence of William Smellie,* 2 volumes (Edinburgh: Alex. Smellie, 1811);

James Mackay, *Burns: A Biography of Robert Burns* (Edinburgh: Mainstream, 1992).

Papers:

William Creech's letterbook, accounts, and manuscripts are in the Edinburgh Room of the Edinburgh Public Library; his correspondence with Lord Kames (1772–1777) is in the Dalguise Muniments, Scottish Record Office, Edinburgh; and the Smellie-Creech correspondence is in the archives of the Society of Antiquaries in Edinburgh.

– Stephen W. Brown

Edmund Curll

(London: 1706 – 1747)

Edmund Curll was probably the most notorious publisher of his era. Frequently in legal trouble for his shady practices, which ranged from printing pornography to pirating the works of nearly every major author of his day, Curll was twice imprisoned and once made to stand in the pillory. Outraged authors, especially Alexander Pope, took matters into their own hands from time to time, and Curll found himself sued, beaten, tossed in a blanket by schoolboys, and otherwise humiliated on several occasions. Such incidents have helped Curll pass into myth as the comically unscrupulous publisher, the philistine buffoon and profiteer feeding upon the noble products of maltreated authors. Curll's twentieth-century biographer, Ralph Straus, presents Curll as a clown at best, a villain at worst. But the truth is more complex than the popular myth and more complex than the portrait Straus paints, for Curll was not always the victimizer: for example, he was at least as much used by Pope as Pope had ever been by him. And that Curll maintained a successful enterprise for more than forty years, publishing, by one estimate, some one thousand different titles, indicates that he had good business sense. But the myth is a compelling one, and disentangling the man from it is not easy. Curll's contributions to publishing history can, at least, be put in a negative way: lawsuits against him resulted in important rulings regarding obscenity and copyright. And some modern scholars are coming to see him as a significant figure in the development of eighteenth-century capitalism, a proletarian hero of sorts who was instrumental in the democratization of publishing and who helped shape the modern notion of authorship.

Appropriately enough for a man who lived such a murky legal existence, his personal origins are obscure. In his will he gives his birth date as 14 July 1683, but newspaper obituaries at his death in 1747 listed his age as seventy-two. He was born in the west of England, perhaps near Maidenhead, Berkshire; in later life he referred to himself as the son of a tradesman, but no further information is available. He evidently had a solid classical education, for his writings reveal a sound knowledge of Greek and Latin. Curll is described in Thomas Amory's autobiographical novel, *The Life of John Buncle, Esq.* (1756, 1766), as pale, tall, thin, and awkward; "His eyes were a light grey, large, projecting, goggle, and purblind. He was splayfooted and baker-kneed." Amory is obviously indulging in satiric exaggeration, but no nonpartisan description of Curll exists.

In 1698 or 1699 Curll was apprenticed to a London bookseller named Richard Smith – probably the Richard Smith who had set up his business only in 1698, published the works of Bishop William Beveridge of St. Asaph (who became something of a patron to him) and other religious writings, and underwent bankruptcy proceedings in 1706 but would stay in business until his death around 1720. Assuming that Curll remained with Smith for the traditional seven-year apprenticeship, he would have been ready to go out on his own by 1705. He was buying book collections and selling them at auction by January 1706; a catalogue for these auctions refers to his shop at the sign of the Peacock, near St. Clement's Church in the Strand.

Curll continued to work in partnership with Smith and other relatively small booksellers, including Robert Halsey, Charles Smith, John Baker, and Benjamin Bragge, who were either trying to establish themselves in the business, like Curll, or were undergoing financial difficulties. When Richard Smith entered bankruptcy in May 1706, Curll was one of the appraisers of his stock (Smith would later claim that Curll had knowingly undervalued some of his books; Curll's answer to the complaint has never come to light). One of the earliest titles with Curll's imprint is a 1706 republication of Smith's 1705 edition of *Caesar's Commentaries of His Wars in Gaul,* translated by Martin Bladen. The title page says that it is an "improv'd" second edition; the only difference, however, is the title page itself, according to which the book was "printed for R. Smith, sold by Cha. Smith and E. Curll."

Curll remained involved in auctioning for some time; but his main interest was publishing, and he began to acquire manuscripts – not always in an aboveboard manner. Another of his earliest titles (of which no copies seem to exist today) was another "second edition," this time of John Dunton's

C. *Julius Cæsar's*
COMMENTARIES
OF HIS
WARS in *Gaul,*
AND
CIVIL WAR with *Pompey.*
To which is Added
Aulus Hirtius, or *Oppius's* Supplement of
the *Alexandrian, African* and *Spanish*
Wars.

With the AUTHOR'S LIFE.
Adorn'd with Sculptures from the Defigns of the
Famous *PALLADIO.*

Made *Englifh* from the Original *Latin*
By Captain *MARTIN BLADEN.*

The SECOND EDITION Improv'd,
With Notes explaining the moft difficult Places, the Ancient and
Modern Geography exactly compar'd, and *Dionyfius Voffius's*
Supplement collected from *Plutarch, Appian, Dion,* &c. which
makes a Connexion between the Wars in *Gaul* and Civil War
with *Pompey.*

LONDON,
Printed for *R. Smith* without *Temple* Bar; and Sold
by *Cha. Smith* at the *Buck* between the Two *Temple* Gates in *Fleetftreet,* and *E. Curll* at the *Peacock*
near St. *Clement's* Church in the *Strand.* 1706.

*Title page for one of the first books to bear Edmund
Curll's imprint*

Athenian Spy (1706), bound with *The Way of a Man
with a Maid.* Exactly what the latter work was is uncertain, but given Curll's later reputation one can
guess that it was at least semipornographic. If so,
then at the outset of his career Curll was already
publishing scandalous material. In this endeavor he
was hardly alone; even the thoroughly respectable
Jacob Tonson had published a version of a popular
pornographic tale, *Aloisia,* when he was becoming
established in 1681. And Curll's list at this time
shows the tremendous diversity that it would maintain throughout his career: in 1707 he published
such serious religious titles as Robert Warren's *The
Devout Christian's Companion,* John Conant's *Sermons
on Several Subjects,* Joseph Harrison's *An Exposition of
the Church-Catechism,* and the anonymous *The Danger
and Folly of Evil Courses.* Many of these works were
produced in partnership with other publishers, but

Curll soon began to produce, without partners, a
succession of pamphlets selling for three- or sixpence.

Curll, like other booksellers of the period,
quickly realized the value of advertising in the
newspapers that were then becoming widely popular. In January 1707 he advertised a forthcoming
collection of poems by Matthew Prior. Tonson,
Prior's publisher, placed a letter in the *Daily Courant*
for 24 January avowing that he owned anything
Prior had written and that any works claimed to be
by that poet but put out by other publishers must be
spurious. (Tonson also says that he will "very
speedily" publish a corrected version of Prior's
works, but no such edition was forthcoming for the
next two years.) Evidently undaunted by the prospect of engaging in battle with the great Tonson,
Curll published Prior's *Poems on Several Occasions*
within the week. The poems were genuine, though
Prior tried to disown some of them; how Curll obtained the manuscript is unknown. This confrontation with the most respected and prestigious publisher of the day was bold – and perhaps foolhardy:
the episode could have made an enemy of Tonson
and might have marked Curll as a shady character
in the eyes of the established publishing world; in
an age when authors rarely owned copyright to
their own works, Prior's feelings on the matter were
not an issue. Curll's partners, Baker and Richard
Burrough, also appeared on the title page, so they
would have shared with him both the expense of the
volume and any blame it might have generated. As
it turned out, Tonson seems to have harbored no
grudge, and he even engaged in some limited partnerships with Curll. The two joined forces in 1709,
for example, to produce a book of Latin poems by
Thomas Hill and again in 1714 when Curll published the ninth volume in Tonson's edition of the
works of William Shakespeare, an octavo and a
duodecimo version of Shakespeare's nondramatic
poems. In 1716, when Curll let it be known that he
was going to print a second collection of Prior's
poems, the poet objected in an advertisement. Curll
had an advertisement printed in reply, stating that
the first advertisement had been placed by an im-
postor, and went forward with *A Second Collection of
Poems on Several Occasions.*

In his early years at the Sign of the Peacock,
Curll also sold patent medicines. In 1708 he published *The Charitable Surgeon,* by "T. C., Surgeon,"
on curing venereal disease. The book attacked John
Spinke, who had recently written on the subject,
and it noted that the best drugs for curing the illness
were to be purchased in Curll's shop. Spinke re-

sponded in several pamphlets in quick succession, the first of which, *Quackery Unmask'd* (1709), claimed that "T. C." was in fact John Marten, a longtime rival of Spinke's. Curll replied in the *Post Boy* newspaper, denying Spinke's charges and deriding his education and background: he offered Spinke five guineas if he could translate any five lines of Latin. Spinke stormed over to the sign of the Peacock, translated five lines from Virgil on the spot, and demanded the five guineas. Curll went on to publish further editions of *The Charitable Surgeon,* and Spinke kept up his pamphlet war against the book and its theory that the mercury treatment – which Spinke advocated – was not effective against venereal disease. Spinke had the last word – rare for one of Curll's adversaries – when he had an analysis done on T. C.'s pills and found that they contained mercury. Curll continued to publish medical books from time to time, including *A New Method of Curing, without Internal Medicines, that Degree of the Venereal Disease, called a Gonorrhea, or Clap* (1709) and *The Generous Surgeon* (1710). Both were probably the work of Marten, who was prosecuted by the Queen's Bench for producing pornographic material in 1709 – though not, evidently, for the work he produced for Curll; the charges were ultimately dismissed. As late as 1736 Curll would publish a translation of Girolamo Fracastoro's sixteenth-century poem *Syphilis.*

In 1710 Curll moved from the Sign of the Peacock to the Sign of the Dial and Bible, and in 1712 he opened a branch shop in Tunbridge Wells. Controversies like those with Prior and Spinke clearly did him no harm, for his business was thriving, and he began to work with more-established booksellers. He published some twenty-five titles with Egbert Sanger, including a set of Nicolas Boileau-Despreaux's works (1711–1713) translated by various hands. With Robert Gosling he produced about the same number of titles between 1710 and 1713. He and John Harding published some auction catalogues, along with Nicholas Bernard's *The Case of John Atherton* (1710), about a seventeenth-century bishop arraigned on charges of bestiality, and the anonymous *The Case of Sodomy, in the Tryal of Mervin Lord Audley, Earl of Castlehaven* (1710). The books were prurient only in their titles, the contents being mostly reports of the trials; but they helped establish Curll in the public mind as a purveyor of unsavory materials. John Morphew worked in close partnership with Curll from 1710 to 1713; he printed rejoinders to Curll and Harding's trial purporting to give the full story – probably a scheme to increase sales of both versions. Morphew was in-

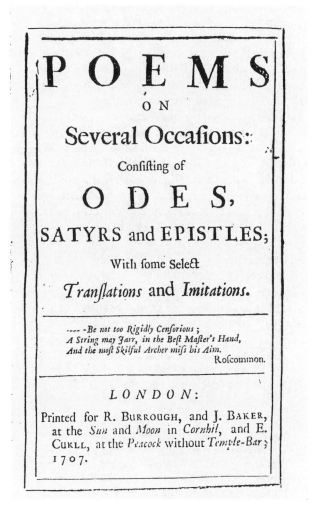

Title page for the volume of poems by Matthew Prior that Curll published in defiance of Jacob Tonson, the powerful publisher who owned the copyrights to Prior's works (Courtesy of the Lilly Library, Indiana University)

volved with the Tory government of the time, and he and Curll produced pamphlets concerning the major issues of the day. Curll felt that the imprisoned fiery preacher Henry Sacheverell was being grossly mistreated by Whig interests, and he attacked Bishop Gilbert Burnet for his role in the controversy in tracts such as *Some Considerations Humbly Offer'd to the Right Reverend the Lord Bishop of Salisbury* and *A Search after Principles,* both "printed for J. Morphew" in 1710. Morphew employed a writer, George Sewell, who also wrote material against Burnet that was jointly published by Morphew and Curll. After 1713 Sewell stayed on to write for Curll.

In April 1710 Curll published an unauthorized edition of Jonathan Swift's *Meditation upon a Broom-Stick;* Curll's note on the copy in the British Library says that he was given the manuscript by John

Cliffe, a lodger at the Dial and Bible. The book was quite popular, so Curll followed it with explanatory "keys" to it and to other works of Swift's. In these keys Curll revealed Swift as the author of "A Tale of a Tub" and "The Battle of the Books," which had been published together in 1704 and enlarged in 1710. Swift had desired to remain anonymous for the sake of his career in the church, and Curll's revelations enraged him. But Swift had little recourse, since Curll had broken no law. Curll later published a key to *Gulliver's Travels* (1726). The key's nominal author was "Signor Corolini, a noble Venetian now residing in London"; *corolini* is Italian for curl, but whether the key was entirely written by Curll himself is unproved. The key is in the form of four letters addressed to Swift – again giving away Swift's anonymity. It is of some interest to the modern reader, for it provides a valuable view of how a contemporary might have read *Gulliver's Travels* – identifying Gulliver, for example, with Robert Harley, earl of Oxford. Swift himself never saw any good in Curll or any of his work; references to his anger toward Curll continue throughout his life, culminating in his *Verses on the Death of Dr. Swift* (1739). Swift describes the events that will follow his death:

> Now *Curll* his shop from rubbish drains:
> Three genuine tomes of Swift's remains!
> And then, to make them pass the glibber,
> Revised by Tibbalds, Moore and Cibber,
> He'll treat me as he does my betters,
> Publish my will, my life, my letters:
> Revive the libels born to die;
> Which Pope must bear, as well as I.

The fatalism of the last line reflects Swift's unfulfilled lifelong wish for revenge against Curll.

Curll also got into a public quarrel with the poet Edward Young in 1717, but in this case Curll was in the right. In May Young sent Curll a poem by his friend Thomas Newcomb with a letter suggesting that it be published; in August Curll printed *An Ode Sacred to the Memory of the Countess of Berkeley* together with Young's commendatory letter. But within days of the publication Young announced in the *London Evening Post* that the letter was not his. Curll placed an indignant rebuttal in that paper as well as in two others. The facts confuted Young, and the newspaper carried a retraction and an apology in which he claimed that he had not wanted to be perceived as dictating public literary taste. His explanation was disingenuous; it is now known that Young issued his denial because, the political winds having shifted, he was anxious not to be publicly as-

sociated with James, the third earl of Berkeley (from whom Joseph Addison, Young's chief patron, had recently distanced himself). Young may have felt that Curll's reputation was such that his denial would be believed. In 1739 Curll and Young corresponded in a friendly manner; on 18 December Young wrote, "Be assur'd I bear you no Illwill," and Curll published an edition of Young's works the following year.

But if Curll had been able to handle the resentments of Prior, Swift, and Young, he met his match when he published unauthorized work by Pope. In March 1716 Curll acquired a manuscript of three poems – one each by Pope, John Gay, and Lady Mary Wortley Montagu. Pope was a good friend of Swift's, and he would have known about Curll's treatment of Swift and would have shared Swift's resentment; furthermore, he would have been acutely conscious of the monetary value of his own work. Accordingly, he sent word to Curll, warning him not to print the poems; but this action only made Curll more determined to do so because it proved that Pope was the author of one of them. Curll brought out the thin volume with the title *Court Poems*. The book's imprint does not name Curll, saying only "Printed for J. Roberts"; James Roberts was a printer and bookseller who often shared imprints with Curll and with many others in the period. Nor did the book explicitly name the authors: it only referred to "A Lady of Quality." Curll's newspaper advertisement, however, said that one of the poems seemed like the work of "the laudable translator of Homer."

Within a few days of the publication of *Court Poems* Pope got his publisher, Bernard Lintot, to invite Curll for a drink at the Swan Tavern in Fleet Street. On 28 March the three men had what appeared to be an amicable meeting; the only critical thing Pope had to say concerned his fear that the publication of *Court Poems* might damage Gay's interest at court, and even this comment was evidently made without particular acrimony. But Pope had laced Curll's drink with a powerful emetic, and Curll became violently ill after he returned home. The humiliation was, so far, at least private, but Pope went on to publish two pamphlets describing the events. The title of the first gives an indication of the satiric thrust Pope could use so well: *A Full and True Account of a Horrid and Barbarous Revenge by Poison, on the Body of Mr. Edmund Curll, Bookseller; with a Faithful Copy of His Last Will and Testament*. The device of declaring one's adversary already dead had been used by Swift some nine years before, in pamphlets that have become known as the Bickerstaff papers, in dealing with the astrologer John Partridge, and the whole episode has a Swiftian spirit about it. The opening of the pamphlet gives a good sense of its flavor: "History furnishes us with Examples of many Satyrical Authors who have fallen Sacrifices to Revenge, but not of any Booksellers that I know of, except the unfortunate Subject of the following Paper; I mean Mr. Edmund Curll, at the Bible and Dial in Fleetstreet, who was yesterday poison'd by Mr. Pope, after having liv'd many years an Instance of the mild Temper of the British Nation." Later Pope refers to himself as being "not the only Instance how Persons of bright Parts may be carry'd away by the Instigation of the Devil." Pope manages the tone in the pamphlet brilliantly, with the result that the reader is led to see his trick not as childish and vicious but as harmless, funny, and – given the provocation – wholly understandable.

Curll fought back, enlisting others in printing attacks on Pope: John Oldmixon wrote *The Catholick Poet,* which was advertised on 31 May 1716, and on the same day Curll printed the critic John Dennis's *A True Character of Mr. Pope, and His Writings.* Attacking Pope on the basis of his religion was particularly powerful rhetoric in the wake of the abortive 1715 Jacobite uprising, and Oldmixon's ballad accuses Pope of being a spy for the Stuart cause; similar charges are leveled in the Dennis pamphlet, along with aspersions on Pope's hunchbacked physique. More audacious than the attacks, though, was Curll's next move: he acquired another manuscript of a poem by Pope, a bawdy translation of the First Psalm, and printed it in full folio format in June as *Version of the First Psalm.* The stately format mocks the sophomoric raunchiness of the poem; the mockery also alludes to Pope's translation of *The Iliad* (1715–1720), his best-known work to that time, which had been produced in a sumptuous and expensive folio. Curll's advertisement for *Version of the First Psalm* included an announcement that he would be printing all of Pope's writings thenceforth. It was a declaration of war – as if one were needed – and the battles between Pope and Curll would continue throughout the rest of their lives.

In late April Curll and his printer, Daniel Bridge, were arrested for publishing an account of the recent trial for treason of George Seton, fifth earl of Winton. Such proceedings were private, and the publication was considered a breach of privilege. Curll and Bridge were released on 10 May after submitting a petition expressing their penitence and asking the House of Lords to have mercy on their families, whose livelihood would be endan-

A FULL and TRUE

ACCOUNT

OF A

Horrid and Barbarous

REVENGE by POISON,

On the Body of

Mr. *EDMUND CURLL*, Bookseller;

With a faithful Copy of his

Laſt WILL and TESTAMENT.

Publiſh'd by an Eye Witneſs.

*So when Curll's Stomach the ſtrong Drench o'ercame,
(Infus'd in Vengeance of inſulted Fame)
Th' Avenger ſees, with a delighted Eye,
His long Jaws open, and his Colour fly;
And while his Guts the keen Emeticks urge,
Smiles on the Vomit, and enjoys the Purge.*

Sold by J. Roberts, J. Morphew, R. Burleigh, J. Baker, and S. Popping. Price Three Pence.

Title page for Alexander Pope's satiric account of a practical joke he played on Curll

gered if the men remained in jail. They were brought in to the lord chancellor and, on their knees, were officially reprimanded.

In July John Barber, the captain of Westminster School, delivered a formal Latin funeral oration for the scholar Dr. Robert South. Curll, who was already planning to publish a life of South, got a copy of the oration and printed it without authorization. Soon he received a polite invitation to visit the school, and on 2 August he did so, no doubt expecting to meet Barber and perhaps be thanked for making his literary effort public. But he was surrounded by the boys of the school, who forced him down on his knees to ask pardon for his act, then whipped him and tossed him in a blanket. The schoolmasters were, of course, in on the scheme: one of them, Samuel Wesley (the elder brother of John Wesley), adopted the persona of the bookseller Dunton to write a mock-heroic poem on the affair, *Neck or Nothing* (1716), which is quite in the spirit of Pope's pamphlets:

This sure might seem enough for once, Oh!
This tossing up, and tumbling down so;
And well thy Stomach might incline
To spue without Emetick Wine.

An author in Curll's employ, Francis Chute, wrote a poem titled *The Petticoat,* and Curll published it in June 1716 under the pseudonym J. Gay. Curll later said that the *J.* stood for Joseph, but the intended confusion with John Gay, whose *Trivia* (1716) was establishing him as a major author, was a device Curll would use again. A farce, *The Confederates* (1717), actually by John Durant de Breval, was published as by J. Gay (1717), as was Breval's *Ovid in Masquerade* (1719).

Curll also continued to publish pornographic books. One of these titles was *Eunuchism Display'd* (1718), whose subtitle promises "many remarkable Cases by way of Precedent." Daniel Defoe wrote an anonymous attack on Curll for the 5 April 1718 *Weekly Journal* in which he coined a term, *Curlicism,* for the publication of such books and called for the government to take action against Curll for his crimes against the virtue of society. Curll took advantage of the publicity by writing a pamphlet in his defense, *Curlicism Display'd* (May 1718), in which he made references to his books and the passages therein to whet the appetites of potential buyers. He welcomed the term *Curlicism* and used it often and with relish.

Curll had a nose for anything that might sell, and he quickly perceived the developing public taste for short biographies of recently deceased public figures. When a well-known person died, Curll would advertise that a biography was already under way and would ask readers to contribute any bits of information they had so as to make the work complete. Often readers would come forward with letters from the deceased; Curll would add some hastily gathered biographical material from the obituaries, along with any previously published work by the deceased, and get his "life" to the market before anyone else. If there was interest, he would follow with second and third editions, sometimes with additions, sometimes without. In 1716, only three months after his humiliation at Westminster School, he went ahead with his life of South; in the next year he produced lives – or, in some cases, simply the last wills and testaments – of Dr. Daniel Williams, Bishop Burnet, and the antiquarian Elias Ashmole. Dr. John Arbuthnot was moved by these lives to remark that Curll's biographies had added a new terror to death. But in the twentieth century Sir Walter Raleigh saw these lives, rough and ready as

they may be by modern standards, as the beginnings of modern biography. Curll's biographies have, however, received little attention from scholars.

For all his shady publications, Curll produced quite a lot of respectable work at extremely low prices – ranging from fiction, such as Sarah Butler's *Irish Tales* (1716) and *Milesian Tales* (1718), to new editions of the poems of Sir Thomas Wyatt and Henry Howard, earl of Surrey (1717); imitations of Ovid such as Richardson Pack's *The Nooning* (1719); and translations from French authors such as René Rapin and François de Salignac de la Mothe Fénelon. Most of these works were produced in cheap – one- or two-shilling – formats. This high level of diversity and output would continue throughout Curll's career.

In 1721 Curll announced his intention of publishing a life of the recently deceased John Sheffield, first duke of Buckingham and Normanby, including a copy of his will. The House of Lords summoned Curll, who had to go down on his knees before it on 31 January. While Curll was there, a standing order was passed making it a crime to publish anything by or about a member of the House of Lords without permission; the order remained in force until 1845.

In 1723 Curll moved to Catherine Street. In October 1724 he published *The Nun in Her Smock,* a somewhat pornographic tale that had been widely printed since 1683 in France, as *Venus dans le cloître,* and in England; its author was probably Jean Barrin. The book is not particularly explicit, but it suggests that it is Christian institutions, not Christ, that have forbidden healthy sexual exploration. An anonymous complaint was lodged against Curll, naming *The Nun in Her Smock* along with *A Treatise of the Use of Flogging in Venereal Affairs* (1718), a translation by Sewell of Johann Heinrich Meibom's *De usu flagorum* (1639) – another widely printed piece of semipornographic prose. While its content is less racy than the title promises (it was apparently first intended as a manual for physicians), the frontispiece of Curll's edition is explicitly sexual; and its title page vividly suggests its genre by saying the book was "Printed for E. Curll, in Fleet-Street . . . where may be had, The Cases of Impotency; and Eunuchism and Onanism Display'd. . . ."

Curll printed a defense of the books, *The Humble Representation of Edmund Curll* (1725), but this pamphlet – and the fact that Curll, sensing the value of publicity, quickly put out a second edition of *The Nun in Her Smock* in February 1725 – seems only to have made the authorities more determined to proceed against him: Curll was arrested on 2

March and imprisoned until July. The trial at the King's Bench dragged on, for there was no law against Curlicism. There had been at least seven obscenity prosecutions in England before Curll's, but the most recent, a 1707 case against James Read and Angell Carter for printing and selling *The Fifteen Plagues of a Maidenhead,* had been quashed because it had been determined that only the ecclesiastical court could try an obscenity case; the civil court could only be invoked in cases of specific libel. The government, therefore, prosecuted Curll under the libel law. Curll tried to help along the sentiment for acquittal by publishing a public apology and by promising to offend no more – by promising, in fact, to retire from publishing. Curll printed his apology in the newspapers for 3 December. Curll's tone in the apology illustrates his indefatigable instinct for advertising:

> I hereby most humbly ask Pardon for these Offences; but being resolved never more to offend in the like Manner, I give this Notice, that so soon as two Books, now in the Press, are finish'd, (viz. 1. The Miscellaneous Works of that Memorable Patriot *Andrew Marvel* Esq.; in Prose and Verse. 2. The *Case* of *Seduction;* being the late Proceedings at Paris against the Rev. Abbe des Rues, for committing Rapes upon 133 Virgins. Written by himself.) I am resolved to retire from all Publick Business....

Not surprisingly, this apology did not satisfy the King's Bench, which announced that Curll would receive sentence in the next term.

In the meantime, however, his shop was raided, nine books were seized, and Curll was rearrested. While being held in the King's Bench Prison he wrote a pamphlet, *The Prisoner's Advocate,* which he arranged to have printed anonymously. The pamphlet describes abuses in the prison system, particularly the bribery prisoners had to practice to survive. Also while in the King's Bench Prison he met an old and dying man, John Ker of Kersland, who showed Curll the manuscript for his memoirs. They were potentially dangerous, containing what might be regarded as state secrets from the previous generation, so Curll – being more cautious than usual – decided to publish them only after sending a copy to Prime Minister Robert Walpole's office and getting approval. Curll took the lack of a reply from Walpole for approval, and from July through November 1726 he published Ker's memoirs in three parts.

When Curll was released, one of his first acts was to place a notice in the *Evening Post* for 5 July that he was not the publisher of Ker's memoirs; he

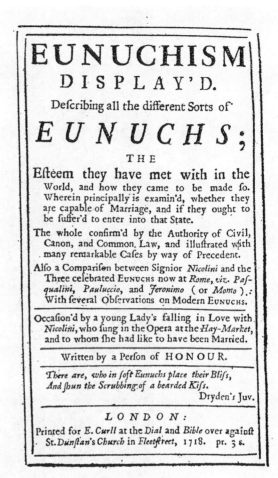

Title page for the pornographic book that led Daniel Defoe to coin the word Curlicism *to refer to the publication of such works*

used the dodge that the memoirs had been printed "for the author." He also insisted that he had kept his pledge to retire. But on 8 July Ker died; Curll had the remaining volumes of the memoirs printed under the imprint of his son, Henry Curll. Shortly after the publication of Ker's third volume, both father and son were arrested. Henry Curll was soon released, but Edmund Curll remained in prison until 12 February 1728. At that time he was fined twenty-five marks apiece for the publication of *The Nun in Her Smock* and the treatise on flogging and was also fined twenty marks and sentenced to an hour in the pillory for Ker's memoirs.

The pillory was far more than a mere indignity; it was often the equivalent of a death sentence, as the crowd was encouraged to beat and maltreat the prisoner in almost any way. On 13 February, the day he was to be pilloried, Curll had a broad-

"The Distressed Poet," by William Hogarth, showing Pope at work on his poem
Of the Use of Riches *(1732) below a picture of himself beating Curll*

side printed and distributed to the crowd stating that he was being punished for printing a book that vindicated the memory of the highly venerated Queen Anne. As a result, not only was he not harmed, but at the end of his hour he was carried away by the crowd in triumph.

Curll had probably not seriously intended to retire, but if he had, his treatment in Pope's *The Dunciad* (1728) would have goaded him back onto the field. In the footrace between the publishers in book 2 Curll slips in some manure, but, like Antaeus touching the earth, he is only made stronger by the experience:

> Vig'rous he rises: from th'effluvia strong
> Inbibes new life, and scours and stinks along.
> Re-passes L[into]t, vindicates the race,
> Nor heeds the brown dishonours of his face.

Curll also competes in the urination contest, where "His rapid waters in their passage burn." There is

no evidence to corroborate the implication that Curll suffered from venereal disease; the line is pure – and highly effective – character assassination. Also, in 1726 Curll had purchased from Elizabeth Thomas some letters from Pope to Thomas's friend Henry Cromwell and had published them without permission from the author. In her youth Thomas's writing had shown such promise that John Dryden had christened her, in the pastoral style of his day, Corinna; but after she sold his letters, Pope savagely satirized her in the *Dunciad* as "Curll's Corinna."

Curll fought back by publishing a pirated version of Pope's poem, a series of keys to it (three in 1728), and by publishing and even writing parts of works such as *The Popiad* (said to have been partly written by Lady Mary Wortley Montagu, who was no longer Pope's good friend), *The Female Dunciad,* and *The Twickenham Hotch-Potch,* all in 1728. Business for these and similar titles, as for the *Dunciad* itself, must have been brisk; the quarrel between Pope and Curll was good publicity for both of them. The next year Pope's *The Dunciad, Variorum,* was published with a note justifying Curll's inclusion in the poem: "if ever [Pope] owed two verses to any other, he owed Mr. Curll some thousands." Curll replied in April 1729 with a thirty-eight-page pamphlet, *The Curliad: A Hypercritic upon The Dunciad Variorum,* in which he gives his side of the story and abuses Pope as a hypocrite and a blasphemer. (The pamphlet is of interest to students of Pope today for its readings of certain lines in *The Dunciad.*) The satiric level of Curll's attack is not high, as may be seen from the couplet on the title page:

Pope, has less Reading than makes Felons 'scape,
Less Human Genius than God gives an Ape.

In 1729 Curll published John Oldmixon's *Memoirs of the Life, Writings, and Amours of William Congreve, Esq.* under the pseudonym Charles Wilson; the volume included Congreve's will and his short prose tale "Incognita." William Congreve, who had just died in a coach accident, was a close friend of Arbuthnot, Pope, and Swift but had not entered into the literary quarrels of the era. There had been rumors before the book was printed that it would include scandalous revelations concerning Congreve's relationship with the actress Anne Bracegirdle, and Arbuthnot and others complained that Curll was overstepping the bounds of decency. In response Curll defiantly declared that his shop would thenceforth be known as the Congreve's Head, and a portrait of Congreve became his device for a time.

In 1731 he moved the shop to Burleigh Street, where he published lives of Gay and the actor Robert Wilks. In August 1733 he published the life and will of Matthew Tindal; the chief beneficiary of the will, Eustace Budgell, who had attacked Curll in the July 1733 issue of *The Bee,* was upset at having his personal business made public by Curll. A series of attacks and counterattacks in the newspapers had a dramatic end result: Budgell, it turned out, had forged the will. Curll was completely vindicated.

Also in 1733 Curll conceived the idea of publishing a biography of Pope, even though he was still living; not only would such a work be profitable, but it also would taunt Pope. An advertisement in the 30 March 1733 *Daily Journal* announced that the biography would be "Embellish'd with Dissertations, Digressions, Notes, and all Kinds of poetical Machinery, in order, to render the Work compleat. Nothing shall be wanting but his (universally desired) Death. Any Memoirs, &c. worthy of his Deserts, if sent to Mr. Curll, will be faithfully inserted."

Soon Curll began receiving tantalizing letters, signed only "P. T.," promising much material; the material turned out to be letters from Pope to various people. P. T. mailed Curll some letters but claimed to have more; he would agree to meet Curll and then call off the meeting. In March 1735 Curll sent Pope word of what was going on; Pope coldly replied in a newspaper advertisement that he did not know any P. T. and that the letters must be forgeries. Soon a man named Smythe, introducing himself as P. T.'s agent, came to Curll and said that Curll could have the letters but that P. T. must see to the printing of them. Curll did not like the arrangement, but he had no choice, and on 12 May 1735 copies that had been printed by John Wright were delivered to Curll. But since some material in the letters was said to concern members of the House of Lords a complaint was lodged, and most of the books were seized. Curll was summoned, but the lords found nothing of offense, and the books were returned to him. (Curll brought his quarrel with Pope even into the hearing, where he allowed that Pope had "a knack for versifying" but that he was Pope's match in prose.) It is now known that Pope was "P. T." and that "Smythe" was an actor he had hired and coached. Pope wanted his letters printed for posterity and had been keeping copies of his letters, or inducing correspondents to return them, since 1712; but it would have been presumptuous for a living author to have his own letters published. Therefore, he manipulated Curll into doing it for him. Better yet, the existence of Curll's version provided Pope with justification for publishing a "corrected edition" of the letters, edited to show himself in the light in which he wanted posterity to see him; the edition came out in 1737 with the imprint of James Roberts.

Pope had another motivation in the affair: he manipulated events so that the pirated copy of his letters would come out while a bill was being debated in Parliament to extend the term of copyright, a measure that would have benefited booksellers far more than authors; Curll, Pope hoped, would become a symbol of the unscrupulous bookseller preying on the unprotected author. The bill was defeated, but it is unlikely that the episode of Pope's letters had much to do with the vote.

Whether Curll ever learned the truth is uncertain; he announced that Pope had given him the letters, but he may not have realized that such was, in fact, the case. But in 1735 he moved to a new shop

Caricatures from the Grub Street Journal *in 1732, showing Curll in his "Literary" and a two-faced Curll with his band of authors*

in Rose Street, by Covent Garden, and changed his sign to the Pope's Head. And he continued to publish Pope's correspondence, producing a four-volume set in 1736 and a fifth volume in 1737. He claimed that his edition was a great deal more accurate than Pope's – and he was right, since Pope was heavily doctoring his own version of his letters.

In May 1741 Curll published the unauthorized *Dean Swift's Literary Correspondence, for Twenty-Four Years.* In early June Pope brought a suit in the court of chancery claiming that he had copyright in his letters to and from Swift. The court found that he did own rights to the letters he had written but not to those written to him, and an injunction was granted prohibiting Curll from selling any further copies of the book. The case is generally regarded as a seminal one in copyright law, for it more clearly established the rights of authors than had any previous law or decision. *Pope* v. *Curll* is seen today as a pivotal case in the transition from a literary culture based on patronage to one based on commercial rights.

Curll finally published *Memoirs of the Life and Writings of Alexander Pope,* consisting of extracts, re-

views, and letters, along with some passages of disguised autobiography, in 1745. He wrote it under an assumed name, William Ayre, though no one was fooled. Curll's sense of humor about himself is evident in passages such as one that is cribbed almost verbatim from Pope's footnote about him in *The Dunciad, Variorum:* "This leads us to a Character of much Respect, that of Mr. *Edmond* Curl: Of whom we may say, that he carried on the Trade to Lengths beyond what it ever before arriv'd at. He possess'd himself of a Command over many Authors, and caus'd them to write what he pleased; they could not call their very names their own. He has been taken Notice of by the *Church,* the *State,* and the *Law,* and received particular marks of Distinction from each." His tone is also remarkable as he tells the story of acquiring Pope's correspondence:

> This is a Practice frequent with Booksellers, to swell an Author's works . . . with any Trash that can be got from any hand; or where they have no such Works, to procure some. *Curl* has in the same Manner advertised the Letters of Mr. *Prior* and Mr. *Addison.* A Practice highly

deserving some check from the Legislature; since every such Advertisement, is really a *Watch-word* to every *Scoundrel* in the Nation, and to every *Domestick* of a Family, to get a Penny, by producing any Scrap of a Man's Writing . . . or by picking his Master's Pocket of Letters and Papers. . . .

Curl was tamper'd with, but nothing was to be done with him, he had got fast hold of a valuable Book; nay he us'd such Means by practising with several People, and talking and writing backwards and forwards, that he by Prying, by Art, by Money, got greater insight into Mr. *Pope's* Correspondence. . . .

Curll concludes by asserting his innocence in the matter and refers to his renaming his shop the Pope's Head as "an Honour we do not remember to have seen done to any Poet whilst living."

Curll continued printing and selling his usual wide variety of titles, including a popular series of pornographic books beginning in 1740 with Thomas Stretser's *A New Description of Merryland* and including imitations and additions to it, such as Charles Cotton's *The Potent Ally; or Succours from Merryland,* published in the same year. Other publishers pirated or produced imitations of the Merryland books, and the printer Thomas Read was arrested in 1745 for printing a series of engravings titled *Complete Set of Charts of the Coasts of Merryland.* Curll owned the copyright to Stretser's original Merryland book, but he was never prosecuted for it or its imitators. Alongside the pornographic works in Curll's lists were Robert Nixon's *Cheshire Prophecy at Large* (1739), which reached its seventeenth edition by 1745; William Beckett's *Practical Surgery Illustrated and Improved* (1740); Thomas Betterton's *The History of the English Stage* (1741); a translation of René Aubert de Vertot D'Aubeuf 's *History of the Revolution in Sweden* (1743); the anonymous *Presbyterian Persecution Exemplified* (1745); and Thomas Simon's *Peruvian Tales* (1745). During the last decades of his life he developed a strong interest in English history and antiquarianism, befriending the Oxford scholar Richard Rawlinson and producing in the 1730s a twenty-volume set of county histories titled *Anglia Illustrata.* John Nichols praised Curll for such works, which preserved "our national remains."

Curll added a rhymed codicil to his will in 1742 that provides some information about his family:

> I have no relatives, my son is dead,
> He left no issue, and his wife's rewed;
> Therefore no legacies at all I leave,
> But all I've got to my dear wife bequeathe.

He died on 11 December 1747.

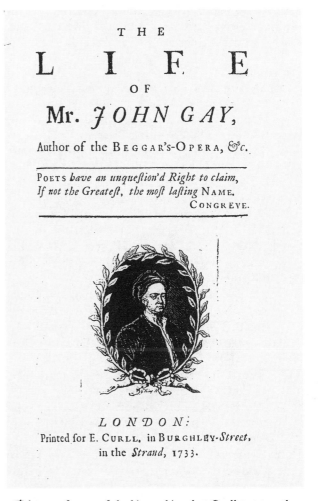

THE
LIFE
OF
Mr. *JOHN GAY,*
Author of the BEGGAR'S-OPERA, &c.

POETS *have an unquestion'd Right to claim,*
If not the Greatest, the most lasting NAME.
CONGREVE.

LONDON:
Printed for E. CURLL, in BURGHLEY-*Street,*
in the *Strand,* 1733.

Title page for one of the biographies that Curll put together from letters and reminiscences solicited from acquaintances of the subject. In earlier years Curll had published works by other authors under the pseudonym J. Gay to capitalize on the playwright's popularity (Courtesy of the Lilly Library, Indiana University).

The image of Curll created by Pope of a shoddy, immoral parasite is vivid, compelling, and hard to dislodge, and Curll's pornographic productions and powerful instinct for self-promotion make it tempting to acquiesce in Pope's view. As a result many aspects of his output — especially his own writings — have never received serious scholarly attention. But any discussion of the developing literary marketplace must include him. For Curll, like his nemesis Pope, epitomizes an age balanced precariously between the older patronage-based system and the as-yet-unshaped age of literature as commodity and author as entrepreneur. In his quarrels with Pope and his troubles with the authorities Curll turned publishing, for a time, into something of a spectator sport, but he — inadvertently — had much to do with clarifying the author's rights to literary property and the limitations that would be placed on the entrepreneurial bookseller.

References:

Norman Ault, *New Light on Pope, with Some Additions to His Poetry Hitherto Unknown* (London: Methuen, 1949; New York: Archon, 1967);

Alan Boehm, "The Poetics of Literary Commerce: Popular and Patrician Bookselling and the Rise of Publishing, 1700–1825," dissertation, Indiana University, 1992;

Edmund Curll, *The Curliad: A Hypercritic upon the Dunciad Variorum* (London: Printed for the author, 1729);

Curll, *Memoirs of the Life and Writings of Alexander Pope,* as William Ayre (London: Printed for the author, 1745);

David Foxon, *Libertine Literature in England, 1660–1745* (New Hyde Park, N.Y.: University Books, 1965);

Foxon, *Pope and the Early Eighteenth-Century Book Trade* (Oxford: Clarendon Press, 1991);

J. V. Guerinot, *Pamphlet Attacks on Alexander Pope, 1711–1744* (London: Methuen, 1969);

Robert L. Haig, " 'The Unspeakable Curll': Prolegomena," *Studies in Bibliography,* 13 (1960): 220–223;

Peter Murray Hill, *Two Augustan Booksellers: John Dunton and Edmund Curll* (Lawrence: University of Kansas Libraries, 1958);

Helen Leek, "The Edward Young–Edmund Curll Quarrel: A Review," *Papers of the Bibliographical Society of America,* 62 (third quarter, 1968): 321–335;

Maynard Mack, *Alexander Pope: A Life* (New Haven: Yale University Press, 1985);

J. McLaverty, "The First Printing and Publication of Pope's Letters," *Library,* sixth series 2 (September 1980): 264–280;

John Nichols, *Literary Anecdotes of the Eighteenth Century: Comprizing Biographical Memoirs of William Bowyer, Printer, F.S.A., and Many of His Learned Friends* (London: Printed for the author, 1812–1816);

Dirk F. Passman, "William Symson, *Gulliver's Travels,* and 'Curllicism' at Its Best," *Etudes Anglaises,* 40 (July–September 1987): 301–312;

Henry Pettit, ed., *The Correspondence of Edward Young* (Oxford: Clarendon Press, 1971);

Sir Walter Raleigh, "Early Lives of the Poets," in his *Six Essays on Johnson* (Oxford: Clarendon Press, 1910), pp. 98–127;

Harry Ransom, "The Personal Letter as Literary Property," *Studies in English,* 30 (1951): 116–131;

Pat Rogers, "The Case of Pope v. Curll," *Library,* fifth series 27 (December 1972): 326–331;

Rogers, *Hacks and Dunces: Pope, Swift and Grub Street* (London: Methuen, 1980);

Mark Rose, "The Author in Court: *Pope v. Curll* (1741)," *Cardozo Arts and Entertainment Law Journal,* 10, no. 2 (1992): 475–493;

Edward L. Ruhe, "Edmund Curll and His Early Associates," in *English Writers of the Eighteenth Century,* edited by John H. Middendorf (New York: Columbia University Press, 1971), pp. 69–89;

David Saunders and Ian Hunter, "Lessons from the 'Literary': How to Historicise Authorship," *Critical Inquiry,* 17 (Spring 1991): 479–509;

Lance Schachterle, "The First Key to Gulliver's Travels," *Revue des langues vivantes,* 38 (1972): 37–45;

Ralph Straus, *The Unspeakable Curll* (London: Chapman & Hall, 1927);

Roger Thompson, *Unfit for Modest Ears: A Study of Pornographic, Obscene and Bawdy Works Written or Published in England in the Second Half of the Seventeenth Century* (London: Macmillan, 1979);

William John Thoms, *Curll Papers: Stray Notes on the Life and Publications of Edmund Curll* (London: Privately printed, 1879);

Peter Wagner, *Eros Revived: Erotica of the Enlightenment in England and America* (London: Secker & Warburg, 1988);

James Anderson Winn, *A Window in the Bosom: The Letters of Alexander Pope* (Hamden, Conn.: Archon, 1977).

Papers:

Papers concerning Edmund Curll's accounts and copyright assignments, along with some letters, are in the British Library.

– Raymond N. MacKenzie

Thomas Davies

(London: 1762 – 1776)

See also the Davies entry in *DLB 142: Eighteenth-Century British Literary Biographers.*

Those interested in Samuel Johnson and his circle will remember Thomas Davies for his famous introduction, in the back parlor of his bookshop at 8 Russell Street, Covent Garden, of Johnson and Davies's fellow Scot James Boswell on the afternoon of Monday, 16 May 1763. Others know Davies as an actor turned bookseller and author whose *Memoirs of the Life of David Garrick, Esq.* (1780) serves as one of the principal contemporaneous accounts of Garrick's life and career; his *Dramatic Miscellanies* (1783–1784) also adds to the store of knowledge of the eighteenth-century theater. Davies earned Boswell's admiration for his "liberal education" and "good understanding"; John Nichols, who wrote the best account of Davies's life and career, described his "uncommon strength of mind," as well as the "rational and improving conversation" enjoyed in his company. Isaac D'Israeli, in his *Calamities of Authors* (1812), praised Davies's efforts as a bookseller whose beautiful editions of English writers twice ruined him financially. Davies, then, surely deserves to be remembered for more than allegedly being driven from the stage by Charles Churchill's biting satiric portrait in *The Rosciad*:

> With him came mighty Davies. On my life,
> That Davies hath a very pretty wife.
> Statesman all over – in plots famous grown,
> He mouths a sentence as curs mouth a bone.

Little is known of Davies's early life: Nichols surmises, on the basis of a remark in *Dramatic Miscellanies,* that he was born in 1712. He became an actor ("player" or "comedian") after he left the University of Edinburgh in 1729. In 1736 he became the original Young Wilmot in George Lillo's *The Fatal Curiosity,* at the Haymarket Theatre in London; in 1775 Davies would edit the complete plays of Lillo. Shortly after his performance in *The Fatal Curiosity* he attempted and failed at bookselling at Duke's Court and Round Court. Becoming a traveling or "strolling" player, in York he met and married the actress Susanna Yarrow, the daughter of Joseph

Yarrow, an actor who was also an amusing writer. In Edinburgh, where Davies managed the unlicensed theater, some of the other actors thought that he was reserving the best parts for himself. He and his wife appeared opposite each other as Horatio and Calista in Nicholas Rowe's *The Fair Penitent* (1703) and as Romeo and Juliet and Lear and Cordelia in William Shakespeare's plays; and they joined the Drury Lane Company in London in 1753. At the peak of their acting careers, the Davieses were each earning five hundred pounds a year. In 1762, however, Thomas Davies left acting, despite what Nichols calls "the good estimation with the Town," to return to bookselling.

On Christmas Day of that year Davies introduced Boswell to Oliver Goldsmith; a few months later came the celebrated meeting of Boswell and Johnson. Knowing of Johnson's antipathy toward the Scots, Davies teasingly announced that Boswell had come from Scotland, thereby setting up Johnson's response: "That, Sir, I find, is what a great many of your countrymen cannot help." After Johnson had left, Davies told Boswell, "Don't be uneasy. . . . he likes you very well"; Davies encouraged Boswell to call on Johnson a week later.

In 1769 Davies published *A Catalogue of Valuable and Curious Books, Including Several Libraries and Collections Purchased at Home and Abroad,* a list of around eight thousand titles that included, at the end, works in which he was a part shareholder. Among the latter were Gilbert Burnet's *Bishop Burnet's History of His Own Time* (1724, 1734), Samuel Richardson's *Clarissa* (1747–1748), and the works of Shakespeare, William Congreve, John Dryden, John Gay, Ben Jonson, Thomas Otway, and Edmund Waller. Davies also published Benjamin Victor's *The History of the Theatres of London and Dublin* (1761–1771); James Granger's popular *A Biographical History of England* (1769–1774); the poetry of William Browne (1772) and Sir John Davies (1773); the works of Dr. John Eachard (1772) and Philip Massinger (1779); and Davies's own *The Characters of George the First, Queen Caroline, Sir Robert Walpole, Lord Hardwicke, Mr. Fox and Mr. Pitt, Reviewed. With Royal and Noble Anecdotes: and A Sketch of Lord Chesterfield's Characters* (1777). Although Davies

Thomas Davies

angered Johnson by publishing without permission Johnson's *Miscellaneous and Fugitive Pieces, by the Author of 'The Rambler'* (1774) while Johnson and Boswell were touring the Scottish Highlands and the Hebrides, Johnson quickly forgave him. In 1777 Davies was one of the group of booksellers who persuaded Johnson to write *Prefaces, Biographical and Critical, to the Works of the English Poets* (1779, 1781).

The witty Davies was popular with his fellow booksellers, with whom he met often at the Devil Tavern, the Temple Bar, and the Grecian Coffeehouse. It was he who first compared Johnson's laugh to sounds made by a rhinoceros, and he told his wife that her beauty was the cause of Johnson's compulsively muttering "lead us not into temptation." On the other hand, Boswell claimed that Davies could make social disagreements more dramatic with his presence and that he even stirred up, by acting as an "informer," friction between Johnson and Thomas Percy. Boswell also said that Davies told the mimic and playwright Samuel Foote of Johnson's threat to use an oak stick on Foote if he added Johnson to his "repertoire" of impressions.

(Davies was judged by Boswell to be – along with Boswell himself and Garrick – one of the best imitators of Johnson's distinctive voice and manner.) Davies and Susanna performed many acts of kindness for Johnson – including giving gifts of food – and for others. Davies's benevolent influence was felt by the kindly, though occasionally irascible, Johnson: Davies got Johnson to help James Bennet, an impoverished schoolmaster who was struggling with an edition of the works of Roger Ascham, for example; and he persuaded Johnson to contribute material to the blind Anna Williams's *Miscellanies in Prose and Verse* (1766). Davies, nevertheless, could be patronized by Johnson and his circle: Boswell found him pompous; Topham Beauclerk snobbishly referred to the humiliation of being clapped on the back by Davies; and Johnson himself once criticized Jonathan Swift's *The Conduct of the Allies, and of the Late Ministry, in Beginning and Carrying on the Present War* (1711) by saying that even Davies could have written it.

Davies's letters reveal an unbusinesslike generosity concerning such matters as advertising and

MEMOIRS

OF THE

LIFE

OF

DAVID GARRICK, Eſq.

INTERSPERSED WITH

CHARACTERS AND ANECDOTES

OF

HIS THEATRICAL CONTEMPORARIES.

THE WHOLE FORMING

A HISTORY OF THE STAGE,

WHICH INCLUDES

A Period of THIRTY-SIX YEARS.

By THOMAS DAVIES.

— Quem populus Romanus meliorem virum quam
hiſtrionem eſſe arbitratur, qui ita digniſſimus eſt ſcena propter
artificium, ut digniſſimus ſit curia propter abſtinentiam.
Cicero pro Q. Roſcio Comœdo.

THIRD EDITION.

VOL. I.

LONDON:

Printed for the AUTHOR, and ſold at his Shop in Great
Ruſſell-Street, Covent-Garden.

M.DCC.LXXXI.

*Title page for Davies's biography of the eminent actor-impresario
(Courtesy of the Lilly Library, Indiana University)*

payments to writers; he went bankrupt in 1778. Johnson lent him money, rallied friends to save Davies's furniture from his creditors, and persuaded the playwright Richard Brinsley Sheridan to produce a benefit at Drury Lane, at which Davies gave a final performance as Fainall in Congreve's *The Way of the World* (1700).

After Garrick's death in 1779 Davies began writing his memoirs of the actor; Johnson provided help with Garrick's early life and a memorable opening: "All excellence has a right to be recorded. I shall therefore think it superfluous to apologize for writing the life of a man who, by an uncommon assemblage of private virtues, adorned the highest eminence in a public profession." After Johnson died in 1784, Davies was mentioned in the diary of Johnson's friend Hester Lynch [Thrale] Piozzi (25 January 1785) as one of those who had begun writing biographies of Johnson. Although Davies never completed such a work, he assisted Boswell with his biography of Johnson. Davies also provided assistance to the Reverend William Shaw for his anonymous *Memoirs of the Life and Writings of the Late Dr. Samuel Johnson* (1785).

Davies died on 5 May 1785; his requested interment in St. Paul's, Covent Garden, had to be paid for by friends. Davies had said that he wrote *Dramatic Miscellanies* "with a view to secure a tolerable income to the partner of my life," but Susanna Davies died in a workhouse on 9 February 1801. Davies's epitaph gives a concise summary of his life and career, excluding his work as a publisher and bookseller:

Here lies the Author, Actor, Thomas Davies;
Living, he shone a very *rara avis.*

The scenes he play'd Life's audience must commend,
He honour'd Garrick – Johnson was his friend.

A couplet from a review of Davies's biography of Garrick completes the picture:

If Booksellers thus cleverly can write,
Let writers deal in books and booksellers indite.

References:

James Boaden, ed., *The Private Correspondence of David Garrick,* 2 volumes (London: Colburn & Bentley, 1831, 1832);

James Boswell, *The Life of Samuel Johnson, LL.D.* (2 volumes, London: Printed by Henry Baldwin for Charles Dilly, 1791; revised and enlarged, 3 volumes, 1793); revised and enlarged by L. F. Powell as *The Life of Dr. Samuel Johnson,* 6 volumes, edited by George Birkbeck Hill (Oxford: Clarendon Press, 1934);

C. F. Burgess, "Thomas Davies and the Authorship of *A Genuine Narrative . . . , The Life of John Hen-*derson," *Restoration and Eighteenth Century Theatre Research,* 9 (May 1970): 24–34;

Elizabeth Eaton Kent, *Goldsmith and His Booksellers* (Folcroft, Pa.: Folcroft Press, 1933);

David M. Little and George M. Kahrl, eds., Phoebe deK. Wilson, associate ed., *The Letters of David Garrick,* 3 volumes (Cambridge, Mass.: Harvard University Press, 1963);

J. P. Malcom, ed., *Letters between the Rev. James Granger, M. A., Rector of Shiplake, and Many of the Most Eminent Literary Men of His Time* (London: Longman, Hurst, Rees & Orme, 1805);

Edward Marston, *Sketches of Some Booksellers of the Time of Dr. Samuel Johnson* (New York: Scribners, 1902);

John Nichols, *Literary Anecdotes of the Eighteenth Century,* 9 volumes (London: Nichols, Son & Bentley, 1812–1815);

Sybil Rosenfeld, *Strolling Players and Drama in the Provinces 1660–1765* (Cambridge: Cambridge University Press, 1939; New York: Octagon, 1970).

– Gene Blanton

Edward and Charles Dilly
(London: 1764 – 1779)

Edward Dilly
(London: 1754 – 1764)

Charles Dilly
(London: 1779 – 1803)

The brothers Edward and Charles Dilly were prominent London booksellers and publishers from the 1760s until Edward Dilly's death in 1779; Edward Dilly had been in business for ten years before his brother became a partner in the firm, and Charles continued for fourteen years after Edward died. The firm was best known as the publisher of James Boswell's *The Life of Samuel Johnson, LL.D.* (1791; revised, 1793), but it also brought out many other influential literary works of the period. An important facet of the brothers' business consisted of reprints of American works and book exchanges with American notables such as Benjamin Rush, Benjamin Franklin, Thomas Bradford of Philadelphia, and William and Arthur Lee of Virginia. The Dillys' importation of American religious, historical, medical, and philosophical works into England was unmatched by any other English book dealer. They also arranged for similar British works to be obtained through their American outlets. Active Dissenters, the Dillys dealt heavily in Nonconformist literature and theological works: they reprinted and circulated writings of English Dissenters such as Isaac Watts, Philip Doddridge, and Nathaniel Lardner and brought like-minded American religious reform writings into circulation in Britain, including those of Joseph Bellamy, Charles Chauncy, and Jonathan Mayhew.

Well known for their frequent dinner parties, which significantly advanced their book business, the Dillys hosted the cream of London literary society, including Boswell, Johnson, Catharine Macaulay, Richard Cumberland, Oliver Goldsmith, and Richard Price. The Whig sympathies of the Dillys led them to support political reform, and radicals such as John Wilkes; Thomas Hollis; John Horne Tooke; and London's lord mayor, John Sawbridge, also frequented the Dillys' house. The Dillys sympathized with the American desire for in-dependence from Britain and promoted religious toleration and freedom of the press; they risked their financial and personal security by printing parliamentary debates and the Junius letters.

The second of three brothers, Edward Dilly was born on 25 July 1732 into a yeoman family that had owned land in Southill, Bedfordshire, for two hundred years. The oldest brother, John, born in 1731 and later referred to as "Squire Dilly" by Boswell, was never involved in the book business and remained in Bedfordshire. Charles, born on 22 May 1739, was described by Boswell as "a good, tall, smartish, civil, bowing young man." A sister, Martha, was born in 1740. None of the Dillys ever married.

Edward and Charles Dilly were apprenticed to booksellers in London – Edward to John Oswald and Charles to James Buckland, both of whom specialized in Dissenting literature. In 1754 Edward bought Oswald's shop at the Rose and Crown, Number 22, the Poultry, on Cheapside near Mansion House. He expanded the business to include publishing in 1758, when for £6 3s. 4d. he bought the rights to Goldsmith's translation of Jean Marteilhe's *The Memoirs of a Protestant, Condemned to the Galleys of France for His Religion*. Dilly's successful publication and sale of Thomas Mortimer's *The British Plutarch, Containing the Lives of the Most Eminent Statesmen, Patriots, Divines, Warriors, Philosophers, Poets and Artists of Great Britain and Ireland* (1762) undermined a similar project to mimic Plutarch's *Lives* in which Goldsmith had invested heavily. (In 1770 the Dillys would publish the original *Plutarch's Lives*, translated by John and William Langhorne, in six volumes; the work would go through several editions.) Charles Dilly became a partner in the business in 1764, after returning from a trip to America. Short and stout, Edward was a nonpareil conversationalist and literary socialite; Charles was more

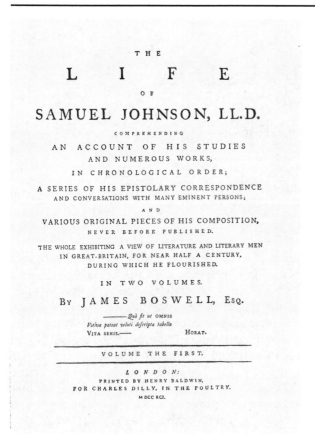

THE

L I F E

OF

SAMUEL JOHNSON, LL.D.

COMPREHENDING

AN ACCOUNT OF HIS STUDIES
AND NUMEROUS WORKS,

IN CHRONOLOGICAL ORDER;

A SERIES OF HIS EPISTOLARY CORRESPONDENCE
AND CONVERSATIONS WITH MANY EMINENT PERSONS;

AND

VARIOUS ORIGINAL PIECES OF HIS COMPOSITION,
NEVER BEFORE PUBLISHED.

THE WHOLE EXHIBITING A VIEW OF LITERATURE AND LITERARY MEN
IN GREAT-BRITAIN, FOR NEAR HALF A CENTURY,
DURING WHICH HE FLOURISHED.

IN TWO VOLUMES.

BY JAMES BOSWELL, ESQ.

————— *Quò fit ut OMNIS*
Votiva pateat veluti descripta tabella
VITA SENIS.—————   HORAT.

VOLUME THE FIRST.

LONDON:
PRINTED BY HENRY BALDWIN,
FOR CHARLES DILLY, IN THE POULTRY.
M DCC XCI.

Title page for the work for which the Dilly firm is best known

circumspect and less verbose than Edward but brought considerable business acumen to the firm.

The Copyright Act of 1709 gave authors copyright protection for fourteen years, with the option for living authors to renew for another fourteen years. Copyright infringement was commonplace in the eighteenth century, but the Dillys were careful to respect copyrights and, whenever challenges arose, were anxious to satisfy claimants. Cumberland observed that the Dilly business was "conducted upon principles of the strictest integrity." The Dillys employed attorneys in London and Philadelphia to steer them through legal matters.

Boswell's relationship with the Dillys, both personal and professional, was unique, similar perhaps only to his relationship with Johnson. Not only did it extend to the dinner parties and after-dinner whist games, but for several years before Boswell established permanent lodgings in London the Dillys reserved a room where Boswell stayed on many extended visits. While the Dillys certainly prospered from their publication of Boswell's writings, the friendship was more meaningful to the Dillys than the monetary gain. Indeed, Charles Dilly lent Boswell several hundred pounds on more than

one occasion. Boswell got to know John and Martha Dilly when they visited London, and on his journeys to and from Scotland he would often stop at the Dilly home in Southill, where he found the familiar Dilly hospitality.

The Dillys, Boswell, and other romantic Britons supported the Corsican struggle for independence, led by Gen. Pasquale Paoli, which would end with the French conquest of the island in 1768. (The Dillys' portrait of Paoli was a conversation piece for their many guests.) Even though the Dillys had, as yet, no outstanding reputation in the publishing trade, Boswell contracted with them to publish his *Account of Corsica, Journal of a Tour to that Island; and the Memoirs of Pascal Paoli* in 1767, granting the copyright for one hundred guineas. The work went through three editions that year, proving quite profitable for the Dillys. The next year Boswell not only agreed to have the Dillys publish a volume he edited, *British Essays in Favour of the Brave Corsicans*, but also invited Edward Dilly to write one of the eight essays in the publication. The Dillys were designated as one of a select group of booksellers to market a new edition of the Anglican Book of Common Prayer in 1767.

In 1768 Edward and Charles Dilly and John Wilkie, publisher of the *London Chronicle*, were reprimanded by the House of Lords for violating the prohibition against printing parliamentary debates. In 1770 the government ordered the editor, Henry Sampson Woodfall, and the printers of *Public Advertiser* arrested for printing the anonymous Junius letters, which criticized the administration of Prime Minister Augustus Henry Fitzroy, third duke of Grafton. As part owner of the *Public Advertiser*, Edward Dilly had approved Woodfall's policy. Dilly testified on behalf of John Almon, the only printer who was convicted in the case. In 1770 Boswell and Edward Dilly purchased one-sixth ownership each in the *London Magazine*, which published many of Boswell's essays. The partners met each month at the Queen's Arms tavern to plan the next edition. The Dillys made the acquaintance of the Scottish poet-philosopher James Beattie through Boswell; Beattie's best-known poem, *The Minstrel; or, the Progress of Genius* (1771), was a Dilly publication.

Much of the bookselling side of the Dillys' business consisted of shipments of Dissenting literature and medical and political tracts to America; the Dillys also offered their shop as an outlet for imported American works. Charles Dilly's trip to America had produced several contacts for book exchanges and reprints, including Bradford, publisher of the *Pennsylvania Journal*. The trip had also established a lifetime liaison with Rush, America's foremost physician. The Dillys used Rush and Franklin as advisers when publishing medical and philosophical writings by Americans. In addition to selling books in America through agents such as Bradford, the Dillys began selling, and often reprinting, American works in Britain. Hollis, the political radical and book collector who endowed Harvard College's library, paid the Dillys to publish American tracts, especially those reflecting opposition to the establishment of an Anglican bishopric in America.

American religious reformers whose works were published by the Dillys included such contemporaries as Bellamy, Chauncy, Mayhew, and Samuel Davies, as well as earlier clergy such as Jonathan Edwards. American political writings were also printed or distributed by the Dillys, including John Lathrop's *Innocent Blood Crying to God from the Streets of Boston* (1771), about the Boston Massacre, and Josiah Quincy's *Observations on the Act of Parliament, Commonly Called the Boston Port-Bill* (1774). Among the works of general American literature circulated in England by the Dillys was James Adair's popular *The History of the American Indians* (1775). Their only unprofitable American publication was Anthony Benezet's *Some Historical Account of Guinea, Its Situation, Produce and the General Disposition of Its Inhabitants: With an Inquiry into the Rise and Progress of the Slave-Trade, Its Nature and Lamentable Effects* (1772), which led the Dillys to refuse similar ponderous tracts thereafter.

The Dillys received many Americans in their London home. In addition to clients and celebrities such as Rush, Franklin, Quincy, the Lee brothers, and Gen. James Oglethorpe, they hosted the Mohican preacher, the Reverend Samson Occom of Connecticut, who was in England to raise funds for an Indian charity school; Dr. John Witherspoon, president of the College of New Jersey (the future Princeton University), who sought funds for his institution; and Reverend John Ewing, who solicited monies for his Presbyterian school in Delaware. The Dillys remained abreast of colonial tensions before and during the American Revolution. Edward Dilly's political radicalism was evident in a letter to John Dickinson of Pennsylvania defending the 1773 Boston Tea Party. While the Dillys realized only a modest income through their American outlets, they fostered a valuable transatlantic exchange of ideas through book shipments, correspondence, and personal visits in their Poultry lodgings.

Catharine Macaulay frequently attended the Dilly dinners, where she regaled the other guests with republican rhetoric. The Dillys printed Macaulay's *Observations on a Pamphlet, Entitled, Thoughts on the Cause of the Present Discontents* (1770), which attacked her fellow Whig Edmund Burke's essay defending political parties, and *An Address to the People of England, Scotland, and Ireland, on the Present Important Crisis of Affairs* (1775), which harshly criticized the administration for its treatment of the American colonies. After Thomas Cadell published the first five volumes of her Whig *History of England from the Accession of James I to That of the Brunswick Line,* beginning in 1763, Macaulay switched to the Dillys for a new octavo edition, which would total eight volumes by 1783; the Dillys paid Macaulay one thousand pounds for each volume. Mutual friends thought that Edward admired the attractive widow as more than a business associate, but in 1778 Macaulay would marry William Graham.

Another cause embraced by the Dillys was religious freedom. As members of the Dissenting minority in England, they were especially sensitive to the issues of toleration and liberty of conscience. In their early careers, they printed and sold many works of Dissenting writers such as Isaac Watts, Philip Doddridge, and Nathaniel Lardner, which were popular in America as well as England. Later the Dillys were acquainted with the Unitarian reformers Richard Price and Joseph Priestly, and Charles Dilly served as a liaison between Price and their American colleague Rush. He also copublished with Cadell the ninth edition of Price's *Observations on the Nature of Civil Liberty, the Principles of Government, and the Justice and Policy of the War with America* (1776), which directly influenced the American Declaration of Independence.

Clergy were perhaps the largest class of Dilly dinner guests over the years; it was rare when at least one religious spokesman did not sit at their table. Among Nonconformists who frequented the Dilly house were Augustus Montague Toplady, whose *Psalms and Hymns for Public and Private Worship* (1776), including "Rock of Ages," was published by the Dillys; John Fell, Dissenting essayist; John C. Ryland, headmaster of Doddridge's Dissenting Northampton Academy; and Thomas Gibbons. But the Dillys also included Anglican divines among their guests, including Samuel Parr, William Robertson, and William J. Temple.

The Dillys' support of parliamentary reform can be traced in large part to their acquaintance with the Dissenting schoolmaster and political moralist James Burgh, which began at least as early as 1761, when the Dillys copublished Burgh's *The Art of Speaking.* Thereafter, Burgh's influence on the Dillys increased through his frequent attendance at their dinners. Burgh and other Dilly associates, such as Price, Franklin, and Andrew Kippis, gathered often for discussions at the "Honest Whig Club." Burgh's preeminent work was *Political Disquisitions: or, An Enquiry into Public Errors, Defects, and Abuses* (1774–1775), published by the Dillys in three volumes at the end of Burgh's career. Many critics regard Burgh's treatise as the most thorough treatment of the reform issue in the era.

Cumberland, whose first publishing agreement with the Dillys was for *The Battle of Hastings: A Tragedy* (1778), remarked in his memoirs (1806) that Charles Dilly sometimes, in jest, offered dinner guests who were fond of using pretentious quotations a list of Greek and Latin phrases, at eighteen pence each, put together by a Dissenting friend of Dilly's. Cumberland was impressed by the way the Dillys could put at ease their varied and often egotistical guests. Boswell used the Dillys' hospitality as an occasion in 1776 to bring together Wilkes, the former editor of the radical newspaper the *North Briton,* and Johnson, a Tory who disdained radicalism; Boswell knew, as he would say in recounting the incident in *The Life of Samuel Johnson, LL.D.,* that "Two men more different could perhaps not be selected out of all mankind." Indeed, in 1770 Johnson had labeled Wilkes "a retailer of sedition and obscenity." Yet, because Johnson often dined at the Dilly house and "always found a good dinner," it was easy for Boswell to bring Johnson and Wilkes together. When Edward Dilly learned of Boswell's arrangement, he feared that Johnson would never forgive him; but Boswell assured Dilly that Johnson was unruffled at the prospect of Wilkes's attendance.

When Boswell and Johnson arrived at the Dillys, Edward Dilly introduced Johnson to Wilkes; Arthur Lee of Virginia; John Miller, printer of the *London Evening Post,* who had been acquitted in 1770 for printing Junius's letters; and the Quaker physician-philanthropist John Coakley Lettsom, whose *Medical Memoirs of the General Dispensary in London, for Part of the Years 1773 and 1774* (1774) was published by the Dillys. Johnson was uncomfortable at first in the midst of what he called the Dillys' "patriotic friends," but Wilkes, who was seated next to Johnson, behaved impeccably during dinner. The conversation turned to the theater and the actors David Garrick and Samuel Foote, who was Johnson's favorite. Further repartee ranged from Johnson's telling a story about planning the biography of John Dryden to Wilkes's and Johnson's comparing passages from Horace. After dinner the party was joined by the merchant William Lee,

Arthur's brother and a London alderman, and another Quaker, Mary Morris "Molly" Knowles, who sparred with Johnson about women's rights and religious toleration. In 1781 Johnson would instruct Charles Dilly to dispatch a copy of his *Prefaces, Biographical and Critical, to the Works of the English Poets* (1779, 1781) to Wilkes with his compliments.

In 1777 the Dillys were among the forty members of a booksellers' cooperative that met at the Shakespeare Tavern to plan an edition of the works of British poets, to be accompanied by biographical sketches of each author by Johnson. The edition was intended to compete with *The Poets of Great Britain: Complete from Chaucer to Churchill,* which had begun publication in Edinburgh that year and would run to 109 volumes when it was completed in 1783. The three members who negotiated with Johnson for the biographies – Thomas Davies, William Strahan, and Thomas Cadell – allowed him to dictate his own terms; he asked for only two hundred guineas, whereas the consortium had been prepared to pay several thousand pounds. Johnson's biographical sketches would ultimately prove to be so extensive that they would be published separately from the works, in ten volumes, as *Prefaces, Biographical and Critical, to the Works of the English Poets.*

The firm published the two volumes of *Miscellaneaous Works of the Late Philip Dormer Stanhope, Earl of Chesterfield: Consisting of Letters to His Friends, Never Before Printed, and Various Other Articles* in 1777 and 1778. In 1778 the Dillys printed *Essays, Moral and Literary,* by their friend and frequent guest Vicesimus Knox, the master of Tunbridge School. When Knox informed the Dillys that they were selling a work by Philip Withers that slandered Knox, they immediately removed the book from their stock.

Boswell and Johnson's 1779 visit to Southill found an ill and dying Edward Dilly, who was visiting John Dilly. Edward died at Southill on 11 May and was buried in the parish church cemetery, with the gravestone describing him as "citizen and bookseller of London."

Charles Dilly continued to support parliamentary reform through his membership in the Society for Constitutional Information. Founded in 1780 by Major John Cartwright, the society included radicals such as Horne Tooke, a former ally of Wilkes, and the Unitarian Kippis, a member of the "Honest Whigs" and editor of the *Biographia Britannica* (1747–1766), which highlighted the contributions of Nonconformists. Dilly also retained his interest in American affairs, publishing Charles Henry Wharton's *Poetical Epistle to His Excellency George Washington* (1780) and the second edition of Thomas Paine's *A Letter Addressed to the Abbe Raynal, on the Affairs of North America* (1782).

Nominated to fill the alderman's vacancy for the ward of Cheap in 1782, Dilly yielded the honor to his fellow publisher John Boydell, who later served as lord mayor of London. Charles was excused from serving as sheriff of London, an onerous and expensive duty, on a plea of Nonconformity. Catharine Macaulay Graham and her husband visited America in 1784–1785, a trip prepared in part by Charles Dilly's correspondence with American confreres such as Rush.

In 1785 Dilly published Boswell's *A Letter to the People of Scotland on the Alarming Attempt to Infringe the Articles of Union, and Introduce a Most Pernicious Innovation, by Diminishing the Number of the Lords of Sessions* and David Ramsay's *History of the Revolution of South Carolina from a British Province to an Independent State.* Rush persuaded Dilly to publish his medical colleague Benjamin Smith Barton's *Observations on Some Parts of Natural History* in 1787. Many others contracted with Dilly for publications ranging from history to gardening to poetry, as revealed by the thirty-two-page *Catalogue of Books Printed for and Sold by Charles Dilly, in London* (1787). William Vans Murray's *Political Sketches* appeared in 1787, John Adams's *A Defence of the Constitutions of Government of the United States of America* in 1787–1788, and William Gordon's *The History of the Rise, Progress, and Establishment of the Independence of the United States of America* in 1788.

The Dillys had always seized opportunities to publish Johnson items, and Charles Dilly continued to do so after Johnson's death in 1784. He arranged for the printing of Boswell's *The Journal of a Tour to the Hebrides with Samuel Johnson, LL.D.* (1785), which quickly went into a second edition, and John Courtenay's *A Poetical Review of the Literary and Moral Character of the Late Samuel Johnson, LL.D.* (1786). Even before Johnson's death Dilly had prodded Boswell to undertake a biography of Johnson; Dilly's insistence played a major role in Boswell's decision to pursue the project. While Boswell was completing his biography Dilly published *The Celebrated Letter from Samuel Johnson, LL.D. to Philip Dormer Stanhope, Earl of Chesterfield* (1790) and *A Conversation between His Most Sacred Majesty George III and Samuel Johnson, LL.D.* (1790), both edited by Boswell. Boswell's "Ode to Mr. Charles Dilly," in which he recalls their social activities, which included good food and drink and stimulating conversation, appeared in

the *Gentleman's Magazine* in 1791. *The Life of Samuel Johnson, LL.D.*, published by Dilly in two volumes in 1791, was followed in 1793 by *The Principal Corrections and Additions of the First Edition of Mr. Boswell's Life of Johnson* and by the three-volume second edition. The book became one of the most popular works in the history of English literature and a model for modern biographies.

Dilly published Cumberland's five-volume collection of essays, *The Observer* (1786–1790). The firm also published Catharine Macaulay Graham's *Observations on the Reflections on the Right Hon. Edmund Burke, on the Revolution in France, in a Letter to the Right Hon. the Earl of Stanhope* (1790) and *Letters on Education* (1790). Dilly published two of Cumberland's comedies after their presentation at the new Drury Lane Theater: *The Jew* (1794) and *The Wheel of Fortune* (1795); the latter was so popular that it went through five editions within the year. In 1798 Dilly published *Dr. Johnson's Table-Talk,* consisting of selections from Boswell's biography.

Dilly succeeded Cadell as master of the Stationers Company from 1800 to 1803. He sold the family firm in 1803 to Joseph Mawman, a bookseller from York. Dilly then moved from the Poultry to a house in Brunswick Row at Queen's Square, Holborn, where he continued to host dinner parties. He died in 1807 during a visit with Cumberland at Ramsgate and was buried in the St. George-the-Martyr cemetery at Queen's Square. Dilly left a fortune of sixty thousand pounds, which included a model farm at Clophill, Bedfordshire. After Dilly's death Cumberland wanted to purchase Dilly's Queen's Square residence, but it was too expensive for him.

Edward and Charles Dilly made a significant contribution to the publishing profession in eighteenth-century England. The breadth of subjects and authors they published was impressive. Their promotion and circulation of Dissenting literature through printing, sales, and book exchanges may have been the greatest in the combined English and American markets of the second half of the century and helped to spread the principles of religious freedom and liberty of conscience. The Dillys practiced integrity in their business dealings, whether negotiating publication agreements or making arrangements for the sale of books, and they earned the respect and friendship of authors and rival booksellers. Their dinner parties in the Poultry nurtured old clients and recruited new ones, and the assistance and encouragement they gave to budding authors may have been the most noteworthy in their profession.

References:

Sylvester H. Bingham, "Publishing in the Eighteenth Century with Special Reference to the Firm of Edward and Charles Dilly," dissertation, Yale University, 1937;

Colin Bonwick, *English Radicals and the American Revolution* (Chapel Hill: University of North Carolina Press, 1977);

James Boswell, *The Life of Dr. Samuel Johnson,* 6 volumes, edited by George Birkbeck Hill (New York: Harper, 1891);

Boswell, "Ode to Mr. Charles Dilly," *Gentleman's Magazine,* 61 (April–June 1791): 367;

Lyman H. Butterfield, "The American Interests of the Firm of E. and C. Dilly, with their Letters to Benjamin Rush, 1770–1795," *Papers of the Bibliographical Society of America,* 45 (1951): 283–332;

Richard Cumberland, *Memoirs of Richard Cumberland: London, 1806,* edited by Henry Flanders (London: Blom, 1856);

Charles Dilly, *A Catalogue of Books Printed for and Sold by Charles Dilly* (London: Printed for Charles Dilly, 1787);

Carla H. Hay, *James Burgh, Spokesman for Reform in Hanoverian England* (Washington, D.C.: University Press of America, 1979);

"Journal of Josiah Quincy, Jun. During his Voyage and Residence in England from September 28th 1774, to March 3, 1775," *Proceedings of the Massachusetts Historical Society,* 50 (1916–1917): 433–471;

Ralph M. Wardle, *Oliver Goldsmith* (Lawrence: University of Kansas Press, 1957).

Papers:

There is no official collection of Dilly papers or correspondence. Letters from the Dillys can be found in the Benjamin Rush Papers and the John Dickinson Papers at the Library Company of Philadelphia; the Josiah Quincy, Jr., Papers and the Jeremy Belknap Papers at the Massachusetts Historical Society in Boston; the Jedidiah Morse Papers at the New York Historical Society in New York City; and the Morse Papers at the Yale University Library.

– Daniel W. Hollis III

Anne Dodd

(London: 1711 – 1739)

Anne Dodd, "at the Peacock without Temple-Bar," was the best known of all the London mercuries for nearly thirty years before being succeeded by her daughter, also named Anne, who carried on the business for almost two decades more. Such was the nature of a mercury's business, however, that although she was known by name to everyone both in the London book trade and among the reading public of her day, Dodd was merely the distributor and not the actual publisher of the hundreds of items that bear her imprint.

Dodd was born Anne Barnes; nothing is known of her antecedents, and while the age supplied on her marriage-license application in 1708 is the conventional "upwards of 22 years," it is likely that she was, indeed, born in the mid 1680s. At the time of her marriage she was living in the London parish of St. Bride, Fleet Street, and it was in the parish church that her wedding to a man the license identifies as Nathaniel Dodd, of Enfield, Middlesex, stationer, took place on 18 March 1708. Her husband was almost certainly the Nathaniel Dodd who had been made free of the Stationers' Company by redemption (that is, by purchase) on 9 February of that year. There was another Nathaniel Dodd in the Stationers' Company during this period, but he was still an apprentice at the time of the marriage and did not gain his freedom – which included the freedom to marry – until the following July; since he was apprenticed to a printer, he is presumably the Nathaniel Dodd who was active as a master printer in the early 1720s.

The Dodds appear to have lived in St. Bride's parish for three and a half years following their marriage; the parish registers record the baptisms of their daughter Elizabeth in December 1708 and of a son, Richard, in September 1711. Their address at the latter date was New Street, off Shoe Lane, north of Fleet Street. How the couple were employed during this period is not known, but shortly after Richard's birth they moved a few hundred yards west to the Peacock, a shop in the Westminster parish of St. Clement Danes, just outside the boundary of the City proper at Temple Bar. The Peacock was a common sign at this date, but the similarity of the addresses, all of which read "without Temple Bar," makes it likely that this was the same shop that had been occupied from 1706 to 1710 by the not-yet-notorious Edmund Curll and from 1710 to 1711 by William Dolphin.

The business Anne Dodd carried on at the Peacock was the conventional one of a mercury. As early as 1714 the bookseller Timothy Goodwin recorded that he received his copies of *The Post Boy* newspaper from "one Dod, a Mercury woman," and in 1721 one of the couple's employees testified that he served Mr. Dodd, "the said Dodd's Wife being a Retailler of News Papers & Pamphlets commonly called a Mercury." Mercury women were normally widows, like Elizabeth Nutt, or the wives of tradesmen – often printers – like Anne Croom. What is unusual in the Dodds' case is that although Anne Dodd was the mercury, the business as a whole seems to have been Nathaniel Dodd's, its servants being his servants.

It is, however, Anne Dodd's name that appears in imprints, not her husband's; no more than two or three "N. Dodd" imprints are known – some of which belong to the printer – compared to the many hundreds that survive for Anne Dodd. This wealth of surviving imprints constitutes a second unusual aspect of the Dodds' business, since the names of most mercuries appear only rarely, if at all, in imprints, and none but Nutt comes even close to Anne Dodd in numbers at this period. What made the Dodds' business so successful – and so conspicuous – is hard to determine. Perhaps the shared management was an advantage, or perhaps the key was simply that the shop was conveniently located to supply the burgeoning West End trade. The frequent use of Anne Dodd's name in imprints testifies to the publishers' desire to let the public know that their paper or pamphlet was available at what was obviously one of London's best-known shops.

The Dodds were not themselves publishers in the modern sense of the word since they neither initiated nor financed the publication of the papers and pamphlets in which they dealt, being merely intermediaries in the distribution process. There is no evidence, for example, that they ever owned a copyright in whole or in part. Neither ever entered a

THE
DUNCIAD,
VARIORVM.
WITH THE
PROLEGOMENA of *SCRIBLERUS.*

·DEFEROR IN VICVM·

VENDENTEM THVS ET ODORES

LONDON.
Printed for A. DOD.1729.

*Title page for the revised and enlarged version of Alexander
Pope's mock-heroic satire on the reign of "Dulnes." The original
edition was also published by Anne Dodd (Courtesy of
the Lilly Library, Indiana University).*

copyright in the Stationers' Registers (though their daughter would do so twice in the 1750s), and there is also no evidence that either ever attended the regular booksellers' trade sales of books and copyrights – sales to which they probably would not have been admitted, given the distinctly inferior level on which they traded. Instead, their business consisted for the most part of picking up large numbers of copies of popular London periodicals and pamphlets direct from the printers for redistribution to booksellers or hawkers or for sale direct to the public.

Because of the scale of their operations the Dodds were subject to being taken in for questioning whenever the government took exception to a particular issue of one of the many papers they handled. It is from their testimony on such occasions, preserved among the papers of the secretaries of state in the Public Record Office, that most of the information about the details of their business affairs is derived. Their relative insignificance, as well as the fact that they handled publications from both sides of the political fence, seems, however, to have

protected them from severe harassment, and there is no evidence that they ever faced a serious attempt to interfere with what, by its sheer scale, must eventually have become an extremely lucrative business. Not only did the business survive occasional official displeasure; it also survived the relatively early disappearance of Nathaniel Dodd, who died intestate in October 1723. Anne Dodd, who was granted the administration of his estate, continued the business as before. In fact, Nathaniel Dodd's death would not have been particularly evident to the general public, since it was Anne's name that had always appeared, and that naturally continued to appear, in imprints.

Among the periodicals the Dodds handled were *The Post Boy;* Nathaniel Mist's *Weekly Journal,* of which they regularly took between 1,200 and 1,500 copies per issue in 1718; *The London Journal,* of which they took more than 2,500 copies in 1721; *The Craftsman,* of which Anne Dodd was taking 1,500 copies by 1731; and *Common Sense,* of which she took about 750 copies later in the 1730s. By modern standards these numbers are modest, but for eighteenth-century periodicals whose pressruns were often less than a thousand and only extremely rarely as many as ten thousand, these were large numbers indeed, often amounting to a quarter of the entire output.

Among the pamphlets they handled were some of every sort: political titles such as *Reasons against Impeaching the Late Ministry* (1715); literary polemics such as *Mr. Dennis's Observations upon Mr. Pope's Translation of Homer* (1717); poems such as *The Pettifoggers, a Satyr* (1723); and miscellaneous items such as *None but Fools Marry* (1730). The most celebrated of all these works was, of course, Alexander Pope's *The Dunciad;* of the imprint, "DUBLIN, Printed, LONDON Reprinted for A. DODD, 1728," it has, however, rightly been said that everything in it is false but the date.

At the time of her husband's death Anne Dodd had at least three children living, since three daughters survived her; but she had also borne at least two sons and may have had other children who were living in 1723 of whom nothing is known. Of the three girls whose existence is certain, Elizabeth was fourteen when her father died, Anne was seven, and Sarah was no more than four.

How Anne Dodd managed to run so large a business under such circumstances is not clear, but help was cheap in the eighteenth century, and she was obviously an extremely competent manager. The business seems to have continued to thrive and even to have grown under her single-handed control; by the time of her death in April 1739 Dodd had provided for her eldest daughter's marriage to the London surgeon Mileson Hingeston, and she bequeathed six hundred pounds, as well as plate and jewelry, to each of her unmarried daughters and five hundred pounds divided among her three grandchildren, as well as ten guineas to the servant who had been with her for fifteen years. She left the

business to her two younger daughters provided that they carried it on jointly, failing which it was to pass to their elder sister on the condition that the latter carry it on for at least a year. She would have been gratified to know that the business was carried on in the name of her second daughter and namesake until well into the 1750s. Moreover, the bookseller Mileson Hingeston, who flourished in the 1760s and 1770s, although not her son-in-law – he had died in 1764 – must have been a relative. Finally, the oft-quoted autobiography *The Life of Mr. Thomas Gent* (1832) refers regularly to "Mrs. Dodd" at this period, but the references are to Mary and Elizabeth Dodd, wives of Nathaniel Dodd the printer, and not to Anne Dodd.

References:

Thomas Gent, *The Life of Mr. Thomas Gent, Printer, of York* (London: Thomas Thorpe, 1832);

Michael Harris, *London Newspapers in the Age of Walpole* (Cranbury, N.J.: Associated University Presses, 1987);

D. F. McKenzie, *Stationers' Company Apprentices 1701–1800* (Oxford: Oxford Bibliographical Society, 1978);

Henry R. Plomer and others, *A Dictionary of the Printers and Booksellers Who Were at Work in England, Scotland and Ireland from 1668 to 1725* (Oxford: Bibliographical Society, 1922);

Plomer and others, *A Dictionary of the Printers and Booksellers Who Were at Work in England, Scotland and Ireland from 1726 to 1775* (London: Bibliographical Society, 1932 [i.e., 1930]);

Michael Treadwell, "London Trade Publishers 1675–1750," *Library,* sixth series 4 (June 1982): 99–134.

– *Michael Treadwell*

R. Dodsley
(London: 1735 – 1753?)

R. and J. Dodsley
(London: 1753? – 1764)

J. Dodsley
(London: 1764 – 1797)

See also the Robert Dodsley entry in *DLB 95: Eighteenth-Century British Poets.*

Robert Dodsley was mid–eighteenth century London's premier publisher of belles lettres, his list of authors reading like a "who's who" of the age. Literary history is indebted to him for preserving the texts of ancient dramas in his *A Select Collection of Old English Plays* (1744–1745), as well as for recording the poetic taste of his age in *A Collection of Poems. By Several Hands* (1748–1758). Taking over the business in early 1759, his brother and successor, James Dodsley, carried the firm almost to the end of the century, becoming a major figure in the London book monopoly and one of the wealthiest booksellers of the day.

Robert Dodsley took an unusual route to the book trade. Born on 13 February 1703, he was the first son of a dissenting Mansfield schoolmaster of the same name whose lineage can be traced to a Midlands family of the thirteenth century. What education the elder Dodsley imparted to his son and pupil is not known, but the former's penchant for mathematics and the writing of poetry would certainly have had an impact on young Robert. The father seems not to have had literary aspirations for his eldest son, for, apparently having as-

sessed the profitable opportunities in the expanding Mansfield woolen market, he apprenticed Robert to a local stocking weaver.

Dodsley's apprenticeship must have proved stifling, for he left his master before completing the seven-year indenture, preferring to take his chances on the road. Given the inflexible attitude toward apprenticeship contracts at the time — masters would offer rewards for runaway apprentices — it is likely that Dodsley had somehow managed to cancel his bonds. Whatever the terms, his departure apparently displeased his father, for when the latter died in 1750, he left all of his property to Robert's younger brother John, who had opted to carry on a family tradition as farmer and maltster in the Mansfield area.

Biographical data for the period immediately after Dodsley's exit from Mansfield is unavailable, but at some point in his early twenties he seems to have been taken on as a footman by Charles Dartiquenave, a well-known epicure, friend of Jonathan Swift and Alexander Pope, member of the Kitcat Club, and contributor to the *Tatler*. But Ralph Straus notes slight evidence in Dodsley's collection of poems *A Muse in Livery* (1732) that Dodsley was also employed in the house of Sir Richard Howe of Gloucestershire during this period; whether it was before or after his service to Dartiquenave is not clear. About 1728 Dodsley became footman to Jane Lowther in Whitehall, London.

Dodsley's first published poem, *Servitude* (1729), addressed the same subject as did the popular *Every-Body's Business, Is No-Body's Business* (1725), written by Daniel Defoe under the pseudonym Andrew Moreton; it also anticipated Swift's *Directions to Servants* (1745), a work that Dodsley would later publish. Despite Dodsley's expressed regret at its "mean subject," *Servitude* must have enjoyed some success, for in 1731 the publisher Thomas Worral put out a second edition with the more appropriate title *The Footman's Friendly Advice to his Brethren of the Livery*. The preface, introduction, and six pages of small talk concerned with *Every-Body's Business, Is No-Body's Business* were supposedly written by Defoe. Evidence is lacking as to whether or not Dodsley had met Defoe, or what, if any, influence Defoe exerted on the footman's behalf.

Dodsley's most significant early publication shows that he had already earned the patronage, if not gained the acquaintance, of a host of Lowther's fashionable friends: *A Muse in Livery, or the Footman's Miscellany* included among its more than two hundred subscribers Sir Robert Walpole; Frances Seymour, countess of Hartford; and Catherine Powlett, Anne Wriothesley, and Anne Palmer, the duchesses of Bolton, Bedford, and Cleveland, respectively. Within five months a second edition was called for; this time the author's name appeared on the title page: "By R. Dodsley, now a Footman to a Person of Quality at Whitehall." The frontispiece by Paul Fourdrinier reflects the age's fascination with the idea of genius trapped in low station, a growing moral and social consciousness that would open the way to the kind of rags-to-riches story that Dodsley's career would illustrate so well. The cut shows a young man in a rough tunic whose left arm is lifted skyward by a winged bracelet toward the words *Happiness, Virtue, and Knowledge;* his right arm is handcuffed to a chain labeled "Poverty" that stretches downward to the words "Misery, Folly, and Ignorance," while his right foot is manacled to a large block labeled "Despair." At the top of the engraving a full-faced sun looks on with an expression of total indifference. Privileged society's haughty repression of natural genius would become a theme of Dodsley's own writings and early publications. For the moment, however, he seems willing to appear politically innocent; only the anomaly of his situation marks the verses he chose for the title page:

Robert Dodsley; painting attributed to William Alcock (National Portrait Gallery, London)

You laugh, and think 'twill be a jest,
To see a muse in Livery dress'd:
But when I mount behind the coach,
And bear aloft a flaming torch;
Methinks on Pegasus I fly,
With fire poetick blazing thro' the sky.

On 14 February 1732 Dodsley married Catherine Iserloo, the "Kitty" who is the subject of some of the most tender verses he wrote while in Lowther's service. Around this time, close on the heels of his success with *A Muse in Livery,* he sent Pope a manuscript for a one-act play; in his letter of response of 5 February 1733 Pope said that although he doubted that the play had enough action for the stage, he would recommend it to John Rich, the manager of the Covent Garden theater. Pope closed with an offer to "shew you my friendship in any instance."

Whether or not Dodsley was still in Lowther's employ at this point is not clear; he would set up his bookshop in Pall Mall only a little more than two years later, and it seems reasonable to assume that he must have had some exposure to the operation of this multifaceted trade in the interim. Since Pope would be his sponsor during the early years of the business, and since Dodsley's next three published poems – *The Modern Reasoners* (1734), *An Epistle to Mr. Pope, Occasion'd by his Essay on Man* (1734), and *Beauty, or the Art of Charming* (1735) – were published by Pope's own publisher, Lawton Gilliver, it is possible that Dodsley spent some time as an assistant to Gilliver.

Pope proved faithful to his word: Rich produced Dodsley's *The Toy-Shop* on 3 February 1735. This moralistic afterpiece, satirizing dissipated luxury, was published by Gilliver the same year and proved as successful in print as on the stage; it would pass through eleven editions in an equal number of years. More important, it supplied Dodsley with the resources, together with a one-hundred-pound contribution from Pope, to open his bookshop at the sign of Tully's Head in Pall Mall, probably in March or April 1735. Not surprisingly, Dodsley's first publication was *The Works of Alexander Pope, Volume II;* his name is linked in the imprint with those of Gilliver and James Brindley.

The first site of Tully's Head is not known, except that it was in Pall Mall. Dodsley's name does not appear in the Westminster rate books until three years later, when he had taken over the former quarters of Sir William Younge in Pall Mall. Straus identifies the site as a large house at the end of a passageway opposite Marlborough House. Westminster was away from the center of the book trade in the City of London: because he had not served an apprenticeship in the trade, did not come from a trade family, and did not have a trade connection to pay the redemption fee, Dodsley did not qualify for membership in the Stationers Company; lacking that credential, he did not enjoy the "freedom of the City of London" – that is, he could not conduct business within the city's limits. On the other hand, locating in Westminster offered certain advantages. At hand were fashionable St. James customers, who patronized such noted local coffee houses as the St. James, White's, and the Smyrna. Likewise, it placed Tully's Head within easy reach of Parliament and the government offices in Whitehall. Moreover, in Westminster Dodsley had no serious competition in the trade except, perhaps, for Brindley in New Bond Street.

With little or no experience and with no trade roots, Dodsley might not have succeeded without Pope's help. Besides the Pope works in which Dodsley collaborated with other booksellers, by 1739 the poet had channeled seven of his other pieces to Tully's Head for Dodsley's sole imprint. The mere appearance of Dodsley's imprint on the distinguished poet's works brought the new bookseller favorable attention in the literary world. Impressed with a bookseller to whom Pope entrusted his works, other authors began to make inquiries at Tully's Head. Moreover, from the beginning Pope

recommended Dodsley to his friends. Writing to William Duncombe on 6 May 1735, for instance, Pope said that Dodsley had just set up as a bookseller, "and I doubt not, as he has more sense, so will have more honesty, than most of [that] profession."

Although the available evidence indicates that in 1736 Dodsley produced only two poems by John Lockman, one by John Dalton, an anonymous collection of love poems, and a new edition of Thomas Norton and Thomas Sackville's *Gorboduc,* in 1737 he published nine books, including a volume of Pope's letters together with Gilliver, Brindley, and John Knapton; an edition of still another of his own plays, *The King and Miller of Mansfield;* and the year's most popular work, Richard Glover's epic *Leonidas.* The next year saw twenty-one new works, as well as new editions of others. The former included *London,* by the not-yet-famous Samuel Johnson; an edition of François Fénelon's *Telemaque;* a translation of Torquato Tasso's *Jerusalem;* a few more poems by Pope; and another of his own plays, *Sir John Cockle at Court.*

Whereas in previous years Dodsley's minimal resources required the collaboration of other booksellers to publish works that exceeded pamphlet size, in 1739 several multivolume works appeared under his own imprint. Although the year opened with another collaboration with Knapton, Gilliver, and Brindley, for Pope's *Poems,* Dodsley published on his own the second volume of Pope's *Works,* as well as two-volume editions of *The Miscellaneous Works in Prose and Verse of Mrs. Elizabeth Rowe,* Francesco Algarotti's *Sir Isaac Newton's Philosophy Explain'd for the Use of Ladies,* and *The Dramatic Works of Roger Boyle.*

It was also in 1739 that Dodsley was prosecuted for publishing Paul Whitehead's satire *Manners,* which assaulted various court figures, politicians, and prelates for serving their own ends at the expense of the country's welfare. One of its victims, Thomas Sherlock, bishop of Salisbury, persuaded the House of Lords to summon both author and publisher to Westminster Hall. Whitehead absconded to avoid prosecution, but Dodsley was reprimanded for publishing this "scandalous" reflection on certain members of the Lords and was ordered detained until further notice in a sponging house in Butcher's Row. Dodsley's friend Benjamin Victor prevailed on another of Whitehead's victims, William Capel, third earl of Essex, to file a petition for his release. Dodsley was released after a week in custody on payment of a seventy-pound fine.

On the surface it would seem that Dodsley was merely a stooge who absorbed the brunt of the rage that the Lords should have directed at White-head, but merely writing a scurrilous work was not considered as serious an offense as publishing that work for public consumption. Moreover, a closer examination of Dodsley's own political attitudes now suggests otherwise. When he was serving as a footman, Dodsley's verses tended to be light-hearted, self-conscious pieces of an aspiring poet tied to a livery. His exposure to the noble and fashionable set during this period, however, seems to have dispelled the awe that a Mansfield apprentice would ordinarily have for his betters, and he began to understand that title, family, wealth, or social position were no assurance of genius or quality and to resent the haughty imposition of a privileged social class. His struggle to reconcile his sense of his own genius with the humiliations he was forced to endure as a footman were first expressed in his essay "Miseries of Poverty" in *A Muse in Livery:* "The miseries of a thinking man are intolerably aggravated by . . . the contempt with which the world looks upon him in a mean and despicable habit . . . and the many insults, inconveniences, and restraints which he undergoes . . . are themes which afford him a great many melancholy reflections." In *The Toy-Shop* Dodsley targeted the pretensions of aristocrats and clergymen; his cynical shopkeeper directs a customer: "You shall find Infidelity mask'd in a Gown and Cassock . . . Oppression is veil'd under the Name of Justice. . . . In short, Worthlessness and Villainy are oft disguis'd and dignified in Gold and Jewels, whilst Honesty and Merit lie hidden under Raggs and Misery." Dodsley's second play, *The King and Miller of Mansfield,* reflects the same theme. King Henry II, separated from his party and lost in Sherwood Forest after a day of hunting, reflects: "Of what Advantage is it now to be a King? Night shows me no Respect: I cannot see better, nor walk so well as another Man. . . . in losing the Monarch, I have found the Man." Saved by a local miller, the king lodges at the miller's house. There he hears a report from the miller's son of a recent trip to London. The young man claims that the court proved to be the "disappointment of all my hopes and expectations"; to be a courtier, one must be a "master of the arts of flattery, insinuation, dissimulation," and bribery. Fools had titles and knaves, pensions. When the king is informed of a local nobleman's deceptive debauching of the young man's beloved, he punishes the lord and rewards the humble miller with a knighthood and pension.

It is reasonable to assume, then, that Dodsley's courting of Pope during the period of the

Frontispiece by Paul Fordrinier for a collection of poems Dodsley wrote during his early career as a footman

latter's scathing satires on a corrupt court and political figures was triggered by more than potential professional advantages. Whitehead's *State Dunces* (1733) had called on Pope to give over his naive social satires and take up the cause of a patriot in days when England was threatened by corruption in court and government. Pope did take up the cause, and it was not long after Dodsley opened Tully's Head's doors that he was publishing Pope's *The First Epistle of the First Book of Horace, Imitated* (1737), a severe attack on court corruption and the age's "Lust of Gold," and *The Second Epistle of the Second Book of Horace, Imitated* (1737), wherein Pope arraigns both the country's laws and the age's cultural degradation as undermining the art of poetry. Even more significant, Dodsley published Pope's *One Thousand Seven Hundred and Thirty Eight,* the poet's most caustic and cynical assessment of the age, just seven months before Whitehead's *Manners.*

Dodsley, then, knew what he was doing when he published Whitehead's "scandalous" piece: *Manners* reflected Dodsley's own sentiments. Some months before its publication he had told Johnson that he had purchased the poem from Whitehead; he had probably let it lie while debating the wisdom of publishing it. He knew – as Whitehead himself complained in his poem – that Pope's powerful reputation would allow Pope to go unscathed for the same lines that would cause Whitehead to be prosecuted; consequently, whereas Dodsley had felt safe with Pope's satires, publishing Whitehead's took some courage. As Johnson later commented, "The whole process was probably intended rather to intimidate Pope than to punish Whitehead."

Except for an unexplained falloff in 1740, Dodsley's list of authors grew through the first half of the 1740s. During that period he brought out the first poems of Mark Akenside, John Brown, John Gilbert Cooper, William Shenstone, Joseph and Thomas Warton, and William Whitehead, all of whom, except the contentious Brown, would maintain long-term publishing relationships with him. He also began publishing the poetry of William Collins, Stephen Duck, and William Thompson, and he brought out the first six volumes (1742–1744) of Edward Young's *The Complaint; or, Night-Thoughts on Life, Death, and Immortality* (1742–1746). Additionally, he published the last works of Swift, including *Directions to Servants* and the tenth volume of *Miscellanies* (1745), as well as various editions of Pope's *Works*. In 1745 he brought out forty separate works, all of which, except for three second editions, were new on the market. The subjects and types of works also expanded during this period: new poetry was joined by editions of classics; historical works; books on architecture, travel, and science; and even some antipapist propaganda. Among them were an edition of the Clerk's Tale from Geoffrey Chaucer's *Canterbury Tales* (1739), the sixth edition of William Cheselden's *The Anatomy of the Human Body* (1741), John Wood's *The Origin of Building* (1741), James Spilman's *A Journey through Russia into Persia by Two English Gentlemen* (1742), Henry Baker's *The Microscope Made Easy* (1742) and *An Attempt towards a Natural History of the Polype* (1743), Christopher Pitt's translation of Virgil's *Æneid* (1743), Edward Pococke's *A Description of the East* (1743–1745), John Downes's *A Popish Prince the Pest of a Protestant People* (1745), and translations of works by Callimachus and Sallust, of Giovanni Boccaccio's *The Decameron* by Charles Balguy (1741), and of Miguel de Cervantes's *Don Quixote* by Charles Jarvis (1742).

In 1741, apparently to compete with Edward Cave, who had pioneered the magazine format with the *Gentleman's Magazine* ten years earlier, Dodsley began the *Public Register, or Weekly Magazine*. The threepenny weekly included essays and fresher news than Cave could supply in his monthly. Cave exerted his influence to squelch the new weekly, and, despite dropping the news to avoid the stamp tax and then resuming it but cutting the size of the periodical, Dodsley was forced to announce in the twenty-fourth number: "the additional expense I was obliged to in stamping it, and the ungenerous usage I have met with from one of the proprietors of a certain monthly pamphlet, who has prevail'd with most of the common newspapers not to advertise it, compel me for the present to discontinue it."

For some, Dodsley is best remembered for his twelve-volume *A Select Collection of Old Plays*. His love of the theater, which began with his own successes on the stage during the 1730s, generated an interest in collecting old English plays. In volume one of the collection Dodsley claims that the "Harleian Collection of old Plays, consisting of between 6 and 700 . . . are now in my possession." From these he selected sixty-one plays, ranging back to 1647, "to snatch some of the best pieces of our old Dramatic Writers from total Neglect and Oblivion." The history of English drama will always be indebted to him for this extraordinary service.

Dodsley had cultivated an extensive circle of poets by 1747, including Thomas Gray and William Mason, and was ready to produce his second major contribution to English literary history and the one for which he is probably best known. With something of the foresight that had generated *A Collection of Old Plays* Dodsley decided "to preserve to the public those poetical performances, which seemed to merit a longer remembrance than what would probably be secured to them by the Manner in which they were originally published." The first three volumes of *A Collection of Poems. By Several Hands* appeared in mid January 1748. Four editions had been called for by March 1755, when Dodsley added another volume to the collection. Three years later two more volumes were added, completing the set.

The extraordinary and enduring success of *A Collection of Poems. By Several Hands* (or "Miscellanies," as it came to be called) is largely attributable to its unique and comprehensive nature. The last attempt to present a collection of poems by several authors had been John Dryden's one-volume *Poems on Various Occasions* (1701); and when, in the early nineteenth century, it was proposed that George Gordon, Lord Byron, compile a similar miscellany, he recalled that Dodsley's was the last decent performance of the kind. Dodsley's collection set the canon for mid–eighteenth century poetry, and sub-sequent compilers of poetry in the century implicitly acknowledged its stature by merely supplementing the original with additional volumes.

Not only did the collection enjoy broad appeal in its time, but modern scholars look on it as an index to the age's poetic taste. Despite the collection's imbalance, caused by Dodsley's heavy representation of friends such as Shenstone, the six volumes offer a wide sampling of contemporary poetic production; except in the cases of perhaps a half-dozen figures, it includes selections from nearly all known major and minor practicing poets. Notably missing are poems by Swift and Young, but these poets hardly risked losing "remembrance" – Dodsley's criteria for inclusion – for regular editions of their works were appearing from the press during these years.

Extracting contributions from ever-revising and tardy poets, making judicious selections as well as "delicate" emendations, convincing printers to keep large sections in standing type while awaiting last-minute submissions and revisions, and publishing the work "in season" and timing advertisements accordingly are among the problems with which Dodsley was forced to deal when producing the collection. Probably they are no better illustrated than in Dodsley's correspondence with Shenstone when the bookseller was attempting to complete the last two volumes in late 1757 and early 1758. Two months before the volumes appeared, for instance, Dodsley wrote pleadingly for Shenstone's final revisions: "Ah, dear Mr. Shenstone! consider what a situation I am in – big with *twins,* at my *full time,* and no hopes of your assistance to *deliver* me!"

Shenstone was a major contributor to several of the bookseller's undertakings. Shenstone's circle of poets supplied many poems for the *Collection.* (One of these poets, Richard Graves, as coexecutor with Dodsley of Shenstone's will, would collaborate with the bookseller in a final tribute to their mutual friend, an edition of Shenstone's works in 1764.) Dodsley's frequent summer jaunts to Shenstone's farm, Leasowes, in Halesowen, Shropshire, in the late 1750s were always used for consultation on his current publishing project. His own pieces, *Melpomene* (1757) and *Cleone* (1758), underwent much revision at Shenstone's hands; and for Dodsley's last major collection, the three-volume *Select Fables of Esop and Other Fabulists* (1761), Shenstone translated Antoine Houdar la Motte's discourse on fables, advised on the fables themselves, supplied illustrations, and even compiled the table of contents. It was also on one of these visits that Shenstone intro-

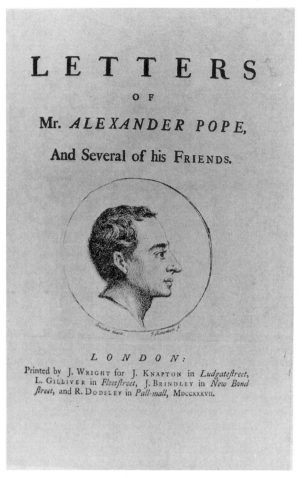

Title page for the collection of Pope's correspondence published by Dodsley in collaboration with others, including Pope's regular publisher, Lawton Gilliver. Pope sponsored Dodsley during his early years in the book trade.

duced Dodsley to the then unknown Birmingham type founder and printer John Baskerville. Baskerville's letters to the bookseller during the mid 1750s suggest that Dodsley served as Baskerville's London agent both for his new typeface and for his experiments in the production of writing paper.

In the same year that Dodsley published the first volumes of *A Collection of Poems. By Several Hands* he also compiled and published another work of wide-ranging utility, *The Preceptor: Containing a General Course of Education,* which comprises two volumes. Remembering his own rudimentary education and with a shrewd eye to the needs of the public, Dodsley aimed *The Preceptor* at youths whose education was likely to be carried on at home. Johnson provided the introduction to the work, which comprises extended essays by various authors on such topics as mathematics, architecture, geography, rhetoric, drawing, logic, ethics, trade and commerce, and law and government. The book passed through many editions during the century and even became a textbook in colonial American colleges.

With much literary talent on call, Dodsley made another run at the periodical market. Engaging Akenside as editor, he began the fortnightly *Museum: or, Literary and Historical Register* in March 1746. Regularly running forty pages, the periodical drew contributions from such writers as Johnson, Collins, Soame Jenyns, Robert Lowth, George Lyttelton, Joseph Spence, Horace Walpole, the Warton brothers, and William Whitehead. Given the predominantly literary character of the *Museum*, it is not clear why Cave should have felt threatened by the periodical, but he printed in the preface to the collected edition of the *Gentleman's Magazine* in 1747 a smug celebration of the demise of the "super-excellent Magazine" after thirty-nine numbers.

In the 1750s Dodsley reached the zenith of his career: his production outstripped all previous years, he published some of his most significant works, he introduced some major new talent, he solidified his publishing relationship with prominent authors, and his own reputation as author enjoyed a few major triumphs. Dodsley opened the decade with a work of his own, *The Oeconomy of Human Life* (1750) – a compilation of more than a hundred pages of moral aphorisms supposedly written by an "Ancient Bramin." Translated into five languages within as many years, *The Oeconomy of Human Life* became the most frequently printed work of the eighteenth century. In 1751 Dodsley introduced Gray's *Elegy Written in a Country Church Yard* and Richard Owen Cambridge's *Scribleriad*, which passed through four and three editions, respectively, in that year alone. In 1752 he published the first editions in England of Voltaire's *Age of Louis XIV*, three in the original French and two in English.

In 1753 Dodsley launched his third periodical, the *World*, employing Edward Moore as conductor. A lively, lighthearted weekly satire on contemporary fashionable life, the *World* was immediately successful and ran for a full three years. Among its contributors were Jenyns; Cambridge; William Pulteney, first earl of Bath; Philip Dormer Stanhope, fourth earl of Chesterfield; Sir David Dalrymple, Lord Hailes; John Boyle, fifth earl of Cork; Sir Charles Hanbury Williams; Joseph Warton; William Whitehead; and Horace Walpole. Dodsley was soon printing twenty-five hundred weekly copies, and by the time of its conclusion it had earned Moore the astounding sum of £858 for three years' work.

During the 1750s Dodsley also owned a share in the chief rival to the *Gentleman's Magazine*, as well as in two of the most influential thrice-weekly newspapers: he had purchased a minor share in the *London Evening Post*, regarded as the most influential newspaper in the provinces, by May 1747; and although he appears to have played little or no role in its production, it seems appropriate that Dodsley, after having been harassed by Cave in his two earlier periodical enterprises, should have bought a quarter share in the established *London Magazine* in 1748. The *London Chronicle*, however, was his major undertaking in newspapers. Begun with the printer William Strahan in 1757, the paper opened with an introduction by Johnson, included many contributions from James Boswell, and ran to the end of the century.

Highlights of 1753 and 1754 included Christopher Pitt and Joseph Warton's edition of the works of Virgil (1753), William Duncan's translation of Julius Caesar's *Commentaries* (1753), William Melmoth's translation of Cicero's *Letters to Several of His Friends* (1753), William Popple's translation of Horace's *Ars Poetica* (1753), Samuel Richardson's *Sir Charles Grandison* (1753–1754), and Thomas Warton's *Observations on the Fairie Queen of Spencer* (1754). Also during these years Dodsley realized the wisdom of earlier decisions as he reaped profits on the third edition of Voltaire's *Age of Louis XIV*, the fourth editions of Melmoth's *Letters on Several Subjects* (first published in 1748 and 1749) and Nathaniel Cotton's *Visions in Verse* (first published in 1751), the fifth editions of Akenside's *The Pleasures of Imagination* (first published in 1741) and George Lyttelton's *Observations on the Conversion and Apostleship of St. Paul* (first published in 1747), and the ninth edition of Gray's *Elegy*.

The year 1755 was a banner one for Dodsley both in terms of total publications and of significant works. Among at least fifty-four credits for the year, the most notable was Johnson's *A Dictionary of the English Language*, a collaborative effort with five other booksellers. Dodsley had published all of Johnson's significant works – *London* (1738), *The Vanity of Human Wishes* (1749), and *Irene* (1749) – and had printed Johnson's pieces in his *Museum, Preceptor*, and *A Collection of Poems. By Several Hands*. Appreciative of his early benefactor, Johnson referred to Dodsley as "my patron, Doddy" and acknowledged (in a letter of 8 April 1755 to Charles Burney) that it was Dodsley who gave him the idea for the dictionary and encouraged him to pursue it. Other important publications of the year included Young's *Centaur Not Fabulous*, the fourth volume of Dodsley's

A Collection of Poems. By Several Hands, and a collaborative edition of *The Works of Jonathan Swift.*

Probably Dodsley's greatest disappointment of these years stemmed from being closed out of a share in the publication of the collected works of his patron and friend Pope. Pope's literary executor, William Warburton, although an early friend and contributor to Dodsley publications, had become estranged from the bookseller because he resented the criticism of his own works that had emanated from Dodsley's press in books such as John Gilbert Cooper's *Life of Socrates* (1749) and *Cursory Remarks* (1751). When Warburton prepared his grand edition of Pope in 1751, he purposely excluded Dodsley from a share in its publication. As late as 1755, when Dodsley apparently made another offer, Warburton rejected it, disingenuously charging the bookseller with not having been "very regardfull of the memory" of Pope.

In 1758 Dodsley began publication of the *Annual Register,* for which he hired Edmund Burke as editor and compiler. This four-hundred-page volume chronicled the previous year's major events and included literary, historical, and topographical essays, as well as poetry and reviews. Although Burke discontinued his services some time in the mid 1760s, James Dodsley continued the publication until 1791, when it was taken over by the Rivingtons. It passed through various hands before being discontinued in 1953.

Tully's Head continued its rapid pace from 1756 through 1758, churning out approximately fifty titles a year, although a portion were new editions of earlier works. The years' distinguished first editions included James Hampton's translation of *The General History of Polybius* (1756), Thomas Blacklock's *Poems* (1756), a collected edition of the *World,* John Dyer's *The Fleece* (1757), Jenyns's *Free Inquiry into the Nature and Origin of Evil* (1757), Burke's *A Philosophical Enquiry into the Origin of Our Ideas of the Sublime and Beautiful* (1757), Gray's *Odes* (1757), volumes five and six of Dodsley's *A Collection of Poems. By Several Hands* (1758), and Thomas Stona's *Remarks upon the Natural History of Religion by Mr. Hume* (1758).

During 1759, Dodsley's last year as master of Tully's Head, the firm continued its high rate of production, publishing such works as Oliver Goldsmith's *An Enquiry into the Present State of Polite Learning in Europe,* Johnson's *The Prince of Abissinia* [*Rasselas*], and Charlotte Lennox's translation of *The Greek Theatre of Father Brumoy.* Although Dodsley officially surrendered the reins to his brother in late March or early April, the familiar imprint "R. and J.

THE

COMPLAINT:

OR,

Night-Thoughts

ON

LIFE, DEATH, & IMMORTALITY.

Sunt lacrymæ rerum, & mentem mortalia tangunt. VIRG

LONDON:
Printed for R. DODSLEY, at TULLY's Head in *Pall-Mall.* 1742.

Title page for the first volume of Edward Young's six-volume work published by Dodsley

Dodsley" continued to appear on Tully's Head publications almost exclusively until Robert's death in 1764. Since Robert Dodsley continued to be active in the business until his death, it is difficult to determine how much of the product during these years was attributable wholly to James's connections and efforts. It is known that Robert put the third edition of his tragedy *Cleone* (1759) to press, hectored authors for contributions to his *Select Fables of Esop and Other Fabulists,* secured support for Baskerville's edition of *Horace* (1762), mollified John Hoadly for errors in his poems in the 1763 edition of *A Collection of Poems. By Several Hands,* prepared an edition of Shenstone's correspondence (1764–1769), interceded with the bookseller Charles Bathurst for John Hawkesworth, responded to Laurence Sterne's offer of the manuscript for *Tristram Shandy* (1760–1767) in late 1759, and advised his brother on such proffered works as Thomas Percy's *Reliques of Ancient English Poetry* (1765).

The last two works caused Robert Dodsley some embarrassment among his peers and some discredit (perhaps unjustly) among modern scholars.

James Dodsley's foot-dragging on *Reliques of Ancient Poetry* gave rise to Percy's long unanswered charge that Robert, behind the scenes, was playing "too much of the bookseller" – that is, that he was too much driven by the market. Even Percy's patron and Dodsley's intermediary, Shenstone, however, acknowledged the manuscript's shortcomings and admitted that he abandoned efforts to convince his protégé to make adjustments. In Sterne's case, Dodsley's balking at buying the first volume of *Tristram Shandy* for £50 was obviously a blunder; its immediate popularity required his brother to pay £250 for the copyright of the first two volumes less than a year later. Robert had clearly been interested in the work, for he had taken the trouble to respond to Sterne with proposed revisions. As even his York friends had advised Sterne, however, it was unlikely that any bookseller would have purchased this crackbrained novel outright; they probably would have offered to serve as his publishing agent, as Dodsley did.

As much as can be discovered from Robert Dodsley's extant correspondence is that his relationships with authors, except in a few cases, were cordial, graceful, and usually moderated by practical business considerations. His extant publishing agreements (instances where he purchased the copyright) show him to have been consistently fair, though not overly generous. The prices he paid authors for manuscripts seem to reflect the standard rates for such works: ten to fifteen guineas for a pamphlet-size poem, a hundred pounds for a recently acted play, fifty to a hundred pounds for fiction, and one hundred fifty to two hundred pounds for translations (especially of Latin authors) and for substantial works in science and medicine. The range of payments reflected anticipated market appeal, which, of course, was projected on the basis of a work's subject and its author's reputation. The unknown Johnson, for instance, was paid ten guineas for his poem *London* in 1738 but fifteen guineas for *The Vanity of Human Wishes* eleven years later. Gray, whose *Elegy Written in a Country Church Yard* had gone through many editions by 1757, was paid forty guineas for only two odes in that year. In the same year the newcomer Burke received twenty guineas for *Philosophical Enquiry into the Origins of our Ideas of the Sublime and Beautiful,* whereas two years earlier the long-popular Young had earned two hundred pounds for *The Centaur Not Fabulous.* Reflecting the same logic, unsolicited manuscripts usually brought less than commissioned works.

Payments also varied in mode and scheduling. In the case of completed works, the most common

agreement called for an outright purchase of the copyright from the author. For works that had already been published by another bookseller, agreements usually required authors to surrender any copies of plates in their possession. Authors of large commissioned works were frequently paid by the sheet on delivery, obviously a method calculated to encourage the work's completion. Sometimes agreements called for payment, either partial or full, in the form of copies of the work, which the author could then present to friends or resell for profit. Although no author was paid in full at the signing of an agreement for a work to be completed, Dodsley would occasionally make small advances at that point. An exception occurred in the case of the proposed translation of Cicero's letters: Melmoth was paid a hundred pounds on signing. The most common procedure, for both commissioned and unsolicited works, was a partial payment either on delivery of the manuscript or on publication, the remainder to be paid three to six months after publication. Still other clauses provided additional payments for subsequent editions (an early form of royalty) or reserved to the author the right of one future impression, usually to allow for a collected edition of the author's works.

By the time of his retirement as head of the firm, Robert Dodsley's name had appeared in imprints as "publisher" of first editions of at least 468 titles. He was, however, the *sole* publisher – the imprint read simply, "Printed for R. Dodsley" – in only 233 of these cases. Beginning in 1753 James Dodsley's initial is linked with Robert's – the imprints read "Printed for R. and J. Dodsley" – in 124 instances, and one or both of their names are linked with other booksellers in 111 imprints. Robert Dodsley was, therefore, publishing or collaborating in the publication of a new volume on an average of every two and a half weeks. His production was surely even more frequent, however, for these figures do not take into account subsequent editions, works published surreptitiously (for example, through Mary Cooper), works that are no longer extant, and works that have not been located.

Robert Dodsley – frequently with James – is listed in the imprints of another 135 titles merely as "seller." Although he did not have a direct share in the profits of such works, the appearance of his name in these imprints suggests the value authors and other booksellers placed on having their wares sold at his shop. In all, then, Robert Dodsley's name appeared, either as publisher or seller, in at least 603 titles during his career.

Dodsley was surely London's leading publisher of belles lettres in the midcentury. During his

Title pages for the first volumes of two popular collections edited and published by Dodsley (Courtesy of the Lilly Library, Indiana University)

twenty-five years at Tully's Head he published at least 87 editions of Greek or Roman classics or imitations of them by Englishmen and 18 works of literary criticism. Moreover, his long list of poets had been responsible for the most common genre issued from Tully's Head, which amounted to at least 238 poems. Other significant genres included biographies, memoirs, and diaries (21 works); dramas (33 works); and fiction (23 works). A loose category of prose works including essays, dissertations, and tracts numbered 208.

On the other hand, Dodsley's business was broad-based; he targeted the main interests of the gentleman reader. As might be expected in an age where religion permeated every aspect of life, Dodsley published no fewer than fifty-seven works on God, the Bible, and the clergy; closely related are another twenty-four books on morality and ethics. He also published at least thirty-eight texts on government and politics, both practical and theoret-

ical; twenty-nine publications concerned with monarchs and nobility; nineteen on patriotism; and thirty-two on war and the military. Two other areas of broad contemporary interest are also substantially represented among his publications: Dodsley's publications include twenty-two works concerned with commerce, trade, economics, and agriculture and about forty dealing with science, mathematics, and medicine. Still other subjects that gained attention at Tully's Head, with at least six publications each, include America, architecture, marriage and the domestic scene, education, geography and topography, philosophy, aesthetics, social criticism and reform, and women. It seems that there was hardly a reader interest to which Dodsley did not respond.

Not all of these publications were put out under Dodsley's exclusive imprint; some were joint undertakings with other booksellers, especially in the case of multivolume works that required the risk of large sums. Early in his career the thrifty Dodsley had tended to stay with slighter publications – pamphlet poems – that could be managed on his slender resources: 72 percent of his business during the 1740s concerned publications of ninety-six pages or fewer that could be carried on without the financial assistance afforded by joint publication. On the other hand, joint publication was not a ready option at the beginning of his career. As an "outsider" to the trade, it is not likely that he would have found willing collaborators among the major booksellers on "bread and butter" works. Consequently, at the outset, he associated with booksellers of the second rank for expensive undertakings, the usual advice offered newcomers. For that reason his early joint publications involved such partners as Gilliver and Brindley.

As he made his mark in the trade, he found prominent booksellers more agreeable to collaboration. Although the vast majority of his publications continued to be solo productions, by the end of the 1740s his name had been linked in imprints with no fewer than fifty-three London booksellers and printers, including Charles Bathurst, William Bowyer, Charles Hitch, Andrew Millar, Samuel Richardson, the Knaptons, the Rivingtons, and the Tonsons. In the first three years of the 1750s, 35 percent of his publications were joint undertakings; curiously, in 1753, when his brother James's name began to appear in Tully's Head imprints, the percentage dropped back to 23, and it remained there for the rest of the decade.

On his known 110 joint undertakings, Dodsley shared the imprint with sixty-nine other booksellers and publishers. His most frequent collaborators were Andrew Millar with twenty-one publications, Thomas and Mary Cooper with eighteen, John or James Rivington or both with ten, and John Whiston and Benjamin White with eight. At least four imprints each showed Dodsley's name linked with Bathurst, John Clarke, John and Paul Knapton, and William Owen. Other collaborators included Bowyer, Somerset Draper, William Johnston, T. and T. Longman, and Charles Marsh. On still other occasions Dodsley joined with provincial booksellers such as Joseph Bentham, George Woodfall, John Woodyer, and W. Thurlbourne of Cambridge and John Barrett, Richard Clements, and James Fletcher of Oxford.

Of all these firms, none was more frequently joined with Dodsley's name than the publishing house of Thomas and Mary Cooper, Dodsley's sales agent in the City. Prior to his death in 1742, Thomas Cooper's name showed up in Dodsley imprints as the solitary "seller" on twenty occasions. From 1743 until 1759 his widow and successor functioned in the same capacity in no fewer than 167 of Dodsley's imprints. Together the Coopers are identified in imprints as the sellers in more than 50 percent of Dodsley's solo publications. Mary Cooper also served as Dodsley's "shadow" publisher on at least four occasions when he preferred to conceal his connection with a work: in the cases of John Gilbert Cooper's *Cursory Remarks,* the first volume of Joseph Warton's *An Essay on the Writings and Genius of Pope* (1756), Burke's *A Vindication of Natural Society* (1756), and his own *Oeconony of Human Life.*

At least thirteen printers served Dodsley during his years at Tully's Head; but because printers' names seldom appeared in imprints, evidence of his dealings with this component of the trade is limited. The most extensive documentation is found in the extant business ledgers for the firms of Bowyer and Strahan. Even here, however, the record blurs because more often than not Bowyer and Strahan were printing parts of works farmed out to them by the printer with whom Dodsley had contracted. John Nichols claims that Dodsley's principal printer was John Hughs, whose shop was near Great Turnstile, Lincoln's Inn Fields. Hughs's name appears in fourteen imprints that cover almost Dodsley's entire career at Tully's Head. Moreover, he was the printer for some of Dodsley's major works, including Pitt's translation of the *Æneid,* Hampton's of *The History of Polybius,* and all six volumes of *A Collection of Poems. By Several Hands.*

As their correspondence reveals, Dodsley served as Baskerville's London promoter when the Birmingham printer was developing his famous typeface in the early 1750s. Baskerville's letters acquaint Dodsley with practically every step in his progress toward the completion of the typeface that would mark England's break with the "old style" of William Caslon and that Dodsley would use for his *Select Fables of Esop and Other Fabulists.* Dodsley also functioned as the London distributor for Baskerville's experiments in the production of writing paper, although the scheme seems not to have been particularly successful.

Through most of the 1750s, while Dodsley's friend Richardson was rallying the London trade against the Dublin "pirates," the master of Tully's Head seems to have quietly carried on a publishing alliance with the Dublin printer-bookseller George Faulkner. As early as 1749 works for which Dodsley held the copyright had appeared simultaneous or even earlier in Dublin without the suggestion of piracy. Even after Faulkner had been blackballed by the Society of Arts (doubtless through Richardson's influence) in 1757, Dodsley was forwarding his *Melpomene* and unpublished sheets of the fourth and fifth volumes of *A Collection of Poems. By Several Hands* for printing in Dublin.

The full complement of illustrators that Dodsley employed will not be known until all of his publications have been examined individually. Available information shows at least twenty-three contributors, some of them the best-known contemporary artists and engravers. Among those providing drawings were Francis Hayman, William Hogarth, William Kent, and Samuel Wale; the engravers included Charles Grignion, Simon François Ravenet, Isaac Taylor, and Gerard van der Gucht. Louis Philippe Boitard and Hubert François "Gravelot" Burguignon produced both drawings and engravings. Boitard, Grignion, Hayman, Walker, and Wale were Dodsley's most frequent illustrators.

Evidence is available to identify three apprentices at Tully's Head, and a fourth is possible. James Dodsley seems to have served his elder brother through most of the 1740s. John Hinxman and John Walter advertised themselves as former Dodsley apprentices when they opened their own shops, Hinxman taking over John Hildyard's business in York in 1757 and Walter setting up at Homer's Head in Charing Cross in 1759. Finally, in 1761 an "L. Lewis" signed a receipt on behalf of James Dodsley, acknowledging a payment for books received.

In 1755 Dodsley's concern for the progress of English commerce, and for the book trade in particular, led him to join the newly formed Society for the Encouragement of Arts, Manufactures, and Commerce, which would become the Royal Society of Arts. His years in book production had made him aware that England was too dependent on paper imported from France and Holland. Consequently, he served with Hogarth, Richardson, and Jacob and with Richard Tonson on several society committees whose goal was the improvement of native English papermaking. Dodsley's committees devised specifications for various kinds of paper, advertised awards for prospective papermakers, and judged the submissions. For his expertise and services, Dodsley was named the society's first official printer and stationer in 1757.

Dodsley's outstanding success in the bookselling trade can be largely credited to a blend of skills: literary sensitivity, an ability to detect new talent, and a keen sense of the market. The number of "first works" of notable authors that he brought to the market is remarkable, but the real proof of his

THE

VANITY

OF

HUMAN WISHES·

THE

Tenth Satire of *Juvenal*,

IMITATED

By *SAMUEL JOHNSON.*

LONDON:

Printed for R. DODSLEY at Tully's Head in Pall-Mall, and Sold by M. COOPER in Pater-noſter Row.

M.DCC.XLIX.

Title page for one of the many works by Johnson that Dodsley published. Johnson credited Dodsley with giving him the idea for his dictionary and referred to Dodsley as "my patron, Doddy."

market sensitivity rests in the multiple editions that resulted from these judgments. At least 24 percent of all the works he published passed through multiple editions during his lifetime. At least 45 of these 113 works reached three or more editions, and 10 of them reached five. His special payoffs were Gray's *Elegy Written in a Country Church Yard* with eleven editions and Young's *Night Thoughts* with twelve; he had been the original publisher for both.

Dodsley died of complications arising from gout on 23 September 1764 while visiting Durham with his old friend Spence, who held a prebend in that city. It is ironic that he should die there, for, after his only other trip to Durham, he had described it to Shenstone as "one of the most romantic places I ever saw." Dodsley was buried in the Durham Cathedral churchyard, his plot marked by a large brown stone on which Spence's inscription can still be deciphered:

If you have any respect
For uncommon industry and merit

Regard this place
In which are interred the remains
of
Mr Robert Dodsley
Who as an author raised himself
Much above what could have been expected
From one in his rank of life
And without a learned education.
Who as a man was scarce exceeded by any
In integrity of heart
And purity of manners and conversation.
He left the world for a better
September 23rd 1764
In the 61st year of his age

Given his enormous success during a quarter of a century in the bookselling business, it is surprising that the largest bequest in his will, that to his brother and successor at Tully's Head, James Dodsley, amounted to only five hundred pounds. The bequest was a pittance compared to what James would leave his descendants at the end of the century. Moreover, Moore had earned almost twice that sum over a three-year period for conducting Dodsley's *World*. A thrifty person, Dodsley certainly had not squandered his money. Among the causes of his relatively small estate could have been the narrow profit margins of early–eighteenth century booksellers, Dodsley's reinvestment of profits in the business, or his generosity to his authors.

Reinvestment is perhaps the most reasonable explanation: besides the five hundred pounds, Dodsley left his brother a fortune in copyrights. Robert had owned outright copyrights to at least fifty works, including continuing favorites by Burke, Gray, Johnson, Spence, the Warton brothers, and Young, as well as exclusive rights to his own *Annual Register, A Collection of Poems. By Several Hands, The Oeconomy of Human Life, The Preceptor, A Select Collection of Old Plays,* and *Select Fables of Esop and Other Fabulists.* He also held extremely valuable shares in Johnson's dictionary, Swift's works, Baker's books on the microscope, the *London Chronicle,* the *London Evening Post,* and the *London Magazine.* Also, although James would pay for the copyrights, Robert had first attracted and negotiated with Sterne for *Tristram Shandy* and with Percy for *Reliques of Ancient English Poetry.*

Although he spent many more years than Robert both as a bookseller and as master of Tully's Head, James Dodsley has yet to attract a biographer or even an extended biographical account. Lacking the innovative publishing credits and the human interest of Robert's rags-to-riches story, James has suffered the fate of most sequels to outstanding performances. Moreover, James had none of his brother's literary talent (the British Library Catalogue shows not one work under his name); Robert, coming to the business as a published poet and successful playwright, had an advantage in attracting prospective authors. The list of significant authors Robert introduced to the literary scene finds no counterpart during James's reign at Tully's Head.

James also seems to have been more timid and private than Robert; despite what must have been a key role in the operation of the shop during Robert's time, he seems to have kept a low profile even after his name joined the firm's imprint. Although correspondents writing to Robert in the 1750s include their compliments to his brother, only one letter written by James survives from the seventeen years that he worked under Robert at Tully's Head. Stranger still, Robert's extant letters do not mention James's name until 20 July 1757, less than two years before he left the business to his brother. This impression of James's social reticence is confirmed by Nichols, who knew him later in his career: Nichols's obituary of James in the *Gentleman's Magazine* says that James favored a secluded life that led to some peculiarities; for instance, after he bought a carriage, he never ventured east of Temple Bar so that his friends would not know that he had one.

It is not clear when James came to London to work in Robert's shop, but his name first appears on a Tully's Head document on 3 June 1742, when he witnessed an agreement his brother had concluded for the purchase of the copyright for Baker's *The Microscope Made Easy.* Nothing is known of James before that time, except that he had been born in Mansfield in 1724, the youngest of Robert's four brothers and two sisters. According to existing records it was on 2 May 1753, with the publication of Henry Jones's poem *Merit,* that James's name first joined Robert's in the well-known imprint "Printed for R. and J. Dodsley"; whether James began to invest in the firm at that time is not known. With few exceptions, this imprint would continue on Tully's Head publications until 1764, well after Robert's retirement. Although Robert never became a member, on 3 December 1754 James was admitted to the Stationer's Company by redemption – that is, in lieu of his serving an apprenticeship, his admittance was purchased. This event certified that the Dodsley firm, once an intruder on the London trade scene, had made sufficient impact to be accepted by the City booksellers. Whereas Robert had confined his business to Westminster, using the Coopers as his City agents, James would later open a warehouse in Lincoln's Inn Fields.

During his first years as the master of Tully's Head, James relied on authors who had been developed by his brother. In the first half of the 1760s he purchased Robert Lowth's *Short Introduction to English Grammar* (1762) with Millar, Percy's *Reliques of Ancient English Poetry,* the first four volumes of Sterne's *Tristram Shandy* and the first two of his *The Sermons of Mr. Yorick* (1760), as well as Joseph Warton's *Essay on the Writings and Genius of Mr. Pope* and Thomas Warton's *Observations on the Fairie Queen of Spencer.* He continued to publish works by Akenside, Cooper, Jenyns, Mason, Melmoth, Moore, Thomas Sheridan, Christopher Smart, and William Whitehead, as well as a host of lesser lights.

Several of Robert's circle would carry on with James for many years. The last two volumes of Robert's tribute to his friend Shenstone, an edition of the latter's works, would be completed by Richard Graves and Richard Jago in 1769. Jago's own *Edge-Hill* would be published at Tully's Head in 1767, and Graves's *The Spiritual Quixote* in 1773. Another of Robert's friends, John Scott Hylton, would edit Jago's works under the title *Poems, Moral and Descriptive* in 1784. One of the writers longest with the Dodsleys produced James's most profitable work: Burke's *Reflections on the Revolution in France* (1790) passed through seven editions and eighteen thousand copies in the year of its publication alone and earned Burke a payment of one thousand pounds within the year. Finally, as late as 1794 Melmoth sold James the copyright to his *Translator of Pliny's Letters Vindicated,* which had first been published in Bath the previous year by R. Cruttwell.

Given Robert's extensive connections in the literary world, his continuing presence at Tully's Head after retirement, and the retention of the "R. and J. Dodsley" imprint until his death, it is impossible to determine which of the brothers was responsible for attracting certain new authors to Tully's Head between 1759 and 1764, although extant agreements for the period always show James Dodsley as the copyright purchaser. During these years appeared Goldsmith's *An Enquiry into the Present State of Polite Learning in Europe* (1759), Daniel Webb's *An Inquiry into the Beauties of Painting* (1760), Frances Sheridan's *Memoirs of Miss Sidney Bidulph* (1761) and *The Discovery* (1763), James Boswell's *The Cub at Newmarket* (1762), Frances Brooke's *The History of Lady Julia Mandeville* (1763), and James Macpherson's *The Battle of Lora* (1763), as well as poems by Edward Jerningham, George Keate, and James Scott.

Many works for which James had inherited either whole or partial copyright continued to be pop-

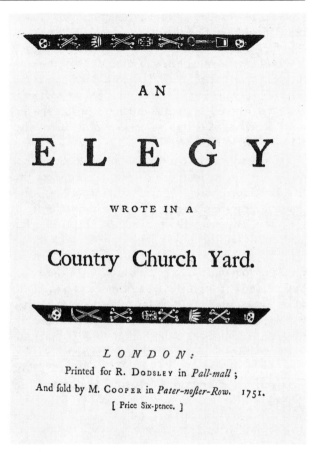

AN

ELEGY

WROTE IN A

Country Church Yard.

LONDON:
Printed for R. Dodsley in *Pall-mall*;
And sold by M. Cooper in *Pater-noster-Row.* 1751.
[*Price Six-pence.*]

Title page for Thomas Gray's best-known poem, first published by Dodsley

ular throughout the century; among those that reached a fourth or later edition during James's years were Melmoth's translation of Cicero's *Letters,* Spence's *Polymetis* (1747), Thomas Gataker's translation of Henri François Le Dran's *Operations in Surgery* (1749), and William Whitehead's *The Roman Father* (1750). Similarly, many individual issues of the *Annual Register,* beginning with that for 1758, passed through four and five editions into the 1790s. William Duncan's *The Elements of Logick* (1748), Brooke's *The History of Lady Julia Mandeville,* and Robert's *World* and *The Preceptor* all achieved eight editions by 1787, 1788, 1790, and 1793, respectively. Melmoth's translation of Pliny's letters (1747) reached its ninth edition in 1796. Johnson's *Rasselas* (1759), in which James had a half share, reached a ninth edition in 1793, and the dictionary went into its tenth edition in 1792, although by that time James was a partner in the work with fifteen other booksellers. Sterne's *Sermons of Mr. Yorick* reached its tenth edition as early as 1771, Melmoth's *Letters on Several Subjects* achieved its tenth edition in 1795, and Gray's *Elegy Written in a Country*

Church Yard reached a thirteenth edition in 1771. To these must be added the many editions of Robert's *The King and the Miller of Mansfield*, *The Oeconomy of Human Life* (the most often printed work of the century), *A Collection of Poems. By Several Hands*, *Select Fables of Esop and Other Fabulists,* and *A Select Collection of Old Plays,* as well as such enduring favorites shared with other booksellers as Swift's *Miscellanies* and Young's *Night Thoughts.*

James was not wholly reliant on Robert's endowment; he had the good fortune to attract the first produced play, *The Summer's Tale* (1765), of a major rising playwright, Richard Cumberland, as well as Cumberland's musical *Amelia* (1769). He also published the most popular poetic work of the last half of the century, Christopher Anstey's Horatian *The New Bath Guide* (1766); by 1776 the book had passed through eleven editions and had made Dodsley so much profit on his £250 investment that he is said to have returned the copyright to the author. Other works he published in the 1760s include Richard Bentley's tragedy *Philodamus* (1767), George Frere's *A Short History of Barbados* (1768), Goldsmith's anonymous "History of England" in *The Geography and History of England* (1765), Lennox's comedy *The Sister* (1769), Horace Walpole's *Historic Doubts on the Life and Reign of King Richard the Third* (1768), and John Leland's *Discourses on Various Subjects* (1769).

The 1770s show the breadth of Dodsley's publishing interests. His titles include such varied works as Arthur Young's *A Course of Experimental Agriculture* (1770); William Cadogan's *Dissertation on the Gout* (1771); and *Letters Written by the Late Right Honourable Philip Dormer Stanhope, Earl of Chesterfield, to His Son, Philip Stanhope, Esq.* (1774), for which Dodsley paid Eugenia Stanhope, the son's widow, the unprecedented sum of fifteen hundred pounds and for which he would still be reaping profits in 1793 with the tenth edition. He also published new editions of Lennox's translations of Louise Françoise de la Baume le Blanc, Duchess de Vallière's *Meditations and Penitential Prayers* (1774) and of Pierre Mathurin de L'Ecluse des Loges's *Memoirs of Maximilian de Bethune, Duke of Sully* (1778). Thomas Warton's *The History of English Poetry* (1774–1781) was published by Dodsley in conjunction with six other booksellers. Dodsley also published the *Speech of Edmund Burke, Esq. on American Taxation* (1775); Jenyns's *A View of the Internal Evidence of the Christian Religion* (1776), which reached a seventh edition in 1785; the first (and only) volume of John Berkenhout's *Biographia Literaria* (1777); an edition of Pindar's odes (1778); Philip

Thicknesse's *The New Prose Bath Guide* (1778?); and William Marshall's *Experiments and Observations Concerning Agriculture and the Weather* (1779). The range is extended with further echoes of the first master of Tully's Head: a collection of Robert Dodsley's works (1777) and Thomas Hull's *Select Letters between the Late Duchess of Somerset, Lady Luxborough, Mr. Whistler, Miss Dolman, Mr. R. Dodsley, William Shenstone, Esq., and Others* (1778). At the end of Hull's edition appears an advertisement listing forty-one publications currently available from Tully's Head.

In the late 1770s Isaac Reed, who is mainly known today for his 1785 edition of Shakespeare's works, began to play a valuable role for the Dodsley firm. Besides editing an edition of Robert's *A Select Collection of Old Plays* in twelve volumes (1780), Reed provided notes for new editions of both Dodsley's *A Collection of Poems. By Several Hands* (1782) and George Pearch's four-volume supplement to the latter (1783). Reed's most vital contribution to publishing history was his preservation, in handwritten notes, of extracts of the Dodsleys' publishing agreements with authors. The extracts were made from the original Dodsley ledgers, which are no longer extant and which Reed received from James's executors a few months after the latter's death.

At some point Dodsley became a member of the Congeries, a booksellers' club that afforded him a share in two consequential productions: Johnson's *Prefaces, Biographical and Critical, to the Works of the English Poets* (1779–1781) and the first complete edition of Johnson's works (1787). Before the latter appeared, however, he seems to have decided to retire: Nichols says, without dating the occasion, that James announced his retirement, then changed his mind two weeks later and advertised that he was back in business. Most likely Dodsley's brief departure from business occurred in late 1786, for in a letter to Dodsley on 11 November of that year Anstey assured Dodsley that he has a right to retire after such long service.

On 7 June 1787 Dodsley lost twenty-five hundred pounds worth of uninsured stock in a fire that began in a cabinetmaker's shop in Little Wild Street, Lincoln's Inn, and spread to the warehouse Dodsley kept in the area. The additional business location suggests the growth his business had enjoyed in recent years, as does his nomination the following year to the office of sheriff of the City and of Westminster, a duty he escaped by paying a fine. It was probably also during these years (Nichols provides no date) that Dodsley bought an estate between Cheslehurst and Bromley.

The nature of James's publications in the 1780s clearly reveals the changes that had come about in the Dodsley firm, both in terms of the proprietor's business interests and his status in the trade. Whereas Robert's business and reputation had been built on publishing poetry and the classics, James was publishing considerably fewer works in these areas; it seems that belles lettres was no longer central to the house plan. Even more revealing are the imprints for James's publications. Since he had become a member of the Congeries, much of his business involved joint undertakings with the City's major booksellers. Consequently, more often than not one finds James's name linked with many others in imprints of large printings of multivolume editions of works by established authors. For instance, he appears with six other booksellers in the imprint of Thomas Warton's *History of English Poetry,* with a like number for the thirteenth edition of Cheselden's *The Anatomy of the Human Body* (1792), with fifteen booksellers for the tenth edition of Johnson's dictionary (1792), with twenty-three booksellers for Vicesimus Knox's *Extracts, Elegant, Instructive, and Entertaining, in Prose* (1791) and John Milton's *Paradise Lost* (1793), and with twenty-seven booksellers for an edition of the *Spectator* in 1788. These collaborations also led to the frequent appearance of his name in imprints as a seller of works published by others.

In short, by the 1780s James had become a wealthy businessman at the center of the London publishing trade; unlike Robert, who had come to the trade as an inexperienced interloper and gradually earned eminence outside of the monopoly, James had become part of the establishment. Also, in contrast to Robert's literary sensitivity and enthusiasm for new projects, James seems to have contented himself with capitalizing on the prosperity that an established name continued to produce.

During the early 1790s Dodsley seems to have turned over the retail portion of his business to George Nichol, bookseller to George III, and to have operated as a wholesaler of his own product. The *Annual Register* was taken over by the Rivingtons in 1791. Dodsley's name continued to appear in imprints, but his solo publications were considerably fewer.

James Dodsley died on 19 February 1797 and was buried in St. James Church, Westminster. On an open book of marble in the chancel he is remembered as a "man of retired and contemplative turn of mind" who was "upright and liberal in all his dealings" and a "friend to the afflicted in general, and to the poor of this parish in particular." His estate, estimated to be worth seventy thousand

Title page for Thomas Percy's collection of old popular ballads, published by Robert Dodsley's brother James. Robert Dodsley retired from the firm in 1759 and died in 1764.

pounds, was distributed principally to his nephews and nieces. His stock and copyrights were sold at the Globe Tavern, Fleet Street, on 18 October 1797, bringing an end to the house of Dodsley.

Letters:

The Correspondence of Robert Dodsley 1733–1764, edited by James E. Tierney (Cambridge: Cambridge University Press, 1988).

Biographies:

Alexander Chalmers, "Life of Dodsley," in *The Works of the English Poets, from Chaucer to Cowper,* volume 25 (London: Whittingham, 1810), pp. 313–323;

Ralph Straus, *Robert Dodsley: Poet, Publisher and Playwright* (London: John Lane, 1910).

References:

R. W. Chapman, "Dodsley's *Collection of Poems*," *Oxford Bibliographical Society: Proceedings and Papers,* 3, no. 3 (1933): 269–316;

Thomas W. Copeland, "Edmund Burke and the Book Reviews in Dodsley's *Annual Register,*" *PMLA,* 57 (June 1942): 446–468;

William Prideaux Courtney, *Dodsley's Collection of Poetry, Its Contents and Contributors: A Chapter in the History of English Literature in the Eighteenth Century* (London: Humphreys, 1910);

Austin Dobson, "At Tully's Head," in his *Eighteenth Century Vignettes,* volume 2 (New York: Dodd, Mead, 1894), pp. 28–56;

Donald D. Eddy, "Dodsley's *Collection of Poems by Several Hands* (Six Volumes), 1758 Index of Authors," *Papers of the Bibliographical Society of America,* 19 (1966): 9–30;

Eddy, "Dodsley's *Œconomy of Human Life,* 1750–1751," *Modern Philology,* 85 (May 1988): 460–479;

James Gray, "More Blood than Brains: Robert Dodsley and the *Cleone* Affair," *Dalhousie Review,* 54 (Summer 1974): 207–227;

Raymond Havens, "Changing Taste in the Eighteenth Century: A Study of Dryden's and Dodsley's Miscellanies," *PMLA,* 44 (March–June 1929): 501–536;

Roger P. McCutcheon, "Johnson and Dodsley's *Preceptor,* 1748," *Tulane Studies in English,* 3 (1952): 125–132;

John Nichols, *Literary Anecdotes of the Eighteenth Century,* 9 volumes (London: Nichols, Son & Bentley, 1812–1815);

Dale Randal, "Dodsley's *Preceptor* – A Window into the Eighteenth Century," *Journal of Rutgers University Library,* 22 (1958): 10–22;

James E. Tierney, "*The Museum,* the 'Super-Excellent Magazine,'" *Studies in English Literature,* 13 (1973): 503–515;

Tierney, "Responses to Tyrants: Robert Dodsley to William Warburton" and "Robert Dodsley to David Garrick," in *Sent as a Gift: Eight Correspondences from the Eighteenth Century,* edited by Alan T. McKenzie (Athens & London: University of Georgia Press, 1993), pp. 109–128, 215–219;

Tierney, "Robert Dodsley: First Printer and Stationer to the Society," in *The Virtuoso Tribe of Arts and Sciences,* edited by D. G. C. Allan and John L. Abbot (Athens & London; University of Georgia Press, 1992), pp. 281–292;

William B. Todd, "A Bibliographical Account of the *Annual Register, 1758–1825,*" *Library,* fifth series 16 (June 1961): 104–120;

Todd, "Concurrent Printing: An Analysis of Dodsley's *Collection,*" *Papers of the Bibliographical Society of America,* 46 (January–March 1952): 45–57;

Richard Wendorf, "Robert Dodsley as Editor," *Studies in Bibliography,* 31 (1978): 235–248;

John C. Weston, "Burke's Editorship of the Historical Articles in Dodsley's *Annual Register,*" *Papers of the Bibliographical Society of America,* 51 (July–September 1957): 244–249;

George P. Winship Jr., "The Printing History of *The World,*" in *Studies in the Early English Periodical,* edited by Richmond P. Bond (Chapel Hill: University of North Carolina Press, 1957), pp. 183–195.

Papers:
Holograph letters to and from Robert and James Dodsley are in the British Library; the Bodleian Library, Oxford; the Birmingham Public Libraries; the Somerset County Record Office; the Houghton and Harvard College Theatre Collection at Harvard University; the Harry Ransom Humanities Research Center, University of Texas at Austin; and the James M. Osborn Collection at the Beinecke Library, Yale University. Extracts of publishing agreements with authors, copied from the original Dodsley ledgers (no longer extant) by Isaac Reed are in the New College Library, Edinburgh; a copy of the Reed extracts made by Edmund Malone is in the James M. Osborn Collection, Beinecke Library, Yale University.

– *James E. Tierney*

James Edwards

(London: 1784 – 1815)

The leading antiquarian book dealer in England, if not in the world, in the late eighteenth century, James Edwards amassed a great private collection of rare books and manuscripts and a small but choice collection of ancient Greek vases. Today he is best known for the distinctive bookbindings and the fore-edge paintings with which he embellished many books. His name also appears as publisher on the title pages of more than a hundred books, usually together with those of other publishers such as Joseph Johnson, Edward and Silvester Harding (especially for illustrated books), George G. and John Robinson, James Robson, Robert Faulder, and Thomas Payne. He was fluent in French and Italian, and he published books in both languages. On a few occasions he obtained the original plates or woodcuts for books that had been published earlier and republished them, sometimes with the original date of publication on the title page.

About 25 percent of Edwards's publications were literary works, and about half of these were books of poetry. Although his publishing output was rather small, it was distinguished by its quality, in terms of both textual importance and physical beauty. Edwards employed the best printers and book illustrators, and he sometimes had a few copies of books he published printed on vellum, silk, or satin and had the illustrations colored by hand. Some of his books rank among the finest produced during the last fifteen years of the eighteenth century, a golden age of British printing and publishing.

Edwards was born in Halifax, Yorkshire, on 8 September 1756, the third of eight children of William and Jane Edwards. His father was a successful bookseller, bookbinder, and publisher, and James and three of his brothers entered the family business. The Edwards firm had a close connection with that of the prominent London publisher Johnson; when Edwards was sent to London on business he stayed at Johnson's home, where he would have become acquainted with such members of Johnson's circle as William Blake, Henry Fuseli, Thomas Paine, Joseph Priestley, and Mary Wollstonecraft.

In 1784 William Edwards helped two of his sons, James and his younger brother John, open a bookshop in London's fashionable Pall Mall. They soon published an impressive catalogue that established them as dealers in the finest rare books and manuscripts. This catalogue, of which no copy is known to survive, listed books from the libraries of N. Wilson of Pontefract, Henry Bradshaw of Marple Hall, Cheshire, and two eminent antiquaries; presumably these books came from the stock of William Edwards and Sons in Halifax. In *The Sexagenarian* (1818) William Beloe says that James Edwards "was the introducer of a new aera, in the profession of which he was so successful a member" and that he was "the first person who professedly displayed in the metropolis shelves of valuable books in splendid bindings." The shop, according to Beloe, "became the resort of the gay morning loungers of both sexes," where students, scholars, and persons of taste were invited to examine the rare books and manuscripts. At some point John moved to Paris, where he died in 1793, and James carried on the business alone.

On 28 January 1785 Edwards received a patent for a method of rendering vellum transparent, which made possible a new type of bookbinding: a drawing or painting would be made on the vellum, and the vellum would be used to bind a book with the painting on the underside; thus, the painting could be seen but would not be damaged by handling. This type of binding had been produced in Halifax at least since 1781; it is not known whether James Edwards was the actual inventor. Some credit his father with the invention.

The "Edwards of Halifax" bindings, as any binding by or for a member of the Edwards family has come to be known, were done in a variety of styles in addition to those with paintings under the vellum. The most common is the "Etruscan" style, a brown calf binding in which the center panels of the front and back covers are stained with acid in a tree-like pattern known as "tree calf" and with borders based on the designs on Greek vases.

The "Edwards of Halifax" name is also associated with fore-edge paintings, pictures painted on the fore-edge of the book's pages and which are revealed only when the leaves of a book are fanned. The origins of this curious art form are unknown,

James Edwards (The Book Collector, *Winter 1984*)

but some of the finest examples were produced by the Edwards family. James Edwards also sometimes had the title pages and initial letters of early printed books illuminated before selling them.

On 24 May 1785 Edwards outbid King George III's agent for the Bedford Missal (or Book of Hours), a magnificent illuminated medieval manuscript, at the auction of the collection of Margaret Cavendish Holles Harley, Duchess of Portland. He bought it for £213 3s. and kept it for his personal library. He added many more treasures to his library, especially incunabula and other early books printed on vellum. One of his prized possessions was the only known copy of the first edition of the works of Livy on vellum.

Edwards made a specialty of importing both new and antiquarian books from Europe, and he often made bookbuying trips to the Continent. In his *Reminiscences of a Literary Life* (1836) the Reverend

Thomas Frognall Dibdin wrote that Edwards "is said on more than one occasion to have followed in the rear of Bonaparte's armies — and leaving that renowned warrior to the capture of cities, and the discomfiture of armies, Mr. Edwards preferred a conquest over a *vellum Livy* and a *Capo di Monte Vase*." He sold some of the books through his catalogues, some at public auctions, and some in his shop. In 1787 he traveled to France, Switzerland, and Italy with three other London book dealers: James Robson, Robert Faulder, and Peter Molini. Their main purpose was to examine the library of Maffeo Pinelli in Venice, of which a six-volume catalogue had recently been published. Edwards and Robson purchased the library in 1788, shipped it to London, and sold it at a series of auctions from 2 March 1789 until 8 March 1790. The Pinelli sale was barely profitable, but the publicity it generated enhanced Edwards's reputation. He sold at least five other collections at auction, sometimes in combination with other dealers: the *Bibliotheca Paitoni* of Giovanni Battista Paitoni, bought in Venice and sold in London between 22 November 1790 and 17 February 1791; the *Bibliotheca Parisiana,* of uncertain ownership, to which was added some books from the library of Cardinal Etienne Charles de Loménie de Brienne, the French prime minister and a collector of incunabula and books printed by Aldus Manutius, which was sold in London on 26 March 1791 and "the Five Days following," according to the sale catalogue; the library of a Signor Santorio, which was sold in Paris on 12 to 14 May 1791; the library of William Wootton, which was sold from 24 February to 2 March 1795; and a collection of books from a monastery in Bamberg, which was sold anonymously at Leigh and Sotheby's on 15 June 1799.

In the autumn of 1789 Edwards traveled to Italy, where he purchased the choicest portions of the libraries of "Cavaliere Zanetti" of Venice and Natale Salichetti, the papal physician, of Rome. He spent the next several months preparing a catalogue of these acquisitions, and he published it in 1790; he considered it his finest catalogue. Edwards published at least seven catalogues of rare books – in 1784 (or perhaps early January 1785), 1787, 1789, 1790, 1794, 1796, and 1800 – and in 1790 a catalogue of gold coins. Apparently, he did not put out a catalogue of his own publications, but at the end of some of the rare-book catalogues are several pages of advertisements for books that he had recently published and new European books that he had imported.

In 1791 Edwards's brother Richard, the youngest of the family, opened a bookshop in London's New Bond Street. He also did some publishing, and today he is best known for having commissioned Blake to illustrate an edition of Edward Young's *The Complaint, and the Consolation; or, Night Thoughts,* which he published in 1797. The prospectus for this book says that copies may be obtained not only from Richard Edwards but also from "Mr. Edwards of Pall Mall" and from the Historic Gallery, also on Pall Mall. When the book came out, however, only Richard was listed as publisher. James and Richard Edwards collaborated in publishing several other books.

As a publisher James Edwards is best known for bringing out an edition of Horace Walpole's *The Castle of Otranto* (1791) printed by Giambattista Bodoni of Parma, Italy, and of William Roscoe's *The Life of Lorenzo de' Medici* (1795). Although Bodoni's printing was handsome, the book was so full of mis-

takes that Walpole thought it unfit to be sold in England. Corrections were made by the insertion of cancel leaves. According to Arthur Young, Edwards also commissioned Bodoni to print 250 copies each of the works of the Greek poets Pindar, Sophocles, Homer, and Theocritus; the Latin poets Horace, Virgil, Lucretius, and Plautus; and the Italian poets Dante, Petrarch, Ludovico Ariosto, and Torquato Tasso. These editions, however, never appeared. With several other publishers Edwards did publish Ariosto's *Orlando Furioso* (1789), Virgil's *Opera* (1793), an Italian translation of Walpole's *The Castle of Otranto* (1795), and a five-volume edition of Walpole's works (1798). He also arranged to have Pierre Didot in Paris print an edition of the Book of Common Prayer in 1791, but because of the troubled times Didot was not able to ship copies to England until 1802; according to the title page it was "sold by W. Edwards & Sons, Halifax."

Roscoe's *The Life of Lorenzo de' Medici* was a huge success, and the firm of Thomas Cadell and William Davies bought the copyright from the author soon after the first edition appeared. A second edition came out in 1796 with the imprint of A. Strahan, Cadell and Davies, and J. Edwards; a third edition in 1797; and a fourth in 1800. It was one of Edwards's most profitable publishing ventures. Another success was George Ellis's *Specimens of the Early English Poets* (1790); three editions were published in 1790 alone.

In 1791 Johnson and Edwards released a prospectus for an edition of John Milton's poems, with notes and a translation of the Latin and Italian poems by William Cowper and illustrations by Fuseli. Although Edwards was to be the copublisher, the book was Johnson's idea, and he was the one who dealt with Cowper. Johnson and Edwards were no doubt inspired by Alderman John Boydell's celebrated Shakespeare Gallery, an art gallery and publishing venture that was also on Pall Mall and in which Edwards and Johnson may have had a financial interest. The Milton edition was to have consisted of a large volume with thirty plates engraved by Blake, Bartolozzi, Holloway, Sharp, and other artists and two smaller volumes of text, smaller plates, and vignettes. The book was never published, partly because Cowper kept putting off the completion of the notes and translations and partly because Boydell objected to it on the grounds that it would compete with an illustrated edition of the works of Milton that he planned to publish.

Four books that Edwards published using the plates from an earlier edition were Thomas Worlidge's *A Select Collection of Drawings from Curious An-*

Examples of "Edwards of Halifax" bindings: (top) paintings under transparent vellum on the covers of a copy of a 1783 edition of William Mason's The English Garden; *(bottom) an "Etruscan" binding (Saint John's Seminary, Camarillo, California)*

Example of a fore-edge painting, a technique associated with the Edwards family. This one depicts Coghill Hall in Yorkshire and is on a copy of a prayer book published in Paris by Didot in 1791 and bound by Thomas Edwards circa 1802 (Courtesy of Henry E. Huntington Memorial Library and Art Gallery, San Marino, California).

tique *Gems,* dated 1768; volume one, part 1 of Samuel Butler's *Hudibras* (1793), with Hogarth's original copperplates used for printing the illustrations (the second volume was published by Benjamin and John White of Fleet Street); Hans Holbein's *The Dance of Death* (1794?), with notes by Francis Douce and illustrations printed from Wenceslas Hollar's original copperplates, which were carefully rebitten before being reused; and the third edition of Maximilian I's *Triumphs* (1796), with notes by Adam von Bartsch, printed from Hans Burgkmair's original woodblocks.

Edwards and his neighbors on Pall Mall, Edward and Silvester Harding, commissioned Lady Diana Beauclerk to illustrate editions of Gottfried August Bürger's *Leonora* (1796) and John Dryden's *Fables* (1797). Both works were printed by Thomas Bensley, one of England's best printers. Fuseli provided the frontispiece for Edwards's edition of Sir Brooke Boothby's *Sorrows, Sacred to the Memory of Penelope* (1796), a handsome folio with several illustrations by other artists.

Other illustrated books published by Edwards were William Hodges's *Select Views in India* (1786, 1788) and *Travels in India* (1793); William Birch's *Délices de la Grande Bretagne* (1791); French and English versions of Moses Harris's *The Aurelian* (1794), a republication of a beautiful book on butterflies first published in 1766; John Gabriel Stedman's *Narrative, of a Five Years' Expedition, Against the Revolted Negroes of Surinam* (1796), some of the plates of which were engraved by Blake; Joseph Strutt's *A Complete View of the Dress and Habits of the People of England* (1796, 1799) in two volumes with 143 plates; James Edward Smith and John Abbot's *The Natural History of the Rarer Lepidopterous Insects of Georgia* (1797), another beautiful book on butterflies, which

Fuseli said would immortalize Edwards; George Vancouver's *A Voyage of Discovery to the North Pacific Ocean, and Round the World* (1798) in three volumes, with a fourth volume of maps and plates; Jean-François de Galaup, comte de La Pérouse's *Voyage de La Pérouse Autour du Monde* (1799), a reprint of the first edition (1797), and the first complete English translation of the work, *A Voyage Round the World* (1799), in two volumes with an atlas of sixty-nine charts and plates.

A trip to the Continent in 1797 seriously undermined Edwards's health, and he decided to retire. Late that year he started to dispose of his stock of books and had his shop converted into a private residence. By the end of 1798 he had turned over the business to Robert Harding Evans, an auctioneer. He did not completely retire, however, for he continued to seek out books for a few of his best customers, among them Francis Douce, Roscoe, and George John, second Earl Spencer. In 1800, through an exchange with the Vienna library, he brought to England some books from the library of Prince Eugène de Savoie. In 1802 he purchased eleven pieces of ancient Greek pottery that had belonged to the king of Naples; the collection included the "Capo di Monte" vase, the largest ancient Greek vase then known, for which Edwards is reputed to have paid a thousand pounds. (It is now in the Metropolitan Museum of Art in New York.) He also published a few books after 1798; according to diarist Joseph Farington's entry for 22 January 1804, he was then planning to publish a continuation of Walpole's *Anecdotes of Painting in England* (1762–1771), although this continuation never appeared.

At an anonymous sale at Christie's on 25 to 28 April 1804 Edwards disposed of some books from his personal library and dealer's stock. On 10 September 1805 he married Katharine Bromhead, daughter of the Reverend Edward B. Bromhead, rector of Reepham, near Lincoln. In 1807 he bought a mansion and 121 acres of land in Harrow-on-the-Hill from his friend Lord John Rushout Northwick, an art collector he had met on the Continent. Edwards and his wife moved into the mansion in the autumn of 1808 and raised five children there. In 1811 he negotiated the sale of several books printed by the first English printer, William Caxton, from the library of Lincoln Cathedral to Earl Spencer.

In June 1814 Edwards went to Paris – mainly, it seems, to see the effects of the Napoleonic Wars on the city. While there he bought some books, which he offered to a few of his longtime customers. The following year, prompted in part by failing health and in part by the high prices brought at the Roxburghe and Stanley sales, he decided to sell his remaining rare books and manuscripts. Early in 1815 the books were shipped to a house in George Street, Hanover Square, and Edwards and his family took up residence there so that he could supervise the preparation of the catalogue. The auction was conducted by his successor, Evans, from 5 to 11 April, at Evans's shop in Pall Mall. The Bedford Missal brought £687 15s. from George Spencer, Marquis of Blandford; the Livy on vellum fetched £903 from Sir Mark Masterman Sykes. Both books are now in the British Library. The sale, which also included the Greek vases (only four of the lesser ones were sold), realized a total of £8,432, or somewhat more than £10 per lot, a result that Dibdin calls "unprecedented in the annals of book-sales!"

Leaving instructions that his coffin be made from the shelves of his library, Edwards died on 2 January 1816 and was buried in the churchyard at St. Mary's Church, Harrow. On a wall of the church, next to the organ, is a marble bas-relief with his portrait and representations of the Livy edition, the Bedford Missal, the Capo di Monte and two other vases, and a short eulogistic inscription.

In *The Sexegenarian* Beloe refers to Edwards's manners as "courteous and courtier-like" and says that some complained that "his enunciation was affectedly soft, and that he had too much the air and grimace of a Frenchman." Edwards had a wide circle of friends and business associates, among them Blake, Fuseli, Walpole, Roscoe, Dibdin, Thomas Johnes, Queen Maria Carolina of Naples, and Sir William and Lady Emma Hamilton. Dibdin wrote parts of his *Bibliomania* (1809) and *The Bibliographical Decameron* (1817) while a guest at Edwards's Harrow estate; the two men had a falling-out, however, be-

cause Dibdin disparaged some of Edwards's books shortly before the 1815 auction.

Despite the relative brevity of his career, James Edwards obtained a secure place in the history of English bookselling, bookbinding, book collecting, and publishing, and he carried out all of these activities with flair and consummate good taste. In *The Bibliographical Decameron* Dibdin says, "no man ever did such wonderful things towards the acquisition of rare, beautiful, and truly classical productions in the shape of a BOKE: and it is truly observed upon his monument in Harrow church . . . that 'to his skilful research and liberal spirit of enterprize his country is indebted for the rarest specimens, biblical and classical, in the typographic art. . . .' " He might also have said that it is to Edwards that England is indebted for the publication of some important and beautiful books and for really splendid bookbindings and fore-edge paintings.

References:

William Beloe, *The Sexegenarian; or, The Recollections of a Literary Life,* second edition (London: Rivington, 1818);

G. E. Bentley Jr., "The Bookseller as Diplomat: James Edwards, Lord Grenville, and Earl Spencer in 1800," *Book Collector,* 33 (Winter 1984): 471–485;

Bentley, "The Edwardses of Halifax and Bibliomania," *Bibliographical Society of Australia and New Zealand Bulletin,* 11 (1989): 141–156;

Bentley, "The 'Edwardses of Halifax' as Booksellers by Catalogue 1749–1835," *Studies in Bibliography,* 45 (1992): 187–222;

Bentley, "The 1821 Edwards Catalogue," *Blake: An Illustrated Quarterly,* 17 (Spring 1984): 154–156;

Bentley, "The Great Illustrated-Book Publishers of the 1790's and William Blake," in *Editing Illustrated Books: Papers given at the fifteenth annual Conference on Editorial Problems, University of Toronto, 2–3 November 1979,* edited by William Blissett (New York: Garland, 1980), pp. 57–96;

Bentley, "Richard Edwards, Publisher of Church-and-King Pamphlets and of William Blake," *Studies in Bibliography,* 41 (1988): 283–315;

"Bibliotheca Edwardsiana," *Gentleman's Magazine,* 85 (March 1815): 254–255; (April 1815): 359;

William Clarke, *Repertorium Bibliographicum; or, Some Account of the Most Celebrated British Libraries* (London: Clarke, 1819);

Thomas Frognall Dibdin, *The Bibliographical Decameron,* 3 volumes (London: Printed for the author by W. Bulmer & Co. Shakespeare Press, sold by G. & W. Nichol, Payne & Foss, Evans, John & Arthur Arch, Triphook, and J. Major, 1817);

Dibdin, *Bibliomania* (London: Printed for Longman, Hurst, Rees & Orme, 1809);

Dibdin, *Reminiscences of a Literary Life,* 2 volumes (London: Major, 1836; New York: AMS, 1970);

Rosa P. Edwards, "A Group of Stuart Miniatures and Their History," *Notes and Queries,* new series 31 (September 1984): 352–356;

Edwards, "James Edwards, Giambattista Bodoni and the Castle of Otranto," *Publishing History,* 18 (1985): 5–48;

Joseph Farington, *The Diary of Joseph Farington,* edited by Kenneth Garlick and Angus MacIntyre (New Haven & London: Published for the Paul Mellon Centre for Studies in British Art by Yale University Press, 1979), pp. 2223–2224;

William Younger Fletcher, *English Book Collectors* (London: Kegan Paul, Trench, Trübner, 1902);

John E. Grant, Edward J. Rose, Michael J. Tolley, and David V. Erdman, eds., *William Blake's Designs for Edward Young's* Night Thoughts, volume 1 (Oxford: Clarendon Press, 1980), pp. 4–8, 85–87;

Frank Haigh, "Edwards of Halifax," *Librarian and Book World,* 35 (July 1946): 185–188;

Haigh, "Edwards of Halifax," *Printing Review,* 13 (1947): 27, 30;

T. W. Hanson, "Edwards of Halifax," *Bookbinding Trades Journal,* 2, no. 6 (1911): 84–87; no. 7 (1911): 100–103;

Hanson, "Edwards of Halifax, Bookbinders," *Book Handbook,* 1, part 6 (1948): 329–338;

Hanson, "Edwards of Halifax: Book Sellers, Collectors and Book-Binders," *Reports, &c. Read before the Halifax Antiquarian Society, 1912* (Halifax, 1913), pp. 142–200;

Hanson, "Richard Edwards, Publisher," *Times Literary Supplement,* 8 August 1942, p. 396;

Hanson, *The Story of Old Halifax* (Halifax: King, 1920);

G. Bernard Hughes, "Edwards of Halifax and His Technique," *Country Life,* 102 (12 December 1947): 1219–1220;

Hughes, "English Fore-Edge Paintings," *Country Life,* 122 (26 September 1957): 602–603;

"James Edwards, Esq. of Harrow," *Gentleman's Magazine,* 86 (1816): 180–181;

Ian Jenkins, "Adam Buck and the Vogue for Greek Vases," *Burlington Magazine,* 130 (June 1988): 448–457;

Joseph Johnson and James Edwards, *Milton. Sept. 1, 1791. Proposals for Engraving and Publishing by Subscription Thirty Capital Plates, From Subjects in Milton* (London: Printed for J. Johnson & J. Edwards, 1791);

Bernard C. Middleton, *A History of English Craft Bookbinding Technique* (New York: Hafner, 1963);

Richard J. Moore-Colyer, ed., *A Land of Pure Delight: Selections from the Letters of Thomas Johnes of Hafod, Cardiganshire, 1748–1816* (Llandysul, Wales: Gomer, 1992);

A. N. L. Munby, *Connoisseurs and Medieval Miniatures, 1750–1850* (Oxford: Clarendon Press, 1972);

Howard M. Nixon and Mirjam Foot, *The History of Decorated Bookbinding in England* (Oxford: Clarendon Press, 1992);

Sir Thomas Phillipps, comp., *MSS. in Edwards's Sale 1815. with the Purchasers Names* (Middle Hill: Middle Hill Press, 1861?);

Seymour de Ricci, *English Collectors of Books and Their Marks of Ownership* (Cambridge: Cambridge University Press, 1930);

H. P. Rohde, "De etruskiske Bogbind; A propos en Gave fra Horace Walpole," *Bogvennen, Ny Raekke,* 9 (1954): 1–28, 85–86;

Nancy Christenson Swan, "A Study of Modern Fore-Edge Painting," thesis, Catholic University of America, 1956;

Carl J. Weber, *Fore-Edge Painting; A Historical Survey of a Curious Art in Book Decoration* (Irvington-on-Hudson, N.Y.: Harvey House, 1966);

Weber, *A Thousand and One Fore-Edge Paintings* (Waterville, Maine: Colby College Press, 1949);

Arthur Young, *Travels, during the Years 1787, 1788, and 1789, Undertaken More Particularly with a View of Ascertaining the Cultivation, Wealth, Resources, and National Prosperity, of the Kingdom of France* (Bury St. Edmunds: Printed by J. Rackham for W. Richardson, London, 1792).

Papers:

T. W. Hanson's unpublished biography, "Edwards of Halifax," together with his extensive notes on, and correspondence concerning, James Edwards, are in the Modern Manuscripts Reading Room of the Bodleian Library, Oxford. Edwards's contract with Joseph Strutt for *A Complete View of the Dress and Habits of the People of England* is in the British Library (Add. 38,729, fol. 230).

– Philip J. Weimerskirch

George Faulkner

(Dublin: 1724 – 1775)

Although critics often measure George Faulkner's contributions to the British print trade of his era in terms of his publication of the works of Jonathan Swift, his career featured forays into a variety of social and political issues. The wide range of historical and literary volumes that he published, alone or in collaboration, warranted Swift's description of Faulkner as "the Prince of Dublin Printers." In his newspaper, the *Dublin Journal,* Faulkner recorded for more than fifty years the events that marked the city of Dublin during the eighteenth century. His pursuit of the truth in the editorial pages of his newspaper, together with his interest in effecting social change in Ireland, often fostered conflict between the printer and the authorities. He was also involved in a celebrated clash with Samuel Richardson over the issue of copyright infringement.

Although the date of Faulkner's birth remains uncertain, most sources list it as 1699. The son of a butcher, Faulkner attended the academy of Dr. Lloyd, the most eminent Irish schoolmaster of his era. He was apprenticed at fourteen to the printer Thomas Hume of Essex Street, serving as a copy editor and compositor for Hume's newspaper, the *Dublin Courant.* At the conclusion of his apprenticeship Faulkner proposed marriage to Hume's daughter, but she declined. Faulkner migrated in the early 1720s to London, where, as a journeyman printer, he joined the print shop of William Bowyer Sr., the father of an acquaintance of Faulkner's.

In 1724 Faulkner returned to Dublin; purchased two newspapers, the *Dublin Journal* and the *Dublin Post Boy;* and established a printing business at Pembroke Court, Castle Street. Later that year he printed for the bookseller George Ewing his first pamphlet, *A Defence of the Conduct of the People of Ireland, in Their Unanimous Refusal of Mr. Wood's Copper-Money.* The first issue of the *Dublin Journal* appeared on 27 March 1725, and in May he published one of his earliest subscription enterprises, an unauthorized reprint of Swift's *Fraud Detected; or, The Hibernian Patriot.* The *Dublin Post Boy* first saw publication during Christmas week of 1725. The following year Faulkner and James Hoey opened a bookshop and printing house at the corner of Christ Church Lane in Skinner's Row. In the summer Faulkner traveled to London, where he met and married Mary Taylor, an English widow. Faulkner's biographers attribute the early success of Faulkner and Hoey's printing ventures to Hoey's organizational acumen, although Hoey lacked any formal training in the trade. They moved in 1729 to a more prestigious location, "the Pamphlet Shop, opposite the Tholstel," but dissolved their partnership in 1730; the nature of their dispute was never divulged.

Faulkner established a new shop on Essex Street after purchasing Hoey's interest in the *Dublin Journal.* Early in 1730 Faulkner informed Swift that he intended to publish Swift's works by subscription in Ireland. Although Swift was skeptical about Faulkner's proposition, later that year Faulkner published, with the author's apparent blessing, Swift's *A Vindication of His Ex – y the Lord C – , from the Charge of Favouring None but Toryes, High-Churchmen, and Jacobites.* Presumably angry over his former partner's good fortune in forging a potentially lucrative business relationship with Swift, Hoey inaugurated a battle of words in the Dublin press, reporting – among other rumors – that Faulkner planned to cease publication of the *Dublin Journal* and permanently relocate to England. Faulkner answered Hoey's salvos with a vengeance in the *Dublin Journal* and then – fearing prosecution for libel – fled to England in September 1730. As he embarked on his voyage Faulkner injured his shin, and he ignored the wound until his arrival in London. According to the *Hibernian Magazine* (1775), "he then found his error in not having paid a proper attention to his hurt, for the journey had so inflamed it to so violent a degree that the best assistance could not prevent a Gangrene, which spread so rapidly, that he had no other means of saving his life, but by the loss of his limb." On his return to Dublin in June 1731 Faulkner announced in the *Dublin Journal* that a "dangerous and tedious indisposition" had necessitated his lengthy absence.

Skillful at procuring subscribers for his publications, Faulkner maintained a profitable business in a city rife with printers and booksellers, including such luminaries as Hoey, George Grierson, George and Alexander Ewing, and Samuel Fairbrother. Employing smaller typefaces enabled Faulkner to in-

George Faulkner (Courtesy of Providence Public Library)

crease substantially the amount of advertising copy in the *Dublin Journal,* and by the 1740s he enjoyed annual profits of at least nine hundred pounds from the newspaper's advertisements alone. Faulkner's fondness for the Elzevir typeface earned him the nickname "the oaken-footed Elzevir."

In February 1731 Faulkner published in the *Journal* excerpts from Swift's pamphlet *Considerations upon Two Bills Sent down from the R- H- the H— of L— to the H—ble H— of C— Relating to the Clergy of I*****d* (1732) in an effort to influence a vote on bills that would have resulted in the creation of a powerful voting bloc of bishops in both houses of Parliament. Likely responsible for the defeat of the bills, Faulkner's publication of the excerpts warranted his arrest under Irish libel laws. In October 1733 he was censured before the House of Lords and discharged without the assessment of a fine. As Robert E. Ward notes: "Faulkner quickly learned that print-

ing material which concerned public figures, whether true or false, violated the public peace."

On 9 February 1733 Faulkner agreed to print a collected edition of Swift's works. On the publication of the three-volume edition in January 1735 Faulkner proclaimed that "in all other Editions that have been publish'd in London and in Dublin are very many gross Errors and Mistakes . . . so that it may be truly said, a genuine and correct Edition of this Author's Works was never publish'd till this time." Including more than two hundred items of Swift's poetry and prose, the edition proved to be a substantial financial success for Faulkner, as is evidenced by an anonymous couplet Faulkner published in the *Dublin Journal* in February 1735: "Poor, Honest George, Swift's Works to print, / Thy Fortune's made or nothing in't."

The increasingly close association of Faulkner and Swift caused difficulties between Swift and Benjamin Motte, Swift's London publisher, who objected to

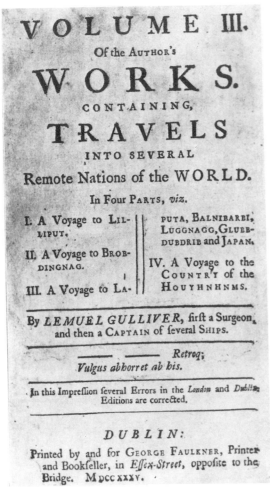

Title page and illustration from Faulkner's "genuine and correct Edition" of the works of Jonathan Swift

the author's inattention to the British editions of his work in favor of Faulkner's Irish editions. In November 1735, the London Chancery Court awarded Motte an injunction against the importation of any of Faulkner's editions of Swift's works into England, abrogating the right of Irish printers to sell their wares in the lucrative English market. Additional legal difficulties followed in 1736, when on Swift's recommendation Faulkner printed *A New Proposal for the Better Regulation and Improvement of Quadrille,* an anonymous pamphlet by Josiah Hort, archbishop of Kilmore. The pamphlet's satiric attack on the legal acumen of Richard Bettesworth, a member of the Irish House of Commons, resulted in Faulkner's conviction for libel before the house on 3 March. Faulkner won his release from Dublin's Newgate Prison on 9 March by paying his fine with copies of Swift's collected works.

In the late 1730s and early 1740s Faulkner's establishment, which typically included seven journeymen and three apprentices, continued to pro-

duce profitable editions, often through collaborative efforts with other Dublin printing houses, as well as with London firms. In September 1737 Faulkner and Hoey – their feud of the early 1730s behind them – collaborated on the publication of a volume of erotic poetry, *The Cupid: A Collection of the Most Beautiful Love Songs in the English Language.* In December 1740 Faulkner joined Robert Owen in the subscription publication of John Thurloe's *State Papers.* Faulkner sold Irish subscriptions for the London publisher Thomas Meighan's edition of Nicholas Plunket's *Faithful History of the Rebellion* (1741), and in 1742 and 1743 he printed *The Life of Marianne,* a three-volume translation of Pierre Carlet de Chamblain de Marivaux's novel *La Vie de Marianne* (1731–1741).

In 1740 Alexander Pope tried to procure Faulkner's services to publish what he surreptitiously planned to be a "pirated" edition of his correspondence with Swift. Since it was at that time considered unseemly for a living author to have his own correspondence published, in 1735 Pope had similarly duped the London publisher Edmund Curll into publishing his letters, resulting in a "pirated" edition that Pope then denounced as error-ridden and revised as an authoritative edition (1737). After receiving copies of the correspondence from an anonymous donor in Bath, Faulkner attempted to secure the permission of the correspondents to publish the letters. Swift agreed, but Pope, to preserve his ability to disown the edition later, declined. Faulkner's refusal to publish the correspondence without Pope's permission defeated the poet's scheme.

After Swift's death on 19 October 1745 Faulkner wrote his obituary for the *Dublin Journal*: "His Genius, Learning and Charity are so universally admired that for a Newswriter to attempt his Character would be the highest Presumption. Yet as the Printer hereof is proud to acknowledge his infinite Obligations to that Prodigy of Wit, he can only lament, that he is by no means equal to so bold an undertaking." The following month he published Swift's *Directions to Servants*.

In 1744–1745 Faulkner published the seven-volume *An Universal History, from the Earliest Account of Time to the Present: Compiled from Original Authors,* which had originally been published in London from 1736 to 1744, but only after an extended legal battle with members of the Dublin printing establishment who had attempted to pirate copies of his edition. A group of Dublin booksellers led by George and Alexander Ewing helped him defeat the pirates in exchange for shares in his latest printing venture.

During the 1740s Faulkner entered into an initially profitable business relationship with Richardson that would eventually jeopardize Faulkner's reputation among his English publishing counterparts and result in substantial financial losses for his Irish colleagues. Faulkner paid Richardson seventy pounds for the right to reprint his first novel, *Pamela; or, Virtue Rewarded* (1740), and in February 1741 Faulkner and George Ewing advertised their edition. Faulkner also published an Irish edition of Richardson's second novel, *Clarissa* (1747–1748), but only after difficult negotiations over the cost of the rights. When Richardson approached Faulkner about the Irish publication of his next novel, *The History of Sir Charles Grandison* (1753–1754), he demanded that the printer agree to limit the distribution of his edition to Ireland and to advertise it only when stipulated by Richardson. In August 1753 Faulkner informed Richardson that three Irish pirates were planning to publish the novel, and realiz-

LECTURES

CONCERNING

ORATORY.

Delivered in

TRINITY COLLEGE, DUBLIN,

By JOHN LAWSON, D. D.
LECTURER in ORATORY and HISTORY, on the Foundation
of ERASMUS SMITH, Efquire.

Videmus quid deceat, non affequimur.
CICERO de Oratore.

DUBLIN:
Printed by GEORGE FAULKNER in Effex-ftreet.
M DCC LVIII.

Title page for a popular book published by Faulkner during the later part of his career

ing that its appearance would irrevocably usurp his rights, Faulkner halted production of the work. Convinced that Faulkner had tacitly agreed to the piracy of his novel, in September Richardson published and distributed *The Case of Samuel Richardson of London, Printer; with Regard to the Invasion of His Property in The History of Sir Charles Grandison, by Publication, by Certain Booksellers in Dublin,* and in February 1754 he published *An Address to the Public, on the Treatment Which the Editor of the History of Sir Charles Grandison Has Met with, from Certain Booksellers and Printers in Dublin,* in which he implicates Faulkner in the piracy. Richardson's erroneous accusations against Faulkner exacerbated the copyright dilemmas that the pirates caused for the legitimate eighteenth-century Irish publishing houses and also tarnished forever Faulkner's reputation as an ethical printer and bookseller.

In January 1755 Faulkner's wife died after a lengthy illness. In 1756 the Dublin Society admitted Faulkner as a member, but unfortunately for his rebounding reputation, Samuel Foote's vulgar satiric play *The Orators,* which opened in London in April 1762, offered a vicious attack on the printer's character. In the play Foote appeared as "Peter Paragraph," a farcical representation of Faulkner that ridiculed the printer's handicap. When the play opened in Dublin in October, Faulkner successfully sued Foote for libel. Foote responded with an equally farcical and libelous theatrical rejoinder, *The Trial of Samuel Foote, Esq. for a Libel on Peter Paragraph* (1763). In 1766 Foote himself lost a leg after falling from a horse, prompting Faulkner's patron Philip Dormer Stanhope, fourth earl of Chesterfield, to write to the printer: "I can not help observing with some satisfaction that Heaven has avenged your cause, as well and still more severely than the courts of temporal justice in Ireland did, having punished your adversary Foote in the part offending."

Among the works Faulkner published in the 1750s and 1760s were John Boyle, fifth earl of Cork and Orrery's *Remarks on the Life and Writings of Dr. Jonathan Swift* (1752); John Lawson's popular *Lectures Concerning Oratory* (1758); and *To the Public* (1766), in which the journeymen printers of Dublin outlined their struggle to reduce the growing number of poorly trained apprentices and unemployed journeymen. When his eleven-volume edition of Swift's works appeared in 1762–1763 Faulkner employed his editorial introduction to answer critics and competitors who questioned his relationship with Swift, replying particularly to the criticisms of John Hawkesworth, editor since 1755 of the London editions of Swift's works. To provide further proof of his association with Swift, Faulkner also included selections from their correspondence. By 1769 Faulkner's edition of Swift's works had increased to twenty volumes and included a large selection of the author's correspondence. Faulkner also published a variety of other literary and historical works, including Charles O'Conor's *Dissertations on the History of Ireland* (1766); Archbishop Hugh Boulter's *Letters* (1770); George, Baron Lyttelton's *The History of the Life of King Henry the Second* (1768–1772); Lord Chesterfield's *Letters to His Son* (1774); and Roderic O'Flaherty's *The Ogygia Vindicated* (1775).

In addition to Lord Chesterfield's demands for a knighthood for Faulkner – an honor he declined – the printer enjoyed a host of other accolades during his final years. In July 1768 his waning health and desire to complete Swift's works forced him to decline his election to the office of high sheriff; in an open letter to the citizens of Dublin, Faulkner expressed his gratitude for their attempt to honor his service to Ireland. He did accept election as an alderman in 1770, however. In August 1775, after dining with friends at a recently painted tavern, Faulkner developed a respiratory ailment; he died on 30 August.

While rancor and litigation characterize many of Faulkner's professional dealings throughout his career, his nurturing of Ireland's embryonic national literature – particularly through the preservation of Swift's canon – more adequately defines his contribution to the print trade of the eighteenth century. Moreover, Faulkner showed great courage in the face of the forces that challenged his right to publish in an era before modern copyright legislation.

Letters:

Prince of Dublin Printers: The Letters of George Faulkner, edited by Robert E. Ward (Lexington: University Press of Kentucky, 1972).

References:

"Authentic Memoirs of the Late George Faulkner, Esq.," *Hibernian Magazine,* 5 (September 1775): 503–505; (October 1775): 567–571;

F. P. Lock, "The Text of *Gulliver's Travels,*" *Modern Language Review,* 76 (July 1981): 513–533;

Joseph McMinn, "Printing Swift," *Eire-Ireland,* 20 (Spring 1985): 143–149;

Robert Munter, "George Faulkner," in his *A Dictionary of the Print Trade in Ireland, 1550–1775* (New York: Fordham University Press, 1988), pp. 96–98;

Charles O'Connor, S.J., "George Faulkner and the Irish Catholics," *Studies: An Irish Quarterly,* 28 (1939): 485–502;

M. Pollard, "George Faulkner," *Swift Studies,* 7 (1992): 79–96;

Catherine Coogan Ward and Robert E. Ward, comps., *A Checklist and Census of 400 Imprints of the Irish Printer and Bookseller, George Faulkner, from 1725 to 1775* (Birmingham, Ala.: Ragnarok Press, 1973).

– *Kenneth Womack*

Robert and Andrew Foulis
(Glasgow: 1742 – 1776)

Robert Foulis
(Glasgow: 1741 – 1742)

Andrew Foulis the Younger
(Glasgow: 1776 – 1777)

Andrew Foulis and James Spottiswood
(Glasgow: 1777 – 1781)

Andrew Foulis and Company
(Glasgow: 1782 – 1787)

Andrew Foulis
(Glasgow: 1788 – 1800)

That simplicity is the classical source of beauty in all the arts was a chief tenet of the Scottish Enlightenment, whether in the architecture of Robert Adams, the political economics of Adam Smith, the poetry of Robert Burns, or the portrait painting of David Allan. Simplicity was as much a moral as an aesthetic value for Scots artists and intellectuals and no doubt had its source in the extreme poverty and Protestant perseverance that distinguished the small urban centers of Glasgow and Edinburgh in the early eighteenth century. Glasgow, a country town of twelve thousand in 1710, would grow to a population of more than eighty thousand by 1800 but in the mid eighteenth century was still small enough to be without direct mail or coach contact with London (everything came by way of Edinburgh); its university, however, was the focus for an increasingly distinguished community of scholars. No small part of the strength of Glasgow University in the mid to late eighteenth century lay in its printing and publishing practices, designed with the double purpose of producing inexpensive textbooks for an increasing student body and of providing the most meticulous and error-free editions of the works of classical authors. The university press was operated and largely reconceived at this time by Robert Foulis and his younger brother Andrew, who developed typographical designs of a simple beauty that radically changed the look of the printed page in the eighteenth century. The Foulis press was in many ways the heart of the Scottish Enlightenment in the city.

Robert Faulls was born in Glasgow on 20 April 1707, Andrew on 23 November 1712; there were two other brothers, John and James. Their father, Andrew, was a maltster who later operated a small tavern; their mother, Marion Paterson Faulls, provided their early education at home, although all four brothers would attend the university. As the eldest, Robert was destined for a trade and was apprenticed to a barber, Alexander Leggat, in 1720. He was granted permission to enter freeman before the expiration of the indentures, but he did not act on the opportunity and was admitted to the incorporation on 12 January 1727. Andrew enrolled as a divinity student at the university in 1727, and on completing the course he taught Latin, Greek, and French.

In 1730, when Francis Hutcheson joined the faculty at Glasgow University, Robert enrolled as one of his students in moral philosophy. By that time Andrew and Robert were sharing rooms in Glasgow College, where they would continue in private or professional quarters throughout their lives. During the 1730s they changed their name from Faulls to the more aristocratic Foulis (pronounced "Fowls"); Robert probably made the change when he left the barber trade in 1737 ("Robert Faulls of Glasgow" is listed as a subscriber to James Duncan's

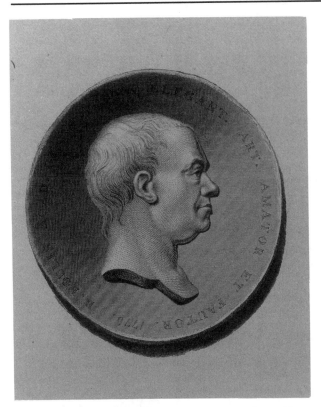

Robert Foulis; engraving by John Horsbugh after a medallion by James Tassie (Courtesy of Special Collections, Thomas Cooper Library, University of South Carolina)

Miscellany Poems in 1734 but appears as "Robert Foulis of Glasgow" in lists after 1737). Both brothers used "Foulis" in 1738 as signatories to the pamphlet *A Vindication of Mr. Hutcheson from the Calumnious Aspersions of a Late Pamphlet.* Hutcheson was one of Robert Foulis's financial benefactors, and the appointment of the Foulis brothers as university booksellers and printers owes much to him. His works would appear most often among the titles published by the Foulis press, comprising twenty-eight items.

The brothers made a tour of England and the Continent in 1738; letters of introduction to the Scots community in France gained access for them to the best libraries in Paris. Robert Foulis was also commissioned by the senate of Glasgow University to obtain important records and to make copies of manuscript documents in the possession of the Scots College at Paris. The fathers of the college wrote a commendation naming Robert and Andrew Foulis for their diligence and efficiency in restoring relations between the university and the college, and that success, more than anything else, appears to have secured their reputations with the governing body of Glasgow University. The Foulis brothers purchased a collection of classical Greek

and Latin texts "sufficient to fill seven hogsheads," which they sold on returning to Glasgow in 1739 to underwrite a second journey to the Continent for the purpose of buying books for auction in Glasgow and London. At this time Robert Foulis met Dr. James Douglas, whom he assisted in amassing a collection of Horace editions. Those twelve months or so of buying and selling books brought both brothers a reputation as bookmen that, in a few years, would protect them alone among Scottish booksellers from a general prosecution over copyright brought from England.

Most of the books they collected during their second Paris trip were sold in London in the spring of 1740. On returning to Glasgow, Robert Foulis, at the urging of a group of professors headed by Hutcheson, established himself as university bookseller within the college premises and as one of only two booksellers then operating in Glasgow. Foulis's first advertisement, in the *Glasgow Journal* in 1741, listed him as a dealer in "scarce and valuable editions of the classics and books proper for the Grammar School and University." Throughout his career Robert would keep a large stock of old and new books at a wide range of prices; when he began to publish he would print unusually long runs, and on his death the shop would carry a backstock of more than seven thousand pounds worth of titles printed by the press. Such extravagance was hardly a responsible fiscal policy in so small a market as Glasgow, even with its voracious university bibliophiles.

Foulis published thirteen works, most of which were printed by Robert Urie, between 1740 and 1742. The most important was an edition of the works of Terence in 1742 that was sold under the imprint of Robert Foulis and Alexander Carlile, also of Glasgow. There is a notable increase in the quality of the printing done for Foulis during this two-year period in terms of accuracy, size of type, simplicity of layout, quality and size of paper, and binding, all indicative of Foulis's ambition to produce fine and collectible editions. Such quality had never been a hallmark of Scottish printing, especially in the limited Glasgow market, where cheapness and utility had been the foremost considerations. The first works printed by Foulis after he added a printing press to his bookselling premises are, however, less than attractive — particularly an edition of the works of Juvenal done all in italic type. In 1743 Foulis applied for the position of university printer, providing a list of seventeen titles with the imprint "Robert Foulis, bookseller in Glasgow" that included editions of Cicero's works and Phaedrus's fables and two works by Hutcheson.

Foulis was granted the appointment on 31 March with the stipulation "that he shall not use the designation of University printer without allowance from the University meeting in any Books, excepting those of ancient authors." On 4 April the first Greek text printed in Glasgow was produced by Foulis in his new capacity. At this time he began to sign his name "Robert Foulis, *academiae typographus*." By 1744 operations had grown to such an extent that Robert brought Andrew into partnership, principally to oversee the retail end of the business. At that point the company's name became Robert and Andrew Foulis or R. and A. Foulis. Its first catalogue, in 1744, included the Byzantine Historians, the Benedictine edition of Saint John Chrysostom, and the Elzevir Cicero. Attempts to establish a University printer and bookseller in Glasgow can be traced back to at least 1640, with Robert Sanders (father and son), James Watson, Hugh Brown, Donald Govan, and Alexander Carmichael holding the position irregularly and at various times; but the Foulis brothers held the position for the longest and only successful tenure. The properties on the west side of the High Street opposite the college grounds that the Foulises purchased in 1747 to expand their operations were bought by the university at public sale in 1782 and continued thereafter to be part of the academic buildings.

Between 1742 and 1776 at least 589 works, by Philip Gaskell's count, were printed by Robert and Andrew Foulis as university printers. The Foulises never produced fewer than 9 works in any year; their production peaked between 1750 and 1755, when they printed 174 titles: 40 in 1750, 43 in 1751, 29 in 1752, 21 in 1753, 10 in 1754, and 31 in 1755. As Gaskell points out, the Foulises' average yearly production of almost 17 works over their thirty-five-year career exceeds Samuel Richardson's average of 13 over forty-three years, with the Foulises' maximum of 43 titles in one year easily surpassing Richardson's top production of 31. The size of the Foulis printing house makes these totals all the more impressive: by Gaskell's calculations, "the Foulises normally used no more than two presses and a proofing press" and the full staff of the establishment never exceeded ten, including Robert and Andrew Foulis. The brothers favored the Printing Demy typeface for textbooks; but they printed an unusual number of variant issues – Gaskell claims that "variant issues were the rule rather than the exception at the Foulis Press" and cites the 1747 *Iliad,* which was issued in Foolscap octavo, Greek with Latin; Pot octavo, Greek with Latin; Foolscap octavo, Greek only; Pot octavo, Greek only; Foolscap quarto, Greek; Pot quarto, Greek; and finally vellum folded octavo in Greek only. Copper-

plate and woodcut illustrations were used by the press, increasingly so after Robert's establishment of the Glasgow Academy of Fine Arts in 1753.

Robert Foulis's obsession with raising the art of printing in Scotland far above anything previously known brought him into an artistic partnership with Dr. Alexander Wilson, who, after training as a physician, established with John Baine a type foundry in St. Andrews. In 1744 he became the University of Glasgow's first professor of astronomy and oversaw its first observatory; at that time he moved the foundry to the college grounds, making Glasgow the only university with its own type foundry. Baine left the partnership that year to set up on his own in Ireland. Prior to the relocation of the foundry to Glasgow, the Foulis press had imported its type from Holland, and the quality of the work printed under those conditions was never more than adequate: entire texts were printed in italics, and broken and irregular type were common. Once Robert Foulis had access to Wilson's foundry he began to conceive his most ambitious projects, and the Foulis style began to take shape. The Foulises purchased all their type from Wilson after 1744, and Robert regularly commissioned special designs – particularly ever-increasing sizes, such as double-pica Greek and roman. The type styles Wilson produced for Foulis were bold and simple, avoiding flourishes and embellishments. This plainness was no doubt urged by Robert Foulis, whose page layouts eschewed ornamentation; a Foulis page is strong, clear, and simple, and in even the smallest formats a regular reading line is emphasized. Foulis makes the eye's work as easy as possible. Foulis's title pages are singular for simplicity: they display no ornaments, no italics, only occasional red lines, uniform use of type, and uniform use of capitals within each line. Foulis laid out the page with a classical symmetry and simplicity that did in print for the book what Adams did in stone for architecture.

Two values of the Scottish Enlightenment are implicit in the works printed by the Foulises: to make learning and the arts as widely accessible as possible and to promote beauty through simplicity. The brothers printed works of philosophy and classical literature in abundance; their modern authors were chiefly the great English poets, with the exception of a few French and Italian texts – notably the 1763 editions of Torquato Tasso's *La Gerusalemme liberata* and Battista Guarini's *Il Pastor fido.* They also undertook to simplify the page by limiting or eliminating printer's devices, ornaments, and italics and developing clear and readable typefaces. Cheap textbooks cannot often be specimens of printing beauty, however, and many of the duodecimo editions produced by the Foulises were neither beautiful nor particularly easy on the reader's eye. Nevertheless, the Foulises' 1749 edition of the works of Cicero in twenty volumes was praised for its combination of utility and elegance, and it continued to be the most practical edition of Cicero's works into the early twentieth century. Accuracy is the greatest hallmark, however, of a Foulis text, a reputation the brothers first earned with their edition of Horace in 1744. Called the "immaculate Horace," the text has only six inaccuracies; the proof sheets were displayed in the college, and students were rewarded for finding those errors.

The choice of works printed at the press was much influenced by Professor George Rosse, who functioned as editor of Latin texts, and Professor James Moor, Robert Foulis's brother-in-law, who edited Greek works. Each also served as proofreader; Robert Foulis is usually credited with being the first Scottish printer to employ a full-time proofreader. Foulis texts were often corrected half a dozen times by as many as three readers and have remarkably few canceled sheets by eighteenth-century standards. Although the Foulis press did not publish authoritatively edited classical texts, and while their ambition to make the works of the major authors affordable to students further limited them, the brothers endeavored to produce works of scholarly significance based on manuscripts and the oldest editions to which they could gain access. They worked throughout their lives compiling material for an edition of the complete works of Plato; their research included transcriptions of the oldest Plato manuscripts, held in the Vatican. The Plato edition was never published, but the materials they collected are now in the Bodleian Library in Oxford and attest to the Foulises' high standards as printers of classical texts. A 1756 edition of Euclid edited by Robert Simson, professor of mathematics at the university, was intended to be used as a textbook; it was printed in Latin and English, indicating that the vernacular had become the language of instruction in geometry. The Foulis Euclid continued to be used as a textbook throughout the nineteenth century.

The great achievement of the press in classical literature was the double-pica folio Homer: the *Iliad,* published in two volumes in 1756, and the *Odyssey,* published in two volumes in 1758. Here beauty and accuracy exceed anything else that the press produced. Robert Foulis commissioned a new font of double-pica Greek type to be designed and produced by Wilson; among the many compliments paid to the quality of the type is Edward Gibbon's: "As the eye is the organ of fancy, I read Homer with more pleasure in the Glasgow edition. Through that

fine medium, the poet's sense appears more beautiful and transparent." Robert Foulis himself designed and supervised the binding of the large-paper edition and selected the paper for the folio copies. But the proofing exceeded all these other efforts for its fastidiousness. Every sheet was read twice and collated by the proofreader James Tweedie, then corrected again by Andrew Foulis; finally, Moor and Muirhead each read through the text on his own, then sat down together for a joint correction of the text. The only error that has been noted in the text is the omission of an iota subscript.

In 1759 the press undertook a forty-one-volume complete series of the Greek historians, beginning with Thucydides and following with Herodotus in 1761 and Xenophon in 1762. The volumes are octavo but use a large typeface that is more common in the folio editions of other printers. The texts have facing Latin translations and are as noteworthy for their correctness as the earlier Horace and Homer. The Foulises received Edinburgh Select Society silver medals in 1755 for their edition of Callimachus, in 1756 for the Horace, and in 1756, 1757, and 1758 for various states of the folio Homer. Some of the classical works printed by Foulis may have had runs of more than two thousand copies, but the quality remained consistently high, and the work of the press was often reprinted in England. The Foulis edition of *Aesop's Fables* (*Fabulae Aesopicae*) published in 1754, for example, was reprinted at the Clarendon Press in 1757 for the Oxford bookseller James Fletcher.

Foulis editions of the works of English authors increased in the 1760s; the press's finest printing of a book by a contemporary author was Thomas Gray's *Poems,* published in quarto in 1768. James Beattie described the volume as "one of the most elegant pieces of printing . . . ever produced," and Gray, who had been eager to commit his collected works to Robert Foulis's care, described Foulis's achievements as "surpassing his predecessors, the Etiennes and the Elzevirs." As with the 1756 Homer, Foulis commissioned a new set of type for Gray's *Poems,* and Wilson responded by producing the largest roman character he had yet designed: a double-pica font cut with a plainness like that of the Homer Greek. The aesthetic success of the Gray book led, at the urging of Beattie, to the publication of a folio edition of John Milton's *Paradise Lost* in 1770, to which the brothers once again committed expense that could not be adequately recovered. Robert Foulis's sense of the printed book as an art form led his press to extravagances that no other eighteenth-century printing operation would undertake without endowment; his commitment to aesthetic values in printing the great texts of classical and contemporary poetry brought reputation but insufficient income to R. and A. Foulis, and the Milton volume was the last venture of that kind.

Indeed, the Foulises redoubled their efforts to make authors accessible to students and the common reader in Glasgow, turning from an emphasis on beauty to one on the utility of the text. From at least the early 1750s the Foulis press had published pocket editions of works by popular English writers, and their 1771 edition of the poems of William Collins resumed that practice. The Collins and Gray editions placed side by side provide a perfect image of the high and low end of the Foulis trade. Cheap though the low end was, it was in no way inferior in accuracy, as Samuel Johnson attests in a letter to James Boswell requesting some of the Foulis pocket editions. Availability and affordability were the objectives of the duodecimo editions, and an advertisement in the 1775 reprint of the Collins *Poems* lists forty titles then available in the series. The books sold for a shilling a volume, and extant correspondence between Robert Foulis and William Warburton over the inclusion of Alexander Pope's letters among the proposed titles indicates that the brothers had principally a student market in mind for these works. The Foulis editions of the works of William Shakespeare provide the best example of the firm's commitment to its common readership. In 1752 the Foulises began publishing the plays in individual volumes with uniform printing and continuous pagination; the canon was completed in 1757. The series was also bound into a set of sixteen octavo volumes. The Shakespeare texts were republished in 1766 in eight volumes that were sold individually as part of a renewed attempt by the Foulis press to develop a wider market for cheap editions of works by English authors. The "shilling poets," as the Foulis cheap editions are commonly known, did not bring in much money because the profit margins were deliberately kept low while the printing was still exacting; but, beginning in 1759, they contributed to the prosecutions for copyright violations brought by English publishers and to the decision by the English trade to publish an edition of the works of the English poets with introductory lives by Johnson that became *Prefaces, Biographical and Critical, to the Works of the English Poets* (1779, 1781).

Whatever alarm the Foulises caused their English counterparts, they never cast much of an eye to the market in England; their shilling poets and other inexpensive editions were not intended for buyers be-

M. TULLII

CICERONIS

O P E R A

QUAE SUPERSUNT

O M N I A.

AD
FIDEM OPTIMARUM EDITIONUM
DILIGENTER EXPRESSA.

VOLUMINIBUS
XX.

G L A S G U A E,

IN AEDIBUS ACADEMICIS

EXCUDEBANT ROB. ET AND. FOULIS

ACADEMIAE TYPOGRAPHI
M.DCC.XLIX.

Title page for an edition of the works of Cicero published by Robert and Andrew Foulis (Courtesy of the Lilly Library, Indiana University)

yond Glasgow, and they were much aware of the copyright laws. Andrew delivered a paper in 1766 on intellectual property to the Literary Society of Glasgow, and Robert addressed the question of copyright law twice in 1770 alone. When the House of Commons passed a bill modifying the law in 1774 (it was defeated in the House of Lords), Robert Foulis was asked to draw up a document on behalf of the Scottish booksellers presenting the other side of the question of making intellectual property perpetual. On the occasion of the original crisis over intellectual property in 1748, when disaster for the Scottish trade was only narrowly averted, Robert Foulis was the only Scottish printer not named – even though he had reprinted the *Guardian* in 1746 and the *Tatler* in 1747, both of which were works liable for inclusion for damages in the suit filed by the English bookmen. It has often been asserted that Foulis's reputation for honesty, and especially his dealing with Andrew Millar, who was a principal pursuer of the action, were sufficient to exempt him. It was his practice to secure a release for anything he intended to print that might jeopardize another book dealer's earnings, but he also defended and exercised his right to print whatever he felt was common property, especially works of cultural significance. He clearly valued the dissemination of fine literature above personal profit, and he resented attempts to limit readership for the sake of financial gain. Foulis's letter to Sir William Murray in November 1754 sets out his business ethic: "I know the most Learned and worthy men in this country think we do public service in reprinting whatever we can *according to Law,* that is in any way calculated to do good."

Robert Foulis's impact on the intellectual life of Glasgow between 1750 and his death in 1776 cannot be overestimated. His printing offices were the center of the university's activities, and he published the work of its most distinguished faculty. Foulis not only printed the institution's textbooks but, through his intimate connections with many of the professors, he helped shape its curriculum – contributing, for example, to the use of English for lecturing. Both Foulises participated in local learned societies, with Robert delivering at least seventeen papers before the Literary Society. The Foulises also founded the *Glasgow Courant* and printed it for fifteen years, providing the city with a second newspaper, and were prime movers in promoting financial support for the arts and learning in Glasgow. Robert Foulis's most ambitious contribution to Glasgow's cultural maturation was his establishment of the Glasgow Academy of Fine Arts: in 1752 he persuaded the spirit merchants John Glassford and Archibald Ingram to contribute toward a trip he took to the Continent to purchase paintings and drawings by the Masters, which would serve as the nucleus of a collection for a school of the fine arts; the works were housed in a building Foulis leased, and he also employed a painter, engraver, and copperplate printer at his own expense. The academy was only a modest success, and it attracted less and less interest and financial support in the course of its twenty-three-year existence. It did, however, produce such skilled graduates as David Allan and James Tassie.

The academy is the most significant demonstration of Foulis's dedication to the visual arts; he wrote of his belief that there is "a connection and mutual influence of the Arts and Sciences upon one another and upon Society," observing that all manufacturers so depend for their inventions on the influence of drawing and modeling that "a nation [that] leads in fashion must previously have invention in drawing." Foulis's interest in design reveals itself in his attention as a printer to paper selection, binding, and especially the type fonts he used for his fine folio editions. Curiously, however, although Foulis used engravings and woodcuts, he was sparing and seemingly uninterested in illustrating his texts. He seemed to conceive of the text as its own illustration

and to prefer to commit his financial resources to commissioning new type rather than to the more expensive engraving process.

The Foulis bookshop would remain the fulcrum of college life throughout the careers of the brothers; it served as a lounge and reading room for students, professors, and any others who shared an interest in philosophy and literature. A committee of professors assisted the Foulises in stocking the shop, which often operated as if it were a university library. In the evenings the brothers conducted book auctions, about which several sources report similar anecdotes illustrating Robert Foulis's generosity and commitment to the university community: he is said to have given books gratis to students who could not afford to place bids and to have withheld from auction volumes that students or professors were reading in the shop during the day. Andrew had a better sense of the necessities of conducting a profitable business and assumed control of the auctions early in the partnership. The auctions were held in the Old Coffee House on the west side of the Saltmarket, at the corner of the Trongate. Catalogues and advertisements for these auctions appeared regularly throughout the partnership's lifetime in the *Glasgow Journal* and the *Glasgow Courant.*

The lives of Andrew and Robert Foulis ended suddenly and tragically; their printing firm suffered a much longer and lingering but equally tragic demise under the mismanagement of Robert's feckless son. Always on the brink financially, the Foulis press was in a particularly precarious condition in 1775, when, on 18 September, Andrew died of a stroke while on a day's outing at the Duke's Lodgings in Drygait. Robert went into an immediate decline. Under the duress of creditors' claims he decided to close the academy and to sell its central collection of paintings and drawings to save the printing business. He traveled to London with an apprentice printer, Robert Dewar, who would later marry his daughter Elizabeth; they arrived in April 1776, having missed the auction season. James Christie, the auctioneer, advised against proceeding with the sale, citing the disappointing outcomes of previous late-season auctions in which buyers offered little more than a half-crown on items listed at twenty pounds. Foulis, however, insisted on going ahead, and the sale was an unmitigated disaster: after costs, he took away only fifteen shillings. His spirits broken, Foulis died at Edinburgh on 2 June on his return journey to Glasgow.

Robert Foulis contracted debts on a regular basis to sustain his printing shop; he had borrowed

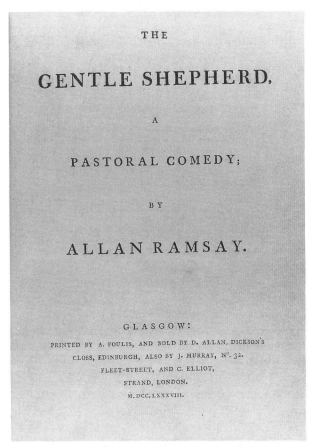

THE

GENTLE SHEPHERD,

A

PASTORAL COMEDY;

BY

ALLAN RAMSAY.

GLASGOW:

PRINTED BY A. FOULIS, AND SOLD BY D. ALLAN, DICKSON'S
CLOSS, EDINBURGH, ALSO BY J. MURRAY, Nº. 32.
FLEET-STREET, AND C. ELLIOT,
STRAND, LONDON.
M. DCC, LXXXVIII.

ALAN·RAMSAY SCOTUS

*Frontispiece and title page for one of the books published by Robert Foulis's son Andrew, who inherited his father and uncle's business
(Courtesy of Special Collections, Thomas Cooper Library, University of South Carolina)*

sums from the Edinburgh physician John Stevenson in 1743, 1744, 1749, and 1753, none of which had been repaid at the time of the firm's dissolution and reincorporation under Robert's son, Andrew Foulis the younger, in 1776. Robert Foulis left the firm seventy-five hundred pounds in debt, but his son assumed the premises with no idea that the press was insolvent. Unable to continue the business without assistance, Andrew Foulis was compelled to go into partnership with James Spottiswood, an Edinburgh bookseller with a reputation for engaging in lawsuits. The partnership began on 30 June 1777, at which time Andrew Foulis leased from Glasgow University his father's printing premises at twenty pounds a year and purchased his father's stock, types, and presses. Spottiswood, who owned a paper mill at Penicuik along with his bookselling firm, contributed one thousand pounds, a sum repayable by Foulis.

While conducting business on his own between 1776 and 1778 without the security of being confirmed as the official university printer, Andrew

Foulis published twenty-nine works, almost one-third of his career total of ninety-four editions in twenty-five years. Foulis commenced work as university printer on 18 May 1778 with the republication of the duodecimo edition of the works of the English poets; but disagreements arose between the partners almost immediately, and the printing operations declined significantly. In 1779 production dropped to four books, remaining at that level in 1780. On 9 March 1781 the partnership with Spottiswood was dissolved; that year the firm printed only three works. On 1 January 1782 Foulis formed a new firm, Andrew Foulis and Company, in association with the printers Alexander Tilloch, Hugh Anderson, and James Harvey; production that year, however, fell to two titles. In 1783 and 1784 the firm reached its zenith with the publication of ten and twelve editions, respectively. Litigations with Spottiswood, however, were persistent, and in 1784 they reached an embarrassing denouement: Spottiswood was ordered to settle certain accounts with Foulis, and Foulis immediately sent officers to arrest his former partner. That rash, unnecessary, and legally dubious action brought about further court action and considerable public scandal. Damages of one thousand pounds were brought against Andrew Foulis and Company, and the firm had to bring a counteraction to prevent seizure of its types and presses. The chaos did much to destroy Foulis's second partnership, and the scandal ruined his reputation. Although Tilloch remained loyal, and the firm acquired patents for stereotype printing in 1784 for England, Scotland, and Ireland, the company never published more than four titles – and often only one – in any year after the confrontation with Spottiswood.

Andrew Foulis was neither a stable personality nor a capable businessman, and he managed in only a decade to destroy the international respect and reputation that had been so carefully built up by his father and uncle. When he was effective – only a sporadic condition – he printed works on a level with the earlier efforts of the Foulis press; his folio edition of the tragedies of Aeschylus, on large paper with John Flaxman's illustrations, published in 1795, is perhaps the finest of Andrew Foulis's efforts. Other important publications are his stereotype edition of Xenophon's *Anabasis* (1784) and his edition of Allan Ramsay's *The Gentle Shepherd* (1788) with David Allan's illustrations. These commendable efforts were isolated, however, and the records of Foulis's dealings as university printer are replete with examples of procrastination and misrepresentation. The new catalogue of the university's library was delivered to him in late 1786 and published in 1791, part of the delay being due to seizure of his type by Spottiswood. The octavo edition of Aeschylus was begun in 1794 and not completed until 1806, six years after Foulis had given up printing, when it was brought out by the London firm of Payne and Mackinlay in cooperation with John Cook of Oxford.

On 10 June 1795 legal proceedings were brought by Glasgow University to remove Andrew Foulis from the printing operations and other facilities he held by lease; in April 1796 he was paid a settlement of seventy pounds and dismissed. Foulis continued as an independent printer until 1800, publishing only two works in those four years – one of which, however, was an important large-paper edition of the works of Euripides that he printed in London in 1797 because he could get no credit in Glasgow or Edinburgh. After closing his printing business Foulis first turned to public recitations as a source of income and

later sold prints and paintings in partnership with Robert Anderson of Aberdeen. In a contemporary record Andrew Foulis is described as "cheating like [a] horse jock[ey]," a sad notoriety for the son of Robert Foulis. Andrew Foulis the younger died in the Edinburgh poorhouse in 1829.

Between 1740 and 1800 the name Foulis appeared in a half-dozen partnerships and some 794 different editions. "R. and A. Foulis" is the imprint on the works for which the family firm is justly remembered as one of the most influential eighteenth-century printers and publishers. The Foulis press is best known for its immaculate editions of the works of classical authors and for its development of type fonts and title-page layouts that brought a new aesthetic of simplicity to the printing practices of the period; Andrew Foulis the younger also experimented with stereotype. While the firm never printed first editions of contemporary literature, its cheap reprints of the works of standard English authors brought new respectability to the concept of the pocket edition. As was the case with other significant movers in eighteenth-century Scottish printing, notably William Smellie and William Creech, for all its influence and success the Foulis firm did not survive for more than a generation and did not persist as a force in publishing in the nineteenth century.

Letters:

Some Letters of Robert Foulis, edited by David Murray (Glasgow: Maclehose, 1917).

Bibliography:

Philip Gaskell, *A Bibliography of the Foulis Press,* second edition (Winchester: St. Paul's Bibliographies, 1986).

References:

William James Duncan, *Notices and Documents Illustrative of the Literary History of Glasgow* (Glasgow: Hutchison & Brookman, printers, 1831; New York: AMS Press, 1973);

John Ferguson, *The Brothers Foulis and Early Glasgow Printing* (London: Dryden Press, 1889);

Philip Gaskell, "The Early Work of the Foulis Press and the Wilson Foundry," *The Library,* fifth series 7 (June 1952): 77–110; (September 1952): 149–177;

David Murray, *Robert and Andrew Foulis and the Glasgow Press* (Glasgow: Maclehose, 1913).

– Stephen W. Brown

M. J. Godwin and Company

(London: 1806 – 1825)

The Juvenile Library

(London: 1805 – 1825)

T. Hodgkins

(London: 1805 – 1806)

See also the William Godwin entries in *DLB 39: British Novelists, 1660–1800; DLB 104: British Prose Writers, 1660–1800;* and *DLB 142: Eighteenth-Century British Literary Biographers.*

The political journalist, philosopher, and novelist William Godwin operated one of the most effective publishing outlets for educational and children's literature of the early nineteenth century. With the assistance of his second wife, Mary Jane Clairmont Godwin, he established simultaneously a publishing house and The Juvenile Library, a London stationery store and bookshop that specialized in selling the material produced by the publishing house. At first Godwin published under the name T. Hodgkins, but after a year he settled on M. J. Godwin and Company. The ruse of using his shop assistant's name for the imprint was designed to circumvent the anti-Jacobin hysteria that in 1805 still identified Godwin with an unsavory radicalism that was, to say the least, not commercially helpful. After Godwin caught Thomas Hodgkins stealing the store's money, he used his wife's initials, M. J., before what he hoped everyone would regard as a common English name, Godwin.

Godwin was a victim of his spectacular successes in the 1790s, accomplishments he could not repeat. The stunning novelties of *An Enquiry Concerning the Principles of Political Justice, and Its Influence on General Virtue and Happiness,* which was published in three editions (1793, 1796, and 1798), captivated the attention of the liberal and radical intelligentsia, from artisans in the London Corresponding Society such as Francis Place to poets such as Samuel Taylor Coleridge and William Wordsworth. The bold political essay *Cursory Strictures on the Charge delivered by Lord Chief Justice Eyre to the Grand Jury, October 2, 1794* (1794) protested against the treason trials so persuasively that one of the defendants, Horne

Tooke, claimed that his life had been saved by Godwin's eloquence. And the innovative "Jacobin" novel and psychological thriller *Things as They Are: or, The Adventures of Caleb Williams* (1794) would go into five editions by 1831. Married in March 1797 to England's most prominent feminist author, Mary Wollstonecraft, Godwin was a leading figure in the revolutionary decade. Although he would be a productive writer for the next three and a half decades, he never came close to achieving the fame he had enjoyed in the 1790s. Consequently, his later career, of which publishing was an important part, has tended to be ignored – as Coleridge, for example, pointed out at the time (according to Henry Crabb Robinson's diary entry of 30 March 1811).

Godwin had always had an interest in education – in 1783 he had tried to start a school at Epsom, Surrey – and in his mature philosophy nothing was more important than educating children in accordance with the principles of political justice. Even before the establishment of The Juvenile Library, Godwin wrote, as William St. Clair has discovered, a children's book for the publisher Richard Phillips titled *Bible Stories* (1803). Nevertheless, Godwin was clearly more interested in writing for adults; it was primarily economic necessity that impelled him into publishing and writing educational and children's literature.

Only after a series of severe disappointments did Godwin turn to children's publishing. Those disappointments began on 10 September 1797, when his wife died giving birth to their daughter Mary, the future author of *Frankenstein* (1818) and future wife of Percy Bysshe Shelley. The widower also had to care for Fanny Imlay, his wife's child by Gilbert Imlay. The domestic tragedy coincided with a massive cultural and political reaction against everything associated with the French Revolution and its English sympathizers. Especially after the publi-

William Godwin circa 1816; drawing by G. Harlow
(location of original unknown)

cation of Godwin's painfully honest *Memoirs of the Author of a Vindication of the Rights of Woman* (1798), which disclosed details about his late wife's extramarital love life, both of them became targets of abuse, ridicule, satire, and slander. From the pulpit and the press came a deluge of invective between 1798 and 1805 not only by longtime reactionaries but also by former friends and fellow liberals such as Samuel Parr, James Mackintosh, and Amelia Opie. So thorough was the attack on Godwin that in 1812 his future son-in-law Shelley would be surprised to learn that he was still alive.

In 1801 Godwin married Mary Jane Clairmont, who brought to the marriage two children, Charles and Jane (who would be known to Shelley and George Gordon, Lord Byron, as Claire). In 1803 the couple had a son, William Jr. Even after the relative successes of Godwin's biography of Geoffrey Chaucer (1803) and his Romantic novel *Fleetwood* (1805), Godwin could not support his family adequately from his writing for adults. His wife,

a skilled translator who had been working in the children's book trade for Benjamin Tabart before her marriage to Godwin, urged that they pool their skills and try to exploit the relatively new and highly lucrative market of educational and children's literature. Godwin agreed, and thus in 1805 were born The Juvenile Library and the publishing enterprise that supplied it with books.

Godwin's notoriety was a serious obstacle in trying to reach the children's book market, which was dominated by strict propriety and pious moralism. Sarah Trimmer, for example, in her magazine *Guardian of Education,* sifted through children's literature for unorthodoxy, which, once detected, was mercilessly condemned. As a symbol of the revolutionary subversion of the established order in sexual morality, politics, religion, and manners, Godwin could not be publicly connected with the business: his earliest publications have the imprint T. Hodgkins, but after he fired Hodgkins in 1806, the imprint became M. J. Godwin and Company; furthermore, Godwin rarely ventured into the bookshop, where the public could see him. Another ploy was the use of pseudonyms: Godwin wrote more than a dozen children's books, in none of which did his name appear as author. Edward Baldwin was his favorite nom de plume, but he also used Theophilus Marcliffe. He seems to have used his first pseudonym, William Scolfield, only for *Bible Stories.*

The Juvenile Library was located on Hanway Street, where the shop sold books published by T. Hodgkins, M. J. Godwin and Company, and other children's publishers, as well as school supplies. Godwin acquired the initial financing for the business from Thomas Wedgwood, a liberal philanthropist who had also assisted Coleridge. Although M. J. Godwin and Company and The Juvenile Library were enormously successful, the Godwins were almost always on the brink of catastrophe and debtors prison. Wedgwood's help was not enough, and periodically Godwin had to turn to other wealthy liberals to stave off bankruptcy. Although it is impossible to understand fully Godwin's financial arrangements, it is clear that he tried to keep his family at a high but not extravagant standard of living; was a generous host and benefactor, entertaining frequently and giving money to needy friends; and had a casual attitude, at best, toward the bottom line. For the anarchist philosopher wealth had no intrinsic value and was to be used to promote social justice.

The Juvenile Library's first book published by Godwin was "Edward Baldwin's" *Fables, Ancient and Modern* (1805). Like all of Godwin's children's

Portrait of a woman believed to be Mary Jane Clairmont,
who married Godwin in 1801 and became his partner in
his bookstore and publishing firm (artist and location
of original unknown)

books, it is both a potboiler that would not have been composed except for economic necessity and a well-written and seriously thought-out text that embodies his philosophy. Revising and expanding on Aesop's fables, Godwin gives egalitarian and libertarian twists to many of the narratives but never in such a way as to detract from the story or to call down upon the book the wrath of reviewers. At least from the time of Jean-Jacques Rousseau's *Emile* (1762), the formation of children's characters was considered an essential liberal cause; the Enlightenment and the Romantic currents that followed in its wake assumed that the child was either a tabula rasa whose nature was to be inscribed by experience or a genial noble savage whose innate benevolence was typically corrupted by malevolent adults. Another important tradition of children's literature, however, and one that all of Godwin's productions were designed to counter, was the Calvinistic notion of children's innate depravity. Godwin's *Fables, Ancient and Modern,* like most of The Juvenile Library's productions, tried to entertain young readers by appealing to their imagination and intelligence and did

not attempt, as many of the religiously oriented texts did, to terrify children into conformity and obedience. *Fables, Ancient and Modern* could hardly have been better received: by 1821 there were nine English editions and several American editions, as well as a French translation (1806) by Mary Jane Godwin. The book was still in print at midcentury.

For his children's literature enterprise Godwin was able to call on friends who were extraordinarily talented writers. The most prominent were Charles Lamb and his sister Mary, who wrote seven books for T. Hodgkins or M. J. Godwin and Company: *The King and Queen of Hearts* (1805), by Charles; *Tales from Shakespear* (1807), by Charles and Mary; *The Adventures of Ulysses* (1808), by Charles; *Mrs. Leicester's School* (1809) and *Poetry for Children, Entirely Original* (1809), by Charles and Mary; and *Prince Dorus* (1811) and *Beauty and the Beast* (1811), both by Charles. The Lambs' books were handsomely illustrated by such engravers as William Mulready, Mary Ann Flaxman, and William Blake. The Lambs' works, especially *Tales from Shakespear,* went

145

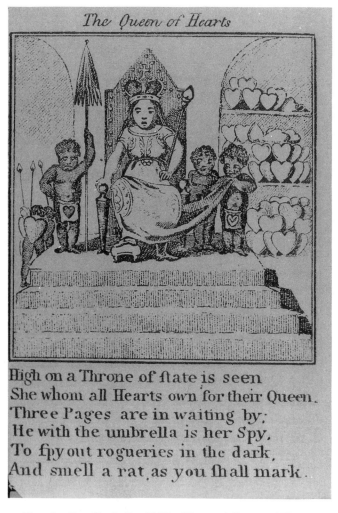

First plate from Charles Lamb's The King and Queen of Hearts, *published by the Godwins (Courtesy of Special Collections, Thomas Cooper Library, University of South Carolina)*

through many editions and are recognized as children's classics.

Godwin drew on other acquaintances and friends as well. His friend Dr. Matthew Raine was headmaster at the Charterhouse school, which purchased texts and supplies from The Juvenile Library, as did the Greenwich school, where the Reverend Charles Burney was headmaster. Margaret Jane King Moore, countess of Mount Cashell, whom Mary Wollstonecraft had educated in her capacity as governess, had remained loyal to her tutor and her tutor's husband even after the political reaction. A rebel in her own right, having left her own husband and children, she assumed the pen name Mrs. Mason and contributed to M. J. Godwin and Company *Stories for Old Daniel; or, Tales of Wonder and Delight,* published in 1808 and continued in 1820, and *Stories for Little Girls and Boys in Words of One Syllable* (n.d.). The sister of the playwright and

Whig politician Richard Brinsley Sheridan, Alicia Lefanu, wrote *Rosara's Chain; or, The Choice of Life: A Poem* (1812). The replacement for the excessively ambitious employee Hodgkins, Eliza Fenwick, contributed *Rays from the Rainbow* (1808) and *Lessons for Children; or, Rudiments of Good Manners* (1808) before defecting to Tabart, the rival publisher for whom Godwin's wife had once worked. Godwin, it seems, was not an easy publisher for whom to work. Lamb complained about his interference on *Adventures of Ulysses,* and although William Hazlitt finished *A New and Improved Grammar of the English Tongne* [*sic*] (1810) for Godwin, the latter's editorial intrusions were so annoying that Hazlitt never again wrote for M. J. Godwin and Company. Godwin asked Wordsworth for a piece, unsuccessfully, and Coleridge promised something but never wrote it.

Godwin's own family contributed to the enterprise. His wife produced the first English translation

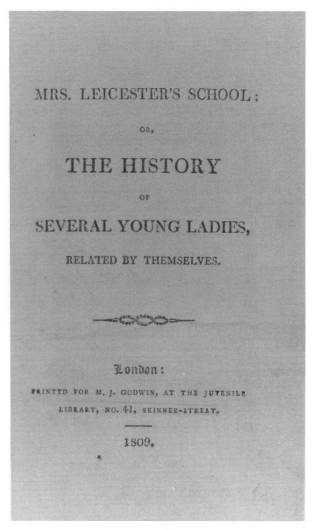

Frontispiece and title page for a children's book by Charles and Mary Lamb (Courtesy of Special Collections, Thomas Cooper Library, University of South Carolina)

of *Der Schweizerische Robinson* (1812–1813), by Johann Rudolf Wyss: *The Family Robinson Crusoe* was immensely popular both in the abridged (1814) and the complete (1816) editions. Mary Jane Godwin also produced *Dramas for Children; or, Gentle Reproofs for Their Faults* (1809) and, no doubt, other Juvenile Library books. Mary Wollstonecraft Godwin precociously created *Mounseer Nongtongpaw* (1808). According to Emily W. Sunstein's hypothesis, she also wrote – under the pseudonym of Caroline Barnard – *The Parent's Offering; or, Tales for Children* (1813) and *The Prize; or, The Lace-Makers of Missenden* (1817).

No one, however, was as prolific as Godwin himself. After *Fables, Ancient and Modern* he wrote, as Theophilus Marcliffe, *The Looking-Glass* (1805), an inspirational biography of Mulready's early years. In 1806 he produced four titles. *The Pantheon,* a book on Greek mythology of which the poet John Keats was especially fond, had four editions by 1814. When Burney, the headmaster of Greenwich, complained that some of the pictures were too erotic, Godwin had the offending plates reengraved to add more clothing. The book's sympathetic portrait of the Greeks' pagan mythology was congruent with the Hellenism of the younger Romantics. *The History of England* went through many editions and was being printed well into the 1850s; an equally popular abridged version, *Outlines of English History,* was published in 1814. Godwin's strong libertarian, Whiggish bias is apparent, but the book is objective enough that it could be used as a school text. *The Life of Lady Jane Grey, and of Lord Guildford Dudley, Her Husband,* a poignant story Godwin used to promote religious tolerance, was reprinted in 1824.

Written for his son, William Jr., *Rural Walks* was also published in 1806.

For 1809 there is *The History of Rome,* which naturally depicted Roman republicanism sympathetically; it went through six editions by 1835, and a new edition would appear in 1862, long after Godwin's death. Also published in 1809 was the popular *Mylius's School Dictionary of the English Language,* of which more than one hundred thousand copies were sold. William Frederick Mylius had composed *The Christ's Hospital Dictionary of the English Tongue* (1809), which became *Mylius's School Dictionary;* Godwin, however, seems to have supervised the dictionary at every step and contributed a preface and various other additions that reflected Enlightenment assumptions. Shortly after Hazlitt's grammar book appeared, Godwin wrote *Outlines of English Grammar, Partly Abridged from Mr. Hazlitt's New and Improved Grammar of the English Tongue* (1810). Godwin's book stressed efficiency and clarity, as it was designed to teach students as quickly and as painlessly as possible. *Mylius's School Dictionary,* Hazlitt's *New and Improved Grammar,* and Godwin's *Outlines of English Grammar* were sometimes published as one text. Godwin expanded his grammar book in 1814, and a new edition appeared in 1824. His last children's book seems to have been the Romantically Hellenistic *The History of Greece* (1821), complementing his histories of England and Rome; it, too, enjoyed many editions, being republished as late as 1862. Other titles that are possibly Godwin's, according to Peter H. Marshall, are Mylius's *The Junior Class-Book* (1809), *The Poetical Class-Book* (1810), and *The First Book of Poetry* (1811).

In 1807 The Juvenile Library and the Godwin household moved to 41 Skinner Street in Holborn, not far from the Old Bailey gallows and the Smithfield meat market. The building's five floors graciously accommodated the Godwin family, and it was conveniently near Godwin's printer, Macmillan, and his stationer, Curtis. Due to uncertainty over the ownership of the building, Godwin paid no rent for years. Despite the low rent at the bookshop's first location and the even lower rent at 41 Skinner, and although the shop was clearing around eight hundred pounds a year, Godwin was plagued by money problems. His friends, including Whig politicians and liberal publishers, organized subscriptions of more than a thousand pounds in 1806 and 1808 to pay off some of Godwin's debts.

The building at 41 Skinner Street served not only as a bookshop but also as a kind of intellectual salon, as did the houses of the publishers Joseph Johnson and Richard Phillips. In his diary Crabb Robinson wrote of Godwin's shop in 1810: "I now and then saw interesting persons at his house; indeed, I saw none but remarkable persons there." In addition to the British notables who visited Godwin there were foreign visitors such as Aaron Burr and Madame de Staël. Perhaps it was the many liberal visitors to 41 Skinner Street that provoked the interest of the spy who submitted a secret report to the Home Office in June 1813 on the sinister intentions of The Juvenile Library: the report, which apparently was never acted on, portrayed Godwin as a schemer plotting to brainwash children with revolutionary propaganda.

The only danger The Juvenile Library actually presented was to Godwin's friends, who kept lending him money that he never paid back. During a particularly severe crisis in 1810, Place assumed the task of trying to settle Godwin's financial problems. Place determined that the bookshop's assets were worth more than £7,000 and that a £3,000 loan could save the enterprise. Loans were secured — one, of £250, from Place himself — and M. J. Godwin and Company and The Juvenile Library were kept alive once more. By 1813, however, Godwin's finances were again in ruin. By that time Godwin had met a proselyte to the Godwinian philosophy: a young heir to a baronetcy in Sussex named Percy Bysshe Shelley.

The Godwin-Shelley relationship was not a happy one. Godwin was hurt by Shelley's eloping with his daughter and humiliated and frustrated by Shelley's financial assistance, which was never quite enough to establish M. J. Godwin and Company and The Juvenile Library on a secure footing. Shortly before the still-married Shelley ran off to Europe with Godwin's teenaged daughter, accompanied by Godwin's stepdaughter Claire Clairmont, he had given Godwin more than a thousand pounds. The conjunction of the two events was mortifying, giving rise to rumors and jokes about Godwin selling his daughters. Even after Mary and Shelley were married in 1816 the relationship between father-in-law and son-in-law was icy.

In 1817 ownership of 41 Skinner Street was finally established; the landlord was the one creditor Godwin could not circumvent, and in 1822 the Godwins and The Juvenile Library moved to 195 The Strand. The business continued until the financial crash of 1825, which ruined many publishing houses that were far better established than Godwin's. The Juvenile Library and M. J. Godwin and Company were forced into bankruptcy, and the assets were taken over by the publishing firm of Baldwin, Cradock, and Joy. Godwin and his wife moved to 44 Gower Place, Bloomsbury, where they lived until the Reform administration granted the old radical a pension and a residence at 13 Palace Yard in 1833. Godwin lived for three more years, and his wife died in 1841.

Despite his constant financial problems, Godwin had been able to sustain The Juvenile Library and his publishing firm for two decades; only a major economic crisis finally destroyed his business. Although economic necessity motivated his venture into bookselling and publishing, Godwin's firm produced high-quality children's literature that was also remarkably popular. Although Godwin and his fellow writers did not trumpet their political ideology, neither did they conceal it. The children's literature Godwin produced seems to have been the kind he wanted to produce and thought ought to be produced. Godwin's publishing enterprise was an effective outlet for liberal and Romantic ideas.

References:

Peter H. Marshall, *William Godwin* (London & New Haven: Yale University Press, 1984);

Charles Kegan Paul, *William Godwin: His Friends and Contemporaries,* 2 volumes (London: King, 1876);

Burton R. Pollin, *Education and Enlightenment in the Works of William Godwin* (New York: Las Americas, 1962);

Joseph E. Riehl, *Charles Lamb's Children's Literature* (Salzburg: Institut für Anglistik und Amerikanistik, 1980);

Henry Crabb Robinson, *Diary. Reminiscences, and Correspondence,* 2 volumes, edited by Thomas Sadler (London & New York: Macmillan, 1872);

William St. Clair, *The Godwins and the Shelleys: The Biography of a Family* (London & New York: Norton, 1989);

St. Clair, "William Godwin as Children's Bookseller," in *Children and Their Books,* edited by Gillian Avery and Julia Briggs (Oxford: Clarendon Press, 1989), pp. 165–179;

Emily W. Sunstein, *Mary Shelley: Romance and Reality* (Boston: Little, Brown, 1989);

George Woodcock, *William Godwin. A Biographical Study* (London: Porcupine Press, 1946).

Papers:

Many of the letters and manuscripts by William Godwin and his circle are in the Lord Abinger Collection at the Bodleian Library, Oxford. There is also considerable manuscript material in the Carl H. Pforzheimer Collection at the New York Public Library.

– Michael Scrivener

Ralph Griffiths
(London: circa 1746 – 1803)

From the 1740s to the 1760s Ralph Griffiths was a general publisher, most of that time at the sign of the Dunciad in St. Paul's Churchyard. His publications during this period covered almost every field, from religion to distilling and from poetry to medicine; he also started or had a share in several periodicals. It was, however, as publisher and active editor of the *Monthly Review* from its inception in 1749 until his death in 1803 that he made a permanent mark on literary publishing.

Born in Shropshire in 1720, Griffiths became a watchmaker in Staffordshire and then, while still a youth, went to London and worked for the bookseller Jacob Robinson. He was not apprenticed to Robinson — or, at least, was not registered as an apprentice — and the exact nature of his employment is unknown. In his *Dramatic Miscellanies* (1785) the bookseller Thomas Davies indicates that Robinson's publication of the periodical *History of the Works of the Learned* (1737–1743) influenced Griffiths's later founding of the *Monthly Review:* Davies says that Robinson "printed a periodical criticism on the works of the learned, from which work I suppose R. G. borrowed his hint of a Review. . . ."

Little is known of Griffiths's early career as a publisher/bookseller; an anonymous account published in the *Monthly Magazine* eight years after Griffiths's death summarizes these years briskly: "Abandoning his trade [as a watchmaker], he came to London, and turned bookseller, first on Ludgate hill, and afterwards in St. Paul's Churchyard, and in Paternoster-row." Documentation survives chiefly for occasions when he was in legal trouble of one kind or another. In the late 1740s he was living at Hoxton, near London. A letter in the Newcastle papers in the British Library, dated 11 September 1746, and a petition in the Public Record Office show his difficulties over the publication of *Authentic Copies of the Letters, and Other Papers Delivered, at Their Execution, by the Nine Rebels Who Suffer'd Death on Wednesday, July 30, 1746, on Kennington Common* (1746). In the letter Griffiths declares himself to be both author and publisher of the work and gives a good picture of his problem:

on the advertising of [the pamphlet] (before publication) a Warrant came from the Duke of Newcastle's Office, by which I and my Printer were taken into Custody, with the whole impression, before it was ready for Sale: But it appearing that the work was not what it was supposed to be, but the whimsical production of my own Brain, we were discharged, but the Books were never returned. However I was told that I should be payed for them, as was customary in Such Cases, no man's property being ever Injur'd at the Secretary's Office. But tho' I have been at Westminster 13 times, I have not yet obtained the least relief, tho' still kept in hopes of succeeding; and as I live 4 miles from thence, my first loss has been much enhanced by this additional loss of time and expence.

He goes on to offer four points in his favor, in the hope that they will procure him relief: his being "Zealously affected to the present government" and his pamphlet "being intended to mortify the Jacobites"; his having lost at least forty pounds by being prevented from publishing the pamphlet; his having always been "industrious, both with . . . tongue and pen, in vindicating the protestant Succession"; and his restraint in resisting the advice of those who urged him to publish an account of his troubles and losses, "which would indeed make a moving Story." His petition two weeks earlier to Thomas Pelham-Holles, Duke of Newcastle, covers substantially the same ground but emphasizes that he is "a young man of no fortune . . . and no means of subsisting but by [his] Pen."

A few months later Griffiths was in trouble again, this time over the publication at the end of 1746 of the popular and much-reprinted *Ascanius; or, The Young Adventurer,* with Charles Edward Stuart, the Young Pretender, as its hero. Griffiths was the author and William Owen the publisher of this highly risky work; in a Public Record Office document of his legal examination Griffiths, who is described as "Gentleman," presents an entirely different picture of his circumstances than in his earlier letter and petition when he says that "he can live independent of the world, & that this way of writing which he hath taken to for some time past, is a pleasant expedient to pass away the time, & calculated for no bad purposes whatever." He does not attempt to explain the dangerously favorable picture of the Young Pretender in his book; he simply denies that he had any such intention: "He saith, that he hath been author of several Pamphletts on the behalf of the Government, & that he never intended by this Pamphlett of Ascanius to give offence, or to move Compassion on the behalf of the Pr^s Son, against whom He should have thought it his Duty, & would have taken up arms with great Zeal, if it had been required of him. . . ." Griffiths even claims to be working on a counterblast "Pamphlett with the same Title" to "lay open to the world the odiousness of the Rebellion & of the Pretender's Son's Character."

Having survived this second peril, Griffiths next found himself in strife over the publication of John Cleland's *Memoirs of a Woman of Pleasure* (1748–1749), which was possibly a joint enterprise with his brother Fenton (the extent of Ralph Griffiths's involvement in the first edition is not clear, and the only documented career of Fenton Griffiths is that of a sailor), under the fictitious imprint "G. Fenton," and the publication in 1750 under his own imprint of the bowdlerized version, *Memoirs of Fanny Hill.* Several documents concerning this case survive in the Public Record Office, including the examinations of Ralph Griffiths, the printer Thomas Parker, and Owen. There is also a letter dated 15 March 1749/50 (Old Style) from the bishop of London, Thomas Sherlock, begging for action to be taken against the censored version, "the Lewdest thing I ever saw . . ."; the bishop says that he has been told that it is "the same with the other, after leaving out some things, which were thought most liable to the Law and to expose the Author and publisher to punishment." Griffiths, who is described in one document as having threatened with a "large Hammer" the men who came to execute the duke of Newcastle's warrant, reports in his statement of 20 March that as Cleland had owed him some money and was due to go abroad, he had asked Cleland "to strike out the offensive parts of [*Memoirs of a Woman of Pleasure*] & compile a Novel from it which might be inoffensive. . . ." In the end this fuss, too, dissipated. Griffiths's most disingenuous – even plainly untruthful – comments on the book came when he reviewed anonymously (all reviewing during the century was done anonymously) the expurgated version in the March 1750 *Monthly Review,* expressing puzzlement about "the step lately taken to suppress this book" and describing it only as "said to be taken from a very loose work, printed about two years ago," which he claims not to have seen. Griffiths's part in the publication of the work was not soon forgotten; nearly forty years later Davies,

MEMOIRS

OF

Mrs. *Lætitia Pilkington,*

WIFE TO THE

Rev. Mr. *Matthew Pilkington.*

Written by HERSELF.

Wherein are occasionally interspersed,

All Her POEMS;

WITH

Anecdotes of several eminent Persons,
Living and Dead.

Among others,

Dean *Swift, Alexander Pope,* Esq;
&c. &c. &c.

DUBLIN Printed ;

London Reprinted : and Sold by R. *Griffiths,* at
the *Dunciad* in *Ludgate-street,* and G. *Woodfall,*
at the *King's Arms* at *Charing-Cross.* 1748.

*Title page for one of Ralph Griffiths's early publications
(Courtesy of the Lilly Library, Indiana University)*

angered by a review of a work of his own in the *Monthly Review,* wrote: "But how the modest and pious Proprietor of the Monthly Review, *Ralph Griffiths* of Turnham Green, can ever exonerate himself from having been the *first editor* and *Publisher* of the *Memoirs of a Woman of Pleasure,* I am not enough concerned to enquire. It surely did not become this man to put stones into his pocket to throw at his old acquaintance."

The earliest surviving works with Griffiths's imprint are dated 1740, although there are grounds for believing that both may be misdated; next come works published in 1746. The last definitely dated one not having to do with the *Monthly Review* appeared in 1766, but 1762 was his last year of multiple publications. A list of "Books printed for, and sold by R. Griffiths, at the Dunciad in St. Paul's Church-Yard" from 1752, appended to the seventh volume of the *Monthly Review,* gives some idea of the range of books and pamphlets he published. It consists of seventy-two items (the numbering goes only to 71, but there are two items numbered 24) grouped under the headings "History and Memoirs" (nineteen items, including both fiction and nonfiction), "Poetry" (seven items), "Miscellaneous" (thirty items), "Divinity, Morality, and Controversy" (ten items), and "Addenda" (six items). Most date from 1748 to 1752. The first category includes historical or semihistorical works, from *The Revolutions of the Republick of Genoa* (1751), a translation from Louis-Georges-Oudard Feudrix de Bréquigny's French original, to the Abbé de Mably's *Observations on the Romans* (1751), also a translation from the French, and Andrew Henderson's *Edinburgh History of the Late Rebellion* (1752); a group of anonymous "autobiographical" novels, including Tobias Smollett's *Peregrine Pickle* (1751), Sarah Scott's *The History of Cornelia* (1750), and *Memoirs of Fanny Hill*; and some actual memoirs, most notably those of Colley Cibber (1740) and Laetitia Pilkington (1748–1749). The works by Smollett, Scott, Cibber, and others in the list are not described elsewhere as published by Griffiths; perhaps he simply sold them. Notable among the poetry is William Kenrick's satire *The Town* (1748) and George Alexander Stevens's burlesque *Distress upon Distress* (1752). Griffiths's "miscellaneous" category ranges from a translation of the works of Sallust and John Hill's *A Review of the Works of the Royal Society of London* (1751) and his *The Actor; or, A Treatise on the Art of Playing* (1750) to James Illingworth's *A Genuine Account of the Man, Whose Hands and Legs Rotted off, in the Parish of King's-Swinford in Staffordshire* (1750); it also includes works on hare hunting, the herring fishery, and venereal disease. "Divinity, Morality, and Controversy" ranges from the comprehensive *A System of Divinity and Morality, Proper for All Families* (1756), compiled by Ferdinando Warner; Richard Baron's *The Pillars of Priestcraft and Orthodoxy Shaken* (1752); and Thomas Gordon's *A Cordial for Low-Spirits* (1750) to items of more limited focus, such as the anonymous *The Expediency and Necessity of Revising and Improving the Publick Liturgy* (1749) and James Forrester's *Dialogues on the Passions, Habits, and Affections Peculiar to Children, Wherein the Infant State of the Soul Is Fully Displayed* (1748). The "Addenda" include Walter Hodges's *Elihu; or, An Enquiry into the Principal Scope and Design of the Book of Job* (1750) and Jacques Pernetti's *Philosophical Letters upon Physiognomies* (1751).

Griffiths's correspondence in the Bodleian Library shows that his book dealings ranged over a wide geographic area. Letters from the publisher and bookseller James Hoey in Dublin, dated between 1760 and 1763, show that Griffiths was supplying Hoey with books and periodicals. Several letters from John Doughty, on his way to and after his arrival in India, show that he was doing some book dealing on Griffiths's behalf, if only in a small way. "I am in good health and . . . have dispos'd of about fifteen Pounds worth of Books," he wrote from a ship near Madras in February 1762; eleven months later he wrote from Calcutta, "the Books which you sent out by me sold for something better than prime cost such indeed as the Monthly Review Keyslers Traveles and some others at 50 pr cent. . . ." A letter of 1 March 1758 from James Ralph, who was contemplating publishing an edition of the works of John Dryden, shows Griffiths's standing as a fount of knowledge in the trade: "I shall want all the Advice and assistance you can give me in it. Not knowing how to compute the number of vols. they will take up, nor being quite certain as to the works themselves." (The Dryden edition was apparently never published.) Griffiths made an effort to become an official government publisher, but without success; a letter of 5 November 1761 from the politician Charles Jenkinson provides a regretful negative answer to one of the same date in which Griffiths asks Jenkinson to bear his "trusty Operator in the Strand" in mind for some of this work, "which must prove advantageous to whoever is the Bookseller."

Had Griffiths merely been a bookseller for some twenty years, his place in publishing history would have been a small one; he might have been known only as part of the early history of *Fanny Hill*. In May 1749, however, he began the enterprise that was to change the literary marketplace forever: the *Monthly Review*. Griffiths's periodical had predecessors in journals that offered some account – principally by means of abstracts and extracts, with little evaluative comment – of "works of the learned," beginning in France in the seventeenth century; the *Journal des Sçavans,* for example, was started in Paris in 1665. His English predecessors, imitators of the French journals, included *Weekly Memorials for the Ingenious,* started in 1682; *Memoirs of Literature,* started in 1710; and Robinson's *History of the Works of the Learned.* None of these publications made any attempt to cover books for the eighteenth century's version of the educated general reader; they covered works considered to be of intellectual importance. What Griffiths saw, as the advertisement attached to the first number of his journal suggested, was that the increasing audience for an expanding literary market might be persuaded of the necessity for "a summary review of the productions of the press, as they occur to notice" to assist its judgments. He promised "a periodical work, whose sole object should be to give a compendious account of those productions of the press, as they come out, that are worth notice; an account, in short, which should, in virtue of its candour, and justness of distinction, obtain authority enough for its representations to be serviceable to such as would choose to have some idea of a book before they lay out their money or time on it."

A newspaper advertisement said that the new journal would provide simply "an Account, with proper Abstracts, of the new Books, Pamphlets, &c. as they come out"; but the first number took an important step toward expanding the field when the six books reviewed in it included two works of poetry and a play. Two months later the next important step was taken when the journal started a supplementary section of short reviews of less important works and declared: "We propose, for the future, to register all the new Things in general, without exception to any, on account of their lowness of rank, or price. But as it would exceed the limits of our plan, as well as prove disagreeable to many of our readers to give a large detail of some of our new productions, we shall content ourselves with giving a very brief account of them, in the manner following." From this point on, each issue consisted of an average of ten long articles followed by a catalogue of shorter items that often included lists of single sermons, some with comment. From the eighth volume to the end of the first series in 1789 each semiannual volume consisted of six monthly numbers (January to June and July to December) published on the first day of the next month (for example, the January number would be published on 1 February), with an appendix published at the end of the seventh month including the index and other necessary material to complete the volume, together with reviews (the appendix came out on the same date as the first number of the next volume – that is, on 1 February and 1 August). Eventually the appendix was given over entirely to items of foreign literature.

The earliest issues of the *Monthly Review* proclaimed it to be the work of "several hands"; at this time Griffiths and his friend William Rose did most of the reviewing, aided by a few others, such as Cleland. In March 1751 an advertisement in the *London Advertiser* described the authorship as "Six Gentlemen of different Qualifications." By the time of Griffiths's death there would have been 175 contributors, and Griffiths would for some time have reviewed only occasionally.

Despite long-standing claims that the *Monthly Review* failed in its early years – Henry R. Plomer, for example, says that "Business did not prosper with him and he became bankrupt, his *Review* being sold for the benefit of his creditors" – the *Monthly Review* prospered and attracted a host of imitators. Between 1749 and 1760 at least nine review journals were started; most were short-lived (the *Impartial Review,* for example, seems to have lasted for only one number in 1759), and only one, Smollett's *Critical Review,* was successful. Many more general journals started review sections as regular features. Magazines such as *Gentleman's* and *London* had done occasional notices of books, and reviews had appeared in newspapers from time to time, but it was not until the *Monthly Review* established a marketplace for critical opinions on every kind of literary work that other periodicals took the enterprise seriously and began systematic reviewing. By 1769, as the journal *Critical Memoirs of the Times* pointed out in its first volume, the editors of most periodicals found it necessary to give "some account of the productions of the press."

In June 1761 Griffiths sold a fourth share in the *Monthly Review* to Benjamin Collins of Salisbury for £755 12s.6d. This transaction may have come about because of financial need; but the journal's printing run had increased, and it would continue for more than forty years with Griffiths at the helm and another forty after that, ceasing publication in 1845. Collins's executors were paid £900 for the quarter share in December 1789, with another £957 7s. for a quarter share of seven years' profits of the *Monthly Review.* C. H. Timperley reports on the journal's early years: "When the *Monthly Review* started there was no regular established Literary Review in Great Britain; nor was this one very successful on its first publication. Several times it was about to be abandoned, as Dr. Griffiths often told his friends; but patience, perseverance, and attention, surmounted every obstacle, and procured it a firm establishment."

One part of the revolution in the literary world to which Griffiths made such a substantial contribution was his early use of review material in advertisements for books. In the *General Advertiser* for Friday, 14 December 1750, there is an advertisement for the forthcoming *Revolutions of the Republick of Genoa* that quotes from the review of the original French edition of the work in the *Monthly Review,* presenting remarks from three separate passages as a single, connected paragraph and including what was to become a typical footnote: "Vide the Character of the Original, in the Monthly Review, for March 1750." The use of review material in advertisements soon became widely established among booksellers and appeared in newspapers and in the booksellers' advertisements printed at the end (or occasionally at the beginning) of books. The latter kind of advertisement carried review material more often, since newspaper advertisements most commonly appeared before the book concerned had been reviewed.

Griffiths was involved in the publication of other journals, including the *London Advertiser and Literary Gazette* (1751–1753), the *Grand Magazine of Universal Intelligence* (1758–1760), the *Library* (1761–1762), and the *St. James's Chronicle* (which began in 1761 and outlasted Griffiths, ceasing publication in 1866), but it was the *Monthly Review* for which he was known. Many Griffiths publications were reviewed in the *Monthly Review* in the years before Griffiths withdrew from book publishing – since the journal was attempting to cover "all the productions of the press," it could hardly be otherwise. Often the fact that a book under review was a Griffiths publication was passed over in silence, apart from the mention of the publisher's name at the head of the review; to Griffiths's credit – or perhaps as a clever move to preempt criticism – the reviews frequently included some quibble about the work. In October 1750, for example, Griffiths expressed the wish that the editor of *Cato's Letters* "had communicated, in a preface to this volume, the authority upon which he asserts the pieces it contains to be Mr. *Gordon*'s." Sometimes the reviewer made jokes, as when John Berkenhout opened his January 1756 review of Carl Gustaf Tessin's *Letters from an Old Man to a Young Prince:*

> This publication hath procured us the honour of a visit extraordinary from our publisher; who in his own, and his printer's name, earnestly desired, that we would not forget to do justice to them both, in our account of these Letters. – "Gentlemen," says he, "people may talk as they will of your Elzevirs, and your Scotch editions; this" (holding one of the volumes in his hand) "is inferior to nothing that was ever published in Great Britain! Do but observe this margin! Why, Gentlemen, the paper cost me some pounds more than is commonly given. And then the type! – there's a letter for you! Caslon cast it on purpose to let the world see, that we can print in London as well as they do in any other part of Europe. Pray, Gentlemen, apprize your readers of the beauty of this impression."

Berkenhout goes on, mocking Griffiths as "our industrious friend" who knows more about paper and type than about the inside of books and pointing out that the content of the book is more important than its form, however elegant. When, in 1762, Griffiths officially retired from bookselling (in fact, he continued to be involved in publishing for many years, but he no longer had a shop or appeared in the imprints of many publications), most of this problem – if it was a problem – stopped, except for comments from disgruntled authors whose works had been given insufficiently respectful treatment in the *Monthly Review.*

The responses of the generation of writers who were experiencing systematic book reviewing for the first time included personal attacks on Griffiths as the figurehead of the *Monthly Review* (although nothing like the attacks directed at Smollett, who was assumed by many to be the author of everything in the *Critical Review* even years after he had left it). Griffiths had to endure such attacks as the poem "On Mother Griffiths," in the April 1763 number of Francis Fawkes and William Woty's *Poetical Calendar,* which begins, "The race of critics, till of late, were grac'd / With reading, learning, judgment, sense, and taste" and goes on, a few lines later, "But now, oh shame to Britain, and the muse! / Dame Griffiths writes her infamous Reviews. . . ." The reference to "Dame Griffiths" stems from the story, often told by Smollett in the *Critical Review,* that Griffiths's first wife, Isabella, wrote for the journal. Griffiths always said that the story was not true – he wrote, for example, to Edward Thompson on 16 March 1771, "I do assure you, and I have signed my name to it, that she never wrote a line, nor a word, in the Review, nor, to the best of my knowledge, in any other production of the Press" – and it is difficult to see why he should have lied so vociferously when he was an encourager of women writers. A month later Fawkes and Woty claimed in another poem that a poet could not achieve success " 'Till Mother Griffiths has receiv'd a bribe. . . ." Of the "ruffian, GRIFFITHS" Percival Stockdale wrote in his 1773 poem *The Poet* that "monthly readers, ever daily fools, / Adopt his nonsense for true critic rules. . . ."

One of the early attackers of the *Monthly Review* was Arthur Murphy, who conducted a mock trial in September 1754 in his *Gray's Inn Journal.* Murphy provides a typical example of the kinds of general objections made to the review journals when he complains that the reviewers "have presumed to pass their Decision, in a Pamphlet entitled the *Monthly Review,* upon all Performances in Literature" and declares that "a more gross Imposition was never offer'd to the Republick of Letters, than for a Bookseller, whose sign is justly *emblematical* of his Authors, *viz.* the *Dunciad,* to take upon him to dictate to the Public in a Work, conducted by obscure Hirelings, Country schoolmasters, &c." He goes on to demand "whether it is not the highest Presumption in a Set of Hirelings . . . to usurp the Seat of Criticism without declaring who and what they are, without producing their Credentials, to shew the World by what Authority they act, and without previously giving undeniable Proofs of their own Ability and Taste. . . ." It is interesting to note that Murphy later became a reviewer for the *Monthly Review.*

Griffiths maintained the anonymity of his reviewers, and he was followed in this practice by his many eighteenth-century imitators. He wrote on 2 September 1788 to the sister of a reviewer who had been inclined to publicize his reviewing activities, "I have always made it an unalterable rule to keep everything as secret as possible, relating to my literary connexions: and I always blamed your Brother for divulging anything about it." The *Monthly Review* maintained an editorial *we* and tried, as did most of the other review journals (until William Kenrick's *London Review* began appending initials to reviews in the 1770s), to maintain consistency among the reviews and to convey the impression of one large enterprise rather than a collection of individual reviews. Most of the reviewers have been identified thanks to Griffiths's cryptically annotated set of the *Monthly Review,* which survives in the Bodleian Library; the list includes many writers who were well known in the eighteenth century, such as Edmund Cartwright, John Wolcot (Peter Pindar), Thomas Beddoes, William Enfield, John Leslie, and John Langhorne, and many who are still widely known, such as John Hawkesworth, Thomas Holcroft, Anna Laetitia Barbauld, and Richard Brinsley Sheridan. Among those who were the authors of only one or a handful of reviews are Smollett; Frances Burney D'Arblay; George Gordon, Lord Byron; Isaac D'Israeli; and David Garrick. Oliver Goldsmith's employment as a general laborer on the *Monthly Review* in the 1750s and 1760s is well known: he claimed to have been badly treated by Griffiths, and his biographer John Forster's partisan account of the incident presented Griffiths as a monster; but more-recent accounts, such as Elizabeth Eaton Kent's, suggest that any ill treatment may have had some justification. Be that as it may, the *Monthly Review* had little good to say about Goldsmith forever after, a graceless pattern not apparently repeated in the case of any other reviewer who left in a huff; perhaps Goldsmith was the first and last full-time employee of the publication.

THE

MONTHLY REVIEW,

O R,

LITERARY JOURNAL.

BY SEVERAL HANDS.

VOLUME XXI.

LONDON:
Printed for R. GRIFFITHS, in the Strand.
MDCCLIX.

Title page for the groundbreaking literary journal Griffiths started in 1749 (Courtesy of the Lilly Library, Indiana University)

It is clear from Griffiths's correspondence that after the earliest years his corps of reviewers included a variety of experts, each of whom dealt with works of a particular kind. Some reviewers — Samuel Badcock and Owen Ruffhead, for example — turned their hands to most kinds of literature; others, such as Charles Burney the elder for music, Charles Burney the younger for classical literature, and John Touchet for law, were employed as needed to review work in their areas of expertise. Most of the reviewers did not know each other's identities; thus, in their correspondence with Griffiths they refer to each other as "your friend who guides the *philosophic* Helm," "your Mathematical Reviewer," "the customary Reviewer of articles of that Nature," and so on.

Reviewing was not a full-time occupation; the majority of reviewers were clergymen, many of them Dissenters. The pay for reviewing was, however, quite good. The usual rate during the second half of the eighteenth century varied between two pounds and four guineas per octavo sheet (sixteen pages). Griffiths notes on a 1794 letter from Leslie that he has agreed to pay Leslie four pounds per sheet, and in an undated letter to William Taylor of Norwich, written around 1795, Griffiths says that the ordinary rate of pay, "with *allowed exceptions* in favour of the more difficult branches of the business," has remained substantially unchanged in the fifty years of the magazine's life and that Taylor's pay, now that he has "gone through [his] probation" and proved that his "abilities and exertions were above the ordinary level and consequence," will be three guineas. J. Workman mentions in an undated letter (circa 1797) that Griffiths's terms are three guineas per sheet. Archibald Maclaine, the writer of most of the Foreign Literature section from 1775 to 1788, refers to "the five-pound *Doucem*" he has apparently been receiving; but this amount appears to have been a secret, indicating that it was unusually high. In an undated letter to Griffiths, written in 1790, Andrew Becket complains that for 280 articles in the *Monthly Review* he has been paid only forty-five pounds; Becket's father, Griffiths's friend and onetime partner Thomas Becket, then wrote at length to Griffiths expressing his disgust at his son's ingratitude. Andrew Becket appears to have been in a minority; many of the reviewers claimed to have little interest in the pay they would receive.

The reviewers were not allowed to keep the review copies sent to them by Griffiths, who bought or borrowed most of the books — free review copies were only occasionally sent out by publishers, usually at the request of the authors — and returned or sold them back to the booksellers. The *Monthly Review* sometimes notes that a work reviewed earlier and mentioned by a correspondent is no longer on hand; and Griffiths's correspondence has several references by reviewers to formerly reviewed works that are no longer in their possession. The practice of returning the books caused difficulties for reviewers invited by Griffiths to respond to a complaint or other comment concerning a review; for example, Badcock, apparently after a complaint about an "expression relating to Dr. Delaney," points out to Griffiths on 30 January 1780: "I have not that Volume of Swift. I returned it to you." On 24 November 1780 Badcock writes, "Had I imagined that I should again have taken up the pen against Madan, I would not have returned the 2 Vols. to you."

Whether book buyers followed the opinions of reviewers there is reason to doubt — although many authors and booksellers believed that they

did — but it is undoubtedly true that many readers obtained their first detailed knowledge of important publications from the *Monthly Review* and its imitators. The list of notable works given extended attention in the *Monthly Review* includes Samuel Johnson's *A Dictionary of the English Language* (1755), his *The Plays of William Shakespeare* (1765), and his *Prefaces, Biographical and Critical, to the Works of the English Poets* (1779, 1781); Adam Smith's *An Inquiry into the Nature and Causes of the Wealth of Nations* (1776); Edmund Burke's *Reflections on the Revolution in France* (1790); David Hume's *The History of Great Britain* (1754, 1757); Sir William Jones's studies in Oriental languages and literatures; Edward Gibbon's *The History of the Decline and Fall of the Roman Empire* (1776–1788); Charles Burney the elder's *A General History of Music, from the Earliest Ages to the Present Period* (1776–1789); William Wordsworth and Samuel Taylor Coleridge's *Lyrical Ballads* (1798); and innumerable accounts of medical and scientific discoveries.

Griffiths seems to have been on good terms with most of the shifting cast of major and minor literary figures who served him as reviewers, and some clearly regarded him with great affection and esteem. "In his company I took particular delight — Such a fund of anecdote, pleasantry & good nature & with views so liberal & enlarged," wrote Leslie on 29 November 1801 to George Edward Griffiths, Griffiths's son and eventual successor. Some of Ralph Griffiths's letters to Charles Burney the elder indicate that excuses for delays in reviewing were received civilly; on 20 April 1790 he urges Burney not to force himself to work when ill: "of the two evils, I prefer suicide to the murder of my friends." In an undated letter, probably written in December 1791, desperation makes Griffiths only a little more pressing:

> I should be glad to know whether I might venture to sollicit y^r. farther assistance, in y^e. present Emergency? — *Our* Harvest is now growing plentiful, & y^e. reapers are, comparatively, few. — Moreover, our *Enlargement* has increased our labour, but the Labourers are not increased in numbers; wch. they ought to be, lest what should be done with pleasure, should become a *toil.* — If, therefore, you could (& I heartily wish you may) make a truce with y^r. *Rhumacy,* & persuade it to quit y^r. shoulders, that I may lay 2 or 3 octavos on them, *instead,* I sh^d. hope you would not be a Sufferer by the Exchange.

An expectation of a good-humored response is suggested by such remarks as William Enfield's cheerful comment in a letter of 4 June 1795: "I find so many arrears that I have written under some dread of your *Condemned Cell,* which, if I conjecture right, resembles the dark country *from whose bourne no traveller returns."*

The *enlargement* Griffiths mentions in his letter to Burney refers to the one major change he made to the *Monthly Review* after it settled into its format of two volumes a year, each volume consisting of six monthly numbers and an appendix. The "appendix month," when the appendix would appear on or about the first of the month together with the first monthly number of the next volume, was a burden to Griffiths and his son; many letters from Ralph and George Edward Griffiths to both Charles Burneys refer to the appendix in such terms as "insatiable monster" and make such comments as "I am too much distress'd, & hurried, to allow of my going abroad, even for one 1/2 hour!" With the new series, beginning in January 1790, the *Monthly Review* started coming out in three volumes a year of about the same size as before, increasing its yearly quantity of pages by half. An address of more than three pages, "TO THE LITERARY WORLD," prefaces the first issue of the new series, justifying the enlargement and the rise in price with the explanation that the great increase in publications has made it impossible for the journal to keep up: "Thus, like the progressive accumulation of the great national debt, hath been this more insignificant debt of THE MONTHLY REVIEW, which has usually amounted to between two and three hundred publications, of various rank and importance."

The 1811 piece on Griffiths in the *Monthly Magazine* dates his prosperity after the beginning of the second series of the *Monthly Review,* commenting that "he commenced a handsome establishment at Turnham Green; latterly kept two carriages, and lived in style." The article also says that Griffiths "was made a Doctor of Law, by some obscure American University"; Forster refers indignantly to Griffiths, "whom the diploma of some American university as obscure as himself made subsequently *Doctor* Griffiths," and many other biographical sources have been as cavalier. Kent, however, demonstrated in 1933 that it was Dartmouth that awarded Griffiths an LL.D. in August 1790 for services to the American cause, particularly help to the then president of the university, John Wheelock. (The other recipient of this honor at the commencement ceremony was Alexander Hamilton, treasurer of the United States.)

At the end of his life Griffiths was virtually blind, but his control over the *Monthly Review* continued. In a letter of 9 May 1801 to his friend Charles Burney the elder, Griffiths refers cheerfully to his own good health, "all but my poor eyes, which are nearly gone: so that I am obliged to a friendly pen for this expression of what passes in my heart & mind." In this letter, signed "The old blind man of the Green," Griffiths can clearly be seen to be still holding the reins of the *Monthly Review:*

> I want now to make a little over-hauling of the acc^t. betwen you & me; & as soon as this hurry skurry App^x. month is over, I hope to set about it. – Mean time, I trouble you with a few literary *somewhats* to amuse your leisure hours. – Moore's Anacreon seems to call for a preference in point of time & dispatch, both as most important & as having waited longest; tho' perhaps your old friend Hoole will dispute precedency with the merry old Grecian. M^r. H. however should remember that the modern Italian has been already handed to the public by us in the 37th. Vol. of our *old* Series: – as you will have the goodness to observe in its proper place.
>
> I find in your book that two publications were sent to you in *May 1799,* which have never been *notticed* viz. Corse's treatise on Singing. folio. sewed. Texier – *l'ami des Meres,* Vol. 1. 8vo.sewed. with regard to the last, as it has been so long overlooked, & is only a first vol. not followed (as far as I know) by others, it may as well sleep in peace: but should not some account yet be given of the first?

Griffiths's death on 28 September 1803 was mentioned in many publications; the most extensive notice, in the *European Magazine* for January 1804, comments mainly on the novelty of and need for the review journal he established. The writer says that little is known of "either the literary life or domestic habits of Dr. Griffiths" but anticipates with pleasure the publication of his father's memoirs by George Edward Griffiths because

> in the variety of situations where this venerable critic and valuable member of society has resided, from the Dunciad in St. Paul's Church-yard, 1747, to the Dunciad near Catherine-street, 1772, where we perfectly remember his shop to be a favourite lounge of the late Dr. Goldsmith, he must have become acquainted with more characters, anecdotes, and circumstances, many of which we hope he has preserved, than, perhaps, any other Critic from Dionysus of Halicarnassus, who, we gather from Polybius and others, was the first reviewer, downward, or indeed any other person of the bibliopolical or literary professions.

The memoirs were, however, never produced.

From his early employment with Robinson to his death sixty years later, still at the helm of the revolutionary review journal he had founded, Ralph Griffiths played an increasingly important part in the literary world. His main interest was book publishing for only a relatively short period, but with the *Monthly Review* he was involved with most aspects of the publishing world and was the originator of permanent changes in it. The publishing equation had previously consisted of author, publisher, and public, with the occasional entry of the patron; now the professional critic had a part to play too.

References:

Thomas Davies, *Dramatic Miscellanies,* 3 volumes (London: Printed for the author and sold at his shop, 1785);

"Extracts from the Portfolio of a Man of Letters," *Monthly Magazine,* 32 (January 1812): 566–567;

Francis Fawkes and William Woty, *The Poetical Calendar; Containing a Collection of Scarce and Valuable Pieces of Poetry: With Variety of Originals and Translations,* 12 volumes (London: Printed by D. Leach for J. Coote, 1763);

John Forster, *The Life and Times of Oliver Goldsmith,* 2 volumes (London: Bradbury & Evans, 1848);

Walter Graham, *English Literary Periodicals* (New York: Nelson, 1930);

Elizabeth Eaton Kent, *Goldsmith and His Booksellers* (Ithaca, N.Y.: Cornell University Press, 1933);

Lewis M. Knapp, "Griffiths's 'Monthly Review' as Printed by Strahan," *Notes and Queries,* 203 (May 1958): 216–217;

Knapp, "Ralph Griffiths, Author and Publisher, 1746–1750," *Library,* fourth series 20 (September 1940): 197–213;

Charles Knight, *Shadows of the Old Booksellers* (London: Peter Davies, 1927);

Roger Lonsdale, "Dr. Burney and the *Monthly Review,*" *Review of English Studies,* new series 14 (1963): 346–358; 15 (1964): 27–37;

Lonsdale, *Dr. Charles Burney: A Literary Biography* (Oxford: Clarendon Press, 1965);

"Memoir of Ralph Griffiths, LL.D.," *European Magazine,* 45 (January 1804): 3–4;

Arthur Murphy, *Gray's Inn Journal,* 2 volumes (London: Printed by W. Faden for P. Vaillant, 1756);

Benjamin Christie Nangle, *The Monthly Review First Series 1749–1789: Indexes of Contributors and Articles* (Oxford: Clarendon Press, 1934);

Nangle, *The Monthly Review Second Series 1790–1815: Indexes of Contributors and Articles* (Oxford: Clarendon Press, 1955);

Norman Edwin Oakes, "Ralph Griffiths and the Monthly Review," dissertation, Columbia University, 1961;

Henry R. Plomer and others, *Dictionary of Booksellers and Printers Who Were at Work in England, Scotland, and Ireland from 1726 to 1775* (Oxford: Bibliographical Society, 1932);

John W. Robberds, *A Memoir of the Life and Writings of the Late William Taylor of Norwich,* 2 volumes (London: John Murray, 1843);

Derek Roper, *Reviewing before the* Edinburgh *1788–1802* (London: Methuen, 1978);

Robert Donald Spector, *English Literary Periodicals and the Climate of Opinion During the Seven Years' War* (The Hague: Mouton, 1966);

Spector, "The Monthly and Its Rival," *Bulletin of the New York Public Library,* 64 (March 1960): 159–161;

Percival Stockdale, *The Memoirs of the Life, and Writings of Percival Stockdale,* 2 volumes (London: Longman, Hurst, Rees & Orme, 1809);

Stockdale, *The Poet: A Poem* (London: Printed for W. Flexney, 1773);

W. Denham Sutcliffe, "English Book-Reviewing 1749–1800," D.Phil. thesis, Oxford University, 1942;

C. H. Timperley, *Encyclopaedia of Literary and Typographical Anecdote,* second edition (London: Bohn, 1842);

Thomas Griffiths Wainewright, *Essays and Criticisms by Thomas Griffiths Wainewright Now First Collected With Some Account of the Author,* edited by William Carew Hazlitt (London: Reeves & Turner, 1880);

Charles Welsh, *A Bookseller of the Last Century: Being Some Account of the Life of John Newbery, and of the Books He Published, with a Notice of the Later Newberys* (London: Griffith, Farran, Okeden & Welsh, 1885).

Papers:
Letters to and from Ralph Griffiths, and other documents related to him, are in the Bodleian Library, Oxford, Add. Mss. C89, C90; the British Library, Newcastle Papers and Liverpool Papers; the Beinecke Library, Yale University, Burney Papers; and the Public Record Office, London.

— Antonia Forster

Joseph Johnson

(London: 1761 – 1809)

Joseph Johnson was among the leading figures in London's liberal and dissenting intellectual circles, whose members included William Godwin, Mary Wollstonecraft, Thomas Paine, Henry Fuseli, Joseph Priestley, and Erasmus Darwin. In his forty-eight years as a publisher and bookseller he produced twenty-seven hundred titles, averaging fifty-six a year. His reputation as a literary publisher and patron of belles lettres was assured by his publishing and promoting of the works of the popular poet William Cowper. Religious publications constituted the largest category of works put out by Johnson, followed by literature, medicine, politics, and science. He commissioned more than a hundred engravings from William Blake, providing Blake's principal source of income while Blake labored on his own creative works. Johnson published two important periodicals: the *London Medical Journal,* the first of its kind published in London, and the *Analytical Review,* an important periodical for dissenting religious, artistic, and political points of view. Contemporary testimonies stress his activities as a publisher and bookseller who promoted inexpensive editions of literary and scientific writings, and religious and political pamphlets.

Johnson's liberalism was balanced by a sense of fairness and willingness to deal with various sides of intellectual debates. Despite the controversial positions of his friends and authors, such as the radical American poet and politician Joel Barlowe (1754–1812), Godwin, Wollstonecraft, and Paine — whom Johnson lodged when he was being sought by the authorities for treason — Johnson left few letters and no documents that reveal his personal political or religious beliefs. Characteristic of the variety of views he was able to accommodate in times of fierce partisan debate is that while he was the official London publisher and distributor for the Unitarian Church and the distributor of dissenting sermons and polemics, his oldest and dearest friend in London was the outspokenly agnostic painter, scholar, and wit Fuseli.

The younger of two sons of John Johnson, a Baptist farmer at Everton, near Liverpool, Johnson was born on 15 November 1738. In 1752 he went to London, where, two years later, he was apprenticed

to George Keith at the Bible and Crown on Gracechurch Street. Keith specialized in publishing and selling Baptist tracts, including the works of his father-in-law, the prominent Baptist theologian Dr. John Gill. Johnson completed his apprenticeship in 1761 and set up his own shop at the Golden Anchor in Fenchurch Street before moving to Lombard Street, finally settling later in 1761 at the sign of Mead's Head at 12 or 14 Fish Hill Street. The shop at Mead's Head was convenient for medical students and doctors to visit on their way to local hospitals; Johnson thus established bookselling and publishing ties with the medical community that he would maintain throughout his career.

In 1765 Johnson entered a partnership with Benjamin Davenport, with whom he moved to 8 Paternoster Row later that year. Davenport's name, when it did appear in imprints, was always second; more often it was subsumed under the imprint "J. Johnson and Co." During his partnership with Davenport, Johnson brought out the short-lived *Monthly Record of Literature* (January–December 1767), a magazine of reviews he took over from William Tooke, another bookseller on Paternoster Row.

In the early years Johnson's publishing and bookselling trade centered on three types of publications: dissenting religious works, works connected with intellectual life in Liverpool, and medical texts. Among the first religious writers whose works Johnson published and distributed was John Newton, an evangelical minister and former slave-ship captain whose *Authentic Narrative of Some Remarkable and Interesting Particulars of the Slave Trade* (1764, with many editions published by Johnson through 1792) was one of the earliest accounts of the slave trade between the west coast of Africa and Liverpool. Johnson also published Newton's collected sermons in 1767. In 1779 Johnson published Newton's *Olney Hymns,* written between 1771 and 1772, to which Cowper contributed sixty-seven hymns; eleven editions of *Olney Hymns* appeared under Johnson's imprint between the first edition and 1810, the year after Johnson's death. Also of note among the religious works published by Johnson during his association with Davenport are editions of two books by the American theologian Jonathan Edwards. In

Joseph Johnson; engraving after a portrait by Moses Haughton, circa 1800 (Courtesy of Providence Public Library)

1766, in association with Keith, Johnson published Edwards's *The Great Christian Doctrine of Original Sin Defended* and *A Careful and Strict Enquiry into the Modern Prevailing Notions of That Freedom of Will, Which Is Supposed to Be Essential to Moral Agency, Vertue and Vice, Reward and Punishment, Praise and Blame*. Johnson became increasingly identified with dissenting causes, most consistently with the Unitarians. The bookseller provided inexpensive editions of sermons and other materials for Unitarian congregations, and he was involved with the Reverend Theophilus Lindsey in establishing the first Unitarian chapel in London in 1774. According to Thomas Rees, "he held the same position among the dissenters that the Rivingtons did with members of the Church of England."

Johnson began his close association with the theologian and scientist Priestley in the 1760s. Johnson and Davenport published Priestley's *Essay on the*

Course of a Liberal Education in 1765 with a consortium that included the dissenting publisher Charles Henderson, Thomas Becket, and Peter Abraham de Hondt. With Robert Dodsley and Thomas Cadell the elder, Johnson and Davenport published Priestley's *History and Present State of Electricity* (1767) and his *Essay on the First Principles of Government* (1768). Priestley, who chose Johnson from among these important booksellers to be his exclusive publisher in London, was the first member of the dissenting academy at Warrington to publish with Johnson.

The ecumenical Warrington Academy, established in 1757, attracted as students the sons of aristocrats, commercial magnates, tradesmen, and impoverished divines from every part of the British Isles, the West Indies, and the American colonies. Johnson became the main London bookseller for the works of the men and women associated with

Warrington, among them the naturalist and folklorist Johann Reinhold Forster; the theologian John Aiken the elder; Aiken's daughter, the poet Anna Letitia Aiken Barbauld; his son, the poet and physician John Aikin; the theologian William Enfield; the chemist Matthew Turner; the physician Thomas Percival; the political economist Thomas Robert Malthus; and the radical Gilbert Wakefield, whose offending pamphlet resulted in the arrest of Johnson in 1789.

Johnson spread his business among various printers in London and the provinces. In the case of radical or dissenting pamphlets and publications he relied on printers in the provincial cities where the authors resided; many of Priestley's works, for example, were printed in Birmingham during the time he lived there. Most of the textbooks published for the Warrington Academy, and other works written by the faculty, were printed by William Eyres in Warrington. Eyres also printed maps, charts, and classical, literary, and homiletic publications for general circulation, and Johnson was Eyres's London agent for many of these publications; the best known was the reformer John Howard's *The State of Prisons in England and Wales* (1777), published by a consortium including Johnson, Cadell, Charles Dilly, and J. Taylor. In 1789 this same group of booksellers published Howard's exposé of Continental hospitals, *An Account of the Principal Lazarettos in Europe.*

From the time Johnson ended his association with Davenport in 1767 until June 1768 he published forty-one titles independently or in connection with Cadell. At the end of June Johnson formed a partnership with John Payne, who had published Samuel Johnson's *Rambler* (1750–1752). Johnson, Payne, and Cadell published Fuseli's polemic pamphlet *Remarks on the Writings and Conduct of J. J. Rousseau* (1767), the first comprehensive treatment of Rousseau to appear in England. With Johnson acting as the senior partner, he and Payne published almost fifty titles in the second year of their partnership, sometimes participating in congeries with one or two other booksellers and sometimes in larger ones – such as the one associated with the Chapter Coffee House, where Johnson and more than thirty other bookmen gathered to enlist Samuel Johnson to write *Prefaces, Biographical and Critical, to the Works of the English Poets* (1779, 1781).

In 1769 Johnson began publishing, collecting subscriptions for, and distributing Priestley's *Theological Repository,* the first Unitarian periodical; the project proved unprofitable, and the scientist abandoned it at Johnson's urging with the third volume

in 1771. Johnson continued to publish Priestley's writings, many of them short religious tracts; by the end of his career, according to Leslie Chard, Johnson published 138 works by Priestley. During this same period he published writings by more than a score of Priestley's antagonists, including the Roman Catholic Alexander Geddes; the Jewish controversialist, linguist, and translator David Levi; and the Calvinist and founder of the "Johnsonian Baptist" sect John Johnson.

In 1770 Johnson's shop and residence were destroyed by fire. The catastrophe ended his partnership with Payne, and later that year, with the assistance of friends, Johnson set up without a partner at 72 St. Paul's Churchyard, where he remained until the end of his life.

The shop was on the first floor of the three-story, trapezoid-shaped building and Johnson's living quarters on the two top stories; he also owned an adjacent apartment. The upstairs rooms were a regular meeting place for liberal intellectuals from the beginning of his residence there. John Knowles, Fuseli's biographer, attended Johnson's dinners there "at least once a-week for some years" and commented on Johnson's hospitality and "the good sense which he exercised, and the prudence with which he allayed the occasional contests of his irritable guests, many of whom were distinguished men of letters, of various characters, and conflicting opinions." The best description of the dinners at 72 St. Paul's Churchyard in the 1790s is recorded in the memoirs of Godwin, who met his future wife, Wollstonecraft, at one of them.

In 1779 Johnson published a handsomely printed collection of Benjamin Franklin's essays titled *Political, Miscellaneous, and Philosophical Pieces.* Franklin approved of the project and cooperated with the editor, the diplomat and economist Benjamin Vaughan, who gathered in this edition all of Franklin's extant political writings and "such of his *Miscellaneous and Philosophical* pieces as are not elsewhere in print."

In addition to Fuseli, Darwin, Priestley, Barlowe, Paine, Wollstonecraft, and Godwin, the group now known as the "Johnson Circle" included the writer and translator George Gregory, the politician and philologist Horne Tooke, the mathematician John Bonnycastle, and the painter John Opie. These men and women were among the writers who became involved in Johnson's periodical, the *Analytical Review,* which flourished through twenty-eight volumes from May 1788 until December 1799.

William Cowper, the poet with whom Johnson was closely associated; crayon drawing by George Romney, 1792 (National Portrait Gallery, London)

Gerald Tyson links the birth of the *Analytical Review* to the demise of Priestley's *Theological Repository* and Paul Henry Maty's *A New Review,* which ran from 1782 to 1786. These periodicals had attempted to provide forums for dissenting liberal viewpoints and broad coverage of published works. The idea for the new literary journal came from Thomas Christie, a young Scottish Unitarian who had originally come to London to study medicine and whose purpose in starting the review was to "give such accounts of new publications, as may enable the reader to judge of them for himself." The first advertisement for the *Analytical Review* concluded: "This New Journal will appear monthly. It will have more of an analytical cast in it than any other, and on that account we shall call it, the *ANALYTICAL REVIEW.*" In addition to reviews, the new "encyclopedic" journal contained literary news, original essays, and articles on foreign literature, natural history, medicine, music, chemistry, geography, travel, and commerce. Johnson also used the *Analytical Review* to review, advertise, and promote his own publications.

It was Christie's intention that reviews and articles be signed and not anonymous, but most reviewers chose to write under pseudonymous initials: Dr. John Aikin, for example, wrote under the initials "DM" (Doctor of Medicine), his sister Mrs. Barbauld under "DMS," and his daughter Lucy Aikin under "DMD." Working closely with Christie and Johnson was the Catholic priest Alexander Geddes. Under the signature "S.A.," Anthony Robinson, a Baptist converted to Unitarianism, controlled the Department of Politics and Economics. Wollstonecraft was an important contributor to the *Analytical Review* from its earliest days, usually under the signatures "M," "W," or "T." Cowper and Fuseli also contributed reviews. The magazine's contemporary reputation for radicalism — confirmed in the judgment of modern scholarship — rested not on the reviews and articles on literature, which reflected rather conventional moral judgments, but on its religious and political reviews. Theologically, the periodical supported a wide range of dissenting views; politically, the *Analytical Review* was critical of the English government and supportive of revolutionary ideas in America and France.

In 1789 Dr. Richard Price, a nonconformist minister and intimate friend of Franklin's, published the pro–French Revolution "Sermon to the Revolutionary Society," which was favorably reviewed by Wollstonecraft in the *Analytical Review.* Edmund Burke's *Reflections on the Revolution in France* (1790), a response to Price's sermon, was given extensive coverage in the review, with several objections to his position and attacks on his conservatism. In the same year Johnson published one of the first answers to Burke's book, Wollstonecraft's *A Vindication of the Rights of Men.* In the pamphlet war that followed, 127 works supporting or opposing the French Revolution appeared, at least 13 of which Johnson published and sold.

Johnson's association with Cowper reveals much about the bookseller as a judge of literature, as a businessman, and as a patron and popularizer of belles lettres. For nineteenth-century commentators such as Charles Knight, Johnson's importance rested almost exclusively upon his relationship with the poet. It is Johnson's "being honorably connected with the fame of Cowper" that Knight has in mind when he calls Johnson the "herald of a new era in literature." Johnson acted as editor and adviser to Cowper in the publication of his *Poems* (1782), suggesting additions and deletions; in a letter to Newton of 28 August 1781 the poet wrote: "I do not know where I could have found a bookseller who could have pointed out to me my defects with more discernment." One editorial suggestion was the suppression of a preface to the poems written by Newton; the preface was included in some copies of editions after 1793 – Norma Russell, Cowper's modern bibliographer, was able to locate fewer than eight. In 1781 Johnson published Cowper's anonymous mock-Spenserian allegory *Anti-thelyphthora,* a satiric response to the Reverend Martin Madan's advocacy of a return to polygamy. This anonymous quarto pamphlet of twenty pages is now the rarest of all of Cowper's writings; the poem was not included in Johnson's editions of his *Poems* or in William Hayley's *The Life, and Posthumous Writings, of William Cowper, Esqr.* (1802–1804) and did not appear in any anthology of his works until Robert Southey's edition (1835–1837). Johnson published *Poems* at his own risk; in return, Cowper gave him the copyright and all potential profits, which turned out to be considerable. The first edition was initially advertised at three shillings, but after the addition of more poems the price was raised to four shillings. According to Russell, most of the editions of *Poems* Johnson produced during Cowper's lifetime were "undistinguished productions, printed on poor-quality paper"; this situation may be explained by Johnson's desire to provide affordable editions to a growing reading public. In 1785 Johnson published Cowper's *The Task,* which, unlike *Poems,* was hailed as a masterpiece; after this success it was sold as volume two of *Poems.* Editions of the set were produced each year for the next three years; Johnson gave Cowper the entire profits from the fifth edition of 1793. The diarist Henry Crabb Robinson estimated Johnson's profits from the sales of Cowper's poetry at ten thousand pounds. The editions of 1806, 1808, and 1811 include illustrations by Fuseli, engraved by Blake and others. Johnson's successors would begin to sell off shares of the copyright in 1812, and by 1815 at least twenty-one partners would be involved in the publication of Cowper's poems.

Cowper began to translate the *Iliad* as a diversion soon after *The Task* went to press; he then turned to a translation of the *Odyssey.* Johnson reluctantly accepted Cowper's wish to publish the translations by subscription. Fuseli, a formidable classicist, served as editor, supplying corrections, revisions, and emendations to Cowper's manuscript. *Proposals for Printing by Subscription, A New Translation of the Iliad and Odyssey of Homer into Blank Verse* was published in 1791. Cowper retained the copyright and received a thousand pounds for an edition of 700 copies. In July 1791 Johnson published Cowper's renderings of the *Iliad* and the *Odyssey* in

two volumes, with a subscription list of 498 names. In spite of unenthusiastic reviews, all of the non-subscription copies sold out in a few months. Johnson published a cheaper octavo version of the same edition in 750 copies in 1793. In 1796 Cowper began revising both poems; he finished the revisions in 1799, but by that time mental illness had severely affected his ability to work. He died the next year. As a result of the impairment of the poet during his last years, Johnson's second edition of 1802, in four octavo volumes, relied more on the 1791 edition than on the erratic corrections and revisions of a later date. This edition was reissued in 1809, after Johnson's death, and in 1810 Johnson's successors put out another printing, with fifty plates that had originally been engraved after drawings by Fuseli and other Royal Academicians for Du Roveray's edition of Alexander Pope's *Homer* (1805–1806). Russell has established that these plates were also published separately under Johnson's imprint in four parts in 1810.

Another project that Johnson planned for Cowper in the early 1790s also involved Fuseli. Johnson devised a grand scheme to publish a "Milton Gallery" along the lines of the series of paintings and subsequent engravings in the *Shakespeare Gallery* (1789) commissioned from British artists by the engraver and printer John Boydell. Johnson planned a series of paintings inspired by the life and works of John Milton, the majority to be painted by Fuseli, that would be exhibited in a gallery; engravings based on the paintings would be sold separately and as part of a fine new edition of Milton's poems to be edited by Cowper. According to Knowles, Johnson intended that his edition of Milton's poems should not just rival Boydell's *Shakespeare Gallery* "but, in point of letterpress, designs, and engravings, surpass any work which had previously appeared in England." In 1791 Johnson advertised his edition of Milton, "with copious notes on his English poems, and translation into verse of those in Latin and Italian" by Cowper. Cowper completed the translations of the Latin poems in February 1792 and the Italian poems in March, but the notes were never completed because of Cowper's "serious mental indisposition." Furthermore, since early 1792 Boydell and the bookseller George Nicol had been working on a rival Milton project, employing the acamedician George Romney as the principal painter and the poet William Hayley to write a life of Milton to complement the paintings. Because of Cowper's infirmities and the competition from Boydell, Johnson abandoned his ambitious Milton enterprise. Fuseli, however,

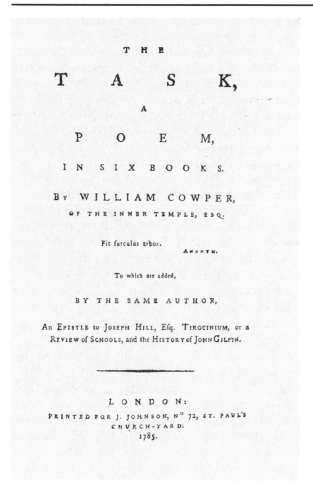

THE

T A S K,

A

P O E M,

IN SIX BOOKS.

By WILLIAM COWPER,
OF THE INNER TEMPLE, ESQ.

Fit furculus arbor.
ANONYM.

To which are added,

BY THE SAME AUTHOR,

An EPISTLE to JOSEPH HILL, Esq. TIROCINIUM, or a
REVIEW of SCHOOLS, and the HISTORY of JOHN GILPIN.

LONDON:
PRINTED FOR J. JOHNSON, Nº 72, ST. PAUL'S
CHURCH-YARD.
1785.

*Title page for the work generally regarded as Cowper's
masterpiece*

who had been commissioned by Johnson to paint thirty pictures, continued the project on his own, producing almost fifty canvases over a period of more than ten years. He exhibited his "Milton Gallery" in 1799 and again, with additional paintings, in 1800 but gained little from sales of the paintings, entrance tickets, or catalogues. The Milton project was the biggest disappointment of his life.

One of the ironies of the failed Milton project is that it was responsible for bringing Hayley and Cowper together. Hayley, an admirer of Cowper, wrote a conciliatory letter to his fellow poet in 1792 in which he denied that his involvement in the Boydell project constituted a rivalry between them. Thereafter, Cowper and Hayley corresponded frequently. When Hayley's life of Milton was completed he brought the manuscript to Cowper, and they made final revisions together. A shortened version of the life appeared as the first volume of *The Poetical Works of John Milton,* published in three im-

perial folio volumes by John and Josiah Boydell between 1794 and 1797. In 1800 Harriot, Lady Hesketh, Cowper's cousin and the executor of his estate, asked Hayley to write a life of the poet. Hayley requested that Johnson be the publisher, and in 1802 Hayley approached Johnson with the idea. He enlisted Blake, who at that time was living near him in Felpham, to contribute six engravings. The two-volume *The Life, and Posthumous Writings, of William Cowper, Esqr.* was printed in Chichester by Hayley's protégé, J. Seagrave, and published in an elegant quarto edition in 1803 with a second edition the same year; a third volume, comprising Cowper's letters, was published by Johnson in 1804. In 1806 Johnson published an octavo edition in four volumes, including some new material. In 1809, the year of Johnson's death, Johnson's successor, Rowland Hunter, published yet another edition with a few omissions and corrections under the imprint "J. Johnson and Co." Hayley profited by his work on behalf of his friend Cowper: Tooke claimed that Hayley realized eleven thousand pounds from the various editions.

Just as Johnson's name was kept before the public in the nineteenth century because of his publication of the poems of Cowper, twentieth-century studies of Wollstonecraft have aroused interest in the bookseller for his encouragement of her when she was a young and unproven author. Her correspondent and patron since his publication of her first work, *Thoughts on the Education of Daughters* (1787), Johnson provided a house for her on her arrival in London to embark on a literary career. Between 1787 and 1790, while living in this house on George Street, Wollstonecraft worked on her novel *Mary, A Fiction,* which Johnson published and offered for sale in 1788. In the same year Johnson published Wollstonecraft's *Original Stories, from Real Life,* with engravings by Blake. This work went through several editions, including a reprint in 1791 with newly added engravings by Blake. In the late 1780s and early 1790s Johnson employed Wollstonecraft as a translator of French, German, Dutch, and Italian works, including a translation of Jacques Necker's *On the Importance of Religious Opinions* (1788); an abridged translation from the Dutch of Maria de Cambon's *Young Grandison* (1790); and *Elements of Morality, for the Use of Children* (1791), "compressed" from the German of the Reverend Christian Gotthilf Salzmann. For two subsequent editions of the Salzmann translation, published in 1791 and 1799, Johnson commissioned Blake to engrave designs based on the original engravings by Daniel Nikolaus Chodowiecki. Wollstonecraft compiled a series of extracts in verse and prose on the model of William Enfield's *The Speaker* (1774) – also published by Johnson – titled *The Female Reader,* which Johnson published under the pseudonym "Mr. Creswick, Teacher of Elocution" in 1789. In 1792 Johnson published her *A Vindication of the Rights of Woman.* Her final work to be published by Johnson during her lifetime was *Letters Written during a Short Residence in Sweden, Norway, and Denmark* (1796). The work was rapidly translated into German, Dutch, Swedish, and Portuguese and had at least one American edition (1796). Johnson published a second edition in 1802. In October 1797, a month after Wollstonecraft's death, Godwin began to draft *Memoirs of the Author of a Vindication of the Rights of Woman.* Johnson published the memoirs together with the four-volume *Posthumous Works of the Author of A Vindication of the Rights of Woman,* edited by Godwin, in January 1798.

Because of its impact on his career, Johnson's most important radical connection was his association with Paine, whose business he had managed while Paine was in exile in France. According to Tyson, Paine approached Johnson in the winter of 1790–1791, at the urging of mutual friends, to publish Paine's *Rights of Man.* For reasons that are not clear, Johnson withdrew his publication of the work; only the first dozen copies of the pamphlet carried his name on the title page, and few of those made it to public sale. Publication of the pamphlet was taken over by an obscure Fleet Street bookseller, Jeremiah Samuel Jordan. Johnson was not named as publisher of *Rights of Man* at Paine's trial for sedition in 1792, but his association with the radical was well established.

Johnson was, however, charged with sedition in 1798 for selling a pamphlet by the radical theologian Gilbert Wakefield attacking bishop of Llandaff Richard Watson's defense of Prime Minister William Pitt, the war with France, and war taxes. Prosecuted along with Johnson were Wakefield; the publisher of the pamphlet, radical Scottish-born bookseller John Cuthell; the printer of the pamphlet; and Jordan, in whose shop copies of the offending work were found. John Aikin would insist in his obituary of Johnson that "turbulence and sedition were abhorrent from his nature" and point out that the Wakefield pamphlet was a reply to another pamphlet, of which Johnson "had sold a much larger number." The statesman Charles James Fox wrote to Priestley in March 1799: "The liberty of the press I considered virtually destroyed by the proceedings against Johnson and Jordan. . . ." Although he was represented by the eminent lawyer

(and future lord chancellor of England) Thomas Erskine, Johnson was convicted on 11 February 1799 and sentenced to six months under house arrest. He spent the time entertaining literary and scientific figures such as Bonnycastle, Fuseli, Godwin, Crabb Robinson, and Maria Edgeworth at weekly dinners and tending to neglected financial affairs. The *Analytical Review* ceased publication with the December 1798 number; it was succeeded during the first half of 1799 by the *Analytical Review (New Series),* sold by T. Hurt of Paternoster Row, but there is no evidence that Johnson or any of his regular reviewers had any part in this periodical.

Johnson published the feminist writer Mary Hays's call for women's rights, *Appeal to the Men of Great Britain* (1798), and her second novel, *The Victim of Prejudice* (1799). Johnson was also the first publisher of Malthus's *An Essay on the Principle of Population* (1798) and of Edgeworth's *Letters to Literary Ladies* (1795).

Johnson's early interest in publishing medical works continued throughout his career. He published and sold George Fordyce's lecture series *Elements of the Practice of Physic, Part II,* followed by *Part I* in 1770. The work on the causes of and treatments for diseases went through six editions by 1791. In 1771 Johnson brought out the first independent publication by John Hunter, a Scottish surgeon, medical researcher, and one of the outstanding scientific writers of the eighteenth century: *The Natural History of the Human Teeth* is widely credited with establishing dentistry as a medical science. The work included sixteen plates by three of the most highly regarded engravers of the time: Robert Strange; William Wyne Ryland; and Charles Grignon Sr., William Hogarth's engraver, whom Johnson employed frequently. Johnson republished *The Natural History of the Human Teeth* in 1778 in two parts, the second part being a supplement. After 1778, when Hunter began publishing his works at his own print shop, Johnson turned to commissioning and selling reprints, or "second editions," of works originally printed by Hunter. In the case of these "second editions" Johnson sometimes acted as the sole agent, as for *Anatomical Description of the Human Gravid Uterus and Its Contents* (1794), and sometimes in partnership with J. Nichol, as with *A Treatise on the Venereal Disease* (1786).

Johnson was the proprietor of the first medical periodical, *Medical Facts and Observations,* which he published and sold irregularly between 1791 and 1800 and which was edited by Dr. Samuel Foart Simmons, physician extraordinary to George III. *Transactions of a Society for the Improvement of Medical*

RIGHTS OF MAN:

BEING AN

ANSWER TO MR. BURKE's ATTACK

ON THE

FRENCH REVOLUTION.

BY

THOMAS PAINE,

SECRETARY FOR FOREIGN AFFAIRS TO CONGRESS IN THE
AMERICAN WAR, AND
AUTHOR OF THE WORK INTITLED *COMMON SENSE.*

LONDON:
PRINTED FOR J. JOHNSON, ST PAUL's CHURCH-YARD.
MDCCXCI.

Title page for one of the few copies of Paine's pamphlet to bear Johnson's imprint

and Chirugical Knowledge, put out by Johnson between 1792 and 1800, consisted of papers presented to the society founded by Hunter and Fordyce. Johnson joined with the firm of Bell and Bradfute and that of T. Duncan in Edinburgh to bring out Alexander Monro's *Experiments on the Nervous System* in 1793. Other important medical writings published and sold by Johnson included the pioneering epidemiologist John Haygarth's *An Inquiry How to Prevent Small-Pox (1784)* and its sequel, *A Sketch of a Plan to Exterminate the Casual Small-Pox from Great Britain* (1794).

Johnson's good friend John Aikin the younger, for whom he published 130 poems, is representative of the "poetical" doctors who used Johnson as proprietor not only for their medical and scientific works but also for their nonmedical writings. Aikin's best-known works published by Johnson were *Essays on Song Writing* (1772), *Translation of the*

Germania and the Agricola of Tacitus, and *Biographical Memoirs of Medicine in Great Britain* (1780).

Aikin was the literary editor of the *Monthly Magazine and British Register,* begun in 1796 by John Phillips of Leicester. When Phillips moved to London in 1796, he used Johnson's shop and facilities to bring out his digest of scientific and literary articles; historical, moral, and critical essays; notices of books published; biographical notices; news from abroad; and correspondence on practical and statistical matters such as disease, population, commerce, and manufacturing. Among the contributors to the *Monthly Magazine* were the satirist "Peter Pindar" (pseudonym of John Wolcot), the poet and translator Capel Lofft the elder, and the pedagogical writer Dr. William Fordyce Mavor. Phillips himself wrote articles opposing government policies under the signature "Common Sense." With volume three in 1799 Phillips moved to his own shop, 71 St. Paul's Churchyard, next door to Johnson, where he took over publication of the magazine.

Perhaps best known of the physicians whose works were sold by Johnson was Erasmus Darwin, five of whose works were published by the bookseller. Darwin's *The Botanic Garden: A Poem, in Two Parts* appeared in seven editions between 1789 and 1806, and *Zoonomia* appeared in three editions between 1794 and 1801. For the copyright of part 2 of *The Botanic Garden, The Loves of Plants,* which was published first, Johnson paid Darwin three hundred pounds; on publication of part 1, *The Economy of Vegetation,* which appeared in 1791 with the second edition of part 2, Darwin received four hundred pounds. Fuseli provided two illustrations for this edition of part 2: the frontispiece and the *Fertilization of Egypt,* the latter engraved by Blake. Blake also executed three engravings of the Portland Vase included in part 1; according to G. E. Bentley, Johnson saw to it that Blake obtained access to the vase itself, or to a Wedgewood copy, for that purpose. The 1791 quarto edition is among the few deluxe editions published by Johnson. The engravings were reengraved for the octavo editions of *The Botanic Garden* (1799) and Darwin's *Poetical Works* (1806). Darwin's other works published by Johnson were *A Plan for the Conduct of Female Education in Boarding Schools,* which included a catalogue of 307 recommended titles for young female readers; *Phytologia* (1800); and the posthumous *The Temple of Nature* (1803). Johnson commissioned Anna Seward, the "Swan of Litchfield," to write *Memoirs of the Life of Dr. Darwin* (1804).

Johnson's publication of juvenile literature between 1782 and 1806 made a significant contribution to the development of that market. In addition to Wollstonecraft's works for children, Johnson published original books by Sarah Trimmer, commissioned translations of popular children's works by French and German authors, and elicited juvenile books on educational subjects from authors whose other works he had published. Works with a moral tone, such as Wollstonecraft's translation and condensation of Salzmann's *Elements of Morality,* formed a large part of the juvenile literature published by Johnson. These works included titles by Edgeworth, whose books for children from the beginning reader to the adolescent comprised genres ranging from plays to scientific texts to novels. Edgeworth's works were published exclusively by Johnson and his successors and earned slightly more than eleven thousand pounds for the firm. Johnson published Mrs. Barbauld's *Lessons for Children, from Two to Three Years Old* (1787) and *Lessons for Children of Three Years Old* (1788) in a large-type format that was extremely popular. A special category of juvenile literature offered by Johnson was the book introducing the youthful reader to a specific subject. The mathematician Bonnycastle, a good friend of Johnson's, wrote *An Introduction to Mensuration, and Practical Geometry,* which Johnson published with a frontispiece by Blake; it went through eleven editions between 1782 and 1812. Textbooks of this sort written by the faculty at Warrington were plentiful in Johnson's catalogues and included Ralph Harrison's *Institutes of English Grammar* (1783); Dr. John Aikin's *England Delineated* (1788); and *The Speaker,* an anthology of essays "with a view to facilitate the Improvement of youth in Reading and Speaking," and *Exercises in Elocution* (1787), both by Enfield. When Godwin and his second wife, Mary Jane Clairmont Godwin, opened their bookstore, The Juvenile Library, in 1805, Johnson was their main source of encouragement and professional contacts in London publishing circles.

Johnson was briefly involved in publishing works by William Wordsworth and Samuel Taylor Coleridge, and he at least contemplated publishing one poetic work by Blake. Johnson published Wordsworth's *Descriptive Sketches* and *An Evening Walk* in 1793; the works went largely unsold, and Tyson's check of the *London Chronicle,* where Johnson placed most of his advertisements, failed to find notice of either work. Wordsworth never used Johnson again after the publication of those two works. Johnson met Coleridge through his Unitarian connections while he was out on bail in the Wakefield case, and in 1798 he published in one volume Coleridge's poems "Fears in Solitude," "France, An Ode," and "Frost at Midnight." Although the volume was favorably reviewed in the December 1798 *Analytical Review,* Coleridge wrote to Southey that "there were not above two hundred copies sold." When Coleridge traveled to Germany in September 1798 with Wordsworth and the latter's sister, Dorothy, he carried letters of introduction from Johnson and an order for thirty pounds to the Hamburg bookseller James Remnant. There is no evidence of further contact between Coleridge and Johnson.

Johnson's connection with the poetry of Blake is equally tenuous and, to a degree, mysterious. Although Blake, who was probably introduced to Johnson by Fuseli, worked as an engraver for Johnson for more than twenty years, beginning with his engravings for Bonnycastle's *An Introduction to Mensuration and Practical Geometry* in 1782 and ending with his engraved plates for Hayley's life of Cowper in 1804, there is little evidence that Blake was a regular member of the "Johnson Circle" or that he was taken seriously by its members as a poet. Blake's biographer, Alexander Gilchrist, mentions that Johnson "tried to help him, as far as he could help so unmarketable a talent." Bentley identifies this attempt to help Blake as a reference to Blake's poem "The French Revolution," proofs of the first seven books of which were run off under Johnson's direction in 1791. The poem was never registered at Stationer's Hall, nor was it advertised in Johnson's *Analytical Review.* Whether publication of the poem was withdrawn by the author or by the bookseller remains a matter for speculation.

Johnson had a particular interest during the 1790s in publishing contemporary German literature in translation. Notable among these works is Johann Wolfgang von Goethe's *Iphigenia: A Tragedy* (1793), translated by William Taylor of Norwich. Johnson also published two works of the popular Hamburg writer "Viet Weber" (G. P. L. L. Wachter), *The Sorcerer* (1795) and *The Black Valley* (1796), translated by George Dyson. In 1796 Johnson published Friedrich Schiller's *Fiesco; or, The Genoese Conspiracy* in a translation by Sir John Stoddart.

In addition to the contemporary authors encouraged by Johnson, Leslie Chard asserts that "of all the major English authors still published by the share system at the turn of the century, Johnson was the majority or exclusive shareholder of virtually every one." This impressive list includes the Edmond Malone and George Steevens edition of the works of William Shakespeare and the works of Pope, Milton, Dr. Johnson, Joseph Addison, Richard Steele, and all of the novelists except Samuel Richardson. In addition, Johnson participated with Wilkie and Robinson, the Rivingtons, Longman and Company, and Cadell and Davies in a consortium, "The Friends of Literature," that put out new editions of Milton's *Paradise Lost,* James Thomson's *The Seasons,* Jacob Bryant's *A New System, or, An Analysis of Ancient Mythology,* and Daniel Defoe's *Robinson Crusoe.* Johnson left his shares in this consortium to his successors. Other best-sellers in which Chard has found Johnson to the major shareholder include works by Isaac Watts and, "of the four major dictionaries of the period . . . the three biggest sellers: [Robert] Ainsworth's Latin, [Abel] Boyer's English-French, and Dr. Johnson's."

Toward the end of his life Johnson suffered from a series of debilitating asthmatic illnesses, his "frame worn to a shadow." He died on 20 December 1809. Johnson, whose fortune at the time of his death is estimated at sixty thousand pounds, never married and left no direct heirs. His business passed to his grandnephews Rowland Hunter and John Miles, both of whom had been admitted to the Stationer's Company in 1808; the elder of the two, Hunter, had lived with and been trained by Johnson. Edgeworth's memoirs record that while Miles was respected, Hunter was difficult, and Miles soon parted company with him. Hunter published under the imprint "Johnson and Co." from 1810 to 1815, when he changed it to "R. Hunter, Successor to J. Johnson." As copyrights lapsed, Johnson's titles were taken over by others, and Hunter gradually sold off the old shares. Hunter continued to use Johnson's name in his imprint until 1828, at which time Edgeworth, the last of Johnson's longtime and popular authors, left him. Johnson's shop at 72 St. Paul's Churchyard was sold at a bankruptcy auction in 1838.

Johnson's generosity and the fairness of his dealings with authors is captured in his obituary in the December 1809 *Gentleman's Magazine* by Dr. John Aikin, who describes his friend, "for some years past considered as the Father of the Trade," as a man of remarkable character whose "literary connexions have lain in great part among the free Enquirers both on religious and political topicks," but also as one who "at the height of party animosity, so little was he regarded personally as a party-man that he continued to number among his intimate friends, several worthy persons of opposite sentiments and connexions, who, with himself, were capable of considering a man's performance of the duties of life apart from his speculative opinions."

The most eloquent tribute to Johnson's character remains the epitaph composed by his dearest friend, Fuseli. The inscription is on his gravestone in the churchyard of Fulham Parish, where he had a country house:

A MAN

EQUALLY DISTINGUISHED BY PROBITY, INDUSTRY, AND DISINTERESTEDNESS IN HIS INTERCOURSE WITH THE PUBLIC, AND EVERY DOMESTIC AND SOCIAL VIRTUE IN LIFE; BENEFICENT WITHOUT OSTENTATION, EVER READY TO PRODUCE MERIT AND TO RELIEVE DISTRESS; UNASSUMING IN PROSPERITY, NOT APPALLED BY MISFORTUNE; INEXORABLE TO HIS OWN, INDULGENT TO THE WANTS OF OTHERS; RESIGNED AND CHEERFUL UNDER THE TORTURE OF A MALADY WHICH HE SAW GRADUALLY DESTROY HIS LIFE.

References:

M. Ray Adams, "Mary Hays, Disciple of William Godwin," *PMLA,* 55 (June 1940): 472–483;

John Aikin, "Biographical Account of the Late Mr. Joseph Johnson," *Gentleman's Magazine,* 79 (December 1809): 1167–1168;

Lucy Aikin, *Memoir of John Aikin, M.D.* (Philadelphia: Small, 1824);

R. C. Alston, F. J. G. Robinson, and C. Wadham, *A Check-List of Eighteenth-Century Books Containing a List of Subscribers* (Newcastle: Avero, 1983);

G. E. Bentley, *Blake Records* (Oxford: Clarendon Press, 1969);

Walter Brouwer, "Joshua Toulmin in the *Analytical Review,*" *Notes and Queries,* 30 (June 1983): 209–212;

Brouwer, "Mary Imlay, Analytical Reviewer," *Notes and Queries,* 29 (June 1982): 204–206;

Marilyn Butler, *Maria Edgeworth: A Literary Biography* (Oxford: Clarendon Press, 1972);

Leslie Chard, "Bookseller to Publisher: Joseph Johnson and the English Book Trade, 1760–1810," *Library,* fifth series 32 (June 1977): 138–154;

Chard, "Joseph Johnson: Father of the Book Trade," *Bulletin of the New York Public Library,* 78 (Autumn 1975): 51–82;

William Cowper, *The Letters and Prose Writings of William Cowper,* volume 3, edited by James King and Charles Ryskamp (Oxford: Clarendon Press, 1982);

Erasmus Darwin, *The Letters of Erasmus Darwin,* edited by Desmond King-Hele (Cambridge: Cambridge University Press, 1981);

Maria Edgeworth, *Chosen Letters,* edited by F. V. Barry (Boston: Houghton Mifflin, 1931);

Andrea Alta Engstrom, "Joseph Johnson's Circle and the *Analytical Review:* A Study of English Radicals in the Late Eighteenth Century," dissertation, University of Southern California, 1986;

Henry Fuseli, *The English Letters of Henry Fuseli,* volume 2, edited by David H. Weinglass (New York: Kraus International, 1982);

Alexander Gilchrist, *Life of William Blake, "Pictor Ignotus,"* 2 volumes (London & Cambridge: Macmillan, 1863);

William Godwin, *Memoirs of the Author of the Vindication of the Rights of Woman* (London: Printed for J. Johnson & G. G. & J. Robinson, 1798);

William Hayley, *The Life, and Posthumous Writings, of William Cowper, Esqr.,* 3 volumes (Chichester: Printed by J. Seagrave for J. Johnson, London, 1803–1804);

Peter Haywood, *Joseph Johnson, Publisher 1738–1809* (Aberystwyth: College of Librarianship, 1976);

Gae Holladay, introduction to *The Female Advocate: A Poem. Occasioned by Mr. Duncombe's Feminead,* by Mary Scott (Los Angeles: William Andrews Clark Memorial Library, 1984);

James King, "An Unlikely Alliance: Fuseli as Revisor of Cowper's Homer," *Neophilologus,* 67 (July 1983): 468–469;

Desmond King-Hele, *Doctor of Revolution: The Life and Genius of Erasmus Darwin* (London: Faber & Faber, 1977);

Charles Knight, *Shadows of the Old Booksellers* (London: Bell & Daldy, 1865);

John Knowles, *The Life and Writings of Henry Fuseli, Esq., M.A.R.A.,* volume 1 (London: Colburn & Bentley, 1831);

Don Locke, *A Fantasy of Reason: The Life and Thought of William Godwin* (London & Boston: Routledge & Kegan Paul, 1988);

Phyllis Mann, "Death of a London Bookseller," *Keats-Shelly Memorial Bulletin,* no. 15 (1964): 8–12;

H. McLachlin, *Warrington Academy: Its History and Influence* (Manchester: Cheatham Society, 1943);

Maureen McNeil, "The Scientific Muse: The Poetry of Erasmus Darwin," in *Languages of Nature: Critical Essays on Science and Literature,* edited by J. G. Jordanova and Raymond Williams (New Brunswick, N.J.: Rutgers University Press, 1986);

McNeil, *Under the Banner of Science: Erasmus Darwin and His Age* (Manchester: Manchester University Press, 1987);

Frank Arthur Mumby, *Publishing and Bookselling* (London: Cape, 1947), pp. 243–247;

John Newton, *The Letters of John Newton* (Carlisle, Pa.: Banner of Truth Trust, 1976);

Henry R. Plomer and others, *A Dictionary of the Printers Who Were at Work in England and Scotland from 1726 to 1775* (London: Oxford University Press, 1932);

Thomas Rees, *Reminiscences of Literary London from 1779 to 1853* (London: Suckling & Galloway, 1896; New York: Harper, 1896);

Norma Russell, *A Bibliography of William Cowper to 1837* (Oxford: Oxford Bibliographical Society, 1963);

Sally N. Stewart, "Mary Wollstonecraft's Contributions to the *Analytical Review,*" *Essays in Literature,* 11 (Fall 1984): 187–199;

Lloyd Paul Stryker, *For the Defense: Thomas Erskine* (New York: Doubleday, 1947);

Alan Sullivan, *British Literary Magazines. The Augustan Age and The Age of Johnson* (Westport, Conn.: Greenwood Press, 1983);

Jane W. Symser, "The Trial and Imprisonment of Joseph Johnson, Bookseller," *Bulletin of the New York Public Library,* 77 (Summer 1974): 418–435;

Michael Treadwell, "London Trade Publishers 1675–1750," *Library,* sixth series 4 (June 1982): 99–134;

Gerald Tyson, *Joseph Johnson, an Eighteenth-Century Bookseller* (Iowa City: University of Iowa Press, 1979);

R. M. Wardle, "Mary Wollstonecraft, *Analytical Reviewer,*" *PMLA,* 62 (December 1947): 1000–1009;

Paul M. Zall, "The Cool World of Samuel Taylor Coleridge: Joseph Johnson or the Perils of Publishing," *Wordsworth Circle,* 3 (Winter 1972): 25–30.

                                                                          – Carol Hall

J. J. and P. Knapton
(London: circa 1730 – 1736)

J[ames]. Knapton
(London: 1690 – circa 1722)

J. and J. Knapton
(London: circa 1722 – circa 1730)

J. and P. Knapton
(London: 1736 – 1755)

J[ohn]. Knapton
(London: 1755 – 1776)

James, John, and Paul Knapton undertook some of the most ambitious publishing projects in London during the first half of the eighteenth century, yet in comparison with the booksellers with whom they occasionally cooperated – the Dodsleys, Lintots, Longmans, and Tonsons – surprisingly little has been written about them. The father and his two sons published a wide variety of mainstream and obscure, long-term and ephemeral, significant and trivial works and built up a fine line of historical, poetical, and theological titles. In sources that do refer to the Knaptons, family connections have often been confused. F. T. Wood and Ambrose Heal follow Henry R. Plomer's error in claiming that James, John, and Paul Knapton were all brothers; William Warburton's biographers John Selby Watson and A. W. Evans have mistaken John for Paul, lopping fifteen years off John's life; and Louise Lippincott was uncertain whether John and Paul Knapton were brothers or cousins of the artists Charles and George Knapton (John Knapton appointed his cousin, George Knapton, as one of the executors of his will).

James Knapton was the son of William Knapton of Brokenhurst, Hampshire. He served his apprenticeship under the London bookseller Henry Mortlock from 2 August 1680 until 5 September 1687, after which he opened a bookshop at the Queen's Head in St. Paul's Churchyard. He moved to the nearby Crown in St. Paul's Churchyard in 1690. Knapton's wife, Hester, bore twelve children between 1693 and 1709; John, the third child and first son to survive infancy, was baptized on 23 April 1696; Paul, the eighth child, on 20 January 1703.

In the first decade of the eighteenth century, the name James Knapton appeared in 265 imprints. He became a leading member, second in seniority to Daniel Browne, in the Wholesaling Conger, a small group of copyright-owning booksellers that wielded formidable control in the period following the Copyright Act of 1710. He was the sole seller of such diverse works as William Dampier's *New Voyage round the World* (1697–1703), the anonymous *Sir Giddy Whim; or, The Lucky Amour* (1703), and *Dictionarium Sacrum seu Religiosum: A Dictionary of All Religions, Ancient and Modern* (1704), attributed to Daniel Defoe. John Dunton characterizes Knapton as a shrewd bookseller with a reputation for sound judgment, especially when it came to acquiring copyrights: "He is a very accomplished person; not that thin sort of animal that flutters from Tavern to Playhouse, and back again; all his life made up with wig and cravat, without one dram of thought in his composition; – but a person made up with sound worth, brave, and generous; and shews, by his purchasing of 'Dampier's Voyages,' he knows how to value a good Copy." When William Bowyer's printing shop and warehouse were destroyed by fire in 1713, Knapton contributed to the fund to assist the ruined but badly needed printer.

Knapton took on nine apprentices in the course of his career, one of whom was his eldest son: John Knapton's apprenticeship lasted from 4 February 1712 to 2 March 1719. Paul Knapton served his apprenticeship under Arthur Bettesworth in Paternoster Row from 1 May 1721 until 7 March 1728. Paul's term overlapped with that of Charles Hitch, who left Bettesworth in 1725; Hitch's name would later follow the Knaptons' in the imprint of Samuel Johnson's *A Dictionary of the English Language* (1755). Bettesworth and James Knapton first appeared together in the imprint of the third edition of Susanna Centlivre's *The Gamester* (1714). The two other names in this imprint were Edmund Curll and Robert Gosling; Knapton and Curll share half a dozen imprints between 1714 and 1743, including Nicholas Rowe's 1714 edition of the works of William Shakespeare. Knapton and Bettesworth increased their copublications in the 1720s with sixty-eight titles, compared to four in the previous decade. In the 1730s the number went up to eighty-one. The association ended with Bettesworth's death in 1738.

James Knapton was elected renter warden for the Stationers' Company in 1710, under warden in 1721 and 1722, upper warden in 1725 and 1726, and master in 1727 and 1728. When the wholesaling congeries started breaking up in the 1720s, Knapton became the senior member of the Castle Conger. His name is given first place in the imprints of most books published by the Castle Conger between 1728 and 1737, such as the fifth edition of Nathan Bailey's *An Universal Etymological English Dictionary* (1731). Between 1723 and 1734 there are nine imprints in which the first three names are Knapton, Robert Knaplock, and Daniel Midwinter; the names occur in a different order elsewhere, as in a 1731 Latin edition of Terence that lists Knaplock, J. & J. Knapton, D. Midwinter & A. Ward, A. Bettesworth & C. Hitch, F. Fayram, and ten others.

Frequent reprinting of works for which no authors' fees had to be paid, such as Edmund Wingate's *Arithmetique Made Easie,* was one key to success in publishing. In the case of this popular book, originally published in 1630, James Knapton's name first appeared in the second "ninth" edition in 1696 (there had been five "eighth" editions), following J. Phillips. The eleventh through fourteenth editions were printed for J. Phillips, J. Taylor, and J. Knapton in 1704, 1708, 1713, and 1720. The fifteenth edition (1726) added John Knapton's name to his father's, and J. Taylor was replaced by the executors of *W.* Taylor. For the sixteenth edition (1735) Taylor's executors disappeared, and Paul Knapton's name was added to his father's and brother's. For the seventeenth (1740) and eighteenth (1751) editions John and Paul Knapton held seniority, followed by J. Hodges.

With John Nicholson and Benjamin Tooke, James Knapton published a translation of Giovanni Boccaccio's *Decameron* (1702); he also published several titles with John Stephens at Oxford that were printed by Leonard Lichfield III and by the Cambridge University Press. Knapton's most prolific authors of the earlier part of the century were the theologians Thomas Bennet; Edward Wells; and Samuel Clarke, a one-time apprentice to Knapton who became the rector of St. James's, Westminster. Knapton developed various lines, including historical biographies such as David Jones's *Life of James II* (1702); drama, such as the sixth edition of John Dryden's *Conquest of Granada* (1704) and George Farquhar's *The Inconstant* (1710?); and law, such as the anonymous *Considerations Touching our Way of Tryal by Juries and the True Difference between Murder and Manslaughter* (1702).

John Knapton first appeared on the same title page as his father in 1722 in the second edition of William Camden's *Britannia.* James, John, and Paul appeared together for the first time about 1730 in the imprint to the fourth edition of William Hawney's *Compleat Measurer,* which was also the first imprint that the Knaptons shared with Hitch. Hitch would copublish more than two hundred titles with the Knaptons until his death in 1764. An advertisement in the *Daily Courant* suggests that he had opened a new shop, at the Crown in Ludgate Street, by 3 January 1735.

As substantial copyright owners, the Knaptons joined the long struggle to protect literary property. In 1734, when Samuel Powell printed an edition of Clark's *Sermons* for the Dublin bookseller Stearne Brock and then sold copies in London that undercut James Knapton's price, Knapton and others petitioned the House of Commons to make changes to the Copyright Act. In 1744 John Knapton joined Andrew Millar in the unsuccessful struggle to control Scottish reprints of London editions in the Edinburgh Court of Session. John and Paul Knapton published Warburton's *A Letter from an Author to a Member of Parliament Concerning Literary Property* (1747), defending the principle of perpetual monopoly. Knapton alerted Warburton, the editor of Alexander Pope's works (and later urged him to be lenient), when he learned of John Sayer's Latin *Essay on Man,* which borrowed from Pope's text without permission. In 1754, when Warburton was considering taking action against the Glasgow printer Robert Foulis over a Scottish edition of Pope's letters, Knapton, backed by Atty. Gen. William Murray, persuaded the editor to drop his suit.

Dear Sir

I have the favour of yours of the 7.

I desire you would send Bowyer the inclosed proofe sheet. I have inclosed too, a little more copy.

I shall be glad to see Mr. Mason's Trag: If there be any thing left for me with you to make up a packet you may send it the usual way. I have looked over the 1st vol. of Pope large 8o. now printing. if the 3d 4th & 5th vols. (in which there are the most notes) be printed off you may send me these three stitched for the same purpose

I am Dear Sir, with the most regard your most affect. friend & faithfull Serv

P. P. March 14.   W. Warburton

Rec'd 3 mo. Sheets Page 31. to 42 and send them to Mr Bowyer Mar 16

Letter from William Warburton to John Knapton, probably written in 1751, with a note by Knapton at the bottom (British Library)

The Knaptons were influential in advertising book titles along with their prices in the journals and magazines of the day; advertisements of their stock also appeared in one out of every ten books they published. Michael Treadwell has used advertisements from the *London Magazine* to determine that 51 percent of the Knaptons' stock was priced at 2s. 6d. or more; the Knaptons thus aimed their books at the upper end of the market, taking on large, costly editions that often took years to appear on the shelves.

As the eldest son of a successful London bookseller, John Knapton was expected to follow in his father's footsteps in the administrative roles of the publishing establishment; he was elected renter warden of the Stationers' Company in 1723, under warden for 1735 and 1736, upper warden in 1739 and 1740, and master in 1742, 1743, and 1744. On the other hand, Paul Knapton seems to have held no position with the Stationers' Company, and Warburton's correspondence suggests that he had little to do with the day-to-day running of the shop: when it came to acting as a go-between for Pope's editor and his overworked printer, shipping books to Prior Park or Germany, or keeping an eye out for scurrilous satires, John Knapton was the one Warburton addressed. Unfortunately, none of Knapton's replies to Warburton's seventy-three letters survives.

James and John Knapton shared the imprint on the fifteen-volume translation of Paul de Rapin-Thoyras's *The History of England* between 1728 and 1733. When sales of the edition proved much higher than originally expected, the Knaptons rewarded the translator, Nicolas Tindal, with an honorarium of two hundred pounds. On completion of the translation, Tindal was presented with a medal by the Prince of Wales. Terry Belanger has followed the changes in the imprint of George Stanhope's translation of Thomas à Kempis's *De Imitatione Christi, The Christian's Pattern,* from "J. [James] Knapton" in 1721 to "J. J. & P. Knapton" in 1733 to "J. & P. Knapton" (the two sons) in 1738, the father having died on 24 November 1736.

Pope had a long acquaintance with the Knapton family. George Knapton, who studied under Pope's friend Jonathan Richardson, made an oil painting of Pope after Sir Godfrey Kneller. Charles Knapton collaborated with Arthur Pond on the medallion for *An Essay on Man* (1733–1734) as well as on a series of sixty-nine engravings from 1732 to 1736. The Knaptons thus played an integral part not only in publishing Pope's works but also in the creation of his visible image.

The first work published by the Knaptons that was directly connected with Pope was Joseph Spence's *Essay on Pope's Odyssey* (1726). James Knapton's name appeared in the list of subscribers to Pope's six-volume edition of Shakespeare's works (1725), and James and John Knapton headed the long list of booksellers on the general title page for the 1728 reprint. In 1737 John Knapton copublished the authorized text of Pope's letters, the firm's first direct venture with the poet. That same year James Watson printed a pirated edition of the letters under the name of Thomas Johnson, a Scottish printer in The Hague who had died in 1735. The piratical printer maintained that he had not infringed the copyright law and said that the most Pope "can expect in Equity, is an Injunction." Watson was, however, anxious to make an out-of-court settlement and wanted John Knapton to mediate. An agreement was reached quickly: Pope dined with Knapton in Marsh-gate (now the Sheen Road) on 29 November, and by 1 December Watson was arranging to put the books in Knapton's hands "as soon as they can be press'd and ty'd up." Pope was quite satisfied with Knapton's handling of the affair, and when Warburton's bookseller, Fletcher Gyles, died late in 1741 Pope recommended Knapton's services, writing on 22 November: "But in particular I think you should take some care as to Mr G[yles]'s Executors. and I am of Opinion no man will be more Serviceable in setling any such accounts, than Mr Knapton, who so well knows the trade & is so acknowledged a Credit in it."

Between 1751 and 1754, 10,750 sets of Pope's *Works* were produced, at a net profit of £5,203 18s. 6 1/2d. The large octavo editions were outnumbered three-to-one by the cheaper crown and pot octavo editions. Shares were calculated on the number of sheets assigned: Warburton held 50.5 percent; the Knaptons 25.2 percent, Tonson and Company 6.7 percent; Bernard Lintot 12.9 percent; and Charles Bathurst 4.7 percent; Bathurst's name did not appear on the title page, perhaps because he had published Thomas Edwards's *Canons of Criticism,* attacking Warburton's 1747 edition of Shakespeare, in 1750. Warburton seems to have left much of the management of his controlling share in Knapton's hands.

Booksellers were occasionally named in the criticism of their authors and editors. Edwards concluded "SONNET XL. *To* SHAKESPEAR" with a satiric glance at two of the sellers of Warburton's 1747 edition.

O what a sea of idly squander'd ink,
  What heaps of notes by blundering critics penn'd
    [The dreams of ignorance in wisdom's guise]

Had then been spar'd! nor *Knapton* then, I think,
And honest [Somerset] *Draper* had been forc'd to
　　send
Their dear-bought rheams to cover plums and spice.

At the height of the scandal surrounding Pope's surreptitious printing of Henry St. John, Viscount Bolingbroke's *The Idea of a Patriot King* (1740?), which broke in the January 1749 issue of the *London Magazine,* Bolingbroke concluded *A Familiar Epistle to the Most Impudent Man Living* (1749), a fierce reply to Warburton's defensive pamphlet, *A Letter to the Editor of the Letters on the Spirit of Patriotism, The Idea of a Patriot-King and The State of Parties, &c., Occasioned by the Editor's Advertisement* (1749), with a mock apology to his customary bookseller: "Having reproved you with no more Acrimony, and advised you with more Charity than you deserve, it is time I should put an End to this familiar Epistle, and ask Mr. *Knapton's* Pardon beforehand, if it become a Pretence, which it may very probably, to Get five or ten Pounds more from him for the Copy of an Answer to it."

Warburton took his revenge by attacking David Mallet's edition of Bolingbroke's works in his anonymous *A View of Lord Bolingbroke's Philosophy; in Four Letters to a Friend,* published by the Knaptons in 1754–1755.

The Knaptons' account with their main printers, the two William Bowyers, stretches from 1725 to 1764. During the late 1740s Bowyer printed the works of various authors for the Knaptons: Pope, Warburton, and sermon writers such as Clarke, Benjamin Hoadly, and Sharp. Around this time the Knaptons were falling behind in their payments to William Strahan for the printing of Johnson's dictionary. The Knaptons missed their first payment to Strahan and were late on their installment of £38 on 9 November 1753. These comparatively minor lapses occurred at the same time as their debt to Bowyer was soaring well over the £1,300 the Knaptons made from Warburton's edition of Pope's works.

John and Paul Knapton had been part of the group of booksellers who agreed on 18 June 1746 to pay Johnson £1,575 to prepare the dictionary within three years. Nine years later, within three months of the much-delayed release date of the dictionary, Johnson wrote to Thomas Warton that "two of our partners are dead": one was Thomas Longman, the other Paul Knapton, who had died on 12 June 1755. The imprint of the dictionary – "London, Printed by W. Strahan, For J. and P. Knapton; T. and T. Longman; C. Hitch and L.

Hawes; A. Millar; and R. and J. Dodsley. MDCCLV" – proved to be the Knaptons' swan song. Within days of his brother's death John Knapton faced bankruptcy. Rumors spread that Bowyer was going to shut down the Knapton business, but the printer wrote to assure his longtime associate of his goodwill. Like most booksellers, the Knaptons juggled thousands of pounds in credits and debits; most of their capital was tied up in their stock of thousands of books, which could take decades to sell. The Knaptons' outstanding account with Bowyer had risen to nearly £1,500 three days before Paul's death; within a few days some two dozen members of the book trade paid £475 4s. into the account. Business carried on, but John Knapton was forced to part with his copyrights and much of his trade sale at the Queen's-Head Tavern, Paternoster Row, on 25 September 1755. The copyrights alone realized £4,642 11s. 9d., which was more than enough to pay off Knapton's debts to his two largest creditors, Bowyer and Warburton; but he had to sacrifice the copyright to such works as Dampier's *A New Voyage Round the World* (1697–1703), which had been the lifeblood of the business since his father's time. A trusteeship made up of T. and T. Longman, Charles Hitch, Andrew Millar, Robert Dodsley, and Knapton himself administered the business, and within three years Knapton's debts were paid in full. Bowyer continued to work as a printer for Knapton.

Following his brush with bankruptcy, Knapton published Shakespeare's *Hamlet* in 1756 and Ben Jonson's *The Alchemist* in 1770 and kept William Mason as an author: his *Elfrida* (1752) went into a sixth edition in 1759. In 1761 Knapton sold a one-third share in the copyright for Charles Shadwell's *The Fair Quaker of Deal* to Thomas Loundes for two guineas. The bookseller who would eventually take over Knapton's premises, Robert Horsfield, shared six imprints with Knapton: the third edition of Mason's *Caractacus* (1760); Sir John Comyns's *A Digest of the Laws of England* (1762–1767); the sixth and seventh editions of Hoadly's *A Plain Account of the Nature and End of the Sacrament of the Lord's-Supper* (1761–1767); volumes eight through ten of Jean Baptiste Louis Crevier's *The History of the Roman Emperors from Augustine to Constantine* (1755–1761), translated by John Mills; and *A Description of Ancient Rome . . . Drawn from an Actual Survey, by Leonardo Bufalino, in the Year 1551; Reduced to a Smaller Scale by J. B. Nolli, in 1748 . . .* (1761).

John Knapton died in 1770, leaving £4,000 in trust and almost £2,500 in bequests (including £50 to his servant, Robert Eve; £10 to each of his maid-servants; and £10 to his coachman). Horsfield was appointed one of Knapton's three executors and received a bequest of £500. John Knapton had remained single; Paul Knapton had married Elizabeth Chalwell of Stevenage in 1741, but they had had no children. Thus, the Knapton publishing dynasty crumbled after two generations. Six years after his death, the name of John Knapton made its last known appearance in the twenty-fourth edition of Bailey's *An Universal Etymological Dictionary*.

The Knaptons have been largely overlooked by book-trade scholars because they were respectable, sober-minded, mainstream booksellers, not flamboyantly successful like Millar (whom Samuel Johnson alternately praised as a Maecenas and chastised as a drunk). After 1755 they were overshadowed by the Longmans and the Dodsleys.

References:

Terry Belanger, "Booksellers' Trade Sales, 1718–1768," *Library,* fifth series 30 (December 1975): 281–302;

John Dunton, *The Life and Errors of John Dunton,* 2 volumes (London: Nichols & Bentley 1818; New York: B. Franklin, 1969), I: 217–218;

A. W. Evans, *Warburton and the Warburtonians* (Oxford: Clarendon Press, 1932);

David Foxon, *Pope and the Early Eighteenth-Century Book Trade,* edited by James McLaverty (Oxford: Clarendon Press, 1991);

Ambrose Heal, "London Booksellers and Publishers, 1700–1750," *Notes and Queries,* fifth series 161 (7 November 1931): 328;

Louise Lippincott, *Selling Art in Georgian England: the Rise of Arthur Pond* (New Haven: Yale University Press, 1983);

Maynard Mack, *Collected in Himself* (Newark: University of Delaware Press, 1982), pp. 491–501;

D. F. McKenzie, *Stationers' Company Apprentices, 1701–1800* (Oxford: Oxford Bibliographical Society, 1978);

Donald W. Nichol, ed., *Pope's Literary Legacy: The Book-Trade Correspondence of William Warburton and John Knapton with Other Letters and Related Documents (1744–1780)* (Oxford: Oxford Bibliographical Society, 1992);

Henry R. Plomer, G. H. Bushnell, and E. R. McC. Dix, *Dictionary of the Printers and Booksellers Who Were at Work in England, Scotland and Ireland from 1726 to 1775* (London: Bibliographical Society, 1932);

George Sherburne, ed., *The Correspondence of Alexander Pope,* 5 volumes (Oxford: Clarendon Press, 1956);

James E. Tierney, ed., *The Correspondence of Robert Dodsley 1733–1764* (Cambridge: Cambridge University Press, 1988);

Michael Treadwell, "London Trade Publishers 1675–1750," *Library,* sixth series 4 (June 1982): 99–134;

John Selby Watson, *The Life of William Warburton, D.D.* (London: Longman, Green, Longman, Roberts & Green, 1863), p. 473;

W. K. Wimsatt, *The Portraits of Alexander Pope* (New Haven & London: Yale University Press, 1965);

F. T. Wood, "London Booksellers and Publishers, 1700–1750," *Notes and Queries,* fifth series 161 (September 1931): 186.

Papers:

The little correspondence of the Knaptons that survives is in the British Library.

– Donald W. Nichol

T. Longman
(London: 1724 – 1725; 1734 – 1745; 1747 – 1753; 1755 – 1797)

J. Osborn and T. Longman
(London: 1725 – 1734)

T. Longman and T. Shewell
(London: 1745 – 1747)

T. and T. Longman
(London: 1753 – 1755)

M. and T. Longman
(London: 1755)

T. N. Longman
(London: 1793 – 1797)

Longman and Rees
(London: 1797 – 1799; 1800 – 1804)

T. N. Longman and O. Rees
(London: 1799 – 1800)

Longman, Hurst, Rees and Orme
(London: 1804 – 1811)

Longman, Hurst, Rees, Orme and Brown
(London: 1811 – 1823)

Longman, Hurst, Rees, Orme, Brown and Green
(London: 1823 – 1825)

Longman, Rees, Orme, Brown and Green
(London: 1825 – 1832)

Longman, Rees, Orme, Brown, Green and Longman
(London: 1832 – 1838)

Longman, Orme, Brown, Green and Longmans
(London: 1838 – 1840)

Longman, Orme and Company
(London: 1840 – 1841)

Longman, Brown and Company
(London: 1841 – 1842)

Longman, Brown, Green and Longmans
(London: 1842 – 1856)

Longman, Brown, Green, Longman and Roberts
(London: 1856 – 1859)

Longman, Green, Longman and Roberts
(London: 1859 – 1862)

Longman, Green, Longman, Roberts and Green
(London: 1862 – 1865)

Longmans, Green, Reader and Dyer
(London: 1865 – 1889)

Longmans, Green and Company
(London and New York: 1889 – 1926)

Longmans, Green and Company Limited
(London and New York: 1926 – 1959)

Longmans
(London and New York: 1959 – 1961; London: 1961 – 1968)

Longman
(London: 1968 –   )

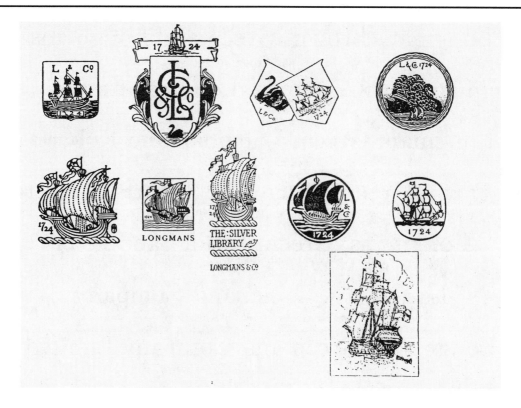

See also the Longmans, Green and Company entry in *DLB 49: American Literary Publishing Houses, 1638–1899.*

The oldest surviving English publishing house was founded on 6 August 1624 when Thomas Longman I acquired the business of William Taylor at the sign of the Ship in Paternoster Row for £2,282 9s. 6d. The sign of the Ship had first been seen over a bookseller's shop when it appeared over that of John Crooke in 1740 in the old St. Paul's Churchyard. Crooke died in 1669, and his business was taken over by his apprentice Benjamin Tooke, who sold the shop to William Taylor's father. John Taylor traded there successfully until 1706, when he was succeeded by William, who had been his apprentice. In 1711 William Taylor moved the sign of the Ship to Paternoster Row. Eight years later he took in an adjacent property, the sign of the Black Swan, which had been owned by Awnsham Churchill, an influential bookseller and publisher.

Born in Bristol in 1699, Longman was the son of Ezekiel Longman, a soap maker. Longman was orphaned when he was eight; his guardians dispatched him to London to be apprenticed, at the relatively late age of seventeen, to the bookseller John Osborn on 9 June 1716. In 1720 he inherited some of his father's West Country properties, and it was through this inheritance that Longman was able to acquire the Taylor assets from Taylor's executors, one of whom was Osborn.

The price Longman paid Taylor's executors covered the shop, a house with top-floor bedrooms for apprentices and servants, a warehouse, and "books both bound and in sheets." Acquiring shares of rights in titles was crucial if a publishing business was to survive, and the titles had to be chosen wisely. On 31 August Longman paid a further £230 18s. for Taylor copyrights that included several works published jointly with leading publishers such as Jacob Tonson and Bernard Lintot; nine of the titles included Osborn as a shareholder. One of the first titles to bear the name Longman, along with those of other publishers, was William Beveridge's two-volume *Private Thoughts upon a Christian Life,* which appeared on 2 September 1724; other Beveridge volumes would also bear his imprint. In 1725 Osborn's son, also named John, became Longman's partner, forming the firm of J. Osborn and T. Longman; the younger Osborn's sister, Mary, would become Longman's wife in 1731.

Arabian Nights' Entertainments figured in the Osborn and Longman list as early as 1725; in that year Osborn and Longman published John Locke's *Some Thoughts Concerning Education.* A highly profitable long-term investment was the guidebook that would run through regular new editions, and Osborn and Longman were shrewd enough to secure the whole share in the fourth edition of W. W. Gibson's *The Farrier's New Guide* in 1725. A year later they published the second edition of Gibson's *The Farrier's Dispensatory* and the first edition of his *The True Method of Dieting Horses*. In the age of the horse there was an obvious demand for such guides, as there would be later for guides to gardening and cookery.

John Quincy's *Lexicon Physiocomedium* appeared in 1726, with J. Osborn and T. Longman as the sole publisher. Also in 1726 Alexander Monro's *The Anatomy of Human Bones,* printed in Edinburgh for William Monro, was sold in London by J. Osborn and T. Longman. That same year Osborn and Longman acquired a share in a projected edition of the complete works of the chemist Robert Boyle, in which the elder Osborn also held shares. The editor was Peter Shaw, who, as Longman's doctor, was to help his wife through a serious illness in 1739; he would also become a favorite Longman author. A month after joining the Boyle project Osborn and Longman acquired a one-third share in the profitable Delphin *Virgil*. Other publishing ventures of Osborn and Longman include Capt. George Shelvocke's *A Voyage round the World by Way of the Great South Sea* (1726) and Joseph Warder's *The True Amazons; or, The Monarchy of Bees* (1726). The title page of a book published in Boston in 1727, *Indian Converts; or, An Account of the Living and Dying Speeches of a Considerable Number of the Christianized Indians of Martha's Vineyard,* lists J. Osborn and T. Longman as its sole seller in London. The Boyle edition was followed by other scientific works, some of them translations; among the latter were Herman Boerhaave's *A New Method of Chemistry* (1727) and G. E. Strahl's *Philosophical Principles of Human Chemistry* (1730), a digest prepared by Shaw. Professional groups were in special need of guides at a time when professional qualifications were in increasing demand, and Longman and Osborn was the sole publisher of Gen. Douglas James's *The Surveyor's Utmost Desire Fulfilled; or, The Art of Planometry, Lagenetry and Altemetry* (1727) and of Thomas Norman's *Philosophical Principles of Medicine* (1730). In cooperation with other publishers the firm produced Isaac Keay's *The Practical Measurer, His Pocket Companion* (1730) and William Bohun's *The Practising Attorney; or Lawyer's Office, Comprehending the Business of the Attorney in All Its Branches* (1732). Later in the century Longman would publish works in English and Latin for the Royal College of Surgeons.

The Longman firm was to specialize in dictionaries and encyclopedias, and in 1728 Osborn and Longman were involved in the publication of Ephraim Chambers's *Cyclopaedia,* a pioneering work

that was to encourage Denis Diderot and Jean Le Rond d'Alembert to start work on their *Encyclopédie* (1751–1780) and provide Samuel Johnson with a useful source for his dictionary (1755). When the project proved successful, Longman gave Chambers a gift of five hundred pounds. In 1730 Osborn and Longman paid forty pounds for a one-twentieth share in Robert Ainsworth's Latin dictionary, a valuable property. In the same year the firm was among the publishers of Nathan Bailey's *An Universal Etymological English Dictionary,* thirty editions of which would be brought out between its first publication in 1721 and 1802. Some of Osborn and Longman's books were copiously illustrated, such as William Dugdale's *The Antiquities of Warwickshire* (1730), "with maps, prospects and portraitures . . . from the original copper plates." John Horsley's *Britannia Romana; or, the Roman Antiquities of Britain* followed in 1732.

The younger Osborn died in 1733, bequeathing to Longman a half share of the patent rights as "printer to the king in Latin, Greek and Hebrew." John Osborn Sr. drew up his will immediately after his son's death, leaving almost the whole of his estate to "my dear and loving son-in-law Thomas Longman and daughter." In 1736 Longman, along with S. Buckley, purchased "The royal Grant and Privilege" of printing William Lily's sixteenth-century Latin grammar; their "revised and improved" edition was published in the hope that it would win "the approbation and Encouragement of those Gentlemen who have the Care and Instruction of Youth." Longman was first listed in a London guide of 1740 as a bookseller living and working in Paternoster Row; also appearing in the list was Charles Rivington, the founder of the business that would be the oldest surviving publishing house until the Longman firm acquired it in 1890. Thomas Shewell, another former apprentice of John Osborn Sr., was Longman's partner between 1745 and 1747. Thomas Longman II, the son of Longman's younger brother Henry, was then serving his apprenticeship with the firm.

When Johnson and a consortium of publishers agreed in 1746 to proceed with the dictionary, it was Thomas Longman I to whom Johnson wrote to suggest that the contract be signed at a breakfast. The prospectus for the dictionary was published in 1747, with Longman's name among the projectors. In 1751 Longman acquired a one-third share in the project to carry the *Universal History,* begun in 1729, forward into "modern times." He would be dead when the first eight octavo volumes — at two pounds "one of the cheapest works ever offered to

Thomas Norton Longman III, who headed the firm from 1797 to 1842; portrait by Thomas Phillips, circa 1830 (from Asa Briggs, Essays in the History of Publishing in Celebration of the 250th Anniversary of the House of Longman 1724–1794, *1976)*

the public" – appeared in 1759. The history, which Edward Gibbon found "plodding," was to be studied by Thomas Jefferson and summarized by the young John Stuart Mill. When Longman bought Taylor's assets he had not acquired a share in the best-known title on Taylor's list, Daniel Defoe's *Robinson Crusoe* (1719), from which Taylor was said to have made a profit of a thousand pounds. It was not until the tenth edition, in 1753, that the name Longman appeared on the title page (along with those of eight other publishers), after Longman acquired a one-twentieth share in the work. This title page was also the first to bear the names of two Longmans: Longman had taken his nephew, Thomas Longman II, into partnership that year, giving him two thousand pounds to acquire his initial share of the firm. The total capitalization of the firm at that time was five thousand pounds.

Longman died on 18 June 1755, two months after Johnson's *A Dictionary of the English Language* ap-

peared. Religion had figured prominently in Thomas Longman I's lists, and by the time he died he had a major stake in the publications of Isaac Watts, the great dissenting hymn writer. Thomas I and his wife were childless; thus, what became a publishing dynasty might have ended in 1755. In his will, however, Longman stipulated that after his wife's death his share of the business should pass to his nephew; he specifically mentioned the right to Lily's grammar. In 1756 Longman's widow's name appeared with that of Thomas II on the title page of Johnson's *Proposals for Printing, by Subscription, the Dramatick Works of William Shakespeare*. His widow gave Thomas Longman II all control of the business four years before she died in 1762. It was during his long and enterprising regime that the house of Longman would come to be considered a publishing leviathan.

The firm continued to publish guidebooks: Philip Miller's *The Gardener's Kalendar; Directing*

What Works Are Necessary to Be Performed Every Month in the Kitchen, Fruit and Pleasure Gardens as Also in the Conservatory and Nursery appeared in 1760 with fourteen other publishers listed as booksellers for a work that was "printed for the author"; eleven years later Thomas Hitt's *The Modern Gardener; or Universal Kalendar* was published. Hannah Glasse's *The Art of Cookery Made Plain and Easy* (1770), which went through several editions, had no fewer than twenty-eight publishers' names attached to it. The sign of the Ship over the Paternoster Row premises disappeared by 1770 because of an act of Parliament decreeing that all signs had to be removed or placed flat against the wall. From then until 1940 the Longman address was simply 39 Paternoster Row.

Thomas Longman I had had a share in the 1749 edition of Miguel de Cervantes's *Don Quixote;* the firm participated in the publication of a 1775 translation of the work by Tobias Smollett "with twenty-eight new copper plates . . . elegantly engraved." Thomas Longman II was one of the six London publishers of Adam Smith's *The Theory of Moral Sentiments* (1776). Chambers's *Cyclopaedia* had gone through five editions by 1746, and a supplement had been published in 1753. Late in the century Thomas Longman II began a difficult search for the right person to update it, finally settling on Abraham Rees. The first number, in folio, was published in 1778; the work sold well and was continued weekly until it was completed in 418 numbers. In 1760 Thomas Longman II had married Elizabeth Harris, the sister of Thomas Harris, the proprietor of Covent Garden Theatre from 1767 to 1799. Longman published many plays and had a one-seventh share in *The Dramatic Works of Colin Cibber* (1777). While he supported the foundation of the *Times* in 1788, he was not involved in the launching of literary periodicals.

Thomas II was the first of the Longmans to live away from the shop in Paternoster Row: in 1792 he moved to Greenhill House, Hampstead. Thomas II also established what was to be an important family link with a related business when his second son, George, went into partnership with the paper maker John Dickinson. The main contributions to the firm made by Thomas Longman II were to extend its provincial networks at a time when the provincial booktrade was increasing in importance and to develop foreign business. During the last decades of the century he both joined in the publication of books that originated with provincial publishers and sold books that were published in the provinces. The initiative sometimes came from

Longman, sometimes from an enterprising provincial printer or bookseller. One provincial item in the Longman list was John Baskerville's *Vocabulary or Pocket Dictionary,* printed by Baskerville in Birmingham and sold by eight London booksellers; another was Richard Harvey's *The Farmers' and Corn-buyers' Assistant* (1764), printed in Norwich "by the author" and sold by three London booksellers. In creating his provincial networks Longman was assisted by William West, future historian of the book trade, who saw him "almost daily" during the mid 1780s to discuss "books for country orders."

Thomas Longman II's interest in overseas markets anticipated the firm's twentieth-century emphasis on the internationalism of the publishing business. This interest is reflected in his correspondence with Henry Knox of Boston. Longman sent books that he urged Knox to sell at a fair price, avoiding "underselling." He also sent periodicals, among them the *Gentleman's Magazine,* the *London Magazine,* the *Monthly Review,* and the *Critical Review,* all of which promoted the culture of the book. Their friendship was not broken by the American Revolution, and when the war was over Knox, who had become a general in the American army, was punctilious in meeting his debts to Longman while insisting that he could not be held responsible for the earlier destruction of books in transit.

Thomas Longman II died on 5 February 1797. He had asked for a simple funeral, saying "I hate the foolish parade of pompous funerals." He was described in his obituaries as a "very considerable bookseller"; although his business obviously involved much more than merely selling books, the term *publisher* in its modern sense was still not used. At the time of his death his business was worth around £103,000.

Thomas Norton Longman III, who inherited the business, had more capital at his disposal than any of his predecessors. He also had a non-Longman partner of skill and enterprise whose background and experience were complementary to his own. Born in 1770, Owen Rees had been made a partner in 1797, before Thomas Longman II died. The son of a Welsh Unitarian minister, he had served his apprenticeship not in London but in Bristol, the city from which Thomas Longman I had come, and had set up shop there in Wine Street, a center of the local booktrade, in 1791. Before he joined Longman, Rees had published in Bristol Romaine Joseph Thorn's poem "Retirement" (1793), which bore on its title page "sold in London by T. N. Longman and J. Parsons." The imprint after the Longman-Rees partnership was "Longman and

Rees"; it was changed in 1799 to "T. N. Longman and O. Rees" and in 1800 back to "Longman and Rees."

In 1798 Thomas Norton Longman III married Mary Slater; they had three sons and four daughters. Mrs. Longman was the cousin of the Reverend Sydney Smith – a useful connection for Longman, who gave the unusual Christian name Smith to the youngest of his daughters. In 1799 a textbook, Lindley Murray's *English Grammar,* sold nearly fifty thousand copies; it would remain in the Longman catalogue for more than a hundred years. During 1800 no fewer than ninety titles were published, among them *Reflections on the Political State of Society of the Commencement of the Year 1800,* by John Bowles, which was also sold by William Cobbett in New York. There were several plays, for the relationship with Covent Garden remained close; one was *Management,* a comedy in five acts by Frederick Reynolds.

One book on the 1800 list would, in the view of later generations, dominate all the rest, and it appeared on the list because of the Bristol connection. William Wordsworth and Samuel Taylor Coleridge's *Lyrical Ballads* had been commissioned by the Bristol publisher Joseph Cottle, who had offered Wordsworth ten guineas in 1795 for an unfinished poem. Cottle was in serious financial difficulties, however, when the *Lyrical Ballads* appeared anonymously in five hundred copies with the imprint "Bristol: printed by Biggs and Cottle for T. N. Longman, Paternoster-row, London, 1798." Cottle sold 108 of his copyrights to Longman and Rees for £210; they included works of poetry and religion, a medical lecture by Thomas Beddoes, and Robert Southey's *Joan of Arc* (1796), but not *Lyrical Ballads.* Cottle set down the value of the *Lyrical Ballads* as nil; sales had been slow, and he had disposed of his remaining copies to J. and A. Arch of Gracechurch Street, London, who in 1798 produced a new title page bearing their name and neither Cottle's nor Longman's. Meanwhile, Longman and Rees published Coleridge's translation of Friedrich Schiller's *Wallenstein* (1800), for which he was paid fifty pounds in advance. The first Longman and Rees edition of the *Lyrical Ballads* appeared in 1800; Wordsworth received eighty pounds for the rights, out of which he paid Coleridge thirty pounds. Longman and Rees published two further impressions of the *Lyrical Ballads* in 1802 and 1805. In 1807 the firm published one thousand copies of Wordsworth's *Poems.* These did not sell as well as *Lyrical Ballads* had, and the critical reaction to the collection reduced Wordsworth to despondency and affected the future relationship between Wordsworth and Longman. Southey, however, became a Longman author. Income from his last epic poem, *Roderick* (1814), enabled him to pay his debts to the firm, and eight years later he claimed that his account with Longman and Rees was bringing him around two hundred pounds a year.

Abraham Rees, who had updated Chambers's *Cyclopaedia,* was invited by Thomas Norton Longman III to produce his own *New Cyclopaedia; or, A Universal Dictionary of Arts and Sciences* in 1802. It appeared, a symbol both of continuity and change, at irregular intervals until it was completed in 1820. The tradition of publishing plays started by Thomas Longman II was continued by Longman and Rees, who in 1806 launched the publication of a series of plays that had been performed at Covent Garden, Drury Lane, and the Haymarket, the three Theatres Royal. They were printed from the prompt books by permission of the managers of the theaters.

Longman and Rees paid a great deal of attention to their authors. They traveled frequently to Scotland and Ireland as well as to the provinces, and when in London they gave literary parties at Paternoster Row and in Hampstead that were attended by a wide variety of guests. One of the guests was Washington Irving, who described Rees as "the laughing partner" and Longman as "the carving partner who attends to the joints." Henry Crabb Robinson called the latter "a quiet gentlemanly man."

One of the most momentous visits was that of Thomas Norton Longman III to Scotland in 1802, when he reached the arrangement with Archibald Constable that led to his firm's becoming a joint publisher of the *Edinburgh Review;* he also negotiated with Sir Walter Scott for the third volume of *Minstrelsy of the Scottish Border* (1803). Later, Scott's novel *Guy Mannering* (1815) was jointly published by the Longman and Constable firms.

Rees never married; he was able, therefore, to devote all his time to the development of the business, and when he died in 1837, just after returning to his native Wales, his relatives claimed that "his unremitting attention to business had undermined his constitution." He had become a rich man, however. By the time Rees died the firm had so many partners listed on its title pages that Scott described it as "the long firm." The partners carried out specialized tasks that included selling old books of other publishers as well as their own lists. Their main publishing rival in London was John Murray, to whom George Gordon, Lord Byron, turned after

Longman refused to publish his *English Bards, and Scotch Reviewers* (1809). Thomas Moore became a major Longman author, although it was to Murray that he had to turn for the publication of his edition of *Letters and Journals of Lord Byron: With Notices of His Life* (1830). New publishers entered the scene, but Longman and Murray were the two main ones. Both were to grow and to survive, on quite different lines, deep into the twentieth century.

In 1823 Longman's son Charles, following the example of his Uncle George, was apprenticed to Dickinson, the papermaker. There was a family link with the printing trade, too, for in 1819 Longman's daughter Mary married Andrew Spottiswoode, who was to become printer to Queen Victoria; he was the grandson of William Strahan, the favorite printer of Thomas Longman I. Thomas Norton Longman III died in 1842 and was succeeded by his sons Thomas IV and William, who had become partners in the firm in 1832 and 1839, respectively. Among the works published under their regime were Thomas Babington Macaulay's *The History of England from the Accession of James II* (1848–1861), Herbert Spencer's *The Principles of Psychology* (1855), Sir Richard F. Burton's *Personal Narrative of a Pilgrimage to El-Medinah and Meccah* (1855–1856), Henry Gray's *Anatomy, Descriptive and Surgical* (1858), John Henry Newman's *Apologia pro Vita Sua* (1864), and James Anthony Froude's *The English in Ireland in the Eighteenth Century* (1872–1874). The Paternoster Row premises were destroyed by fire in 1861 but were rebuilt and reopened in 1863. William Longman died in 1877 and Thomas IV in 1879. Their successors were Thomas Norton Longman V and George H. Longman, the sons of Thomas IV, and William's sons, Charles J. Longman and Hubert H. Longman. A New York branch was opened in 1887, and a Bombay branch in 1890. The firm's offices were destroyed again in German air raids in December 1940 and January 1941. After that, there was to be no return to Paternoster Row. The New York branch of the firm was dissolved in 1961. Mark and William Longman became cochairmen in 1963;

with William's death in 1967, Mark was left as the last Longman to head the firm. In 1968 the firm's independence came to an end when it was purchased by the Financial and Provincial Publishing Company, which later became Pearson PLC; it also moved into new offices in Harlow, Essex. In 1970 Longman merged with the Penguin Publishing Company; within the next few years its general publishing list was transferred to the Penguin imprint, leaving Longman to concentrate on educational publishing. Mark Longman died in 1972. A new New York branch was opened in 1973. The firm now has branches and associate companies all over the world; its main office is Longman House, Burnt Mill, Harlow, Essex. The chairman and chief executive is Paula Kahn.

References:

Cyprian Blagden, *Fire More than Water* (London: Longmans, 1967);

Asa Briggs, ed., *Essays in the History of Publishing in Celebration of the 250th Anniversary of the House of Longman 1724–1974* (London: Longman, 1976);

Harold Cox and J. E. Chandler, *The House of Longman* (London: Longmans, Green, 1925);

Francis Espinasse, *Critic* (24 March 1860); (7 April 1860); (21 April 1860);

Andrew Pettigrew and Richard Whipp, *Managing Change for Competitive Success* (Oxford: Basil Blackwell, 1993);

Thomas Rees and John Britton, *Reminiscences of Literary London, 1779–1853* (London: Suckling & Galloway, 1896).

Philip Wallis, *At the Sign of the Ship* (Harlow, U.K.: Longman, 1974).

Papers:

The Longman archive at Reading University contains little eighteenth-century material; many Longman papers were destroyed by fire in 1861 and 1940–1941.

– Lord Asa Briggs

Andrew Millar

(London: 1729 – 1767)

Andrew Millar, one of the most successful publishers of belletristic titles in eighteenth-century London, was characterized by Samuel Johnson as the "Maecenas of the age" and as the bookseller who "raised the price of literature," although his success was attributed by his contemporaries to his business and marketing acumen rather than to his literary taste and judgment. Publisher and friend of the poet James Thomson, the novelist Samuel Richardson, and the dramatist and novelist Henry Fielding, Millar was the bookseller chiefly responsible for seeing Johnson's *A Dictionary of the English Language* (1755) through the press. David Hume's *The History of England* (1756) and William Robertson's *The History of Scotland, During the Reigns of Queen Mary and of King James VI* (1759) are among the important nonliterary books published by Millar.

In spite of Millar's eminence in the book trade, only scant biographical information about the bookseller's personal life is available; it is found in scattered references in John Nichols's *Literary Anecdotes of the Eighteenth Century* (1813), the letters of David Hume, and James Boswell's *The Life of Samuel Johnson, L.L.D.* (1791). The printer William Strahan, Millar's friend and associate in the London trade, made an entry in his ledger that gives Millar's date of birth as 19 October 1706. All sources agree that Millar was born in Scotland, but no specific place of birth or information about Millar's parentage is noted. Strahan's entry records that on 4 May 1730 Millar married a woman named Jane, who was born on 24 February 1709, and that three children born to the couple died in infancy.

In the early 1740s Millar moved from that establishment to the house formerly occupied by the elder Jacob Tonson at the Shakespeare Head, opposite Catherine Street. In this house, which Millar renamed Buchanan's Head, he worked for the rest of his long and profitable career.

Millar's involvement with Thomson's works dates to 1728, a year before he set up shop at 141 The Strand, and is paradigmatic of his skill as a marketer of books and his encouragement of literature. Thomson's *Winter* (1726), *Summer* (1727), and

A Poem Sacred to the Memory of Sir Isaac Newton (1727) had been published by another Scottish bookseller in London, John Millan. In a letter written in 1728 Thomson lists Millar along with George Strahan and John Millan as handling the subscriptions for *The Seasons*. The earliest reference to *Spring: A Poem* in the Stationer's Register was entered by Millar on 23 January 1728; the first publication of *Spring,* with the imprint "Printed and sold by A. Millar and G. Strahan," was advertised in the newspapers on 5 June 1728. George Strahan's name was dropped from newspaper announcements after 12 June 1728. Court records in an action brought by Millar in a piracy case ten years later show that "Andrew Millar in the year 1729, purchased this work called the Seasons . . . of James Thomson, the author and proprietor . . . for £160." In 1729 Thomson transferred to Millar for £137 the copyrights in perpetuity of *Spring* and *The Tragedy of Sophonisba* (1730), along with "all additions corrections alterations and amendments whatsoever which shall or may at any time hereafter be made into or concerning them." In April 1730 an advertisement appeared in the *Daily Post* soliciting subscribers for a quarto edition of *The Seasons* and listing Millar, William Innys, and George Strahan as booksellers prepared to receive subscriptions. Copies of the book were to be delivered by Thomson, Millar, and the bookbinder John Brindley. The printer was Millar's friend Richardson, who had also printed the first edition of Thomson's *Britannia* (1730) for T. Warner. In June 1730 Millar advertised a second edition of *Britannia* in quarto, bound with the subscription edition of *The Seasons*. This combined edition was offered for sale by Millan and Millar for the next eight years.

In 1736 Millar, together with the booksellers J. Gray and John Nourse, entered into a contract to sell books for the Society for the Encouragement of Learning, which had been founded by William Bowyer, the "learned printer" of the Society of Antiquaries. Thomson and another poet, Paul Whitehead, were the literary representatives of a group of noblemen, learned doctors, and professors. The organization was seen by many booksellers as in competition with the regular trade. During the three years that Millar was associated with the society it published only four books. The organization lasted for twelve years, sometimes contracting with booksellers such as Millar, sometimes publishing from its own house. No profit came to authors or booksellers from this enterprise, and the project left a legacy of a two-thousand-pound debt.

In 1738 Millar's role as Thomson's sole publisher was confirmed when he purchased the remainder of Millan's Thomson copyrights. "The Seasons and Other Poems" was entered in the Stationer's Register for Millar on 24 June 1738. Millar did well in his purchase, acquiring the rights for £105, the same price paid by Millan in 1729. As soon as he acquired the copyrights Millar brought action against booksellers in Scotland who were pirating editions of Thomson's works. By 12 June 1738 Millar was selling the first octavo edition of *The Works of Mr. Thomson* under the imprint "Printed for A. Millar." Millar continued to act as the exclusive publisher of Thomson's works until the poet's death. In May 1748 Millar published Thomson's *The Castle of Indolence,* with a second posthumous edition following Thomson's death in August of that same year. Millar published Thomson's last play, *Coriolanus. A Tragedy,* in 1749. In 1750 Millar published *The Works of James Thomson,* edited by George Lyttleton, and a small collection of previously unpublished poems, *Poems on Several Occasions.*

Millar's friendship with Richardson dates to the beginning of Millar's career in London, when he acted as a bookseller, either independently or in congers, for books printed by Richardson. After 1747 Millar's imprint began to appear regularly on Richardson's books. Richardson recommended Millar to others: "he has great Business, and is in a way of promoting the Sales of what he engages in. . . . He is a man of Courage as well as of handsome Spirit; and single hearted." The few extant letters exchanged between the two men suggest a considerable degree of intimacy.

Millar's first involvement in selling Richardson's works seems to have concerned Richardson's edition of Daniel Defoe's *A Tour Thro' the Whole Island of Great Britain* (1738). The work, which went through six editions, lists Millar as fifth in a group of booksellers. Between 1747 and 1748 Richardson's *Clarissa* was published in three installments by Millar with J. and J. Rivington, J. Osborne, and John Leake. The first complete edition of *Clarissa* sold out in 1749, four months after the last three of the seven volumes appeared. By 1759 the work had run to a fourth edition in eight volumes. Millar was

THE

CASTLE

OF

INDOLENCE:

AN

ALLEGORICAL POEM.

Written in

IMITATION *of* SPENSER.

By

JAMES THOMSON.

LONDON:

Printed for A. MILLAR, over againſt *Catherine-ſtreet,* in the *Strand.*

M DCC XLVIII.

Title page for the last completed work by Scottish poet James Thomson, published by Andrew Millar a few weeks before Thomson's death (Courtesy of the Lilly Library, Indiana University)

involved in a conger of five in the publication of *The History of Sir Charles Grandison* (1754). Richardson's friendship with Millar was instrumental in bringing Charlotte Lennox's *The Female Quixote* to Millar's attention; Richardson printed the work, and Millar offered it for sale in 1751. So close was the friendship between Millar and Richardson that in 1758 Richardson added Millar to the list of executors of his will.

Another popular poet whose works Millar published early in his career was the Scottish physician John Armstrong. Armstrong was a friend of Thomson, who portrayed him in *The Castle of Indolence.* Armstrong's licentious poem *The Economy of Love* was printed for Thomas Cooper in 1736 but was registered to Andrew Millar in the Stationers' Register. Millar's business relationship with the booksellers Thomas and Mary Cooper appears to have begun with *The Economy of Love.* Thomas Cooper's, and subsequently Mary Cooper's, imprints appear on several works to which Millar held the copyright in the Stationers' Register. The poem for which Armstrong is remembered today, the didactic *Art of Preserving Health,* was entered in the Stationers' Register for Armstrong but was entered in William Strahan's printing ledger for Millar in April 1744. This situation means that Armstrong retained ownership but Millar paid or arranged for the printing of the book. A second edition, "printed for A. Millar," was published in 1747, and a third edition came out in 1748.

Thomson advised Fielding to bring his novel *Joseph Andrews* to Millar in 1742. Millar paid £199 6s. for *Joseph Andrews* and a farce and pamphlet by Fielding. Two editions of the novel were published anonymously in 1742, and a third with copper plates in 1743. In 1743 Millar published a second edition of Fielding's *Miscellanies* in three volumes. In 1744 Millar published Fielding's sister Sarah's novel *The Adventures of David Simple,* which included a preface by Henry Fielding.

In 1748 Henry Fielding contracted with Millar for a novel titled "The History of a Foundling in Eighteen Books." This was Fielding's great novel, *Tom Jones,* for which Millar purchased the entire copyright for six hundred pounds. *Tom Jones,* published under Fielding's name, was first advertised by Millar in the *General Advertiser* on 28 February 1749. The advertisement illustrates Millar's selling technique, announcing that the publisher was "pressed to be able to provide sufficient copies to keep up with the demand" but that "such Gentlemen and Ladies as please, might have them sew'd in Blue Paper and Boards at the Price of 16s. a Set." There were at least two printings of the six-volume first edition, with another edition in 1749 and yet another, with the author's corrections, in 1750. Millar, on finding the novel such a success in its first edition, was moved to pay Fielding another one hundred pounds.

In 1751 Millar published Fielding's *Amelia* in four volumes. Once again, Millar's advertisement of the novel was calculated to excite interest in the work, claiming that four presses were at work in order to satisfy the "earnest Demand . . . but the Proprietor notwithstanding finds it impossible to get them bound in Time, without spoiling the Beauty of the Impression, and therefore will sell them sew'd at Half-a-Guinea." Sir Walter Scott, in his preface to Fielding's collected works in 1800, reports that Millar paid a thousand pounds for the copyright of *Amelia.* Scott also says that, at a prepublication sale for booksellers, Millar, fearing that *Amelia* would not enjoy the success of *Tom Jones,* offered his other publications "on the usual terms of discount; but when it came to *Amelia,* he laid it aside, as a work in such demand, that he could not afford to deliver it to the trade in the usual manner. His ploy was successful and, to Millar's relief, the impression was quickly bought up." Millar evidently was not involved in publishing Fielding's *Covent-Garden Journal* (1752), although he advertised in its columns and Fielding went out of his way to puff books published by Millar in the journal. The last work of Fielding's that Millar published was *The Journal of a Voyage to Lisbon* (1755), which appeared one year after the death of the author.

Millar's involvement with Johnson's *A Dictionary of the English Language* reveals another aspect of the bookseller's business ventures. Copyrights for dictionaries were among the most valuable in the trade. The publishers who formed a partnership to bring out Johnson's dictionary included, in addition to Millar, John and Paul Knapton, Thomas Longman, Charles Hitch, and Robert Dodsley. Millar took charge of the publication of the work and dispersed payments to the writer. The original price paid to Johnson was £1,575. In describing final arrangements for publication James Boswell reports: "When the messenger who carried the last sheet to Millar returned, Johnson asked him, 'Well, What did he say?' – 'Sir,' (answered the messenger) he said, thank GOD I have done with him.' 'I am glad (replied Johnson) that he thanks GOD for anything.'" Millar was among the acquaintances who rallied around Johnson after his wife's death in 1752.

Millar's successful marketing techniques also benefited his countryman David Hume to no small degree. Hume's association with Millar dates as early as 1742, when the bookseller handled the London sales of *Essays, Moral and Political,* which was published in Edinburgh. Between 1748 and 1749 Millar became the main agent for Hume in London, publishing three collections of essays, including *Philosophical Essays Concerning Human Understanding* (1748). In 1751 Millar published Hume's *An Enquiry Concerning the Principles of Morals.*

Hume's *History of England* was first published as *The History of Great Britain* in Edinburgh in 1754. After the first volume of the work failed to sell, arrangements were made through Hume's Edinburgh publisher, Gavin Hamilton, for Millar to take fifty copies of the first volume. One version of how Millar gained copyright to Hume's history is recorded in a 1777 life of Hume by Samuel Jackson Pratt. Millar did not sell the book to customers when they requested it but described it as "incomplete, another volume is coming out soon. 'You are welcome,' Millar assured his customers, 'to the use of this in the mean time.'" In this manner Millar "circulated"

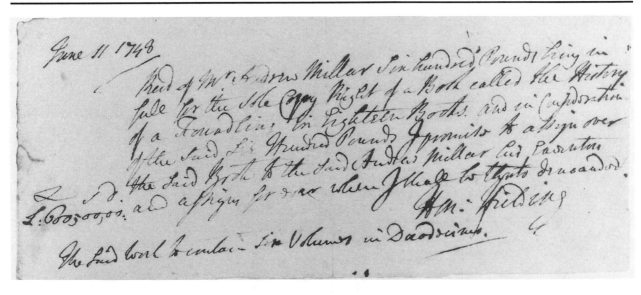

Receipt from Henry Fielding acknowledging that Millar paid six hundred pounds for the copyright of Fielding's Tom Jones *(Pierpont Morgan Library MA 789)*

volume one among "some hundred readers" without selling one. Using this ploy, Millar got Hamilton to sell him the copyright to the work for "a trifle." Millar then contracted to publish volume two, which was well advanced by November 1754, for £750. Once Millar had charge of the publication of the second volume he "pushed the sale of the first." The second volume, printed by Hume's friend and correspondent William Strahan for Millar in 1756, was a success and, in Hume's words, "helped to buoy up its unfortunate brother." In 1757 Hume began negotiating the final sale of all the author's rights to both volumes of *The History of England.* Hume, who did not want to be burdened with business affairs associated with his books, profited despite his relinquishing of the copyright; within seven years his income from the work reached £3,400. A decade after the failed debut of the first volume, Hume's *History of England* had become the most popular and best-selling history published to that date. The Hume-Millar correspondence reveals two unrealized literary projects that they were considering: a translation of and commentary on Plutarch by Hume, to be paid for and published by Millar, and a weekly paper in London to be edited by Hume and published by Millar.

A 1759 letter from Hume to a Glasgow associate reveals that, despite his reputation as a businessman, Millar was not immune to financial trouble. "Poor Millar is declared bankrupt," writes Hume, "his debts amount to £40,000, and it said that his creditors will not get above three shillings in the pound." Hume placed the blame for the setback out-side the bounds of the trade: "All the world allow him to have been diligent and industrious; but his misfortunes are ascribed to the extravagance of his wife, a very ordinary case in this city." It is likely that the bankruptcy was a temporary measure on Millar's part to protect his assets, for in the 1760s his business was certainly thriving.

The capstone of Millar's involvement with the publishing and marketing of Thomson's work came in 1762, thirteen years after the death of the poet, when the bookseller brought out a beautiful two-volume subscription edition titled *The Works of James Thomson.* An "Account of the Life and Writing of Mr. James Thomson," by the Scottish mathematician and author Patrick Murdoch, was included in the first volume. Millar contributed the profits from the edition to the erection of a monument to Thomson in Westminster Abbey. Millar would hold the exclusive copyrights to the works of Thomson until his death in 1768; his executors would sell the whole copyright to the trade for £505.

It was also in 1762 that Millar published the complete works of Henry Fielding, edited by the author, actor, and biographer Arthur Murphy. The edition included a life by Murphy and an engraved frontispiece portrait of Fielding by William Hogarth. The works of no other English novelist of that time had received so complete a treatment. The edition was republished in varied formats by the purchasers of Millar's copyrights and their successors from 1771 to 1821.

Millar has been credited with introducing in 1753 a new practice in booksellers' trade sales: in-

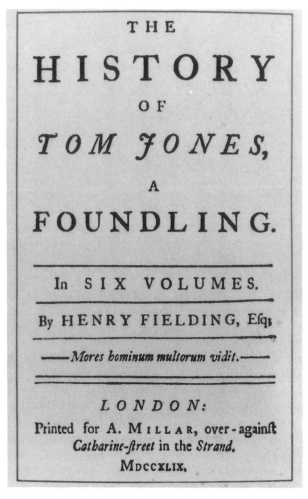

THE

HISTORY

OF

TOM JONES,

A

FOUNDLING.

In SIX VOLUMES.

By HENRY FIELDING, Eſq;

———— *Mores hominum multorum vidit.* ————

LONDON:

Printed for A. MILLAR, over-againſt
Catharine-ſtreet in the *Strand.*
MDCCXLIX,

Title page for Fielding's novel Tom Jones, *which was so successful
that Millar paid the author one hundred pounds over and
above the copyright price*

stead of offering the whole or remaining stock of a publisher he would offer parts of the current stock of one or more booksellers. Such sales, which would become a widespread practice in the nineteenth century, were used both for subscriptions and for the remaindering of books, as "current stock" meant either titles that were offered year after year according to demand or titles that were considered "dead or moribund." Millar has been identified as the proprietor or partial proprietor of eleven trade sales between 1753 and 1768. In the catalogues of such sales printed by Strahan between 1759 and 1765, works by Millar's authors Fielding, Hume, and Thomson appear regularly in editions of 250 copies each.

In 1764 J. H. Füßli, who would change his name to Henry Fuseli, traveled to England in the company of Sir Andrew Mitchell, the British envoy to Berlin. It was through Mitchell and the poet John Armstrong, who had acted as physician to the British army in Prussia and had met the young Swiss exile in Berlin in 1763, that Fuseli was introduced to Millar, who launched Fuseli's career as an art historian by commissioning him to translate six essays by Johann Joachim Winckelmann as *Reflections on the Painting and Sculpture of the Greeks: with Instructions for the Connoisseur and An Essay on Grace in Works of Art* (1765). The collection of essays, published by subscription, sold poorly; after a year not even all of the subscribers had bothered to collect their copies from Millar, who had turned over all of the proceeds from the sale of the work to Fuseli. In 1766 Millar advertised a "second edition," with the word *corrected* added to the title and with the name of Thomas Cadell, who would be Millar's successor, added to the imprint. The conjecture that Millar, who was on the eve of retirement at this time, was "cleaning house" of unsold liabilities for Cadell is reinforced by the fact that this "edition" was sold for one shilling less than the first edition.

In 1767 Millar brought a legal action concerning copyright infringement that had ramifications beyond the intent of the original suit and results that the bookseller did not live to see. The case, *Millar* v. *Taylor,* was brought by Millar against the bookseller James Taylor, who had printed an edition of Thomson's *The Seasons.* When Thomson had conveyed the rights to Millar in 1729 he had included the "benefit of all additions, corrections, and amendments which should be afterwards made in the said copies." The Court of King's Bench decided that Thomson had an assignable right in *The Seasons* under common law, and that the 1709 Statute of Anne had not taken the right away. The ruling retained authorial creative rights to correct, add, and revise. In this case the author, Thomson, was deceased, but he had assigned those authorial rights to Millar and Millar's agents. Thus, no new or "improved" edition of *The Seasons* could be put out by another publisher. Millar died while the case was pending. *Millar* v. *Taylor* lasted as precedent for five years but was overturned in a suit brought by Alexander Donaldson, another bookseller, against Thomas Beckett and fourteen partners who bought the Thomson works at auction in 1769. *Millar* v. *Taylor* and *Donaldson* v. *Beckett* are considered landmark cases in English copyright law.

In 1767 Millar had turned over his business to his associate Cadell, a man described by Nichols as a "striking instance of the effects of a strong understanding when united to unremitting industry." Cadell, who had been apprenticed to Millar in 1758 and had been his partner since 1765, carried on Millar's legacy as a patron of literature; indeed, according to Nichols, he exceeded his predecessor in his enterprise at "publishing the works of the celebrated writers that have ornamented the age in which we live."

In describing Millar as "artificer of his own fortune," Nichols stresses that Millar's success in the book trade lay not in his own learning or literary judgment as much as in his "nice discrimination in selecting his literary counsellors" and his wise business dealings. Millar enjoyed a year of retirement in a villa at Kew Green, where he died on 8 June 1768. He left legacies to David Hume and to William and Allen Fielding, the sons of Henry.

References:

Hugh Amory, "Andrew Millar and the First Recension of Fielding's *Works* (1762)," *Transactions of*

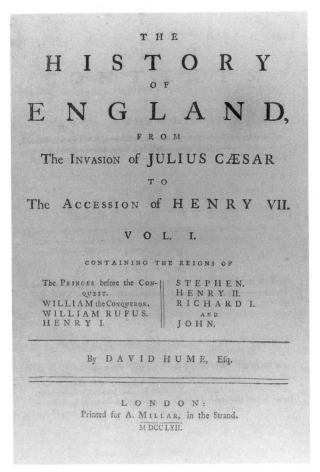

Title page for Hume's history, which failed when the first version was published in Edinburgh in 1754 but became a best-seller for Millar (Courtesy of Special Collections, Thomas Cooper Library, University of South Carolina)

the Cambridge Bibliographical Society, 7, part 1 (1981): 57–78;

Martin C. Battestin and Ruthe R. Battestin, *Henry Fielding. A Life* (London & New York: Routledge, 1989);

Terry Berlanger, "Booksellers' Trade Sales, 1718–1768," *Library,* fifth series 30 (December 1975): 281–302;

Cyprian Blagden, "Booksellers' Trade Sales 1718–1768," *Library,* fifth series 5 (March 1951): 243–257;

James Boswell, *Boswell's Life of Johnson,* edited by George Birkbeck Hill, revised by L. F. Powell (Oxford: Clarendon Press, 1934);

John Hill Burton, ed., *Life and Correspondence of David Hume,* 2 volumes (Edinburgh: William Tait, 1846);

Hilbert H. Campbell, *James Thomson (1700–1748): An Annotated Bibliography of Selected Editions and the Important Criticism* (New York & London: Garland, 1976);

John Carrol, *Selected Letters of Samuel Richardson* (Oxford: Clarendon Press, 1964);

Arthur E. Case, *A Bibliography of English Poetical Miscellanies 1521–1750* (Oxford: Bibliographical Society, 1935);

W. B. Coley, Introduction to Henry Fielding, *The Jacobite's Journal and Related Writings* (Oxford: Oxford University Press, 1974);

W. L. Cross, *History of Fielding* (New Haven: Yale University Press, 1918);

Culloden Papers (London: T. Cadell & W. Davies, 1815);

Frederick H. Dudden, *Henry Fielding: His Life, Works, and Times* (Oxford: Clarendon Press, 1952);

T. C. Duncan Eaves and Ben D. Kimpel, *Samuel Richardson Biography* (Oxford: Clarendon Press, 1971);

H. George Hahn, *Henry Fielding: An Annotated Bibliography* (Metuchen, N.J.: Scarecrow Press, 1979);

David Hume, *The Life of David Hume, Esq. Written by Himself* (London: Printed for W. Strahan and T. Cadell, 1777);

R. Austen Leigh, "William Strahan and His Ledgers," *Library,* fourth series 3 (March 1923): 261–287;

William H. McBurney, *English Prose Fiction 1700–1800 in the University of Illinois Library* (Urbana: University of Illinois Press, 1965);

John Nichols, *Literary Anecdotes of the Eighteenth Century,* 7 volumes (London: Nichols & Bentley, 1813);

Nichols, *Minor Lives. A Collection of Biographies by John Nichols,* edited by Edward L. Hart (Cambridge, Mass.: Harvard University Press, 1971);

Lyman Ray Patterson, *Copyright in Historical Perspective* (Nashville, Tenn.: Vanderbilt University Press, 1968);

Samuel Jackson Pratt, *An Apology for the Life and Writings of David Hume, with a Parallel between Him and the Late Lord Chesterfield* (London: Fielding & Walker, 1777);

Allen Reddick, *The Making of Johnson's Dictionary 1746–1773* (Cambridge: Cambridge University Press, 1990);

William Merritt Sale Jr., *Samuel Richardson. A Bibliographical Record of his Literary Career with Historical Notes* (New Haven: Yale University Press, 1936);

James Sambrook, Introduction to *The Seasons,* by James Thomson (Oxford: Clarendon Press, 1981);

James H. Sledd and Gwin J. Kolb, *Dr. Johnson's Dictionary. Essays in the Biography of a Book* (Chicago: University of Chicago Press, 1955).

– Carol Hall

The Minerva Press
(London: 1790 – 1820)

William Lane
(London: circa 1770 – 1790)

William Lane founded The Minerva Press in 1790 and, using his great entrepreneurial skills, especially in advertising and marketing, made it the largest publisher of fiction of its time. Over a thirty-year period The Minerva Press published more than eight hundred works, mainly Gothic fiction, which were cheaply produced and much criticized for their lack of literary excellence. Lane was the first to employ mass-marketing techniques for producing and distributing fiction: along with his presses he set up circulating libraries and filled them with his own products.

Born in 1738 Lane was the son of John Lane, a poulterer who lived in Whitechapel. It is not known what education he received. Lane originally followed his father's trade (for which he was later condemned as being the "printing poulterer" and "chicken-butcher"). By about 1770 he was using half of his father's shop for a bookselling business. Three years later his business occupied 13 Aldgate High Street, and he published his first book, *The Ladies Museum, or Complete Memorandum Book for the Year 1774,* and advertised an edition of Hugh Stopley's *Christiani Cultus.* In 1775 he moved to 33 Leadenhall Street. For the next few years he built up the business, particularly engaging in the publication of songs and jest collections. He applied for membership in the Stationers' Company and was granted freedom by redemption on 2 December 1777. In February 1778 he paid twenty pounds to become a liveryman.

From 1779 to 1784 Lane spent much of his time serving in the London militia and helped suppress the Gordon Riots of 1780. Because of his appointment as captain, he received the right to style himself "Esquire." By 1784 he was back to concentrating on business and advertised "several Novels in manuscript for publishing the ensuing Season." By this time he probably had a small press of his own and employed other printers. In 1785 he printed at least thirteen original works of fiction. In 1786 he took Richard Slatter as an apprentice in his bookselling business and was elected partner in the Stationers' Company.

By 1790 Lane was calling his business The Minerva Press and had a bust of Minerva over the door. He purchased 31 and 32 Leadenhall Street, buildings he described in his prospectus of 1794 as "constructed in an elegant and commodious manner, to answer the purposes of printing in all its various branches, and on a principle, it is presumed, [which] will ensure encouragement and protection. The printing materials are entirely new, the types from the most celebrated foundaries." More than likely, however, the offices were converted dwellings with inadequate lighting and accommodation for printing. The type Lane used before 1800 shows some Caslon-like letters, but their general origin is hard to distinguish. In 1791 Lane advertised for publisher's readers and booksellers, and in 1792 he employed John Plummer as superintendent of the Minerva printing office.

After the publication of Horace Walpole's *The Castle of Otranto* (1765), Gothic fiction became enormously popular. Stories set in ancient castles or abbeys in which young women are pursued by villains and frightened by supernatural occurrences were devoured by the reading public, which did not seem to mind that many of these tales followed the same formula and became almost indistinguishable. Lane saw great opportunity for profit in providing cheap fiction for the literate public that had emerged in the eighteenth century. He employed at least thirty men working on four presses to print thousands of vol-

Frontispiece for Eliza Parsons's Gothic novel, The Castle of Wolfenbach, *published by The Minerva Press in 1793*

umes of Gothic horror and romance. In the 1794 prospectus he promised that Minerva Press publications would have such subjects "as tend to public good – the pages shall never be stained with what will injure the mind, or corrupt the heart – they shall neither be the Instrument of Private Defamation or Public Injury."

Lane's volumes, the majority of which were duodecimos, were quickly but not carefully made. Even later volumes, produced when the business was successful, were printed on coarse, yellowish or gray, machine-made paper, using small type. Most are full of typographical errors.

In many ways Lane followed the printing practices of John Bell. The only ornaments he used were rules, sometimes a combination of a double rule and a thick and thin rule. In the 1790s the text of Minerva volumes was often set with double space between paragraphs, and each chapter began on a new page. Unlike Bell, Lane retained the fashion of the long or swash *s* until 1800.

Minerva volumes had no printed spine label, but it is difficult to ascertain the style of binding because they usually were re-bound by their owners or by circulating libraries. Before 1800 they were is-

sued in sheets or with a plain paper wrapper; afterward they had printed labels on paperboard.

The novels were seldom illustrated, though they sometimes were embellished with a frontispiece. Mary Charlton's *Phedora; or, the Forest of Minski* (1798), for example, has a wild, stormy scene with the hero clutching a tree on the edge of a precipice while supporting the fainting heroine. The most extensively decorated books were produced in the mid 1790s. Some had Gothic letters, small ornaments like a vase of flowers at the end of chapters, or large margins. Italics were also used, and sometimes a word or short phrase would be printed in a separate line of capitals for effect.

In 1790 the average price of a Minerva volume was half a crown. By 1820, with a steady rise in printing costs, the price had risen to 5s. 6d. Reviewers condemned Lane productions for their "wretched paper and imperfect letter," for being "carelessly written and printed." But the economies of the books' production made them affordable to a wider reading public.

To create a cheap source of material for his presses Lane turned his readers into writers. He advertised that he had deposited five hundred pounds with an "eminent" banker for the purpose of purchasing literary works. The going rate for first novels at the time was between five and ten pounds, but Lane advertised that he would pay as much as thirty pounds; in fact, he rarely paid that much — ten to twenty was more common. He was able to get away with paying small sums by appealing to the vanity of first-time writers, often women, who were gratified at seeing their works in print. Lane even used novels as advertisements for authors. *The Follies of St. James's Street* (1789) has a minor character who is trying to publish her second novel and is treated well by a Lane-like figure, and in Catherine Harris's *Edwardina* (1800) a character is tempted to turn novel writer by the "liberal encouragement" that Minerva offers.

Another source of material for Lane's presses was American fiction, for the rights to which he probably did not pay. Lane published the British editions of all of the novels of Charles Brockden Brown, including *Wieland, or Transformation* (1800), *Edgar Huntly* (1803), and *Ormond* (1800). H. Caritat served for a time as the New York agent for Minerva publications.

Still other money-saving practices Lane used to feed the enormous demand for books were postdating novels so that they continued to be "new" until the end of the following year, binding remainder sheets with a new title page, and refurbishing older works to make them seem new. *The Magdalen, or History of the first Penitent received into that charitable Asylum* (1783), by the Reverend William Dodd, seems to have been pieced together from one of Dodd's sermons at Magdalen House and an anonymous novel published in 1759 by Rivington and Dodsley titled *The Histories of Some of the Penitents in the Magdalen-House.*

Another way Lane found to feed the demand for books was to publish collections that resemble eighteenth-century versions of *Reader's Digest.* In 1783 he published *The Polite and Pleasing Instructor* and in 1786 *Lane's Annual Novelist: A Collection of Moral Tales, Histories, and Adventures Amusing and Instructive;* there is no record of any further issues of the annual. In 1791–1792 Lane published *The Polite Repository; or, Amusing Companion.*

Although Minerva Press fiction was cheap in price and quality, it was still too expensive for many readers. Lane had two solutions to the expense problem. One was to publish the even cheaper and more efficient bluebooks, which were thirty-six four-by-seven-inch pages stitched into a flimsy paper cover and sold for six pence. Lane was far from alone in this practice: other well-known publishers of bluebooks were Thomas Tegg, Langley and Belch, and T. and R. Hughes. Lane's other solution was circulating libraries. Before Lane, libraries were few and restricted: only a select group could obtain permission to borrow books. Lane organized and supported lending libraries in which the subscriber, for a small periodic fee, could borrow a book and, when finished, exchange it for another. From the early days of his business in the 1770s Lane operated a circulating library next to his bookselling and printing business. In 1791 he advertised that he had nearly six hundred thousand volumes. By 1800 the Minerva Library contained some fifteen thousand of Lane's own productions.

As early as 1786 Lane was advertising that he would advise any person desirous of establishing a circulating library and would provide the volumes for it. In one early advertisement he calls the circulating libraries "Nurseries of Entertainment, of Arts, and of Science" and asserts that they have been "not more the Business than the Pride of my Life." He claims that The Minerva Press is busy printing "Works of Merit . . . to supply the fanciful and the studious with the best Efforts that Ingenuity can form, or Imagination embellish." To attract readers he includes a seven-page Gothic tale made up of many of the titles currently sold by The Minerva Press. He closes his advertisement with an offer to authors whose "eminent talents will be liberally, though proportionably, encouraged from their earliest Dawn to their meridian Splendour." Lane thus encouraged the founding of provincial libraries, greatly increased the audience for and influence of Minerva Press fiction throughout England, and aided the growth of widespread literacy. In "Our English Watering-Place" (1851) Charles Dickens describes a typical Minerva Press library, in this case one attached to the Assembly Rooms, Nuckell's Place, Broadstairs: "This is the library for the Minerva Press. If you want that kind of reading, come to our watering-place. The leaves of the romances, reduced to a condition very like curl-paper, are thickly studded with notes in pencil: sometimes complimentary, sometimes jocose."

Lane found other ingenious ways to help market his product. He became proprietor of a newspaper, *The Star and Evening Advertiser,* the first evening daily, which he used as a vehicle to promote his publications from 1788 to 1792. It came out at 3:00 P.M. and was printed by Peter Stuart at 31 Exeter Street. Lane also used *The Star* to promote his political views supporting William Pitt's administration,

Frontispiece and title page for a Minerva Press catalogue

and he fired Stuart when the printer would not favor them. Lane's beliefs became entwined with his publishing business on at least one other occasion: in 1792 John Kimber, the captain of a slave ship, was acquitted of the murder of a young African girl; Lane supported him by publishing *The Trial of Captain John Kimber* (1792) and giving copies of the pamphlet away.

Lane did not publish first editions of the best Gothic fiction, such as works by Ann Radcliffe, Matthew Lewis, or Charlotte Smith, though he did print later editions of their works. His stable of authors included Eliza Parsons, Agnes Maria Bennett, Mary Meeke, and Regina Maria Roche. Parsons was a skillful narrator whose plots, unlike many Gothic tales, were plausible. From 1791 to 1795 Minerva published six of her works, including *Errors of Education* (1791), *The Castle of Wolfenbach* (1793), and *Lucy* (1794). Bennett was celebrated for her depiction of character, though her novels were

immoderately long, with too many digressions and unnecessary characters. At her death in 1808 her work was ranked with that of Henry Fielding and Samuel Richardson. Minerva published her *Ellen, Countess of Castle Howard* (1784), *Juvenile Indiscretions* (1786), and *Agnes de-Courci* (1794). Meeke, though not subtle in characterization, told lively stories in works such as *Count St. Blancard* (1795); Roche wrote lurid, sentimental romances such as *The Children of the Abbey* (1796), which would reach eleven editions by 1832 and would be reprinted throughout the nineteenth century.

The most distinguished novelist associated with The Minerva Press was Robert Bage, whose *Man as He Is* Lane published in 1792, followed by *Hermsprong* in 1796. Bage wrote not Gothic horror tales but incisive satires of the absurdities of society and the foibles of human nature. He was unusual in that he invoked equal social standards for men and women, so that a woman's loss of chastity did not

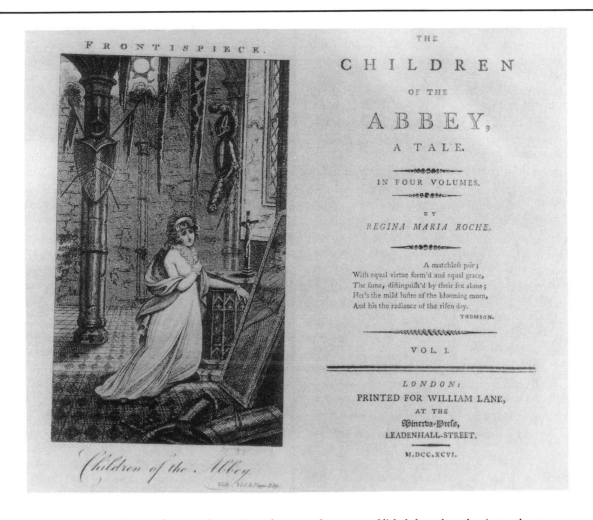

Frontispiece and title page for a popular sentimental romance that was republished throughout the nineteenth century

mean ruin or death. His heroines are strong and intelligent.

Most works of minor fiction in the eighteenth century were published pseudonymously; all thirteen of the novels Lane published in 1785 follow this practice, and only two of these works were later claimed by their authors. In 1800 pseudonymous books made up about half of Minerva's annual output, and twenty years later the proportion was almost one-third. The author of *Ill Effects of a Rash Vow* (1789) carried anonymity to an extreme: Lane had to carry on communications with her through newspaper columns. In most cases concealment was attributed to female delicacy, though curiosity about authorship certainly stimulated sales. The most common pseudonym was "A Lady," though some pseudonyms were more original and appropriate to the work: for example, Jane West chose Mrs. Prudentia Homespun for her *The Advantages of Education*

(1793). Not all writers who assumed the title "A Lady" were, in fact, female. Some grubstreet scribblers disguised themselves as women because reviewers were sometimes kinder to female writers.

Though not works of care and art, Minerva Press publications were widely read. At least two of the books Jane Austen's Gothic-crazed heroine Catharine Morland mentions in *Northanger Abbey* (1818) were Minerva publications. Bennett's works were particularly popular: her *Anna; or, Memoirs of a Welsh Heiress* (1785) went through four editions by 1805 and was twice translated into French, and her *Vicissitudes Abroad; or, The Ghost of My Father* (1806) sold two thousand copies on the day of its publication, at thirty-six shillings for the six-volume set.

As a whole, Minerva fiction was throwaway literature – quickly written, read, and forgotten. Reviewers gleefully condemned it, as in the review in the *Monthly Mirror* (July 1797) of *Eloise Montblanc:* "We have contrived to get through this novel ourselves; but we do not mean to be revenged on the author by recommending the same duty to any one of our readers." The August 1797 *Monthly Mirror* comments on another Lane production: "If we merely apprize our readers that there exists a novel bearing the title above mentioned, we think we shall do sufficient honour to the *Wanderer of the Alps* [1796], and the author ought to thank us for not proceeding any further."

Some Minerva fiction received good reviews, however. Francis Lathom's *The Impenetrable Secret* (1805) and *The Mysterious Freebooter* (1806) were praised for their artful construction, interesting situations, and lively conception. But Lathom did not write exclusively for Lane, and, like many Minerva authors, he wrote too much too quickly, producing twenty-three novels between 1798 and 1830. Meeke's novels were favorites of Thomas Macaulay and Mary Mitford. Walter Scott owned three of Bennett's novels, and Samuel Taylor Coleridge on one occasion said that Scott's comic characters could not stand comparison with Betty Brown in Bennett's *The Beggar Girl and Her Benefactors* (1797).

Nonetheless, The Minerva Press gained a reputation for and became a symbol of lightweight popular fiction. The term was even used as an insult. Thomas Love Peacock said in "An Essay on Fashionable Literature" (1818) that the works of The Minerva Press were "completely expurgated of all the higher qualities of mind," and Charles Lamb condemned them in "Sanity of True Genius" (1826) as "those scanty intellectual viands of the whole female reading public."

Though most of the works published by The Minerva Press were Gothic fiction, there were exceptions. Eugenia de Acton, for example, wrote Gothic novels for Minerva, but Lane also published her *Essays on the Art of Being Happy* (1803), which included such essays as "Economy of Times" and "Simplicity of Manners."

Lane also published travel books, the most prominent of which was *Travels through the Interior Parts of America; in a Series of Letters* (1789), written by "an officer" – Thomas Anburey, formerly an officer in Gen. John Burgoyne's army. The work consists of two volumes of about five hundred pages each. Unlike most of Lane's books, it was sold by subscription and lists nineteen pages of distinguished subscribers, including royal and noble names. Also unlike most of Lane's productions was the large number of illustrations in the book: it includes eight copper engravings, such as "An Indian Warrior entering his Wigwam with a Scalp" and "The Section and Plan of a Block-house." Lane also published

translations of travel books, such as Elizabeth Helme's translation of François Vaillant's *Voyage de Monsieur le Vaillant dans l'Interieur de l'Afrique, par le cap de Bonne-Esperance* (1790) as *Travels from the Cape of Good Hope into the Interior Parts of Africa.*

In the early days of the business Lane also printed music and songbooks, some in conjunction with Oliver and Boyd of Edinburgh. In 1780 he published *The Festival of Momus,* a collection of comic songs; and between 1780 and 1794 he published at least twenty collections of songs or jest. Many of these were extremely popular. His first humor book, *Historical and Entertaining Anecdotes; or The Pocket Remembrancer,* was published in 1775.

Lane also capitalized on his military experience. When England became involved in the Napoleonic Wars, The Minerva Press published an illustrated forty-page handbook titled *The Soldier's Companion* (1803). It was "intended for the use of the volunteers of this country" and included instructions for military drill, dress, and haircut. At sixpence each, two hundred thousand copies were sold in a few days, and there are sixty-five known editions.

Lane became wealthy from his various enterprises. A contemporary recalls him riding around town in a "splendid carriage" accompanied by "footmen with their cockades and gold-headed canes." Lane created his own seal, with a griffin and the motto *Perseverando.*

Around 1800 Lane separated the printing and publishing departments of The Minerva Press. In 1802 he took on a partner, Anthony King Newman, who had been freed from his indentures as the publisher's apprentice in 1801. From 1803 to 1809 the publishers' imprint was "Lane, Newman, and Co." Lane engaged another partner, John Darling, in the printing business in 1806, and books from then to 1813 appear with the imprint "Lane, Darling, and Co." After that Darling, as sole owner of the Minerva Printing Office, continued to undertake general business and also to print books for Newman. In 1839 his son Daniel became his partner, and John appears to have retired ten years later. In 1853, 31 Leadenhall was still occupied by "Daniel A. Darling and Son."

Sometime between 1803 and 1809 Lane retired to Brighthelmstone (modern Brighton), where he died on 29 January 1814. He had been married twice but left no children. By 1811 books from The Minerva Press were listed as being published by A. K. Newman and Company, successors to Lane,

Newman and Company, and for ten years Newman made few changes in the publishing procedures of The Minerva Press. In 1820, however, Newman, once styled "a patron of undeveloped fictional genius," dropped the name Minerva and concentrated on children's books and remainder publishing. Lane had published a few collections of fairy tales – *The Palace of Enchantment* (1788) and *Pleasing Companion* (1794) – but nothing on the scale of Newman.

Newman retired in 1848 at the age of eighty and sold his stock to Robert S. Parry, who was also a remainder publisher. In 1854 the premises were put to various uses, including Parry's firm (he styled himself a "commission merchant") and a wholesale boot warehouse. By 1862 there were no longer any representatives of the old firm, though as late as 1888 Parry was still carrying on business at 31 Eastcheap. The Minerva Press buildings on Leadenhall Street had been torn down in 1859.

References:

J. Ardagh, "The Minerva Press," *Notes and Queries,* 162 (9 April 1932): 268;

Dorothy Blakely, *The Minerva Press (1790–1820)* (London: Oxford University Press, 1939);

Michael Sadleir, "Minerva Press Publicity: A Publisher's Advertisement of 1794," *Library,* fourth series 2 (September 1940): 207–215;

Montague Summers, "A. K. Newman and the Minerva Press," *Notes and Queries,* 175 (17 December 1938): 438;

Summers, *The Gothic Quest: A History of the Gothic Novel* (London: Fortune Press, 1938);

Martin Tropp, *Images of Fear: How Horror Stories Helped Shape Modern Culture (1818–1918)* (Jefferson, N.C. & London: McFarland, 1990), pp. 15–19.

                                                          – Ann W. Engar

Benjamin Motte Jr.
(London: 1715 – 1723)

Samuel Tooke and Benjamin Motte
(London: 1724)

Benjamin Motte
(London: 1725 – 1735)

Benjamin and Charles Motte
(London: 1730)

Benjamin Motte and Charles Bathurst
(London: 1735 – 1738)

Benjamin Motte Jr., printer, bookseller, publisher, and scientific writer, packed many diverse activities into a life of just over forty-four years. In his own time he was known as a cultured and relatively successful bookseller who was respected without being celebrated. To later generations, however, he has become much better known because of his connection with Jonathan Swift: he published the first —and, indeed, all the earliest London (as opposed to Dublin) – editions of *Gulliver's Travels* (1726), Swift and Alexander Pope's *Miscellanies* (1727, 1728, 1732), and Swift's *Polite Conversation* (1738).

Motte was born in November 1693 in the London parish of St. Botolph Aldersgate, the eldest of at least three surviving sons of the master printer Benjamin Motte Sr. The elder Motte, the son of a glover of St. Alban's, had been apprenticed to the trade and freed in 1675. For the next decade he seems to have worked as a journeyman, rising to the position of overseer in the printing house of Mary Clarke, widow of the master printer Andrew Clarke, whose daughter Anne he married in 1692. The printing house was a large and prosperous one, and Benjamin Sr. bound more than a dozen apprentices after taking control of the business, several of whom – George James, Samuel Palmer, and Edward Say – became successful master printers in their own right. He also enjoyed a reputation for erudition and in 1700 printed a curious edition of the Lord's Prayer "in above a hundred languages, versions, and charac-

ters [typefaces]," partly, of course, to advertise the capacities of his press. Soon after his death in December 1710, his books were catalogued for sale; unfortunately, they were mixed with those of another owner, the Reverend Robert Ferguson. There were more than a thousand titles in all, more than two thirds of them in Latin and Greek, and while it is impossible to know whose were whose, it was the printer rather than the clergyman who was identified on the title page of the catalogue as "learned."

Benjamin Jr. was only seventeen at the time of his father's death, so it was his mother who took over the direction of the printing house and to whom apprentices were bound until 1715, when he was of age to be made free of the Stationers' Company by patrimony. Thereafter, he presumably took a larger part in the business, but printing certainly did not occupy the whole of his time. He seems to have inherited some of his father's intellectual interests, to which he added mathematics and science, and he compiled a massive two-volume abridgment of the *Philosophical Transactions* of the Royal Society from 1700 to 1720. Motte seems also to have printed the work, which was published in 1721. It was good enough to earn Edmund Halley's testimony that it was done "with due Care and Judgment," but it involved Motte in a dispute with Henry Jones, whose rival abridgment appeared in the same year. In his *Reply to the Preface Published by Mr. Henry Jones with His Abridgment* (1722) Motte defends his conduct (and, incidentally, the priority of his work) with considerable grace and modesty. He

Cover letter from Jonathan Swift to Benjamin Motte Jr. that accompanied the manuscript for Swift's Gulliver's Travels. *The letter is in the handwriting of the playwright John Gay, and the signature is a pseudonym (Pierpont Morgan Library MA 563).*

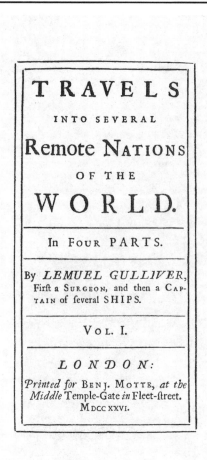

TRAVELS

INTO SEVERAL

Remote Nations

OF THE

WORLD.

In Four PARTS.

By *LEMUEL GULLIVER*,
Firſt a SURGEON, and then a CAP-
TAIN of ſeveral SHIPS.

VOL. I.

LONDON:

Printed for BENJ. MOTTE, *at the
Middle* Temple-Gate *in* Fleet-ſtreet.
MDCCXXVI.

Title page for the first edition of Gulliver's Travels

claims, for example, merely to have been following the pattern of John Lowthorp's earlier abridgments, though his achievement is, nevertheless, considerable. He also points out that he is a mere printer, and, as such, his abridgment was published for him by a conventional grouping of booksellers: Richard Wilkin, Ranew Robinson, Samuel Ballard, William and John Innys, and John Osborn.

Two years later, however, Motte gave up the printing business in Aldersgate Street, which had been his family's for more than thirty years, and went into business as a bookseller and publisher at the Middle Temple Gate in Fleet Street. The reasons for his giving up printing are not known, nor is it known who took over Motte's presses and other equipment. A good deal is known, however, about the circumstances under which he joined the bookselling business at the Middle Temple Gate. That business was a long-established and flourishing one that had been set up about 1695 by Benjamin Tooke Jr., Swift's first publisher, who ran it until

his death in May 1723, at the age of fifty-one. A few months before his death Tooke had taken into partnership his brother, Samuel, who was then thirty-two. Perhaps, however, because of Samuel Tooke's uncertain capacity, or perhaps because Samuel's health was already visibly failing, Benjamin Tooke left the controlling interest in the business not to him but to an older brother, the Reverend Andrew Tooke, Fellow of the Royal Society, who was simultaneously a master at the Charterhouse school and professor of geometry at Gresham College.

There had been a longstanding friendship between the Mottes and the Tookes: a fourth Tooke brother, Robert, had been apprenticed to Benjamin Motte Sr. from 1692 to 1699, and the elder Motte had stood surety for Benjamin Tooke Sr. when the latter was appointed steward of St. Bartholomew's Hospital in 1705. Moreover, the members of the younger generation of Mottes and Tookes seem to have been brought together by their common intellectual interests: not only did Benjamin Motte Jr. share Andrew Tooke's interest in the sciences, but his younger brother, the engraver Andrew Motte, was a distinguished mathematician who, later in the 1720s, would deliver the Geometry Lecture at Gresham College presumably under Andrew Tooke's patronage. Andrew Tooke was almost twenty years older than his brother Samuel, and since his was the controlling interest in the bookselling business, it seems likely that it was he rather than Samuel who in late 1723 or early 1724 invited Benjamin Motte Jr. to join Samuel in partnership. The partnership lasted only a year, however, for in December 1724 Samuel Tooke died, leaving Motte in sole operating control of the business. Andrew Tooke remained as a silent partner and in 1729 still held the lease of the shop; Motte would owe Andrew Tooke the greater part of £1,645 at the time of the latter's death in January 1732.

Motte was also engaged in two other partnership arrangements, though in these he was the senior partner. The first seems to have been not a full partnership, covering the entire business, but rather a limited agreement covering only a few works that he published jointly in 1730 with another younger brother, the bookseller Charles Motte. Charles had been apprenticed to the bookseller Ranew Robinson from 1712 to 1719 and had been in business in some small way since the early 1720s, though precisely where he was and what he was doing are not known. Charles Motte died in 1731, leaving his copyrights to his mother, his books to his brother Andrew, and his bound and unbound pamphlets to Benjamin. One of those who swore to the authentic-

A N

IMITATION

OF THE

SIXTH SATIRE

OF THE

SECOND BOOK

O F

H O R A C E.

Hoc erat in Votis, &c.

The firſt Part done in the Year 1714,

By Dr. S W I F T.

The latter Part now firſt added,
And never before Printed.

L O N D O N:
Printed for B. MOTTE and C. BATHURST
in *Fleet-Street,* and J. and P. KNAPTON in
Ludgate-Street, MDCCXXXVIII.

(Price one Shilling.)

*Title page for a work published in the final year of Motte's life.
Although it was attributed only to Swift, the work was
coauthored by Alexander Pope (Courtesy of the Lilly
Library, Indiana University).*

ity of Charles Motte's will was Benjamin's young apprentice Charles Bathurst, who had paid the princely premium of eighty pounds to be bound to Benjamin in 1727. After Charles Motte's death Benjamin spent three years in business alone before entering into partnership with his former apprentice Bathurst for the final three years of his life.

Of all the works Motte published, by far the most celebrated was *Gulliver's Travels,* which appeared in two octavo volumes on 28 October 1726. Swift had used Benjamin Tooke Jr. as his publisher during Queen Anne's reign (1702 to 1714), and on his return to London in 1726 after twelve years in Ireland he offered the work, with characteristic loyalty, to Tooke's successor for two hundred pounds. To conceal the authorship, the manuscript was dropped off at Motte's house under cover of darkness, with a letter purportedly written by Lemuel

Gulliver's cousin, "Richard Sympson." Motte, too, was cautious and had Andrew Tooke make alterations in the work. Motte resisted Swift's attempts to have his original text fully restored, but Swift seems to have forgiven him: in 1727 Swift added his signature to Pope's on the contract for the three original volumes of the *Miscellanies,* and he corresponded on generally friendly terms with Motte until the latter's death. In 1732, when Pope seemed to be maneuvering to exclude Motte from the publication of the fourth volume of the *Miscellanies* in favor of his own publisher, Lawton Gilliver, Swift lent his support to Motte; as a result, Motte and Gilliver shared in the undertaking. Moreover, short works, particularly poetry, that Swift gave to friends for publication in London in the early 1730s tended to be offered first to Motte, presumably on Swift's recommendation. Motte's relatively distant involvement with one such piece, *An Epistle to a Lady* (1733), led to his being taken into custody in 1734, though no harm came of it in the end.

The only time relations between Motte and his most distinguished author seem to have been strained was in 1735, when the publisher's protest over the importation into England of George Faulkner's Dublin edition of Swift's *Works,* which included many pieces to which Motte held the English copyright, led to an outburst from Swift on the cruel oppression of Ireland by England in this as in other areas of trade. Motte obtained an injunction against the sale of Faulkner's edition, but Swift did not retaliate and seems to have continued to channel work to Motte for London publication and to use the publisher as his unofficial London banker, particularly for the payment of the annuity with which he supported his sister, Jane Fenton.

In addition to *Gulliver's Travels,* the *Miscellanies,* Swift and Pope's *Imitation of the Sixth Satire of the Second Book of Horace* (1738), and Swift's *Polite Conversation* (1738), Motte's publishing involved a mixture of new works and new editions of older works whose copyrights he had inherited from Benjamin Tooke. The latter were generally steady-selling works such as some of the Delphin editions of classical texts used in schools, Edward and John Chamberlayne's *Magnæ Britanniæ Notitia: or, The Present State of Great Britain* (first published in 1669), and Giovanni Paolo Marana's *Letters Writ by a Turkish Spy* (first published in eight volumes from 1687 to 1694), in all of which Tooke had owned a share of the copyright. The new works Motte published were, with the exception of those of Swift and his circle, considerably more modest. Many were sermons, and many were works of authors with connections to Motte or to his various partners. Among these were books by Philip Bearcroft and Lewis Crusius, Andrew Tooke's colleagues at the Charterhouse school, and Andrew Motte's *Treatise of the Mechanical Powers* (1727) and his translation of Sir Isaac Newton's *Principia* (1729).

Benjamin Motte died intestate in April 1738. His mother had died in 1737, and both of his younger brothers had predeceased him, but he was survived by his wife, Elizabeth Brian Motte, whom he had married in 1725; a daughter, Elizabeth; and a son, Thomas. Administration of his estate was granted to his brother-in-law, Thomas Brian, who was described as Motte's creditor – presumably because he had advanced some of the £1,645 due to Andrew Tooke's heirs at Tooke's death. Meeting the estate's obligations required the liquidation of some of Motte's assets, and at a trade sale on 9 December 1740 "the Copies [copyrights] of the late Mr. Robert Knaplock, and part of Mr. Benjamin Motte's" were auctioned off to an inner circle of London's copyright-owning booksellers. The copyrights realized more than £1,000, and a second sale, on 15 December 1743, which included several items listed but not sold in 1740, produced a further £225. While several copyrights or shares of copyrights are known to have been Motte's, others belonged to Knaplock or other booksellers; it is, therefore, impossible to determine the Motte estate's share of the total receipts.

Neither Motte's widow nor his children seem to have had any further connection with bookselling or publishing. There remained, however, a family connection with the trade, for in October 1739 Motte's sister-in-law, Mary Brian, married Bathurst, who had carried on the business at the Middle Temple Gate after his partner's death and was to do so with considerable success until his own death in 1786.

References:

Terry Belanger, "Booksellers' Sales of Copyright: Aspects of the London Booktrade 1718–1768," dissertation, Columbia University, 1970;

Donald Cornu, "Swift, Motte, and the Copyright Struggle: Two Unnoticed Documents," *Modern Language Notes,* 54 (January 1939): 120–121;

Irvin Ehrenpreis, *Swift: The Man, His Works, and the Age. Volume Three: Dean Swift* (London: Methuen, 1983);

D. F. McKenzie, *Stationers' Company Apprentices 1641–1700* (Oxford: Oxford Bibliographical Society, 1974);

McKenzie, *Stationers' Company Apprentices 1701–1800* (Oxford: Oxford Bibliographical Society, 1978);

Henry R. Plomer and others, *A Dictionary of the Printers and Booksellers Who Were at Work in England, Scotland and Ireland from 1668 to 1725* (London: Bibliographical Society, 1922);

Jonathan Swift, *The Correspondence of Jonathan Swift,* 5 volumes, edited by Harold Williams (Oxford: Oxford University Press, 1963–1965);

Michael Treadwell, "Benjamin Motte, Andrew Tooke, and *Gulliver's Travels,*" in *Proceedings of the First Munster Symposium on Jonathan Swift,* edited by Hermann J. Real and Heinz Vienken (Munich: Wilhelm Fink, 1985), pp. 287–304.

– Michael Treadwell

John Murray

(London: 1768 –)

The firm of John Murray was founded in November 1768 when John MacMurray, a twenty-three-year-old marine lieutenant retired on half pay, purchased for approximately four hundred pounds the bookselling establishment of William Sandby under the Sign of the Ship at 32 Fleet Street, London. With some financial assistance from his father in Edinburgh, Murray — who had dropped the Scottish prefix from his name — announced himself to the public as selling "all new Books and Publications. Fits up Public or Private Libraries in the neatest manner with Books of the choicest Editions, the best Print, and the richest Bindings. Also, executes East India or foreign Commissions by an assortment of Books and Stationery suited to the Market or Purpose for which it is destined; all at the most reasonable rates." He began by publishing new editions of George, Baron Lyttelton's *Dialogues of the Dead* (1768) and *The History of The Life of King Henry the Second,* as well as of Horace Walpole's *The Castle of Otranto.* In 1770 Murray published what was to become the standard translation of *Plutarch's Lives,* by John Langhorne, and Edmund Cartwright the Elder's poem *Armine and Elvira* (1771) went through seven editions. John Millar's law books were also well received. Murray sought connections with booksellers and authors in Ireland and Scotland, but it took a legacy of more than four thousand pounds from an uncle's estate in 1775 to provide the capital for him to be more adventuresome.

In 1777 Murray published three passages, totaling fifty lines, of poems by Thomas Gray in a *Poetical Miscellany* without seeking the permission of William Mason, Gray's literary executor; Mason won an injunction stopping the sale of the work despite Murray's offer to settle out of court. Shortly thereafter, Murray determined that Mason had used considerably more copyrighted material, which was held by Murray, in his *The Poems of Mr. Gray. To Which Are Prefixed Memoirs of His Life and Writings.* Murray presented these facts in a pamphlet, *A Letter to W. Mason, A.M., Precentor of York, Concerning His Edition of Gray's Poems, and the Practice of Booksellers.*

Murray's first wife died childless in 1776; Murray married her sister, and on 27 November 1778

John Murray II was born. In June 1782 Murray had a stroke that temporarily paralyzed his left side. In 1783, at the suggestion of Gilbert Stuart, Murray began the *English Review of Literature, Science, Discoveries, Inventions and Practical Controversies and Contests,* one of many periodical ventures that would be associated with the firm. In July 1783 he took legal action against the publishers of the *Encyclopaedia Britannica* because of a verbatim abridgment of two books by Stuart on which Murray held copyrights. He published medical books on cures for puerperal fever (1787), the duties of a regimental surgeon (1787), the case of a boy who had been mistaken for a girl (1787), and preventing fatal consequences of diseases contracted by Europeans in hot climates (1788); Jane Timbury's novel *The Male Coquet* (1788); Mitford's *History of Greece;* John Leslie's works on natural science; and a translation of Johann Kaspar Lavater's work on physiognomy. He was also one of two London booksellers of the 1788 edition of Allan Ramsay's *The Gentle Shepherd* (1725) and one of seven to bring out *The Interesting Narrative of the Life of Olaudah Equiano, or Gustavus Vassa, the African, Written by Himself* (1789). By the time of his death on 6 November 1793 he was regarded as the leading publisher of belles lettres.

Samuel Highley, dubbed the "faithful shopman" in Murray's will, was appointed to carry on the business for the benefit of Murray's widow and family while John II continued his schooling at Dr. Roberts's Loughborough House in Kennington. Previously he had attended the Royal High School in Edinburgh and Dr. Burney's Gosport school, where his writing master, while repairing his pen, accidentally ran his penknife into the boy's right eye, destroying the sight in that eye.

His mother remarried in September 1795 and left London with her two daughters. Thus, although still a minor, John Murray II became Highley's partner and began paying his mother for the business, which she had inherited. Highley, a cautious manager, ignored publishing in favor of bookselling. Murray dissolved the partnership on 25 March 1804, retaining the premises while Highley kept the principal part of the firm's medical works. Like his contempo-

John Murray, founder of the John Murray publishing house

raries and rivals, Thomas Longman and Charles Rivington, Murray disposed of his retail stock and concentrated on publishing – especially works of "solid character," which for him meant travel accounts and medical and philosophical works; but he was also interested in drama and poetry. Difficulties in collecting payment, however, curtailed publication of new works, and Murray began a policy requiring payment within six months of shipment. Murray and Archibald Constable and Company of Edinburgh became agents for each other's publications, beginning with Isaac D'Israeli's *Flim-Flams!* (1805) and resulting in considerable business for each. On a business trip to Scotland in 1806 Murray proposed to Anne Elliot, the daughter of an Edinburgh publisher who had been a friend of his father. They were married on 6 March 1807 in Edinburgh. Their first child, John Murray III, was born on 16 April 1808.

The connection with Constable brought Murray a one-fourth interest in the copyright of Sir Walter Scott's *Marmion* (1808) and an opportunity to meet Scott. After a breach between Constable and Thomas Norton Longman III in 1807, Murray briefly became the London publisher of Constable's *Edinburgh Review* and joint publisher, from January 1808 to June 1811, of the *Monthly Mirror*. Murray, however, decided that there was a need for a conservative periodical to balance the liberal bias of the *Edinburgh Review*. Such Tories as John Hookham Frere and John Wilson Croker (who was to write nearly 260 articles for the new venture) concurred, as did Scott (who was smarting from the attack by the *Edinburgh Review* on his *Marmion*), George Ellis, and George Canning. The *Quarterly Review* would favor traditional English morality, paternalism, aristocratic authority, and the supremacy of the Anglican Church. It would have such close ties with the Tory government that Sir Robert Peel; Arthur Wellesley, first duke of Wellington; and Edward George Geoffrey Smith, Lord Stanley, would become contributors.

The first number of the *Quarterly Review* appeared in February 1809 with William Gifford, who had started reading for the house in 1808, as editor.

Murray instructed Gifford to "Publish the best information, the best science, the best literature; and leave the public to decide for themselves." Murray worked hard to make the magazine a success; he wrote Gifford, "My mind is so entirely engrossed, my honour is so completely involved in this one thing that I neither eat, drink, nor sleep upon anything else." Although Gifford's inability to provide material on time increasingly caused the magazine to appear late, by 1811 the *Quarterly Review* had rising sales and such contributors as the poet laureate, Robert Southey, who became a regular with the February issue – which appeared in March – and Admiralty Secretary John Barrow, who, with Croker, was responsible for obtaining Murray's appointment as publisher to the admiralty. On 15 February 1817 Southey wrote a friend, "The Review is the greatest of all his [Murray's] works, and it is all his own creation; he prints 10,000, and fifty times ten thousand read its contents in the East and in the West." During 1817 circulation increased to 14,000. The magazine became known for its attacks on Percy Bysshe Shelley but especially for Croker's condemnation of John Keats's *Endymion* (1818), an attack that was accused of hastening Keats's death in 1821. Even Scott was subject to less than favorable reviews, and Samuel Taylor Coleridge thought the review of his tragedy *Remorse* (1813) so objectionable that he may have begun writing *Biographia Literaria* (1817) in response; the anonymity of the reviewers prevented Coleridge from knowing that the harsh critic was none other than his nephew, John Taylor Coleridge.

The author most associated with the house of Murray is George Gordon, Lord Byron. Murray published the first two cantos of the phenomenally successful *Childe Harold's Pilgrimage,* for which he paid Byron six hundred pounds, in 1812. Thus began a stormy relationship between the two men. Among the points of contention were the publisher's failure to answer the poet's letters and the inaccurate printing of Byron's works; the latter problem stemmed from Byron's sometimes illegible handwriting and his refusal to read proofs. Byron also refused to recast parts of the poem that Murray deemed unsuitable for the British public.

When *Childe Harold's Pilgrimage* proved an immediate success Murray purchased the lease, copyrights, and stock of the bookseller William Miller for £3,822 12s. 6d. and moved to Miller's former Mayfair address, 50 Albemarle Street. There he hosted political and literary discussions from two to five o'clock in the afternoon in the drawing room. At this period the drawing room was frequented by Scott, Gifford, Southey, Thomas Campbell, Ugo Foscolo, Henry

Hallam, H. H. Milman, and Giovanni Belzoni; in 1823 the Athenaeum Club would grow out of these gatherings at Murray's. Byron's letters from abroad frequently provided entertainment for the drawing-room assembly, and many compilations of his letters have been published by the Murray firm. Murray brought about a reconciliation between Byron and Scott at Albemarle Street on 7 April 1815. These two authors, and the publishers Constable and Murray, were responsible for the radical change in the profession of authorship in which the eighteenth-century patronage system was replaced by relationships of authors with entrepreneurial publishers.

In April 1817 the Blackwood firm introduced the Tory *Edinburgh Monthly Magazine,* which came to be known as *Blackwood's Magazine;* Murray shared in publishing the October 1817 issue, and in August 1818 he paid one thousand pounds for a half share in the magazine. But a month later Murray wrote William Blackwood expressing disapproval of the magazine's slashing criticisms. On 3 September 1818 Murray wrote Scott: "Barrow, as the head of all my most respected friends, has told me that it would be utterly detrimental to my character to continue my name any longer; and there is no occasion for its use, for if the writers direct their minds to higher objects to which they are fully competent, the journal will sell ten times better. I have already raised the sale 500 copies since I have joined in it." (At the same time Murray reaffirmed his commitment to the *Quarterly Review* and Scott's contributions to it.) Murray's name appeared for the last time on number 22 of *Blackwood's Magazine,* for January 1819; the following issue listed no London publisher. On 17 December 1819 the thousand pounds Murray had advanced was returned to him. Murray thereupon transferred his Scottish agency to the firm of Oliver and Boyd.

Jane Austen's dissatisfaction with the publisher Thomas Egerton over the terms for a second edition of her novel *Mansfield Park* (1814) led her to offer *Emma* to Murray in 1815. His reader, Gifford, wrote positively of *Emma,* and Murray offered £450 for the copyrights for that work as well as *Sense and Sensibility* (1810) and *Mansfield Park.* According to Marghanita Laski, Henry Austen, who handled Jane Austen's publishing arrangements, countered "that his sister had made more out of 'one very moderate edition of *Mansfield Park* . . . and a still smaller one of *Sense and Sensibility.*' Eventually Mr. Murray agreed to publish a first edition of *Emma* and a second edition of *Sense and Sensibility* on profit-sharing terms. Jane Austen said of her new publisher, 'He is a rogue of course, but a civil one.' " At the suggestion of the Prince Regent's librarian, the Reverend James Stanier Clarke, Austen dedicated the novel to the prince and arranged for presentation copies to be specially bound in scarlet with the prince's insignia on the spine. Scott's review of *Emma* in the *Quarterly Review* delighted the author. After her death on 18 July 1817, her *Northanger Abbey* and *Persuasion* were published together by Murray at the end of the year but dated 1818.

The appearance of the first cantos of Byron's *Don Juan* in 1819 caused one of the biggest literary stirs of the decade. The demand for copies was so great that Murray's front door had to be barricaded against the clamoring agents of the nation's booksellers; the stock was passed through the dining-room windows into their hands. After the first five cantos, however, Murray refused to publish any more, returning them to Byron's agent, Douglas Kinnaird, on 17 October 1822.

The popularity of Byron's poems and Austen's novels resulted in Murray being inundated with manuscripts; some poets wished the honor of having Lord Byron's publisher named on the title pages of their works. The manuscripts were read by Gifford, Croker, and Barrow, initiating the practice of house readers. Coleridge and Leigh Hunt were briefly Murray authors; another of the few poets whose works Murray published was the popular Felicia Hemans. In December 1818 Murray purchased the copyrights for George Crabbe's *Tales of the Hall* (1819) and all his previous works for three thousand pounds; Longmans had more correctly estimated their value at one thousand pounds. Campbell's seven-volume *Specimens of British Poets* appeared in 1819. Murray also published works by Madame de Staël, Thomas Moore, the explorer Sir John Franklin, Gabriele Rossetti, and Caroline Bray. In 1842 Caroline Norton, whose poem *A Voice from the Factories* was published by Murray in 1836, wrote a tribute to him:

> John Murray! Dare I call thee John?
> Yes: for who calls thee Mister Murray?
> The first familiar name's the one
> Which puts us authors in a flurry:
> The first familiar name is that
> Long linked with memories bright and pleasant;
> With hours of intellectual chat
> O'er claret, venison, grouse, and pheasant;
> And all the sunshine, clouds, and blame
> Which hang round Byron's chequered story,
> Whom THY discernment led to Fame
> When fools denied the wreath of glory!

The firm began early to publish educational books. In 1824 Murray bought the copyright for Elizabeth Cartwright Penrose's *Mrs. Markham's His-*

tory of England, which had been remaindered by Constable; it became a mainstay of British girls' schools for nearly a century. Another of his most consistent sellers was *Little Arthur's History of England* (1835), by Maria Dundas Graham, later Lady Callcott, who also wrote travel books for Murray, advised him about books (she was an excellent critic), and became godmother to one of the Murrays' daughters. The history continued to sell for 130 years. Maria Eliza Rundell's *Domestic Cookery* (1806), the first cookbook to emphasize home rather than institutional cooking, proved to be a perennial best-seller with at least ten thousand copies sold each year; its sixty-fourth edition appeared in 1840. At one point she tried to have the work published by Longmans; but Murray's claim held, and he paid her two thousand pounds for the copyright.

A longstanding relationship with D'Israeli contributed to the success of the house of Murray. John Murray I had published the original volume of D'Israeli's *Curiosities of Literature* in 1791, when the author was twenty-five; by 1823 it would run to five volumes in the seventh edition. In 1803 John Murray II brought out his *Narrative Poems* and in 1805 *Flim-Flams! or, The Life and Errors of my Uncle and His Friends! With Illustrations and Obscurities by Messieurs Tag, Rag, and Bobtail,* which ran to two editions only because it was rumored to include libelous material. D'Israeli's *The Literary Character, Illustrated by the History of Men of Genius* (1818) was a more critically acclaimed work.

Murray eagerly entertained foreign visitors, especially Americans; in 1815 George Ticknor became the first American intellectual to write about Murray's hospitality, but the American most frequently associated with the firm was Washington Irving, who first visited 50 Albemarle Street on 16 August 1817 with a letter of introduction from Campbell. Murray invited Irving to dine with him that evening. At dinner Irving proposed to arrange a system whereby American and British publishers would provide prepublication copies to each other to circumvent literary piracy from the other country's publishers. Murray said that the idea had possibilities but did not volunteer the information that Theobald Wolfe Tone had failed with just such a plan. Irving, who misread Murray's politeness for agreement, went ahead with his scheme. After the unauthorized publication of essays from Irving's *The Sketch Book of Geoffrey Crayon, Gent.* (1819–1820) in the *Literary Gazette* and a rumor that a London publisher planned to collect the essays, Irving approached Murray; but Murray chose not to publish *The Sketch Book* because British copyright law only

John Murray II; engraving after a portrait by Pickersgill

protected works that were first published in Britain. Irving turned to John Miller, whom he had met at Murray's, but Miller's business failed just after he had published the first four parts of Irving's book as a single volume in 1820. Murray admired the work – Irving wrote to his friend Henry Brevoort on 9 September 1819, "Among the admirers is Murray, the 'prince of booksellers' so famous for his elegant publications" – but he required a push from Scott before he would agree to publish volume two of *The Sketch Book* in 1820. At Irving's insistence Murray paid 250 guineas for the copyright rather than the equal share of the profits the publisher preferred. That same year Murray also published *A History of New York* (1809; revised, 1812), which had finally been noticed in the British press, and he expressed the hope that Irving's future efforts would be published first in England under the Murray imprint.

Murray was most important to Irving's career: being the "first American writer to be a notable success in Britain" enhanced his status and the size of his American reading public. The Murray imprint, according to George H. Putnam, Irving's final American publisher, marked a book with literary importance, resulting in a growing reputation and more money at home. Murray's imprint also discouraged pirating publishers in England; or, when Murray's name was not sufficient, the publisher used speed – getting Irving's *A History of New York* through the press before William Wright's unauthorized edition could appear, for example. Unfortunately, in his haste Murray used the second edition, not the third, which Irving had prepared for the American public. Appreciating the effort, Irving reproved Murray only mildly in a letter of 26 October 1820.

Because sales of *The Sketch Book* were so great, Murray gave Irving an additional hundred guineas and had his portrait painted and hung next to Byron's in the drawing room. In a 29 June 1822 letter Murray offered Irving an advance of one hundred pounds for a work that turned out to be *Tales of a Traveller* (1824); Murray initially proposed to pay twelve hundred guineas for the book, but Irving eventually received the fifteen hundred he desired.

At this time Byron's relationship with Murray was deteriorating due to the poet's ingratitude toward the publisher, which was expressed in verbal and written abuse. Despite their differences, Murray paid two thousand guineas for Byron's autobiography, to be published posthumously. Instead, the manuscript was placed, page by page, into the drawing-room fireplace on 17 May 1824, almost a month after Byron's death, following deliberations by Murray, Moore, Byron's friend John Cam Hobhouse, and representatives of Lady Byron and Byron's half sister Augusta Leigh – all of whom feared for the author's reputation if it had been published. Still wishing to bring out a biography of Byron, in 1826 Murray approached Moore; his edition of *Letters and Journals of Lord Byron: with Notices of His Life* was published by Murray in 1830.

Gifford had suffered several years of ill health, and Croker had stepped in to help edit the *Quarterly Review.* By December 1824 Gifford's declining health forced his resignation as editor; he had published only two issues that year. He continued to act as general literary adviser to the periodical until his death in 1826. Murray made John Taylor Coleridge the editor of the *Quarterly Review;* after a brief sojourn in the post he was replaced by John Gibson Lockhart, Scott's son-in-law, who would retain the position until 1853.

In 1820 Murray and Croker had briefly been proprietors of the *Guardian,* which was printed by Charles Knight at Windsor. Murray had continued to desire to publish a newspaper, and the first issue of the *Representative,* which he financed and operated in partnership with Benjamin Disraeli, appeared on 25 January 1826, priced at 7d. It supported the government of Robert Banks Jenkinson, second earl of Liverpool, and was concerned with commerce and finance. Murray failed to acquire a suitable editor for the *Representative* and was deserted by his partner; the last issue appeared on 29 July with Murray more than twenty-six thousand pounds poorer. The resulting rift in the Murray-Disraeli relationship was further aggravated by Disraeli's novel *Vivian Grey* (1826–1827), published by Henry Colburn, in which the character of the Marquis of Carabas, a vain, ambitious, elderly nobleman, was commonly thought to be patterned after Murray, although Disraeli denied the charge. It required the skills of Sharon Turner, Murray's legal adviser and a mutual friend, to soothe their feelings. After refusing Disraeli's *The Young Duke* (1831), Murray published Disraeli's *Contarini Fleming* (1832), but it was not a financial success.

In 1828 the publisher began the Murray's Family Library series to make copyrighted works cheaper and accessible to a wider circle of readers. It would include history, biography, travel, science, natural history, and general literature by the leading authors of the day. The first volumes were John Gibson Lockhart's *The History of Napoleon Bonaparte* (1829), a life of Alexander the Great, and Allan Cunningham's *The Lives of the Most Eminent British Painters, Sculptors, and Architects* (1829–1833). Gross typographical errors had prevented Irving's *History of the Life and Voyages of Christopher Columbus* (1828) from becoming the standard reference source Murray intended, and a revised and abridged edition appeared in 1830 as part of the Family Library. The Family Library did not do as well as Murray had expected, and on 4 December 1834 he wrote Lockhart that he was completing the sale of ten thousand copies of the forty-seven volumes to Thomas Tegg, the remainder man, for a shilling each. The sale brought Murray only a marginal profit. During this period he thought of starting a new popular magazine, but he dropped the idea when Irving rejected the post of editor.

Murray was a member of the Society for the Diffusion of Useful Knowledge; in 1828 he agreed to act as publisher for its Library of Entertaining Knowledge but quickly changed his mind, not wanting to become too closely associated with popular literature. He was also a leader of the London Booksellers' Committee, which on 9 December 1829 decided to force controls on retail book prices.

In 1831 declining sales of the *Quarterly Review* caused Murray to retrench by reducing the number of titles scheduled to appear in the fourteen-volume edition of Byron's complete works and in a six-volume collection of Gifford's essays. After expressing some interest in Thomas Carlyle's *Sartor Resartus,* he ultimately refused it, resulting in bitterness on Carlyle's part (it was published by James Munroe in Boston in 1836 and by Saunders and Otley in London in 1838). Another disgruntled author was Irving, who once again mistook Murray's listening to his ideas for acceptance and was outraged when Murray denied agreeing to payment for manuscripts sight unseen. Irving's *Mahomet and His Successors* (1850) was barely begun, and *The Alhambra* (1832) was only contemplated and depended on additional funding for Irving to do the research. Tempers cooled, and Irving once again appeared in the Murray lists after defecting to Colburn and Bentley for *The Alhambra.* But despite such setbacks, Murray published many enduring works, including revised editions of Thomas Robert Malthus's *An Essay on the Principle of Population* (1817, 1826), Mungo Park's *Travels in the Interior Districts of Africa* (1816, 1817),

Sir John Ross's *A Voyage of Discovery* (1819), and Sir William Parry's journals of his voyages in search of a northwest passage (1821–1826).

John Murray II died on 1 July 1843; John Murray III took over a leading publishing firm, but one that, due to his father's generosity with authors, was not in a strong financial position. His widow inherited £50,000, the sum total of the estate. Murray III had attended the Charterhouse School and received an M.A. from the University of Edinburgh. Before joining his father's firm in 1829, he had filled many notebooks with descriptions of his travels, and he used them to build up the firm's first series of guidebooks for Continental travelers. The *Handbooks,* as they were called, were so thorough that they included the sanitary conditions of hotels and cities. Murray wrote, "I made it my aim to point out things *peculiar* to the spot. . . . I did not begin to publish until after several successive journeys and temporary residences in Continental cities, and after I had not only traversed beaten Routes, but explored various districts into which my countrymen had not yet penetrated." The first guide covered Holland, Belgium, and north Germany and appeared in 1836, preceding the first Karl Baedeker guide by three years; subsequent volumes also anticipated each of Baedeker's. There were *Handbooks* to the counties and the cathedrals of the British Isles as well. Murray, however, brought out new editions too slowly, so the information was sometimes outdated. *Punch* found them important enough to notice in a poem:

> So well thou'st played the hand-books' part,
> For inns a hint, for routes a chart,
> That every line I've got by heart.
>   My Murray.

> Once I could scarce walk up the Strand;
> What Jungfrau now could us withstand,
> When we are walking hand in hand,
>   My Murray?

From 1829 until he took over the firm, all of Murray III's longer holidays were spent traveling and writing the *Handbooks.*

In 1845 Murray began the Home and Colonial Library, an inexpensive series similar to his father's Family Library; the volumes were priced at 2s. 6d. each. Reprints of Southey's *The Life of Nelson,* originally published in 1813, and George Borrow's *The Bible in Spain,* first published in 1843, began the series. Borrow, who served as an agent for the Bible Society, had brought his first book-length manuscript to Murray II in 1840; *The Zincali, or, An Ac-*

count of the Gypsies of Spain (1841) had been well received. Murray later published Borrow's *Lavengro* (1851) and *Romany Rye* (1857). Irving's *Bracebridge Hall,* first published in 1822, was included in the series, as was Herman Melville's *Typee* (1846), for which the author received one hundred pounds for the English copyright. Because Murray read only Scott's novels and did not care to publish fiction, Herman Melville had to provide proof that he had sailed the South Seas before Murray would publish *Omoo* the following year. Author and publisher were to split the profits evenly, but since the book lost money Melville received nothing. The firm never even considered *Moby-Dick,* which was published by Bentley in 1851 as *The Whale.*

In 1848 Sir Austen Henry Layard, who was to write regularly for the *Quarterly Review,* offered Murray the copyright for his book *Nineveh and Its Remains* (1849) for £250. Because Murray did not approve of authors parting with their copyrights, he offered to pay the expense of publication and give Layard the larger share of the profits. The first year Layard's share was £1,500 pounds, and he continued to receive a check every succeeding year until Murray's death.

Irving's final dealings with the firm came in the 1850s when Murray commenced proceedings against Henry George Bohn, who had begun publishing an unauthorized collected edition of Irving's works based on Putnam's American edition (1848–1855). After accumulating £850 in legal expenses, Murray sold Irving's copyrights to Bohn. Murray declined to publish Irving's five-volume *Life of George Washington* but did act on his behalf and secured from Bohn, according to Irving, "a promise of £50 and a hope of something more if he can keep the field to himself." Overall, Irving was treated well by the Murrays, having received £9,767 10s. in his lifetime from the firm.

Lockhart's last *Quarterly Review* issue was the one for June 1853. Although he lingered until the following year, the editor's declining health forced him to resign in July, at which point he repeated his predecessor Gifford's verse about his own experience as editor and literary adviser: "Over-worked and over-worried / Over-Croker'd, over-Murray'd." Under Lockhart the magazine had attained renown as a reliable judge of literature that placed increased emphasis on realism and displayed an appreciation for German writers. He required of his contributors temperance of style and eschewed poetical flights of fancy. During Lockhart's tenure Croker's review of Alfred, Lord Tennyson's *Poems* (1832) had contributed to the poet's ten-year silence, after which the

Chilbe Harold's Pilgrimage.

A ROMAUNT.

BY

LORD BYRON.

L'univers est une espèce de livre, dont on n'a lu que la première page quand on n'a vu que son pays. J'en ai feuilleté un assez grand nombre, que j'ai trouvé également mauvaises. Cet examen ne m'a point été infructueux. Je haïssais ma patrie. Toutes les impertinences des peuples divers, parmi lesquels j'ai vécu, m'ont réconcilié avec elle. Quand je n'aurais tiré d'autre bénéfice de mes voyages que celui-là, je n'en regretterais ni les frais, ni les fatigues.

LE COSMOPOLITE.

LONDON:

PRINTED FOR JOHN MURRAY, 32, FLEET-STREET;
WILLIAM BLACKWOOD, EDINBURGH; AND JOHN CUMMING, DUBLIN.
By Thomas Davison, White-Friars.
1812.

Title page for the first of George Gordon, Lord Byron's works to be published by Murray

magazine had praised the improvements in the 1842 volumes. The staff regulars were Croker, who wrote ninety-nine articles for the first one hundred issues; Abraham Hayward, for half a century beginning in 1834; Irving; Henry Hart Milman; and Elizabeth Rigby, Lady Eastlake, who for many years was the only woman contributor. Lockhart had written Murray about Eastlake, "I have no doubt she is the cleverest female writer now in England, the most original in thought and expression too, and she seems *good* besides, which after all has its charms for old sinners like you and me." Although she contributed to the *Quarterly Review* for half a century, Eastlake is most remembered for her December 1848 attack on Charlotte Brontë's *Jane Eyre* (1847). Furious with John Ruskin for devaluing some Old Masters, she reviled his *Modern Painters* (1843–1860) in the *Quarterly Review*.

The Reverend Whitwell Elwin, a country parson from a remote Norfolk village who had begun writing for the review a decade earlier, replaced Lockhart as editor at a salary of £250 per quarter and £100 extra for articles he wrote. Steeped in knowledge of English literature, he published nearly two dozen fine pieces while editor, but he worked in spurts. Correspondence was a major burden for him, and rejected manuscripts sometimes went astray. He preferred his work in his parish and found irksome the ten days he had to spend in London each quarter, and the review was frequently late. To remedy the problem Murray unsuccessfully offered Elwin an extra £200 a year if he would move to London. A relative unknown, Elwin had the difficult job of dealing with much more experienced writers. Nevertheless, he set high standards and rewrote all the submitted articles, regardless of authorship. When Croker wrote an article attacking France, England's ally in war against Russia, Elwin rejected it and Croker resigned. After Croker's departure subscribers complained about the lack of conservative political articles, and sales fell off somewhat.

When David Livingstone returned to England from Africa in 1856, Murray offered him two thousand pounds in advance of two-thirds of the profits for his first book, *Missionary Travels and Researches in South Africa* (1857). On the day of publication all twelve thousand copies were sold. Also in 1856 Isabella Bird's *The Englishwoman in America* was brought out by Murray.

Since 1845, when he bought *The Voyage of the Beagle* (1839) from Colburn for £150, Murray had been Charles Darwin's publisher, and in 1859 the firm published Darwin's *On the Origin of Species by Means of Natural Selection*. The book came to the firm recommended by Sir Charles Lyell, and Darwin received two-thirds of the net profits for it. Murray brought out an edition of 1,250 copies at 15s., all of which sold at his annual sale despite Bishop Samuel Wilberforce's unflattering comments in the *Quarterly Review*.

During the summer of 1859 Elwin wrote Murray asking to be relieved of the editorship of the *Quarterly Review* because he was unable to meet deadlines and preferred his other work. Murray asked for time to find a successor, and on 27 June 1860 he wrote Elwin that he had found one in his old friend William Macpherson, who had held a judicial post in India. To show his appreciation, Murray sent six dozen bottles of the finest old port to his departing editor and asked him to continue writing regularly for the *Quarterly Review*. That request was denied, but Elwin would serve as an honorary literary adviser for many years and would write some of the more delicate reviews regarding theologically dangerous works. Lord Robert Cecil's article "The Conservative Reaction" in the last issue edited by Elwin attracted considerable notice.

Murray's cousin and partner, Robert Cooke, engineered the purchase of the freehold next door on Albemarle Street for £4,100 plus £150 for fixtures. The building would serve as a warehouse until 1930, when that part of the business was moved to the Clerkenwell Road. Macpherson's administrative talents were appreciated by contributors, but subscribers complained that the articles were less readable than they had been under Elwin's meticulous revision. Macpherson resigned as editor of the *Quarterly Review* in March 1867 and was succeeded by Dr. (later Sir) William Smith, known as "Dictionary Smith." During their fifty-year association Smith and Murray planned and produced dictionaries of Greek and Roman antiquities (1842) and biography (1850, 1851), Latin-English (1855), and the Bible (1860–1863), as well as a classical atlas that caused an expense to the firm of £150,000 with a protracted delay in recouping the investment. During the Franco-Prussian War, Murray encouraged military articles since, as he wrote to Cooke, nothing else was read. The aesthetes came in for censure in the conservative journal until the end of the century. In 1862 Murray published Darwin's *On the Various Contrivances by Which British and Foreign Orchids Are Fertilized by Insects;* the first edition of fifteen hundred copies sold immediately. Also in 1862, for the first anniversary of Prince Albert's death, a volume of the prince consort's speeches and addresses was scheduled for publication by a house that failed to produce it. Murray was called in, had the book reset, and brought it out on the scheduled date. Queen Victoria was so grateful that ten years later, when the Albert Memorial in Hyde Park was nearing completion, Murray was asked to produce a sumptuous folio volume describing the structure.

In 1864 Murray lifted his ban on poetry to publish Edward George Geoffrey Smith Stanley, fourteenth earl of Derby's translation of Homer's *Iliad;* the first edition of three thousand copies was quickly followed by a second large edition. Encouraged by the success of the classic, Murray risked publishing his friend Sir Edward Bulwer-Lytton's *Lost Tales of Miletus* (1866), which was based on classical myths, but it did not do well. Works by the clergy remained prominent on the Murray lists.

On 9 October 1869 Charles Appleton, an Oxford don, launched a new Murray journal, the *Academy,* to provide serious readers with reliable judgments on issues of high culture. Murray had long desired to publish a weekly literary organ, but he wanted a broader audience than too scholarly a periodical could provide. He rejected the first proposed issue. The first published issue attracted readers because it included the first publication of

Byron's explanation for his separation from his wife, but by the third number the circulation had dropped from twenty thousand to six thousand, and advertising pages from twenty to four. Appleton and Murray clashed when Appleton wanted to include an article titled "The Historic Jesus," which Murray regarded as detrimental to the Christian faith, resulting in Appleton going off on his own after one year and Murray paying a large sum to free himself from the agreement.

Murray had a lifelong interest in geology and mineralogy, and in 1877 he published his own *Scepticism in Geology and the Reason for It: An Assemblage of Facts from Nature Opposed to the Theory of Causes Now in Action and Refuting It,* as "Verifier." An attack on the theories of Lyell, whose books the firm had published, the work was praised by the Royal Geographical Society. When *The Descent of Man* appeared in 1871, Murray asked Elwin to write the review in the *Quarterly Review* because he was uneasy about a coarse passage in the book. It sold extremely well, and Murray paid eight hundred pounds for a second edition in March and the same for a third in May.

In July 1879 Murray III wrote to Samuel Smiles, encouraging the latter's projected life of Murray II: "My Father, I venture to think, deserves a Biographer. I know not where he would find so good and appreciative an one as you, and I think I may venture to assure you that the materials for it are copious and most interesting. If you undertook it, it would be the pleasure and duty of my son, Robert Cooke and myself to aid and assist you in every way in our power. . . . We are prepared, therefore, to offer you for this Life, which I suppose will extend to two volumes 8vo, either One Thousand Guineas for the copyright, payable on completion of the printing, or, if you prefer it, one half-share of every edition." Smiles took the thousand guineas. The biography was published in two volumes in 1891.

In 1887, to fulfill a project of his father's, Murray began *Murray's Magazine,* a 144-page shilling magazine, with Edward Arnold as editor. The prospectus declared, "The aim of the Magazine, then, will be to provide popular articles on social and political topics of the day, and to give the newest and best information on Literature and Art, Natural History, Science, Geography, Travels etc. In matters controversial it is not proposed to represent one side only, but to invite discussion from representatives of opposing views. A special feature will be communications from Correspondents Abroad and in the Colonies furnishing authentic intelligence on subjects of general interest." The first issue included Byron's "Lines to Lara" and a previously unpublished 1816 letter from John Murray II to Byron in which the publisher outlines just such a magazine and expresses the hope that the poet will contribute to it. The *Times* review of the first issue praised the firm as one of the oldest and most powerful publishing houses but found that not everything in the number was solid. The first year ended in financial loss. Later issues included Margaret Woods's *Esther Vanhomrigh,* for which she was paid £150 for the serial rights and two-thirds net profit for each edition; pieces by Lady Eastlake, Theodore Roosevelt, Marie Belloc, Matthew Arnold, Alfred Austen, W. E. Norris, and Edna Lyall; William Gladstone's "The Impregnable Rock of Holy Scripture"; and John Murray III's piece on the origin and history of his handbooks. There was not enough to distinguish this offering from its many rivals or to appeal to changing tastes, and its appearance was bland; it ceased publication a few months before Murray's death on 2 April 1892.

Murray III was succeeded by his sons John IV and Alexander Henry Hallam; the other partner, Cooke, had died a year earlier. John Murray IV had attended Eton and Magdalen College, Oxford, before diligently passing through all the departments of the firm beginning in 1873. On returning from his honeymoon in 1878 he had been made a junior partner. Hallam Murray had joined the firm in 1884; he was an accomplished watercolorist who exhibited at the Royal Academy and illustrated several books, including his own *The High Road of Empire* (1905). He improved book production, especially the bindings and the use of color in printing. Murray IV edited *The Autobiographies of Edward Gibbon* (1897) and wrote a short biography of his father (1919). He served as editor of the *Quarterly Review* from October 1893 to January 1894, succeeding Smith until Rowland Prothero, later Lord Ernle, took over for five years; Prothero was, in turn, succeeded by his brother, Sir George Prothero, who had been a professor of history at Edinburgh University. Under Sir George the *Quarterly Review,* although far from the formidable presence it had been in the nineteenth century, produced some fine essays, such as Percy Lubbock's assessment of Edith Wharton and John Middleton Murry's review of Marcel Proust. In 1916 Arthur Waugh castigated "The New Poetry" for its emphasis on everyday language and realism. The majority of the pieces were on social, political, and historical subjects with an enlightened conservative bias. Articles appeared by J. B. Bury, T. Sturge Moore, Evelyn Underhill,

Edmund Gosse, and Sir James Frazer; there were many biographical pieces on Byron because of the interests of the firm and the Protheros. Beginning in 1920 film criticism emerged in the pages of the *Quarterly Review* with Bertram Clayton's column "The Cinema."

In October 1900 Murray IV introduced another magazine, persuading Henry Newbolt to edit the *Monthly Review.* The periodical achieved a distinguished reputation due to the contributions of Newbolt's friends, including Roger Fry, Arthur Thomas Quiller-Couch, Edith Sichel, Arthur Symons, Walter de la Mare, William Archer, and Havelock Ellis. Newbolt resigned in 1904 because his focus on the free-trade issue caused Murray embarrassment. The *Monthly Review* ceased publication with the June 1907 issue.

That John Murray IV was careful in his management of the family firm can be seen in a series of letters to Sir Edward Hamilton, author of *Gladstone: A Monograph* (1898). Every detail about the production process was carefully explained to Hamilton — when the price would be fixed, the kind of paper that would be used, where and when the announcement of the forthcoming work was to appear, the date of publication, the color of the binding and lettering, when to expect reviews from the advance copies sent out to reviewers, why good leather bindings take longer, how many copies would be printed, why a delay occurred, the type and frequency of advertising, and why the third edition had to be delayed until fewer than 140 copies were left of the second — in twenty-two carefully wrought letters written from 17 October 1898 to 6 January 1899 mostly by John Murray, with one by Hallam when John was away.

Murray IV played an important role in the "Book War" between the *Times* Book Club, which was selling almost-new books to its members at a steep discount, and the publishers, who agreed among themselves in October 1906 not to supply any more books to the club. The *Times* complained that book prices were too high and that publishers were making excessive profits. When, in the fall of 1907, Murray refused to supply the newly published *The Letters of Queen Victoria,* the *Times* Book Club was obliged to buy the three-volume work at three guineas. The *Times* reviewer accused Murray of extortion and coupled his name with Judas Iscariot; Murray sued for libel and was awarded seventy-five hundred pounds in damages. This financial blow forced the sale of the paper to A. C. W. Harmsworth, Lord Northcliffe, who ended the war by signing the Net Book Agreement in Octo-

*Fireplace in the drawing room of the Murray offices, where the
manuscript for Byron's memoirs was burned on 17 May 1824*

ber 1908. One month later the *Times* and Murray co-published a cheap edition of the queen's letters.

Hallam Murray retired in 1908 and was replaced by John Murray V, who had been born in 1884, attended Eton and Magdalen College, Oxford, and commanded a battalion in Flanders. The Murray firm acquired the publisher Smith, Elder, when Reginald Smith, who owned the latter firm, died in 1916 and his widow, Elizabeth, decided to sell. Murray's representatives soon found that the firm was seriously overvalued; but, not wanting to leave a widow uncared for, the negotiations were handled with delicacy and Murray paid generously. The Murrays also felt a certain loyalty since the two companies were so similar in their publishing and the founder of Smith, Elder, George Smith, had worked days for Murray and evenings for his own firm while Smith, Elder was getting started. Smith, Elder's *Cornhill Magazine* served as a valuable source of new authors. As part of the purchase Murray acquired works by Arthur Conan Doyle, Mary and

Jane Helen Findlater, W. H. Fitchett, F. Anstey, A. C. Benson, Marie Belloc Lowndes, H. Seton Merriman, and Mrs. Humphry Ward. Leonard Huxley, who had been assistant editor of the *Cornhill* and a reader for Smith, Elder, became the editor, succeeding the late Reginald Smith. Huxley contributed more regularly than had any editor of the *Cornhill* since Leslie Stephen in the previous century. Articles of literary history, biography, and criticism concerning Geoffrey Chaucer, William Shakespeare, and eighteenth- and nineteenth-century English literature were the hallmarks of the magazine at this time. After Huxley's death on 3 May 1933 Lord Gorell became the editor; he would have the unpleasant task of ceasing publication in 1939 due to World War II. He was also a partner in the firm for three years.

John Murray IV died in 1928; John Murray V replaced his father as head of the firm and became coeditor of the *Quarterly Review* with C. E. Lawrence. Lawrence had served as coeditor throughout

John Murray IV's tenure, having succeeded Sir George Prothero in 1922, and held key editorial positions in the firm.

Murray V added Axel Munthe, P. C. Wren, and Kathleen Norris to the Murray author list. Being childless, Murray V turned for a successor to his nephew, Arnaud Robin Grey, who took the name John G. "Jock" Murray when he joined the firm to preserve the identity of the house. Educated at Eton and Magdalen College, Oxford, he became assistant editor of the *Cornhill* in 1931 and assistant editor of the *Quarterly Review* two years later. While at Oxford in the late 1920s, Jock Murray had met John Betjeman, who was to become poet laureate and a regular writer for the firm; Betjeman had introduced Murray to Osbert Lancaster, who became the regular illustrator for the poet's books. Murray said about Lancaster, "If he agreed to do a book it would come at a rate of knots. If he lost impetus, wild horses, money, entreaties, nothing would get it out of him." All twenty-six of his books were published by Murray. Also at Oxford at the time were Maurice Bowra, Evelyn Waugh, C. Day Lewis, Isaiah Berlin, Anthony Powell, and Kenneth Clark. All of these Oxford men eventually wrote for the *Cornhill Magazine,* which, after the hiatus due to World War II, Jock Murray cajoled his uncle into restarting in 1944. Peter Quennell produced three issues a year until 1947, when it became a quarterly. As editor Quennell was, he said, "naturally inclined to disregard the fashions of the present day, and determined merely to satisfy, so far as I could, the public's taste for good writing." The *Cornhill* published many pieces by and about Victorian authors such as Tennyson, Charlotte Brontë, John Ruskin, Robert Browning, and Laurence Oliphant; a Crimean War photo supplement carried extra impact from being published at the time of the Korean conflict.

In 1950 Jock Murray, who had served as assistant editor of the *Cornhill* under Quennell, anonymously took the helm as coeditor with Osyth Leeston, who gradually retired. In 1951 John Murray changed from a partnership to a limited-liability company with a five-member board to avoid death duties and to keep the firm independent. The *Cornhill* served to showcase Murray authors and to advertise Murray titles, balancing a consciousness of tradition with an intense awareness of modern times. The *Sunday Times* of 18 July 1954 said that it provided "sensibility, good taste, a feeling for tradition and a zest for adventure. . . . Not in the least political, not much concerned with literary experiment, it reflects and caters for the diversions of civilized minds, and deserves hearty congratulations upon its achievement." By the 1960s the *Quarterly*

Review was competing with scholarly journals for academic readers and with other magazines for a general readership; thus, soon after John Murray V died on 6 October 1967 so did the venerable *Quarterly Review* in 1968. Betjeman appeared nineteen times into the early 1970s; Lancaster contributed twenty-four times. In addition to the Oxford group Max Beerbohm, Elizabeth Bowen, André Gide, Margaret Lane, Rose Macaulay, and W. Somerset Maugham appeared with some frequency. In 1975 Jock Murray made the difficult decision to shut down the *Cornhill Magazine;* other magazines of the type had long ceased publication, unable to compete with the Sunday supplements of newspapers. In the last two decades pieces by May Sarton, X. J. Kennedy, Betty Miller, Frank O'Connor, Sylvia Townsend Warner, Ruth Prawer Jhabvala, Freya Stark, Dervla Murphy, and Nadine Gordimer had been included, along with retrospective articles honoring the centenaries of the birth of Henry James and Ward. Patrick Leigh Fermor, who contributed nine articles beginning in the summer of 1949, is still writing travel books for Murray. *Advertiser's Weekly* placed circulation at twenty thousand in 1954, but the next year it was recorded as half of that; reading habits had changed, and there were many competing forms of entertainment.

From the early 1970s to 1981 one of Jock Murray's personal preoccupations was the twelve volumes of *Byron's Letters & Journals* (1973–1982), edited by Leslie A. Marchand, for which Murray helped acquire previously unknown letters. Murray had asked Marchand to work on the letters after Marchand came to 50 Albemarle Street to do research for his 1957 biography of Byron. No longer worried about damage to Byron's reputation, as his grandfather had been, Murray was anxious to publish the letters to offset the burning of Byron's memoirs. Marchand worked on the manuscript at the Murray offices – just as, in the nineteenth century, many authors had written works while staying at 50 Albemarle.

Under Kenneth Pinnock, who retired in 1985, Murray became one of the leading educational publishers for secondary schools and colleges; its list spanned the whole curriculum but displayed particular strength in science, thanks to a long collaboration with the Association for Science Education. Typical of the firm's innovative approach to textbooks in the 1960s was D. G. Mackean's *Introduction to Biology,* a strikingly designed large-format book. First published in 1962 and still a best-seller, it has sold more than four million copies and has been translated into many languages. Later in the 1960s the firm developed, with W. and R. Chambers, the

Nuffield Mathematics Project. The textbook list continued to thrive in the 1970s and 1980s; best-selling authors included Tom Duncan, whose physics books were sold throughout the English-speaking market, and F. E. S. Finn, a widely respected apostle of English grammar and a noted poetry anthologizer. The firm has further strengthened its position as a leading history publisher with the series Discovering the Past for ages five to sixteen, published in conjunction with the Schools History Project.

Jock Murray gradually turned over the management of the company to his son, John R. Murray, in 1987–1988. Until his death on 22 July 1993 he remained a director and continued to work two days per week. With John R. Murray as chairman and director of the General Books Marketing Division, Nicholas Perren as managing director, Grant McIntyre as editorial director, and Judith Reinhold as education director, John Murray Publishers began the 1990s by publishing 60 general titles, down from 103 the previous year – a prodigious number for the fifty-four employees. The firm produces a twice-yearly illustrated catalogue announcing its new offerings, which include travel books, cartoons, collected letters, literary companions to various cities, biographies, intellectual histories, sports, military and general history, architecture and design, cookbooks, wines and spirits, crafts and hobbies, economics, fiction, art history, gardening, history, linguistics, literary criticism, mathematics and statistics, medical, reference, and scientific and technical; many of these areas have been staples of the firm throughout its history. Murray shares general sales representatives with Robert Hale and also represents the American art publisher Abbeville Press throughout the United Kingdom. Murray books have been distributed by Grantham Book Services since the firm sold its Clerkenwell Road warehouse in 1989. The drawing room remains a meeting place for authors and for the John Betjeman Society, which occasionally gathers on Sunday afternoons. The firm continues its wariness about publishing poetry, although it has brought out the poems of George Mackay Brown. As it has for more than two centuries, the company appeals to the lover of good books who appreciates what is enduring in the British heritage.

References:

Richard Boston, *Osbert: A Portrait of Osbert Lancaster* (London: Collins, 1989);

Kenneth Clark, *The Other Half* (London: John Murray, 1977);

Pierre Irving, ed., *The Life and Letters of Washington Irving,* 4 volumes (New York: Putnam, 1864);

Marghanita Laski, *Jane Austen and Her World* (New York: Scribners, 1969);

Raymond N. MacKenzie, "The Quarterly Review," in *British Literary Magazines: The Modern Age 1914–1984,* edited by Alvin Sullivan (Westport, Conn.: Greenwood Press, 1986), pp. 389–392;

Ben Harris McClary, ed., *Washington Irving and the House of Murray: Geoffrey Crayon Charms the British 1817–1856* (Knoxville: University of Tennessee Press, 1969);

Caroline Moorhead, ed., *Over the Rim of the World: Freya Stark Selected Letters* (London: Murray & Russell, 1988);

John Murray III, "The Origin and History of Murray's Handbooks for Travellers," *Murray's Magazine,* 6 (September 1887): 623–629;

John Murray IV, *John Murray III, 1808–1892: A Brief Memoir* (New York: Knopf, 1920);

George Paston [Emily M. Symonds], *At John Murray's: Records of a Literary Circle 1843–1892* (London: John Murray, 1932);

Peter Quennell, *The Wanton Chase* (London: Collins, 1980);

Carol de Saint Victor, "The Monthly Review," in *British Literary Magazines: The Victorian and Edwardian Age 1837–1913,* edited by Sullivan (Westport, Conn.: Greenwood Press, 1984), pp. 229–246;

Samuel Smiles, *A Publisher and His Friends: Memoir and Correspondence of the Late John Murray,* 2 volumes (London: John Murray, 1891);

Anna M. Stoddard, *Life of Isabella Bird* (London: John Murray, 1906);

Patrick Taylor-Martin, *John Betjeman: His Life and Work* (London: Allen Lane, 1983);

Gaye Tuchman and Nina Fortin, *Edging Women Out* (New Haven & London: Yale University Press, 1989).

Papers:

Correspondence and other documents about the firm are in the John Murray Archives.

– Barbara Quinn Schmidt

John Newbery
(Reading: 1740 – 1743; London: 1743 – 1767)

Thomas Carnan
(London: 1750 – 1791)

Francis Newbery (the Elder)
(London: 1765 – 1781)

Francis Newbery (the Younger)
(London: 1768 – 1780)

Newbery and Carnan / Carnan and Newbery
(London: 1768 – 1781)

Elizabeth Newbery
(London: 1772 – 1814)

Francis Power
(London: 1789 – 1793)

John Newbery has often been described as the first publisher for children. In reality he had predecessors, but as Sydney Roscoe asserts in his bibliography of Newbery's publications, "John Newbery's achievement was not to invent . . . juvenile books, not even to start a fashion for them, but to so produce them as to make a permanent and profitable market for them, to make them a class of book to be taken seriously as a recognised and important branch of the book trade." Newbery was the first children's publisher to employ an in-house staff of illustrators to create a quality product and the first to publish separate lists for "Children" and "Young Gentlemen and Ladies" – what would now be called "young adult" books. He is commemorated by the John Newbery Medal, awarded annually since 1922 for the best children's book published in the United States by an American author. The marketing profession also owes a debt of gratitude to Newbery for the ingenious sales techniques he developed. Even following Roscoe's rather broad definition, only about one-fifth of the five hundred–odd books Newbery published were for juveniles: he also published works by Oliver Goldsmith, Samuel Johnson, and Christopher Smart.

Newbery was born in 1713 to a Berkshire farmer. At age sixteen he began an apprenticeship with the *Reading Mercury and Oxford Gazette*. In 1737 the proprietor of the paper, William Carnan, died and left his estate to his brother Charles and Newbery; in the summer of 1739 Newbery married his late employer's widow, Mary.

The following summer Newbery went on an extended tour of England to search for business opportunities. His diary of the trip is a fascinating document of social history; it is also full of ideas for new commercial ventures, many of which he successfully carried out. By 1743 he had deployed a corps of forty-three salesmen to sell the *Reading Mercury* in Southampton, Bicester, Hastings, and elsewhere; he had set up a local lending library; and had become a wholesaler of draper's goods. In 1746 he would patent, manufacture, and sell Dr. James's Fever Powder, a profitable patent medicine advertised as being effective against gout, rheumatism, scrofula, scurvy, leprosy, and distemper in cattle. Seventeenth- and eighteenth-century booksellers commonly purveyed nostrums as a sideline, and Newbery was able to sell books and pills through the same national marketing networks.

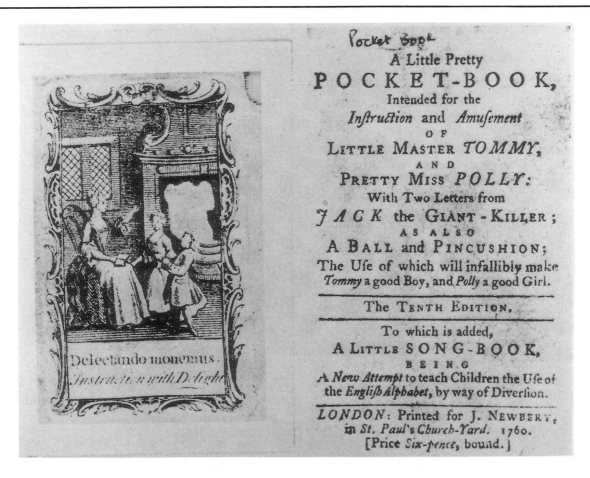

Frontispiece and title page for a later edition of the first children's book John Newbery published after moving from Reading to London. He may have been the author.

Newbery's diary for 1740 also records his ideas for publishing and marketing books, including a translation of the Koran and Richard Allestree's *The Whole Duty of Man*. Later that year Newbery published the latter, as well as *Miscellaneous Works Serious and Humerous [sic] In Verse and Prose* – the first two books to appear under his imprint.

Late in 1743 Newbery departed for London, leaving his stepson John Carnan in charge of the Reading business. Newbery established a shop at the Bible and Crown near Devereux Court, outside of Temple Bar. In 1745 he moved to the Bible and Sun at 65 St. Paul's Churchyard, the center of London's book trade.

The first book Newbery published in London was also his first children's book, *A Little Pretty Pocket-Book* (1744). Though published anonymously, the book may have been written by Newbery. The inscription on its frontispiece, *Delectando monemus* (Instruction through Delight), was to be the hallmark of the Newbery list. The publisher had been strongly influenced by John Locke's *Some Thoughts Concerning Edu-*

cation (1693), in which the philosopher argued that "children may be cozened into a knowledge of the letters; be taught to read, without perceiving it to be anything but a sport, and play themeselves into that which others are whipped for." When a child begins reading, Locke said, "some easy pleasant book, suited to his capacity, should be put into his hands, wherein the entertainment that he finds might draw him on and reward his pains in reading, and yet not such as should fill his head with perfectly useless trumpery, or lay the principles of vice and folly." Locke suggested books of "pictures of animals with printed names to them." Such is precisely what *A Little Pretty Pocket-Book* offered its readers, and it cost only sixpence – or eightpence for an edition with a ball and pincushion.

Locke lamented that there were few entertaining children's books available other than *Aesop's Fables* and *Reynard the Fox* (the first children's edition of Aesop in English had been published only in 1692). But "Instruction through Delight" would soon become the credo of the English Enlightenment. Popular scientific lecturers, equipped with microscopes

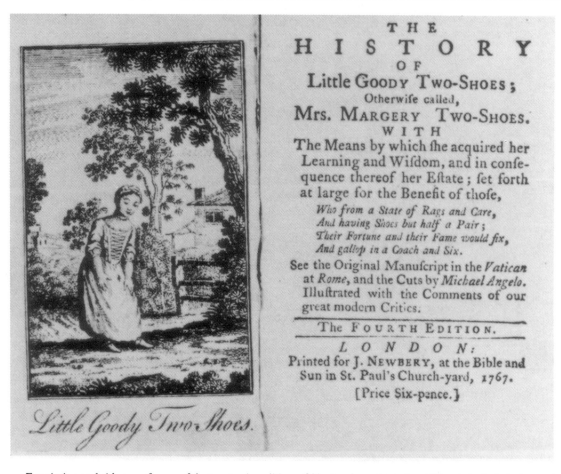

Frontispiece and title page for one of the twenty-nine editions of Newbery's most popular children's book that appeared between its first publication in 1765 and the end of the century

and vacuum pumps, would offer entertaining public demonstrations to parents and children alike. Samuel Richardson helped create the form of the English novel, designed for the twin purposes of amusement and moral instruction, and Newbery's nephew Francis Newbery would publish abridged children's editions of Richardson's *Clarissa* (1768), *The History of Sir Charles Grandison* (1768), and *Pamela* (1769).

Juvenile literature changed with those cultural trends. The title of one popular book suggests the grimness of seventeenth-century children's literature: *A Token for Children; Being an Exact Account of the Conversion, Holy and Exemplary Lives, and Joyful Deaths of Several Small Children* (1671), by the Puritan cleric James Janeway. In Janeway's account seven-year-olds talk like preachers, reject play for piety, and read nothing but Scripture and devotional works. Isaac Watts's *Divine Songs, Attempted in Easy Language for the Use of Children* (1715), on the other hand, includes the usual admonitions about hellfire but softens them with assurances of God's love; Watts also

makes an effort to entertain his young readers and write from their point of view. In 1730 Thomas Boreman began to publish his instructional books for children, most notably his ten *Gigantick Histories* (1740–1743). "During the Infant-Age, ever busy and always inquiring, there is no fixing the attention of the mind, but by amusing it," Boreman advised. He bound his books in Dutch flowered paper boards, and advertisements for his general list were shamelessly inserted into his stories: both techniques were adopted by Newbery, who published successful imitations of Boreman's books. Newbery may have also taken his cue from Thomas Cooper of Paternoster Row, who published *The Child's New Play-thing* (1742) with the stated goal of making "learning to read a *Diversion* instead of a *Task*." Cooper also published the first nursery-rhyme book for English children, *Tom Thumb's Song Book for All Little Masters and Misses,* written by "Nurse Lovechild" and advertised by Cooper's widow, Mary, in March 1744.

That May or June *A Little Pretty Pocket-Book* appeared. It includes an illustrated songbook that

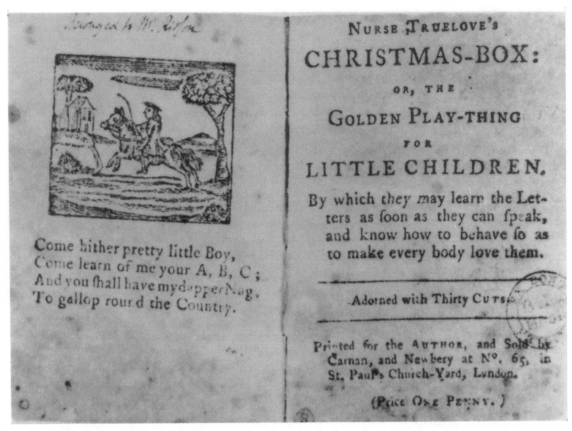

Frontispiece and title page for a book Newbery used for promotion. Fourteen thousand copies were distributed to children who paid only a penny for the cost of the binding (Bodleian Library, Oxford).

promises "to teach Children the Use of the English Alphabet, by Way of Diversion." It cites John Dryden, Alexander Pope, and "the great Mr. Locke" to the effect that the child is a tabula rasa who can be made virtuous and rational by an enlightened learning environment. It prescribes proper diet and exercise along with just enough exposure to hardship to build character. It asserts that through "Reasoning and mild Discipline" children can be taught to subdue their passions and control their appetites.

The Newbery gospel offered not threats of damnation but a cheerful appeal to rational self-interest. Learn your lessons, promises *A Little Pretty Pocket-Book,* and one day you will ride in a coach and six. Children are advised that saying their prayers "makes God Almighty love and bless them"; studying hard "makes every Body admire them"; and giving to the poor "makes the whole World love them." In Newbery's universe work is always rewarded and altruism pays dividends as reliably as Isaac Newton's laws of motion – another Newbery children's book was *The Newtonian System of Philosophy,* by "Tom Telescope," which ran through seven

editions between 1761 and 1787. In the realm of juvenile literature, the Age of Reason had arrived.

That was the message of Newbery's most popular book, *The History of Little Goody Two-Shoes* (1765). With the exception of Sarah Fielding's *The Governess* (1749), it was the first English children's novel, running through twenty-nine editions between 1765 and 1800. (The first edition was considered lost until 1965, when the British Museum announced that it had obtained a copy and placed it on permanent display.) It was published anonymously, as were most of Newbery's children's books, but the brothers Giles and Griffith Jones were probably the authors.

Goody Two-Shoes is Margery Meanwell, who is orphaned when her father is "seized with a violent fever in a place where Dr. James's Fever Powder was not to be had, and where he died miserably." Margery is reduced to wearing rags and a single shoe until she is given a complete pair (hence her nickname) by the charitable Reverend Smith. As a child of the Enlightenment, Margery appreciates that Smith is good because he is learned, so she educates herself and other children through

Die Martis, ad senatum superiorem accessit majestas regia, more solito stipata &, post duodecim articulos assensu regio stabilitos, hujusmodi orationem benevolam habuit.

Barones mei & Generosi.

HUIC sectioni Senatoriae haud licet finem prius statuere, quam mea in vestram consiliorum prudentiam benevolentia exprimatur. Illa pietas & fortitudo, quarum, in imperii salutem, singuli ad unum specimina edidistis, ut rueret nefandus nuperrime conjurantium exercitus, & noxii justitiae tela non effugerent, quae inter agenda, subditorum jurata fides tantum attulit auxilii, non solum ex opinione de vestro senatu efformata evenere, verum etiam ejusmodi sunt, ut mihi suadeam, res praeclare adeo gestas pace optima domi stabilita, Pseudo-principis & sociorum spem futuram amovente, vobis esse perficiendi consilium.

Illa agendi autoritas, quam mihi in re tam ardua minime negandam censuistis, non frustra nec inaccurate adhibita, illa sola spectavit, quae potissimum vobis in votis fuerant; & nostris consiliis quam evidentissime clementia divina favit: non ignoro u ta adhuc stabilienda superesse, quo salus nostra magis diuturna fiat, & sceleri futuro locus nullus pateat: quoniam vero res illae sapientur agitatae sunt, quae in senatu postero fusius sunt evolvendae, vos e vestris comitatibus diutius non detinendos censui, dum intempestivum adeo anni tempus volvitur. Non sine laetitia vos certiores facio, rerum adversarum fortunam secundiorem videri, quam cum antehac ad vos orationem habui. Simul ac per triplicis imperii salutem licuit, manum pro viribus numerolam ad Belgas expedii, quae exercitui foederato cum provinciis foederatis subsidio foret, & Gallos audaciora meditantes repellerent. Haec, aliaque subsidia a vobis concessa, vires multo ampliores illis copiis addidere, quam inorunte anno vel spes potuisset pingere. Hic rerum exitus, cum feliciori utriusque exercitus Austriaci & Sardonici fortuna, aliisque casibus causae publicae pergratis, evidentius innuere videtur, hostes nostros tandem rationis normam necessario secuturos, & fines Britannicos pacem tutam & illustrem exornaturam. Haec mihi potissimum in votis habeo.

Generosi e senatu inferiori,

Vestra inter in annum insequentem subsidia concedenda alacritas, gratias a me benigniores postulat. Non me latet anxia illa difficultas, quam temporis ordo & huic officio subsidiario & etiam fidei publicae miscuit, quanque sola vestra sapientia evincere potuit. Subsidia concessa ex votis vestris eroganda curabo; nec vos fugere potest meus impensus publicas minuendi animus, jusso dato, ne legiones subditorum nobiliorum pietate conscriptae, stipendia merere pergerent.

Barones mei & generosi,

Tot in mecoque fidei vestrae inconcussae amoris & observantiae specimina ob oculos habeo, ut de vestra in posterum pietate minime dubitandum censeam, persuasum omnino habeo, singulos, pro varia vestra autoritate, &c. omnes vias persecuturos, quibus, & pacem genti reddatis, & redditam conservetis; conjurationis iniquissimae vulnera fugetis; apud animos subditorum in imperium pietatem a nuperrima haud alienam colendam curetis. Nunquam illa animo excidet; nostra sollicitudo regia semper imperii saluti & subditorum (quantum in me erit) felicitati invigilatura, memorem animum probabit.

Dein, Ornatissimus Cancellarius, Rege imperante, in hunc modum loquutus est.

Barones mei & Generosi,

Volunt Regia monita & mandata, Senatum

hunc Parliamentarium, ad Martis diem, Septembris instantis trigesimum prorogandum. Unde Senatus hic Parliamentarius, utque ad Martis diem, Septembris instantis trigesimum, prorogatur.

Ducem Somersetiensem mortuum esse falso rumor asserebat.

Nobilis admodum Baro Hobart, Magnae Britanniae comes, sub titulo comitis Buckinghamiensis (fertur) brevi constituetur; necnon

Nobilis aomodum Baro Fitzwilliams, Vicecomes, & Comes, sub titulo vice Comitis Milton, in agro Northamptoniensi, & Comitis Fitz-Williams, de Norborough, in eodem.

Die Mercurii, nob. admodum Senatus inferioris prolocutor, Majestatem regiam invisit, ab eadem quam humanissime acceptus.

Die Saturni, Jacobus Stewart, Baronettus, in novum carcerem Sudovicensem traditus est.

Literae e Munimento Augustensi datae asserunt, Dominum de Moor, cum septingentis aliis rebellibus, nuper in custodiam esse traditum.

In rebellium numero, non ita pridem mari ad Londinenses advecto, est Glenbucketius, junior.

Die Saturni, Comes de Traquair in turrem Londinensem tradebatur.

Eodem die, Comitisse Cromartie, cum filio Barone Mac Leod, apud turrem captivo, & filiabus ternis, Comitem invisendi & una cum eodem prandendi veniam obtinuit.

Die hesterno, hora fera tertia, Baro Lovat, cujus fama, ne dicam infamia in singulorum ore versatur, turrem Londinensem attigit; stipante militum corona. Ipse inter caeteros Londinum ingredientem utroque oculo lustrabam; vultum mirabar Fallaciis natum, pro varia occasione et sceleris et pietatis larva indutum. *O prudentiam senilem!* Clamans, ad calamum Latinum redii.

CONNUBIO JUNCTI.

Baro Petersham, comitis de Harrington filius natu maximus, cum Domina Carolina Fitzroy, Clementiae suae, Ducis Graftonensis, filia natu maxima.

Georgius Goatly, Arm. de Alsford, apud Cantianos, cum Domina Mills, Cantuariensi, et auro et Pulchritudine dotata.

Dom. Michael Batt, apud collem Margaretatem Sudovicensem, Mercator ferrarius, cum Domina Wicks, vidua bene locupletata.

Neomagi, apud surrienses, Joannes Fuller, Arm. cum Domina Dorrel,—Dorrel apud cantabrigienses Armigeri filia, virgine formosa et dotem honestam numerante.

MORTUI.

In vico Piccadilly, Thomas Smith, Arm. aleatorum cohorti bene notus.

Nob. Joannes Brudenell, Arm. morbo apoplectico sublatus.

N. B. Uni et alteri epistolae a viris eruditis de lingua Gallica, &c. acceptae fusius brevi responsum dabitnr. Interea probo utriusque consilia.

N. B. In Mercurio 22. in col. 2. pro *fatebat*, lege *fatebatur*: non sine horrore illum errorem inspexi: non autem in singulos irreperat, sed in ultimis lineis literae saepius manu incauta inter excudendum e loco suo deturbantur. Interea vix sibi in animum inducet lector noster assiduus, in re tam aperta ipsum *Agricolam* peccasse. In eodem Mercurio, in col. 1 pro *manum.* lege *manuum.* Hos & hujusmodi errores facile legentis calamu fugare poterit & juventutis captui accommodare.

GEORGE R.

GEORGE the Second, by the Grace of God, King of Great Britain, &c. to all to whom these presents shall come, Greeting. Whereas our Trusty and Well-beloved *John Newbery*, of *London*, Bookseller, hath, with great Expence and much Labour, compiled a Work, intitled, *The Circle of the Sciences*; or, *The compendious Library*; digested in a Method entirely new, whereby each Branch of *Polite Literature* is render'd extremely easy and instructive. We being willing to encourage all Works of public Benefit, are graciously pleased to grant him our Royal Priviledge and Licence, for the sole Printing, Publishing, and Vending the same. Given at St. *James's* the 8th of *December* 1744. By his Majesty's Command, HOLLES NEWCASTLE.

To the PUBLIC.

THIS Work, which is principally intended to lead CHILDREN from the very Cradle thro' the most polite and useful of the *Literary Arts and Sciences*, is render'd as instructive and entertaining as possible.

In the first Place, a proper Method is taken to open their tender Minds, and give them a Taste for Letters aft r which their Ideas are enlarg'd by familiar, easy, and progressive Steps, till they arrive at a tolerable Knowledge of *Books* and *Men*.

Nor will th's Work (as the Author humbly conceives) be less useful to those who are advanced in Years; there being as much said on each Science as is necessary for any Gentleman to lay up in his Memory, who does not intend to make that Science his particular Employment. And as the whole is made entertaining, the fair Sex ('tis presum'd will find something to engage their Attention, especially under the Heads, *Rhetoric, Poetry, Criticism, Geography, Chronology, History, Philosophy*, &c. as well as in the Preface or Introduction to each Book, which contains a short Historical Account of the Science.

Of this novel and useful Undertaking seven Volumes are now publish'd, *viz.*

Vol. I. An easy and entertaining *Spelling Book.* Price bound 6d.

Vol. II. A Compendious *Grammar* of the *English* Tongue. Price 6...

Vol. III. A *Spelling Dictionary*, on a new Plan. Price 1s.

Vol. IV. The Art of *Writing* illustrated with Copper Plates; to which is added a Collection of useful Letters, and Directions for addressing Persons of Distinction either in *Writing* or *Discourse*. pr 1s.

Vol. V. The Art of *Arithmetic* made familiar and easy. Price 1s.

Vol. VI. The Art of *Rhetorick* laid down in an easy entertaining Manner and illustrated with several beautiful Orations from *Demosthenes, Cicero, Sallust, Homer, Shakspear*, &c. &c. &c. Humbly inscribed to his Royal Highness Prince *George*. Price 1s.

Vol. VII. The Art of *Poetry* made easy, and embellish'd with a Variety of the most shining Epigrams, Epitaphs, Songs, Odes, Pastorals, &c. &c. &c. from the best Authors. Humbly inscrib'd to her Royal Highness the Princess *Augusta*. Price 1s.

N. B. The Arts of *Logick, Criticism, Geography, Chronology, History*, and *Philosophy*, are in the Press, and will be publish'd with all Expedition.

Also may be had,

MAturini Corderii Colloquia Selecta; or, Select Colloquies of *Maturin Cordier*: Better adapted to the Capacities of Youth, and fitter for Beginners in the Latin Tongue, than any Edition of those Colloquies, or any other Book yet publish'd. Containing, Part I. The Colloquies in Latin, from a correct Edition publish'd at the *Hague*; but for the Ease of Beginners, the Words are placed in the Order of Construction. Part II. An *English* Literal Translation, in a New Method: By the Help of which the young Scholar may with Ease attain to the rendering of the *Latin* Colloquies into *English*; and cannot mistake what *English* Words which answer to the *Latin* Part III. An Analysis, or Grammatical Resolution of the *Latin* Words in the Colloquies. By *Samuel Loggon*, M. A. For the use of Schools. The second Edition, with Improvements. Price 1s.

LONDINI: Typis GULIELMI FADEN, in viculo Sarisberiensi, vulgo Salisbury-Court, in vico de Fleet-street, ubi venalis prostat & epistolae ad Autorem accipiuntur. Prostat pariter apud Joannem Newbery, ad insigne Bibliorum & Solis, in coemiterio Sancti Pauli; necnon apud G. Jones, ad insigne Flabelli & Syderis, in vico vulgo dicto Compton-street, Soho, J. Fletcher, bibliopolam Oxoniensem, & circumforaneos Mercuriopolas.

N. B. *Advertisements in any Language are taken in by the Printer of this Paper, at Three Shillings each. Care is likewise taken to disperse this Paper, throughout* Scotland, Ireland, Germany, *and* Holland.

Page from the 16 August 1746 issue of Newbery's Mercurius Latinus, *in which the news was reported in Latin. The third column includes an announcement in English of the publication of Newbery's* The Circle of the Sciences, *the first children's encyclopedia.*

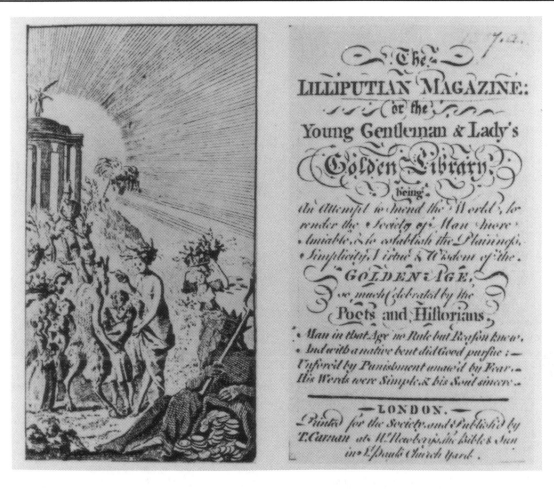

Frontispiece and title page for an issue of the first children's magazine in England

spelling games, several of which are reproduced in the book. She studies so diligently that she rises to become a school headmistress – the reader is told that her pupils have read forty-two Newbery books, all of which are conveniently listed at the back of the third edition. Through the power of reason, Margery resolves domestic quarrels, teaches children to accept the fact of death, arbitrates legal disputes so effectively that lawyers are pauperized, and shows superstitious villagers that ghosts and witches do not exist. She even teaches animals (who, according to the book, are endowed with reason) to spell. Ultimately Margery becomes a lady by marrying a gentleman, who dies of a fever and leaves her a fortune. In *The History of Little Goody Two-Shoes* God the Father does not terrify his children with hellfire; instead, God the Indulgent Uncle rescues his nephews and nieces from calamity. And he awards points for effort: "God Almighty protects not only those who are good, but those who endeavour to be good."

Newbery was an enthusiastic exponent of capitalism and consumerism – "Trade and Plumb-cake

for ever! Huzza!" proclaims *The Twelfth-Day Gift* (1767), which includes frequent advertisements for other Newbery books. He unabashedly appealed to rising middle-class parents who wanted their children to rise still further. The bourgeoisie were developing a new and less punitive approach to child rearing, but at the same time they were eager to inculcate the work disciplines and intellectual skills necessary for career success. They worried (as parents have worried throughout history) about declining moral values, and Newbery's advertisements spoke directly to that concern: "At a time when all complain of the depravity of human nature, and the corrupt principles of mankind, . . . the only way to remedy these evils is to begin with the rising generation, . . . impressing on their tender minds proper sentiments of religion, justice, honour, and virtue."

Newbery's adult list displayed an equally keen sense of his market. *The Ladies Complete Pocket-Book*, published annually from 1750 to 1789, includes tables for recording household expenses and marketing, as well as songs and dances fashionable in London high society. It successfully targeted middle-class urban housewives who had to manage a budget but, at the same time, aspired to gentility. Newbery established himself early as a publisher of useful guidebooks for that class of readers, such as *The Accomplish'd Housewife* (1745) and *A Dictionary Explaining the Most Difficult Terms* (1745). He also published a few best-sellers, such as Isaac Bickerstaffe's *Love in a Village* (1763), which ran through at least eight editions in the year of its publication.

Newbery advertised heavily in the *Universal Chronicle* and, for the export market, in the *Pennsylvania Gazette*. He frequently used his own books to promote his other wares: long before Goody Two-Shoes plugged Dr. James's Fever Powder, Benjamin Martin's *Micrographia Nova* (1742) reminded the reader that the microscopes depicted therein were on sale at Newbery's shop in Reading. Likewise, *The Art of Poetry on a New Plan* (1762), probably written by Newbery, praised Smart and other Newbery poets. Newbery offered discounts to teachers and booksellers who bought in bulk, and there were promotional giveaways: around 1750 he had fourteen thousand copies of *Nurse Truelove's Christmas-Box* printed for almost free distribution, with children "only paying one penny for the binding." Newbery also devised educational games to teach spelling, reading, writing, and arithmetic; these were often sold together with books.

His marketing techniques paid off. *The Royal Primer,* copublished with Benjamin Collins of Salisbury around 1751, sold twenty thousand copies in twenty years. Newbery published eleven titles in 1748, twenty-five in 1760, and thirty-four in 1766. Because his books were frequently pirated, Newbery ardently supported copyright legislation and urged his customers not to accept inferior imitations, "that he, who has entered so heartily into their service, and been ever studious of their improvement, may, at least, reap some of the fruits of his labour."

In *The Idler* (19 August 1758) Johnson affectionately and not inaccurately caricatured Newbery as "that great philosopher Jack Whirler, whose business keeps him in perpetual motion, and whose motion always eludes his business; who is always to do what he never does, who cannot stand still because he is wanted in another place, and who is wanted in many places because he stays in none." Newbery was a model of the New Entrepreneurial Man, always concocting new business schemes, overloading his personal schedule, and racing through life: "He calls often on his friends to tell them he will come again to-morrow; on the morrow he comes

again to tell them how an unexpected summons hurries him away," Johnson wrote. "When he enters a house his first declaration is that he cannot sit down; and so short are his visits that he seldom appears to have come for any reason but to say he must go.... But, overwhelmed as he is with business, his chief desire is to have still more. Every new proposal takes possession of his thoughts; he soon balances probabilities, engages in the project, brings it almost to completion, and then forsakes it for another, which he catches with the same alacrity, urges with the same vehemence, and abandons with the same coldness."

In the transformation of the book trade from aristocratic patronage to mass-market capitalism, Newbery was clearly in the vanguard; but he was neither an ungenerous man nor a supporter of the status quo. Even modern children's writers, who pride themselves on their uncompromising realism, would be startled by *The History of Little Goody Two-Shoes:* though it includes large helpings of treacle, it is also a brutally frank exposé of social injustice. Margery's enemy is the evil Sir Timothy Gripe, who is enclosing the land and evicting his peasants. His crony, the corrupt churchwarden Graspall, abuses the paupers in his charge "in a Manner too horrible to mention ... and judge, oh ye Christians, what State the Church must be in, when supported by a Man without Religion or Virtue." Margery's father tries to defend the rights of the poor, "but to what Purpose are Complaints, when brought against a Man, who can hunt, drink, and smoak with the Lord of the Manor, who is also the Justice of the Peace?" Sir Timothy illegally tries to force Meanwell off his land, and though Meanwell successfully defends himself, he is bankrupted by his legal costs. "Ah, my dear Reader, we brag of our Liberty, and boast of our Laws: but the Blessings of the one, and the Protection of the other, seldom fall to the Lot of the Poor; and especially when a rich Man is their Adversary. How, in the name of Goodness, can a poor Wretch obtain Redress, when thirty Pounds are insufficient to try his Cause? ... when our Laws are so obscure, and so multiplied, that an Abridgement of them cannot be obtained in fifty Volumes in Folio?"

The History of Little Goody Two-Shoes taught children – including "Children of six Feet High" – a harsh and sophisticated view of power structures in Augustan England. When the Reverend Smith tries to protect Margery, Graspall threatens to reduce his tithes. This is a world where relatives are too proud and greedy to take in the orphaned Margery and where money that should be spent to help the poor is wasted on lavish aristocratic funerals. There is even an attempted rape. Only when Margery acquires wealth and "power" is she able to have Sir Timothy dismissed from his post as justice of the peace – she knows when to stop being Little Goody Two-Shoes. The story may end happily, but it does not describe the best of all possible worlds: it cries out for slum clearance, education for the poor, and an end to cruelty to animals. *Little Goody Two-Shoes* reads like a curious hybrid of Eleanor Porter's *Pollyanna* (1913) and Voltaire's *Candide* (1759) – in fact, Newbery had published the works of Voltaire in twenty-five volumes (1761–1765), translated by Tobias Smollett and others.

Newbery also published what might be called the first children's encyclopedia, *The Circle of the Sciences* (1745–1748). Its seven volumes cover grammar, arithmetic, rhetoric, poetry, logic, geography, and chronology. The set was priced at seven shillings. He published abridged children's editions of *Plutarch's Lives* (1762) and the Bible (fourteen editions between 1757 and 1791). In early 1751 he launched the first children's periodical in England, if not in the world: the *Lilliputian Magazine,* which was probably written largely by Smart and edited by Newbery. Its initial press run was four thousand copies and was sold for threepence a month. It was discontinued after three issues, and no copies of the first printing survive; but it was successfully marketed as a bound volume, with seven editions between 1752 and 1772.

Newbery was also involved in several periodicals. Perhaps the most extraordinary was *Mercurius Latinus,* which reported the news in Latin. Though it was willing to take "Advertisements in any languages," it lasted for only thirty-one issues in 1746. He also had interests in *The British Magazine* (edited by Smollett), *The London Chronicle, Lloyd's Evening Post, Owen's Chronicle or the Westminster Journal, The Sherborn and Yeovill Mercury, The Christian's Magazine,* and probably *The Literary Magazine.* Newbery's weekly *Universal Chronicle* lasted only two years (1758–1760), but in that time it published Johnson's *Idler* letters. In 1760 Newbery launched the *The Public Ledger,* the oldest continuously published daily newspaper in Britain, though it survives today only as a commercial gazette. Goldsmith contributed to *The British Magazine* and, for one guinea each, wrote his 125 "Chinese Letters" for *The Public Ledger.* The latter were collected and published by Newbery as *The Citizen of the World* (1762).

In 1750 Charles Burney introduced Newbery to Smart, a promising young poet fresh from Cambridge University. Smart won the university's

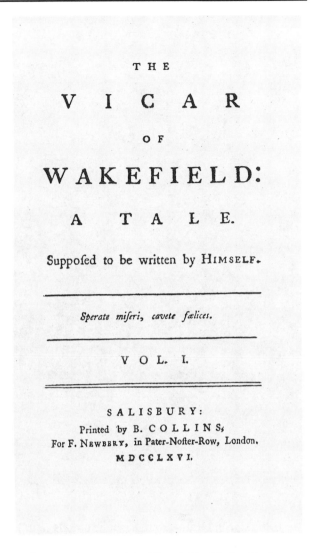

THE

VICAR

OF

WAKEFIELD:

A TALE.

Suppofed to be written by HIMSELF.

Sperate miferi, cavete fælices.

VOL. I.

SALISBURY:
Printed by B. COLLINS,
For F. NEWBERY, in Pater-Nofter-Row, London.
MDCCLXVI.

Title page for the novel by Oliver Goldsmith that Newbery, at the request of Samuel Johnson, invested in to keep Goldsmith out of debtors' prison

Seatonian prize five times, and all five poems would be published by Newbery: *On the Immensity of the Supreme Being* (1751), *On the Eternity of the Supreme Being* (1752), *On the Omniscience of the Supreme Being* (1752), *On the Power of the Supreme Being* (1754), and *On the Goodness of the Supreme Being* (1756). Smart contributed to one Newbery magazine, *The Student* (1750–1751); as Mary Midnight he edited and almost entirely wrote another, the Rabelaisian *The Midwife; or, The Old Woman's Magazine* (1751–1753). In 1750–1751 Smart exchanged satiric barbs with a fellow Newbery author, William Kenrick. Such slanging matches were a popular sport in Grub Street, and this one may well have been staged for the sake of publicity. Smart then became embroiled in a similar public squabble with

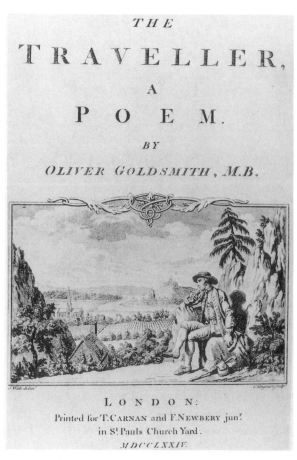

Title page for the first book to appear under Goldsmith's name

the critic John Hill, whom he lampooned in *The Hilliad* (1753).

In 1752 Smart married Newbery's stepdaughter, Anna Maria. Smart suffered bouts of insanity, and his father-in-law had him committed to St. Luke's Hospital in 1757 and later to a private asylum. Newbery continued to publish Smart's works and to supply him with loans and literary work.

He was equally generous in advancing money to Johnson and Goldsmith. In the summer of 1762, when Goldsmith faced arrest for debts to his landlady, he summoned Johnson for help. Johnson discovered that Goldsmith had enormous liabilities and only one unrealized asset: the uncompleted manuscript for *The Vicar of Wakefield* (1766). Johnson offered it to Newbery, who was reluctant to take it (he rarely published novels) but bought a one-third share for twenty pounds – the remaining shares were later bought by Benjamin Collins and William Strahan. That Christmas, to allow him to write undistracted, Newbery put Goldsmith up at Canonbury Tower in Islington, paying his room

and board and charging the costs to his account, which was always in arrears. Newbery paid Goldsmith thirty pounds for writing introductions to Richard Brookes's *New and Accurate System of Natural History* (1763), forty-two pounds for a two-volume children's *History of England* (1764), twenty-one pounds for *The Traveller* (1764) – the first book actually published under Goldsmith's name – and sixty guineas for *A Survey of Experimental Philosophy* (the earliest surviving edition of which is dated 1776).

When *The Vicar of Wakefield* was finally published, it included a well-earned and oft-quoted tribute to Newbery. It may be found in the episode where Dr. Primrose falls deathly ill at a roadside tavern, is stranded there for three weeks, and on his recovery has no money to pay his expenses. "It is possible the anxiety from the last circumstance alone might have brought on a relapse," the character recounts, "had I not been supplied by a traveller who stopped to take a cursory sort of refreshment. This person was none other than the philanthropic publisher in St. Paul's Churchyard, who has written so many little books for children. He called himself their friend, but he was the friend of all mankind. He was no sooner alighted but he was in haste to be-gone, for he was ever on business of the utmost importance and was at the time actually compiling materials for the history of one Mr. Thomas Trip. I immediately recollected this good-natured man's red-pimpled face, for he had published for me against the Deuterogamists of the age, and from him I borrowed a few pieces to be paid at my return."

It was thoughtful of Goldsmith to employ the Newbery method of puffing books – in this case *A Pretty Book of Pictures for Little Masters and Misses; or, Tommy Trip's History of Beasts and Birds* (1752), but the author borrowed more than a few pieces: when Newbery died, Goldsmith still owed him about two hundred pounds. *The Vicar of Wakefield* would not turn a profit until its fourth edition (1770).

Nevertheless, Newbery died a wealthy man on 22 December 1767. His money had primarily come not from publishing but from the sale of Dr. James's Fever Powder and at least thirty other patent cures. He left his drug interests to his son Francis, who had been sent to Oxford and Cambridge Universities but completed degrees at neither. In partnership with Thomas Carnan, Francis also took over the book business at 65 St. Paul's Churchyard. They published variously as Newbery and Carnan, as Carnan and Newbery, or under their individual names. Together they published Hannah More's *A Search after Happiness* (1773) and *The Inflexible Captive*

224

(1774). A rise in the price of leather prompted New-bery and Carnan to experiment with a new type of binding – half green vellum and stout dark green paper boards with a paper label on the spine. It was first used in the publication of Goldsmith's *A Survey of Experimental Philosophy* (1776).

In 1770 Francis earned a dowry of three thousand pounds by marrying Mary Raikes, sister of Robert Raikes, the owner of the *Gloucester Journal* and founder of the Sunday School movement. Carnan and Newbery quarreled, and by 1780 the latter had given up publishing for patent medicines, the profits from which allowed him to live as a prosperous Sussex gentleman. The Newbery family would continue in the wholesale drug business into the twentieth century via the firm of Francis Newbery and Sons.

Carnan, whose first imprint appeared in 1750, carried on publishing at St. Paul's Churchyard until his death in 1788. He published Smart's *Hymns, for the Amusement of Children* (1771), but the bulk of his output consisted of almanacs. He published the *Ladies Complete Pocket-Book* (beginning in 1750); *Goldsmith's Almanack, Poor Robin's Almanack, Rider's Almanack, Vincent Wing's Sheet Almanack, Baldwin's Daily Journal,* and his own version of Francis Moore's popular *Vox Stellarum* (all beginning in 1776); and *Baldwin's Daily Journal* (beginning in 1776). He also put out almanacs for each of the counties of England, usually a broadsheet to hang on a wall, priced at between six and eight pence.

Carnan challenged and broke the almanac monopoly that had been enjoyed by the Stationers' Company since the time of James I. The monopoly was worth two thousand pounds a year in clear profit to the company, which secured an injunction against him on 25 November 1773. On 4 February 1774 Carnan replied that King James had no right to grant the monopoly. His case was strengthened on 22 February, when the House of Lords ruled against the notion of perpetual copyright, and on 29 May 1775 the Court of Common Pleas upheld him. The company's almanac sales were halved, from 544,000 in 1775 to 268,000 in 1777; by 1781 Carnan was selling more than 100,000 a year. His almanacs were more accurate, better printed, and far better advertised than the Stationers', and the competition forced them to improve their product. The company tried and failed to restore their monopoly by act of Parliament, but in 1781 they succeeded in doubling the stamp tax on sheet almanacs, which seriously cut Carnan's profits and forced smaller publishers out of the field. After Carnan's death the Stationers bought his almanacs from Francis Newbery

and Anna Maria Smart for fifteen hundred pounds and halted their publication.

Francis Power, the son of John Newbery's daughter Mary and Michael Power, published books from St. Paul's Churchyard until 1793, when he became a wine merchant. Power published the earliest surviving copy of *Mother Goose's Melody* (1791), though it was advertised in 1780 and had been dated as far back as 1765. In any case, it was one of the first Mother Goose books in English and a model for many later British and American editions.

In addition to his son Francis, John Newbery had an older nephew named Francis Newbery, whom he set up in the publishing business in 1765 at the Crown at 15 Paternoster Row. It was he, together with Benjamin Collins, who published *The Vicar of Wakefield,* though Francis was clearly acting for his uncle. In 1768 he moved to 20 Ludgate Street; the address was also given as "The Corner of St. Paul's Church Yard" and "No. 20 St. Paul's Church Yard." He probably owned a share of *The Gentleman's Magazine.* An increasingly hostile rivalry developed between his firm and Carnan and Newbery, with each disparaging the other's books in advertisements. To compete with Carnan's *Ladies Complete Pocket-Book,* Francis Newbery published *Newbery's Ladies Pocket-Book* beginning in 1772.

In 1771–1772 Goldsmith, still in debt to John Newbery's estate, secured from Francis the nephew a further advance of two hundred to three hundred pounds to write a novel. He never produced an acceptable novel, but he persuaded Francis to accept instead the rights to *She Stoops to Conquer* (1773), which sold four thousand copies in three days and earned three hundred pounds more than the advance amount.

After Francis's death in 1780, his firm was carried on by his widow, Elizabeth. Even after she remarried, she continued to use the Newbery name as an imprint: it was a selling point, valuable enough to be pirated by others. Approximately 520 books were published by Elizabeth, the majority of them for children. She often copublished with Vernor and Hood, and she ran a bookshop that sold the works of other publishers, as well. She developed a new line of educational games and puzzles, including a *New Game of Human Life* (1790), the *Royal Genealogical Pastime of the Sovereigns of England* (1792), and *A New Geographical Game Exhibiting a Complete Tour through Scotland and the Western Isles* (1792).

A fire forced the business to relocate temporarily to 37 Ludgate Street in 1786–1787. Abraham Badcock managed the firm for Elizabeth Newbery

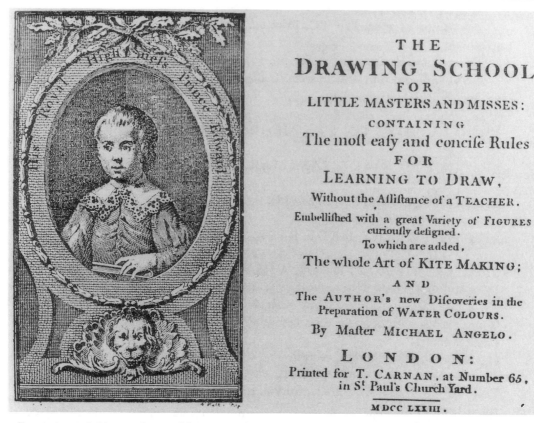

Frontispiece and title page for one of the many works produced by Richard Johnson for Thomas Carnan, who took over Newbery's business in partnership with Newbery's son Francis

until 1797, when he was succeeded by John Harris. In 1802 Elizabeth Newbery sold the business to Harris in return for an annual income of five hundred pounds, though her name appeared occasionally as an imprint up to 1810.

Harris continued the Newbery tradition of publishing fine children's books, including *The Dog of Knowledge* (1801); *Mother Bunch's Fairy Tales* (1802); *Dame Partlet's Farm* (1804); *Old Mother Hubbard and Her Dog* (1805), written and illustrated by Sarah Catherine Martin; *The Butterfly's Ball and the Grasshopper's Feast* (1807), illustrated by William Mulready and written by William Roscoe; *Marmaduke Multiply's Merry Method of Making Minor Mathematicians* (1816); *The Paths of Learning Strewed with Flowers* (1820); the first book of limericks, *The History of Sixteen Wonderful Old Women* (1820); and a collection of fairy tales, *The Court of Oberon* (1823). Harris was succeeded by Grant and Griffith, which eventually became the firm of Griffith, Farran, Okeden and Welsh. One of the partners was Charles Welsh, who in 1885 would publish (with the same company at the same address) his biography of John Newbery, *A Bookseller of the Last Century*.

Roscoe estimates that the Newbery family published a total of about twenty-four hundred books. Some of these are known only through newspaper advertisements – though, as Roscoe notes, it is not always safe to assume that all books announced in eighteenth-century newspapers were actually published.

The Newberys were loyal to their authors. For example, John Newbery published the first three editions of Johnson's *The Idler* (1761, 1762, 1767); the fourth appeared under Carnan's imprint (1783), the fifth under that of Francis Power (1790). Elizabeth Newbery published several editions of Johnson's *Lives of the Most Eminent English Poets* (1781–1801), *Prefaces to the Works of the English Poets* with Francis Newbery the nephew (1779–1781), and the *Works of Samuel Johnson* in eleven volumes with Carnan (1787). Several members of the family produced editions of *The Rambler* (1761–1789).

A fascinating record of the economics of eighteenth-century authorship is found in the account books of the Grub Street writer Richard Johnson, who did a vast variety of hackwork for about forty booksellers; about one quarter of his business was with the Newbery family. Francis Newbery Sr.

bought his *A New Roman History* (1770) for eight guineas, or just over five shillings per thousand words. From Elizabeth Newbery, Johnson received two guineas for his children's book *The Village Tatlers* (1786). His working relationship with Carnan began in 1769, when he was paid five guineas for *Letter between Master Tommy and Miss Nancy Goodwill* (1770), which was largely cribbed from Sarah Fielding's *The Governess* (1749). In 1785 Carnan filed a lawsuit against Daniel Paterson and Carington Bowles, claiming that *Paterson's British Itinerary* (1786) violated Carnan's copyright for Paterson's *A New and Accurate Description of All the Direct and Principal Cross Roads in Great Britain* (1771). Johnson took on the paperwork, drawing up documents comparing the two books, replying to the defendants' claims, preparing briefs, attending the Court of Chancery, and correcting subsequent editions of Paterson's *Roads*. For Carnan, Johnson also occasionally edited *Lloyd's Evening Post* (at a half guineas per edition); and he wrote some creditable children's books, notably *The Drawing School for Little Masters and Misses* (1773) and *Juvenile Sports and Pastimes* (1773), both published under the pseudonym Master Michel Angelo. He produced most of Elizabeth Newbery's Christmas lists for 1786 and 1787, and she paid him ten guineas for *Newbery's Familiar Letter Writer* (1788) and *Newbery's New Spelling Dictionary of the English Language* (1788). Johnson followed the Newbery tradition of using his books to plug his other books: in *The Toy-Shop* (1787) the Toyman recommends Johnson's *The Adventures of a Silver Penny* (1786), *Juvenile Rambles* (1786), *The Little Wanderers* (1786), *The Little Moralists* (1786), *The Flights of a Lady-Bird* (1786), and *The Looking-Glass for the Mind* (1787).

Before the Newbery publishing dynasty came to an end, the tone of children's literature had taken a new turn. Compared with John Newbery's list, Elizabeth Newbery's juvenile books were more expensive, more moralizing, and less entertaining. The book-buying public, frightened by the French Revolution and braced by the rise of Evangelicalism, was less receptive to the liberalism of the old Newbery volumes. Maria Edgeworth was advising parents to take up their pens and scissors and cut the nasty bits out of their children's books – Wilbur Macey Stone found just such a mutilated copy of a 1795 edition of *Little Goody Two-Shoes,* not published by the Newberys, in which the attempted rape was inked out. In 1802 Charles Lamb complained to Samuel Taylor Coleridge that "*Goody Two-Shoes* is almost out of print. Mrs. [Anna Laetitia] Barbauld's stuff has banished all the old

classics of the nursery, and the shopman and Newbery's hardly deigned to reach them off an old exploded corner of a shelf, when Mary asked for them." Lamb recalled wistfully "that beautiful interest in wild tales, which made the child a man, while all the time he suspected himself to be no bigger than a child. Science has succeeded to poetry no less in the little walks of children than with men. Is there no possibility of averting this sore evil? Think what you would have been now, if instead of being fed with Tales and old wives' fables in childhood, you had been crammed with geography and natural history." Death threats were back in fashion in children's literature: in the first part of Martha Mary Sherwood's *The Fairchild Family* (1818) children are shown, as a moral lesson, the corpse of a murderer hanging from a gibbet.

Nevertheless, Newbery books had won great popularity in America, where they were imported by Benjamin Franklin and reprinted by Hugh Gaine of New York, Mein and Fleeming of Boston, and Isaiah Thomas of Worcester. A Dutch edition of Newbery's *The Renowned History of Giles Gingerbread* (1764) was published in Amsterdam in 1781.

In England these books were fondly recalled by a generation of authors, among them Charles Knight and Robert Southey. In a 1787 issue of the Eton student magazine *The Microcosm* (possibly the first periodical published by children) young George Canning praised Newbery's volumes in Homeric terms. Leigh Hunt called him "the most illustrious of all booksellers in our boyish days, not for his great names, not for his dinners, not for his riches that we knew of, not for any other full-grown celebrity, but for certain little penny books, radiant with gold and rich with bad pictures." Actually Newbery set a high standard for children's book illustrations in his day, and Hunt conceded that "we preferred the uncouth coats, the staring blotted eyes, and round pieces of rope for hats, of our very badly-drawn contemporaries, to all the proprieties of modern embellishments."

Bibliography:

Sydney Roscoe, *John Newbery and His Successors 1740–1814: A Bibliography* (Wormley: Five Owls Press, 1973).

References:

John Alden, "Pills and Publishing: Some Notes on the English Book Trade, 1660–1715," *Library,* fifth series 7 (March 1952): 21–37;

Cyprian Blagden, "Thomas Carnan and the Almanack Monopoly," *Studies in Bibliography,* 14 (1961): 23–43;

John Dawson Carl Buck, "John Newbery and Literary Merchandising 1744–1767," dissertation, University of California, Berkeley, 1977;

Buck, "The Motives of Puffing: John Newbery's Advertisements," *Studies in Bibliography,* 30 (1977): 196–210;

F. J. Harvey Darton, *Children's Books in England,* third edition, revised by Brian Alderson (Cambridge: Cambridge University Press, 1982), pp. 120–139;

Jill E. Grey, "The Lilliputian Magazine – A Pioneering Periodical?," *Journal of Librarianship,* 2 (April 1970): 107–115;

Elizabeth E. Kent, *Goldsmith and His Booksellers* (Ithaca, N.Y.: Cornell University Press, 1933);

E. Jennifer Monaghan, "For Spiritual or Pleasurable Ends: The Portrayal of Children's Reading in Children's Books, 1670–1785," in *Reading: A Literary Feast,* edited by Malcolm P. Douglass (Claremont, Calif.: Claremont Reading Conference, 1989), pp. 80–92;

Arthur Le Blanc Newbery, *Records of the House of Newbery from 1274 to 1910* (Derby & London: Bemrose & Sons, 1911);

William Noblett, "John Newbery: Publisher Extraordinary," *History Today,* 22 (April 1972): 265–271;

Julian Roberts, "The 1765 Edition of *Goody Two-Shoes,*" *British Museum Quarterly,* 29 (Summer 1965): 67–70;

Dorothy M. Rogers, "John Newbery: His Entry into the No-Man's-Land of Children's Books," thesis, State University of New York at Geneseo, 1977;

Arthur Sherbo, *Christopher Smart: Scholar of the University* (East Lansing: Michigan State University Press, 1967);

Wilbur Macey Stone, "The History of Little Goody Two-Shoes," *Proceedings of the American Antiquarian Society,* 49 (October 1939): 333–370;

Mary F. Thwaite, *From Primer to Pleasure in Reading* (London: Library Association, 1972);

Thwaite, Introduction to *A Little Pretty Pocket-Book* (New York: Harcourt, Brace & World, 1967);

John Rowe Townsend, *John Newbery and His Books: Trade and Plumcake for Ever, Huzza!* (Metuchen, N.J.: Scarecrow Press, 1995);

M. J. P. Weedon, "Richard Johnson and the Successors to John Newbery," *Library,* fifth series 4 (June 1949): 25–63;

Charles Welsh, *A Bookseller of the Last Century* (London: Griffith, Farran, Okeden & Welsh, 1885).

Papers:

The Free Library of Philadelphia has records of John Newbery's business dealings with Oliver Goldsmith.

– Jonathan Rose

Samuel Richardson

(*London: 1721 – 1761*)

See also the Richardson entry in *DLB 39: British Novelists, 1660–1800.*

As a writer Samuel Richardson was the progenitor of the epistolary novel. As a printer and editor he published travelogues by Daniel Defoe and Jonathan Swift, historical works by Nathanael Salmon and Thomas Birch, and a host of newspapers devoted to the promulgation of free speech and enlightenment in eighteenth-century England. Richardson also published political tracts by Philip, duke of Wharton; Francis Atterbury; and George Kelly, while promoting the works of women writers such as Sarah Fielding and Jane Collier. The wisdom in Richardson's *The Apprentice's Vade Mecum: or, Young Man's Pocket-Companion* (1733), as well as his careful attention to the artistry and precision of his craft, reveal his desire to employ his vocation as a means of effecting social, ideological, and literary change in the England of his day.

Richardson was baptized in Mackworth, Derbyshire, on 19 August 1689. His daughter Anne's correspondence suggests that he was born on 31 July; few details regarding Richardson's early life are extant, however, for he rarely shared his memories with his family and friends. For this reason, Richardson's biographers often look to his letter of 2 June 1753 to Johannes Stinstra, his Dutch translator, for information concerning his formative years. Richardson's father, Samuel Richardson Sr., traveled to London in 1667, where he was apprenticed to Thomas Turner, a joiner; he married Richardson's mother, Elizabeth, in 1682. Richardson's letter to Stinstra dates his own initial foray into the printing world to 1704, when his father urged him, "at the Age of 15 or 16," to choose a vocation after the elder Richardson proved unable to fund his son's education for the clergy. "I chose that of a printer," Richardson wrote, "tho' a stranger to it, as what I thought would gratify my Thirst after Reading." On 1 July 1706, according to Stationers' Company records, he began his apprenticeship with John Wilde, a printer whose specialties included almanacs and works of popular fiction.

In his letter to Stinstra, Richardson recalls his tenure under Wilde as a "diligent Seven Years . . . to a Master who grudged every Hour to me, that tended not to his Profit, even of those Times of Leisure and Diversion, which the Refractoriness of my Fellow-Servants *obliged* him to allow them, and were usually allowed by other Masters to their Apprentices. I stole from the Hours of Rest and Relaxation, my Reading Times for Improvement of my Mind." His apprenticeship expired on 2 July 1713, and less than two years later, on 13 June 1715, he became a freeman of the Stationers' Company and a citizen of London. During this period Richardson worked as an "Overseer of a Printing-House" and as a compositor. "But *that* failing, I began for myself, married, and pursued Business with an Assiduity that, perhaps, has few Examples."

In the early 1720s Richardson's life begins to emerge from the shadows of what biographers refer to as his "lost years." By early 1721 Richardson was assisting the widow of John Leake with her printing business, and on her death in April he inherited a small legacy. He purchased Leake's printing business later that year and shortly thereafter printed his first volume, Jonathan Smedley's *Poems on Several Occasions.* On 23 November he married Martha Wilde, the daughter of his former master, and he rapidly became a prosperous tradesman. He was admitted to the livery of the Stationers' Company in 1722.

The London booksellers who controlled the printing trade of the day operated in much the same manner as twentieth-century publishers – purchasing copyrights from authors, paying printing costs, distributing books, and reaping the profits from their sale. In his correspondence with Stinstra, Richardson expresses pride regarding his collegial association with the booksellers, as well as his independence from them: "Some of them even thought fit to seek me rather than I them, with writing Indexes, Prefaces, and sometimes, abridging, compiling, and giving my Opinion of Pieces offered them." Richardson did not confine himself to printing for booksellers, often printing for individual authors, on government contracts, for periodicals, and by subscription.

Richardson's interest in politics especially marks his early years as printer. He printed works

Samuel Richardson; portrait by Joseph Highmore, circa 1754 (Stationers' Hall, London)

for several Tory authors during this period, including Atterbury, Kelly, the duke of Wharton, and Archibald Hutcheson. For participating in the Jacobite plot of 1722 – an alleged attempt to seize important public buildings in London and kidnap George I – Atterbury was banished for treason and Kelly was imprisoned in the Tower. Shortly after Atterbury's banishment, Richardson printed an edition of Atterbury's *Maxims, Reflections and Observations* (1723), apparently without the author's knowledge or consent. The first subscription edition Richardson is known to have printed is the translation of Michel de Castelnau's *Mémoires* (1724) composed by Kelly while in the Tower. Richardson printed in 1723 the duke of Wharton's *True Briton,* a periodical harshly critical of the government of Robert Walpole. The title page of the magazine listed "T. Payne" as the printer, and following Thomas Payne's arrest for sedition later that year Richard-

son posted a sizable portion of the printer's bond. In 1728 the notorious bookseller Edmund Curll attempted to avoid prosecution for obscenity by naming Richardson as the author of an essay critical of George I, George II, and Walpole that appeared in the 24 August 1728 *Mist's Weekly Journal.*

Along with such politically charged works Richardson also produced in the 1720s several books of significant literary import, including the works of Sir Philip Sidney (1724–1726), an abridged edition of Jonathan Swift's *Gulliver's Travels* (1727), Richard Savage's *The Wanderer* (1729), and James Thomson's *Britannia* (1729). He also published several volumes by Defoe, including *A Tour thro' the Whole Island of Great Britain* (1724–1725), *A New Voyage round the World* (1725), *A New Family Instructor* (1727), and *Religious Courtship* (1729). Richardson continued to publish subscription works, including Nathanael Salmon's *The History of Hert-*

230

fordshire (1728) and *A New Survey of Great Britain* (1728–1730). Richardson also printed a variety of periodicals, including Aaron Hill and William Bond's biweekly *The Plain Dealer,* which ran from 23 March 1724 through 7 May 1725.

On 11 April 1727 the members of the Stationers' Company elected him to the office of renter warden, the principal duty of which was the collection of dues. On 2 February 1731 he purchased a £40 yeoman's share in the Stationers' Company, followed by similar acquisitions in 1736 and 1746, and culminating in his 1751 purchase of an assistant's share for £320. While these figures reflect Richardson's escalating prosperity, the growing number of his apprentices provides an additional indicator of his success as a printer: in his incipient years as a printer Richardson kept three apprentices, but by the 1740s he maintained as many as five.

A broadside titled *Rules and Orders to Be Observed by the Members of This Chapel* affords a rare window into Richardson's printing establishment. Dated 30 August 1734, the broadside includes the signatures of twenty compositors and pressmen – a fairly large number during that era of the English printing trade – and lists a variety of fines for such offenses as fighting, swearing, and insobriety. The appearance during the late 1720s and early 1730s of advertisements for volumes printed at Richardson's press further underscores his success as a printer. His workmanship attracted the attention of such publishing luminaries as Arthur Bettesworth, John Osborn, Thomas Longman, Charles Rivington, and George Strahan.

Richardson's printing activities extended to the popular press through his association with the *Daily Journal* in the mid 1730s. During that era printers had proprietary control over the newspapers they printed and were responsible for adhering to licensing, libel, and stamp laws. In 1735 the paper expressed support for Matthew Tindal, a suspected deist and the author of the much-maligned "Philosopher's Prayer," and included several advertisements for the volume in which Tindal's prayer was printed, as well as letters written in defense of the prayer. The *Grub-Street Journal* criticized the *Daily Journal* for attacking priests and supporting Tindal, and even another of Richardson's periodicals, the *Weekly Miscellany,* denounced Tindal. Following the scandal the popularity of the *Daily Journal* subsided dramatically, and the newspaper ceased publication on 15 January 1737.

Richardson fathered six children with his first wife, Martha, all of whom died in infancy or as tod-

THE

APPRENTICE's

VADE MECUM:

O R,

Young Man's Pocket-Companion.

In THREE PARTS.

PART I. Containing useful Comments and Observations on the Covenants entered into between Master and Servant, by way of *Indenture* ; wherein that wise Obligation is considered Article by Article. With some occasional Remarks on *Play-houses* ; and particularly on one lately erected.

PART II Containing general Rules and Directions for a young Man's Behaviour in his Apprenticeship. Familiarly addres'd to the Youth himself.

PART III. Some brief Cautions to a young Man against the Scepticism and Infidelity of the present Age, which insnare the Minds, and debauch the Morals of the Youth of this Kingdom: Wherein the essential Principles of Christianity are laid down and vindicated in so intelligent and forcible a Manner, as may serve for a Preservative against the contagious Infidelity of the present Age, and enable a young Man to give a *Reason* for his *Faith.*

Addressed to the Right Worshipful the Chamberlain of *London.*

The Whole calculated for the mutual Ease and Benefit both of Master and Servant ; and recommended to the serious Consideration of all Parents, *&c.* who have Children that they design to put out Apprentice.

LONDON:

Printed for J ROBERTS in *Warwick-Lane* ; and Sold by J. LEAKE at *Bath.* 1734.

Title page for the first complete work known to have been written by Richardson. It was printed on his press.

dlers; Martha Richardson died on 23 January 1731. On 3 February 1733 Richardson married Elizabeth Leake, the daughter of his former employer.

The first of Richardson's known compositions, *The Apprentice's Vade Mecum,* appeared in 1733, although the title page dates the pamphlet's publication as 1734. Printed at Richardson's press, the work finds its roots in a letter the author had written two years before to his nephew, Thomas Verren Richardson who had been apprenticed to Richardson on 1 August 1732 but had died on 8 November of that year. The first part of the pamphlet features Richardson's observations regarding the apprentice's duties and his commentary on the pitfalls of gaming, fornication, and taverns. The author also devotes particular attention to the dangers of the theater: "A good Dramatick Writer, is a Character that this Age knows nothing of; and I would be glad to name the Person living who is fit to be made an Exception to this general Censure." In the second

Title page for Richardson's revision of Sir Roger L'Estrange's seventeenth-century edition of Aesop's tales. The book was printed by Richardson at the end of November 1739.

part Richardson offers "general Rules and Directions for a young man's Behaviour in his Apprenticeship," warning against foppery and self-indulgence and extolling the virtues of generosity and friendship. Richardson reminds the reader to respect the journeyman and his fellow apprentices: "And let it always be remembered, that no man is to be ill used by you, if he happens to be poor or low in the world; for, how can you tell what your own fate will be?" The volume concludes with the third part, giving additional advice about morality, faith, and other virtues lost amid the "Scepticism and Infidelity of the present Age, which insnare the Minds, and debauch the Morals of the Youth of this Kingdom."

In 1735 Richardson printed another pamphlet, titled *A Seasonable Examination of the Pleas and Pretensions of the Proprietors of, and Subscribers to, Play-Houses, Erected in Defiance of the Royal Licence.* Largely an ad-

dendum to his comments on the theater in *The Apprentice's Vade Mecum,* the treatise offers arguments for moral censorship of the theater. On 17 January 1736 a rare verse composition by Richardson appeared in *The Gentleman's Magazine.* William Bowyer Jr. and Edward Cave, two stewards for a proposed feast for London printers, had sent Richardson a poetic invitation to the gathering. Richardson composed his poem as a "humorous" response to their invitation, which he was forced to decline. The poem concludes: "So wishes he, who, pre-ingag'd, can't know / The pleasures that wou'd from your meeting flow."

Richardson supplemented his printing business in the late 1730s by printing bills and reports for the House of Commons. Although the work was time-consuming and laborious, this enterprise afforded him the opportunity to establish vital contacts on the British political scene while also allowing him to work independently of the booksellers. Richardson maintained his association with the House of Commons for the remainder of his life, printing between four and twenty-six bills per year and forging a friendship with the speaker of the House, Arthur Onslow. Onslow's influence likely led to the lucrative contract Richardson received in 1742 to print all the journals for the House of Commons. Onslow attempted to obtain a station at court for Richardson, but the printer refused to consider such an appointment.

In 1735 Richardson began the last newspaper he is known to have printed: intended to provide objective reportage of the British political scene, the *Daily Gazetteer* appeared until 1748. Richardson revised and edited the second edition of Defoe's *A Tour thro' the Whole Island of Great Britain* (1738), correcting errors and appending a useful selection of statistical information about the British Isles.

On 20 November 1739 Richardson printed a version of *Æsop's Fables* based on Sir Roger L'Estrange's popular 1692 edition. He included a preface in which he acknowledges his alterations of L'Estrange's text. He omitted 266 fables — 58 being deemed repetitive or lacking a suitable moral and 208 "rather to be deemed witty Conceits, facetious Tales, and sometimes ludicrous Stories, than instructive Apologues" — appended new morals to 95 and substantially altered 34.

In the late 1730s Richardson joined the Society for the Encouragement of Learning, a select group of scholars and patrons founded in 1736 to promote the printing of serious works that the typical London bookseller would not print. The society sponsored the publication of eleven volumes, but its inability to sell the books it printed forced it to suspend operations in early 1749. One of three printers employed by the society, Richardson published *The Negotiations of Sir Thomas Roe* (1740), the papers of the seventeenth-century British ambassador to Constantinople. Richardson prepared the volume's preface and table of contents – a laborious and exacting task, for the latter ran to nearly ninety thousand words. Richardson's textual apparatus included tables, cross-references, and editorial explanations. In a letter of 27 September 1739 Richardson's friend Aaron Hill remarked on the volume's impressive front matter: "Good God! What a Task have you had and what a comprehensive and satisfactory Abstract have you made of his matter! It is such a *Part* of his work, as a Chymical Quintessence is of a Vegetable – It increases ye Virtue by diminishing the Bulk." Despite its relentless advertisement in the London press and an enthusiastic review in the periodical *The History of the Works of the Learned* (May 1740), *The Negotiations of Sir Thomas Roe* sold poorly – perhaps because of its prohibitive price of seventeen pounds. In the 1740s Richardson was also associated with the Society of Booksellers, an organization led by Thomas Osborne that devoted itself to printing works on favorable terms to the authors. Before the society suspended operations it commissioned Richardson to print Robert James's *Medicinal Dictionary* (1743–1745).

In 1739 Richardson's friends Rivington and Osborn persuaded him to write "a little Volume of Letters, in a Common Style, on such Subjects as might be of Use to those Country Readers who were unable to indite for themselves." Richardson began composing *Letters Written to and for Particular Friends, on the Most Important Occasions,* or *Familiar Letters* in September or October 1739 and published it on 23 January 1741. In the interim Richardson composed his first novel, *Pamela; or, Virtue Rewarded,* in a mere two months. An epistolary novel, *Pamela* was published on 6 November 1740 and met with unqualified commercial success, becoming a forerunner of the modern best-seller. The novel had appeared in five editions and a French translation by October of the following year.

Richardson's next novel, commonly known as *Pamela, Part II,* appeared on 7 December 1741. Although it was a best-seller in the tradition established by *Pamela,* the sequel failed to replicate the critical success of its forebear, and was criticized for a lack of structure and banal plot. Along with his budding career as a novelist, Richardson continued his printing activities. On 1 December 1741 he was elected to the ruling body of the Stationers' Com-

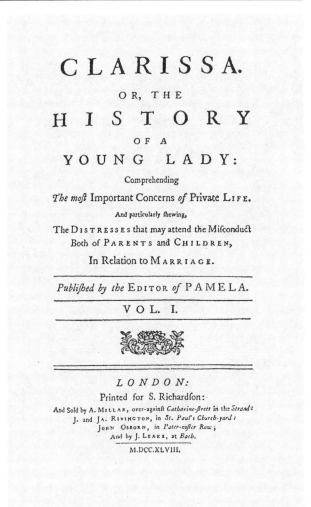

CLARISSA.
OR, THE
HISTORY
OF A
YOUNG LADY:
Comprehending
The *most* Important Concerns of Private L I F E.
And particularly shewing,
The D I S T R E S S E S that may attend the Misconduct
Both of P A R E N T S and C H I L D R E N,
In Relation to M A R R I A G E.

Published by the E D I T O R *of* P A M E L A.
VOL. I.

LONDON:
Printed for S. Richardson:
And Sold by A. M I L L A R, over-against *Catharine-street* in the *Strand:*
J. and J A. R I V I N G T O N, in *St. Paul's Church-yard:*
J O H N O S B O R N, in *Pater-noster Row;*
And by J. L E A K E, at *Bath.*
M.DCC.XLVIII.

Title page for the first volume of the longest novel in English, written and published by Richardson

pany, the Court of Assistants. Despite generally poor health during this period he printed James Hervey's popular *Meditations among the Tombs* (1746), George Lyttelton's *To the Memory of a Lady Lately Deceased* (1747), and Edward Young's *Night-Thoughts* (1748). In 1749 Richardson published David Hartley's *Observations on Man,* Thomas Birch's *An Historical View of the Negotiations between the Courts of England, France, and Brussels, from the Year 1592 to 1617,* and Sarah Fielding's *The Governess.*

Richardson published the first two volumes of his next novel, *Clarissa; or, The History of a Young Lady* – the longest novel in the English language at well over a million words – in December 1747. The third and fourth volumes appeared in April 1748, followed by the fifth, sixth, and seventh in December 1748. Richardson published a revised edition in 1749 and yet another revision in 1751. Richardson's next novel, *The History of Sir Charles Grandi-*

Page from Richardson's 2 June 1753 letter to his biographer Johannes Stinstra (Gemeentelijke Archiefdienst, Amsterdam)

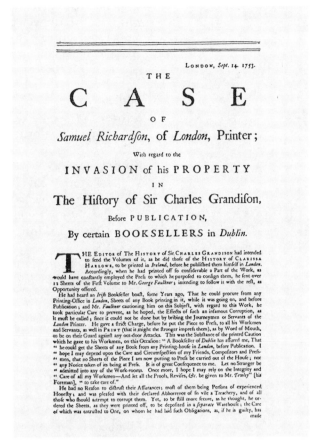

LONDON, *Sept. 14. 1753.*

THE

CASE

OF

Samuel Richardſon, of London, Printer;

With regard to the

INVASION of his PROPERTY

IN

The Hiſtory of Sir Charles Grandiſon,

Before PUBLICATION,

By certain BOOKSELLERS in *Dublin.*

*First page of one of the two pamphlets Richardson wrote and
printed to protest the piracy of one of his novels by
Irish publishers*

son (1753–1754), was pirated in 1753 by Irish publishers. In September 1753 Richardson published and distributed a statement of his grievances, *The Case of Samuel Richardson of London, Printer; with Regard to the Invasion of His Property in The History of Sir Charles Grandison, by Publication, by Certain Booksellers in Dublin,* and in February 1754 he published *An Address to the Public,* in which he accuses his Irish bookseller, George Faulkner, of pirating the work. Richardson published the first four volumes of *The History of Sir Charles Grandison* in November 1753, the fifth and sixth volumes in December 1753, and the seventh in March 1754. Johnson offered unqualified praise for the book, writing to Richardson in the spring of 1753: "To wish you to go on as you have begun would to many be a very kind wish, but you, Sir, have beyond all other men the art of improving on yourself."

Richardson continued to pursue his printing concerns, publishing Jane Collier's *An Essay on the Art of Ingeniously Tormenting* (1753) and Sarah Fielding's *Lives of Cleopatra and Octavia* (1757) and

The History of the Countess of Dellwyn (1759). Richardson probably assisted in the publication of the English translation of Marguerite de Lussan's *Vie de Louis Balbe-Berton de Crillon* (1760) and the revision of the manuscript for Anna Meades's *The History of Sir William Harrington* (1771), published more than a decade after the printer's death. Richardson also assisted Young with his manuscript for *The Centaur Not Fabulous* (1754) and with his *Conjectures on Original Composition in a Letter to the Author of Sir Charles Grandison* (1759), a precursor of Romantic criticism in which, following Richardson's advice, Young questions the originality of Alexander Pope.

In September 1752 Richardson's printing shop, which was located beneath his living quarters, caught fire, requiring him to construct a new facility at a considerable cost. Richardson was honored for his printing achievements by being made a master of the Stationers' Company in 1754. By the end of the following year the author relinquished any notions of writing additional novels; in a letter of 21 October 1755 Richardson wrote to Lady Dorothy

THE

HISTORY

O F

Sir CHARLES GRANDISON.

I N A

SERIES of LETTERS

Publifhed from the ORIGINALS,

By the Editor of PAMELA and CLARISSA.

In SEVEN VOLUMES.

VOL. I.

LONDON:

Printed for S. Richardfon ;

And Sold by C. HITCH and L. HAWES, in *Pater-nofter Row* ,
By. J. and J. RIVINGTON, in *St. Paul's Church-Yard* ;
By ANDREW MILLAR, in the *Strand* ;
By R. and J. DODSLEY, in *Pall-Mall* ;
And by J. LEAKE, at *Bath* ;

M.DCC.LIV.

Title page for Richardson's edition of his 1754 novel

Bradshaigh: "I have, or seem to have, an unconquerable Aversion to the Pen! My Imagination on which you kindly compliment me, seems entirely quenched."

Illness plagued Richardson for the remainder of his life, and in 1760 "Paralytic Fits" forced him to suspend the sizable personal correspondence from which he had derived much pleasure. He suffered a stroke on 28 June 1761 and died on 4 July, leaving an estate of about fourteen thousand pounds – a testament to his success as printer and novelist.

Letters:

Selected Letters of Samuel Richardson, edited by John Carroll (Oxford: Clarendon Press, 1964).

Bibliographies:

William Merritt Sale Jr., *Samuel Richardson: A Bibliographical Record of His Literary Career with Historical Notes* (New Haven: Yale University Press, 1936; London: Oxford University Press, 1936);

Richard Gordon Hannaford, *Samuel Richardson: An Annotated Bibliography of Critical Studies* (New York: Garland, 1980).

Biography:

T. C. Duncan Eaves and Ben D. Kimpel, *Samuel Richardson: A Biography* (Oxford: Clarendon Press, 1971).

References:

Elizabeth Bergen Brophy, *Samuel Richardson: The Triumph of Craft* (Knoxville: University of Tennessee Press, 1974);

Carol Houlihan Flynn, *Samuel Richardson: A Man of Letters* (Princeton: Princeton University Press, 1982);

William Merritt Sale Jr., *Samuel Richardson: Master Printer* (Ithaca, N.Y.: Cornell University Press, 1950).

– Kenneth Womack

Charles Rivington
(London: 1711 – 1742)

John Rivington
(London: 1742 – 1745; 1756 – 1775)

John and James Rivington
(London: 1745 – 1756)

John Rivington and Sons
(London: 1775 – 1792)

F. and C. Rivington
(London: 1792 – 1810)

F., C., and J. Rivington
(London: 1810 – 1822)

C. and J. Rivington
(London: 1822 – 1827)

C., J., G., and F. Rivington
(London: 1827 – 1831)

J., G., and F. Rivington
(London: 1831 – 1836)

J., G., F., and J. Rivington
(London: 1836 – 1841)

G., F., and J. Rivington
(London: 1841 – 1842)

F. and J. Rivington
(London: 1842 – 1859)

J. and F. H. Rivington
(London: 1859 – 1866)

F. H. and S. Rivington
(London: 1867 – 1889)

F. H. Rivington
(London: 1890)

See also the James Rivington entry in *DLB 43: American Newspaper Journalists, 1690-1872.*

The firm of Rivington, an important London publishing house throughout the eighteenth and nineteenth centuries, remained in family hands from 1711 to 1890. While the Rivingtons were known in the eighteenth century primarily as theological publishers and in the nineteenth as both theological and educational publishers, the first two generations in the bookselling business – Charles and his sons John and James – were involved in the publication of significant literary works, among which were Samuel Richardson's *Pamela, or Virtue Rewarded* (1740) and Tobias Smollett's *Complete History of England* (1758). The family was influential in the London book trade and was closely connected with the Stationers' Company: four of the masters of the company, as well as the clerks from 1800 to 1956, were Rivingtons.

Charles Rivington, the founder of the Rivington publishing house, was baptized on 15 November 1688 at Chesterfield, in Derbyshire. His father, Thurston, was a butcher, and the family was involved in the leather trade. Charles was apprenticed in 1703 to Emanuel Matthews, a bookbinder in Paternoster Row, London. On 6 October 1707 he was turned over to the bookseller Awnsham Churchill. Rivington was freed 4 September 1710 and in 1711 purchased the premises and trade of the recently deceased Richard Chiswell, an eminent London bookseller who had been in business at the Rose and Crown, St. Paul's Churchyard, since 1663 and, like Churchill, had become an important member of the Wholesaling Conger. Charles Rivington's descendants Christopher and James

Rivington have speculated about the source of the young bookseller's capital for such a purchase: "It is possible that, with the recent death of his elder brother Thurston in 1710, Charles was now able, as the eldest son, to call upon greater financial backing from his family in Derbyshire. We do not know how much Rivington had to pay; however, thirteen years later, Thomas Longman had to pay over £2000 for a well established business."

In 1714 Rivington moved his shop to the north side of St. Paul's Churchyard and continued business under the sign of the Bible and Crown (later designated number 62 St. Paul's Churchyard). These premises remained in the Rivingtons' possession until 1853.

From 1716 to 1736 Charles Rivington's name appeared on the imprints of an average of ten titles per year, about half of which he published jointly with other booksellers. After 1730 many of these were theological works, such as the second edition of John Veneer's *An Exposition on the Thirty-Nine Articles of the Church of England* (1734), and sermons commissioned by their authors. Rivington, however, was clearly not rigid in his support of the established church, for he also published works for John Wesley and George Whitfield, leaders of the Methodist movement. In 1735 he brought out Wesley's edition of Thomas à Kempis's *The Imitation of Christ,* described by Septimus Rivington in 1919 as "a book that has, after the Bible, gone through more editions than any other."

Charles Rivington became the leading theological bookseller in London, but he did not restrict himself to religious works. Trade dictionaries were profitable, and in a four-year span he published John Nott's *Cook's and Confectioner's Dictionary* (1723),

Charles Rivington, founder of the Rivington firm

Philip Miller's *The Gardeners and Florists Dictionary* (1724), Richard Neve's *The City and Country Purchaser, and Builder's Dictionary* (1726), and N. B. Philippos's *The Farrier's and Horseman's Dictionary* (1726). In 1725 and 1727 Rivington published Daniel Defoe's popular two-volume *The Complete English Tradesman.*

Rivington also published fiction. He was a member of the Castle Conger, one of the two most important congers of the 1720s. Norma Hodgson and Cyprian Blagden define a conger of this period as "a little joint-stock company with about ten shareholders, who print their books together for their mutual, and normally equal, advantage and publish their names at the foot of their title-pages and in their advertisements." The Castle Conger established ties with Penelope Aubin, whose fiction influenced the works of Richardson and the Abbé Prévost. The title page of Aubin's *Life of Madam de Beaumont, a French Lady* (1721) carries the names of the members of the Castle Conger: Elizabeth Bell

(widow of Andrew Bell), John Darby, Arthur Bettesworth, Francis Fayram, John Pemberton, John Hooke, Charles Rivington, Francis Clay, Jeremiah Batley, and Edward Symon; the order of their names was determined by their seniority as freemen of the Stationers' Company. During the 1720s Rivington's name, along with those of the other conger members, appeared on the title pages of six of Aubin's novels and three of her translations.

Rivington's connection with Richardson dates back at least to 1724, when both men were involved in the publication of the second edition of Nathan Bailey's *Universal Etymological English Dictionary:* Richardson was one of its two printers, and the Castle Conger owned the property. Christopher and James Rivington have traced some thirty titles published by Rivington and printed by Richardson in the 1730s. Richardson continued to print for the Rivington family at least until 1753.

In 1739 Rivington and John Osborn Sr. urged Richardson to write a book of familiar letters to

The sign of the Bible and Crown, under which the Rivington firm did business from 1714 until 1890

serve as models for the use of country people. As he composed letters intended "to instruct handsome Girls, who were obliged to go out to Service," Richardson remembered a story of a servant girl who married her master; soon he interrupted his work on *Letters Written to and for Particular Friends, on the Most Important Occasions* (1741) and turned his attention to writing a novel. *Pamela,* published late in 1740 but dated 1741 on the title page, was an instant success, and went through four more editions in 1741.

Rivington died on 22 February 1742; Richardson, one of the executors of his will, wrote Aaron Hill on 24 September that he had suffered "A dreadful [nervous affliction], partly occasioned by the shock of Mr. Rivington's sudden death." Charles and Eleanor Pease Rivington had thirteen children, eight of whom were sons. John, James, and Charles Jr., the three sons who outlived their father, all entered the book trade. John was twenty-two at the time of his father's death; James was eighteen. John had been apprenticed to his father on 6 May 1735; James on 4 September 1739. John and James Rivington each inherited half of the bookselling business from their father. John was freed by patrimony on 1 June 1742, and on 6 July, James was turned over to him as an apprentice. Until James turned twenty-one, John managed their affairs, for which duty he was paid twenty pounds a year out of James's share. James was freed by patrimony on 3 December 1745; the two brothers were then in formal partnership until 1756. Charles Jr., who had been born in 1731, was apprenticed to Richardson on 9 August 1746; he was freed on 4 September 1753 and opened his own printing office in Staining (or Steyning) Lane. He took over some of the printing Richardson had been doing for John and James Rivington.

Given the different temperaments of John and James, the ten years they were partners were not tranquil ones, and although they shared equally in the literary property acquired by their father, they also went their separate ways in cultivating and conducting business relationships. John was the eminently respectable theological bookseller; according to Septimus Rivington, he was "of dignified and gentlemanly address, going with gold-headed cane and nosegay twice a day to service at St. Paul's . . . and breakfasting every alternate Monday with Archbishop Secker at Lambeth." In his orthodoxy John differed significantly from his father: he forced Wesley and Whitfield to change booksellers, and in 1752 he published Richard Hurd's sermon *The Mischiefs of Enthusiasm and Bigotry.* Around 1760 he was appointed publisher to the Society for the Promotion of Christian Knowledge. He was also a director of the Amiable Society and the Union Fire Office and a governor of Christ's Hospital.

While John quietly built on his father's established business, following the conventions of the London trade, James took risks and looked farther afield in hopes of turning a large profit in a short time. His most ambitious aim was to corner the American book market by underselling the members of the London trade who had established themselves as suppliers of books for American booksellers. Both John and James Rivington were active in the Stationers' Company: James was renter warden in 1752; and although rather than serve as renter warden John paid a fine of £24 10s. 6d. on 25 March 1749, he eventually rose to master of the company in 1775. By that time his brothers James and Charles and his four sons were all members of the Livery.

The Bodleian Library holds a unique copy of part of Richardson's printing account with John and James Rivington during the 1750s. The document reveals that in 1750 Richardson printed the fourth edition of his *Familiar Letters* and charged the Rivingtons £6 6s., one third of the printing costs, for 1,500 copies. Charles Rivington had owned a one-third share in the work, and his sons thus each possessed a one-sixth share. Other printing jobs done by Richardson for the Rivingtons in 1750 were 750 copies of Patrick Delany's *Twenty Sermons on Social Duties* at a cost of £25 11s. 6d., 2,500 copies of the two-volume eighth edition of James Hervey's *Meditations and Contemplations* at a cost of £67 9s., and 2,000 copies of Miller's *The Gardeners Kalendar* at a cost of £31 14s. 6d.

The Rivington brothers announced their separation in the *London Evening Post* for 6 March 1756:

Charles Rivington's second shop, at 62 St. Paul's Churchyard

The Partnership between JOHN and JAMES RIVINGTON, Booksellers, being this Day dissolv'd by mutual Consent: All Persons who are indebted to the said Partnership are desir'd to pay their respective Debts to John Rivington in St. Paul's Church-yard; and all Persons having any Demands on the said Partnership, are desir'd to bring or send their Accounts to the said Shop, in order to receive Satisfaction for the same.

The Trade continues to be carried on by John Rivington, in St. Paul's Church-yard; and by James Rivington in Paternoster Row. Any Orders which they shall be favour'd with at their respective Shops, will be gratefully receiv'd and punctually executed,

By their most oblig'd, and obedient Servants,
JOHN RIVINGTON,
JAMES RIVINGTON.

Although the advertisement says that anyone who owed money to the partnership should pay John Rivington, James was claiming for himself the money owed by American booksellers. On 17 May 1757 John wrote to John Stevens of Boston, Massachusetts, who owed the firm £81 18s. 7d. for books

ordered on 4 September 1754; James had attempted to collect the payment. John warned Stevens that James's demand was illegal, for a power of attorney of 5 March 1756 prevented James from receiving such payments. He added that James had been making similar demands on other customers' accounts and closed: "I am sorry I am forced to write in this manner in relation to my Brother, but in Justice to my own family I am obliged to do it."

Immediately beneath the announcement in the *London Evening Post* dissolving the partnership, James Rivington had inserted a second notice:

JAMES RIVINGTON, *from St. Paul's Church-yard*, AND JAMES FLETCHER, jun. *from Oxford*, BOOKSELLERS, Beg Leave to acquaint their Friends, THAT they have enter'd into Partnership, and open'd a Shop in Pater-noster Row, near Cheapside; Where their Favours will be most gratefully received.

James Fletcher Jr. was the son of an Oxford bookseller with whom the Rivingtons had been doing business; in 1755 the Rivingtons and James Fletcher Sr. had jointly published seven works, six of them

PAMELA:

O R,

V I R T U E Rewarded.

In a SERIES of

FAMILIAR LETTERS

F R O M A

Beautiful Young D A M S E L,
To her P A R E N T S.

Now first Published

In order to cultivate the Principles of
VIRTUE and RELIGION in the Minds of
the YOUTH of BOTH SEXES.

A Narrative which has its Foundation in TRUTH
and NATURE; and at the same time that it agree-
ably entertains, by a Variety of *curious* and *affecting*
INCIDENTS, is intirely divested of all those Images,
which, in too many Pieces calculated for Amusement
only, tend to *inflame* the Minds they should *instruct*.

In Two VOLUMES.

V O L. I.

LONDON:

Printed for C. R I V I N G T O N, in *St. Paul's Church-*
Yard; and J. O S B O R N, in *Pater-noster Row.*
M DCC XLI.

Title page for Samuel Richardson's first novel, which had its origin
in a suggestion by Rivington and John Osborn. Richardson
printed many of the works published by the Rivington firm
(Courtesy of the Lilly Library, Indiana University).

sermons preached at Oxford. James Fletcher Jr. was freed in April 1756 and remained in partnership with James Rivington at the sign of the Oxford Theatre in Paternoster Row until they were declared bankrupt in January 1760. According to the bankruptcy records, the partnership had favored Rivington from the beginning, when "it was agreed between them . . . that James Rivington was to have two thirds of the Profits arising from such Trade and . . . James Fletcher the Remaining third of the Profits[,] that the management of the Business of the shop was chiefly left to . . . James Fletcher but the Care of the Books and Cash and Raising and paying the money belonging to the . . . partnership were undertaken and conducted by . . . James Rivington."

Before forming the partnership with Fletcher, Rivington had established what was to prove a mutually profitable business relationship with Smollett. On 14 and 19 November 1751, at two sales of the books and shares of copyrights of John Osborn Sr., the Rivington brothers had made their first invest-

ments in Smollett's writings. They paid £17 for a one-eighth share in *Roderick Random* (1748), £13 15s. for a one-eighth share in Smollett's translation of Alain-René Lesage's *Gil Blas* (1749), and £28 10s. for a one-eighth share in Smollett's projected translation of Miguel de Cervantes's *Don Quixote,* which was not published until 1755. On 5 May 1753 Smollett signed an agreement with Robert Dodsley, William Strahan, and James Rivington promising to compile for them *A Compendium of Authentic and Entertaining Voyages,* a seven-volume work that was published in 1756.

Sometime in 1755, apparently at James Rivington's behest, Smollett committed himself to write *A Complete History of England,* which Rivington and Fletcher published in four quarto volumes in 1757 and 1758. It was a resounding success, and in 1758 an octavo edition began appearing in weekly sixpenny installments published by Rivington and Fletcher along with Richard Baldwin. A legend persists that Rivington devised an ingenious method for advertising the new edition, sending a package of the prospectus to every parish clerk in England with a halfcrown enclosed to have them distributed through the pews of the church; the people read the papers instead of listening to the sermon, resulting in a large demand for the work. The publishers also widely advertised the *Complete History* in the newspapers during the two years it appeared in installments. Their efforts at marketing the work paid off: on 28 September 1758 Smollett said in a letter that "the weekly sale of the History has increased to above Ten thousand," and two years later the printer William Strahan claimed that Rivington had made ten thousand pounds from the work. Smollett's biographer Lewis M. Knapp terms such a sale of a historical work "unprecedented."

Probably in 1759 Smollett contracted with Rivington for a long-term project, *The Present State of All Nations,* which was published in 1768–1769, after Rivington and Fletcher's bankruptcy, by Richard Baldwin, William Johnston, S. Crowder, and George Robinson and John Roberts. Another agreement in 1759 concerned plans for a new review-miscellany, *The British Magazine: or, Monthly Repository for Gentlemen and Ladies,* to begin in January 1760. In this case it seems likely that Smollett engaged Rivington, rather than the other way around, as the periodical was in its editor's control rather than the publishers'. Rivington and Fletcher brought in another publisher, the relatively unknown Henry Payne, to join them in the endeavor; his role in the project became prominent when Rivington and Fletcher declared bank-ruptcy on 3 January 1760.

Nineteenth- and early-twentieth-century schol-ars generally attributed the partners' insolvency to James Rivington's unsteadiness of character: he re-portedly gambled away the large profit from Smollett's *Complete History* at the Newmarket races. But James Rivington was more than an engaging scapegrace whose profligacy forced him into bank-ruptcy. According to William Strahan, Rivington engaged in disreputable business practices that so outraged Strahan that he abruptly stopped printing for the young bookseller in 1756. Strahan, who had printed for John and James Rivington since 1749 re-corded his complaints about James Rivington from 1755 to 1761 in a series of letters to David Hall, a Scots friend who had settled in Philadelphia and had become Benjamin Franklin's printing partner in 1748. In 1755 Strahan had learned from Hall that Rivington, still in partnership with his brother John, was trying to make inroads in the American book trade by underselling established London booksell-ers such as Strahan; John Rivington, however, was refusing to cooperate with his brother's scheme and would not ship books at the cheap prices James had been advertising. Hall had pledged to maintain Strahan as his London contact, and Strahan had cautioned him that "such Terms as Mr. Rivington's were never heard of till now." He had advised Hall to wait and see how long Rivington could afford to do American business at a loss.

A year later James Rivington had gone after Strahan's business in Charleston, in the Carolina colony. In September 1756 Strahan told Hall how he had retaliated: "I immediately determined, both for this Reason and for his general indifferent Char-acter, to having nothing further to do with him, and therefore refused even to print a large piece of Work for him (a new History of England in 3 vol. 4to. by Dr. Smollet)." Strahan had printed about two-thirds of the first volume of Smollett's *Complete History* when he halted work. Rivington had most inopportunely found himself in need of a new printer, but he had not had to look far to find one: the competent manager of Strahan's printing office, Archibald Hamilton Sr., had realized that Smollett's *Complete History* was a potentially lucrative job and, according to Strahan, "thought it a good Opportu-nity to begin for himself." Thus, Hamilton had set up his own shop, printing Smollett's *Complete History* and later the *British Magazine* for James Rivington.

In 1758 Strahan had written Hall that James Rivington was taking "the most low, dirty and un-warrantable Methods to supplant his Neighbours

Title page for a work by Daniel Defoe (Courtesy of the Lilly Library, Indiana University)

(his own Brother not excepted)." For two years James Rivington had been exporting books to America, some at lower prices than Strahan knew he must have paid for them in London, yet he did not appear to be losing money. Strahan explained Rivington's strategy: "About a year ago, under Pre-tence of Want of Money, he made a Sale of all his Copies [copyright shares], some of which, I, among others, purchased. His real Drift we could not then dive into, but it since appears, that he is determined to pirate every good Book in the Trade." Only the most influential members of the London trade owned copyrights or, more commonly, shares of copyrights, and they guarded their properties jeal-ously. The splitting-up of copyright shares among several partners helped insure what Terry Belanger has termed "the safeguarding of *de facto* perpetual copyright and the discouragement of piracy": sup-posedly a pirate would be afraid to infringe on a

John and James Rivington, who succeeded their father as heads of the firm

copyright held by many powerful booksellers. When a copyright-owning bookseller went out of business or died, his copies would be offered for sale at an auction to which only the most prominent members of the trade would be invited. Thus, a core of booksellers was able to maintain control of the London trade. Among this elite group were the Rivingtons, who had inherited their positions, and Strahan, who, as an important printer, had bought his way in. The sale of James Rivington's "Books in Quires, and Copies" had been held on 10 November 1757 and had raised between £1,300 and £1,400. While Rivington offered small fractional shares in such well-known works as Richardson's *Pamela,* Smollett's *Roderick Random* (1748), and Defoe's *Robinson Crusoe* (1719) the major proceeds of the auction came from Hervey's *Meditations and Contemplations,* an abridgment of Miller's *Gardeners Dictionary,* and Miller's *Figures of the Most Beautiful, Useful and Uncommon Plants Described in the Gardeners Dictionary* (1760). Rivington offered each of these in seven lots of one-sixteenth share per lot, reserving a one-sixteenth share of each title to himself. The sale of these three titles alone brought James Rivington £1,078. By the summer of 1758 Rivington had set up a system for reprinting the property of many of the most important London booksellers without their consent. In March 1759 Strahan wrote Hall

that titles Rivington had pirated included Bailey's *Universal Dictionary* and Hervey's *Meditations and Contemplations.* He declared that "separate Prosecutions will be commenced against him; so that it [is] not unlikely he will in the End lose as much by this dirty and scandalous Dealing as he once thought to get by it."

Strahan's letters, then, indicate that it was as much the injunctions against Rivington and the losses he sustained in drastically underselling his competitors in America as it was his gambling proclivities that forced Rivington and Fletcher into bankruptcy early in 1760. Strahan must have felt more than a little satisfaction in dispatching the news to Hall on 7 January: "This is to acquaint you that Mr. James Rivington broke last week for £20,000 or rather £30,000. . . . Several Booksellers are great Sufferers, many Printers very deep, and four or five Bookbinders quite ruined. . . . Riv. will hardly pay 10s. in the pound." The catalogue of the bankruptcy auction on 3 April 1760 indicates that James Rivington owned copyrights or shares of copyrights in some three hundred titles; the sale brought in more than £3,500, an impressive figure for a trade-sale auction. Much of the property had been inherited or purchased before Rivington's sale in 1757.

James Fletcher Jr. was able to return to business in July 1761; aided by his father he opened a

Francis Hansard Rivington, the last of the family to head the firm

shop in St. Paul's Churchyard and recommenced publishing the *British Magazine*. But the irrepressible James Rivington had other plans. Less than a week after the bankruptcy sale, Strahan wrote that Rivington intended to set up business in New York, and in June 1760 he added that Rivington was using his wife's annuity of £300 a year to obtain credit for a cargo of books worth more than £3,000 that he planned to take with him; Strahan noted wryly that Rivington "propose[d] to Serve all America with that Commodity." In September 1760 Rivington and his wife immigrated to the colonies. He established himself in the American book trade, enjoyed a checkered career, and died in New York on 4 July 1802.

After 1756 the Rivington family firm continued to flourish under John Rivington's direction. In 1757 John brought into the firm two of his sons: Francis, born in 1745, and Charles, born in 1754. Probably because they were minors, John Riv-

ington's name appeared alone on imprints for some years. Septimus Rivington reports that "in 1760 the value of the shares in trade books held by John Rivington was £3,906; in 1761, £3,909; in 1762, £3,636; and in 1772, £5,324." Miller's *Gardeners Dictionary* continued to be among the most valuable titles. In 1772 Rivington held a one-eighth share, worth £60, in the eight-volume duodecimo edition (1751) of Richardson's *Clarissa* (1747–1748). He also owned a one-sixth share in the *London Magazine,* valued at £200; a one-fifteenth share in the *London Evening Post,* valued at £100; and a one-tenth share in the *Public Advertiser,* valued at £400. Rivington owned shares in many more works, but the account book that Septimus Rivington described has apparently been lost, and it is not easy to determine from perusal of title pages whether Rivington held shares in the copyrights. For example, the imprint of the two-volume *Histories of Some of the Penitents in the*

The Rivington offices at 34 King Street, Covent Garden

Magdalen-House, published anonymously in 1760, reads: "Printed for John Rivington and J. Dodsley," but Rivington and Dodsley did not own any of the property. Richardson, who printed the book at the request of Lady Barbara Montagu, the author, wrote to her: "I put Mr. Rivington's and Mr. Dodsley's Names to the Title Pages as your Ladiship left that to me. The former will obey all the Commands that shall be transmitted to him. It is best that the Account should pass thro' one Hand." In this not-uncommon situation Rivington and Dodsley acted simply as publishers.

Francis Rivington was freed by patrimony on 5 August 1766, Charles on 7 November 1775.

Around 1775 the imprint changed to John Rivington and Sons. John Rivington died on 17 January 1792; in a codicil to his will dated 13 January he left two mourning rings to his brother James and his wife in New York. Beyond this suggestion of amicable relations, it is not known on what terms the two brothers stood after 1760.

Immediately following John's death the imprint of the firm became F. & C. Rivington as Francis and Charles carried on their father's business. In 1810 they brought in Francis's eldest son, John, and continued as F., C., and J. Rivington. Francis was master of the Stationers' Company in 1805, Charles in 1819. Francis Rivington died in 1822. George and Francis, Charles's sons, were brought into the business in 1827. Charles died in 1831.

During the first half of the nineteenth century, Rivington books were primarily theological. One publication of literary note was the first complete edition of Edmund Burke's works (1853) in eight volumes, published by F. and J. Rivington and edited by Francis. The Rivingtons were publishers for John Henry Newman and were caught up in the controversy surrounding the Oxford Movement in the early 1840s. By the 1860s books of sermons were no longer popular because newspapers had begun to report sermons, and it was much cheaper to buy newspapers than books. In 1867 Septimus Rivington joined his elder brother Francis Hansard Rivington in partnership. Sons of Francis, who had retired in 1859, they saw the firm through a period of retrenchment. Francis Hansard looked after the theological side, and Septimus opened up a new area of publishing for the firm, the "Secondary, Public, and Private School educational line," which flourished until poor health and disagreements with his brother forced Septimus to resign in May 1889. Septimus admitted that he had turned the educational side of the business into "an almost entirely personal one," which had created serious friction between the brothers. Francis Hansard Rivington was able to hold the Rivington firm together for another year, but in 1890 he sold the business to Longmans. In 1889 Septimus Rivington had become senior partner in Percival and Company, which was renamed Rivington, Percival and Company in 1893 and Rivington and Company in 1897. Although that firm survived until 1963, the sale to Longmans in 1890 had brought to a close the business that had been in the Rivington family for 179 years.

References:

Terry Belanger, "Booksellers' Trade Sales, 1718–1768," *Library,* fifth series 30 (December 1975): 281–302;

J. A. Cochrane, *Dr. Johnson's Printer: The Life of William Strahan* (Cambridge, Mass.: Harvard University Press, 1964);

T. C. Duncan Eaves and Ben D. Kimpel, *Samuel Richardson: A Biography* (Oxford: Clarendon Press, 1971);

Barbara Laning Fitzpatrick, "The Text of Tobias Smollett's *Life and Adventures of Sir Launcelot Greaves*, the First Serialized Novel," dissertation, Duke University, 1987;

Leroy Hewlett, "James Rivington, Loyalist Printer, Publisher, and Bookseller of the American Revolution, 1724–1802: A Biographical-Bibliographical Study," dissertation, University of Michigan, 1958;

Norma Hodgson and Cyprian Blagden, *The Notebook of Thomas Bennet and Henry Clements (1686–1719) With some aspects of Book Trade Practice*, Oxford Bibliographical Society Publications, new series 6 (Oxford: Bibliographical Society, 1953);

Lewis M. Knapp, "The Publication of Smollett's *Complete History . . .* and *Continuation*," *Library*, fourth series 16 (December 1935): 295–308;

Knapp, *Tobias Smollett: Doctor of Men and Manners* (Princeton: Princeton University Press, 1949);

Ian Maxted, *The London Book Trades 1775–1800: A Preliminary Checklist of Members* (Folkestone: Dawson, 1977);

D. F. McKenzie, ed., *Stationers' Company Apprentices 1701–1800,* Oxford Bibliographical Society Publications, new series 19 (Oxford: Bibliographical Society, 1978);

Septimus Rivington, *The Publishing Family of Rivington* (London: Rivingtons, 1919);

William M. Sale Jr., *Samuel Richardson: Master Printer,* Cornell Studies in English, 37 (Ithaca, N.Y.: Cornell University Press, 1950);

Tobias Smollett, *The Letters of Tobias Smollett, M.D.,* collected and edited by Edward S. Noyes (Cambridge: Harvard University Press, 1926).

– *Barbara Laning Fitzpatrick*

Papers:
A crucial source of information on Charles Rivington is a typescript by C. and J. Rivington, "Charles Rivington Bookseller, Publisher and Stationer 1688–1742: An Interim Note on His 300th Birthday" (1988), a photocopy of which is in the Stationers' Company Library, London. The Bodleian Library, Oxford, has "Agreement for Conger copies of Books" (MS. Eng. Misc. b. 44) and "Rivington Accounts, 1749–59" (MS. Don. c. 66, fols. 17–21). The British Library has "Booksellers' Trade Sale Catalogues, 1718–1768." The Public Record Office, London, has documents related to the bankruptcy of James Rivington and James Fletcher Jr.

James Roberts

(London: 1701 – 1754)

James Roberts, a successful master printer and prolific trade publisher, was one of the leading members of the London book trade in the first half of the eighteenth century. In his day he was known and respected throughout the trade, and his name remains familiar to students of the period for the simple reason that his well-known imprint, "Printed for J. Roberts, near the Oxford Arms in Warwick Lane," appears on more works published in the reign of George I and the early years of the reign of George II than that of any other publisher.

The year of Roberts's birth is unknown. The age he gave at the time of his marriage would put it at about 1672, while that given at the time of his death suggests 1669. His father was Robert Roberts, whose antecedents are unknown but who had been apprenticed to the printer Thomas Lock about 1655 and made free of the Stationers' Company in 1662 by another printer, Matthew Inman, who had married Lock's widow. In 1665 Robert Roberts had married Mary Hewerton; the couple had at least four children, including James and Jasper, born in 1674. Throughout these early years Robert Roberts was a senior journeyman compositor and eventually an overseer in the printing house of the widow Anne Maxwell in Stationers' Court. About 1676 he was taken into partnership, and he succeeded to the business on Maxwell's death in 1684.

Although neither James nor Jasper Roberts was formally bound to the trade, it is clear that they learned their craft in the family business before taking up their freedom in the Stationers' Company by patrimony, James in 1692 and Jasper in 1695. By the latter date the business must have been quite a large one since, in addition to his two adult sons, the elder Roberts had four apprentices, more than were strictly allowed. John Dunton claimed that the elder Roberts printed twenty books for him without a single disappointment and praised the printer for never breaking his word to a bookseller.

In November 1701 Robert and Jasper Roberts died within a week of each other, leaving Mary Roberts in nominal control of the business. The lease of the two houses in which the business was located had been in the process of routine renegotiation between the elder Roberts and the Stationers'

Company at the time of his death. The lease was granted to his widow for twenty-one years from Lady Day 1702 at a rent of thirty-two pounds per annum; but the fact that all of the apprentices were (with one exception) bound to James rather than to his mother indicates who was really in control of the printing house. James Roberts was to have sixteen apprentices over the fifty-three years he ran the business; and it is significant that whenever he is described in the Stationers' records on the binding of an apprentice it is as "of Stationers' Court, printer."

The notice of Roberts's death in the *Gentleman's Magazine,* however, calls him "an eminent printer and publisher." In the eighteenth century those who, having the legal right of reproduction, caused books to be printed and distributed for sale — what would now be called *publishers* — were called *booksellers,* a term now often expanded to *copyright-owning booksellers* to distinguish them from mere retailers. What the *Gentleman's Magazine* had in mind when it called Roberts a publisher was something for which no exact modern equivalent exists and for which scholars have therefore had to coin the term *trade publisher.* This term reflects the fact that it was the principal function of such people to publish (that is, offer to the public) works on behalf of other members of the book trade. Although they frequently put their names on books (or, more often, pamphlets and periodicals) and distributed them for sale, they did so not as owners of the copyright and principal investors but as mere paid agents. In this capacity they were acting on behalf of the real copyright owner and investor, whose name one might normally expect to find on the imprint but who had decided, for whatever reason, to keep his or her name out of the imprint and to commission a trade publisher such as Roberts, John Morphew, or Thomas and Mary Cooper to "publish" the work on his or her behalf.

Thus, while Roberts's name appears on thousands of printed items in the first half of the eighteenth century, he was the publisher, in the modern sense, of almost none of them. The only works of which it can be proved that he was the actual publisher are the eighteen whose copyrights were entered to him in the Stationers' Company registers. It is not a particularly impressive list, although it does include, among the sermons, dying speeches, and pamphlets on the Bangorian controversy, *The Case of Richard Steele, Esq.* (1719), Delariviere Manley's *The Adventures of Rivella; or The History of the Author of the Atlantis* (1714), and a corrected and enlarged edition of Daniel Defoe's *The True-born Englishman: A Satyr* (1716).

Roberts's involvement in trade publishing came about through his marriage to Mary Baldwin, daughter of the successful trade publishers Richard and Abigail Baldwin, in January 1708. The Baldwin shop, which had been opened by Richard Baldwin around 1688 and carried on by his widow after his death in 1698, was near the Oxford Arms in Warwick Lane, less than one hundred yards from the Roberts printing house. At the time of her daughter's marriage Abigail Baldwin was still in control of the business. After bearing three daughters in less than three years, Mary Roberts died in October 1712. She had been an only child; accordingly, when Abigail Baldwin died in November 1713 she left her estate, apart from bequests to a sister and to the Robertses' three daughters, to her "loving son-in-law." Roberts, who must have known the business at close hand and may already have had to run it during his mother-in-law's last illness, decided to keep it, and *The Post Boy* for 24–26 November 1713 carried the announcement that "Books, Pamphlets, &c. are publish'd as usual, at the late Dwelling-House of A. Baldwin deceas'd, in Warwick Lane, by her Son-in-Law, James Roberts." The trade publishing shop was so close to Roberts's printing house that it could be run by a junior employee who could be supervised with ease.

Roberts's mother died in January 1714, and from that date his control over both businesses was complete. His domestic life, like his professional one, if not uneventful, has at least left no record of great events. He seems never to have remarried, and his one run-in with the authorities was due to the fact that the author of a heretical pamphlet had Roberts's name put on the imprint without his knowledge. He was once assaulted at night in Paternoster Row, near his house, "by Four Persons unknown"; but his offer of a reward in the *Daily Courant* of 20 February 1721 makes it clear that he had no idea why.

Only in the Stationers' records is there any detailed evidence of Roberts's steady rise to power and distinction within his livery company. He had been clothed as a liveryman as early as 1695 and in 1701 had fined for the office of renter-warden, a necessary condition of all further advancement in the company. In 1719 he was elected to the Court, or governing body, of the Stationers' Company – a

noteworthy achievement for a printer in a company then dominated by booksellers. He served his turn as under warden from 1723 to 1725, as upper warden from 1727 to 1729, and finally as master for an almost unprecedented four years (two then being the norm) from 1729 to 1733. Election to the Court was for life, and with Stationers' Hall only a few steps from his printing house Roberts attended faithfully until his death, missing only six meetings out of several hundred in the last twenty years of his life.

Roberts died on 2 November 1754. He left no will, and the administration of his estate was therefore granted to his eldest daughter, Mary, who had never married and who had kept house for him. The ultimate fate of Roberts's printing business is not known, but the trade publishing company did not survive him. In the 1730s it was already in decline, and after the mid 1740s it dwindled away to almost nothing, the aging Roberts having long been overtaken by the rising new stars of London trade publishing, Thomas and Mary Cooper at the Globe in Paternoster Row.

References:
Fredson Bowers, "Robert Roberts: A Printer of Shakespeare's Fourth Folio," *Shakespeare Quarterly,* 2 (July 1951): 241–246;

John Dunton, *The Life and Errors of John Dunton* (London: Malthus, 1705; New York: Garland, 1974);

D. F. McKenzie, *Stationers' Company Apprentices 1641–1700* (Oxford: Oxford Bibliographical Society, 1974);

McKenzie, *Stationers' Company Apprentices 1701–1800* (Oxford: Oxford Bibliographical Society, 1978);

Henry R. Plomer and others, *A Dictionary of the Printers and Booksellers Who Were at Work in England, Scotland and Ireland from 1668 to 1725* (London: Bibliographical Society, 1922);

Michael Treadwell, "London Printers and Printing Houses in 1705," *Publishing History,* 7 (1980): 5–44;

Treadwell, "London Trade Publishers 1675–1750," *Library,* sixth series 4 (June 1982): 99–134.

Papers:
Biographical and professional details about James Roberts can be found in the registers of the London parishes of St. Lawrence Jewry (1674) and St. Martin Ludgate (1701, 1708–1714, and 1754) and in the Court Books (1701–1755) and Copyright Registers (1707–1737) of the Stationers' Company.

– Michael Treadwell

Simpkin and Marshall
(London: 1814 – 1828)

Simpkin, Marshall and Company
(London: 1828 – 1889)

Simpkin, Marshall, Hamilton, Kent and Company Ltd.
(London: 1889 – 1941)

Simpkin, Marshall (1941) Ltd.
(London: 1941 – 1955)

While William Simpkin and Richard Marshall are acknowledged as central to the nineteenth-century book trade, little information about their lives is available. It is known that they began their careers as assistants to Benjamin Crosby, a London book wholesaler. Wholesalers were a necessity in a business that, while supplying books and periodicals the length and breadth of Great Britain, was based in London. The rise of wholesaling was rapid, and the chief companies responsible for this side of the business found themselves in great demand throughout the country and the colonies and among the smaller booksellers in London. Simpkin and Marshall were to become, in the words of Henry Curwen, virtually "synonymous with this wholesale supply of the requirements of other houses." The company achieved a virtual monopoly, largely because it was highly successful, efficient, and respected.

Crosby had come to London from Yorkshire and had been apprenticed to James Nunn, a bookseller. Following the completion of his apprenticeship, Crosby found a position with the "King of Booksellers," George Robinson, who had established his wholesale company in the 1760s. Robinson's can be said to be the first modern wholesale book firm, and he is generally regarded as having initiated what John Feather describes as a "revolution in the book trade." After a few years with Robinson, Crosby moved on to another bookseller, a Mr. Stalker of Stationers' Hall Court in London. Although not much is known of Stalker or of Crosby's time with him, it was from his establish-

ment that Crosby was to develop his own business, being one of the first London booksellers to travel throughout Britain looking for custom.

Crosby had begun what was soon to become a national bookselling and distribution service. Soon he was unrivaled in his ability to supply books throughout the country. In addition, he was a regular bulk buyer of remainders at book-trade fairs. At about this time Crosby's assistants Simpkin and Marshall began to be noticed for their diligence and hard work on behalf of their employer.

When Crosby gave up the profession in 1814 due to paralysis, he gave part of his stock and all of his country business connections to Robert Baldwin and another wholesale company, Craddock and Joy, and his Paternoster Row premises and London business to Simpkin and Marshall. He died the following year.

Although Crosby had given his provincial business to outsiders, Simpkin and Marshall were not slow to explore and redevelop these areas. The two men actively sought out new clients throughout the country. Not only did they supply books, but they also became London agents for regional publications. Such connections were particularly strong with Scottish printers and publishers.

Simpkin and Marshall were fortunate in their timing, which accounts for some of their speedy success. The book trade was experiencing a depression in the 1820s, and many titles were being remaindered at low cost. Simpkin and Marshall bought stock at low prices and then sold it to their regional customers at regular wholesale prices, ensuring a significant profit. Although they were not innovators in the book trade, as was W. H. Smith, their commercial success from the 1820s to the 1850s is a sign of a trade in a period of rapid transition.

In 1827 a volume of poetry titled *Poems by Two Brothers,* published by J. and J. Jackson of Louth, was also published under the Simpkin and Marshall imprint. This was the first London publication for a young poet named Alfred Tennyson and one of the few truly notable publications by the company. The following year a Mr. Miles bought Simpkin's share of the firm, which changed its name to Simpkin, Marshall and Company. Simpkin would die in 1863.

Simpkin, Marshall and Company was in the habit of lending its name to the publications of its country clients, a practice that afforded the firm profits with minimum expenditure. While not illegal, it did leave them open to lawsuits for libel: although, technically, Simpkin, Marshall was not the publisher, the appearance of its name on a book made the firm liable for the contents. One case that attracted much attention was brought about by a story in *Tait's Edinburgh Magazine* in 1836 in which a man named Richmond was reputed to have been a spy. Simpkin, Marshall and Company was cited as the London agent of the magazine, and Richmond demanded the unprecedented sum of five thousand pounds in damages. Richmond, however, lost the case. In October 1837 the companies to which Crosby had assigned his country connections went bankrupt, and the connections reverted to Simpkin, Marshall and Company.

In 1855 Marshall retired at sixty-seven, and Simpkin, Marshall and Company was entirely in the hands of the Miles family. Simpkin died in 1857. In 1859 the Miles brothers rebuilt and enlarged the premises in Paternoster Row, locating the entire business in one warehouse and incorporating time-saving management techniques. Agents were employed with responsibility for particular areas of the country, and regular customers were allotted pigeonholes for correspondence. The latter practice was particularly helpful on what was known as "magazine day," when all periodicals were printed and distributed every week. Such changes may seem obvious today, but at the time they greatly improved the speed and efficiency with which business was carried out – customers were no longer viewed as individuals but as part of an interrelated and interdependent system of production and marketing. Another noteworthy innovation in 1859 was the decision to close at 2:00 P.M. on Saturdays, allowing employees extra leisure time. Presumably

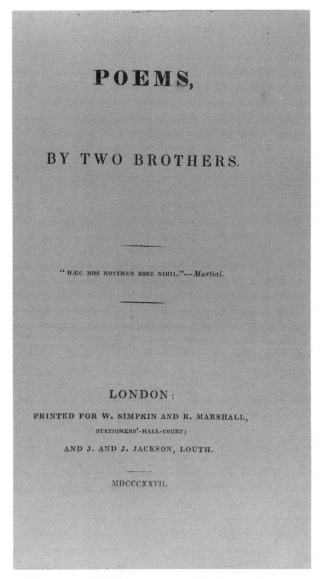

POEMS,

BY TWO BROTHERS.

" HÆC NOS NOVIMUS ESSE NIHIL."---*Martial.*

LONDON:

PRINTED FOR W. SIMPKIN AND R. MARSHALL,
STATIONERS'-HALL-COURT;

AND J. AND J. JACKSON, LOUTH.

MDCCCXXVII.

Title page for Alfred Tennyson's first published book. His brothers Frederick and Charles wrote some of the poems (Courtesy of Special Collections, Thomas Cooper Library, University of South Carolina).

this change came about because of improved efficiency through effective time management.

Business continued in much the same manner, with a steady and significant growth in colonial trade for the rest of the nineteenth century. In 1889 three wholesale houses amalgamated to form Simpkin, Marshall, Hamilton, Kent and Company. One of the companies bought was the wholesaler Hamilton, Adams and Company.

Many people worked for Simpkin, Marshall who subsequently pursued successful independent careers in the various areas of the book trade. One was the publisher Grant Richards; another was Frank Hanson, who became a partner with Joseph

Truslove in the well-known bookstore chain Truslove and Hanson.

In 1920 the Associated Booksellers appointed a full-time paid secretary, and Simpkin, Marshall, Hamilton, Kent donated a room for the organization's offices. The first secretary was W. J. Magenis, who was succeeded by Hilda Light in 1930. Light had been secretary to H. E. Alden, the managing director of Simpkin, Marshall, Hamilton, Kent.

Simpkin, Marshall, Hamilton, Kent was affected by a three-month strike in 1925 and by the General Strike in 1926. The effects of these strikes were not as detrimental to book firms as to other businesses, however, because book-trade employees were generally ill organized.

In 1933 the technical publisher Crosby, Lockwood and Company was sold to Simpkin, Marshall, Hamilton, Kent. On the night of 29 December 1941 a German air raid completely destroyed Paternoster Row. All of Simpkin, Marshall, Hamilton, Kent's buildings, records, and stock were lost. Following this event Sir James Pitman, representing a group of publishers, bought the firm from the Miles family, forming Simpkin, Marshall (1941) Ltd. and placing the company in temporary premises on the North Circular Road and then in St. John's Wood. In 1951 the firm was bought by Robert Maxwell, who moved it to the Marylebone Road. Maxwell was himself in difficulties by 1954, and Simpkin, Marshall (1941) Ltd. went into voluntary liquidation on 2 May 1955. The British book trade suffered from the loss of this powerful, centralized wholesale and distribution organization, which had served the needs of publishers and retailers alike; its functions have not been replaced.

It is probably impossible to compile a list of everything published by Simpkin, Marshall and Company, in its various guises, over 140 years. Of the more than six thousand works, however, relatively few are of literary merit or interest. Few publishing houses today could afford to indulge in such a cornucopia of trivia. The company published self-help books on astrology and spiritualism; swimming instruction; popular history and science books; school crammers and primers; religious and doctrinal pamphlets; guides to spiritual aid and comfort, morality, and ethics by countless headmasters, rectors, clergymen, and spinsters; minor collections of verse and fairy tales for children; books on grammar, calisthenics, and agriculture; gardening; fishing; chess; and so on. From the mid nineteenth century the firm was the principal publisher of Thomas Cook and Son's travel publications, including maps, guidebooks, and foreign-language phrase books. The company primarily published inexpensive reprints of canonical works, along with collections of excerpts designed to cash in on the popularity of an author, such as *Through the Year with Dickens* (1909). Reprints of works such as those of John Bunyan indicate the company's eye for a supplement to its religious tract and doctrinal-pamphlet market. George Gordon, Lord Byron's *The Prisoner of Chillon* (1816) is a rare first edition for Simpkin, Marshall, although it was a copublication, demonstrating that the company's success was built not on risk taking but on its ability to pursue adroitly the more profitable areas of the book market.

References:

Henry Curwen, *A History of Booksellers, the Old and The New* (London: Chatto & Windus, 1873), pp. 412–420;

John Feather, *A History of British Publishing* (London: Routledge, 1991);

F. A. Mumby and Ian Norrie, *Publishing and Bookselling,* fifth edition (London: Cape, 1974);

Norrie, *Mumby's Publishing and Bookselling in the Twentieth Century* (London: Bell & Hyman, 1982).

— Julian Wolfreys

William Smellie
(Edinburgh: 1760 – 1765; 1790 – 1795)

Auld, Auld, and Smellie
(Edinburgh: 1765 – 1767)

Balfour, Auld, and Smellie
(Edinburgh: 1767 – 1771)

Balfour and Smellie
(Edinburgh: 1771 – 1780)

Creech and Smellie
(Edinburgh: 1781 – 1790)

Although he retained no important copyrights and his printing firm did not survive a second generation, William Smellie is considered preeminent among Scottish printers and publishers during the second half of the eighteenth century. In the thirty-five years that comprised Smellie's career – 1760 to 1795 – the number of paper mills in the neighborhood of Edinburgh quadrupled from three to twelve, the quantity of paper manufactured increased from sixty-four hundred to more than a hundred thousand reams, and printing houses in Edinburgh grew from six to sixteen. Smellie's activities in the book trade and as an author involved him closely with all the major figures of the Scottish Enlightenment. Alone among contemporary printers and publishers, Smellie established himself as an original intellectual force contributing significantly to journalism, natural history, and literature. His press was established at the foot of the Anchor Close (the present site of the offices of the *Scotsman*), where it remained throughout his lifetime and many partnerships, until the business was dissolved on the death of his son Alexander. None of the firm's accounts is extant, and the only description of the business premises is an anecdotal narrative variously titled "Reminiscences of Anchor Close" or "A Visit to Mr. Smellie's Printing-Office, Foot of the Anchor Close" that was published in several magazines in the early 1840s.

William Smellie was born in 1740 in the Edinburgh suburb of Pleasance and educated at the grammar school in the neighboring village of Duddingstone until the age of twelve. The family were Cameronians, a politically suppressed Presbyterian sect, which may account for the absence of Smellie's birth date from the records in his parish. His father, Alexander Smellie, was a master builder who designed and constructed the Martyrs' Tomb in Greyfriars' Churchyard at Edinburgh. On 1 October 1752 Smellie was apprenticed to the printing firm of Hamilton, Balfour, and Neil in Edinburgh. Hamilton oversaw printing operations, Balfour was a bookseller, and Neil was a papermaker at Collington on the Waters of Leith. This combination of all the branches of book manufacture in a single partnership was peculiar to the Scottish trade at that time, according to Robert Kerr.

Four years into his apprenticeship Smellie was appointed corrector of the press at a weekly salary of ten shillings. In this capacity he oversaw the printing of an edition of Terence, which the Edinburgh Philosophical Society chose in 1758 as the most accurate classical language edition. No doubt in acknowledgment of that distinction, Smellie was released early from his indentures, and in 1759 he joined the Edinburgh printers Sands, Murray, and Cochrane at a salary of sixteen shillings per week. There he chiefly worked editing, correcting, and preparing abstracts for the *Scots Magazine,* arguably the most important periodical publication in Scotland at the time. Smellie's early experience with the *Scots Magazine* contributed significantly to shaping his literary bent and publishing preferences. The magazine's eclectic interests complemented and con-

William Smellie

firmed Smellie's wide-ranging curiosity and willingness to blur the lines of distinction between the arts and sciences. The magazine format remained crucial to Smellie's ideas about publishing, and throughout his career he would involve himself in more ventures of that kind than any other Edinburgh printer; even his original concept for the first edition of the *Encyclopaedia Britannica* would be essentially an adaptation of Smellie's notions about periodical publications.

Smellie began his career as an essayist when he accepted his position with Sands, Murray, and Cochrane. He was at that time also a student at the University of Edinburgh, and his work collecting and abstracting essays for the *Scots Magazine* no doubt encouraged and quickly taught him much about current periodical and polemical rhetoric. Four essays appeared in quick succession in 1759 and 1760, among which "An Essay on the Means of

Supporting and Promoting Public Spirit" was awarded a competitive prize by the Select Society of Edinburgh; the section on self-love shows considerable influence by early–eighteenth century writers such as Joseph Addison and Alexander Pope, and a curious dialogue with a fetus is an obvious imitation of Laurence Sterne's *Tristram Shandy* (1759–1767), the first two volumes of which had just appeared. This mixture of the philosophical and the satiric in a prose reminiscent of the great English periodical writers of the early decades of the century would remain typical of Smellie's style and tone throughout his career.

In 1763 Smellie married Jean Robertson; they would have thirteen children. Smellie's marriage and growing family made his position with Sands, Murray, and Cochrane financially inadequate, and he left the firm to form, on 25 March 1765, a new partnership with William and Robert Auld, the former having been a fellow apprentice. Smellie's first establishment as a master printer was underwritten in part by two of his professors at the University of Edinburgh, Dr. John Hope and Dr. James Robertson, who lent him seventy pounds. Hope had guided Smellie through his studies in botany, which laid the groundwork for his later achievements in natural history, and Robertson's Hebrew grammar had been set and corrected for the university by Smellie. This partnership, Smellie's first, experienced difficulties from the outset, and in its financial mismanagement and constant bickering among the partners was typical of the business relations and alliances that would follow and determine Smellie's career in the book trade. Smellie was no easy man to deal with. Standard lives have created an image of Smellie as a precocious, thoughtful, prudent, and ethical printer who sacrificed economic security to his pursuit of literary excellence in the trade. But a more careful examination of what survives from Smellie's correspondence with his partners reveals a man who, however intellectually gifted, was unreliable and even devious in his business dealings and who escaped censure in large part because of a gift for retaining favor with men who carried authority in Edinburgh's rather small literary and academic circles. That pattern begins with the Auld partnership, which lasted less than two years. Smellie began to draw on the company's operating funds and to contract personal loans from William Auld almost immediately in 1765 and continued to do so through December of the following year, at which time Robert Auld withdrew from the firm and was replaced by Balfour, formerly master to both William Auld and Smellie. Balfour and Smellie had already joined forces in 1765, when they were appointed printers to the University of Edinburgh, in which capacity they continued until 1795, being chiefly responsible for the printing of medical theses in Latin.

Among Smellie's most important literary efforts in his partnership with Balfour and Auld was the revising and editing of William Buchan's *Domestic Medicine; or, The Family Physician* (1769). Smellie discouraged Buchan's plan to publish the work in parts in the north of England, advising him to seek subscriptions in Edinburgh for publication there. Between 1765 and 1769, when the first edition of *Domestic Medicine* appeared in five thousand copies, Smellie rewrote the text, for which he received a fee of one hundred pounds. Nineteen editions of the book were published before the end of the century, and it was translated into a dozen languages.

William Auld had brought with him ownership of the *Weekly Journal,* a newspaper that had been founded in 1757. The *Journal* became one of the causes of the reorganization of the partnership. Smellie's personal papers indicate that he forced Auld's withdrawal from the partnership. Smellie also refused to assist Auld when the latter fell into financial difficulties brought on by an illness in 1769, even though Auld had extended considerable charity to Smellie and his family in their earlier difficulties. Smellie also reneged on a written agreement to take Auld's nephew William Rogers as apprentice, and he persistently declined to acknowledge Robert Auld as legal factor in William's absence. Smellie ultimately demanded that the company break its association with the *Weekly Journal.* As would be the case in Smellie's disagreements with William Creech later in his career, the issue finally came down to Smellie's manipulation of the company's books. Thus, William Auld wrote in a letter dated Tuesday, 16 October 1770: "there is no cause for such an immense hurry as Mr. Smellie seems to be in. Indeed every transaction in our Company has been hurried thro' with too much rapidity. But that must not be the case here. He has constantly had the Books by him, to satisfy himself and we must have an equal opportunity to be satisfied and also time to deliberate upon it." It is further obvious from an exchange of correspondence in late October 1770 that Smellie used the opportunity of Auld's illness to force the firm's hand where the *Weekly Journal* was concerned.

On 12 November 1771 the partnership of Balfour, Auld, and Smellie was dissolved, and that of Balfour and Smellie commenced business. Smellie had succeeded in removing Auld from the firm and in persuading Balfour to give up the company's interest in the *Weekly Journal;* the newspaper continued to appear until 1780, suggesting that Auld was correct in charging that Smellie had been too hasty in discounting its value. Smellie did, however, gain a more beneficial agreement with Balfour. The former partnership had brought both Auld and Smellie an irregular salary, often as low as twelve shillings per week. The new agreement allowed Smellie ninety pounds per year, in return for which he superintended the whole work of printing, correcting, and posting all items published by Balfour, while overseeing the accounts of the printing house. This contract marks the real beginning of Smellie's career as a master printer.

Financial problems nonetheless continued for Smellie, who, within two years of the formation of Balfour and Smellie, wrote to Henry Home, Lord

Kames, seeking surety for a credit of three hundred pounds with the Royal Bank of Scotland. Lord Kames signed the bond on 28 May 1774 and continued as surety for Smellie's various business interests until 1782. As was often the case with Smellie's impressive political and financial alliances, the printer had approached Lord Kames anonymously while acting in his capacity as corrector for the firm of Sands, Murray, and Cochrane, which had printed the first edition of Kames's *Elements of Criticism* (1762). Smellie's talents for self-promotion served him well throughout his career.

This was a particularly crucial period in Smellie's business life, and his apparent obstinacy in dealing with the Aulds (Robert Auld described Smellie's maneuvers in 1769 as "Declarations of War") was at least in part instigated by his increased acquaintance with the community of Scots printers and publishers in London. Surviving correspondence suggests that Smellie approached William Strahan in late 1769 or early 1770 about the possibility of relocating in London. Smellie was at the time engaged in compiling the first edition of the *Encyclopaedia Britannica* for the partnership of Andrew Bell and Colin Macfarquhar for two hundred pounds, a venture he seems to have undertaken with no clear sense of the work it could entail or of the limitations imposed by the deadlines in his contract. At any rate, the final product bears little relation to his proposal for the encyclopedia as he printed it in 1768. The first edition began to appear in parts in 1771; remaining unbound sheets were sent to London, at which time Smellie supplied a new preface. This preface provides a critical statement on the concept of encyclopedia making that is implicitly opposed to the methods of both Ephraim Chambers and the French Encyclopedists.

Smellie also became involved in periodical publication during this period. He seems to have had in mind the example of Addison and the style of *The Spectator* from his first attempt at a periodical project until his last. Thus, he wrote to Samuel Charteris in 1764: "I design to sift the Spectator, and endeavour to discover wherein he excels, and wherein he falls short of the mark." Smellie would play a major role in seven of the forty newspapers, literary reviews, and magazines that appeared in Edinburgh between 1760 and 1790, as well as developing proposals for three periodicals for which he could not raise interest sufficient to proceed to publication. His notions of what could be achieved through the periodical press far outstretched the derivative eclectic methods of his apprenticeship with the *Scots Magazine,* the country's longest-running

magazine. Beginning as early as 1758, in letters to Charteris and others, Smellie described a periodical ideal combining a newspaper's daily interests with long essays on topics both literary and scientific. Correspondence with readership was always central to these speculations, but Smellie did not manage to bring together a partnership willing to commit to his vision of what a periodical might be until 1773, when the *Edinburgh Magazine and Review* began its three-year run under the editorship of Gilbert Stuart.

The idea of combining magazine and review formats seems to have come from Smellie, according to a correspondence exchanged by John Murray, the London publisher for the *Edinburgh Magazine and Review,* and Stuart in 1774. The venture would ultimately comprise forty-seven numbers in five octavo volumes published between October 1773 and August 1776. In "To the Public," an introductory essay in the first issue, Stuart sets out an ambitious model for an editorial policy that stresses an almost infinite variety of interests for the magazine from academic research to anecdotal histories, touching on contemporary politics, trade, medicine, law, memoirs, and poetry – or, in Stuart's words, the "discoveries and views in all the different branches of philosophy and science." Stuart and Smellie were joined in their efforts by Alexander Kincaid, His Majesty's Printer and Stationer for Scotland; Creech; and William Kerr, Surveyor to the General Post Office for Scotland. The magazine fulfilled its ambitious promise to its public because of the respect commanded by its partners, and especially because of the unique intellectual abilities and wide-ranging interests of Smellie and Stuart.

Smellie and Stuart, however, possessed aggressive and satiric natures that, while they made for unusually frank and insightful essays and reviews, also inflamed much of the readership. The publication quickly became singular both for its intellectual distinction and for the notoriety of its opinions. Smellie's regular column on history was often given to satiric comment, and he carried on a strikingly abusive correspondence with a Reverend Nisbet of Montrose over the latter's support of the colonies at the outbreak of the American Revolution. Typical of Smellie's capacity for a literary duplicity equal to his double-dealing in business was the ironic preface he wrote for the *Treatise on Falconry* (1775). The author did not detect Smellie's irony, and the book with its preface was given by Smellie to Dr. Thomas Blacklock to review for the October 1773 issue of the magazine. But it was left to Stuart to make an enemy of James Burnett, Lord Monboddo, in his review of the latter's incompetent *On the Origin and Progress of Language* (1773-1792). The *Edinburgh Magazine and Review* disintegrated under the pressures brought to bear in response to Stuart's personal attack on Monboddo.

Smellie managed to escape the affair without damaging his personal and political connections with Lord Monboddo, and one of the four portraits of the printer in the National Portrait Gallery of Scotland shows him in a group at a literary evening with Monboddo. Once again Smellie's instinct for surviving crises brought on by his own illiberality preserved him almost miraculously. Smellie, however, kept alive his vision of a Scottish periodical venture that would express the characteristics of a newspaper, magazine, and review in a single publication. His prospectus in September 1788 for the proposed but never published *Scottish Chronicle* reads remarkably like the address "To the Public" that prefaced the initial number of the *Edinburgh Magazine and Review*.

Between the publication of the prospectus for the encyclopedia in 1768 and the encyclopedia's appearance under the imprint of Bell and Macfarquhar in 1771, Smellie exchanged three letters with Strahan in which it was proposed that Smellie go to London to manage Strahan's shop. Smellie wrote a lengthy autobiographical letter outlining his qualifications and setting his own printing concern's income at two hundred pounds per annum. Strahan abandoned the correspondence, however, and Smellie was never to leave Edinburgh. Smellie's career by that time was almost inextricably bound up with the Edinburgh political and intellectual elite through his founding membership in the Society of Antiquaries, of which he was both first recorder and official printer; in 1781 he was elected keeper and superintendent of the Museum of Natural History. It is as difficult to imagine Smellie without Edinburgh as it would be to separate Samuel Johnson from London.

If Strahan had considered hiring Smellie to manage his operations on account of the younger Scot's intellectual reputation and meticulousness as a printer and corrector, his dealings with Smellie between 1783 and 1785 over the London sale of Smellie's translation of Georges-Louis Leclerc de Buffon's *Histoire naturelle* (1749-1788) as *Natural History, General and Particular* (1780-1785) must have corrected any overestimation on his part of the printer's skills as a businessman. Strahan and Thomas Cadell purchased half of the copyright of the Buffon translation while continuing to bicker with Smellie over the completion of imperfect cop-

ies, the settlement of accounts, and Smellie's miscalculation of the costs and schedules for the engravings. Such errors had plagued both the encyclopedia project and the *Edinburgh Magazine and Review*. Strahan wrote to Smellie on 26 March 1785 that "so many disagreeable circumstances have arisen from this transaction, that we almost wish we had not engaged in it." There were no further inquiries about Smellie's relocation to London; even in the highly irregular financial world of the Edinburgh trade, the printer was remarkable for his mishandling of money matters — the most notable instance being his receipt of two hundred pounds for the first edition of the *Encyclopaedia Britannica,* while Bell and Macfarquhar would go on to amass a profit of forty-two thousand pounds from the second and third editions of the work. Smellie claimed that he was not involved in later editions of the encyclopedia because of Macfarquhar's decision to include biographical essays; yet Smellie contributed the essay on Lord Kames to the second edition. It is more likely that Smellie was excluded from the second edition because of his misjudgments over format, engravings, and the printing schedule during the preparation of the first edition; Smellie proved too unreliable for the astute partnership of Bell and Macfarquhar. Throughout his career Smellie either mismanaged or sold too quickly and too cheaply the rights to his best literary properties.

Between 1780 and 1781 Smellie was casting about for a new and financially more-secure partnership. The firm of Balfour and Smellie was experiencing difficulties brought on by a glut of cheap printing in Edinburgh, but Balfour's lack of interest in pursuing new literary properties also negatively affected the firm's income. By the 1780s Balfour had expanded his own business associations to include paper manufacture, which, according to Kerr, proved "extensive and thriving," and he continued to be an important bookseller in Edinburgh. But Creech was fast becoming the most innovative of that city's publishing booksellers and owned literary properties that included some of the most distinguished achievements of the 1780s. Creech was also the only Edinburgh bookseller of the time who was not a printer, and thus he presented Smellie with the opportunity for a realignment that would benefit both partners.

Throughout their partnership, Smellie had been Balfour's exclusive printer while also contracting business of his own. On dissolving his ties with Balfour, Smellie elected to continue as the latter's printer until their indebtedness was cleared. The terms of this settlement took four years to fulfill, during which time Smellie continued to take assignations from Balfour – a demand on Smellie's printing operations that occasionally caused Creech considerable vexation and often interfered with the bookseller's most important undertakings, including the first Edinburgh printing of Robert Burns's poems in 1787. Smellie set and corrected the Burns volume for Creech, but not according to the demands of his partner's schedule.

For a long while Smellie concealed from Balfour his negotiations with Creech, even though there is no indication that Balfour would have opposed releasing Smellie from the partnership – nor did Balfour balk when negotiations became open. The subterfuge and conniving seem simply to reflect Smellie's character: all his partnerships and most of his business dealings seem to have been made unnecessarily difficult by the printer's suspiciousness and undependability. At any rate, Balfour's proved the most congenial of Smellie's four career partnerships when the company's disbanding was negotiated. Smellie feigned shock at Balfour's compliance when he wrote to Creech, "Considering the prodigious quantity of business now carrying on, and the debts due to the printing-house, together with the hardness of Mr Balfour, his offer, and the terms of payment, are surprisingly moderate." Smellie concludes the letter with unintended irony: "I can fully rely on the peaceableness of my own disposition [, and] I cannot help thinking that neither of us will ever have occasion to repent, far less quarrel." Within four years the "peaceable" Smellie roused the volatile Creech to a pitch of frustration that forced their partnership to be dissolved in December 1790. As in previous instances, the disagreement between Smellie and his partner was occasioned by Smellie's mishandling of the printing office's books.

After the partnership Creech continued to employ Smellie's Anchor Close printing operation extensively, an indication of Smellie's abilities as a printer; throughout his career he had no superior where the setting of type and the correcting of a text were concerned. He worked quickly and with unsurpassed accuracy and continued not only to supervise but also to set and correct much of his shop's work until illness prevented him from doing so late in his life. But as a businessman he lacked the interest to be similarly punctilious. Creech's last business correspondence with Smellie in November 1792 is typical of the complaints against Edinburgh's finest printer: "I have been going over your Accounts, and shall continue at them every evening till they are finished. With a man capable of such . . . confused statements of Accounts I never wish to have any transactions. Your strange conduct to me has put many hundred pounds out of your way, and with no other printer had I ever the smallest difficulty. You have driven me to employ people I never would have thought of. I wish you well, but henceforth, all business between us is at end."

To survive as an independent, Smellie had to turn to Lord Gardenstone to act as his security with the banking house of Sir William Forbes and Company, a credit that he had exhausted by late 1794, despite the sale of the copyrights to his own works. Smellie's 1 February 1795 response to Forbes, after the bank called in the printer's credit, details the complex disputes over printing accounts with booksellers that vexed Smellie's final years. His son Alexander was put to considerable difficulty to keep the Anchor Close printing operation going after his father's death in 1795. A final dispute with Creech was not settled by the estate in the courts until 1798.

If Smellie's business skills contrasted his genius as a printer, his talent as an author did a great deal to supplement his income and brought both respect and trade to the press at the foot of the Anchor Close. Smellie's best-known association as a writer was with Burns, but he also numbered among his literary acquaintants much of the intellectual elite of Edinburgh at the height of the Scottish Enlightenment. Smellie commanded respect from the likes of Lord Kames, Stuart, Adam Smith, David Hume, Adam Fergusson, Hugh Blair, James Beattie, and Alexander Munro. He wrote literary lives of Smith, Hume, and Kames as part of a proposed project to do for Scottish authors what Johnson had done for English ones, but death prevented his carrying his "Biographia Scotia," *Literary and Characteristic Lives* (1800), beyond that early stage.

Smellie's achievements and influence as a printer and writer are unsurpassed in the eighteenth-century Scottish book trade. His influence in scientific writing extends from his involvement in the first popular handbook for home medicine, Buchan's *Domestic Medicine,* to his important translation of Buffon and his own *Philosophy of Natural History.* His single-handed authorship of the first edition of the *Encyclopaedia Britannica* is a performance on a level with Johnson's *A Dictionary of the English Language* (1755). As a printer Smellie was associated with both Balfour and Creech, two of Edinburgh's leading booksellers, and his sale of the copyrights for his personal works alone brought him several thousand pounds. Still, he died poor because, for all his intellectual gifts and his capacity for hard work, he was incapable of lasting personal success. Perhaps his closest literary friendship was with Burns, with whom he shared a gift for self-destruction. Kerr destroyed the bulk of Smellie's intimate correspondence with Burns because Kerr was determined to produce a respectable biography for the family man Smellie by overlooking the dissipation that constantly undermined him and that he had in common with both Burns and Stuart. Smellie introduced each of those friends to a drinking club he had helped establish called the Crochallan Fencibles, a contrast to the many learned societies Smellie assisted in founding. Even among the Fencibles, Smellie took upon himself the role of recorder and printer, keeping a journal of club meetings with informed irony.

References:

Mary Elizabeth Craig, *The Scottish Periodical Press 1750–1789* (London: Oliver & Boyd, 1931);

Sir William Jardine, "Memoir of William Smellie," in *Naturalist's Library* (Edinburgh: W. H. Lizars, 1843);

John Kay, *A Series of Original Portraits and Caricature Etchings* (Edinburgh: H. Paton, Carver & Gilder, 1837–1838);

Robert Kerr, *Memoirs of the Life and Writings of William Smellie,* 2 volumes (Edinburgh: J. Anderson, 1811).

Papers:

A collection of William Smellie's correspondence is in the archives of the Society of Antiquaries of Scotland; all quotations from the correspondence are from the letters in this collection with the permission of the secretary to the society.

– Stephen W. Brown

Smith, Elder and Company
(London: 1824 – 1916)
Smith and Elder
(London: 1816 – 1824)

George Smith was born in 1789 in Moray-shire, Scotland, to a farmer whose early death left his family ill provided for. He became an apprentice to Isaac Forsyth, a bookseller and banker in Elgin, but soon sought greater challenges in the London publishing world, first at Rivington and then at John Murray. He was chosen on one occasion to deliver proof sheets to George Gordon, Lord Byron, from Murray, who also relied on Smith's assistance at evening sales to booksellers.

In 1816 Smith and Alexander Elder, another Scot a year younger than he, founded Smith and Elder at 158 Fenchurch Street; the firm specialized in exporting books and stationery to officers in the service of the East India Company. At first Elder worked alone during the day, Smith joining him in the evenings after working at Murray's. On 19 July 1819 they entered their first publication as members of the Stationers' Company, *Sermons and Expositions on Interesting Portions of Scripture,* by Dr. John Morison, a congregational minister. Shortly thereafter Smith married Elizabeth Murray, daughter of an Elginshire glassware manufacturer; they lived over the shop. Following the birth in 1824 of the second of their six children, George Murray Smith, the business and home were moved to larger quarters at 65 Cornhill. By this time the firm had a third partner, Patrick Stewart, and engaged in banking, underwriting, and colonial shipping as well as in bookselling and publishing, and its name was changed to Smith, Elder and Company; Elder was responsible for the publishing department. Stewart's guardian headed a Calcutta firm and was a valuable connection for the India business.

In 1826 the firm published James Donnegan's *A New Greek and English Lexicon* jointly with Chalmers and Collins of Glasgow. The following year Smith, Elder and Company brought out Richard Thomson's *Chronicles of London Bridge.* Gift books, called keepsakes, were popular with wealthy readers in the 1820s and 1830s; therefore, Smith, Elder produced *Friendship's Offering,* which, despite the twelve-shilling price, sold between eight thousand and ten thousand copies a year from 1824 to 1844. Not all ventures were so successful: in 1833 Smith and Elder began the Library of Romance, a series of novels priced at six shillings each. After four months and four novels the firm discontinued the series and returned to three-volume novels at prices the circulating libraries required to make a profit. This failure resulted in a more conservative publishing department and a policy of never publishing novels in parts.

George Murray Smith joined the firm in 1838 and spent the next five years learning the business from the ground up: making up parcels, bookbinding, bookkeeping, composing type, copying letters in the letter book, and mending quills. At nineteen he became head of the publishing department. Previous managers had failed, in part because Elder did not pursue a consistent policy. Young Smith was given fifteen hundred pounds to use as he saw fit. He began a thirty-year professional relationship with John Ruskin by bringing out the first volume of the latter's *Modern Painters* (1843–1860); Ruskin's father stood willing to cover any loss on the work, an important consideration at this point in the firm's history. He read Richard Henry (Hengist) Horne's *A New Spirit of the Age* (1844) both in manuscript and in proof and poured suggestions on the patient author. He later rejected a novel by Horne in which a philanthropist, believing the world to be overpopulated, advocates murdering as many people as possible. Smith next acquired Leigh Hunt's *Imagination and Fancy; or, Selections from the English Poets with an Essay in Answer to the Question What Is Poetry* (1844) for one hundred pounds, but he naively agreed to pay the prolific G. P. R. James six hundred to seven hundred pounds for the first edition of each of his novels. Because he did not want to saturate the market, he soon had three James novels awaiting publication. The experience taught Smith the importance of writing workable agreements and considering publication schedules.

Frontispiece and title page for the Christmas annual that Smith, Elder took over from another firm in 1828 and published until 1844
(Courtesy of Special Collections, Thomas Cooper Library, University of South Carolina)

George Murray Smith took over the firm in 1845 when both his father and Elder retired; George Smith died the following year. In 1848 George Murray Smith discovered that Stewart, the remaining partner, had embezzled thirty thousand pounds from the firm. To avoid bankruptcy, Smith looked for ways to cut expenses; for example, he discovered a more economical arrangement for purchasing paper. He also avoided publishing risky works; thus, he refused submissions by the then-unknown Robert Browning. (For *The Ring and the Book* [1868–1869] Browning would receive four hundred pounds for one edition – more than for any of his other books – and all of his subsequent works would be published by Smith.) To prevent public knowledge of the firm's near ruin, Smith kept Stewart on – but in a menial capacity, where he handled no money. Smith worked out arrangements with the firm's creditors and repaid all the debts ahead of schedule, but it took ten years to repair the damage.

When William Smith Williams, the main reader for the firm, read the manuscript for *The Professor,* he wrote such a kind rejection letter that the author submitted her next novel, *Jane Eyre* (1847), to the firm. Williams and Smith brought the novel out in only six weeks – in time for the Christmas trade – and gave it proper advertising. Charlotte Brontë was amazed, especially considering the treatment her sisters' novels had received at the hands of Thomas Cautley Newby. Smith encouraged Brontë to visit him in London and invited her to travel with him and his widowed mother, since he appreciated how isolated her life was in Yorkshire. She began to suspect, however, that he was interested in her not as a woman but only as a novelist, and then only when she was writing a novel; the boxes of books he had sent to her were not as carefully chosen when she was in a fallow period. Smith was supportive, however, while she was writing *Shirley* (1849), a period during which her brother Branwell and her sisters Emily and Anne died. She included him under the guise of Dr. John Graham Bretton in her novel *Villette* (1853). The firm published *The Professor* in 1857, two years after Brontë's death. Elizabeth Cleghorn Gaskell received one thousand pounds for *The Life of Charlotte Brontë* (1857), which she wrote to honor the memory of her friend.

The first book by William Makepeace Thackeray that Smith, Elder published was *The Kickleburys on the Rhine,* an 1850 Christmas book. Although the work was successful, Thackeray returned to Chapman and Hall for *Rebecca and Rowena* (1852). Then his *Henry Esmond* (1852) was brought out by Smith, Elder under a contract that required Thackeray, for the only time in his career, to complete the novel before publication rather than have it appear serially as he was writing it. Smith also had Brontë critique it in manuscript. Its appearance was elegant, with antique Queen Anne print, witty running titles, and fine paper and binding, and the firm mounted a clever advertising campaign for it. Charles Edward Mudie took 430 copies of the first edition, an unusually high number, for his circulating library.

In 1854 the firm founded a paper of English news for Britons in India, the *Overland Mail;* seeing that the same transportation system could be used in both directions, it founded in the next year a paper of Indian news for Britain, the *Homeward Mail.* The Indian Mutiny of 1857 severely reduced the firm's nonpublishing business. In February 1859 Smith, who had failed to acquire the *North British Review,* decided to start a monthly magazine, and Thackeray agreed to provide a serialized novel for it. When Thomas Hughes and others refused the editorship, Thackeray agreed to serve if he could be responsible only for editorial, not business, matters. Smith sought the most brilliant contributors and offered lavish payments, often double what the authors had received before. As Smith remembered it, "No pains and no cost were spared to make the new magazine the best periodical yet known to English literature." Smith rightly thought that there was a market for a shilling magazine that would contain a serial novel by Thackeray, a second serial, poetry, and informative articles. Thackeray commissioned Anthony Trollope to write the second serial and even specified the subject matter. The *Cornhill Magazine* made its debut in December to catch the Christmas trade but was dated January 1860 – inaugurating a new year and decade – to emphasize its freshness. The initial issue opened with the first installment of Trollope's *Framley Parsonage,* for which he was paid one thousand pounds, twice as much as he had ever previously received. It was followed by

"The Chinese and the Outer Barbarians"; part 1 of Thackeray's *Lovel the Widower*; the first installment of George Henry Lewes's *Studies in Animal Life*; an ode to the author of *Vanity Fair* (1847–1848), "Our Volunteers," by Thackeray's friend "Father Prout" (Francis Sylvester Mahony); "A Man of Letters of the last Generation," Thornton Hunt's article on his father, Leigh; "The Search for Sir John Franklin"; "The First Morning of 1860"; and the first of Thackeray's familiar essays that became known as the *Roundabout Papers.* The inclusion of the poem by Prout guaranteed that all would know that the "anonymous" editor was Thackeray, a master at entertaining. The magazine's sophisticated, urbane tone was aimed at the prosperous middle class. The issue was attractively packaged with several illustrations, decorative initials beginning new items, and a distinctive orange cover, drawn by Godfrey Sikes and engraved by W. J. Linton, showing the four seasons from the planting to the harvesting of the corn crop. Thackeray was so anxious that he fled to France before the first issue appeared, but it was an instant success: 109,274 copies of the first issue (including those contained in the bound volume of the first six issues) were sold by the end of 1861. Smith doubled Thackeray's salary and puffed the sales as 120,000. On 14 January Smith held the first of his monthly *Cornhill* dinners for contributors.

Lewes was paid twenty-five shillings a page for *Studies in Animal Life* and would receive half the profits when the articles were published in book form (1862), but when he introduced some of Charles Darwin's ideas Smith ended the series after six numbers. During the first year works by Alfred Tennyson, John Ruskin, Elizabeth Barrett Browning, Thomas Hood, Richard Monckton Milnes, G. A. Sala, Washington Irving, Fitzjames Stephen, Anne Thackeray, George Macdonald, Eliza Lynn Linton, E. S. Dallas, and Frederick Greenwood appeared in the *Cornhill,* along with the posthumous publication of a poem by Emily Brontë and the opening chapters of the uncompleted novel "Emma" by Charlotte Brontë with an introduction by Thackeray. Thackeray, however, had the unpleasant tasks of rejecting an Elizabeth Barrett Browning poem wherein a wife feigns infidelity and a Trollope story that mentions illegitimate children and of stopping publication of Ruskin's *"Unto This Last"* because the work was too socialistic for a family magazine (Smith published the completed work in book form in 1862, however).

Sales of the magazine began dropping with the second number; only the February and March 1860 issues sold in six digits, and through the second half of that year and the first half of 1861 each issue sold 87,500 copies. The print run was reduced to 72,500 in September. Expenses had risen in the area of payments to contributors, which ranged during the year from almost six hundred pounds to more than seven hundred pounds for the December issue. A large portion of these payments went to Thackeray; for example, in September he received two-thirds of the seven hundred pounds paid to contributors. Harriet Beecher Stowe's *Agnes of Sorrento,* on the other hand, earned her only fifty pounds per part, partly because women novelists usually received less and partly because the novel failed utterly to replicate the success of its predecessor, *Uncle Tom's Cabin* (1852). Although Smith did attract Trollope while the latter was rising in popularity, he often had the misfortune of publishing a lesser-quality work that followed one of an author's best works. Having the subsequent work by the author who was credited with starting the American Civil War, however, provided positive publicity for the magazine and its ability to capture the famous as well as the best. Illustrators included John Everett Millais, Frederick Leighton, George Du Maurier, and Frederick Walker, whose work was reprinted in the *Cornhill Gallery* in 1864. Richard Doyle produced "Birdseye Views," a series of foldout illustrations of social satire, beginning in April 1861.

Early in 1862 Smith approached Lewes about resuming *Studies in Animal Life,* but Lewes declined. Smith was also interested in publishing the new novel by Lewes's companion, George Eliot, to offset the effect of the disappointing *Agnes of Sorrento,* which would be ending its serialization soon. *Romola,* which began in the July 1862 issue, was not popular because it was so densely packed with history and ideology. The publicity gained by Smith's offer of ten thousand pounds to Eliot for the novel (although she actually received seven thousand) added to the prestige, if not the sales, of the *Cornhill.* Lewes, who also began writing for the *Cornhill* again in July and who was aware of the financial problems, asked for five thousand pounds for Eliot's next novel, *Felix Holt;* after Smith read some of it to his wife, the Smiths concluded that it would not be profitable. It was published by Blackwood in 1866.

The issue for May 1862, of which only sixty thousand copies were printed, was Thackeray's last as editor. He disapproved of some of the novels Smith had acquired, such as Stowe's (Thackeray was sympathetic with the South). And Smith's extravagant offer for *Romola* strained relations with Thackeray, who was not a party to the negotiations. He most resented Smith's intrusions into editorial

JANE EYRE.

𝔄n 𝔄utobiograph𝔶.

EDITED BY

CURRER BELL.

IN THREE VOLUMES.
VOL. I.

LONDON:
SMITH, ELDER, AND CO., CORNHILL.
1847.

Title page for the first of Charlotte Brontë's novels to be published by Smith, Elder

matters, despite Thackeray's own absentmindedness, impatience with detail, frustration at the effect of constant interruptions on his own writing, and anguish over rejecting manuscripts. He found it especially difficult to reject the appeals of indigent women writers to publish their inferior works, and he often enclosed money in the rejection letters.

No replacement for Thackeray was found. Robert Browning, who had returned to England from Italy following the death of his wife, and Lewes both declined Smith's offer. Lewes's poor health and his desire to finish his history of science led him to accept six hundred pounds to act as chief literary adviser, but not editor. Instead, an editorial committee, which varied from two to three members until 1871, was formed. It included Smith; Lewes through 1864; Frederick Greenwood, who did a large share of the editorial work and who was

THE INTERIOR OF HADES.

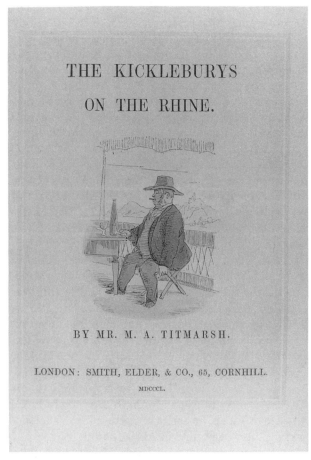

THE KICKLEBURYS
ON THE RHINE.

BY MR. M. A. TITMARSH.

LONDON: SMITH, ELDER, & CO., 65, CORNHILL.

MDCCCL.

Frontispiece and title page for the first book by William Makepeace Thackeray to be published by the firm (Courtesy of Special Collections, Thomas Cooper Library, University of South Carolina)

later replaced by J. F. W. Herschel; and, later, Edward Dutton Cook. In July 1862 Lewes and Greenwood began a semiregular series, "Our Survey of Literature, Science, and Art," which evolved in 1863 into "Notes on Science." Even though the magazine lost money, it brought new writers to the firm; with the exception of Charles Dickens, Smith could and did claim that he had published all the major writers.

He made more money from enterprises other than publishing, such as self-insuring his less-risky overseas routes; shipping guns to Australia after the discovery of gold there; owning a dozen sailing ships from 1870 to 1879 under the name Smith, Bilbrough and Company, with offices at 36 Fenchurch Street (the one he kept the longest, the *Old Kensington,* was named after an 1873 novel by Anne Thackeray), and becoming part owner of the Aylesbury Dairy. The greatest part of his fortune, a million and a half pounds, came from table water. When he found a safer way to ship it from Ger-

many and lowered the price per bottle by buying it in volume and bottling it in England, thereby reducing breakage, he created a demand for Apollinaris, "the Queen of Table Waters." (After more than two decades of ownership, Smith sold the water enterprise in 1898.) He used his financial acumen to assist genius: among those he helped were Thomas Hughes, Browning's son Pen, Matthew Arnold, and Thackeray and his daughters. Smith handled their affairs, lent them money, and bought them presents. Arnold was once a full year late in repaying a loan, but Smith said nothing; Smith obtained for Mrs. Gaskell a large discount on furniture for her new house (to her great annoyance, however, he did not pay her on a par with male novelists; nevertheless, she far preferred to write for Smith rather than for Dickens's magazines). The portraits of Charlotte Brontë and Thackeray that he commissioned for their loved ones later adorned their collected works.

By the summer of 1863 the magazine was losing money; therefore in November Gaskell's *Cousin*

Phyllis brought her only £25 per part. During the next year there was a brief increase in circulation of a few thousand copies to forty-five thousand when Thackeray's posthumous novel *Denis Duval* ran; Smith paid Thackeray's heirs £250 per part for it. Gaskell's *Wives and Daughters* began in August 1864; she received £78 15s. per installment, in contrast to Wilkie Collins's £250 for *Armadale,* which increased sales for November to forty-one thousand. The early installments of these two novels only briefly halted the decline. The last installment of *Wives and Daughters* had to be completed by Greenwood from Gaskell's notes after she died suddenly on 12 November 1865. Charles Lever's *The Bramleighs of Bishop's Folly,* beginning in December 1867, brought him only £60 per installment, while *Put Yourself in His Place,* which ran from March 1869 through July 1870, earned Charles Reade £153 17s. each month, reflecting the relative popularity of the two authors. George Meredith's *The Adventures of Harry Richmond* (1871) followed Reade's novel. Smith rejected Meredith's *Beauchamp's Career* in 1874 as unreadable.

In spite of the erosion of the magazine's circulation to below twenty-four thousand, the *Cornhill* outsold its rivals by more than twice. Smith concluded that readers were attracted as much by novelty as quality and that they wanted more fiction and lighter matter. Rival shilling magazines provided those ingredients, beginning in 1860 with the *Temple Bar,* edited by Sala, which lured thirty thousand buyers. The shilling magazines virtually eliminated the shilling part-issue of serial novels, which had been popular for more than a quarter of a century. Such magazines soon became so numerous that each had a circulation of only twelve to fifteen thousand. In 1867 Trollope became the first editor of *Saint Paul's Magazine,* and the publisher William Tinsley, who had just started his own house organ, *Tinsley's Magazine,* lamented, "there were more magazines in the wretched field than were blades of grass to support them."

When Smith felt blocked in one direction, he usually began a new endeavor. In 1865 it was the *Pall Mall Gazette* (the firm had acquired additional office space at 45 Pall Mall in 1861), an evening newspaper with an emphasis on literature and art. Thackeray had first conceived of such a paper in his novel *The History of Pendennis* (1848–1850), published by Bradbury and Evans, where the prospectus stated that it was addressed to the higher circles of society and was written by gentlemen for gentlemen. The *Gazette* surfaced again in Thackeray's *The Adventures of Philip* (1862), which first appeared in

the *Cornhill,* where the paper was described as having passed through several hands. The connection to Thackeray, whose reputation remained high, was an important advertising tool. With the *Pall Mall Gazette* Smith sought to bring into daily journalism the thought and culture normally found only in the quarterly or monthly reviews. The enterprise was too liberal for Smith's partner, Henry S. King, who did participate in it.

The first issue of the paper appeared on Tuesday, 7 February 1865, in eight folio pages priced at twopence, and sold 3,897 copies. Greenwood was the editor, and Lewes was adviser and drama critic and wrote occasional articles. Lewes's reviews were collected as *On Actors and the Art of Acting* in July 1875, and his three review articles on Darwin's *The Variations of Animals and Plants under Domestication* (1868) were considered so knowledgeable by Darwin that the two men began a correspondence. Lewes severed connections with the *Pall Mall Gazette* in October 1868 because of a hostile review of Eliot's *The Spanish Gypsy.* Smith, however, went on to publish the third edition of Lewes's *The Life of Goethe* (1875).

The *Pall Mall Gazette* provided an epitome of the news, culled from the morning papers, and two or three articles on political and social questions but without political bias. Occasional "Notes" became a distinguishing mark of the paper. Editors included W. T. Stead and Edward Cook, and contributors included Fitzjames and Leslie Stephen, Trollope, Arnold, Meredith, Ruskin, Eliot, Milnes, John Morley, Reade, Sir Arthur Helps, James Hannay, Laurence Oliphant, R. H. Hutton, Thomas Hughes, Herman Merivale, John Morley, Thomas Henry Huxley, Richard Jefferies, and Meredith Townsend. Friedrich Engels wrote approximately sixty "Notes on the War." In 1866 the three installments of Greenwood's brother James's "A Night in the Casual Ward: By an Amateur Casual" caused an upswing in circulation; under Smith and Frederick Greenwood the highest circulation was nine thousand. The *Pall Mall Gazette* became the forerunner of the cheap evening press in 1869, when it briefly reduced its price to one penny and then returned to two pence. On 1 May 1880 Smith sold the paper to his son-in-law Henry Yates Thompson, a liberal; Frederick Greenwood, who had grown conservative, resigned, fearing that it would become a ministerial journal, and was replaced by Morley. Thompson kept it until 1892, when he sold it to William Waldorf Astor.

In 1868 Smith retired from the foreign agency and banking businesses and identified himself solely

THE HISTORY

OF

HENRY ESMOND, Esq.

A COLONEL IN THE SERVICE OF HER MAJESTY
Q. ANNE.

WRITTEN BY HIMSELF.

Servetur ad imum
Qualis ab incepto procefferit, et fibi conftet.

IN THREE VOLUMES.
VOLUME THE FIRST.

LONDON:
PRINTED FOR SMITH, ELDER, & COMPANY,
OVER AGAINST ST. PETER'S CHURCH IN CORNHILL.
1852.

Title page for the only novel Thackeray was ever required to complete before publication. The rest were serialized as he wrote them (Courtesy of the Lilly Library, Indiana University).

with publishing. His partner took over the agency and banking enterprises under the name Henry S. King and Company at both the Cornhill and Pall Mall addresses. Smith, Elder and Company moved to a renovated private residence at 15 Waterloo Place in January 1869.

In 1871 Thackeray's son-in-law, Leslie Stephen, who had written for the *Pall Mall Gazette* starting with the second number, as well as for the *Cornhill* (beginning with "American Humour" in 1866), sought Smith's advice about accepting the editorship of *Fraser's Magazine*. In a spur-of-the-moment decision Smith offered him five hundred pounds a year to edit the *Cornhill*, and Stephen accepted. Recognizing the author's potential with rural stories, Stephen encouraged Thomas Hardy to submit a novel and received *Far from the Madding Crowd;* the novel ran throughout 1874 and was illustrated by Helen Patterson (later Helen Allingham), whom Hardy was to praise as his best

illustrator. It was followed by the radically different and disappointing *The Hand of Ethelberta* (1876), an urban satire. Stephen found *The Return of the Native* (1878) too dangerous for a family magazine, so it appeared in *Belgravia,* which specialized in sentimental and sensational fiction. Henry James's *Daisy Miller* (1879) was well received by the *Cornhill* audience, but his *Washington Square* (1881) was less popular because readers found it lacking in event. Arnold's *Culture and Anarchy* (1869) and *St. Paul and Protestantism* (1870) had appeared in the magazine before Stephen assumed the editorship; Stephen faced the unpleasant duty of abruptly terminating Arnold's *Literature and Dogma* (1873) because its chapter on miracles exceeded the wide latitude that was accorded virtually only to Arnold. Although Stephen was personally sympathetic to Arnold's position, he was easily influenced by reader complaints.

Stephen excelled as an author of literary essays, writing more than sixty pieces that established the intellectual tone of the magazine, and as an editor in his meticulous correction of manuscripts and painstaking work with writers. He published contributions by Edmund Gosse, Andrew Lang, John Addington Symonds, Frances Power Cobbe, Sidney Colvin, Eliza Lynn Linton, Margaret Oliphant, and William Black and discovered Robert Louis Stevenson. But changing tastes caused sales to drop to twelve thousand in 1882. When Stephen learned about the decline in circulation, he resigned. Smith, who always separated editorial from business affairs, may have leaked the figures in an attempt to alter the direction of the *Cornhill.*

Because he admired Stephen's talents and dedication, Smith offered him the editorship of a new venture, *The Dictionary of National Biography* (*DNB*), in the fall of 1882 at an annual salary of eight hundred pounds and offices at 14 Waterloo, with a speaking tube to number 15 next door, where Smith, Elder was housed. On the recommendation of Frederick James Furnivall, Stephen offered Sidney Lee the position of subeditor at a salary of three hundred pounds a year. Smith, who estimated that he would lose fifty thousand pounds on the venture, saw it as his contribution to his country since other countries, such as France and Germany, already had national biographies.

On 23 December 1882 "A New Biographia Britannica" was announced in the *Athenaeum* with a statement of its editorial principles: only notable deceased Britons would be included; precise facts and dates would be given, with bibliographies in the case of writers; no philosophical or critical disquisitions or elaborate analyses of character would be permitted, but characteristic anecdotes and statements of subjects' views would be acceptable. Lists of worthy British men and women were compiled; John Murray, who had explored the possibility of such a project in the 1850s but had abandoned it when the cost became clear, gave his list of names to Smith. Sample entries were prepared; Stephen's on Joseph Addison became the model. The initial list was mailed to contributors on 10 January 1883. Stephen's greatest worry was inexperienced writers, who tended to write far too much. *The Dictionary of National Biography* was to be a project in which the community at large was encouraged to feel involved: every October and April lists of nine hundred to one thousand names were printed in the *Athenaeum* for readers' suggestions. The first volume was published on 1 January 1885 and priced at 12s. 6d.; succeeding volumes would appear quarterly until 1900. As the losses grew, Smith demanded more editorial pruning.

Lee became joint editor in 1890 and sole editor in June 1891, when Stephen resigned on doctor's orders. The last list was prepared in the spring of 1897, along with subject indexes to the first fourteen volumes; the following year Lee was planning supplements covering omissions and the newly deceased. On 25 May 1900 the publication of the sixty-third and last volume was celebrated at the Carlton Hotel at a dinner given by Edward, Prince of Wales. The lord mayor of London and Smith also gave dinners. Eighty-seven authors contributed to volume one, including Stephen, Lee, Gosse, Hall Caine, Dutton Cook, Francis Espinasse, Sidney Low, Theodore Martin, and A. W. Ward. In the original sixty-three volumes 27,236 entries were provided by nearly seven hundred writers, including Lee with 757 signed entries and Stephen with 378, many of which were written after he retired as editor; both men also wrote many unsigned entries. Thompson Cooper wrote the most – 1,415. At the end of 1901 the organization was broken up, and many papers were destroyed. In 1903 Lee prepared a summary volume, the *Index and Epitome,* at the behest of Smith's widow; she also insisted that an errata volume be published in 1904. She ultimately bequeathed the *DNB* to Oxford University's Clarendon Press.

Other works published by Smith, Elder during this period included Mrs. Humphry Ward's *Robert Elsmere* in February 1888. Smith offered her a modest advance of two hundred pounds for an edition of five hundred copies, which was quickly followed by six more three-volume editions and a popular

Cover for the magazine Smith, Elder published from 1859 to 1916, when the firm was sold to John Murray. The magazine continued to appear until 1975. Its editors under Smith, Elder included Thackeray, Leslie Stephen, and James Payn.

one-volume edition of five thousand copies that sold out in July, with twenty-three thousand more sold before the end of the year. The shock and indignation of clergy, plus former prime minister William Ewart Gladstone's article "Robert Elsmere and the Battle of Belief" in the *Nineteenth Century* (May 1888) answering the novel's attack on revealed religion, increased sales enormously. Ward, Matthew Arnold's niece, continued to publish regularly with the firm.

James Payn, a popular novelist who had previously edited *Chambers's Journal,* became editor of the *Cornhill* in 1883, succeeding his college friend Stephen, who called him "the best of the journalists." Payn sought new readers by including more-popular material, such as short stories. H. Rider Haggard's *Jess* and a reduced price heralded the start of a new series with the July 1883 issue. The magazine remained too literate for the sixpenny audience, however, and the change offended some of its faithful readers; as a result, circulation declined further. As a cost-saving measure, illustrations were discontinued in 1886.

Payn had been serving as a reader for the firm, thanks to the recommendation of Stephen, since Williams's retirement in 1874. In 1880 Payn had rejected Joseph Henry Shorthouse's *John Inglesant,* which became a great success for Macmillan with more than fifty editions. Later Payn, not realizing that the novel was the one he had turned down, happened to read that Smith, Elder had missed out on it; he stormed into Smith's office insisting that the person responsible be reprimanded. Before telling Payn the truth, Smith calmed him down; then he reassured Payn that he himself still found it a dull book. Smith accepted occasional lapses from hardworking employees.

Because of his uncle Richard Doyle's association with the magazine in its earliest days, Arthur Conan Doyle was eager to contribute to the *Cornhill.* He submitted manuscripts until he got Payn to accept "Habakuk Jephson's Statement," which appeared in January 1884 and launched his writing career. Payn also accepted *The White Company* (January–December 1891), although he normally refused historical novels. He did not, however, accept the first Sherlock Holmes story, *A Study in Scarlet* (1887). Doyle was to go on to build an enormous circulation for the *Strand* magazine. Payn's industry and his ability to attract new talent, including F. Anstey, Stanley Weyman, and Henry Seton Merriman, kept the magazine afloat.

When Payn retired in 1896, John St. Loe Strachey was brought in as his replacement. In July Strachey began a third series that returned to the shilling price and to belles lettres, with memoirs, autobiographies, and diaries, but no major turnaround in circulation occurred. Strachey resigned in December 1897 to become editor of the *Spectator.*

Strachey's successor, Reginald John Smith, had attended Eton and Cambridge and read law before becoming George Murray Smith's son-in-law and partner. Because George Murray Smith's sons were no longer connected with the firm, Reginald Smith had inherited it when the elder Smith retired in 1896. As editor of the *Cornhill* Reginald Smith continued to serialize after many other magazines had ceased to do so. Smith was able to attract some good writers whose works would then be published by Smith, Elder, and he ran many commemorative issues and articles. Works by Hardy, Ward, Lee, Meredith, Lang, George Gissing, Max Beerbohm, A. E. Housman, Arthur C. Benson, Anthony Hope, Alfred Noyes, Robert Bridges, Julian Huxley, Ar-

thur Quiller-Couch, A. I. Shand, and William Butler Yeats appeared. Virginia Stephen Woolf contributed six pieces to her father's former magazine. George Murray Smith's last contribution to *Cornhill* was a series of his reminiscences; only a few of the pieces were completed when he died in 1901, but they ably served to celebrate the forty-year history of the magazine, which had outlasted many of its rivals.

Anne Thackeray Ritchie contributed introductions to the Biographical Edition (1894–1899) and Centenary Edition of her father's collected works (1911). She also wrote reminiscences, beginning with "First Number of the *Cornhill*" for the first issue of the new series in July 1896 (it was reprinted in her *From the Porch,* published by Smith, Elder in 1913), and in December 1900 she began a series of familiar essays, like her father's *Roundabout Essays,* called *Blackstick Papers* after a character in Thackeray's *The Rose and the Ring* (1845); they were published in book form in 1908. She had appeared in the magazine in the first year under her father, and under her brother-in-law Stephen, and she contributed an atmosphere of nostalgia that spoke to many faithful readers who wanted to be reminded of the magazine's past glory.

During World War I the cost of printing labor rose 300 percent, resulting in the magazine's being reduced in length to 128 pages and then to 112 with the price increasing from one shilling ordinary to one shilling net. But circulation rose, according to Leonard Huxley, then assistant editor, because it provided solace with its series of war stories and articles by Doyle, Boyd Cable, C. H. Firth, W. H. Fitchett, and Frank Bullen.

As head of the firm Reginald Smith followed George Murray Smith's model: read everything the firm published and encourage a coterie of loyal authors and experts connected to the magazine and the house. He perfected the charming business letter and kept up a vigorous correspondence with longtime *Cornhill* readers who often praised the new authors whose works appeared on its pages. Smith used these comments, as well as press notices, in encouraging letters to the young writers, many of whom dedicated their books to him in appreciation. Also like George Murray Smith, Reginald Smith won the loyalty of employees as well as authors. John Aitchison served as business manager for forty-five years until 1915, and William Partledge remained in the post of principal accountant for forty years.

The copyrights Smith, Elder owned and the authors who were bound to the firm turned out to be less valuable than would have been imagined when Reginald Smith died suddenly in 1916 and his widow, George Murray Smith's daughter Isabel, decided to sell the firm to John Murray, which had historical ties with Smith, Elder as well as similar publishing philosophies. But after the financial records were examined John Murray IV's negotiators made an offer decidedly below what Isabel Smith's solicitor had sought. The negotiations nearly broke down before Murray made an offer that was higher than the value of the firm justified but that would provide for the family of a colleague and friend. Isabel Smith received a series of payments managed by Partridge that totaled nearly thirteen thousand pounds. Murray was interested in purchasing the *DNB* from her mother, but it proved too expensive.

Letters were written to each of Smith, Elder's authors. Anne Thackeray Ritchie responded that her life was "so associated with the *Cornhill* and the dear and familiar house of Smith Elder & Co I went out into the lane to calm myself and to think it over, and then little by little I realized the deep relief that dear Isabel Smith should have found your help — and friend of her husband — and that it was to such a tradition as yours, that fate had led her. I felt more and more grateful when your kind message came this am. . . ." Among the copyrights owned by Smith, Elder were those for E. W. Hornung's Raffles books and works by Arnold, the Brontës, the Brownings, Doyle, Gaskell, Gissing, Thackeray, Ward, Harriet Parr (Holme Lee), and Eden Philpotts. As many members of the firm as possible were kept on, with the understanding that Murray employees would have preference when they returned from the war. To guarantee the continuation of her father's magazine, Isabel Smith insisted on the right to repurchase it if Murray should ever decide not to keep it. Thus ended an era, but the *Cornhill Magazine,* edited by Leonard Huxley and finally by John G. Murray, survived until rising costs and changing tastes forced its closure in 1975.

References:
Richard D. Altick, *The English Common Reader* (Chicago: University of Chicago Press, 1957);

Rosemary Ashton, *G. H. Lewes: A Life* (Oxford: Clarendon Press, 1991);

A. C. Benson, *Memories and Friends* (London: John Murray, 1924);

Gillian Fenwick, *The Contributors Index to the Dictionary of National Biography 1885–1901* (Winchester: St. Paul's Bibliographies / Detroit: Omnigraphics, 1989);

Sara Ferrell, assisted by Audrey Sheats, "*The Cornhill Magazine,* 1860–1900," in *The Wellesley Index to Victorian Periodicals, 1824–1900,* 5 volumes, edited by Walter E. Houghton (Toronto: University of Toronto Press, 1966–1989; London: Routledge & Kegan Paul, 1966–1989), I: 321–415;

Jenifer Glynn, *Prince of Publishers: A Biography of the Great Victorian Publisher George Smith* (London & New York: Allison & Busby, 1986);

Lindall Gordon, *Charlotte Brontë: A Passionate Life* (London: Chatto & Windus, 1994);

Leonard Huxley, *The House of Smith Elder* (London: Privately printed, 1923);

Barbara Quinn Schmidt, "The Cornhill Magazine," in *British Literary Magazines: The Modern Age, 1914–1984,* edited by Alvin Sullivan (Westport, Conn.: Greenwood Press, 1986), pp. 103–110;

Schmidt, "In the Shadow of Thackeray: Leslie Stephen as the Editor of the *Cornhill Magazine,*" in *Innovators and Preachers: The Role of the Editor in Victorian England,* edited by Joel H. Wiener (Westport, Conn. & London: Greenwood Press, 1985), pp. 77–96;

Schmidt, "The Patron as Businessman: George Murray Smith (1824–1901)," *Victorian Periodicals Review,* 16 (Spring 1983): 3–14;

J. W. Robertson Scott, *The Story of the Pall Mall Gazette, of Its First Editor, Frederick Greenwood, and of Its Founder, George Murray Smith* (London & New York: Oxford University Press, 1950);

George Murray Smith, *Some Pages of Autobiography* (London: Privately printed, 1902);

John Sutherland, "*Cornhill*'s Sales and Payments: The First Decade," *Victorian Periodicals Review,* 19 (Fall 1986): 106–108;

J. Don Vann, "The Cornhill Magazine," in *British Literary Magazines: The Victorian and Edwardian Age, 1837–1913,* edited by Alvin Sullivan (Westport, Conn.: Greenwood Press, 1984), pp. 82–85.

Papers:

Although no complete archive exists for Smith, Elder and Company, the National Library of Scotland has the most extensive holdings; John Murray has records plus the correspondence regarding the sale. The Parsonage Library at Haworth has holdings connected with the publisher and with Charlotte Brontë.

– Barbara Quinn Schmidt

William Strahan
(London: 1738 – 1785)

Andrew Strahan
(London: 1785 – 1818)

Andrew Strahan and William Preston
(London: 1804 – 1815)

Andrew and Robert Spottiswoode
(London: 1819 – 1832)

Andrew Spottiswoode
(London: 1819 – 1855)

Eyre & Spottiswoode
(London: 1855? – 1989)

William Strahan arrived in London in 1736 a journeyman printer and died in 1785 a wealthy and eminent figure, having made his fortune as a printer, publisher, and bookseller and having sat in Parliament from 1774 to 1784. His portrait by Sir Joshua Reynolds hangs in the National Portrait Gallery. He was not only Samuel Johnson's printer but also his friend, and he also counted many other celebrities, including David Hume and Benjamin Franklin, among his friends. The ledgers Strahan kept – showing his clients, expenditures, and receipts – form one of the richest manuscript collections available for the study of eighteenth-century printing and publishing.

Strahan, whose surname was originally spelled *Strachan,* was born on 24 March 1715 in Edinburgh, the son of a customs clerk. After attending high school he was apprenticed to John Mosman and William Brown, the king's printers in Scotland; he then moved to London, where he worked as a compositor for the Bowyer Press from early May 1736 to 25 February 1738. On 20 July 1738 he married Margaret Penelope Elphinston at the church of St. Mary le Bow. An undated document, "Specimen of Printing-Letter by T. Hart and W. Strahan, in Bury Court, Love Lane, Wood St.," implies a printing partnership, probably with the Thomas Hart who had also been employed by the Bowyers; but if such a relationship existed it must have been brief,

for in November 1738 Strahan was in the printing business by himself, with one press.

The location of Strahan's first shop has not been established. During his first year in operation he received payments of £444 14s. 6d. and had expenses of £234 for journeymen's wages, £30 for printing materials, and £149 2s. for living expenses. The net profit of £31 12s. 6d. was quadrupled the following year.

In that first year eight members of the book trade and twelve private clients gave business to Strahan. One of the eight trade clients was George Strahan, who may have been a relative; another was Andrew Millar, a fellow Scot who, until he retired, would be Strahan's best customer. On 12 April 1739 Strahan received an order from Millar to print 750 copies of a translation of Dutot's (first name unknown) *Political Reflections upon the Finances and Commerce of France* for £24 3s.; the following year Millar paid Strahan £167 14s. 6d., which was nearly one-third of all the money Strahan received for printing that year. Millar's orders to Strahan increased steadily over the years, although he never completely stopped using the printing houses of his friends Samuel Richardson and Henry Woodfall.

Millar was a good customer to have: his shop in the Strand was highly successful, and he was atypical of eighteenth-century booksellers in that he paid his bills promptly and in cash. Shortly after

William Strahan; painting by Sir Joshua Reynolds (National Portrait Gallery, London)

Millar became Henry Fielding's publisher in 1742 Strahan began printing most of Fielding's works; by 1779 he would have printed 62,700 copies. Close to Fielding in popularity were the poems of James Thomson, of which Strahan printed 27,000 copies for Millar. He printed almost as many copies of Hume's various essays and of his popular *History of England* (1759–1763).

By 1742 Strahan had moved to Wine Office Court, an alley off Fleet Street. In 1748 he moved to 10 Little New Street, which he remodeled to house both his printing business and his home. Within five years he had outgrown this space and was enlarging it handsomely: he wrote to David Hall in 1753 that "my House and Garden will stand upon a Spot of Ground near 90 feet square, and be beyond Dispute the largest and best Printing-House in Britain." The following year he told Hall that he was keeping nine presses going.

It was through his connection with Millar that Strahan got the order to print Johnson's *A Dictionary of the English Language* (1755), on which he made a substantial profit. The capital for the dictionary was put up by several partners, for whom Strahan acted as paymaster while he was printing the book. Thereafter he apparently served Johnson as both banker and publisher, as well as his host at frequent dinner parties. Strahan appears in James Boswell's letters, where he is described with the epithets "wealthy plumpness" and "good animal spirits."

It was not by printing alone that Strahan made his fortune: he perceived early in his career that his prospects were limited unless he could compete as a publisher and as a bookseller. To have engaged openly in these activities, however, could have antagonized the clients of his printing business. Instead, Strahan astutely exploited certain characteristics of the trade and connections of his own until he was so firmly established in all aspects of the book trade that his preeminence was secure. One connection that Strahan exploited was Hall, a friend and protégé who, like Strahan, had been apprenticed to Mosman and Brown in Edinburgh. Strahan's efforts to secure a place for Hall in America led to a lifelong friendship with Franklin, who took Hall into partnership in 1748. The three men helped each other in various ways. Strahan furnished books, paper, ink, and political news to Franklin and Hall, and they provided him with a market.

Strahan also took advantage of the London booksellers' chronic shortage of cash by accepting payment in books instead of money. Robert Harlan has shown that Strahan accepted several hundred pounds sterling in books and pamphlets in payment of bills from twenty-one clients, all but one of whom were booksellers and publishers. Between 1739 and 1750, according to Harlan's calculations, 15 percent of the total payment Strahan received was in trade. This arrangement encouraged the booksellers to give him printing business and provided him with an inventory from which to supply the American market and, to a lesser extent, a Scottish market as well.

During this period the risks of publishing were distributed by dividing the costs; people who invested money to bring out a book owned "shares," or fractional interests in the copyrights of the works. There was an aftermarket in these shares, which were often offered at sales that could be attended only by recognized publishers. Although he had sometimes received shares in exchange for absorbing printing costs, the first sale Strahan was permitted to attend was that of the shares and stock of John and Paul Knapton, who, when they failed in business, owed the printer the substantial sum of £408 10s. As a result of the debt Strahan was appointed a trustee, in which capacity one of his duties was to superintend the sale.

How Strahan's liabilities were converted into assets is illustrated by the history of the *Grand Magazine of Universal Intelligence and Monthly Chronicle of Our Times* (1758-1760). Planned as a monthly publication with high standards and a variety of features, it was advertised extensively and at first seemed to be successful. In the third year of publication, however, interest declined sharply, and the magazine was discontinued. Strahan had purchased a half share at the outset; but his investment was not a total loss, for he made money printing the magazine. Ralph Griffiths, another partner, was much less fortunate: he owed Strahan for printing both the *Grand Magazine* and *The Monthly Review*. Ulti-

mately, Strahan canceled half the debt in exchange for a one-quarter share in *The Monthly Review,* which was successful from its beginning in May 1749 and proved to be one of Strahan's most reliable sources of income.

Another excellent investment was Strahan's one-ninth share in *The London Chronicle* (1 January 1757 to 28 April 1823), from which he also benefited by being its printer. Boswell said that it was circulated on the Continent more extensively than any other English newspaper. It is supposed to be the only newspaper that Johnson regularly read; he also contributed to it, as did Boswell and Franklin. Strahan estimated that in one year the value of his one-ninth share rose to £350; he had paid £20 for it.

Thomas Becket, a former apprentice of Millar's, who became the chief importer in London of French books, which he sold at Tully's Head in the Strand, chose Strahan as printer of most of his publications, including James Macpherson's *Fingal* (1762), the third edition of Thomas Chippendale's *The Gentleman and Cabinet-Makers' Director* (1762), the letters of Lady Mary Wortley Montagu (1763), *The Poetical Works of Mr. William Collins* (1765), John Wilkes's paper *The North Briton,* and Laurence Sterne's *Sermons of Mr. Yorick* (1760) and parts of his *Tristram Shandy* (1760-1767) and *A Sentimental Journey* (1768).

Strahan's largest purchase of shares at one time was at the sale of Millar's stock and shares in 1769, when he bought forty-two titles, bringing the number of shares he owned to more than two hundred. Science and medicine were the fields most frequently represented. There were three works by James Ferguson: *Astronomy Explained upon Sir Isaac Newton's Principles* (1756), *Lectures on Several Subjects, in Mechanics, Hydrostatics, Pneumatics, and Optics* (1760), and *Tables and Tracts, Relative to Several Arts and Sciences* (1767). Another highly regarded work that Strahan acquired at the Millar sale was Sir John Pringle's *Observations on the Diseases of the Army* (1752), for which the author became known as the "founder of modern military medicine." Strahan also bought shares in several Italian and French grammars and two important works on morals: Richard Price's *A Review of the Principal Questions and Difficulties in Morals* (1756) and Adam Smith's *The Theory of Moral Sentiments* (1759), as well as John Locke's works, Jonas Hanway's *An Historical Account of the British Trade over the Caspian Sea* (1753), Fielding's works, and the poems of Thomson.

Thomas Cadell, Millar's successor, shared the ownership of many titles with Strahan, and after

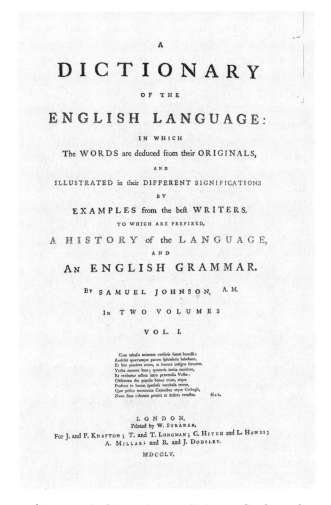

A

DICTIONARY

OF THE

ENGLISH LANGUAGE:

IN WHICH

The WORDS are deduced from their ORIGINALS,

AND

ILLUSTRATED in their DIFFERENT SIGNIFICATIONS

BY

EXAMPLES from the best WRITERS.

TO WHICH ARE PREFIXED,

A HISTORY of the LANGUAGE,

AND

An ENGLISH GRAMMAR.

BY SAMUEL JOHNSON, A.M.

IN TWO VOLUMES

VOL. I.

Cum tabulis animum censoris sumet honesti;
Audebit quaecunque parum splendoris habebam,
Et sine pondere erunt, et honore indigna ferentur,
Verba movere loco; quamvis invita recedant,
Et versentur adhuc intra penetralia Vestae:
Obscurata diu populo bonus eruet, atque
Proferet in lucem speciosa vocabula rerum,
Quae priscis memorata Catonibus atque Cethegis,
Nunc situs informis premit et deserta vetustas.   HOR.

LONDON.
Printed by W. STRAHAN,
For J. and P. KNAPTON; T. and T. LONGMAN; C. HITCH and L. HAWES;
A. MILLAR; and R. and J. DODSLEY.
MDCCLV.

Title pages for Johnson's great dictionary. Strahan, who
received the contract to print it through his connection
with Andrew Millar, made a substantial profit on it.

1770 he was the most important client of Strahan's printing firm. Becoming a share owner increased Strahan's stature and also increased his business: he was able to see to it that many of the books in which he owned shares were printed by his presses.

Another avenue to copyright ownership was direct negotiation with the author. On 4 July 1751 Strahan purchased from Tobias Smollett, for £157 10s., a half share in *A Treatise on the Theory and Practice of Midwifery* (1751), based on lectures given by William Smellie and edited by Smollett. At that point Strahan had already printed several of Smollett's works, including four editions (seven hundred copies) of *Roderick Random* (1748) between 1748 and 1752. The treatise on midwifery went through several editions and allowed Strahan to make a 100 percent profit on his investment. Much less successful was Smollett's novel *Ferdinand Count Fathom* (1753), for which Strahan paid the author

forty pounds for a one-third share. In this, as in many subsequent publishing ventures, Strahan was a silent partner; the imprint said only that the book was "printed for W. Johnson, at the Golden Ball in St. Paul's Courtyard." The association between Smollett and Strahan continued over several publications and was decisive, according to Harlan, in establishing Strahan as a publisher.

Another means to increase business was patent printing, which Strahan took up in 1761 in partnership with Henry Woodfall. The two men bought the patent for law printing from Richardson's widow and Bernard Lintot's granddaughter. It entitled them to print "all manner of law books, which any way relate to the common or statute law of our realm of England," though the privilege was completely defensible only in regard to the common law. A building in Craven Street was extensively remodeled to house the firm. In the seven years that followed the partners grossed sixty-five hundred pounds, enough to cover their initial investment and expenses and provide them a decent profit. When Woodfall died, his share of the patent was inherited by his widow, Mary. Thenceforth books published at Craven House carried the imprint W. Strahan and M. Woodfall, though she was not directly involved in the operation of the business. Strahan scrupulously divided the profits equally between himself and Woodfall until her death in 1781, by which time the partnership had made a gross profit of twelve thousand pounds. By the time Strahan partially retired at the age of sixty-nine he would have divided close to thirty thousand pounds in gross profit with three Woodfalls successively; but there were other benefits as well, such as the prestige of being law printer to the king, of having two printing houses, and of being associated in business with the Woodfalls. Moreover, holding the legal patent enabled Strahan to attract clients to his private printing firm.

Soon after Strahan secured his share in the legal patent he began to pursue an even more desirable patent, that of king's printer, which was due to revert to Charles Eyre in 1770. Strahan paid Eyre five thousand pounds for a one-third share in the patent, and it was agreed that in addition to his share of the profits Strahan was to receive three hundred pounds a year for managing the business (Eyre, a "Wiltshire gentleman," had no actual involvement in printing). The partners agreed to purchase the printing materials of the Baskett family in Blackfriars, the prior holder of the patent, but to house the operation in a new building to be constructed at 8 East Harding Street, Shoe Lane, adjacent to Strahan's New Street firm. Strahan kept the two businesses separate, and the distinction was maintained by his successors.

As the king's printer, the partners had the right to print Bibles and prayer books, acts of Parliament, and any works under the control of the king. Strahan's records reveal that ten years after becoming Eyre's partner, he had received sixty-five hundred pounds in dividends and three thousand pounds in salary. Meanwhile, the value of the patent had increased: in 1780 Strahan estimated that his share of the patent was worth ten thousand pounds, or twice what he had paid for it, and his share of the building, the stock, and the printing materials was worth twenty-five hundred pounds. Beyond that, in becoming the king's printer he had gained the highest title to which a British printer could aspire. By 1770 he had eleven presses in his "private" business and had

opened two "public" printing houses: the Law House, with four presses; and the King's House, with six to nine presses.

When Strahan commenced the king's printing in 1770, he was the leading printer in London. While, as the king's printer, he could not be excluded from parliamentary debates, which he loved to attend, he was often too busy as the king's printer to attend them. Harlan calculates that Strahan's printing came to at least four times as much as the combined output of Richardson and William Bowyer Sr., both of whom were eminent printers.

From 1771 until his death in 1785 Strahan typically put his name in the imprint of the books he published; and he put it first, showing his stature in the trade. Whereas from 1751 to 1770 Strahan's list had been eclectic, in the later period he was associated with many important historical works, including William Robertson's *History of America* (1777), Robert Watson's *The History of the Reign of Philip the Second, King of Spain* (1777), Joseph Nicolson and Richard Burn's *The History and Antiquities of the Counties of Westmorland and Cumberland* (1777), and Philip Yorke's *Miscellaneous State Papers: From 1501 to 1726* (1778). Harlan has calculated that historical works comprised 22 percent of his later publications, science and medicine 12 percent, prose literature 11 percent, biography 9 percent, and philosophy and religion 7 percent. The last grouping had constituted, by a small margin, the largest class of publications in the first half of Strahan's career. In his earliest days as a printer some of his most substantial clients were the Wesley brothers and George Whitefield. In the 1740s Strahan could have been taken for a printer of religious literature.

During the last fifteen years of his life Strahan was involved in three kinds of publishing activities: purchasing shares in works previously published, purchasing copyrights from authors of new works, and ownership of part of the stock of two other publishers, Cadell and Thomas Longman II. Harlan estimates that during this period Strahan published works by seventy authors, of whom twenty-five were Scotsmen; most of the latter were the most popular writers on Strahan's list.

Strahan's one-third share in the *Domestic Medicine* (1772) of the Scots physician James Buchan was among his most successful investments; it was one of the most popular medical manuals of the eighteenth century, and by 1783 Strahan had printed twenty-six thousand copies of it. Smollett's *Travels Through France and Italy* (1766) had been successful for four years when Strahan bought a one-sixth share in it, and it continued to be popular for sev-

THE

HISTORY

OF THE

DECLINE AND FALL

OF THE

ROMAN EMPIRE,

By EDWARD GIBBON, Esq;

VOLUME THE FIRST.

Jam provideo animo, velut qui, proximis littori vadis inducti, mare pedibus ingredi-
untur, quicquid progredior, in vastiorem me altitudinem, ac velut profundum invehi ; et
crescere pene opus, quod prima quæque perficiendo minui videbatur.

LONDON:

PRINTED FOR W. STRAHAN; AND T. CADELL, IN THE STRAND,
MDCCLXXVI.

AN

INQUIRY

INTO THE

Nature and Caufes

OF THE

WEALTH OF NATIONS.

By ADAM SMITH, LL. D. and F. R. S.
Formerly Profeffor of Moral Philofophy in the Univerfity of GLASGOW.

IN TWO VOLUMES

VOL. I.

LONDON:

PRINTED FOR W. STRAHAN; AND T. CADELL, IN THE STRAND.
MDCCLXXVI.

Title pages for two prestigious—and profitable—works published by Strahan in 1776

eral more years. In 1771 Strahan purchased a one-half share in *Fingal* (1762), by "Ossian" (James Macpherson); the high price he paid — £150 — shows how highly the poem was still valued almost ten years after its first publication.

A coup for Strahan was his purchase in 1771 of a half share in Henry Mackenzie's novel *The Man of Feeling* for £25 5s. By the time the eighth edition appeared in June 1783, at least sixty-nine hundred copies had been printed. It was one of Strahan's most profitable publications. Strahan subsequently paid Mackenzie £52 10s. for a half share in his novel *The Man of the World* (1773).

Not everything that Strahan touched turned to gold. He, together with Cadell, made the mistake of paying six thousand pounds for John Hawkesworth's *An Account of the Voyages Undertaken by the Order of His Present Majesty for Making Discoveries in the Southern Hemisphere, and Successively Performed by Commodore Byron, Captain Wallis, Captain Carteret, and Captain Cook, in the Dolphin, the Swallow, and the Endeavour* (1773), which was universally condemned. A happier venture was the publication of *A Tour through*

Sicily and Malta (1773), by Capt. Patrick Brydone, which was recommended to Strahan by Hume. Six editions of 6,750 copies were printed in less than four years.

One of the most successful of all Strahan's publications was *A Father's Legacy to His Daughters* (1774), by John Gregory. The book presented fatherly advice on religion, conduct, amusements, friendship, love, and marriage. For £25 10s. Strahan purchased a half share in both that work and Gregory's *Elements of the Practice of Physic* (first published in 1772). Between April 1774 and October 1775 six editions of one thousand copies each were published of *A Father's Legacy to His Daughters*. Demand then fell off but did not end. The tenth edition appeared in 1784.

Strahan printed and published Johnson's *A Journey to the Western Islands of Scotland* in 1775. The following year the first volume of what was probably his most prestigious publication appeared: Edward Gibbon's *The History of the Decline and Fall of the Roman Empire* (1776–1788). Gibbon wrote in his memoirs that "So moderate were our hopes, that the original impression had been stinted to five hundred, till the number was doubled, by the prophetic taste of Mr. Strahan."

Strahan also owned a substantial share in Smith's monumental *An Inquiry into the Nature and Causes of the Wealth of Nations* (1776). Though it did not sell as well as Gibbon's book, its sale, Strahan wrote to Hume, "has been more than I could have expected from a work that requires much thought and reflection (qualities that do not abound among modern readers) to peruse to any purpose."

A more popular book was Hugh Blair's five-volume *Sermons* (1777–1801), which Strahan turned down when it was first offered to him. After he received a note from Johnson praising one of the sermons he discussed it with Johnson, then sent a letter to Blair, enclosing Johnson's note, and saying that he had changed his mind and would like to publish the *Sermons*. Boswell recorded in his biography of Johnson that in view of the immediate success of the book, Strahan and Cadell voluntarily doubled the price they had paid Blair for the copyright and tripled it for the second volume. By the time Strahan died he had printed a total of 33,500 copies of the *Sermons* — the largest number of copies printed of any publication with which Strahan was associated.

Harlan attributes Strahan's success as a publisher to six factors: his ability to purchase a great many shares; his talent for getting to know important people and for impressing them; his ability to relate cordially to authors and his willingness to compensate them fairly; his insight into the reading tastes of the public; his ethnic identity as a Scot at a time when many of the most popular English authors were Scots; and, finally, the fact that he was a highly articulate man with sound taste and literary judgment. He earned the respect and admiration of Franklin by writing lucid, objective accounts of political events in England, which were printed in the *Pennsylvania Gazette*. He was a fine letter writer; Franklin in one of his letters to "dear Straney" says, "So excellent a manner of writing seems to me a superfluous gift to a mere printer." As a printer he did not produce works that would be valued by posterity for their appearance, but he was careful and conscientious in his craft; Hume several times complimented Strahan on his emendations of the author's texts. Next to a charge for correcting the proofs of John Milton's *Paradise Regained* in 1753 Strahan's ledger included a note by Strahan: "As the most uncommon care was taken in correcting the above Books, every sheet being carefully read by the Printer, no less than ten times over, he hopes that if they really turn out to be the most correct editions hitherto published (not otherwise) the Proprietors will think him entitled to such a Reward for his Labour as they would have given to a person employed on purpose."

In anticipation of lightening his workload Strahan had made his son Billy a partner in his printing business in 1767, but Billy soon decided to go into business by himself. Strahan's second son, George, had no taste for the business, choosing instead to take holy orders; he attended Johnson on his deathbed. Strahan's youngest son, Andrew, had been apprenticed to his father on 4 October 1763 and proved to be a good printer and partner as well as a worthy successor. On William Strahan's death in 1785, Andrew Strahan inherited most of his estate, including the private printing business and half of the king's printer's patent. Like his father, he was a vigorous and successful businessman. According to Richard A. Austen-Leigh, Andrew Strahan inherited "his father's professional eminence, his political attachments, his consistency of public conduct, and his private virtues. By his generous encouragement of genius he attained the very highest rank of his profession, and became equally eminent for the correctness of his typography and the liberality of his dealings." Like his father he was copublisher with Cadell of many important works and a member of Parliament.

To extend his premises, Strahan acquired buildings at 6 and 7 Newstreet Square in 1800. In the following years he acquired adjacent buildings that would be identified with the firm for many decades to come. In 1804 he took William Preston, a former employee, into partnership. Preston died in 1818.

Strahan, who had no children, took into his business the fourth and fifth sons of his sister Margaret and her husband, John Spottiswoode. Andrew and Robert Spottiswoode succeeded their uncle in the management of the business in 1819. Strahan died in 1831.

Robert Spottiswoode, the younger of the brothers, died in 1832. Andrew Spottiswoode was a member of Parliament for Saltash and then for Colchester. He married Mary, the daughter of the publisher Thomas Norton Longman, and had two sons, William and George Andrew. When they inherited the family business on Andrew Spottiswoode's death in 1866, it was formally divided into the two parts in which it had always functioned. The patent was exercised by William Spottiswoode as a partner in Eyre and Spottiswoode, which survived as a publisher until 1989. The private printing, William Strahan's original business, went to George Andrew Spottiswoode as a partner in Spottiswoode and Company, later Spottiswoode, Ballantyne, and Company.

Biography:

J. A. Cochrane, *Dr. Johnson's Printer: The Life of William Strahan* (Cambridge, Mass.: Harvard University Press, 1964).

References:

Richard A. Austen-Leigh, *The Story of a Printing House: Being a Short Account of the Strahans and Spottiswoodes,* second edition (London: Eyre & Spottiswoode, 1912);

O. M. Brack, "William Strahan: *Scottish* Printer and Publisher," *Arizona Quarterly,* 31 (Summer 1975): 179–191;

Robert Dale Harlan, "William Strahan: Eighteenth Century London Printer and Publisher," dissertation, University of Michigan, 1960;

Patricia Hernlund, "Problems of Editing Business and Trade Manuscripts," in *Eighteenth-Century English Books* (Chicago: Association of College and Research Libraries, 1976), pp. 42–81;

Keith I. D. Maslen, "William Strahan at the Bowyer Press, 1736–1738," *Library,* fifth series 25 (September 1970): 250–251.

Papers:

The ledgers of William Strahan's printing firm are held by the British Museum and are available on microfilm. The David Hall Collections of the libraries of the American Philosophical Society and the Historical Society of Pennsylvania hold collections of Strahan's correspondence and business records.

– Sandra Naiman

The Strawberry Hill Press

(Twickenham: 1757 – 1797)

See also the Horace Walpole entries in *DLB 39: British Novelists, 1660–1800,* and *DLB 104: British Prose Writers, 1660–1800, Second Series.*

The Strawberry Hill Press was begun by the novelist, essayist, aesthetician, and eccentric Horace Walpole. Walpole was the fourth earl of Orford, the son of Sir Robert Walpole, Britain's longest-serving prime minister. As a writer Horace Walpole is remembered chiefly for *The Castle of Otranto* (1764), which served to define the key elements of the genre. His letters are still studied, as well.

Walpole established the press, also referred to by him as the *Officina Arbuteana,* in 1757 in two rooms of his Gothic villa, Strawberry Hill, at Twickenham, on the River Thames near London. The press had its origin in his fascination with the processes of printing and publication rather than in some systematic plan to establish a commercially viable business. Many of its publications had small print runs and were never intended for retail sale, and few hold any real literary interest. Walpole's publishing output can be divided into two main categories: books and what Walpole called Detached Pieces.

Walpole's fascination with the Gothic was to find its way into engravings, designs, and typographical embellishments of the press's publications. Gothic elements are especially evident in the work of John Henry Müntz, a Swiss painter and engraver who worked for Walpole from June 1755

until November 1759, when, amid some acrimony, the artist was dismissed. Such disputes were not uncommon, Walpole being neither the easiest nor the most stable of men for whom to work – although his next engraver, Joseph Forrester, remained with Walpole for seven years (albeit as an indentured apprentice). Other engravers were hired for particular jobs; despite Walpole's hobbyist approach and his sometimes careless procedure in record keeping, which makes it hard to establish with accuracy the proceedings of the Strawberry Hill Press, he was an enthusiastic printer and publisher. He actively solicited manuscripts, occasionally from authors who were reluctant to work with him – as was the case with Thomas Gray, whose *Odes by Mr. Gray* (1757) was the first work printed by the Strawberry Hill Press.

Walpole also proofread – though not always reliably – and he chose the papers and types used by the press. The best Dutch and Whatman papers were selected by Walpole and purchased by his agent, Jacob Tonson. For the first print run of Gray's *Odes* the author's regular publisher, Robert Dodsley, supplied the paper. The type used by the Strawberry Hill Press was produced and supplied by William Caslon, the first British manufacturer of type to produce a complete range of high-quality Roman and Italic types. Caslon also produced Greek and exotic scripts. By the time Walpole established his press, Caslon types had become recognized as the profession's standard and had replaced

Horace Walpole, founder and proprietor of the Strawberry Hill Press (after a portrait by Sir Thomas Lawrence)

types imported from Europe. Caslon types allowed Walpole and his printers to produce a consistent quality of reproduction, whether for runs as small as a dozen or as large as seven hundred copies. The title-page fleurons for Strawberry Hill editions were designed by Walpole's friend Richard Bentley, who had contributed extensively to the villa's refurbishment in the Gothic style (Bentley's father, Richard Bentley, edited Lucan's *Pharsalia,* published by the press in 1760).

Walpole hired William Robinson, a flamboyant Irishman, as his first printer. In June 1757 Walpole gave his printing press a public opening and invited many of the leading printers, publishers, and booksellers. Although he was haphazard at best about keeping records of the number of copies printed of any edition (often a number would be chosen arbitrarily and entered long after the event), A. T. Hazen has established that Robinson singlehandedly began the printing of two thousand copies of Gray's *Odes* on 16 July 1757. The first publication should have been Richard Bentley's translation of Paul Hentzner's *A Journey into England* (1757), but Walpole discovered during the typesetting of that book that the volume of Gray's odes was nearing completion, despite Gray's slow composition and

arduous revision process. Walpole virtually bullied Gray and his publisher, Dodsley – who had already paid forty guineas for the rights to Gray's book – into letting the Strawberry Hill Press print the poems. The title page was an advertisement for the press, featuring a vignette of Strawberry Hill. Bentley's translation was delayed only briefly, however. According to Walpole's journal, 220 copies were printed. Walpole wrote the prefatory advertisement, and Hentzner's late-sixteenth-century account was elegantly produced in a bilingual edition, with the original Latin text Bentley's translation on facing pages.

Having been launched in a fairly auspicious manner with two major publications, the Strawberry Hill Press consolidated its reputation in its second year. The press published Walpole's own *Catalogue of Royal and Noble Authors* (1758), consisting of bibliography, criticism, and antiquarian discourse. The first edition had a print run of three hundred copies. It was followed by another collection by Walpole, *Fugitive Pieces in Verse and Prose* (1758), comprising essays and poems, many of which had previously been published in the influential periodical *The World.*

Two other publications of 1758 reveal Walpole's charitable impulses and show that he did

The printing house at Strawberry Hill

not regard the Strawberry Hill Press as a profit-making business. Walpole had borrowed the manuscript for Charles, Lord Whitworth's *An Account of Russia as It Was in the Year 1710* from a neighbor, Richard Owen Cambridge, and had become so enamored of it that he decided to publish it. Of the seven hundred copies of the first edition printed, the proceeds from six hundred copies went to the poor of the parish of Twickenham. The six hundred copies sold within two weeks, after which the book went to be reprinted in London. The charitable object of the publication of Joseph Spence's *A Parallel, in the Manner of Plutarch, Between a Most Celebrated Man of Florence, and One, Scarce Ever Heard of, in England* was the "one, scarce ever heard of" of the title, Robert Hill, a Buckingham tailor with a compendious knowledge of ancient languages, particularly Latin, Hebrew, and Greek. (The "celebrated man of Florence" in the title was Antonio Magliabecchi, a renowned librarian.) Walpole printed seven hundred copies of the work, which was sold by Dodsley, Gray's publisher and one of Walpole's paper suppliers.

In the summer of 1758 Walpole bought forty manuscripts from the widow of the engraver George Vertue, consisting of uncollated notebooks of ill-edited biographical, historical, and critical information on British artists. From this unwieldy collection Walpole compiled the highly significant and influential *Anecdotes of Painting in England* (1762–

1780). As R. W. Ketton-Cremer points out, "It is hardly possible to exaggerate the service that Walpole rendered to the history of art by his rescue of Vertue's manuscripts, and by his extremely competent handling of them in the *Anecdotes.*" Walpole encountered many difficulties in preparing the work from Vertue's notes. He began by compiling the index, and he had completed two volumes by October 1760; but his printer, Thomas Farrer, disappeared, delaying the publication of the first volume until 1762, by which time Walpole had completed volume three of the work.

If 1758 had been for Walpole an annus mirabilis, 1759 was to prove his *annus horibilis,* with a marked reversal of fortune for the press. Work on Bentley's annotated edition of Lucan's *Pharsalia* was under way when, in March, Robinson was let go and replaced by Benjamin Williams, whose tenure at Strawberry Hill was approximately eight weeks. James Lister, his replacement, stayed just one week. Lister was replaced by Farrer, who soon disappeared. Finally, Kirgate was hired, and he remained with Walpole until Walpole's death, with the exception of a three-year hiatus (1765 to 1768) when Walpole was in France.

It is fair to say that the contribution to printing made by the Strawberry Hill Press was due as much to Kirgate as to Walpole. The printer was as zealous a collector and bibliographer as was his master; according to Hazen, he collected anything

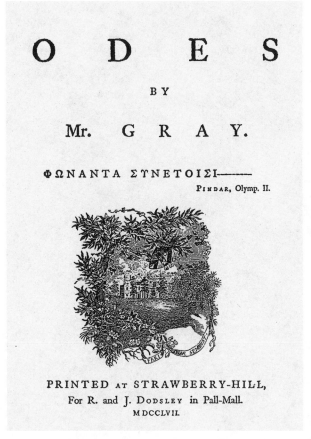

O D E S

BY

Mr. G R A Y.

ΦΩΝΑΝΤΑ ΣΥΝΕΤΟΙΣΙ———
PINDAR, Olymp. II.

PRINTED AT STRAWBERRY-HILL,
For R. and J. DODSLEY in Pall-Mall.
MDCCLVII.

Title page for the first publication of the Strawberry Hill Press

he could find of "Walpolian interest" and "consistently added notes about the rarity or importance of the various pieces."

When Walpole returned from France in 1768, Kirgate was reappointed to his post as printer, along with which he assumed the position of Walpole's secretary. After the reopening of the press, however, Walpole did not publish any works as important as those he had published before his sojourn in France.

During the year of Walpole's return the Strawberry Hill Press produced two hundred copies of Charles Jean Hénault's tragedy *Cornelie Vestale,* along with fifty copies of Walpole's own blank-verse tragedy, *The Mysterious Mother.* The small print run for Walpole's work may be explained by the fact that the author anticipated a negative reception for the play, which dealt with incest. It shocked even Walpole's admirers; nevertheless, it was praised by George Gordon, Lord Byron, who thought it was in the tradition of the greatest tragedies. In the same year Walpole embarked on a plan

of printing a quarto edition of his own works. Although the project remained unfinished in his lifetime, it would form the basis of the posthumously published five-volume edition of Walpole's works (1798).

The year 1769 brought another of Walpole's charitable printings. The recipient of the proceeds was an impoverished clergyman, Francis Hoyland, whose verse the Strawberry Hill Press published in an edition of three hundred copies. In 1772 Walpole saw the completion of a volume that had been on his mind for some twenty years: a new edition of the *Mémoires du Comte de Grammont.* Walpole added comprehensive notes, made corrections to proper names, and wrote a preface. *Miscellaneous Antiquities,* edited by Walpole, was published in the same year.

In 1780 the fourth volume of *Anecdotes of Painting in England,* which had been ready since 1771, was published. Walpole had refrained from publishing the volume because some of the artists who were commented on in a less-than-flattering light were still alive at the earlier date. The fourth vol-

Thomas Kirgate, printer and secretary for the Strawberry Hill Press
(Courtesy of the Providence Public Library)

ume reflected a particular interest of its editor as, in addition to the commentary on British artists, it considered at length the current state of English architecture. The volume closed with Walpole's *Essay on Modern Gardening,* which was subsequently translated into French by Louis-Jules-Barbon Mancini-Mazarini, Duc de Nivernois, as *Essai sur l'Art des Jardins* and reprinted at Strawberry Hill in a bilingual edition in 1785. Kirgate was aided in the printing of this edition by Edward Yardley, who was hired for the month of August at the rate of a guinea per week. In the same year a collection of six fairy tales, titled *Hieroglyphic Tales,* was published. In 1787 Walpole met the sisters Mary and Agnes Berry; by the following year they had become close friends of Walpole's and were addressed by the author in one of his detached pieces.

Little else of any worth was published by the press. Among the more notable of the minor pieces was Hannah More's *Bishop Bonner's Ghost* (1789), probably the last full-length book to be published by the Strawberry Hill Press during Walpole's lifetime.

The best-known work *not* published by Walpole's press was the collection of poems supposedly authored by a fifteenth-century priest, Thomas Rowley. In 1769 Thomas Chatterton sent the manuscripts, which he had, in fact, written himself, to Dodsley and other documents relating to the imaginary Rowley to Walpole, to be published by Strawberry Hill. Walpole was taken in initially but he soon discovered Chatterton's deception with the aid of Gray and withdrew from the project. The suicide of the seventeen-year-old Chatterton followed shortly afterward. Walpole was reviled and blamed for Chatterton's death by William Wordsworth, Samuel Taylor Coleridge, others, but it has since been demonstrated that Walpole was not in any way to blame for Chatterton's suicide. Walpole died in 1797 – ironically, not at Strawberry Hill, the house with which his name is so closely associated, but in his London home in Berkeley Square.

In his will Walpole left Kirgate only one hundred pounds, a pittance for the service and devotion the printer had shown to the often irascible writer. It appears that Kirgate set about reprinting some of the press's pieces, usually selling them as original editions or authorized reprints to raise money for himself. Among the last of Kirgate's republications was the appropriately titled *The Printer's Farewell* (1797). Kirgate, who did not pursue the profession of forgery for long, was responding to the demand for rare books from the Strawberry Hill Press that had arisen almost immediately after Walpole's death.

Bibliography:

A. T. Hazen, *A Bibliography of the Strawberry Hill Press with a Record of the Prices at which Copies have been Sold including a New Supplement* (Folkstone & London: Dawsons, 1973).

Biography:

R. W. Ketton-Cremer, *Horace Walpole: A Biography* (Ithaca, N.Y.: Cornell University Press, 1964).

References:

Austin Dobson, *Horace Walpole, A Memoir* (London: Osgood, McIlvaine, 1890);

W. S. Lewis, "The Genesis of Strawberry Hill," *Metropolitan Museum of Art Studies,* 5 (June 1934): 57–92.

Papers:

The most extensive collection of Horace Walpole materials is at the Lewis Walpole Library of Yale University in Farmington, Connecticut.

– Julian Wolfreys

Effingham Wilson

(London: 1806 – 1931)

The publishing house of Effingham Wilson has nearly escaped the notice of literary historians. There are no articles or chapters devoted to it, and the majority of scholars – even specialists in the nineteenth century – would hardly recognize its name. Yet when Wilson died in 1868 he was memorialized as the dean of London publishers, a brave and independent soul who had defied equally attempts at suppression by authorities and widespread corruption within the book trade itself. He stood as a model of firm principle at a time when, as Thomas Carlyle put it in *Sartor Resartus* (1836), "Puffery and Quackery have reached a height unexampled in the annals of mankind." In 1833 John Stuart Mill told Carlyle of Wilson's enlightened opposition to the common practice of "puffing": "I find both from enquiry and observation that the puffing system has worn itself out, even more rapidly than seemed likely; & a united chorus of praise from all the press will scarcely now sell fifty copies of any work: Effingham Wilson the bookseller is so sensible of this that he has resolved to cease advertising the praises of periodicals and to sell his wares by *samples,* advertising passages of the works themselves." Carlyle replied morosely, "Bookselling even Effingham Wilson finds to be about *dead* – of Puffery." The book trade's exaggerated claims in advertising its products lost credibility with the reading public. Yet amid what Thomas Frognall Dibdin called "bibliophobia," Wilson promoted the genuine merits of his authors and drew into his fold such ascendant literary figures as Alfred Tennyson, Robert Browning, Sarah Austin, and John Sterling to complement a catalogue already enriched by writers of the previous generation such as Jeremy Bentham, William Hazlitt, and Samuel Taylor Coleridge. Though never as dominant among publishers of belles lettres as Edward Moxon, William Pickering, or John Murray, Wilson should be remembered especially for encouraging, in his early years, young literary talent spurned by more-cautious publishers.

Between 1806 and 1931 Wilson published 1,387 titles that were catalogued by the British Library. (British Library holdings of Moxon's publications total 412 titles, of Pickering's 1,112 titles, and of Murray's 5,535 titles.) Extrapolating from a combination of sources, it is possible to estimate Wilson's total output at around 2,500 titles – a highly respectable achievement. Wilson's publisher's device, a cricket or grasshopper in a laurel wreath, was probably adopted from the crest of Sir Thomas Gresham, founder of the Royal Exchange, where the firm's offices were located. (Some historians suggest that the crest was derived from the German word *Grassheim,* homophonous with *Gresham.*) The grasshopper's chirp led to the rescue of an infant in a favorite tale in the "goody magazines" of Wilson's early years.

Wilson was born near Richmond, Yorkshire, in 1783. In 1802 he moved to London, where he learned the book trade under John Sewell and James

Effingham Wilson in 1862

Asperne, who published the *European Magazine* at 32 Cornhill, and Thomas Hurst of Paternoster Row, who had a brief alliance with the house of Longman during Wilson's time with the firm.

In 1805 Wilson went into business as a bookseller, handling political pamphlets. Two pamphlets in the form of letters addressed to the Prince of Wales by "an Englishman" but ascribed to a disgruntled member of Parliament, James Paull, reveal Wilson's desire to promote criticism of Tory interests. Wilson defied a challenge from Attorney General Sir Vicary Gibbs that had dissuaded the rest of the book trade from selling these works. *A Plain Letter to His Royal Highness the Prince of Wales, upon His Plain Duties to Himself, His Wife, His Child, and to the Nation: As Such Duties Arise Out of the Late Investigation of the Conduct of the Princess of Wales. By the Author of A Letter to the Hon. C. J. Fox, upon His Conduct on the Several Motions of Mr. Paull, against the Marquis Wellesley* (1806) was followed by two undated editions and a

sequel, *The Prince of Wales: A Second Plain Letter to His Royal Highness, Wherein His Plain Duties to Himself, His Wife, His Child and to the Country Are More Plainly Shewn than in the First: Also, That His Royal Highness Is an Accomplished Gentleman, a Virtuous Man, a Good Christian, and a Sound Philosopher. With Remarks on the Correspondence upon His Claim for Military Rank and Employment; Which Likewise Prove, the Duke of York to Be a Great Author, a Good Swimmer and an Able General* (1806?).

Wilson's imprint first emerged from Chapter House Court, St. Paul's Churchyard, in 1806, and his satiric proclivities appeared at once in works such as *The Fashionable World Reformed*, by "Philokosmos," and the anonymous *Royal Legend: A Tale of the 14th Century*, published the following year. By the summer of 1812 Wilson had moved his business to 88 Cornhill, the southeast corner of the second Royal Exchange. Criticism of the Prince of Wales entailed considerable risk at the time – John Hunt, for example, was imprisoned on charges of sedition for his *Examiner* articles. Yet the excesses of the Regency demanded reproof, and Wilson gambled in publishing several attacks that became popular and went through multiple editions. The anonymous author of *In Memory of Effingham Wilson* (1869) tells the story of how the Duke of York's aide-de-camp arrived one day at the Royal Exchange with a horsewhip and announced his intention of punishing the publisher for a recent pamphlet: "Mr. Wilson, nothing daunted by the appearance of his military visitor, or the sight of the weapon, but standing bolt upright, requested the Colonel to fulfill his commission, but, he added, 'the moment you lay hands on me, you will find it necessary to make your appearance before the Lord Mayor.'" With a torrent of threats the aide departed, and the episode concludes, "Those who knew Effingham Wilson as we knew him, will feel pretty certain that had the Colonel but raised his arm to strike, something would have occurred prior to his appearance at the Mansion House."

Chief among Wilson's early pamphleteers was George Daniel, whose most celebrated work was the suppressed *R—y—l Stripes: or a Kick from Yar——th to Wa——s; with the Particulars of an Expedition to Oat——ds and the Sprained Ancle: A Poem, by P——P——, Poet Laureat* (1812). One of the few surviving copies, in the British Library, includes Daniel's manuscript note explaining the scandal: "The poem is founded on a report that Lord Yarmouth had horsewhipped the Prince Regent at the Duke of York's (Oatlands) for making certain overtures to his mother-in-law the Marchioness of Hertford." Wilson printed the poem, which, Daniel continues, became "excessively rare – I believe there are not *six copies* in existence (two are in my own possession & one in the hands of a friend to whom I presented it, at Ipswich). It was suppressed and bought up (before it was published) in January 1812 by order of *The Prince Regent* & through the instrumentality of *Lord Yarmouth* and *Colonel McMahon,* a large sum being given to the author for the Copyright. It was advertised & placarded, which drew public attention to it, & a copy was by some means procured by the parties above mentioned who applied to the Publisher before any copies were circulated. The author secured *four* copies only – One of which he sold to a public Institution for five guineas. A man at the west end of the town who had procured a copy made a considerable sum by advertising & selling *manuscript* copies at half-a-guinea each." Such was the succès de scandale that formed Wilson's reputation. Daniel also wrote tamer poetry in a William

Cowperesque mode, and Wilson published a collection of it in 1812 with a portrait frontispiece by Henry Corbould, the draftsman hired by the British Museum to draw the Elgin Marbles. The same year Wilson published Daniel's anonymous triple-decker novel *The Adventures of Dick Distich.* Daniel's satire sometimes ran in an Augustan vein and recommended him to the company of Charles Lamb, whose circle he enjoyed for many years. Wilson published Daniel's further attacks on the prince regent, *The R——l First-Born; or, The Baby out of His Leading-Strings* (1812), *Suppressed Evidence; or, R——l Intriguing* (1813), and a general satire of literary culture, *The Modern Dunciad* (1814), that spared only Cowper, George Crabbe, Robert Southey, and George Gordon, Lord Byron, and went through four editions within a year. This volume included a caricature frontispiece by another satiric artist whose association with Wilson helped shape the firm's reputation: George Cruikshank.

From 1809 to 1848 there are fourteen Wilson titles with Cruikshank illustrations. Sometimes Wilson would obtain a plate for a broadside Cruikshank had published separately; at other times he would commission Cruikshank to illustrate reprints of classics such as Tobias Smollett's translations of *Gil Blas* and *Don Quixote,* both published in 1833 for Roscoe's Novelist's Library. Wilson published separately Cruikshank's illustrations for J. Y. Akerman's *Tales of Other Days* (1830). Cruikshank was joined on occasion by his brother, Robert, who also illustrated Wilson's satires, most notably Anthony Hudson's *The Old Black Cock and His Dunghill Advisers in Jeopardy; or, the Palace that Jack Built* (1820) and the anonymous *The Real Devil's Walk: Not by Professor Porson.* (1830)

Wilson's early success owed no small part to his relations with Bentham. He published Bentham's *Plan of Parliamentary Reform* (1817), *Church of Englandism and Its Catechism Examined* (1818), and *Bentham's Radical Reform Bill* (1819). Wilson's surviving correspondence with Bentham shows the publisher attempting to recover copies of Bentham's earlier works for reprinting or resale. In the early 1820s Wilson published at least four more Bentham titles, the most significant of which marked the only collaboration between Wilson and William Pickering: the third edition of Bentham's first book, *A Fragment on Government* (1823). (Although advertised as the second edition, the Wilson/Pickering edition had been preceded by a pirated, corrupt Dublin edition published in 1776, the same year as the first edition.) Another work in this group, *The Elements of the Art of Packing as Applied to Special Juries* (1821), had, according to *The Bookseller* (1 July 1868), "been refused by Bentham's former publishers, and had lain in MS. for ten years in consequence." Wilson's relations with Bentham reflect the publisher's commitment to reform literature and probably account for his appeal to radicals and young poets of the 1830s.

Wilson also published self-help books, such as H. Le Blanc's *The Art of Tying the Cravat* (1828), Hallifield Cosgayne O'Donnoghue's *Marriage: The Source of Social Happiness* (1828), "An Old Physician's" *Health without Physic* (1829), *Composition and Punctuation Familiarly Explained* (1829), and *Vegetable Cookery* (1829); more than half of his titles in 1829 fell into this category and appeared just in time for the Christmas season. He also published introductions to foreign languages and French-language guides for foreign travelers in England. His location at the Royal Exchange no doubt suggested to him the utility of another sort of companion for foreign visitors and investors, books such as Edward Jenkins's *Value of French and English Measures and Money* (1826) and William Tate's *Manual of Foreign Exchanges* (1829). The portion of his catalogue devoted to travel literature introduced remote corners of the empire and places as exotic as Brazil, Bermuda, and Babylon. He also promoted the study of institutions closer to home with books such as John Iliff Wilson's *A Brief History of Christ's Hospital* (1828?), which went through five editions by 1830. Wilson matured as a publisher in the 1820s, and his radicalism evolved into a liberalism that elevated intellectual debate and self-betterment over anarchy. Even his anticlericalism moderated. Early in the decade he might publish an anonymous satire on George IV, such as Hudson's *The R——l Fowls; or, the Old Black Cock's Attempt to Crow over His Illustrious Mate* (1820) or the immensely popular *A Peep at the P*v****n; or, Boiled Mutton and Caper Sauce at the Temple of Joss* (1820), but by its end he was publishing George E. Biber's *Christian Education, in a Course of Lectures* (1830) and the Dean of St. Paul's Convocation Sermon (1831). Wilson befriended the educator George Birkbeck and supported the Mechanics Institutes, the Society for the Diffusion of Useful Knowledge, and other foundations for the spread of learning to the working classes. Wilson represented a fusion of new Radical and old Whig: he could, all at the same time, appeal for public subscriptions to defray the election debts of Mill's friend, the classical historian and reform member of Parliament George Grote; serve on the council of the London Political Union; and advertise himself in his 1831 catalogue as "Bookseller to the Emperor of all the

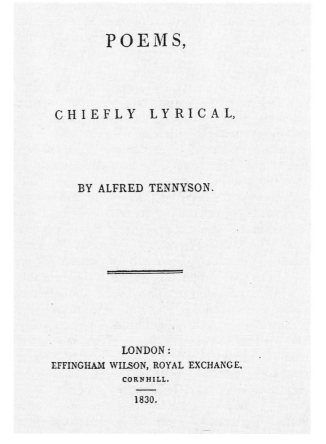

POEMS,

CHIEFLY LYRICAL,

BY ALFRED TENNYSON.

LONDON:
EFFINGHAM WILSON, ROYAL EXCHANGE,
CORNHILL.
1830.

Title page for one of Tennyson's early books, a work that led to a dispute between author and publisher

Russias." In any case, he was no favorite of English Tories, whether at the *Times*, a paper he perpetually annoyed with satires and that snubbed his publications in consequence, or in his guild, the Clothworkers' Company, which withheld from him his rightful vote because he published books "inimical to the State."

One of the enigmas unanswered by Tennyson's biographers is why the young poet would ask Wilson to publish his first independent book, *Poems, Chiefly Lyrical*, early in 1830. Tennyson's fellow Cambridge Apostles, John Sterling and F. D. Maurice, had already joined Bentham's followers in the London Debating Society; through them Wilson must have been known at Cambridge as a reform publisher who also gambled on literature. *Poems, Chiefly Lyrical* was published in June 1830 in six hundred copies, bound in boards, and sold for five shillings. Tennyson complained to Wilson about its restricted distribution and communicated through his friend Arthur Henry Hallam his desire to have it sold in Cambridge, Cheltenham, and Louth. Hallam apparently found Wilson difficult and led Tennyson to his next publisher, Moxon. Moxon probably heard of Wilson's loss on the volume, for his first run of Tennyson's next book, *Poems* (1832), was only three-quarters as large.

Wilson took an active part in the debate over so-called taxes on knowledge, duties on printed products. Much of his trade consisted of pamphlets and occasional tracts directed at the broader reading public. According to *In Memory of Effingham Wilson* (1869), "One of the first cheap periodicals, in 1834–36, entitled *The Parterre [of Fiction, Poetry, History, Literature, and the Fine Arts]*, was his and had for some time considerable success. Mr. Wilson also started in the very earliest days of the railway system, *The Railway Journal [The Railway Magazine*, founded May 1835], but it proved to be, at the period of its first production, before its time. He sold it to Mr. Herapath [in March 1836], who attached his name to the paper, and it became afterwards a great property. [Wilson] published for many years, and his house still publishes, a larger number of pamphlets than any other firm in the trade." To defend these interests, in 1831 Wilson assembled a collection titled *The Moral and Political Evils of the Taxes on Knowledge, Expounded in the Speeches Delivered at the City of London Literary and Scientific Institution on the Subject of a Petition to Parliament against the Continuance of the Stamp Duty on Newspapers, the Duties on Advertisements, and on Printing-Paper.* Without a means of spreading knowledge from Parliament to the people, Wilson feared, the uninformed mob would be left to operate on rumor. On the other hand, Wilson was active in the book trade's attempts to keep its wholesale and retail prices high; Pickering accused Wilson and other booksellers of conspiring to prevent price cutting by ambitious tradesmen. Bookselling was an increasingly risky business, and Wilson was unwilling to jeopardize the profession in the name of competition.

In collaboration with Chapman and Hall, Wilson acquired the rights to William Hazlitt's last work, the four-volume *Life of Napoleon* (1830), from the defunct firm of Hunt and Clarke. This was an especially brave venture, since John Lockhart's and Walter Scott's treatments of the subject were still fresh on the market. Besides the Cruikshanks another young illustrator, Alfred Crowquill, contributed to Wilson's catalogue in the early 1830s. Wilson continued to contribute to reform agitation with works such as John Wade's *The Extraordinary Black Book: An Exposition of the United Church of England and Ireland; Civil List and Crown Revenues; Incomes, Privileges and Power, of the Aristocracy; Privy Council, Diplo-* *matic, and Consular Establishments; Law and Judicial Administration; Representation and Prospects of Reform under the New Ministry. The Whole Corrected from the Latest Official Returns, and Presenting a Complete View of the Expenditure, Patronage, Influence and Abuses of the Government in Church, State, Law and Representation* (1831), an exposé of Parliament sometimes called "The Reformer's Bible." One of the leading ladies of the Bentham circle, Austin, translated the amorous correspondence of the German rogue and fortune hunter, Prince Hermann Pückler-Muskau; when John Murray flinched, Wilson accepted the two-volume work, which became one of the hits of the 1831 Christmas trade. A year later Austin produced for Wilson *Selections from the Old Testament,* and he continued to publish her translations of European literature for several years. When Austin's three-volume *Characteristics of Goethe* appeared in May 1833, only one book in Wilson's career had surpassed its price, the mysterious novel *Fitzgeorge* at 31s. 6d. in June 1832. *Fitzgeorge* was published anonymously, went through two editions, and has been attributed to Sterling, whose triple-decker *Arthur Coningsby* was published anonymously by Wilson in January 1833.

After the passage of the Reform Bill of 1832 a larger proportion of literature accompanied Wilson's perennial interest in politics, finance, travel, and foreign affairs. Charles Cowden Clarke had original work and his editions of the works of Geoffrey Chaucer (1833–1835) published by Wilson. The earliest English translation of Victor Hugo's *Notre Dame: A Tale of the Ancien Regime* was published by Wilson in three volumes in August 1833. Popular editions of works by Crabbe and Byron; Thomas Roscoe's translation of Miguel de Cervantes's *Don Quixote* (1833), illustrated by George Cruikshank; and Thomas Campbell's two-volume *Life of Mrs. Siddons* (1834) also appeared in these years. It might be argued that such works fit into a campaign for the edification of the growing reading public and for the cultivation of their sensibility. In the spring of 1835 the young Browning offered Wilson his verse drama *Paracelsus*. Browning had been dissatisfied with Saunders and Otley's production of his only previous book, *Pauline* (1833), complaining that it had been overpriced and underdistributed; his overtures to Murray met with the response that poetry was no longer marketable, and even Moxon complained of his losses on Tennyson's work and Henry Taylor's verse drama *Philip van Artevelde* (1834). With financial backing from Browning's father, Wilson published *Paracelsus* in August 1835 and within a year was arranging to sell the final copies. The poet later remarked, "The success was much beyond my expectations."

Social criticism became another of Wilson's strengths in the 1830s. Austin translated Victor Cousin's *Report on the State of Public Instruction in Prussia* (1834), and William Howitt's *Popular History of Priestcraft* (1833) went through five editions within a year. Wilson's relations with the conservative *Times* were strained the most during these years. The paper labeled Wilson "the Radical Bookseller of the Royal Exchange" and recommended that its readers boycott his books. Eventually relations were improved between the publisher and the newspaper, and Wilson always enjoyed the friendship of John Black, editor of the liberal *Morning Chronicle*. The social experimentalist Robert Owen had several books published by Wilson, including his autobiography (1857) and part of his *Book of the New Moral World, Containing the Rational System of Society* (1836), the work that most fully expounds his doctrines of industrial reform and social organization. Wilson had established several American affiliates in the 1830s, and when they declined or vanished in the panics of 1836–1837, he suffered serious losses. Still worse circumstances lay ahead, however.

A fire at the Royal Exchange on 10 January 1838 curtailed Wilson's business during the six years of its rebuilding. Although he was ordinarily insured against fire, Wilson's latest premiums had been neglected, and he found himself unprotected. With a temporary location of 18 Bishopsgate, Wilson continued to publish a few political tracts on timely issues such as the Corn Laws, the Canada question, the accountability of the reformed Parliament, colonial policy, and banking laws. Wilson's early concern with the conduct of royalty resurfaced in a popular pamphlet on the future King Edward VII, *Who Should Educate the Prince of Wales?* (1843). During this time he wrote *Wilson's Description of the New Royal Exchange,* published to coincide with the queen's opening of the restored structure 28 October 1844. On that occasion the liberal press greeted his return with lavish tributes (ten of which are extracted in the 1869 memorial volume). Only then did he resume the full range of his offerings, adding such categories as engineering, public transport, agriculture, public health, and art. His literary offerings were never again as strong as they had been in the 1830s, though he published the pseudonymous *Blackwood v. Carlyle by a Carlylian* (1850), ascribed to the journalist and literary editor James Hannay; and the powerful *Speech of Charles Dickens, Esq., Delivered at the Meeting of the Administrative Reform Association at the Theatre Royal, Drury Lane, Wednesday, June 27, 1855* (1855).

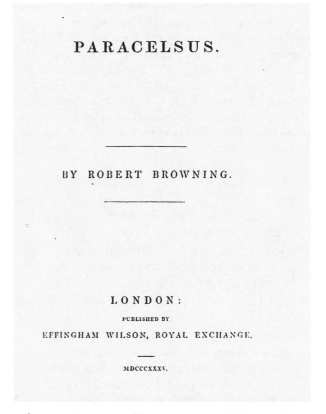

Title page for the successful verse drama that Wilson published after other publishers turned it down (Courtesy of the Lilly Library, Indiana University)

Wilson published an edition of *Railway Property* (1849), by the father of self-help literature, Samuel Smiles, and began a highly influential series, Wilson's Legal Handy Books. Continuing to foster liberal causes, he published Giuseppe Mazzini's attack on French policy, *To Louis Napoleon* (1858), and his pamphlet *The Italian Question and the Republicans* (1861). Wilson lived to see the passage of the Reform Bill of 1867, and after he died in June 1868 the firm was continued under the direction of his son, William Wilson. A long tribute attributed by some to Walter Bagehot appeared in the *City Press* that summer, and dozens of notices were printed in papers on both sides of the Atlantic.

The Effingham Wilson imprint survived and flourished with an increasing concentration on commercial interests; the self-help literature of the reformer became investment advice for the economist of the empire. Treatises appeared on life insurance and underwriting, the postal system and telegraph, railways in India and rates of duty in Russia, and shipping laws and systems of currency exchange. Collaborations with other publishers continued, and the Wilson imprint appeared on publications from New York and Amsterdam in the 1890s. The last volumes displaying the Wilson imprint appeared in 1931, and a 1932 issue of *The Bookseller* carried the announcement, "Sir Isaac Pitman & Sons, Ltd., announce that they have acquired the business of Mr. Effingham Wilson, of 16 Copthall Avenue, London, E.C. 4, and will in future deal with all orders for Mr. Effingham Wilson's publications from their address at Parker Street, Kingsway, London, W.C. 2."

References:

James J. Barnes, *Free Trade in Books: A Study of the London Book Trade since 1800* (Oxford: Clarendon Press, 1964);

Philip A. H. Brown, *London Publishers and Printers: A Tentative List – c. 1800-70* (London: Privately printed by the British Museum, 1961);

Stephen Conway, ed., *The Correspondence of Jeremy Bentham,* 9 volumes to date (Oxford: Clarendon Press, 1989–);

Thomas Frognall Dibdin, *Bibliophobia: Remarks on the Present Languid and Depressed State of Literature and the Book Trade* (London: Henry Bohn, 1832);

June Steffensen Hagen, *Tennyson and His Publishers* (University Park: Pennsylvania State University Press / London: Macmillan, 1979);

In Memory of Effingham Wilson (London: Privately printed, 1869);

Philip Kelley and Ronald Hudson, eds., *The Brownings' Correspondence,* 8 volumes to date (Winfield, Kans.: Wedgestone Press, 1984–);

Jack Kolb, ed., *The Letters of Arthur Henry Hallam* (Columbus: Ohio State University Press, 1981);

Cecil Y. Lang and Edgar F. Shannon Jr., eds., *The Letters of Alfred Lord Tennyson,* 3 volumes to date (Cambridge, Mass.: Harvard University Press / Oxford: Oxford University Press, 1981–);

Harold G. Merriam, *Edward Moxon: Publisher of Poets* (New York: Columbia University Press, 1939);

Francis E. Mineka, ed., *The Earlier Letters of John Stuart Mill, 1812-1848,* 2 volumes (Toronto: University of Toronto Press / London: Routledge & Kegan Paul, 1963);

Charles Richard Sanders and others, *The Collected Letters of Thomas and Jane Welsh Carlyle,* Duke-Edinburgh Edition, 15 volumes to date (Durham, N.C.: Duke University Press, 1970–);

John Sutherland, "The British Book Trade and the Crash of 1826," *Library,* sixth series 9 (June 1987): 148-161.

– Eric W. Nye

Appendix

The Development of the Author's Copyright in Britain

The Development of the Author's Copyright in Britain

Prior to the passage of the Statute of Anne (8 Anne c.19) in 1710, copyright was principally a booksellers' affair, a guild matter organized and administered by the Stationers' Company. Only members of the Stationers' Company – booksellers, printers, and binders – could hold a copyright. But the statute, the world's first copyright law, vested the first ownership of a copyright in the author. Thus, authors became, at least in principle, legally empowered figures in the literary marketplace. The eighteenth century was characterized by a protracted legal struggle over the exact nature of the author's right; in this struggle the modern institution of authorial copyright was born.

The story of the Statute of Anne begins in 1695 with the final lapse of the Licensing Act, the printing statute through which the Crown regulated the content of books and the Stationers' Company derived its power to regulate members' exclusive printing rights. For years the Stationers' Company had lobbied Parliament to restore licensing, but when this attempt failed – neither of the two political parties would trust the other with the power of the censor – the booksellers changed their strategy and sought a bill that would simply secure copyrights. They may have been influenced by Daniel Defoe, who in his *Essay on the Regulation of the Press* (1704) and elsewhere appears to have been the first to advocate a bill to protect authorial property rights. In petitioning Parliament for a law to secure copyright the booksellers, who previously had emphasized the need for regulation of all aspects of the book trade, chose to emphasize the effect that disorder in the trade was having on authors. Many "learned Men have spent much Time, and been at great Charges in composing Books," the booksellers asserted in their petition of 26 February 1707 to the House of Commons, but the uncertainty of literary property was now a "great Discouragement of Persons from writing Matters, that might be of great Use to the Publick." Joseph Addison also took up the author's cause in *The Tatler* (1 December 1709): "All Mechanick Artizans are allowed to reap the Fruit of their Invention and Ingenuity without Invasion; but he that has separated himself from the rest of Mankind, and studied the Wonders of the Creation, the Government of his Passions, and the Revolutions of the World, and has an Ambition to communicate the Effect of half his Life spent in such noble Enquiries, has no Property in what he is willing to produce, but is exposed to Robbery and Want, with this melancholy and just Reflection, That he is the only Man who is not protected by his Country, at the same Time that he best deserves it."

Despite their professed concern for authors, the booksellers' goal was not an author's bill of the sort envisioned by Addison. What they wanted was simply parliamentary confirmation of traditional Stationers' Company practices whereby the great London booksellers were able to claim the works of such authors as Francis Bacon, William Shakespeare, and John Milton as their properties. Parliament, however, was suspicious of the virtual stranglehold that the Stationers' Company had exercised on the book trade. Thus, in two major departures from traditional practice the legislators both limited the term of copyright – setting it at fourteen years, with the possibility of extension for a second term if the author was still living at the expiration of the first – and identified the author as the first holder of copyright. As Lyman Ray Patterson has argued, both innovations were aimed at breaking the great booksellers' monopolistic hold on the trade. The term limits meant that valuable copyrights could no longer be passed from bookseller to bookseller in perpetuity, and the inclusion of the author meant that for the first time one did not have to be a member of the Stationers' Company to hold copyright. Both of these departures figured prominently in the title of the Statute of Anne: "An act for the encouragement of learning, by vesting the copies of printed books in the authors or purchasers of such copies, during the times therein mentioned."

Nevertheless, in practice literary property continued to be a bookseller's rather than an author's concern. In the early part of the eighteenth century authors were reluctant to involve themselves deeply in commerce, and most authors continued to sell their works outright to booksellers. Alexander Pope was an exception: he represented himself as a gentleman and scholar rather than as a professional writer, but he was intimately involved in every aspect of the publication and promotion of his writings and, more than any other writer of his era, was concerned with his legal rights as an author. Pope was not the first well-known English author to go to court: in 1729 his friend John Gay, perhaps in part under Pope's influence, secured an injunction against several booksellers in connection with piracies of his *Polly* (1729). But Pope was the first author to make regular and repeated use of the statute. He did so in consultation with his friend William Murray, later Lord Mansfield, who as chief justice of the King's Bench was to become one of the major figures in the copyright struggle later in the century.

Pope was directly and indirectly involved in many court cases, but by far the most important was his 1741 suit against Edmund Curll over the publication of his letters. *Pope* v. *Curll,* which established that the copyright in a letter belongs to the writer while the ink and paper of the material object belong to the recipient, remains a foundational case in English and American copyright law. It also records a pivotal moment in the production of the concept of intellectual property as essentially immaterial. As Benjamin Kaplan has remarked, the drafter of the Statute of Anne was still thinking of the right to "copy" as a printer would: as the right to print and reprint a physical object – a book. *Copy,* the traditional term for the exclusive right to print a title, also referred to a material object: the manuscript on which the printed edition was based. In the 1730s, however, the new term *copyright,* which suggests an attenuation of this notion of the manuscript as the material basis of the property, came into general circulation. A new and abstract concept of literary property was emerging, a legal claim centered on the idea of the individual author's productive labor rather than on the guild and the ancient practices of book-trade regulation.

This new concept received its first elaboration in a pamphlet titled *A Letter from an Author to a Member of Parliament Concerning Literary Property* (1747). In this publication Pope's friend and literary executor, William Warburton, distinguishes intellectual from material property in order to argue for the absolute nature of the author's right. Warburton's pamphlet is an early document in the legal struggle over the nature of copyright that dominated the middle years of the century. At the heart of the struggle was the limitation of the copyright term specified in the Statute of Anne. This issue was of little consequence to most authors but was of great consequence to the booksellers who purchased copyrights

from authors. Did the statute determine the whole extent of protection, or did it merely supplement an underlying common-law right of property? The great London booksellers who dominated the trade sought to maintain their position by establishing that, despite the statute, copyright was perpetual: their properties, they argued, derived not from the statute but from the common-law right to property. The foundation of this right lay in the author's labor, through which a property came into being that was no different in principle from any other sort of property and that, therefore, lasted forever; ownership of such property could be transferred from the author to the bookseller. Opposed to the London booksellers were the provincial booksellers and printers, in particular an energetic group of Scottish booksellers who were seeking an independent role for themselves as reprinters of popular titles. This party denied that any protection existed beyond the copyright terms specified in the statute. Parliament might grant an author a limited privilege in his or her writings, but such a privilege was not the same thing as an absolute property. How could something as tenuous and difficult to define as an idea be claimed as property?

The question of the author's common-law right could only be resolved by the courts, a process that took many years. The issue was litigated without resolution in *Tonson* v. *Collins* (1760) and again in *Millar* v. *Taylor* (1769). It was finally resolved by the House of Lords in the case of *Donaldson* v. *Becket* (1774) . In *Tonson* v. *Collins,* in which William Blackstone argued for the author's right, the main lines of the argument on both sides of the question were developed. The opponents of common-law copyright maintained that ideas could not be property. Blackstone answered that not ideas but "style and sentiment" were the "essentials of a literary composition," and he restated this formula in authoritative form in 1766 in the second volume of his *Commentaries:*

> When a man by the exertion of his rational powers has produced an original work, he has clearly a right to dispose of that identical work as he pleases, and any attempt to take it from him, or vary the disposition he has made of it, is an invasion of his right of property. Now the identity of a literary composition consists entirely in the *sentiment* and the *language;* the same conceptions, cloathed in the same words, must necessarily be the same composition: and whatever method be taken of conveying that composition to the ear or the eye of another, by recital, by writing, or by printing, in any number of copies or at any period of time, it is always the identical work of the author which is so conveyed;

and no other man can have a right to convey or transfer it without his consent, either tacitly or expressly given.

Thus emerged something like the modern principle that what copyright protects is the expression of ideas, not ideas themselves.

For technical reasons *Tonson* v. *Collins* never came to a decision. In *Millar* v. *Taylor,* however, the highest common-law court in England, the Court of King's Bench, presided over by Pope's old friend Lord Mansfield, ruled that authors did have a common-law right and that copyright was, therefore, perpetual. From what source was the author's right drawn? "From this argument," Lord Mansfield wrote: "Because it is just, that an author should reap the pecuniary profits of his own ingenuity and labour. It is just, that another should not use his name, without his consent. It is fit, that he should judge when to publish, or whether he ever will publish. It is fit he should not only choose the time, but the manner of publication; how many; what volume; what print. It is fit, he should choose to whose care he will trust the accuracy and correctness of the impression; in whose honesty he will confide, not to foist in additions: with other reasonings of the same effect." But Mansfield's strong position in favor of authors' common-law rights was not accepted in Scotland, which followed Scottish rather than English common law and where local interests favored the limited term. For a brief time, therefore, authors had common-law rights in England but not in Scotland. In *Donaldson* v. *Becket,* however, a case pressed by the Scottish reprinter Alexander Donaldson, the House of Lords overruled Mansfield by determining that copyright was limited in term.

The immediate consequence of the Lords' decision was to end the monopoly that the great booksellers of London held on the publication of the works of classic writers. But, even if the struggle was a booksellers' rather than an authors' affair, the notion of the author's common-law right had been elaborated and promulgated. The Lords provided no rationale for their decision in *Donaldson* v. *Becket* — in this period legal decisions were made by a simple vote of the whole House — but in succeeding years an understanding developed that what the Lords had done was to ratify the notion that an author's right existed even while insisting that the common-law right was superseded by the limited term of the statute. In a letter dated 7 March 1774 (probably to the publisher William Strahan), Samuel Johnson called the Lords' decision "legally and politically right." On the one hand, Johnson said, the author had a "natural and peculiar right to the profits of his

own work." On the other, it was "inconvenient to Society that a useful book should become perpetual and exclusive property." Therefore, the author must purchase the protection of society "by resigning some part of his natural right." Johnson favored a longer copyright term than the statute allowed, but, even though he was closely allied with the London booksellers, he did not favor the restoration of the old system.

During the course of the eighteenth century authors' social and economic circumstances had changed greatly, in part as a consequence of the expanded market for books that emerged in this period. At the time of the passage of the Statute of Anne, respectable authors' primary relations were still typically with patrons rather than with booksellers. Hacks might write for money, but authors such as Pope did not acknowledge their professional status. By 1754, however, Johnson's letter rejecting Philip Dormer Stanhope, fourth earl of Chesterfield's belated gesture of patronage in connection with Johnson's *A Dictionary of the English Language* (1755) signaled that professional authorship was becoming both economically feasible and socially acceptable. Alvin Kernan has called Johnson's letter "the Magna Carta of the modern author." In a widely printed speech to the House of Lords in the course of the debate in *Donaldson* v. *Becket,* Sir Charles Pratt, first earl of Camden, argued against perpetual copyright, saying that glory, not money, was the genuine author's reward. His depiction of authors as sublime spirits divorced from the marketplace drew a quick response from the celebrated republican historian Catharine Macaulay in a pamphlet titled *A Modest Plea for the Property of Copyright* (1774), in which she sarcastically pointed out that "literary merit will not purchase a shoulder of mutton, or prevail with sordid butchers and bakers to abate one farthing in the pound of the exorbitant price which meat and bread at this time bear." Plainly, the day of the professional author had arrived.

In the eighteenth century the proponents of perpetual copyright were the London booksellers. By the early nineteenth century, however, the booksellers had adjusted to the limited copyright term, and, indeed, many had a vested interest in the new arrangement. It was authors who took the lead in lobbying Parliament on copyright matters. In 1814 a revised statute extended the copyright term to twenty-eight years after publication or the author's lifetime, whichever was longer. But this term seemed paltry to Robert Southey and William Wordsworth, both of whom maintained that the author's right should be perpetual. "The question is simply this," Southey said in an essay in the January 1819 number of *The Quarterly Review,* "upon what principle, with what justice, or under what pretext of public good, are men of letters deprived of a perpetual property in the produce of their own labours, when all other persons enjoy it as their indefeasible right – a right beyond the power of any earthly authority to take away?" And for two decades Wordsworth was a central figure in a campaign to extend the copyright term that included Thomas Carlyle and Hartley Coleridge as well as Southey and other literary figures. This campaign resulted in the Copyright Act of 1842, which lasted until the twentieth century and which provided a term of the author's lifetime plus seven years, or forty-two years from publication, whichever was longer.

Thus, the legal empowerment of the author in Britain preceded by many years the social and economic development of the author as a respectable professional. By the conclusion of the booksellers' struggle over the validity of term limits, however, the author's status had changed, and it was now authors such as Southey and Wordsworth who were claiming that copyright should be perpetual. Thus, in the course of the eighteenth century the author's copyright was defined and promulgated, and by the end of the century it had become a matter of substance as well as of form.

References:

John Feather, "The Book Trade in Politics: The Making of the Copyright Act of 1710," *Publishing History,* 8 (1980): 19–44;

Feather, "Publishers and Politicians: The Remaking of the Law of Copyright in Britain 1775–1842, Part 1," *Publishing History,* 24 (1988): 49–76;

Feather, "Publishers and Politicians: The Remaking of the Law of Copyright in Britain 1775–1842, Part 2," *Publishing History,* 25 (1989): 45–72;

Benjamin Kaplan, *An Unhurried View of Copyright* (New York: Columbia University Press, 1967);

Alvin Kernan, *Printing Technology, Letters and Samuel Johnson* (Princeton: Princeton University Press, 1987);

James McLaverty, "Pope and Copyright," in *Pope and the Early Eighteenth-Century Book Trade: The Lyell Lectures, Oxford 1975–1976,* by David Foxon, revised and edited by McLaverty (Oxford: Clarendon Press, 1991);

Lyman Ray Patterson, *Copyright in Historical Perspective* (Nashville: Vanderbilt University Press, 1968);

Mark Rose, *Authors and Owners: The Invention of Copyright* (Cambridge, Mass.: Harvard University Press, 1993).

– *Mark Rose*

Books for Further Reading

Barnes, James J. *Free Trade in Books: A Study of the London Book Trade since 1800.* Oxford: Clarendon Press, 1964.

Blagden, Cyprian. *The Stationers' Company, a History, 1403–1959.* Cambridge, Mass.: Harvard University Press, 1960.

Clair, Colin. *A History of Printing in Britain.* New York: Oxford University Press, 1966.

Curwen, Henry. *A History of Booksellers, the Old and the New.* London: Chatto & Windus, 1873.

Dibdin, Thomas Frognall. *Bibliophobia: Remarks on the Present languid and depressed state of literature and the book trade. In a Letter Addressed to the Author of the Bibliomania.* London: Bohn, 1832.

Feather, John. *A Dictionary of Book History.* London: Croom Helm, 1986.

Feather. *A History of British Publishing.* London: Croom Helm, 1988.

Feather. *The Provincial Book Trade in Eighteenth-Century England.* Cambridge: Cambridge University Press, 1985.

Feather. *Publishing, Piracy and Politics: An Historical Study of Copyright in Britain.* London & New York: Mansell, 1994.

Foxon, David F. *Libertine Literature in England, 1660–1745.* New Hyde Park, N.Y.: University Books, 1966.

Foxon and James McLaverty. *Pope and the Early Eighteenth-Century Book Trade: Lyell Lectures in Bibliography, 1975–1976.* New York: Oxford University Press, 1991; Oxford: Clarendon Press, 1991.

Harris, Michael. *London Newspapers in the Age of Walpole: A Study of the Origins of the Modern English Press.* Rutherford, N. J.: Fairleigh Dickinson University Press, 1987; London: Associated University Presses, 1987.

Horne, Thomas Hartwell. *An Introduction to the Study of Bibliography to which is Prefixed a Memoir on Public Libraries of the Antients.* London: Printed by G. Woodfall for T. Cadell & W. Davies, 1814.

Kidson, Frank. *British Music Publishers, Printers and Engravers: London, Provincial, Scottish, and Irish. From Queen Elizabeth's Reign to George the Fourth's, with Select Bibliographical Lists of Musical Works Printed and Published within that Period.* New York: Blom, 1967.

Marston, Edward. *Sketches of Some of the Booksellers of the Time of Dr. Samuel Johnson.* London: Low, Marston, 1902.

Maslen, Keith I. D., and John Lancaster, eds. *The Bowyer Ledgers.* London: Bibliographical Society, 1991; New York: Bibliographical Society of America, 1991.

Maxted, Ian. *The London Book Trades, 1775–1800: A Preliminary Checklist of Members.* Folkestone, U.K.: Dawson, 1977.

Mayo, Robert Donald. *The English Novel in the Magazines, 1740–1815: With a Catalogue of 1375 Magazine Novels and Novelettes.* Evanston, Ill.: Northwestern University Press, 1962.

McCoy, Ralph E. *Freedom of the Press: A Bibliocyclopedia. Ten-Year Supplement (1967–1977).* Carbondale: Southern Illinois University Press, 1979.

McCoy. *Freedom of the Press: An Annotated Bibliography.* Carbondale: Southern Illinois University Press, 1968.

McCoy. *Freedom of the Press: An Annotated Bibliography. Second Supplement, 1978–1992.* Carbondale: Southern Illinois University Press, 1993.

Middleton, Bernard C. *A History of English Craft Bookbinding Technique.* New York: Hafner, 1963.

Mumby, Frank Arthur, and Ian Norrie. *Publishing and Bookselling,* fifth edition. London: Cape, 1974.

Myers, Robin. *The Stationers' Company Archive: An Account of the Records 1554–1984.* Winchester: St. Paul's Bibliographies, 1990.

Myers and Harris. *Aspects of Printing from 1600.* Oxford: Oxford Polytechnic Press, 1987.

Myers and Harris. *Author/Publisher Relations during the Eighteenth and Nineteenth Centuries.* Oxford: Oxford Polytechnic Press, 1983.

Myers and Harris. *Development of the English Book Trade, 1700–1899.* Oxford: Oxford Polytechnic Press, 1981.

Myers and Harris, eds. *Censorship & the Control of Print: In England and France 1600–1910.* Winchester: St. Paul's Bibliographies, 1992.

Myers and Harris, eds. *Economics of the British Booktrade, 1605–1939.* Cambridge: Chadwyck-Healey, 1985.

Myers and Harris, eds. *Sale and Distribution of Books from 1700.* Oxford: Oxford Polytechnic Press, 1982.

Myers and Harris, eds. *Serials and Their Readers, 1620–1914.* Winchester: St. Paul's Bibliographies, 1993.

Sullivan, Alvin, ed. *British Literary Magazine,* 2 volumes. Westport, Conn.: Greenwood Press, 1983.

Contributors

Robert R. Bataille ....*Iowa State University*
Gene Blanton ....*Jacksonville State University*
Lord Asa Briggs...*Ringmer, U.K.*
Stephen W. Brown ....*Trent University*
Ann W. Engar...*University of Utah*
Barbara Laning Fitzpatrick ....*University of New Orleans*
Antonia Forster ....*University of Akron*
Cynthia Guidici ....*University of North Texas*
Carol Hall..*Howard University*
Daniel W. Hollis III..*Jacksonville State University*
Raymond N. MacKenzie ....*University of St. Thomas*
Sandra Naiman ....*Northern Illinois University*
Donald W. Nichol..*Memorial University*
Eric W. Nye ....*University of Wyoming*
Alexander Pettit ....*University of North Texas*
Alan Pratt ....*Embry-Riddle Aeronautical University*
Ruth Robbins ....*University of Luton*
Deborah D. Rogers ....*University of Maine*
Jonathan Rose ....*Drew University*
Mark Rose ....*University of California, Santa Barbara*
Barbara Quinn Schmidt ....*Southern Illinois University*
Michael Scrivener ....*Wayne State University*
Sandra Spencer ....*University of North Texas*
James E. Tierney ....*University of Missouri, St. Louis*
Michael Treadwell ....*Trent University*
Philip J. Weimerskirch ....*Providence Public Library*
Julian Wolfreys ....*University of Luton*
Kenneth Womack...*Northern Illinois University*

Cumulative Index

Dictionary of Literary Biography, Volumes 1-154
Dictionary of Literary Biography Yearbook, 1980-1994
Dictionary of Literary Biography Documentary Series, Volumes 1-12

Cumulative Index

DLB before number: *Dictionary of Literary Biography,* Volumes 1-154
Y before number: *Dictionary of Literary Biography Yearbook,* 1980-1994
DS before number: *Dictionary of Literary Biography Documentary Series,* Volumes 1-12

N

O

ISBN 0-8103-5715-1

Documentary Series